Seoul

timeout.com/seoul

Time Out Guides Ltd
Universal House
251 Tottenham Court Road
London W1T 7AB
United Kingdom
Tel: +44 (0)20 7813 3000
Fax: +44 (0)20 7813 6001
Email: guides@timeout.com
www.timeout.com

Published by Time Out Guides Ltd, a wholly owned subsidiary of Time Out Group Ltd.
Time Out and the Time Out logo are trademarks of Time Out Group Ltd.

10 9 8 7 6 5 4 3 2

This edition first published in Great Britain in 2011 by Ebury Publishing.
A Random House Group Company
20 Vauxhall Bridge Road, London SW1V 2SA

Random House Australia Pty Ltd 20 Alfred Street, Milsons Point, Sydney, New South Wales 2061, Australia

Random House New Zealand Ltd 18 Poland Road, Glenfield, Auckland 10, New Zealand

Random House South Africa (Pty) Ltd Isle of Houghton, Corner Boundary Road & Carse O'Gowrie, Houghton 2198, South Africa

Random House UK Limited Reg. No. 954009

Distributed in the US and Latin America by Publishers Group West (1-510-809-3700)
Distributed in Canada by Publishers Group Canada (1-800-747-8147)

For further distribution details, see www.timeout.com.

ISBN: 978-1-84670-283-9

A CIP catalogue record for this book is available from the British Library.

Printed and bound in Great Britain by Butler Tanner & Dennis, Frome, Somerset.

The Random House Group Limited supports The Forest Stewardship Council (FSC®), the leading international forest certification organisation. Our books carrying the FSC label are printed on FSC® certified paper. FSC is the only forest certification scheme endorsed by the leading environmental organisations, including Greenpeace. Our paper procurement policy can be found at www.randomhouse.co.uk/environment

Time Out carbon-offsets its flights with Trees for Cities (www.treesforcities.org).

Contents

WHENEVER, WHEREVER YOU NEED MONEY..

WE GET IT THERE IN 10 MINUTES*

CHOICE IS IN YOUR HANDS

1. Arrange for the person sending the money to visit a MoneyGram agent near them. After sending the money, they will give you a reference number.

2. Find your nearest MoneyGram agent at **www.moneygram.com** or anywhere you see the MoneyGram sign.

3. Give the reference number and your ID** to the MoneyGram agent.

4. Fill out one simple form to receive your money.

MoneyGram. ®
Money Transfer

www.moneygram.com

Introduction

Few international visitors know too much about Seoul before they arrive – a fact that makes the excitement most travellers feel on arrival all the more palpable. This is one of the largest, busiest and most densely populated cities on earth, yet despite this it manages to hold down an amazingly low crime rate; with so little to fear, it's little wonder that most locals seem extremely content with their lot.

Contentment is also perhaps a legacy of the horrors witnessed here during the catastrophic civil war of the 1950s. The city managed to rebuild itself in a hurry, jumping from poverty to prosperity in just a couple of generations. An understandable absence of town planning during that troubled time means that there are now very few old buildings in the city, and though little architectural coherence has been given even to new constructions, the resultant patchwork of neon-panelled skyline is certainly quite stimulating. The lights are at their brightest in the city's two main business districts – City Hall north of the river, and Gangnam to the south, both of which boast dozens of streets resembling sci-fi film sets. Seoul's wildest nightlife areas, Hongdae and Itaewon, are no slouches either in the visual department.

Trillions of won are passed around every day, making Seoul Asia's fourth-richest city. However, such high-octane commerce seems a world away in and around the city's palace quarter – the focal point of Seoul and, indeed, all Korea for the past six hundred years. Here, and in Insadong just to the south, a gentler Seoul comes into view: look hard enough and you'll find lovingly painted wooden eaves, wafts of incense smoke, tiny stores selling pottery or paintbrushes, and secluded alleyways in which time seems to have stood still for decades.

All this, and so far no mention of the thing that helps bring visitors back time and again – the food. Korea's national cuisine is simply sensational, and even if you can't handle the inevitable spice, you'll be able to fall back on a world's worth of international restaurants. It's no exaggeration to call Seoul one of the world's top food cities – and possibly the only one not recognised as such by the wider world. A fair amount to unearth, then, on a single trip. *Oliver Duke, Editor.*

Get the local experience

Over 50 of the world's top destinations available.

Seoul in Brief

IN CONTEXT

Seoul has a rich dynastic past, and knowledge of its historical layers of Confucian, Buddhist and Christian thought is essential to an understanding of the city. We also examine traditional and colonial architecture, and focus on contemporary Seoul, and the Hallyu Wave of pop culture. Past and present are linked with a look at *makgeolli*, a traditional rice wine now undergoing a surge in popularity.

▶ *For more, see pp16-40.*

SIGHTS

Having been almost entirely levelled in the early 20th century, Seoul is an almost entirely modern city. But some palaces, temples and other structures did remain, evidence of Seoul's five hundred plus years as capital of the Joseon Kingdom. We also look at Seoul's slew of excellent museums, as well as less-heralded sights such as Shamanist shrines and activities such as river cruises.

▶ *For more, see pp42-83.*

CONSUME

Seoul is a capital of consumption. For one thing, it's one of the world's greatest culinary secrets – restaurants serving Korea's rich and varied national cuisine are neatly augmented by a new pack of cosmopolitan eateries, as well as secluded tearooms and funky cafés. You can also try local alcoholic drinks almost unknown outside the country, and sleep in a traditional wooden guesthouse.

▶ *For more, see pp86-159.*

ARTS & ENTERTAINMENT

Seoul's concentration of modern art galleries is quite prodigious; in Insadong and Bukchon, it's hard to turn a corner without running into one (or more). You'll also be able to take in a musical or *pansori* performance, and there are more idiosynratic delights available: snooze with a floorful of locals in a *jimjilbang* spa, watch a movie in a room for two, or sing in a karaoke-style *noraebang*.

▶ *For more, see pp162-198.*

ESCAPES & EXCURSIONS

Seoul may be one of the world's largest cities, but there are many ways to escape: there's a national park within the city itself, while two ancient capitals – each bursting with treasure – are within day-trip distance. Absorb a bit of history in Incheon and Suwon, two cities that are essentially part of Seoul, or take a few cautious steps into North Korea across a demilitarised zone that's anything but.

▶ *For more, see pp200-218.*

Seoul in 48 Hours

Day 1 Exploring Old Seoul

7AM Dawn sees Seoul at its quietest, and you'll be able to enjoy the relative hush with a trip to charming **Bukchon** (*see p46*), which has more traditional wooden *hanok* buildings than anywhere else in central Seoul. Their eaves, slate roof tiles and brass-clad doors catch the morning light in a quite wonderful way. After a good wander around these hilly lanes, it's time for a pick-me-up in one of the dozens of charming cafes – **Books Cooks** (*see p128*) and **Sajingwan** (*see p130*) are two good choices in the area.

10AM Seoul has five royal palaces, and they're all worth a visit – check out the architecturally superb **Changdeokgung** (*see p42*) and its 'Secret Garden', or the more historically fascinating **Changgyeonggung** (*see p43*), connected by walkway to **Jongmyo** (*see p56*), a park-like royal shrine.

1PM Time for lunch, and the options are plentiful. The **Insadong** area (*see p51*) is full of restaurants serving cheap, traditional food – see p112 **A Guide to Korean Cuisine** for a little primer on local dishes. Here you'll also find **Yetchatjip** (*see p134*), a quaint tearoom filled with tiny birds, and dozens of places to go shopping for presents (*see p51* **Souvenir Shopping**).

4PM Tour the palace of **Gyeongbokgung** (*see p44*) and its on-site museums, before catching sunset in the palace grounds. For dinner, head to **Balwoo** (*see p111*) for some good Buddhist temple food, or splash out on a royal feast at **Yongsusan** (*see p111*), before falling into **Pub of the Blue Star** (*see p136*) for a rice-wine nightcap.

10PM After a day soaking up Korean tradition (and food), the Bukchon area's wooden guesthouses (*see p87*) are the most appropriate places to drop into for a night's sleep – typically conducted on the floor, in a sandwich of futons.

NAVIGATING THE CITY

Seoul is absolutely huge, but thankfully the most interesting areas for visitors – from the Royal Quarter in the north to Gangnam in the south – are bound into one tight central zone, bisected roughly from east to west by the Hangang River. This whole area is criss-crossed by a superb and easy to use subway network (*see p221*) – there will always be a station within walking distance, tickets are cheap, and all signs are dual-language. Seoul isn't really a walking city, but the Royal Quarter, home to many of Seoul's most interesting sights, is a pleasing exception. It's a doddle to get around with street maps in hand (*see pp246-255*). And if all else fails, taxis (*see p221*) are always available to take you where you want to go.

SEEING THE SIGHTS

Admission fees for sights in Seoul is very affordable by international standards, and

Day 2 Into the Modern Day

11AM Why not start the day fashionably late? Head south of the river to explore the shopping boutiques of ultra-fashionable **Apgujeong** (*see p74*). **Jardin de Chouette** (*see p147*) is great for womenswear, while **Daily Projects** (*see p151*) is popular for men. Luxury mall **Boon the Shop** (*see p151*) is also well worth a look, both for its wide range of luxury labels and for its central atrium that plays host to rotating art exhibitions. And when you need a break from dashing from shop to shop, duck into the **Café Madang** (*see p131*) at Hermès for a coffee.

2PM It's lunchtime, and there's no better place to head while you're in this area than trendy **Garosugil** (*see p74*). Here you'll find **West Meets East** (*see p134*), a café that specialises in mixing Korean and international ingredients and serves wonderful sweet pancakes, among other treats.

4PM It would be a shame to go the whole day without taking a break from consumerism to enjoy a little culture: the Buddhist temple of **Bongeunsa** (*see p75*) should suffice, as will the regal burial mounds at **Samneung Park** (*see p76*).

7PM Enough culture – it's time for some food. In keeping with the day's contemporary angle, a stab at neo-Korean cuisine would be appropriate. **Jung Sikdang** (*see p122*) or – north of the river – **Poom** (*see p124*) are among the best places in the city to sample new takes on old favourites.

10PM Seoul's nightlife is a pleasure to dive into. North of the river, **Itaewon** has huge number of cosmopolitan places to eat and drink (*see p123, p141*), while **Hongdae**, the university area to the east is a little wilder and more youthful, and also has some great places to catch live music (*see p181*).

students and the elderly can expect reductions, if they remember to bring ID along. Note that most museums, and a fair few galleries, are closed on Mondays, and that you'll usually have to pay entrance fees in cash. The main times to avoid are weekends and holidays, when some sights can get very busy indeed, and the daily rush hours (8am-9.30am, and 6pm-8pm), when public transport is packed and the roads are blocked.

PACKAGE DEALS

Since public transport and entrance tickets for sights are cheap in Seoul, package deals are largely unnecessary. However, the city operates the Seoul Citypass scheme (www.seoulcitypass.com or www.visitseoul.net), which allows up to 20 bus or subway trips per day, as well as free rides on the Seoul City Tour Buses (*see p222*). On the latter, you'll be able to pick up coupons allowing free entry to selected sights.

Seoul in Profile

THE ROYAL QUARTER

The **Bukchon** area is redolent of old Seoul – its small, hilly lanes are lined with wooden housing, and there are occasional views of the area's three wonderful palaces, all dating from the Joseon Dynasty. The adjacent **Samcheongdong** area is similarly relaxed, though its cafes, galleries and restaurants exude a far more contemporary air. In addition, the relatively unexplored area of **Buamdong** lies just around the mountain to the north.
► *For more, see pp42-50.*

INSADONG

Heading south instead, the **Insadong** area is also markedly traditional by Seoul standards, and a firm favourite with locals and visitors. While walking down its appealing main thoroughfare, you'll find it incredibly tempting to delve off into the side alleys. Do so, and before long you'll be sitting (most likely on a heated floor, in the traditional style) in an enchanting restaurant or tearoom.
► *For more, see pp51-57.*

MYEONGDONG, CITY HALL & AROUND

Going further south again, Seoul's vibe takes a distinct turn for the modern. **Myeongdong** is a shopper's paradise, its streets packed to the max from morning until night. Not that all joy to be extracted from the area is commercial in nature: it also has the city's greatest number of colonial buildings, erected during Japanese occupation – the best are dotted between Myeongdong and **City Hall**.
► *For more, see pp58-64.*

DONGDAEMUN

Dongdaemun was the name given to Seoul's eastern gate, at a time when the city was much smaller and surrounded by a forbidding wall. This is still standing, though these days the name is more often used for the market, by far the largest in the land and a delightfully confusing space. South is the **Chungmuro** area, home to a re-created dynastic village, as well as some terrific traditional song and dance performances. Heading south once more will bring you **Mt Namsan**, a small mountain jutting out of central Seoul.
► *For more, see pp65-69.*

THE UNIVERSITY DISTRICT

West of the city centre is Seoul's main university district. The number of students here is quite phenomenal – more than 100,000 at the four largest universities alone. As you'd expect, this is the best area in which to dive into Seoul's edgier side. The area around **Hongdae**,an art university, has attained national renown for its nightlife, though neighbouring **Sinchon** is no slouch ether.
► *For more, see pp70-73*

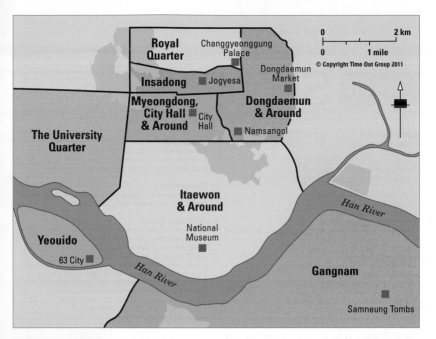

GANGNAM
Royal Quarter
Changgyeonggung Palace
Insadong
Jogyesa
Dongdaemun Market
Myeongdong, City Hall & Around
City Hall
Dongdaemun & Around
The University Quarter
Namsangol
Itaewon & Around
National Museum
Han River
Yeouido
63 City
Han River
Gangnam
Samneung Tombs

0   2 km
0   1 mile
© Copyright Time Out Group 2011

GANGNAM

With a name meaning 'South of the River', the wide area of **Gangnam** is an almost entirely modern district. Bar some regal burial mounds and a superb Buddhist temple, it's largely devoid of sights, and off the radar of most visitors. (And the fact that meals and drinks here cost double what they would north of the river also keeps visitors away.) Still, dedicated shoppers will get a kick out of the boutiques lining **Apgujeong**, an area that tries to play itself up as Korea's Beverly Hills.
► For more, see pp74-77.

YEOUIDO

Though often overlooked by visitors to Seoul, the business district of **Yeouido** is worthy of a quick look. An island in the Hangang River, it's home to Asia's one-time tallest building, the **National Assembly**, and the world's largest church. In addition, there are swathes of riverside parkland, which make good walking or cycling territory; in summer, the open-air swimming pools are great places to cool down.
► For more, see pp78-80.

ITAEWON & AROUND

A short hike over Namsan will bring you to **Itaewon**, an area far more cosmopolitan than anywhere else in Seoul. Embassy staff, American military personnel and thousands of English teachers call this place home, and many more pop by regularly for a meal or a drink, since this is also one of Korea's most happening nightlife areas. Consumption aside, the district is home to an excellent museum, and to art galleries.
► For more, see pp81-83

TimeOut Seoul

Editorial

Editor Oliver Duke
Copy Editor Ros Sales
Listings Checker Oliver Duke
Proofreader Tamsin Shelton
Indexers William Crow, Jamie Warburton

Managing Director Peter Fiennes
Editorial Director Ruth Jarvis
Business Manager Dan Allen
Editorial Manager Holly Pick
Management Accountants Margaret Wright, Clare Turner

Design

Art Director Scott Moore
Art Editor Pinelope Kourmouzoglou
Senior Designer Kei Ishimaru
Group Commercial Designer Jodi Sher

Picture Desk

Picture Editor Jael Marschner
Picture Desk Assistant/Researcher Ben Rowe

Advertising

New Business & Commercial Director Mark Phillips
International Advertising Manager Kasimir Berger
International Sales Executive Charlie Sokol

Marketing

Senior Publishing Brand Manager Luthfa Begum
Guides Marketing Manager Colette Whitehouse
Group Commercial Art Director Anthony Huggins

Production

Group Production Manager Brendan McKeown
Production Controller Katie Mulhern

Time Out Group

Chairman & Founder Tony Elliott
Chief Executive Officer David King
Chief Operating Officer Aksel Van der Wal
Group Financial Director Paul Rakkar
Group General Manager/Director Nichola Coulthard
Time Out Communications Ltd MD David Pepper
Time Out International Ltd MD Cathy Runciman
Cultural Development Manager Mark Elliott
Group Commercial Director Graeme Tottle
Group IT Director Simon Chappell
Group Marketing Director Andrew Booth

Contributors

History Jim Dinsdale. **Architecture** Robert Koehler. **Seoul Today** Oliver Duke, Darcy Pacquet. **Makgeolli Magic** Michael van der Zweep. **The Royal Quarter** Chris Backe, Oliver Duke. **Insadong** Oliver Duke, David A Mason. *Shamanism* David A Mason. **Myeongdong, City Hall & Around** Chris Backe, Oliver Duke. *Christianity in Korea* Brother Anthony of Taizé. **Dongdaemun & Around** Chris Backe, Oliver Duke. **The University Area** Chris Backe, Oliver Duke. *School Daze* Jason Strother. **Gangnam** Oliver Duke, Matt Kelley. *Buddhism in Korea* David A Mason. **Yeouido** Chris Backe. Hotels Oliver Duke. **Itaewon** Chris Backe, Oliver Duke. **Restaurants** Oliver Duke, Dan Gray, Jen Flinn. *Spice World* Jen Flinn. Cafés & **Tearooms** Oliver Duke, Dan Gray, Jen Flinn. *Teas of Korea* Brother Anthony of Taizé. **Bars** Oliver Duke, Greg Curley. **Shops & Services** Oliver Duke, Sara Kim. **Calendar** David Carruth. **Children** Michael van der Zweep. **Film** Oliver Duke. **Directing Talent** Darcy Paquet. **Galleries** Oliver Duke. **Gay & Lesbian** Matt Kelley. **Music** Shawn Despres, Sara Kim. **Nightlife** Greg Curley. **Sport & Fitness** Oliver Duke *Taekwondo* Stream Lee. **Performing Arts** Jen Flinn. **Escapes & Excursions** Oliver Duke, Matt Kelley. *North Korea: Against the Odds* Jason Strother. **Directory** Oliver Duke, Jen Flinn. **Vocabulary** Michael van der Zweep.

The editor would like to thank Seoul Metropolitan Government and Seoul Tourism Organization.

Maps by JS Graphics Ltd (john@jsgraphics.co.uk). Maps are based on material supplied by ITMB Publishing.

Front Cover Photography Masterfile. **Back Cover Photography** Seoul Metropolitan Government and Shutterstock

Photography by Seong Joon Cho, except pages 5, 75 Ragma Images; pages 7, 8, 10, 11 (right), 19, 20, 28, 32, 38, 46, 53, 55, 59, 60, 65, 66, 71 (right), 73, 76, 83, 108, 112, 121, 126, 129, 162, 163, 167, 168, 173, 189, 191, 192, 195, 198, 205 Seoul Metropolitan Government; pages 7 (bottom right), 9, 39, 47, 54, 90, 101, 122, 137, 142, 143, 144, 147, 150, 157, 172, 183, 207, 208, 210, 216, 219 Gijs Bekenkamp; page 15 Jin Young Lee; page 16 Getty Images; pages 31, 41, 62, 113 Shutterstock; page 35 Mika Heittola; page 43 Mary Lane; page 45 (top left) Nikolay Postnikov; pages 45 (top right), 201, 212 Gina Smith/Shutterstock.com; page 45 (bottom), 199, 202 Tatiana Grozetskaya/Shutterstock.com; pages 176, 177, 179, 213 Matt Kelley. The following pictures were supplied by the featured establishments: pages 37, 98, 105, 119.

About the Guide

GETTING AROUND

The back of the book contains street maps of Seoul, as well as overview maps of the city and its surroundings. The maps start on page 244; on them are marked the locations of hotels (❶), restaurants and cafés (❶), and pubs and bars (❶). The majority of businesses listed in this guide are located in the areas we've mapped; the grid-square references in the listings refer to these maps.

THE ESSENTIALS

For practical information, including visas, disabled access, emergency numbers, lost property, useful websites and local transport, please see the Directory. It begins on page 220.

THE LISTINGS

Addresses, phone numbers, websites, transport information, hours and prices are all included in our listings, as are selected other facilities. All were checked and correct at press time. However, business owners can alter their arrangements at any time, and fluctuating economic conditions can cause prices to change rapidly.

The very best venues in the city, the must-sees and must-dos in every category, have been marked with a red star (★). In the Sights chapters, we've also marked venues with free admission with a FREE symbol.

PHONE NUMBERS

The area code for Seoul is 02. You don't need to use the code when calling from within the city: simply dial the seven- or eight-digit number as listed in this guide.

From outside South Korea, dial your country's international access code (011 from the US) or a plus symbol, followed by the country code (82), 2 for Seoul (dropping the initial zero) and the seven- or eight-digit number as listed in the guide. So, to reach the Blue House, dial +82 2 730-5800. For more on phones, including information on calling abroad from the UK and details of local mobile-phone access, *see p228*.

FEEDBACK

We welcome feedback on this guide, both on the venues we've included and on any other locations that you'd like to see featured in future editions. Please email us at guides@timeout.com.

Time Out Guides

Founded in 1968, Time Out has grown from humble beginnings into the leading resource for anyone wanting to know what's happening in the world's greatest cities. Alongside our influential weeklies in London, New York and Chicago, we publish more than 20 magazines in cities as varied as Beijing and Beirut; a range of travel books, with the City Guides now joined by the newer Shortlist series; and an information-packed website. The company remains proudly independent, still owned by Tony Elliott four decades after he launched *Time Out London*.

Written by local experts and illustrated with original photography, our books

also retain their independence. No business has been featured in this guide because it has advertised, and all restaurants, cafés, bars and other venues featured are visited and reviewed anonymously.

ABOUT THE EDITOR

Based in East Asia and a frequent visitor to Seoul, **Oliver Duke** is travel writer and editor.

A full list of the book's contributors can be found opposite. However, we've also included details of our writers in selected chapters and feature boxes throughout the guide.

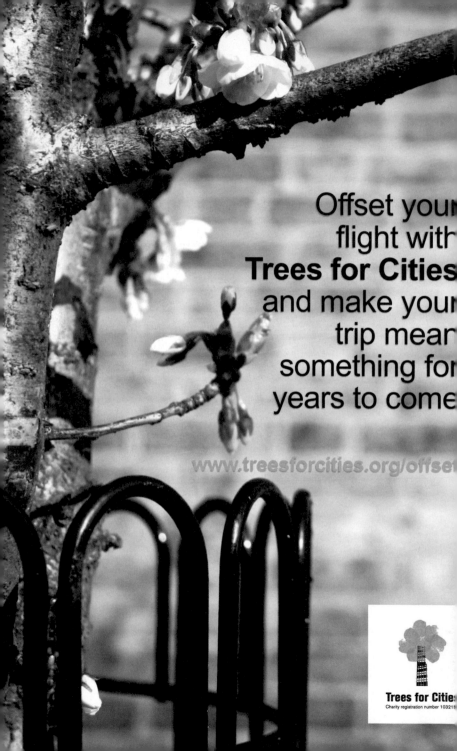

Offset your
flight with
Trees for Cities
and make your
trip mean
something for
years to come

www.treesforcities.org/offset

Trees for Cities
Charity registration number 103218

In Context

History

*Dynastic rule, destructive war
and an economic miracle.*

From its earliest days as an ancient capital to its present-day incarnation as a megacity, the city known today as Seoul has always been a hub of sorts. The city and its hinterland have often been a cultural or political dividing line too: even today the Korean Demilitarized Zone (DMZ), the strip of land acting as a buffer between North and South Korea, is just an hour's drive from central Seoul.

Incredibly for a city that has invested so much in modernity, some basic layout of the medieval city remains, perhaps most notably Jongno, Seoul's main east–west thoroughfare, linking the Great East Gate (Dongdaemun) and Gyeongbokgung Palace. But overlaying this is a cityscape that reflects the recent past of the Korean economic miracle. Much of the city was flattened in the Korean War, and its infrastructure destroyed. It got back on its feet with incredible speed; rebuilding was quick and utilitarian – aesthetics weren't a priority. In the early years of the 21st century, however, Seoulites are beginning to look beyond economic growth and towards sustainability.

IN THE BEGINNING

There are indications that humans have lived in the area that is now Seoul since the Paleolithic age, but it was really in the Neolithic age that full-scale human settlement of the fertile Hangang River valley began. In 1925, flood waters washed away much of the Hangang River's southern bank in what is now the Amsadong district of south-east Seoul, revealing a large number of earthenware shards; subsequent excavations revealed stone tools, building sites and other evidence of a large scale Neolithic settlement dating back 3,000 to 7,000 years. Indeed, the Seoul area, along with the river valleys along the Dumangang, Daedonggang and Nakdonggang rivers, is believed to have been one of Korea's four biggest centres of Neolithic culture.

The Bronze Age developed in Korea from around 1500 BC. As Bronze Age culture took root, the estuary of the Hangang River – including what is now Seoul – became the dividing line between two distinct cultures, one to the north and one to the south, a fact demonstrated by the unearthing of distinct northern and southern styles of pottery in and around the city. In one way or another, the Seoul area would mark a cultural or political dividing line for much of its history; even today, the infamous Korean Demilitarized Zone (or DMZ, *see p204*), which marks the dividing line between North and South Korea, is just an hour's drive from downtown Seoul.

The peoples along the Hangang formed tribal federations, while to the north the first Korean kingdom, Gojoseon, rose up, first in the Liaodong Peninsula and later in the Daedonggang river valley of today's North Korea. In 108 BC, however, the Chinese Han Dynasty conquered Gojoseon, setting up in northern Korea the so-called Four Commanderies of Han. The Seoul area fell under the rule of one of these commanderies, the Zhenfan Commandery.

This foreign occupation met with resistance from the locals, and the Four Commanderies were gradually eaten away until the last of them, the Lelang Commandery, was finally conquered by the Korean kingdom of Goguryeo in AD 313. The Hangang River valley came under the rule of Mahan, a Korean tribal confederation that controlled much of the Korean south-west from the first century BC to the third century AD.

WIRYESEONG AND THE THREE KINGDOMS

The Baekje, one of the tribes that composed the Mahan confederation, established itself in the Seoul area after its founder, King Onjo, moved there from what is now Manchuria. In 18 BC, Onjo established his capital, Wiryeseong, in what is now south-east Seoul. The earthen walls of the ancient capital are still very much around in the form of Pungnap Toseong (Pungnam Earthen Fortress) and Mongchon Toseong (Mongchon Earthen Fortress) in the Songpa-gu district: the walls can be hiked, and in fact, the latter was used as a venue for the pentathlon event of the 1988 Summer Olympic Games.

Under pressure from the other tribes of the Mahan confederation, the Baekje moved its capital north of the Hangang River to an area around Mt Dobongsan around 132 AD, but moved it back south again later – it is from this last relocation that the earthen walls that remain today are believed to date. The kingdom flourished, and in the third and fourth centuries, it expanded to include almost the entirety of western Korea, with the exception of some areas in today's North Korea. Conducting a brisk trade with China, the Baekje adopted many aspects of Chinese culture and administration, not the least of which was Buddhism, which the kingdom adopted as its official state religion in 384. The Baekje also sent many scholars, Buddhist monks and artisans to Japan, where they played a major role in transmitting Chinese and Korean culture to the Japanese. Indeed, according to the Nihon Shoki, a Japanese history text from 720, Buddhism was officially introduced to Japan by a mission sent by King Seong of Baekje in 552.

Unfortunately for Baekje, its expansion came to a screeching halt in the fifth century, when its rival to the north, the kingdom of Goguryeo, went on a conquering spree under

'Yi adopted the royal name of King Taejo and named his new kingdom Joseon, or "Land of the Morning Calm".'

King Gwanggaeto the Great (reigned 391-412). By the end of Gwanggaeto's reign, Goguryeo ruled much of Manchuria and northern and central Korea. King Jangsu, Gwanggaeto's son and successor, continued his father's winning ways. In 475, Jangsu seized upon political instability in Baekje to launch a major invasion, effortlessly conquering the Hangang River region and burning its capital of Wiryeseong to the ground. Baekje's ruler, King Gaero, was captured, brought to Achasan Fortress (its remains still exist, on the south-east outskirts of Seoul) and executed.

Baekje survived the invasion, but stripped of the fertile Hangang River valley, it moved its capital south, first to today's Gongju (*see p215*) and later to the town of Buyeo in the province of Chungcheongnam-do. Plotting revenge against Goguryeo, it entered into an alliance with Silla, an emerging kingdom in south-eastern Korea (today's Gyeongsang provinces). In 551, the two allies invaded Goguryeo with the aim of retaking the Hangang River region. Baekje did the heavy lifting early on, bleeding itself dry attacking Goguryeo's forts defending the area before finally driving Goguryeo from the area. Two years later, however, Silla turned on Baekje and took control of the Hangang valley for itself. This precipitated a war between the former allies that quickly ended with the Baekje king's death in battle.

Now in command of the strategically vital and resource-rich Hangang valley, Silla grew into the strongest player on the Korean Peninsula, benefiting greatly in particular from its now-direct trade access to China, with which it would develop especially close relations. Baekje, on the other hand, went into an interminable decline that ended with the Baekje capital falling to a combined Silla-Chinese invasion in 660. With the fall of Goguryeo to another combined Silla-Chinese invasion in 668, Silla ended the so-called Three Kingdoms Era and unified most of the Korean Peninsula under its rule.

GETTING MEDIEVAL

Silla ruled Korea south of Pyongyang until 935, when a period of provincial uprisings and political instability was brought to end by Wang Geon, a rebel king who established his own dynasty of Goryeo. Goryeo established its capital at Gaegyeong, today's city of Kaeseong in North Korea. The area around what is now Seoul was elevated into a major administrative district, named Yangju-mok, under the reign of King Seongjong (981-97), and in 1067, it was renamed Namgyeong and designated one of the kingdom's three subcapitals. The subcapital's boundaries were roughly those of Seoul of later centuries – Mt Naksan to the east, Mt Ansan to the west, Mt Bugaksan to the north and Yongsan to the south – and for the first time ever, a royal palace was built in the town, likely on the spot now occupied by the presidential mansion of Cheongwadae. Thanks to the town's new importance, nearby locals began flocking to it, and what is now Seoul began to take on the look of a bona fide city. During the reign of King Sukjong (reigned 1095-1105), an attempt was even made to relocate the royal capital to Namgyeong, but the king, who was impressed by the site's superb feng shui properties, died before the plan could be realised.

In 1231, a Mongol army sent by Ögedei Khan invaded Goryeo. The Koreans were overwhelmed, and the royal family fled to the West Sea island of Ganghwado, where they were safe from the notoriously water-shy Mongols. The warriors from the steppe took the rest of the country, though, and Namgyeong became a base for the Mongol army. The Korean court sued for peace and returned to the mainland to rule as Mongol puppets. Under Mongol pressure, Goryeo's subcapitals were abolished and Namgyeong was reduced in status and renamed Hanyang. King Gongmin revived the subcapital system as part of a larger bid to free his kingdom of Mongol influence, and talk of moving the royal capital itself to Hanyang continued to the end of the dynasty itself. In fact, the last king of Goryeo, King Gongyang, briefly relocated the capital to the city before returning it once again to Gaegyeong.

A ROYAL CAPITAL IS BORN

In 1392, the Goryeo court dispatched an army under the command of General Yi Seong-gye to the north with orders to invade China and annex the Liaodong Peninsula, which in ancient times had been ruled by Korean kingdoms. However, when Yi reached the Amnokgang (Yalu) river that marked the border with China, he decided to rebel, and instead marched his troops on the royal capital. With a good deal of official and popular support, Yi seized the capital and deposed King Gongyang, bringing the Goryeo dynasty to an end. Taking the throne for himself, Yi adopted the royal name of King Taejo and named his new kingdom Joseon, or 'Land of the Morning Calm'. Taejo also replaced Buddhism with Confucianism as the kingdom's ruling ideology. (For more on Korean Buddhism, see p77.)

Protected by mountains in all directions and the mighty Hangang River to the south, the city of Hanyang, which had already been discussed frequently as a capital under the previous dynasty, attracted the attention of Taejo's closest advisors, most notably the noted Buddhist monk and feng shui expert Muhak. Muhak urged the king to place the capital of his new kingdom in Hanyang, and in 1393, the government selected the site as the new capital. Work began immediately on constructing the Confucian capital's palace and royal shrines, and in November 1394 the court officially relocated to Hanyang, where the government of Korea would remain, more or less, for the next 600 years. In 1395, the city was renamed Hanseong, and work was completed on Taejo's residence, Gyeongbokgung Palace (see p43). Finally, in 1396, the capital's administrative districts were drawn and its protective ring of fortress walls and gates completed. Hanseong's fortress walls defined the limits of the city – Mt Bugaksan to the north, Mt Namsan to the south, Mt Naksan to the east, and Mt Inwangsan to the west.

IN CONTEXT

Royal clothing for formal occasions, Joseon Dynasty.

Kings of Joseon

The sweet and sour of the Joseon Dynasty.

King Sejong.

세종대왕

IN CONTEXT

The Jeonju Yi family, the royal family of the kingdom of Joseon, ruled Korea in an unbroken line of 27 kings for five centuries, from 1392 to 1910. Royal dynasties with this kind of staying power have been rare, and it provided Korea with 500 years of – mainly – stability.

Still, some kings were better than others, and none were better than the fourth monarch, King Sejong (reigned 1418-50). Sejong is one of only two Korean kings (the other being the fifth century Goguryeo conqueror King Gwanggaeto) who was honoured with the posthumous title *daewang*, meaning 'the great'. The very model of the Confucian ideal of the enlightened scholar-king, Sejong oversaw a golden age in the development of Korean culture and science. He is most remembered for creating Hangeul, Korea's unique, scientifically based alphabet, but his scholarly and policy interests covered a wide range of subjects, including agriculture, astronomy, military science, medicine, agriculture and even music. Sejong filled his government with men selected on the basis of talent. A typical case was that of Jang Yeong-sil, who became one of the greatest scientists in Korean history, despite his low birth.

The king created a royal research institute, the Hall of Worthies, and filled it with the nation's top scholars.

Not all Joseon kings could live up to this, however. Two were forcefully overthrown and denied the posthumous temple names usually given to monarchs, meaning that historically, they weren't even recognised as kings. The son of the very capable King Seongjong, Yeonsangun (reigned 1494-1506) ruled as a hedonistic despot. Truth be told, he didn't start off so bad, but when he learned that his birth mother was a deposed queen who had been poisoned at the suggestion of court officials, he launched two bloody purges of the court literati, had two of his father's concubines beaten to death and even killed his own grandmother. He had a thousand women brought to the palace as court entertainers and turned the Seonggyungwan, the country's highest centre of Confucian learning, into a pleasure ground. Finally, a group of scholar-officials had had enough and deposed Yeonsangun, replacing him with his half-brother. The ex-king was sent into exile and died within the year.

The other deposed not-king, Gwanghaegun (reigned 1608-23), was, in fact, a pretty decent ruler, contributing much to Korea's reconstruction after the Japanese invasions of 1592-98 as crown prince and king. He also pursued a sensible foreign policy, carefully balancing Korea's relations with Ming and Manchu as the two sides fought for control of China. He fell victim to factionalism at the Korean court, however, and was unceremoniously deposed and sent into exile, where he spent the remaining nearly 20 years of his life. His successor, King Injo, was not as wise, and in pursuing an openly pro-Ming policy, provoked two Manchu invasions that left Korea devastated.

REVOLTS OF THE PRINCES

In 1392, King Taejo named Yi Bang-seok, his second son with his second wife, as his successor. This did not go over well with another son from an earlier wife, the highly capable Yi Bang-won, who had been instrumental in bringing his father to power, but who enjoyed a relationship of mutual hatred with Taejo's prime minister, Jeong Do-jeon. Jeong, the chief ideologue of the new kingdom, who is credited with establishing the neo-Confucian basic framework of Joseon, wanted to build a nation run by ministers and Confucian principles. Bang-won, on the other hand, wanted to build an absolute monarchy. Having convinced Taejo to name Bang-seok as the crown prince, Jeong plotted to do away with the ambitious Bang-won.

Bang-won, however, struck first. In 1398, he and his supporters raided Gyeongbokgung Palace, killing Jeong and his half-brothers, including the crown prince, in an incident known as the First Revolt of the Princes. Disgusted by the spectacle of his own sons killing each other for the throne, King Taejo named his eldest son, Yi Bang-gwa, as the new crown prince and abdicated in 1399. Bang-gwa, now King Jeongjong, moved the capital from Hanyang back to the old Goryeo capital of Gaegyeong, now Gaeseong, in a bid to escape the developing power struggle.

Soon after, however, Bang-won was at it again, this time in a conflict with his elder brother Bang-gan, who – like him – had his eye on the throne. The elder Yi, joined by one of Bang-won's disgruntled generals, revolted in the Second Revolt of the Princes in 1400. Bang-won put this revolt down, executing or exiling those responsible. Fearing his brother, King Jeongjong named Bang-won as his successor and abdicated. Taking the royal name King Taejong, Bang-won moved the capital back to Hanseong in 1405. With unpleasant memories of Gyeongbokgung, the sight of the bloodshed of 1398, and already ill-disposed to the palace, whose construction had been championed by Jeong Do-jeon, Taejong had a new palace, Changdeokgung (*see p44*), constructed between 1405 and 1412.

DEVELOPMENT, WAR AND RECOVERY

Taejong oversaw much development of the capital, including the planning and construction of Jongno ('Bell Street', *see p24* **Avoid-Horse Alley**), Seoul's main east–west thoroughfare, linking the Great East Gate (Dongdaemun, *see p66*) and Gyeongbokgung Palace. The Jongno area developed into a major commercial district, with merchants setting up shop on both sides of the road. In front of Gyeongbokgung Palace, another road linking the palace with the Great South Gate was built, this one lined by major government ministries. Amazingly, this arrangement has changed very little over the intervening 600 years: Jongno is still one of Seoul's major commercial districts (*see p54*), while Sejongno, as the road linking the Great South Gate and Gyeongbokgung is now called, is flanked by the Central Government Complex, the Ministry of Foreign Affairs and other major ministries. North of Jongno, between the Gyeongbokgung and Changdeokgung palaces, Korea's neo-Confucian scholar-official aristocracy, or *yangban*, set up their homes in what is today's Bukchon Hanok Village (*see p46*), while the area south of Jongno was home to lower-level officials and scholars. In the east was the shrine of Jongmyo, which housed the royal ancestral tablets, and in the west was the Sajikdan shrine, where the king held regular rites to honour the gods of the soil and harvest. Access to and from the city was strictly controlled by the city gates, whose opening and closing was accompanied by the ringing of the bell that hung in the Bosingak Belfry on Jongno.

In 1428, Hanseong's population was recorded as 103,328. When those living just outside the city walls are included, the population came to 110,000. For the next 200 or so years, the population would hover around the 200,000 mark.

Events in neighbouring countries, however, would have a devastating impact on the kingdom of Joseon, including its capital. In 1590, the Japanese warlord Hideyoshi Toyotomi consolidated his rule over Japan, bringing peace to those war-town islands.

IN CONTEXT

Not content simply to rule over a unified Japan, he determined he should conquer China as well. Hideyoshi requested that Joseon help Japan in its invasion of China; when Korea refused, the Japanese invaded on 25 May 1592. Landing a massive invasion force on the southern coast at what is today Busan, the Japanese launched a multipronged offensive up the Korean Peninsula. Greatly outnumbering the Korean defenders and armed with the arquebus, which had been introduced to Japan by the Portuguese, the Japanese were practically unstoppable. On 8 June, the invaders crushed a Korean army on the plains of Chungju, and two days later they took the Joseon capital of Hanseong. King Seonjo fled with his family to the north (on farm animals, no less, the royal stables having been looted), and the city's slave population burnt the slave registries and the royal palaces before the Japanese could enter the city.

The Japanese continued their race up the peninsula, reaching the border with China. In the waters off Korea, however, the brilliant Korean admiral Yi Sun-sin defeated the Japanese navy in a series of battles, playing havoc with Japanese logistics. Deprived of supplies and reinforcements, the Japanese offensive stalled. The Chinese then intervened on the side of their Korean allies, and the combined Korean-Chinese force went on the offensive, driving the Japanese back to a line just a few miles north of Hanseong before stalling itself. Stalemated, the two sides began negotiations (interestingly, an almost identical situation would play itself out several centuries later during the Korean War). These negotiations failed to produce a peace, however, and the Japanese launched a second invasion. Again, Admiral Yi Sun-sin's command of the seas doomed the Japanese effort, and with the death of Japanese leader Hideyoshi Toyotomi in 1598, the Japanese withdrew from Korea for good. Seven years of fighting left the Korean Peninsula in smoking ruins, however, with the countryside suffering particularly serious deprivations. Many skilled artisans and technicians were captured and taken back to Japan, providing a boost to Japanese civilisation but depriving Korea of their services. In Seoul, most of the government buildings, including the royal palaces and shrines, were burned to the ground, although, fortunately, the memorial tablets of the Joseon kings had been removed from Jongmyo shrine before the fall of the city and safely hidden from the Japanese.

Before Hanseong – and Korea as a whole – could completely recover, the Koreans were faced with another invasion, this time from the north. In 1627, the civil war in China between the Ming Dynasty and the Manchu spilled over into Korea, when a Manchu army invaded Korea with the goal of ending Korean support for the Ming, who had come to Korea's aid during the Japanese invasions of 1592-98. After a quick and relatively painless campaign, the two sides signed a treaty to end the war, but in 1636 the Manchus invaded again, this time demanding Korea submit as a vassal to the Manchus' newly founded Qing Dynasty. Led by the Manchu prince Dodo, the Qing force – composed of Manchu, Mongol and Chinese troops – drove straight to the capital of Hanseong. The Joseon king, Injo, fled to Namhansanseong, a mountaintop fortress south of the Hangang River. The Qing took the capital and laid siege to Namhansanseong. After a 45-day siege, King Injo surrendered and, in humiliating fashion, was forced to kowtow to the Qing emperor Hong Taiji, indicating that Joseon was now a Qing vassal. Before Injo had surrendered, however, the Qing force laid waste to large tracts of northern and southern Korea; in Hanseong, the predominantly Mongol occupation force raped, burned and pillaged as they liked. For the second time in less than 50 years, the country was in ruins, and its capital city devastated.

For the next two centuries, however, Korea enjoyed relative peace. Under the reigns of the highly capable monarchs King Yeongjo (reigned 1724-76) and King Jeongjo (reigned 1776-1800), Korea enjoyed a Renaissance of culture, science and learning. Led by brilliant scholars like Jeong Yak-yong, the *silhak* ('practical learning') movement strove to redirect neo-Confucianism towards social, economic and political concerns. Jeongjo even entertained the idea of moving the capital from Hanseong to an exceptionally designed fortress town south of the Hangang River. This move

IN CONTEXT

'Japan would rule Korea for 35 years, from 1910 to 1945, when Japan was defeated by the Allies in World War II.'

never took place, but the impressive fortress in Suwon (*see p211*), which is now a UNESCO World Heritage Site, is still in good repair and a popular tourist destination.

END OF A DYNASTY AND THE RISE OF MODERN SEOUL

Despite the best efforts of kings like Yeongjo, factionalism – long a characteristic of Korean politics – continued to plague the royal government, depriving the country of the talent needed to deal with what was becoming an increasingly dangerous world. In 1863, the young Gojong took the throne, but authority would remain firmly in the hands of his father, the powerful prince-regent Yi Ha-eung, better known by his formal name and title, Heungseon Daewongun. An arch-conservative, the Daewongun pursued a policy of strict isolationism internationally, and a policy of persecuting Korea's growing Catholic community domestically. This latter policy led to a punitive expedition by the French in 1866 following the execution of nine French missionary priests. Korean rejections of US trade demands also led to a brief clash with US troops in 1871. These clashes, combined with growing European imperialism in China, further convinced the Daewongun of the need to avoid interaction with the West.

In Hanseong, the Daewongun sought to reinforce royal authority through an ambitious building programme. Most notably, he ordered the reconstruction of the Gyeongbokgung Palace, which had been laying in ruins since the Japanese invasions of 1592-98. A massive complex of over 300 buildings was constructed, complete with a majestic throne hall and serene pleasure ponds. Located right in the heart of the capital for all to see, it was intended as a symbol of royal power and national pride. In 1873, Gojong assumed royal authority for himself, and the Daewongun retired to the background, where he remained an influential figure.

The royal dynasty was not much longer for this world, however. Japan, in the midst of its dramatic modernisation and westernisation following the Meiji Restoration, employed western-style gunboat diplomacy to open up Korea to trade in 1876. The Japanese were soon followed by the Americans, British, French, Russians and other western powers that rushed to sign their own trade and diplomatic relations pacts with the Joseon kingdom. The West also sent Christian missionaries to Korea, where they began to open schools, hospitals and, of course, churches. In the Jeongdong district, next to the Deoksugung Palace, westerners began erecting European-style embassies, offices, schools and churches.

Foreign influences in Korea continued to grow, and more ominously, clash. When China dispatched troops to Korea to help the royal government put down a peasant revolt in the Korean south-west in 1894, the Japanese responded by sending their own troops to Korea, who seized the Gyeongbokgung and installed a pro-Japanese government. This, in turn, sparked the First Sino-Japanese War, which ended the following year with China's resounding defeat and the severing of Korea's long-standing vassal relationship with China.

With the help of foreign advisors, the Joseon kingdom undertook a modernisation programme in an effort to hold off the barbarians (or imperialists) at the gate. The previously medieval city of Hanseong was transformed into a semi-modern metropolis with running water, electricity, trams, telephones, modern schools and western-style hospitals. In 1899, the country's first railway began service, linking Hanseong with the West Sea port of Jemulpo (today's Incheon). The following year, the first bridge over the

IN CONTEXT

Hangang was completed, easing access to the capital from the southern provinces. In 1905, service began on the newly completed rail line linking Hanseong and the southern port of Busan. Even the royal palaces began to modernise: Edison General Electric of the United States installed electric lighting at Gyeongbokgung Palace in 1887, and large, western-style buildings were added to Deoksugung Palace (*see p60*). Much of this new infrastructure was built by foreigners: the American duo of Henry Collbran and Harry R Bostwick, for instance, won concessions to build Hanseong's tram system, the city's first commercial electricity system, the city waterworks and the railway to Jemulpo.

Alas, it was all too little, too late. Imperial interest in Korea grew, with the Russians and Japanese taking a particularly keen interest. Weary of Japan's growing influence, Emperor Gojong's powerful and politically wily wife, Myeongseong, sought Russian support to counterbalance Tokyo. The Japanese responded by having Myeongseong assassinated at Gyeongbokgung Palace in October of 1885. Fearful for his own life, Emperor Gojong fled to the Russian Embassy, where he would stay for a full year before relocating to Deoksugung Palace, under the watchful eye of the western embassies. In 1897, Gojong declared that he had elevated the status of his kingdom to that of an empire, but the Daehan Empire, as it was called, could not hold off the

IN CONTEXT

Avoid-Horse Alley

A practical solution to the problems of rigid class stratification.

Jongno ('Bell Street', *see p54*) might have been – and still is – Seoul's major east–west thoroughfare, but in the old days, walking along it could prove something of a pain, at least if you were a commoner. In the socially stratified society of Joseon Korea, commoners were required to prostrate themselves before members of the *yangban* scholar-elite. On a busy street such as Jongno, which passed the royal palaces, *yangban* were moving along all the time, either on horseback or by sedan chair. Any commoners around had to bow head-to-dirt to each and every one. Not only was this tedious and tiring, but to the busy merchants who set up shop along the road, it could prove financially deleterious.

The residents of the neighbourhood came up with a novel solution, however. They created narrow alleyways running parallel to Jongno that allowed commoners to travel to their destination without passing a single aristocrat. Over time, restaurants and taverns congregated in the alleyways, known as Pimatgol ('Avoid-Horse Alley'), catering to the local denizens: those serving *makgeolli* (rice wine), broiled fish and *bindaeddeok* (mung bean pancakes) were particular favourites.

As Korea modernised in the 20th century, commoners were no longer required to bow before grandees along Jongno, but the Pimatgol remained popular as an entertainment area. Its eateries and pubs dished out cheap but delicious food and drink, providing much-needed comfort to an urban population worked to the bone by Korea's post-Korean War development-focused dictators. They also provided a good place to wait out the midnight to 4am curfew that was enforced in Seoul from 1955 to 1982.

However, Seoul's local government viewed the narrow streets as ripe for redevelopment and, in 2009, much of the Pimatgol was demolished to make way for new skyscrapers, amid much controversy. Some of the restaurants have moved into the new buildings erected in the area. But to many, the clean, modern alleys that used to be Pimatgol lack the warmth and charm that made the area such a special place in the past.

real empires chomping at the bit. Japanese and Russian ambitions finally came to a head in February 1904, when the Japanese launched a surprise attack on the Russian Far East Fleet at Port Arthur, marking the start of the Russo-Japanese War. To the world's surprise, the Japanese trounced the Russians, especially at sea. When the war ended in September the following year, Japan was the undisputed master of Korea and the most powerful nation in the Far East. In 1905, Japan strong-armed Korea to sign the Eulsa Treaty, turning it into a Japanese protectorate, and five years later, Japan delivered the *coup de grâce* when it annexed Korea outright in 1910.

SEOUL UNDER THE JAPANESE
Japan would rule Korea for 35 years – from 1910 to 1945, when Japan was defeated by the Allies in World War II. The colonial era was a complex period in Korean history: a good deal of modernisation took place under Japanese rule, but Japan's deprivation of Korean sovereignty, the high-handedness of its rule and its attempts to wipe out an independent Korean cultural identity left feelings of bitterness and resentment that still plague Korea–Japan relations to this day. Colonial rule also exasperated social tensions within Korea itself, tensions that, after Korea regained its independence, developed into outright hostility, national division and war.

The Japanese renamed Korea's cities with Japanese names: Hanseong, now the colonial capital, was rechristened Keijo. Large areas outside of the old city walls, such as the Yongsan district, were incorporated into the city, which administratively now stretched to the north bank of the Hangang River. An influx of new residents and Japanese settlers boosted the population, from just 250,000 in 1905 to 730,000 by 1936. The downtown districts of Jongno, Taepyeongno and Myeongdong was transformed into a bustling commercial district, while northern areas of the city like Cheongnyangni were urbanised, thanks to the extension of the tram service. The Japanese built roads, hotels, cinemas, department stores, banks and other symbols of modernity and Japanese imperial might: the imposing neo-Baroque dome of Seoul Station is a good example of this urban design philosophy. On the northern slopes of Mt Namsan, the Yongsan district and other parts of the city, Japanese settlers established residential districts of their own, full of wooden Japanese homes similar to those found in cities such as Tokyo or Osaka. In what is now the Daehangno area, the colonial authorities built a fully fledged university, one of the most prestigious in the Japanese Empire.

To build their colonial capital, however, the Japanese destroyed much of the city's cultural and architectural heritage. The old city walls, including the Great West Gate, were demolished to make way for tram tracks. Entire neighbourhoods of stately Korean-style homes were demolished. On Mt Namsan, the Japanese built a massive Shinto shrine – to Koreans, an insulting symbol of their cultural subjugation. Even the old royal palaces, the scene of so much history during the 500 years of the Joseon kingdom, were mutilated: one was completely dismantled, while the others were greatly reduced in scale. Gyeongbokgung, the oldest and largest of the palaces, was reduced from 300 buildings to just ten, and in front of it, the Japanese built the headquarters of the colonial Government-General, completely blocking the view of the palace from downtown. Adding insult to insult, the massive neo-classical building was constructed in the shape of the Chinese character for Japan. Between Changdeokgung and the royal shrine of Jongmyo, the Japanese built a road, severing the link between the Korean royal family and their ancestors.

Japanese colonial rule was never pleasant, but as Japan's wars in China worsened and militarists seized greater control over Japan itself, it grew even worse. Korean labour and resources were mobilised for Japan's wars: the most notorious example of this was the mobilisation of Korean women to serve as so-called 'comfort women', treated as sex slaves by the Japanese military. Within Korea, the Japanese enforced a policy of Japanification that some have called cultural genocide: discouraging the use

IN CONTEXT

of the Korean language, encouraging Koreans to take Japanese names, forcing Koreans to pray at Shinto shrines and other policies designed to wipe out Korean national identity. These policies would only come to an end with Japan's defeat in the Pacific War in 1945.

KOREAN WAR, RECONSTRUCTION AND MODERN SEOUL

The end of Japanese colonial rule allowed Korea to regain its independence, but the euphoria would not last very long. The United States and the Soviet Union quickly moved into the peninsula, dividing the nation into two separate zones of occupation, with the Americans in the south and the Soviets in the north. The old royal and colonial capital, now renamed for the last time as Seoul, found itself in the American zone of occupation. As the Cold War set in, these zones of occupation grew permanent, leading to the declaration in 1948 of the pro-western and capitalist Republic of Korea (aka South Korea) in the southern half of the country and the pro-Soviet and communist Democratic People's Republic of Korea (aka North Korea) in the northern half. The South was immediately plagued by political instability, while the North armed itself to the teeth with Soviet weaponry. On 25 June 1950, the mutual hostility between the two states turned to open warfare when North Korea launched a surprise invasion of South Korea.

The Korean War lasted for three years, during which time Seoul changed hands no fewer than four times. By the time the war ended, much of the city was flattened and its infrastructure was in ruins. Aggravating an already desperate situation was the presence of countless refugees from other parts of Korea, swelling Seoul's population to 2.5 million. By the late 1950s, the city was back on its feet, more or less, but Seoul, and Korea as a whole, still faced crippling poverty and housing shortages; the country relied largely on international aid, particularly from its wartime ally and Cold War benefactor, the United States.

In 1961, military leaders led by Lt Gen Park Chung-hee overthrew an elected but unstable government and established a junta of their own. Park, who in 1963 was elected president as a civilian, would rule the country for 18 years. The authoritarian Park sought legitimacy by promoting economic development, and this he did with an almost single-minded focus by promoting exports, first of labour-intensive, light industrial products and later capital-intensive heavy industrial goods. Park was assassinated in 1979, but his successors, both military dictators and civilian presidents after Korea became a multi-party democracy in 1987, largely continued his export-led growth strategy. The results were dramatic. In 1961, Korea's GNP per capita was just US$85. By 1979, it was US$1,500, and by 1996, it was over US$11,000. In 1988, Korea had its big 'coming-out' party when Seoul hosted the Summer Olympic Games.

The impact this development had on Seoul's skyline has been nothing short of dramatic. If the city was more or less a bombed-out refugee camp in 1953, by the 1990s, it was a bustling metropolis of concrete, glass and steel. Initial developments focused on the all-important housing problem. Large concrete apartment complexes were built throughout the city and in suburban areas – they weren't pretty, but they got the job done. Roads were paved, the old tram system abandoned and an ambitious subway system was started in 1974. The Cheonggyecheon Stream, which had become an open sewer lined by shanty towns, was paved over and turned into an elevated roadway. A new national system of highways linked Seoul with other cities throughout the country, bringing more wealth and people to the capital. Most dramatically, the farmland south of the Hangang was incorporated into the city and turned into a wealthy commercial and residential hub. The Hangang, once a meandering river with sandy banks, was deepened and lined with concrete embankments. One of the Hangang's islands, Yeouido (*see pp78-80*), was transformed from a flood-prone sandbar into Seoul's Manhattan, home to towering skyscrapers, financial houses and media companies.

Miracle on the Hangang

From farmland to gold mine in 40 years.

To get a real sense of the so-called Miracle on the Hangang, Korea's economic miracle of the 1960s, '70s and '80s, head south of the Hangang to the neighbourhood now referred to as Gangnam (literally 'South of the River').

Prior to the 1960s, Seoul's confines ended at the north bank of the Hangang river. Most of the south bank was composed of farmland, with the exception of Yeongdeungpo, an industrial neighbourhood in the south-west. In 1963, however, large swathes of the south bank were incorporated into Seoul, and the government and construction companies embarked on the herculean task of transforming rice paddies into a new residential and commercial district to accommodate the city's burgeoning population. The Gangnam Development Program called for the area to be developed in a planned, organised fashion. The opening of the Hannam Bridge in 1969 and the Seoul–Busan Highway in 1970 added further impetus to this development.

To encourage the development of the area, Seoul's government slapped on construction restrictions in areas north of the river. Entertainment establishments such as bars and nightclubs were quick to move to the south, which was free from the taxes and regulations found north of the river. The government moved government offices to the area, too, and built apartments to house city workers. And prestigious academic institutions, including Seoul's top high schools, moved their premises here, taking advantage of the plentiful land.

By the 1980s, the Gangnam district had become *the* place to live in Seoul. Property prices skyrocketed, and speculators had a field day: in 1979, land prices in the ritzy Gangnam neighbourhood of Apgujeongdong were 900 times what they were in 1963. Gangnam had become a place where fortunes were made.

Today, Gangnam is a bustling district of gleaming skyscrapers, luxury apartments, posh shops and prestigious schools. Many of the biggest names in Korean business, including Samsung, have located their headquarters in the district too. To Koreans, Gangnam has become virtually synonymous with wealth, luxury and privilege, not bad for a place populated by ox-drawn ploughs just 40 years ago.

Architecture

The city's buildings tell its story.

TEXT: ROBERT KOEHLER

At first glance, Seoul doesn't appear to be a place of architectural wonder. And to be fair to critics, this is because much of the city does, in fact, leave something to be desired aesthetically. History has not been particularly kind to Seoul's architectural heritage, as first the Japanese imperialists, then the Korean War, and finally post-war urban planning destroyed many of the city's historic buildings and neighbourhoods. In the hardscrabble years following the Korean War, when Seoul had more people than homes to house them, architectural priorities leaned heavily towards the utilitarian; beauty came in a distant second. The result was a city dominated by massive complexes of concrete apartments that, while much more practical than the white elephant monuments erected by many post-colonial states, lent the cityscape a dreary monotony.

Look beneath the concrete, glass and steel, however, and you'll find there's much more than first impressions might indicate. While much of Seoul's architectural heritage has been lost, a lot remains.

A TRANSFORMING CITYSCAPE

In the old downtown area, four grand royal palaces and their lovely gardens stand testament to the beauty of old Korea. Near the palaces, alleyways lined by stately Korean traditional homes seem to resist the march of time, while in the mountains that embrace the city, the medieval city walls stand guard just as they have since the 14th century. Japanese and western missionaries left architectural legacies of their own, and even after the Korean War, a number of local architects managed to transcend utilitarianism to create true works of art that embraced both Korean tradition and the international architectural trends of their era.

It cannot be stressed enough, however, that Seoul's cityscape is transforming by the day. While past administrators emphasised function over form, the leaders of today's Seoul are vigorously pursuing both, as evidenced by the city's selection as the World Design Capital of 2010. Throughout the city, a number of ambitious architectural projects by both internationally renowned and prominent local designers are transforming once gritty and grey neighbourhoods in imaginative and often dazzling ways.

HANYANG, CAPITAL OF JOSEON

People have been living in the Seoul area since the prehistoric era, but the city was truly born in 1394, when the site that is now Seoul was selected as the capital of the newly founded dynasty of Joseon. Work began almost immediately on the new capital, which the dynasty's Confucian rulers based on the Chinese imperial grid system. A palace was built in the north, a shrine to the harvest in the west, and a royal ancestral shrine in the east. Around the capital, a ring of fortress walls and gates was constructed. Incredibly, Seoul's old downtown area remains largely true to the original grid to this day.

The most notable examples of Joseon-era architecture are the royal palaces, of which there are four remaining in downtown Seoul (a fifth, the Gyeonghuigung, is largely a recent reconstruction, the original having been almost completely destroyed during the Japanese colonial era). The largest of these, the **Gyeongbokgung** (*see p45*), is also the oldest, as it was founded right at the start of the Joseon Dynasty. Its history is also typical of the country's architecture: first built in 1394, it – like many of Korea's historic buildings – was burnt to the ground during the Japanese invasion of 1592-98, rebuilt again in the mid-19th century, and largely dismantled by the Japanese during their colonial rule of Korea from 1910 to 1945. Restoration work has been ongoing ever since. Like the Forbidden City in Beijing, it was a city unto itself, a massive complex of halls, gates, pavilions and pleasure gardens, surrounded by walls through which admission was strictly regulated. The palace makes masterful use of its surroundings, especially the mountains that form its backdrop, a harmony best seen in two pleasure pavilions, the massive two-storey Gyeonghuiru and the picturesque Hyangwonjeong.

Joseon Dynasty architecture can be seen at its most sublime at **Changdeokgung** (*see p44*), the longest serving of the royal palaces and a UNESCO World Heritage Site. The palace grounds themselves demonstrate all the typical traits of Korean traditional architecture, such as attention to surroundings and careful consideration of feng shui. The real treasure is its enchanting rear garden, the Huwon, widely regarded as the most outstanding piece of Korean traditional gardening in the country. Similar to English gardens, Korean gardens seek to make maximum use of the existing terrain with a minimum amount of human input to produce landscapes of simple, unforced beauty. Artifice such as pleasure pavilions enhance the surroundings, not dominate them. The Buyeongji Pond, in the heart of the Huwon, demonstrates this perfectly. The square-shaped pond with a single round island in the centre also serves as an architectural expression of the Korean cosmology, which pictured the earth as square and the heavens as a circle. Also in the Huwon is the Yeongyeongdang, a residential complex built in the rustic fashion of a country gentry's home, with its unpainted wooden surfaces and simple buildings tied together by courtyards.

IN CONTEXT

'Jongmyo Shrine was one of the first buildings constructed by the highly Confucian leaders of the Joseon Dynasty.'

Changgyeonggung (*see p45*) is unique in that – unlike the other palaces, which face south – it faces east. It is home to some splendid pieces of Joseon Dynasty architecture, including a stone bridge from 1483 and a front gate and main hall from 1616, which are among the oldest of Seoul's wooden palace buildings. Visitors may be surprised to find in its rear garden a Victorian glasshouse, built in 1907 by a French company and designed by a Japanese architect.

The smallest of Seoul's palaces, the **Deoksugung** (*see p60*), is also one of the most interesting, as it brings together both Korean traditional architecture from the 19th-century and western-style architecture from early years of the 20th century. Of particular note here is the quirky Jeonggwanheon Pavilion, a quirky Romanesque pavilion with Korean traditional motifs built in 1900 by a Russian architect as a place for King Gojong to enjoy the then-exotic drink of coffee, and the imposing neo-classical Seokjojeon Hall, designed by a British architect as King Gojong's living quarters and completed in 1910.

Another representative piece of Joseon Dynasty architecture can be seen at **Jongmyo Shrine** (*see p56*), which like Changdeokgung Palace, has been designated a UNESCO World Heritage Site. The place of interment for the royal memorial tablets, the shrine was one of the first buildings constructed by the highly Confucian leaders of the Joseon Dynasty. The original shrine was burnt down during the Japanese invasions of 1592-98 (the tablets, however, were saved); what you see today dates from 1601. It contains the memorial tablets of 19 kings and 30 queens, and is a model of Confucian simplicity and modesty. The main hall, the Jeongjeon, is one of the longest wooden buildings in East Asia. The shrine grounds are also thickly forested.

Like most Korean cities of the Joseon Dynasty, Seoul was a walled city. About 18 kilometres (11 miles) of walls used to surround the capital; about ten kilometres of the old city walls still remain, largely in the mountains that surround the downtown area, where the walls remained safe from urban planners. More impressive are the imposing city gates, of which three still remain. The most spectacular of these was the southern gate, known as both Sungnyemun and Namdaemun; its wooden superstructure was the oldest wooden structure in Seoul before being tragically burnt down in an arson attack in 2008. The eastern gate, known as Heunginjimun or **Dongdaemun** (*see p66*), survives in its 1869 incarnation, crowned by a two-storey wooden superstructure built in the ornate style of the late Joseon Dynasty. A third, simpler gate, the northern portal of **Sukjeongmun**, is located on the slopes of Mt Bugaksan. Several minor gates still exist, too, including the picturesque **Changuimun**, at the entrance of the Buamdong neighbourhood (*see p50*).

More examples of Joseon Dynasty architecture can be found elsewhere in Seoul. Near the touristy Insadong neighbourhood is the **Unhyeongung 'Palace'** (*see p54*), which was actually the estate of the powerful late-19th-century regent, Heungseon Daewongun. With its hidden courtyards, simple and unpainted wooden halls and division into men's and women's quarters, it is typical of aristocratic residential architecture of the late Joseon Dynasty. In the garden of the Westin Chosun Hotel (*see p93*) is another splendid piece of late Joseon architecture, the **Wongudan Altar**. Built in 1897, the triple-gabled hall is the Korean equivalent of the famous Temple of Heaven in Beijing, upon which it may have been modelled.

IN CONTEXT

Gyeongbokgung. *See p29.*

FOREIGN INFLUENCES

At the end of the 19th century, Korea opened up to the outside world, and in came the Japanese and western diplomats, missionaries and traders, all bringing their distinctive architectural styles. In the old legation quarter of Jeongdong, near Deoksugung Palace, this architectural legacy is very much in evidence. The **Chungdong First Methodist Church** (1897) is a pretty red-brick Victorian chapel built by American missionaries. The same missionaries also built nearby **Pai Chai Academy** (1916), Korea's first modern secondary school: its keystones and dormer windows proved a model for mission school construction in Korea. Also built of red brick, the **Jungmyeongjeon Hall** (1896) was constructed by a Russian engineer as a library for King Gojong. With its verandas and balustrades, it's typical of western architecture in Asian 'treaty ports'. The 'crown jewel' of the Jeongdong district, however, is the lovely **Seoul Anglican Cathedral** (1926). Designed by British architect Arthur Dixon, the church – built in the shape of a Latin cross – is a Romanesque masterpiece that astutely incorporates indigenous Korean elements and harmonises perfectly with the nearby Deoksugung Palace. Another beautiful work is the neo-classical **Salvation Army Central Hall** (1928), modelled on London's Clapton Congress Hall. Although it's not open to the public, the **British ambassador's residence** (1891) – formerly the British consulate – is a lovely Georgian structure built in a style similar to British legations throughout the Far East.

The French contribution to Korean architecture can be seen primarily in Catholic churches. The oldest western-style one in Seoul is **Yakhyeon Catholic Church** (1892), near Seoul Station. Its mixture of Romanesque and Gothic elements served as a model for Catholic churches across Korea. Far more impressive, however, is the landmark **Myeongdong Cathedral** (1898; *see p58*) in the heart of Seoul's commercial Myeongdong district; the towering Gothic edifice, replete with vaulted ceiling, dominated its surroundings when it was first built. Surrounding the cathedral are several other buildings of note, including the old **Bishop's residence** (1890), Korea's oldest existent western-style building. While not nearly as big as Myeongdong Cathedral, the old **Yongsan Seminary** (1892) and its small chapel (1901), now a girls' school in the Yongsan-gu district, reveal a beautiful simplicity and masterful use of the sloping terrain.

Yonsei University and **Ewha Womans University** (*see p72*), founded by American missionaries, are fine examples of Tudor Gothic architecture. Yonsei's old campus was designed in the 1920s by Henry Killiam Murphy, an American architect better known for his work for Chiang Kai-shek in China. Ewha Womans University's old main hall (1935), was designed by William Merrell Vories, an expatriate American in Japan. Its small prayer room on the third floor, with its sublime Gothic roof, is a hidden gem.

The Japanese ruled Korea from 1910 to 1935, so unsurprisingly, it is they who left behind the biggest architectural legacy from that period, both in the positive and negative sense. In the name of modernisation and urban planning, they levelled much of Seoul, destroying much of Korea's cultural and architectural heritage in the process. Not even the royal palaces were safe: one was completely destroyed to make way for a school, while the others were all greatly reduced in size. Once a complex of 330 buildings, Gyeongbokgung was reduced to just ten, the view of which was blocked by a grand colonial edifice, since demolished, that served as the office of the Government-General.

Still, Seoul did modernise substantially under the Japanese, and this can be seen in the architecture they left behind, which exhibits an eclectic mix of European styles. The old **Daehan Hospital** (1907) near Daehangno, built by the Japanese for the Korean royal government at a time of great Japanese influence, is a beautiful neo-Baroque building with an imposing clocktower. In Myeongdong, which the Japanese developed as a commercial district (and are still shopping in today), we can find many examples of Japanese colonial architecture, including the French château-style old **Bank of**

Bukchon Hanok Village.

'Throughout Seoul, huge concrete apartment complexes were built to house the city's burgeoning population.'

Korea headquarters (1912), designed by renowned Meiji architect Tatsuno Kingo; the neo-classical **Korea First Bank** (1935); the Renaissance-style former Mitsukoshi Department Store (1930), now the **Shinsegae Department Store** (*see p142*); and the Chicago School-style **KEPCO Building** (1928). **Seoul City Hall** (1926), currently undergoing a major renovation, mixes Renaissance and art deco elements, while the towering **Cheondogyo Central Temple** (1921) near Insadong, the headquarters of the Korean religion of Cheondogyo, was built in Vienna Secession style by Japanese colonial architect Nakamura Yoshihei. The ornate art nouveau interior of the latter is worth seeing, as the ceiling above the spacious meeting hall is held up without a single pillar. The most impressive colonial edifice, however, is probably old **Seoul Station** (1925), a Palladian structure crowned by a large Byzantine dome. With the construction of a larger, newer station, the old building is now being renovated for use as an arts centre.

While foreigners built many of Seoul's landmarks during this time, Korean architects, too, began learning western architecture. The Tudor Gothic campus of **Korea University** (1934) was designed by Korean architect Park Dong-jin, while the old main hall of **Seoul National University** (1931), a modernist structure with hints of Frank Lloyd Wright, was designed by Korean architecture pioneer Park Gil-ryong. Nor did Korean traditional architecture die: in the neighbourhood between the Gyeongbokgung and Changdeokgung palaces, Seoul's *nouveaux riches* began building, from the 1920s, Korean *hanok* homes not entirely unlike the grander estates found in the countryside, but with shorter eaves and a more fastidious use of space to adapt to urban conditions. When seen from above, the result – **Bukchon Hanok Village** (*see p46*) – looks like a sea of tiled roofs, interrupted only by the empty spaces of each home's inner courtyard.

As Japan's wars in China and the Pacific worsened and the grip of the Japanese military grew stronger both in Japan and in Korea, architectural trends took a turn towards the spartan. The campus of **Seoul Tech** (1941), built by the Japanese as an arms research facility on the outskirts of town, shows the dehumanising scale and rationalism of the contemporary architecture of Nazi Germany and Fascist Italy.

WAR, RECOVERY AND DEVELOPMENT

Korea's liberation from Japanese colonial rule in 1945 was followed by national division and the Korean War. During the war, Seoul changed hands no fewer than four times. When the guns finally fell silent, what emerged was a battered city, largely flattened, flooded by refugees and with few resources to rebuild.

By the late 1950s, however, the city managed to get back on its feet, and with the coming to power in 1961 of the military dictator Park Chung-hee, Korea began its now fabled forced-march of economic development. National priorities focused on the practical, especially housing. Throughout Seoul, huge concrete apartment complexes were built to house the city's burgeoning population. Built quickly and cheaply, they were functional, but certainly not pretty. Public buildings, too, were built as spiritless, utilitarian boxes. Older neighbourhoods were sometimes flattened to make way for this new construction.

The architectural record from this period is not entirely grim, however. Ambitious local architects strove to make the most of the limited resources to create buildings that inspired. The two greatest architects of this period were Kim Swoo-geun (1931-86) and Kim Chung-up (1922-88). Japanese-trained, Kim Swoo-geun was influenced by Le Corbusier and Tange Kenzo, as can be seen in the exposed concrete surfaces of the **Walkerhill Hilltop Bar** (1961), and the **Freedom Center** (1963) on Mt Namsan. Later, however, he developed his own architectural language, one best seen in his masterpiece, the stunning **Kyungdong Presbyterian Church** (1980) in Jangchungdong. The church, built of roughly cut red brick, in the shape of hands put together in prayer, is entered through the back via a flight of meditative steps; inside, the exposed concrete interior recalls the early Christian catacombs. Kim also designed **Seoul Olympic Stadium** (1984; *see p76*), which was built to resemble the graceful lines of Korean porcelain. Kim Chung-up, a student of Le Corbusier, left to Seoul a number of very Corbu-esque structures, including the very under-appreciated former **Seo Gynecology Clinic** (1967), the **Peace Gate** of the Olympic Park (1988) and his masterpiece, the **French Embassy** (1961). Kim also brought the International Style to Seoul when he designed the **Samil Building** (1970), a 31-storey smoked glass skyscraper that was the tallest building in Seoul when it was built (for a review of the buffet restaurant now sitting pretty on its top level, *see p117*).

Other landmarks from Seoul's development years include the beautiful **Hyehwadong Catholic Church** (1960), **Jeoldusan Martyrs' Shrine** (1967; *see p70*) and the **National Theater of Korea** (1973; *see p197*), all designed by architect Lee Hee-tae; the landmark **Sejong Center for the Performing Arts** (1978; *see p198*), which fuses Korean and western architectural elements; **Seoul Arts Center** (1993), which reinterprets Korean traditional motifs in concrete using the latest western architectural techniques; and, of course, the golden tower of Skidmore, Owings and Merrill's landmark **63 City** (1985; see *p79*), briefly the tallest building in Asia when it was first constructed.

THE CONTEMPORARY CITY

Part of this effort has included awarding ambitious redevelopment projects to big-name international architects. In the gritty Dongdaemun district, the historic Dongdaemun Stadium was levelled to make way for the **Dongdaemun Design Plaza & Park** (2011; *see p66*), an entrancing landscape of curving concrete and green gardens created by Pritzker-winning British architect Zaha Hadid. In the likewise gritty Yongsan district, American architect Daniel Libeskind has been selected to redevelop the neighbourhood into an international business district capped by a 150-storey tower. In the multicultural neighborhood of Itaewon, the **Leeum Museum of Art** (2004; *see p82*) features work by three of the world's top architects, Mario Botta, Jean Nouvel, and Rem Koolhaas. Rafael Viñoly was brought in to design the landmark steel-and-glass **Jongno Tower** (1999; *see p55*), and the stately old stone buildings of **Ewha Womans University** have been joined by French architect Dominique Perrault's sunken campus complex of glass and steel (2008; *see p73*).

Even more interesting have been the contributions of local Korean architects. In 2002, SeoAhn Total Landscape put the final touches to **Seonyudo Park** (p000), a lush botanical garden built amid the remains of a disused water treatment plant. Also on the Hangang River, Haean Architecture's **Floating Islands** (2011) is a picturesque complex of three interconnected structures built upon floating bases anchored to the bottom of the river. In 2004, Choi Moon-gyu and Gabriel Kroiz teamed up to create Insadong's **Ssamziegil** (*see p155*), a youthful four-storey complex of shops, galleries and workshops that recalls a hillside road . Cho Minsuk of Mass Studies, a rising star in the world of architecture, has been doing some intriguing work, including the **Ann Demeulemeester** shop (2007; *see p146*) near Dosan Park, immediately recognized by its living façade of vegetation. Also south of the river is Kim In-cheurl's unusual **Urban Hive** (2009), an office tower supported by its concrete, honeycomb exterior, which allows for greater use of interior space.

Seoul Today

Korea looking out, and the world looking in.

TEXT: OLIVER DUKE & DARCY PACQUET

Seoul is one of the world's largest cities. Its positives are manifold, including super-friendly locals, a jaw-droppingly good dining scene, a public transport network among the best on earth, and a near-zero crime rate. It has hosted the Olympic Games, the World Cup and a G20 Summit. Yet for all its size, wealth, importance and uniqueness, Seoul – and, indeed, Korea as a whole – remains a surprisingly unknown quantity on the international scene. Several factors are behind this, including the pariah-state neighbour to the north, the rampant industrialisation that followed the devastating war with that neighbour, and the equally rampant westernisation that accompanied such progress. All served to dilute Korea's unique identity, but things are turning around, and fast.

OPENING UP

The Korea of today could be said to have begun in 1981, when Seoul was awarded the 1988 Olympics. The country was, at that time, comparable to North Korea in GDP-per-head terms, and essentially a dictatorship – almost unbelievably, the Olympics were handed to Seoul just 16 months after a massacre of civilians in the south-west of the country. During Olympic preparations the world belatedly started to pay attention to this neglected peninsula, and applied a little diplomatic pressure; the Games were opened by Roh Tae-woo, the country's first freely elected president just a few months beforehand.

Roh was eventually succeeded by Kim Dae-jung, who had been sentenced to death in 1980 for his role in the uprising that led to the aforementioned massacre. Kim inaugurated the Sunshine Policy of rapprochement with North Korea, and in 2000 held a historic summit in Pyongyang, an event for which Kim was awarded the Nobel Peace Prize. Trade began to flow across the border, though it quickly became evident that much of the money heading to the North was being misused – and that the 2000 peace summit had been 'bought' for hundreds of millions of dollars. Kim's successor, Roh Moo-hyun, continued to pursue the Sunshine Policy, but questions were raised by the North's nuclear tests of 2006; on the election of Lee Myung Bak in 2008, the policy was discontinued, and cross-border relations became ever more frosty. The year 2010 saw the sinking of a military frigate, an act denied by, but attributed to, the North, and a rather more blatant North Korean attack on Yeonpyeongdo, an island west of Seoul. For more on North Korean relations, *see p204* **North Korea: Against the Odds**.

VOYAGE OF SELF-DISCOVERY

From the top down, Korea has, for decades, kowtowed to western principles and styles, specifically those of the USA. The proportion of Seoulites wearing baseball caps and preppy, Ivy League-style clothing is even higher than one would find across the Pacific, and Roman text is everywhere. The English language has long been associated with progress and wealth, the proof being its appearance in marketing campaigns aimed at locals – every major company, and almost every district, city and town, has an English-language slogan. However, a marked shift has taken place since the turn of the millennium, and Korean-ness is becoming cool once more, both at home and abroad.

The fields of food and design have witnessed particularly fascinating changes. Variants on Italian and Indian cuisine have swept across the nation, but of more note is the new-found popularity of 'neo-Korean' cuisine. This wide-ranging term is used to describe dishes that are essentially Korean, but also feature imported ingredients or methods of creation: Jung Sikdang (*see p122*), for example, uses non-native ingredients, while its herbal foams are a good example of new tastes being hauled from native ingredients. Meanwhile, *makgeolli*, a traditional rice wine, has undergone a huge surge in popularity, both in its original version and in various modern permutations. For more, *see p38-40* **Makgeolli**. Meanwhile, handbags from the Stori stable (*see p152*) are made with traditional Korean materials and motifs, and have sold well in Shoreditch and Manhattan, while the purses and ties of Lee Geon Maan (*see p152*), each featuring the Korean alphabet in their patterns, have proven popular enough with Japanese visitors to warrant the building of a huge new store in Tokyo.

In the arts, Korean pop music is popular in much of Asia while the Korean film industry has found worldwide fame (*see right* **Making It Big on the Big Screen**). But perhaps the most visible sign of Seoul's new forward-thinking mindset lies in its architecture. After decade upon decade of monumentally uninspiring creations, Seoul's decision makers have been striving to improve their city's urban landscape through design. For more on the built environment of the contemporary city, *see p34*.

Seoul today is enjoying the fruits of its post-Korean War economic miracle. It's not all about rebuilding any more. Today's Koreans have become confident in their own identity, and are melding their own traditions with other influences, foreign and domestic, to come up with exciting new forms.

Making It Big on the Big Screen

Korean creativity makes its mark in cinema.

Most countries would be quite happy to have a film industry like that of South Korea. Although it hit its commercial peak back in 2006, when local films made up more than 64 per cent of tickets sold, it can still count on an annual share of 40-50 per cent of the market. Given the worldwide strength of Hollywood films, this is no small accomplishment. Cinema occupies a central place on the Korean cultural scene. Big Korean films receive plenty of exposure in the local press and generate a considerable degree of discussion. The local star system contributes a great deal to the energy of Korean cinema, while the best-known Korean directors may themselves become household names (*see p171* **Directing Talent**).

The industry is dynamic and diverse. At one end of the spectrum, it turns out self-styled blockbusters like Kang Je-gyu's World War II drama *My Way*, budgeted at a massive $30 million, and Korea's first 3D blockbuster *Sector 7* (2011), about workers on an oil-rig battling monsters rising up from the sea. Effects-based films have become common, with Korean CGI (computer-generated imagery) companies raising their game to become the most sophisticated in Asia. A film like *Sector 7* may have cost less than $10 million, but it looks considerably more expensive thanks to the technological strengths of local firms. Unsurprisingly, film productions from across Asia – and even Hollywood – are contracting Korean companies to perform effects work.

Just as impressive, in a very different way, is the low-budget, art-house film sector. Hundreds of aspiring directors and film students overcome financial hurdles to produce a dazzling array of films each year. Of the 140-plus Korean films released in cinemas in 2010, more than half were budgeted

at less than $1 million, and it is here that some of the most innovative and surprising works are emerging. The best place to catch them is at one of Korea's major film festivals, which actually take place outside Seoul: Busan's **BIFF** in October (by many measures, Asia's biggest film festival; www.biff.kr); **Jeonju Film Festival** in May (http://eng.jiff.or.kr), or Bucheon's **PiFan** in July (www.pifan.com). The better films also find a not-insignificant audience on commercial release. Successes from early 2011 include *Bleak Night*, about a high school suicide, and *The Journals of Musan*, about the experiences of a North Korean defector in Seoul.

The films may be successful in cinemas, but many within the industry argued that its survival was threatened by the fact that, unlike in the US and Europe, the DVD market has never established itself in Korea, and the practice of illegal downloading had compromised this potentially important source of revenue. The industry attempted to fight back in 2009, when Korea became one of the first countries to establish legal downloading as a widely used option for watching films. With the support of local web portals such as Naver and Daum, legal downloading revenues surged in 2010, giving filmmakers a ray of hope for the future.

PiFan.

IN CONTEXT

Makgeolli Magic

From a drink for old men to young Seoul's favourite tipple.

TEXT: MICHAEL VAN DER ZWEEP

Korea is an individual and interesting place when it comes to alcohol. Locally made beer is poor, and attempts at wine almost laughable, but the country does have a splendid range of indigenous alcoholic drinks. Foremost among these is *makgeolli*, a quaffable rice wine with the colour and complexion of diluted milk, and an ABV content of around six per cent. As recently as the turn of the present century, it was regarded as 'grandfather fuel', and almost exclusively consumed by elderly men – drinking *makgeolli* was seriously uncool. However, it has since undergone a dramatic surge in popularity, one unlikely to dip in a country that's fervently in the process of rediscovering its own traditions.

Chin Chin. See p138.

THE QUINTESSENTIAL KOREAN DRINK

Makgeolli is a traditional Korean drink, made from processed rice and other grains, and usually boasting an alcoholic content of five to seven per cent. Many claim it has special medicinal properties. It's a refreshing drink and easy to quaff, or to imbibe in quantity: watch out, though, as *makgeolli* has a habit of making those consuming too much drunk very suddenly indeed. It's also a little tricky to open a bottle: rice sediment settles at the bottom, so the bottle will have to be shaken, but since the drink is still in the latter stages of fermentation, it'll fizz like milky champagne.

There are hundreds of varieties. Most are near-identical, but ingredients vary by area, with two particularly notable places of manufacture both within day-trip distance from Seoul. The small city of Gongju is famed for its chestnuts, many of which worm their way into the local hooch, while the sleepy lakeside town of Danyang uses the fresh spring waters of the nearby Sobaeksan mountain range to produce over a dozen excellent varieties, some of which incorporate black beans or other local ingredients.

By most accounts, *makgeolli* is Korea's oldest alcoholic drink – its origins can be traced as far back as the Goryeo Dynasty (918-1392), where it was enjoyed by those in all walks of life. The drink had a long heyday during the hundreds of years of the Joseon Dynasty (1392-1910). It was even consumed by the Joseon kings and queens, forming part of the standard royal banquet.

Makgeolli's popularity took a nosedive during the Japanese occupation (1910-45), when producing liquor was banned outright. This was part of the colonialists' strategy of maintaining social control and security, while at the same time it was a handy way of increasing sales of drinks made by Japanese-owned enterprises. Shortly after the Korean War (1950-53) *makgeolli* was again banned, this time because rice was required to produce it – post-war Korea had chronic food shortages, and every last grain was required to feed its population. From that point onwards, *makgeolli* was made from other ingredients, such as imported flour and other grains from abroad. In the 1970s and '80s, the drink was popular because it was cheap, but then sales began to drop year on year, due to increases in sales of *soju* and beer – and the discovery of imported drinks.

REDISCOVERY AND REVIVAL

Nobody seems too sure exactly when drinking *makgeolli* became cool again. Its re-emergence took many by surprise, but it certainly fitted the pattern of what was happening in the new Seoul: after decades of rapid industrial progess and hardcore westernisation, the city suddenly found itself more interested in its own identity, paying more respect to local traditions: clothing, food and architecture have had their own roles to play in this renaissance, so why not alcohol?

There were other reasons behind the re-emergence of *makgeolli*. Low prices certainly helped things along, since in terms of price per millilitre, *makgeolli* is the cheapest Korean alcohol on sale. However, unbeknown to many locals, it's actually among the most expensive drinks to produce – it receives favourable tax rates from the government, on account of its importance to the national heritage.

IN CONTEXT

'Korean students are now becoming fond of home-made makgeolli cocktails.'

There are also the drink's purported health benefits to consider. It has a relatively low percentage of alcohol, and contains proteins and vitamin B, the latter known to promote healthy skin. In addition, it's brewed with natural micro-organisms similar to those found in yoghurts and other fermented foods; these can help to increase blood circulation, help digestion and metabolism. Recent studies have also shown that active (or live) yeast, highly concentrated in *makgeolli*, can prevent various geriatric-related diseases such as high blood pressure, heart problems and arterial sclerosis.

Some Koreans still fear *makgeolli* – if seen drinking it, you may well be asked how you're going to cope with the apparently inevitable hangover the following morning. However – if you'll pardon the pun – this may well be a hangover from dynastic times. *Makgeolli* was once exclusively home-brewed and essentially a moonshine, but with today's legal regulations and cleaner processing methods, headaches seem to occur much less frequently. If questioned, retort that Korean beer is the one you have to watch out for – many local brews contain a preservative similar to formaldeyde.

AN OLD, NEW DRINK

One factor behind the sustained new popularity of *makgeolli* is the fact that so many enterprising locals are giving this old drink new tweaks. It's emerging in a variety of new flavours, some traditional, some not. Speciality taverns opting for the former are selling *makeolli* mixed with the powder of pine needles, mugwort or green tea, or introducing new flavours such as apricot, grape, raspberry, mulberry, pear and even pine nut. Others are mixing the drink with the juice of imported fruits, such as kiwi, strawberry or banana. Korean students are now becoming fond of home-made *makgeolli* cocktails, as evidenced by signs at certain convenience stores, which give not-so-subtle hints of the optimum blends – *makgeolli* shandy is particularly tasty, made with 50 per cent *makgeolli* and 50 per cent Chilsung Cider (not an alcoholic drink, as its name may suggest, but a lemonade).

In fact, who says that *makgeolli* has to remain in its original form at all? It goes with just about anything: successful experiments include *makgeolli* espresso and *makgeolli* sorbet, while *makgeolli* skin packs are now being used in several of Seoul's spas. The next trick is going to be making *makgeolli* popular abroad; it has been sold in Japan for decades, and is particularly popular in Osaka and the wider Kansai region, to which many Korean families moved during the occupation period. However, the nature of the drink makes it hard to export. It contains live yeast that is still fermenting and prone to prise open containers, a problem compounded by the flimsy plastic bottles used by most manufacturers. Some are now using glass bottles, though these varieties typically contain preservatives, and are looked down on by true *makgeolli* connoisseurs. However, it's just one of the new strategies being employed to ensure that *makgeolli* is not a mere *yuhaeng*, or fad, but here to stay.

WHERE TO TRY MAKGEOLLI

Connoisseurs and purists should try **Chin Chin** (*see p138*), a restaurant and bar serving regional *makgeolli* and superb food. More variety, and a great atmosphere, can be found at the **Pub of the Blue Star** (*see p136*), with *makgeolli* infusions including mugwort and green tea, or **Dduktak** (*see p138*), which offers all sorts of 'makocktails'. The party-minded on a tight budget, meanwhile, are well catered for at **Poseokjeong** (*see p138*), which has ultra-cheap all-you-can-drink specials. Or, for a truly local experience, try a **convenience store** (*see p153*). Most sell *makgeolli* and have outdoor seating in summer.

IN CONTEXT

Sights

The Royal Quarter

Seoul at its most dignified.

The kingdom of Joseon declared what is now Seoul as its capital in 1392, and for most of the following half-millennium the country was run from a small band of land below the northern mountains. The machinations of regal rule meant that three separate palaces served as the seat of power within the first century of the dynasty's rule – off-limits for years but now fully open to the hoi polloi, these are among the best sights Seoul has to throw at its visitors. With such history behind it, one would expect this area to be highly developed – the fact that it's Seoul's most traditional district by far is, for many, a pleasant surprise. Charming rows of wooden houses run up and down the hilly lanes, giving visitors a taste of the city as it once was; trendy cafés and restaurants are here too, an indication of the direction the city is taking.

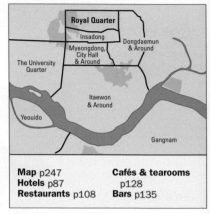

Map p247	Cafés & tearooms
Hotels p87	p128
Restaurants p108	Bars p135

NAVIGATING THE AREA

The three palaces forming the royal quarter's southern edge are all accessible by subway. However, you'll have to put a little effort in to reach other places listed in this section. Bukchon Hanok Village and Samcheongdong are pedestrian-friendly areas, and both a short, pleasant walk from Anguk subway station; however, to reach Buamdong you'll need to walk much further, or take a bus or taxi.

THE PALACES

Seoul's Five Grand Palaces form a major part of the city's tourist appeal – elegant reminders of the long line of Joseon kings that stretched from the dawn of the dynasty in 1392 to Japanese annexation in 1910. The first three palaces to be built are all located within a kilometre-long swathe of land. **Gyeongbokgung** was the first, built with amazing speed and finished in 1395. Completed less than a decade later – unbelievably rapid construction, for the time – was **Changdeokgung**, just to the east; another palace, **Changgyeonggung**, lies just beyond Changdeokgung's eastern

wall, and dates from 1483. Two further palaces were added in the following centuries: **Deoksugung** (*see p60*) and **Gyeonghuigung** (*see p63*), located further to the south and as such featured elsewhere.

Note that 2010 saw the first sales of a combined ticket, allowing entry to all three palaces listed here, plus Jongmyo shrine. Should the scheme be continued, such tickets will cost ₩10,000 – not much of a saving, but they're valid for one month.

★ Changdeokgung Palace

Yulgongno 99 (762-8261, http://eng.cdg.go.kr). Anguk station (line 3), exit 3. **Open** *Apr-Oct* 9am-6pm Tue-Sun. *Dec-Feb* 9am-5pm Tue-Sun. *Nov, Mar* 9am-5.30pm Tue-Sun. *English-language tours* 11.30am, 1.30pm & 2.30pm. **Admission** *Palace* ₩3,000 incl guided tour; *Palace & Huwon* ₩5,000 incl guided tour; ₩15,000 self-guided tour Thur. **Map** p247 G1/2.

Changdeokgung is the second oldest of Seoul's five palaces and a World Heritage Site. According to most observers, it's the city's most beautiful palace, thanks largely to its lovely setting amid gardens, and the way in which the buildings fit so well into the terrain they've been built on. Despite the Joseon

Changdeokgung Palace.

kings already having had a perfectly good palace just to the west in Gyeongbokgung (*see p44*), construction started on Changdeokgung in 1405 and was completed in 1412. As with all of Seoul's royal palaces, it has been attacked, destroyed and restored a number of times.

The buildings here look older and less restored than the ones in Gyeongbokgung. The main palace gate, Donhwamun, was rebuilt in 1608 and features an eight-ton copper bell. Although only 30% of the palace's buildings have been restored so far, there is still plenty to see. Geumcheongyo is Seoul's oldest bridge, originally built in 1411; Injeongjeon, registered as a 'national treasure', was a hall in which coronations took place and where the king received envoys from foreign countries; Juhamnu Pavilion was where people once took state exams as the king looked on.

The real reason to visit, however, is the garden. Once known as Geumwon (Forbidden Garden) and Naewon (Inner Garden), the names of Biwon (Secret Garden) and Huwon (Rear Garden) are commonly used today. The 78-acre garden was originally constructed for the royal family and palace women, and features everything from 300-year-old trees to a lotus pond. It's an intimate place, a spot for reflection, and a chance to take in some nature (although it can be hard to appreciate this with a group on a guided tour).

In order to keep this space beautiful, people are required to join a tour group on most days. Every Thursday, though, people are allowed to wander freely, albeit it for a much larger ticket price. Tours take around 90 minutes; guides are well informed, and share the stories that the walls wish they could tell. You'll walk a couple of kilometres in total, so wear comfortable shoes.

★ Changgyeonggung Palace

Waryongdong 2-1 (481-4650, http://cgg.cha.go.kr). Hyehwa station (line 4), exit 4. **Open** *Apr-Oct* 9am-6pm Tue-Sun. *Dec-Feb* 9am-5pm Tue-Sun. *Nov, Mar* 9am-5.30pm Tue-Sun. **Admission** ₩1,000. **Map** p247 G1/2.

Although separated from Changdeokgung by nothing more than a dividing wall, Changgyeonggung is far less visited than its neighbour. Access is certainly trickier – the palace's eastern gate is a fair walk from the nearest subway stations – but its grassy, verdant setting alone makes a visit worthwhile. Although built in 1483, making it almost a century younger than its neighbouring palaces, Changgyeonggung aguably has the most interesting

---

INSIDE TRACK
FREE GUIDED TOURS

The city runs free guided tours of the palace district. Tours are divided by theme – ancient culture, Korean traditions, modern culture, and a mix of the three. To reserve a spot on one of the tours, check the city website (www.visitseoul.net) and click on 'Walking tours'.

INSIDE TRACK
CHANGING OF THE GUARDS

Got a camera? Your photos of Gyeongbokgung will look most impressive if you time your visit to coincide with the palace's colourful Changing of the Guard ceremonies. These take place on the hour from 10am to 4pm every day but Tuesday, and start in the front courtyard of the palace.

---

history, including one of Seoul's most famous tales: a royal murder. Prince Sado, heir to the throne, was murdered here by his father, King Yeongjo, in 1762. Sado had been behaving strangely, and his father was worried about what might happen should he ascend to the throne. So one day he lured his son into a rice casket near the palace's eastern wall, and placed him under lock and key until he starved to death.

The Japanese annexation saw a zoo and theme park added to Changgyeonggung, an obvious attempt to erode the regal dignity of the palace. However, in a Korea with precious few such facilities, they remained in use for almost 40 years after independence, and were only torn down in the early 1980s. One survivor from this period is an ornate greenhouse, which holds a wide array of plant life. The grounds are lovely too; Seoul strolls are rarely this enjoyable, and it's tempting to linger a while by the lake.

★ Gyeongbokgung Palace

Sejongno 1-1 (3700-3900, www.royalpalace.go.kr). Gyeongbokgung station (line 3), exit 5. **Open** *Mar-Oct* 9am-6pm Mon, Wed-Sun. *Nov-Feb* 9am-5pm Mon, Wed-Sun. *English-language guided tours* 11am, 1.30pm, 3.30pm. **Admission** ₩3,000. **Map** p247 E2.

The 'Palace Greatly Blessed by Heaven', as its name means, has the longest and most storied history of any Korean palace. The story starts in 1395, three years after the beginning of Joseon Dynasty rule. The original main palace of Gyeongbokgung was completed, and the Joseon Dynasty moved its capital from Kaesong (now in North Korea) to this new palace in what was then known as Hanyang (now Seoul). It's sometimes viewed as a Korean version of the Forbidden City in the sense that it was once a self-functioning unit. Later kings of the Joseon Dynasty continued to expand the palace, but much of it was destroyed during a slave rebellion in 1592. Note that signage in the palace blames the Japanese instead; that country did, indeed, devastate much of Korea during repeated invasions in the 1590s.

After the Japanese invasion, the Joseon Dynasty called another palace – Changdeokgung (*see p42*) – (*see p42*)

home for generations. Gyeongbokgung remained unused for almost 270 years. Fast-forward to 1867, when the palace buildings were reconstructed. The new structures, over 330 in all, made up a massive complex with 5,792 rooms, taking up 4,414,000 square feet (410,000 square metres) of land.

Gyeongbokgung's renovations and reconstructions were destroyed when Korea became a vassal state of Japan. The new colonialists demolished all but ten of the buildings, and constructed the Japanese Government General building right in front of the throne hall, a tremendous blow to Korea's national pride. Some even claim that its shape, when viewed from above, resembled the Japanese ideogram for sun – the first character in their local name for the Land of the Rising Sun. The building survived for decades after World War II, but was destroyed in 1995 to make room for more renovations to the palace.

Today, about 40% of Gyeongbokgung's original buildings exist. The absence of those that are no more have made some room for walking – and the massive crowds. This is the most-visited place in all Korea by foreign tourists, and locals love it as well, even more so since the unveiling of the reconstructed front gate, Gwanghwamun, in 2010.

National Folk Museum

3704-3114, www.nfm.go.kr. **Open** *Mar-Oct* 9am-6pm Mon, Wed-Sun. *Nov-Feb* 9am-5pm Mon, Wed-Sun. **Admission** free with entry ticket to Gyeongbokgung. **Map** p247 F1.

Housed in the Gyeongbokgung palace grounds, in a new, though classically styled, tapering structure, the National Folk Museum offers a first-hand look at the Korea of the past – a rather romanticised history, but one colourfully told with thousands of artifacts. Opened by a Japanese curator in 1924 and originally located on the Mt Namsan slopes, the museum opened in 1993 in a building that formerly housed the National Museum of Korea.

National Palace Museum

3701-7500. **Open** *Mar-Oct* 9am-6pm Tue-Sun. *Nov-Feb* 9am-5pm Tue-Sun. **Admission** free with entry ticket to Gyeongbokgung. **Map** p247 E2.

Originally opened in 1992 as the Royal Museum at Deoksugung Palace, this was renamed and relocated to its current location in 2005. The full collection went on display in November 2007, after a complete renovation of all the galleries. It certainly looks fresh and new, and with more than 40,000 artifacts spread over three floors and over 11,000m sq of permanent exhibition space, expect your feet to be moving for a few hours if you want to see it all. While ahead of the curve for family friendliness (few museums in Korea have a nursing room), there are few specifically child-friendly activities. Special exhibitions take place from time to time, and are usually very well put together.

SIGHTS

Gyeongbokgung Palace.

Bukchon Hanok Village.

BUKCHON HANOK VILLAGE

Getting there: Anguk subway (line 3).
Bukchon Hanok Village could be considered
the soul of Seoul, chiefly because it's the most
traditional part of the city. There's a clue in the
name: *hanok* is the term for Korea's old-style
traditional wooden houses, which were once
found all over the country but have now
largely been replaced by concrete structures.

Though beloved by locals today, the area
could have looked quite different had other
plans come to fruition: in the 1960s, as with
more or less everywhere else in what was then
a city with new-found affluence and a booming
population, Bukchon was slated for renovation.

INSIDE TRACK
WOODEN HOMES

Bukchon Hanok Village is the only place
in Seoul in which it's possible to stay in
a *hanok* guesthouse – these traditional
wooden homes once covered the city, but
their numbers have dwindled considerably
in recent decades. However, a fair few
have survived in this area, and they make
for some of Asia's most characteristically
traditional places to stay. For a selection,
see p87.

However, protests from locals (and the nearby
location of the presidential home) persuaded
the government to spare the area, which has
been left distinctly low-rise as skyscrapers
have sprouted to the south. End result: one of
the most visually pleasing places in Seoul, its
winding, hilly lanes a reminder of past times.

The area can eat up several days of
sightseeing. Firstly, it's hemmed in on both
sides by royal palaces – **Changdeokgung**
(*see p42*) to the east, and **Gyeongbokgung**
(*see p44*) to the west. In Bukchon itself there
are a number of interesting museums; clustered
together a ten-minute walk north of Anguk
subway station are the **Donglim Knot
Museum**, the **Hansangsoo Embroidery
Museum**, the **Gahoe Museum** and the bizarre
Seoul Museum of Chicken Art. This is also
the best place to stay in Seoul for traditionally-
minded sorts – some of the area's *hanok* houses
have been converted into miniature guesthouses
(*see left* **Inside Track**).

Donglim Knot Museum
*Gahoedong 11-7 (3673-2778). Anguk station (line
3), exit 2.* **Open** 10am-6pm Tue-Sun. **Admission**
₩2,000. **Map** p247 F1.
Few tourists find their way into this curious
museum – a shame, since some Korean crafts feature such lovely knotwork. Opened in April 2004,
the museum is located inside a traditional wooden
hanok house; most displays are, of course, made up

of *mae-deup*, or knots, but plenty of other materials abound. Just coming to see the beautiful knots is a mere fraction of the fun – try your hand with a full- or half-hour programme to make a necklace or a woven pendant for your cellphone (reserve at least two days in advance).

Hansangsoo Embroidery Museum

Gahoedong 11-32 (744-1545, www.hansangsoo. com). Anguk station (line 3), exit 2. **Open** 10am-5pm Tue-Sun. **Admission** ₩3,000. **Map** p247 F1.
A little off the beaten tourist track, this privately funded museum showcases over 1,000 pieces of embroidery. These include Buddhist embroideries, and pleated sheets with traditional Korean patterns. If you're keen to have a go yourself, drop in for a cheap (₩3,000), hour-long hands-on programme. This starts with an exhibition by the instructor, then you're given a chance to sew on your own handkerchief. Note that Korean is the only language spoken, so you might find yourself appreciating hand gestures – and maybe learning a few words of the local language.

Gahoe Museum

Gahoedong 11-103 (741-0466, www.gahoe museum.org). Anguk station (line 3), exit 2. **Open** 10am-6pm Tue-Sun. **Admission** ₩3,000. **Map** p247 F1.
The Gahoe Museum holds over 1,500 traditional Korean art and craft pieces, including hundreds of time-worn paintings and amulets, as well as beautiful folding screens, shown in two exhibition halls. The primary focuses are on beauty, religion and a

humble lifestyle. Don't forget to try a complimentary cup of green tea, made from leaves grown in the south-western province of Jeollanam-do. This is a museum for craft-lovers, and just like at the Knot and Embroidery museums, there's a chance for visitors to have some crafty fun of their own – various activities are available, including the rubbing of roof tiles on to a piece of paper, or creating a hand-stamp from wooden amulets. If you have a bit more time and ambition, try drawing a fan or painting a picture frame in the traditional style. Instruction is offered, but only in Korean. Guided tours are available in English from Tuesday to Friday.

Seoul Museum of Chicken Art

Gahoedong 12 (763-9995, www.kokodac.com). Anguk station (line 3), exit 2. **Open** 10am-5pm, closed Mon. **Admission** ₩3,000. **Map** p247 F1.
And now, for something completely different. Yes, you read the name right – chicken art. In case you didn't know that chickens could be seen in an artistic way, this museum aims to prove just that. The private collection reveals different portrayals of the humble chicken through culture and art. Start with the permanent exhibit on the first floor, then explore the special exhibitions on the second floor. The museum is one of the main attractions in Bukchon Hanok Village – give it a good hour.

SAMCHEONGDONG

Getting there: Anguk (line 3) is the closest station, but it's around 15mins from Samcheondong itself. However, the walk is quite pleasant: take

Kukje Gallery. *See p48.*

Samcheongdong.

a right-hand turn around 100m from exit 1 of Anguk station, and it's straight all the way. Those visiting Gyeongbokgung can exit the palace through its east gate; turn left and walk to the palace's north-east corner, and Samcheongdong will be just across the road. Simply put, Samcheongdong is one of Seoul's most charming areas. Its name translates as something proximate to 'Three Purities', apparently with reference to the mountains, water and people of yore. Things haven't changed much – Samcheongdong's proximity to both Gyeongbokgung Palace and the presidential residence has kept buildings close to the ground, and things remained surprisingly local until around 2005, when Seoulites discovered the area's appeal. Cafés, restaurants and art galleries have since moved in en masse, albeit with a refined atmosphere in comparison with their counterparts in Insadong, just a walk to the south; indeed, the **Kukje Gallery** (*see p174*) is one of the most esteemed in Korea, with **Gallery Hyundai** (*see p174*) not too far behind.

The Kukje is located just off the western end of **Samcheongdonggil**, the area's main road. Lined with elegant establishments, it heads first north-west, then north, and slopes gently uphill towards the mountains. After around a kilometre you'll find yourself in **Samcheong Park**, one of the capital's most pleasant stretches of parkland, with superb city views.

Up until this point it's wonderful pedestrian territory – go any faster than walking pace and you'll miss out on dozens of distinctive cafés, galleries and shops, which are most interesting on the side street that peels off Samcheongdonggil to the south-east, just 100 metres to the north-east of the Kukje Gallery. Head anywhere west of Samcheongdonggil and you may be questioned by police; there's a large police presence in this area, since the presidential residence – the **Blue House** – is just across the way. The house and its grounds can be visited by tourists, though for understandable reasons this has to be organised in advance. There are also a number of interesting museums in the area: **Toykino** and the **World Jewellery Museum**, respectively full of toys and treasure, are just off the Samcheongdonggil main drag, while further up the hill is the **Silk Road Museum** – worth heading up to for the superlative views over Gyeongbokgung and the city centre.

Blue House

Sejongno 1 (730-5800, www.president.go.kr). Gyeongbokgung station station (line 3), exit 5. **Open** *Tours only* 10am, 11am, 2pm, 3pm Tue-Sat. **Admission** free. **Map** p247 E1.
Located right behind Gyeongbokgung, this is the official home of the Korean president. Officially called Cheongwadae, it's also known as the Blue House on account of its colourful roof tiles – during the Joseon Dynasty, blue tiles signified the seat of power. Tours are available, but as you'd expect in a country still

officially at war with its neighbour, these are strictly controlled, and reservations must be made at least ten days in advance. You'll also need your passport. Photography is only allowed in certain sections, and video cameras are banned. The reward for following the rules is getting about as close to the action as a civilian can get. The hour-long tour, which includes a couple of bus rides, won't let you near any highly sensitive areas. The beautiful presidential garden, Nokjiwon, more than makes up for that.

▶ *Tours must be booked online at least ten days in advance. It's essential to bring your passport for identification.*

Silk Road Museum

Samcheongdong 35-99 (720-9675). Anguk station (line 3), exit 2. **Open** 10am-7pm Tue-Sun. **Admission** ₩2,000. **Map** p247 F1.

A diverting museum on a lofty road, way above central Samcheongdong. The views are superb and the exhibits intriguing – mostly hailing from the westernmost Chinese province of Xinjiang. They're certainly worth a peek for those with any interest in the Silk Road, the ancient highway that once stretched all the way from China to Europe.

Toykino

Samcheongdong 63-19 (725-2690, www.toykino. com). Anguk station (line 3), exit 2. **Open** 10am-6pm Tue-Sun. **Admission** ₩5,000. **Map** p247 F1.

Perhaps more shop than museum, and perhaps more telling about contemporary Japan than contemporary Korea, but Toykino is fascinating nonetheless. It houses a veritable army of figurines – over 30,000 all told, hailing from both Korean shores and abroad. A separate gallery showcases board games and features a few vending machines, enabling visitors to walk away with toys of their own.

World Jewellery Museum

Hwadong 75-3 (730-1610, www.wj museum.com). Anguk station (line 3), exit 2. **Open** 11am-5pm Wed-Sun. **Admission** ₩5,000. **Map** p247 F1.

This small museum houses a personal collection of over 3,000 pieces of jewellery, gathered over the course of three decades. About a third of them are on display here at any one time, though the museum has permanent features that include an 'amber wall' and necklace hall; a fascinating display of masks, rings and ivory objects can be found on the second floor.

BUAMDONG

Getting there: there is no subway station in the Buamdong area, but it's easy to reach by bus or taxi, or a half-hour walk up the western wall of Gyeongbokgung, then around the mountain.

Mt Bugaksan

The forbidden peak.

Most of those who spend a little time in Seoul would come to the conclusion that Mt Namsan (*see p82*) is the city's most important mountain. While it's true that Mt Namsan once book-ended Seoul to the south, its northern counterpart – Mt Bugaksan, whose name means 'Northern Crag Mountain' – has an even more compelling case for recognition. Ever since Seoul first became a capital, in 1392, the city has been ruled from areas around this peak; the Joseon kingdom built not one but three palaces on its southern foothills, viewing the area as the most auspicious feng shui location in the Hangang river valley. Japan annexed Korea in 1910, but on independence in 1945 the area was again selected as Seoul's seat of power: the Blue House, home to the country's president ever since, was built between Mt Bugaksan and Gyeongbokgung in 1948.

Auspicious though it may have been in geomantic terms, the location of the Blue House caused problems in the decades following the Korean War (1950-53). With little bar trees and rocks to the north, it found itself at the mercy of North Korean attacks. The most serious incident occurred in 1968, when a team of North Korean commandos crossed the hill in an attempt to assassinate President Park Chung-hee. They got within 800 metres (2,600 feet) of the Blue House before being rumbled by South Korean police; shooting followed as the group tried to make their way back to the DMZ, leaving over 90 dead.

Mt Bugaksan was placed off-limits immediately after the attack, and it remained so until 2006. But it's now possible to hike along an east–west mountain trail, best accessed from Buamdong (*see above*) – foreigners will need to bring their their passport for identification. This is still a highly secure area: it's unwise to venture from the path, and police will go hunting for those who do not come back down before 3pm. The path opens at 9am, but is closed on Mondays.

SIGHTS

Buses heading to Buamdong include the 1020 from Gwanghwamun subway station (line 5), while a taxi from Gyeongbokgung will not cost more than ₩5,000. Lastly, hourly shuttle buses go to the Gana Art Center and Whanki Museum, but they're hard to track down – it's easier to return to central Seoul on these services, which depart the Gana on the hour (10am-5pm), and reach the Whanki 10mins later.

The district of Buamdong is a mere 30-minute walk from Gyeongbokgung, but feels cut off from central Seoul – you will, in fact, have to go round a small mountain to get here. This is **Bugaksan**, which was for long off-limits to the general public but now makes for a great hike (*see p49* **Bugaksan**). Presidents have stayed on the south side of this mountain since independence; in the following decades, Buamdong to the north also became popular with politicians, businessfolk and others in the upper echelons of Korean society. The 1980s saw most of Seoul's richer inhabitants migrate south of the river to Gangnam, but relics of Buamdong's time in the sun still remain – walking around the hilly lanes, you'll see some of the city's largest houses. Buamdong has also recently found favour with young, arty Seoulites – superb venues such as the **Gana Art Center** and **Whanki Museum** are a delight to explore (once you've tracked them down), and you'll be able to eat and drink well on your way around: **Sanmotunge** (*see p130*) is a hilltop café with a stunning mountain view, while **Art For Life** (*see p108*) combines excellent pasta with regular jazz performances.

Gana Art Center

Pyeongchangdong 97 (720-1020, www.ganaart.com). **Open** 10am-7.30pm daily. **Admission** varies by exhibition.

A visually striking gallery – you'll have seen work by its designer, Jean-Michel Wilmotte, if you landed in Korea at Incheon International Airport. It also has a greater floor-space than any other gallery in Seoul, partly thanks to its remote, near-mountainous location; the on-site pasta restaurant is a boon to those who want to stay a few hours. The art itself is almost always the work of Korean artists, and not always merely visual in nature. Occasional events take place from spring to autumn on a pine-fringed outdoor stage.

Whanki Museum

Buamdong 210-8 (391-7701, www.whanki museum.org). **Open** 10am-6pm, closed Mon. **Admission** ₩3,000.

A shrine of sorts to Kim Whanki, a forward-thinking local artist who joined the Paris avant-garde scene in the 1930s, and in doing so injected oriental elements into western art – and vice versa. The large museum is full of Kim's work and influences, and features rotating art exhibitions in keeping with Kim's philosophies. The building's calm vibe makes it quite tempting to stay a while, as does the coffee available in the main lobby.

Buamdong

Insadong

An artery between old and new

The Royal Quarter (*see pp42-50*) holds the bulk of Seoul's historic sights, while just a short walk to the south, Myeongdong (*see p58-64*) has the city's most concentrated capitalism. Sitting directly in between is the neighbourhood of Insadong, whose main thoroughfare, **Insadonggil**, provides a highly tangible connection between old and new Seoul. The road tumbles gently downhill from north to south, and a short stroll will take you past dozens and dozens of traditional restaurants, tearooms, shops and art galleries, all somehow squeezing into the area's myriad narrow lanes. Also here are delightful wooden pavilions, striking places of Buddhist and Christian worship, and even a miniature palace. Always popular with foreign visitors to Seoul, Insadong is now seething with young locals, eager to lap up the new takes on traditional food, drink and art that the area keeps throwing at them. At its southern edge, and running east to west, **Jongno** has been one of the city's main streets for centuries.

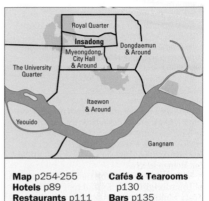

Map p254-255	**Cafés & Tearooms**
Hotels p89	p130
Restaurants p111	**Bars** p135

SIGHTS

NAVIGATING INSADONG

This area can be navigated almost entirely on foot – more enjoyably so, indeed, than anywhere else in Seoul. It is bounded to the north by **Sajikno**, a road underscored for much of its local course by subway line 3; **Anguk** and **Gyeongbokgung** stations are the most useful for the immediate Insadong area, while **Dongnimmun** to the west is handy for a few nearby sights. Subway line 1 likewise barrels under **Jongno** to the south of the area; **Jonggak** and **Jongno 3-ga** stations are the most useful, while the latter is also a stop on line 5. If you're heading to or from Dongdaemun market (*see p67*), it's a good idea to stroll along the banks of Cheonggyecheon, a small stream just to the south of Jongno.

INSADONG

Getting there: Anguk station (line 3), Jonggak station (line 1) or Jongno 3-ga station (lines 1, 3 & 5).
Insadong is Seoul's most popular area with international visitors, and notably low-rise by Seoul standards. Locals from Insadong and its surrounding districts are extremely proud of their maintenance of tradition, which manifested itself in 2000: the city had planned to modernise the area, but was dissuaded from doing so thanks to fierce protests from traditionalist elements. Just a few years later, Starbucks

INSIDE TRACK
SOUVENIR SHOPPING

Insadsonggil is by far the best place in Seoul in which to go hunting for souvenirs. Silk fans, traditional *hanbok* clothing, paper lanterns and tea sets are popular, while some art supplies shops will translate a foreign name into Korean and engrave it on to a name stamp, enabling you to sign for things the old-fashioned way. For handmade trinkets, there's no better place to head than **Ssamziegil** (*see p155*), a market whose few levels of tiny shops are accessible on the same spiralling courtyard walkway.

SIGHTS

INSIDE TRACK
CAR-FREE INSADONGGIL

Traffic merrily courses down Insadonggil throughout the day – rather dangerous, given the fact that this fairly narrow street gets packed. However, each weekend road blocks are put up at the road's north end from 2pm to 8pm on Saturday, and 10am to 8pm on Sunday. Happily, these traffic-free times coincide with colourful musical processions, which take place in late morning and early afternoon on Saturday and Sunday.

opened up a branch at the southern end of the road; a few more protests later, and it agreed to have the name written in local *hangeul* characters only – the first branch of the chain worldwide to have its sign written in anything but Roman letters.

The area is bisected by the diagonal tangent of **Insadonggil**, a delightful road whose every building contains something of interest, whether it be a gallery, restaurant, tearoom, shop, or a combination of all four. This road was once a stream, which led into what is now **Cheonggyecheon**, a gentrified stream whose banks are highly popular walking grounds for visitors and locals. Small, labyrinthine side-alleys known as *golmok* jut from Insadonggil itself, and the temptation to dive into a few of them is hard to resist, especially if you're hungry – a fair few of the restaurants have English-language menus, and others have pictures of the dishes in their windows. Many of the buildings here are the traditional wooden structures known as *hanok* – some are replicas rather than original constructions, but it's hard to tell the difference. One of the most

INSIDE TRACK
WHAT'S THAT SMELL?

While walking along Insadonggil, you may find your nasal cavity assaulted by an awful stench. Its likely source is *bondaegi*, or boiled silkworm larvae, a dish that's often eaten as a street snack and is – to put it mildly – an aquired taste. Try some and you'll win the admiration of any watching local. Those with less brave tastebuds may prefer to hunt down some *hoddeok*, little fried pancakes containing brown sugar and walnut, sold (usually in winter) for ₩1,000 from other stands.

notable such structures is **Minga Daheon**, which now houses Min's Club restaurant (*see p115*). This is not a tourist sight as such and only diners (or wine-tipplers) are welcome inside, but the beauty of the 1930s construction is quite apparent from the outside. Interestingly, despite its rustic appearance, it was designed by one of the more forward-thinking architects of the time and seen as a highly modern *hanok* when built; in fact, it was also one of the first structures in the country to have an inside toilet.

Eating and drinking is an essential part of the Insadong experience: *see p111* **Restaurants** and *p130* **Cafés & Tearooms** for some suggestions. With the exception of wonderful galleries such as the **Sun Art Center** and the **Insa Gallery** (for both, *see p175*), sights themselves are surprisingly thin on the ground, and rather low-key: the mini-palace of **Unhyeongung** (*see p54*) is a fine place for a short stroll, as is **Tapgol Park** (*see p54*) just down the road. The latter was closely related to the famed March 1 Independence Movement against Japanese occupation, as was the **Seungdong Presbytarian Church**, an interesting Romanesque red-brick building opposite Unhyeongung. Both witnessed the formation of anti-Japanese protest groups, and protests still continue several generations later: on the other side of Insadonggil, there are protests outside the **Japanese Embassy** every Wednesday at 1pm, demanding apologies from Tokyo for the colonial-era use of sex slaves, the 'comfort women'. Protests about contemporary issues tend to take place outside City Hall. A short walk from the Japanese Embassy is **Jogyesa** (*see below*), one of Seoul's main Buddhist temples, and a good place in which to get a handle on the fading national religion.

FREE Jogyesa
Gyeonjadong 45 (732-2183, www.jogyesa.org). Anguk station (line 3), exit 6. **Open** 24hrs daily. **Admission** free. **Map** p247 F2.
Jogyesa is the international headquarters of Korea's dominant and unified national Buddhist sect, known as the Jogye Order for eight centuries, a name hailing from a famous Buddhist mountain in southern China. It's one of Korea's few completely urban temples, located in the heart of downtown Seoul rather than on a mountain. It's also one of the newest major Korean temples, built in 1910, but still quite fascinating. It features three of Korea's largest bronze Buddha statues in its Main Hall, and vivid paintings of the life of Sakyamuni Buddha on its outside walls. Two grand old trees dominate its courtyard, in front of a spectacular stone pagoda believed to contain some of Sakyamuni's holy relics brought to Korea

Buddhism in Seoul

Temples, meditation and delicious food.

If **Jogyesa** (*see left*) has given you a taste for things Buddhist, there's a lot more to discover in the immediate vicinity of the temple. Outside its eastern gate are a pack of small shops selling incense, Buddhist figurines and monks' clothing – great to look at, even if you're not intending to buy. On the other side of the road is the large **Templestay** building (www.eng.temple stay.com), where you can book a night's stay at Jogye Order temples across the land; a fair number of suitable locations lie within the periphery of Seoul, or you can go for broke and stay in a remote mountain range. The top floor of the same building

is home to **Balwoo** (*see p111*), one of Seoul's best restaurants; under the same ownership as Jogyesa Temple, it serves delightful Buddhist food. A short walk north of Anguk subway station will bring you to the **Ahnkook Zen Academy** (www.ahnkook zen.org), which offers English-language meditation programmes. Meditation courses are also available elsewhere across the city, most pertinently at the **Shambhala Centre** (www.seoul.shambhala. info), south of the river near Sadang subway station (line 4). Also south of the river is **Bongeunsa** (*see p75*), perhaps a more appealing temple than Jogyesa.

SIGHTS

Jogyesa.

by a Ceylonese monk to commemorate the revival of Korean Buddhism after the oppressive Confucian royal regime had been overthrown. A bell pavilion, funeral hall and Bodhisattva shrine also surround the Main Hall, and the compound is always busy with worshippers. The large stone headquarters office building behind it features a small but excellent museum of Korean Buddhist art in its basement.
▶ *For more on Korean Buddhism, see p77.*

FREE Tapgol Park
Jongno 3-ga station (lines 1, 3 & 5), exit 1.
Open 6am-8pm daily. **Admission** Free.
Map p247 G3.
This small park is a favourite with older locals, who come for a gentle walk and a chat. Much of the park is paved, but it's a pleasant place nonetheless. The 'tap' in Tapgol is Korean for pagoda, and there is indeed a fine one at the park's rear end: built in 1467 as part of what was then a temple, the Wongaksa Pagoda is constructed in ten levels of marble, and is now officially listed as the country's number two National Treasure. Unfortunately it looks somewhat trapped in the ugly glass case put around it for preservation purposes; you'll have to look closely to see the various Buddhas, Boddhisattvas and Buddhist animals carved beautifully on to each level. In 1919, the park was used for the first reading of the Declaration of Independence, making it the place where the March 1 Movement was born.

Unhyeongung
Unnidong 114-10 (766-9090, www.unhyeongung.or.kr). Anguk station (line 3), exit 4. **Open** *Apr-Oct* 9am-7pm Tue-Sun.
Nov-Mar 9am-6pm Tue-Sun. **Admission** ₩700; free noon-1pm. **Map** p247 F2.
Though not officially regarded as such since it was never home to a reigning monarch, this is a palace in all other senses of the word. The site dates from the 14th century, and a small amount of early construction remains. King Gojong lived here until becoming king at the age of 12, at which point he moved into Changdeokgung (*see p42*), just across the way. It was also home to Gojong's father Heungseon, a highly conservative prince regent who pulled the strings behind the scenes. Today, it makes a pleasant visit, its largely unpainted buildings giving off a different air to those found in the five official palaces; some are filled with accoutrements of regal times. Twice a year (in spring and autumn) there are glorious re-enactments of Gojong's marriage to the ill-fated Empress Myeongseong – ask at a tourist office (*see p229*) for the exact dates.

Jongno

Getting there: Gwanghwamun station (line 5), Jonggak station (line 1) or Jongno 3-ga station (lines 1, 3 & 5).
Cutting an east-to-west swathe through the heart of Seoul, Jongno has been one of the city's main thoroughfares for centuries. Lined with thousands of billboards and teeming with lanes of traffic day and night, it's hard to imagine that as recently as the early 20th century it was a wide dirt avenue, peopled by locals wearing loose white cotton clothing and horsehair hats.

Those days now seem very far away, but a few vestiges of dynastic times remain. Most

---

Hangeul: a Korean Script

Inspired by a medieval king, hangeul only found favour after World War II.

Korea's distinctive alphabet, known as *hangeul*, has been around since the 1440s. It was created by the so-called Hall of Worthies, a team led by King Sejong (1397-1450). In those days, as in the west, most people in Korea were illiterate. It took years of study to learn the Chinese ideograms used at the time, but only those with wealth and power were able to do so. However, Sejong's noble vision of a written system accessible to all was shot down by the *yangban* – Confucian scholars who, at the time, rivalled the royal house of Joseon for might. In fact, *hangeul* only truly took off five centuries down the line, after Japanese occupation ended in 1945 – take a look at any photograph, poster or television commercial from the 1960s, and you'll still see Chinese characters all over the place.

Hanbok clothing. *See p51.*

important is **Jongmyo** (*see p56*), large, wooded grounds where the 'spirit tablets' of kings and queens have been kept, and venerated, ever since the dawn of the Joseon Dynasty in the 1390s. Whenever the sun's out, you'll be able to take in a truly absorbing sight in the small, park-like area between the grounds and Jongno itself: dozens and dozens of elderly men dressed to the nines, playing oriental board games. Chinese chess and *baduk* are the games of choice; the latter is almost identical to the Japanese game *Go*, and there's even a local 24-hour television channel devoted to it. Heading west down the road, **Tapgol Park** (*see left*) marks the start of Insadonggil. Cross the road and walk further again, and you'll find **Bosingak**, a glorious wooden belfry. In dynastic times, when central Seoul was under curfew, its bell was rung to announce the daily opening and closing of the city gates; in fact, this is what gave Jongno its name – it translates as 'Bell Street'. These days it's only rung once a year, on New Year's Eve, when its environs are among the most crowded in Seoul. Heading west again, just before **Gwanghwamun Square** (*see right*) you'll see another old structure – the lovingly painted pavilion of **Bigak**. This has stood here since the 40th anniversary of King Gojong's accession to the throne in 1902, though it's now utterly dominated by **Kyobo Tower**, the large building looming up to the rear. This is one of two distinctive towers on Jongno: rising up from Anguk station is the 33-storey **Jongno Tower**, whose highest level is hoisted clear of the building's main body on three steel cylinders. These were added in 1999 by Uruguayan architect Rafael Viñoly, creating one of Seoul's most interesting pieces of modern architecture.

Just to the south, and tracing a parallel line to Jongno, is the man-made

Cheonggyecheon Stream – sunk a few metres below street level and with pedestrian-only paths on both banks, this is probably the best place to walk in central Seoul. Hand-holding couples totter across stepping stones, children jump in for a wade and there are occasional lantern festivals, but all this hides an absorbing history, stretching back to the earliest days of Joseon. The dynasty's first king, Taejo, died in 1408, after ceding power to his quarrelling sons. One of these, Taejeong, is said to have desecrated the tomb of Taejo's wife, and built parts of it into a bridge over Cheonggyecheon. After the Korean War (1950-53), the stream's banks were home to vast shanty towns of incredible squalor. Korea's economy took off in the 1960s and the stream was built over, then almost forgotten about – a point driven home when an elevated highway was erected over it in the 1970s. It was not until 2003 that Lee Myung-bak (then mayor of Seoul, and later president of the country) announced a US$250 million plan for its renovation, one almost shot down by angry local taxpayers. The renovations went ahead, however, and some of those who once grumbled about the cost of the project now saunter happily down the stream every day. It's fronted at its western terminus by *The Spring*, a red-and-blue coiled sculpture designed by Claes Oldenburg.

Gwanghwamun Square

Gwanghwamun station (line 5), follow signs inside station. **Map** p247 E3.

Gwanghwamun Square stretches south from the eponymous gate fronting Gyeongbokgung Palace. Formerly part of a 16-lane thoroughfare, it received extensive renovation in 2009, reopening as a more pedestrian-friendly place with fountains and other water features. Two statues jut from this expanse of concrete. At the southern end is Yi Sun-sin, a famed admiral who ingeniously repelled the Japanese invasions of the 1590s. Nearer the northern end sits King Sejong, one of Korea's greatest rulers and co-creator of the Hangeul script here today (*see p54* **Hangeul: a Korean Script**). Subterranean halls under Sejong's chair give some history of the area, though neither are terribly interesting.

▶ *Much of the square turns into a gigantic ice-skating rink in winter; see p193.*

FREE Ilmin Museum of Art
Sejongno 139 (2020-2055). Gwanghwamun station (line 5), exit 5. **Open** 11am-7pm Tue-Sun. **Admission** Free. **Map** p247 E3.

An interesting art museum in the former headquarters of *Dong-A Ilbo*, one of Korea's main newspapers. The old tile floors complement the art nicely. Almost entirely local, the permanent collection has a particular emphasis on paintings from the Goryeo Dynasty, while there are rotating exhibitions of newer Korean work. There's also a small café on site, which stays open until 10pm.

Jongmyo
Hunjeongdong 1-1. Jongno 3-ga station (lines 1, 3 & 5), exit 11. **Open** 9am-5pm Mon, Wed-Fri; 9am-6pm Sat, Sun. **Admission** ₩1,000, incl entry to Changgyeonggung Palace. **Map** p247 G2.

The large, forested grounds of Jongmyo were where the kings and queens of Joseon came to rest – not their bodies, which were interred in hill-like burial mounds around the city, but their spirits, housed in stone tablets and venerated by generations of descendants. The first hall was built here in 1394 and intended to house the spirits of seven kings and their queens; at the time of construction it was likely the longest building in East Asia. The dynastic line of kings continued far beyond the capacity of these initial plans, necessitating the construction of a larger hall in 1447. Both were damaged during the Japanese attacks of the 1590s, but have stood intact since being rebuilt shortly after.

▶ *For Changgyeonggung Palace, accessible on the same entry ticket as Jongmyo, see p43.*

INSIDE TRACK
JONGMYO JERYE

If you're in Seoul on the first Sunday in May, be sure to hit Jongmyo – this is when it plays host to the *jerye*, a rite held to worship the old kings and queens of Joseon. Dating back to the dawn of the dynasty in 1392, this is by far the most important Confucian ceremony in modern Korea, a slow-moving but highly colourful procedure usually accompanied by traditional court music.

DONGNIMMUN

Getting there: Dongnimmun station (line 3).
A short subway-ride west of Insadong is Dongnimmun, a scruffy area earmarked for development by the local government. It's home to one of Seoul's most interesting sights – **Seodaemun Prison History Hall** (*see right*), built as a prison by the Japanese during colonial times, and used to keep dissenters to their rule behind bars. Jutting up across the road from the prison is **Mt Inwangsan**, a prominent mountain of white and grey crags just to the west of Gyeongbokgung. Its peaks afford some of the best views in Seoul – not only of the palace, but the grand Samgaksan mountains to the north, and the skyscrapers of downtown stretching south. This is Seoul's main centre of shamanic shrines and practices, and also a great place to go hiking. Off the south-eastern foot of the mountain is **Sajik Park**, a small patch of (largely paved) land with some interesting features. Here you'll find old royal altars once used to worship the Earth and the harvest, as well as large statues of a great neo-Confucian philosopher and his mother. Just uphill behind the park there's an archery range – one of Seoul's only such facilities for this traditional practice – and a large modern shrine to Dangun, Korea's mythical founding king. Lastly, there's Korea's own Arc de Triomphe – **Independence Gate**, located rather incongruously next to a flyover south of Dongnimmun station.

Mt Inwangsan
From Dongnimmun station (line 3), exit 2.
The small mountain of Inwangsan is Seoul's centre of shamanic shrines and practices, and has been considered sacred for thousands of years. Its name is suitably auspicious: Inwangsan means 'Benevolent King Mountain', a term that intertwines meanings from Korean shamanism, Buddhism and Confucianism. The pine-lined trails feature some fascinating relics of the Joseon Dynasty: the restored 600-year-old city wall stretches over the long north-south ridge, and a steep (but paved) hiking trail runs all the way along its eastern side, offering an excellent day hike. However, the most interesting place on this mountain is the Inwangsa area halfway up the southern face – the most active site of Korean shamanism that most visitors will ever see. This steeply set compound contains a complex of Buddhist temples and shamanic shrines, which are gradually coming to be regarded as a single temple. They're clustered around Seonbawi, a sacred boulder, and the profound Guksadang spirit shrine. Visitors just might see some live-action shamanism happening up here – colourful performances revealing Korea's indigenous spirituality amid remarkable crags and twisted pines.

Seodaemun Prison History Hall

*Hyeonjeodong 101 (363-9650, www.sscmc.or.kr).
Dongnimmun station (line 3), exit 5.* **Open** *Mar-
Oct* 9.30am-6pm Tue-Sun. *Nov-Feb* 9.30am-5pm
Tue-Sun. **Admission** ₩1,000. **Map** p246 C2.
Though now converted to a museum, the old
Seodaemun Prison still exudes an eerie energy.
This was the main detention centre for dissenters
to Japanese colonial rule – thousands were impris-
oned here, and a fair proportion of those inmates
were tortured with near-drowning or confinement
in incredibly small spaces. Many met their end at

an annex building to the east of the main, red-brick
complex, outside which stands the 'Wailing Tree'.
Those on their way to the gallows often gripped
on to this on their way in, but only succeeded in
delaying the inevitable. Inside this annex is a far
smaller tree, which locals claim is kept stunted by
the souls of those executed just a few metres away.
These days, few Koreans remember that this
actually served as a prison long after the end of
occupation: South Korea was essentially a dictatorship until the 1980s, and thousands of dissenters
ended up here.

Shamanism

Spirits of Seoul.

Belief in a world inhabited and controlled by
spirits is the oldest form of Korean religion.
Shamanism was brought here from the
Siberian forests and Mongolian steppes,
and its practitioners were very powerful
in pre-historic tribal societies and the early
kingdoms. Shamanism merged with Chinese
Taoist ideas, and was then influenced by
Buddhism and Confucianism to evolve into
the unique, colourful and dynamic tradition
that is very much alive today.

Shamanist shrine, Inwangsan.

Korean shamanism was legally
suppressed by neo-Confucian elements
in the Joseon Dynasty (1392-1945); over
the years this led to the tradition being
considered the province of the uneducated
and lower class. The creed was wiped out
by North Korean communists, with many
adherents fleeing to the South before and
during the Korean War (1950-53).

Shamanism has not yet been declared an
official religion in Korea. Some leaders want
it to be recognised as such, but a lack of
organisation and standardisation – and
opposition from Christian groups – remain
obstacles. However, local governments near
some sacred mountains have fully legalised
their shrines, prompting a resurgence of
shamanist identity.

There is a loosely organised pantheon
of dozens of types of gods, spirits and
ghosts, ranging from the 'Great Guardian
Generals' who rule the directions of heaven
to powerful mountain-spirits known as
sanshin. Also included are spirits of
prominent trees, caves, boulders and piles
of stones, as well as agricultural spirits, the
tutelary gods of households and villages,
mischievous goblins, and ghosts. These
spirits are believed to have the power to
influence or change the fortunes of living
people, and Korean shamans communicate

with and supplicate them to solve the
problems of clients or communities.

Korean shamans of old were commonly
male, especially in the southern provinces,
where both skills and status were handed
down in hereditary fashion. Most shamans
now operating in South Korea are women,
known casually as *mudang* or politely as
manshin. They become intercessors between
spirits and human beings, using dances,
costumes, trances and repetitive chants.
They are often accepted or recruited after a
mysterious illness called *shinbyeong*, which
is recognised and cured by a senior *manshin*.

At least 20,000 shamans make a steady
living in Korea, and many more practise part-
time. Shamans are consulted as fortune-
tellers for financial and marital decisions,
and may practice geomancy. Their ritual
dances, featuring colourful robes,
expressive movements, chanting, drums
and ritual weapons, are now emerging as
public-performance arts and motifs, and
some are officially recognised by UNESCO
as forms of Intangible Cultural Heritage.
*The writer, David A Mason, is an author
and professor of Korean cultural tourism
at Seoul's Kyung Hee University.*

SIGHTS

Myeongdong, City Hall & Around

Korean high-rise at its highest.

Chunky business blocks radiate out from City Hall, creating a highly visible contrast with the more traditionally minded district of Insadong, just to the north. This has long been the Korean capital's own capital of commerce: not just for the suits staffing the aforementioned skyscrapers, but for the locals and tourists racing between the shops, restaurants, cafés and massage centres of the fascinating Myeongdong district. However, there's actually more to this area than consumption: it also features two old palaces, a charming cathedral and several fascinating museums.

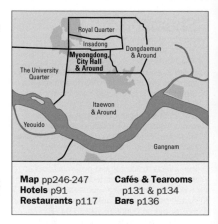

Map pp246-247	Cafés & Tearooms
Hotels p91	p131 & p134
Restaurants p117	Bars p136

NAVIGATING THE AREA

This business district is criss-crossed by subway lines, most pertinently lines 1 and 4, which meet underneath Seoul train station. Line 1 races north to hit City Hall, while line 4 heads east to Hoehyeon and Myeongdong stations. The Myeongdong area itself is largely pedestrianised, but such is the concentration of shoppers during weekends and weekday afternoons that it will still take time to get around.

MYEONGDONG

Getting there: Myeongdong station (line 4), Euljiro 1-ga station (line 2) or Euljiro 3-ga station (lines 2 & 3). It's also within walking distance of Insadong and Dongdaemun, and other places listed in this chapter.

Myeongdong is where Seoul goes to shop – as well as legions of visitors, especially from Japan, China and other Asian countries. The area hums with activity from morning until night; most places open at 10am and close at around 8pm, outside which times the streets can be eerily quiet. There are a few major department stores in this area –

the two most interesting are **Shinsegae** (*see p142*), a gorgeous chunk of colonial Korea and home to its most luxurious contemporary brands, and **Lotte** (*see p142*), a vast complex also featuring spas, cinemas, restaurants and Korea's biggest hotel (*see p93*). Most of the other shops in the area are decidedly smaller affairs, and number in their hundreds; the best time to go shopping here is during the Seoul Summer Sale (www.seoulsale.com), which usually takes place from late summer to early autumn – you can download discount vouchers in advance online.

Myeongdong is certainly more geared towards consumption than sightseeing, but one notable exception is **Myeongdong Cathedral**, which peers haughtily out over the shopping district. Many travellers also use Myeongdong as a base from which to attack the small mountain of Namsan, many choosing to head up by the **Namsan Cable Car** from here.

FREE Myeongdong Cathedral

Myeongdong 1-8 (774-3890, www.mdsd.or.kr). Euljiro 1-ga station (line 2), exit 5. **Open** 9am-9pm daily. **Admission** free. **Map** p247 F4.

Korea's oldest parish church and the main symbol of Korean Catholicism, the cathedral was built in the late 19th century, with King Gojong laying the first stone in 1892. It was consecrated in 1898, but the history of Catholicism in Korea started decades earlier as an academic novelty (*see p61* **Christianity in Korea**). The church has been used for political sanctuary many times in its history: during the Japanese colonial period, the period of the dictatorships that ran Korea in the following decades, and even today in smaller-scale struggles against the law. Indeed, the basement graveyard holds the shrines of several Christians martyred during the purges of the 1860s. Try to meander past the cathedral when the organ plays, usually around lunchtime.

★ Mt Namsan Cable Car

753-2403, www.cablecar.co.kr. Myeongdong station (line 4), exit 3. **Open** 10am-11pm daily. **Tickets** ₩6,000 one-way, ₩7,500 round-trip. **Map** p247 G4.

There are a number of different ways to ascend Mt Namsan (the name means 'South Mountain'), Seoul's small city-centre peak, including several rubberised hiking trails which criss-cross the slopes – see p82 for more details. However, this is undoubtedly the most fun way to reach the summit: a 600m-long cable car trip up from Myeongdong. Views are splendid all the way to the top, a full 140m above the base. The trip only takes three minutes, so even those who are a little afraid of heights should be fine. Each car can hold up to 48 people, and departures are regular; however, the lower base is still a sweaty uphill walk from Myeongdong station.

CITY HALL

Getting there: City Hall station (lines 1 & 2). It's also within walking distance of Insadong and other places listed in this chapter.

The Royal Quarter may have been the de facto centre of Seoul for centuries, but today the real focus of proceedings is based around City Hall. As well as being the administrative hub of the city, this is also an important place for citizens – **Seoul Plaza** (*photo p60*), the circular patch of grass to the south of City Hall, is a venue for major musical performances, protests, and even an ice skating rink in the winter (*see p193*).

City Hall's central political and cultural role is somewhat ironic, since the building itself is actually a colonial-era structure, built by the Japanese in 1926. Many locals would rather see the back of this stately remnant of occupation, but it is, and will remain, a listed structure. However, at the time of writing major changes were afoot: the old City Hall was being gutted and transformed into a

Myeongdong.

library, while a new, futuristic structure was being built alongside it. On its completion, scheduled for 2012, much of it will be open to the public.

Heading south of City Hall will bring you to the Namdaemun market area (*see p145*), but there's plenty to see immediately to the west. Just across the road is **Deoksugung Palace**, one of Seoul's famed five palaces and a disarmingly beautiful place; interestingly, the complex also contains a few colonial-era brick structures, one of which houses the **National Museum of Contemporary Art**. The palace is bounded to the south by **Deoksugunggil**, a road with an interesting secret; *see p60* **Inside Track**. This is one of Seoul's most charming roads – little trafficked, lined with gingko trees and lit

---

INSIDE TRACK
CHANGING OF THE GUARD

Come to Deoksugung Palace at the right time and you'll catch the changing of the guard. This colourful ceremony takes place each day except Monday at 11am, 2pm and 3.30pm, and goes on for around half an hour.

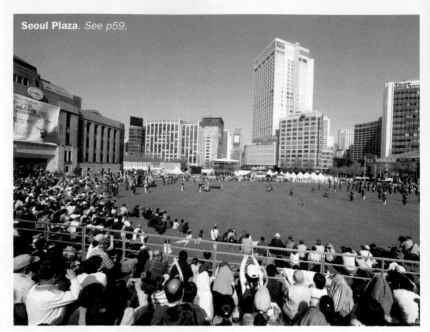

Seoul Plaza. *See p59.*

SIGHTS

up at night with fairy lights. Heading west from the palace, you'll soon see the wonderful **Seoul Museum of Art** to your left – this is where Matisse, Van Gogh and company come to play when they're in Seoul. It's another colonial-era structure, and there are plenty more in the area, most notably the former **Russian Legation**. King Gojong, Korea's last monarch, holed up here for a while during the height of Japanese occupation.

Also on Deoksugunggil is the wonderful **Chongdong Theater** (*see p197*), which hosts some of Seoul's best performances of traditional music.

INSIDE TRACK THE ROAD OF BROKEN HEARTS

Deoksugunggil is a small, relatively traffic-free road running south of Deoksugung Palace. Lined with gingko trees and illuminated at night with fairy lights, it may seem like an ideal date location, but you'll see precious few couples. Seoul's main divorce courts were once located here, and it has long been seen as bad luck for couples to walk along this road: according to local lore, you'll split up even before reaching the end.

★ Deoksugung Palace
Taepyeongno 58 (771-9955, www.deoksugung. go.kr). City Hall station (lines 1 & 2), exit 2. **Open** 9am-9pm Tue-Sun. **Admission** ₩1,000. **Map** p247 E3.

About as close to the heart of downtown as you can get, this palace started life as a residence of the crown prince. After the Japanese invaded in 1592 and destroyed the other royal palaces, Prince Wolsan (older brother to King Seongjong) made it his home. After King Gwanghaegun was enthroned here in 1608, he renamed it Gyeongungung. In 1618, the 'official' palace was moved to newly rebuilt Changdeokgung, and this palace became a back-up or auxiliary building.

Fast forward to 1897, when King Gojong proclaimed the founding of the Korean Empire – and himself as emperor – here. This came despite the advances in Japanese control, and was seen as a break in the hitherto one-way order of things. Emperor Gojong didn't last long, however, as he was forced out by the Japanese and confined to the palace. The palace was renamed Deoksugang.

There are plenty of modern touches here, which you won't see in other Seoul palaces. The first European-style garden and fountain built in Korea were completed here in 1910. The hall of Seokjojeon, which once housed the National Museum of Korea, shows some 19th-century western influences. The west wing of this building houses the National Museum of Contemporary Art (*see p62*).

Christianity in Korea

Seoul's new religion.

Catholicism was introduced to North-east Asia by the Italian Jesuit Matteo Ricci (1552-1610), whose book in Chinese, *The True Meaning of the Lord of Heaven*, reached Korea along with other books introducing western learning. Beginning in 1777, a group of scholars began to meet in a remote hermitage to study Catholicism. Late in 1783, one of the group led a diplomatic mission to Beijing, accompanied by his son, Yi Seung-hun. In 1784, Yi S ng-hun was baptised in Beijing. On returning to Seoul, he baptised the other members of his circle. From the start the believers bridged Korea's class divide. The group of Catholics would meet in a house on the hill where Myeongdong Cathedral now stands.

Catholics began to be persecuted at once, because they refused to celebrate ancestral worship rites, considered by the state to be an essential part of Korean culture, and in 1801 the community was decimated during a fierce persecution. However, the faith survived despite the fact there were no ordained priests in Korea until clergy from France arrived secretly from 1836. Many were martyred. Persecutions continued, the worst being in 1866, in which thousands of Catholics died.

Protestantism came to Korea following the opening of the country in 1882. Methodist and Presbyterian missionaries arrived from Canada and the US, together with a smaller Anglican mission from England. They founded hospitals, schools and other socially useful institutions while encouraging Koreans to establish churches and engage in evangelising. The Bible was translated by a committee of experts. Then came the annexation of Korea by Japan. Many of the leaders of the Independence Movement were Protestants and the Japanese viewed both them and the foreign missionaries with great suspicion. In the later 1930s, many missionaries were forced to leave Korea.

After 1945, the communists who took control of North Korea were deeply hostile to Christianity; thousands of Christians, Protestant and Catholic, fled to the South before or during the war (1950-53) and in North Korea religion was completely abolished. After the Korean War the churches in South Korea grew rapidly. The Catholic Church was slower to increase its numbers but its witness to justice and truth during the years of dictatorship, its integrity and its spirituality have brought many to it in recent decades.

It is impossible to say exactly how many Koreans are active members of a church today. Many sources indicate that there are about eight million Protestants and five million Catholics. The Anglican Church is relatively small and there is also a tiny Orthodox community. The many Protestant churches that term themselves Presbyterian are themselves divided into a large number of competing tendencies. There are a number of mega-churches boasting of tens of thousands of members, while many churches are very small. In short, Christianity in Korea is diverse. And today – In a reversal of the earlier days of Korean Christianity – Korean clergy and lay people of all denominations are being sent overseas as missionaries.

The writer, Brother Anthony of Taizé (www.hompi.sogang.ac.kr/anthony), was born in England and has lived in Korea since 1980. He is currently president of the Royal Asiatic Society Korea Branch (www.raskb.com), which serves as a forum for English-speakers to learn more about Korea through lectures and visits.

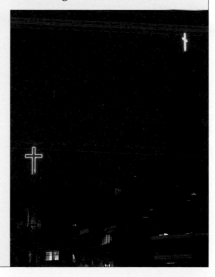

SIGHTS

SIGHTS

Deoksugung Palace. *See p60.*

Deoksugung may lack some of the out-and-out grandeur of the other Seoul palaces, but its modern styling brings a different perspective to Korea's dynastic past. The royal changing of the guards ceremony happens three times a day – *see p59* **Inside Track**.

FREE National Museum of Contemporary Art

Taepyeongno 58 (2022-0600, www.moca.go.kr). City Hall station (lines 1 & 2), exit 2. **Open** 9am-6.30pm daily. **Admission** free; ₩3,000 special exhibitions. **Map** p247 E3.

Don't confuse this with the main Museum of Contemporary Art, which is located south of Seoul in Gwacheon (*see p77*). This is the Deoksugung Annex, which provides an opportunity to take in some modern art without leaving the downtown area. The second floor features rotating exhibitions, while the third floor shows modern pieces selected by the curators. Artists featured during past special exhibitions have included Picasso, Nosoo Pak and Bae Bein-U. JM Brown, the British financial advisor to the Empire of Korea during its dying days, designed the building in 1900, and it was finished by the Japanese in 1910. It's now called Seokjojeon Hall, and the museum is located in its west wing. The museum itself actually started life in Gyeongbokgung in July 1973, and was moved here in 1998.

★ Seoul Museum of Art

Seosomundong 37 (2124-8800, www.seoulmoa. seoul.go.kr). City Hall station (lines 1 & 2), exit 1. **Open** 10am-9pm Tue-Fri; 10am-7pm Sat, Sun. **Admission** Varies; usually ₩12,000 for major exhibitions. **Map** p247 E3.

The Seoul Museum of Art has long prided itself on a good balance of technically proficient art, and modern, popular tastes. When the work of international masters comes to Seoul, this is where they usually end up – Picasso, Matisse and Van Gogh are among those to have featured in exhibitions. The building itself is also notable: a colonial-era structure built in 1938 as an art gallery, it found a new lease of life after independence as the Korean Supreme Court building. It has since been totally remodelled, while the building's façade, in Renaissance style, was retained and preserved. The interior is now bright and spacious, perfect for displaying art. There's a café and snack bar on the premises.

SEODAEMUN

Getting there: Seodaemun station (line 5). It's also within walking distance of other areas in this chapter.

Like Namdaemun and Dongdaemun, Seodaemun is named after one of Seoul's four old city gates – this was the western one, but the structure itself no longer exists. The area that it lent its name to, just west of City Hall, is part business, part residential, and rather unremarkable but for two phenomenal sights, conveniently located right next to each other: the wonderful **Gyeonghuigung Palace** and the gigantic **Seoul Museum of History**.

FREE Gyeonghuigung Palace

Sinmunno 1 (724-0274). Gwanghwamun station (line 5), exit 7. **Open** *10am-6pm Tue-Fri; 9am-6pm Sat, Sun.* **Admission** *free.* **Map** p247 E3.

Of Seoul's five palaces, Gyeonghuigung is certainly the runt of the litter: unlike its four more illustrious siblings, no admission fee is charged, and even the old throne room is open to entry. In addition, it only gets a fraction of the other palaces' visitor numbers, but herein lies its beauty – this is the most relaxing palace in Seoul, and some visitors actually rate it their favourite. Gyeonghuigung may be a little smaller than the other palaces, and its structures slightly less elegant, but it's well worth a visit, especially considering its proximity to the Seoul Museum of History, just down the path.

★ FREE Seoul Museum of History

Saemunangil 50 (724-0194, www.museum. seoul.kr). Gwanghwamun station (line 5), exit 7. **Open** *9am-9pm Mon-Fri; 9am-7pm Sat, Sun.* **Admission** *free (ticket required from reception); ₩700 for most temporary exhibitions.* **Map** p247 E3.

Seoul's main historical museum is very large, very interesting, and one of the city's best places in which to while away a rainy day. The permanent exhibits chart each segment of the city's fascinating past, from the Stone Age to present times. The displays of Joseon-era paintings and earthenware are particularly interesting. A more recent creation is the large floor map of Seoul, which children find particularly riveting. These permanent exhibitions have free entry, but some wings of the museum host temporary exhibitions of art or photography – this is almost always work of extremely high quality, so it's worth giving the museum's website a look to see what's going on. Also on the complex is Kongdu Iyagi, a restaurant serving delectable neo-Korean food.

▶ *For our full review of Kongdu Iyagi, see p118.*

NAMDAEMUN

Getting there: Hoehyeon station (line 4). It's also within walking distance of other places listed in this section.

Lying south of City Hall, Namdaemun provides the southern counterpoint to Dongdaemun. Like its more famous brother, Namdaemun got its name from one of Seoul's old city gates – it means 'South Great Gate'. The portal itself,

also known as Sungnyemun, has a tragic recent history, having been nearly destroyed by an arson attack in 2008. The chunky, elaborately painted gate had stood proudly over the area since 1398, just after Seoul was declared capital of the new Joseon kingdom. It had been awarded official status as the country's most important cultural monument, having been one of the only important structures in the city to emerge unscathed from Japanese occupation, the Korean War and six full centuries of wear and tear. However, in the evening of 10 February 2008, one man and a few cans of paint thinner saw the structure's wooden cap damaged beyond repair – a calamity, in the eyes of most locals. However, Seoul has rich experience of rebuilding – more or less everything else of age in the city is a reproduction – and Namdaemun should be returned to its former glory by 2013.

Namdaemun and Dongdaemun have another interesting parallel – they have both lent their name to gigantic markets. Like its rival to the east, **Namdaemun market** (*see p145*) is absolutely gigantic, a beast that sprawls across several city blocks, both indoors and out. There's little actual sightseeing to be done in the immediate area, but the wonderfully designed **Rodin Gallery** certainly merits a mention, along with the unusual **Bank of Korea Museum**.

FREE Bank of Korea Museum

Namdaemunno 110 (759-4881). Hoehyeon station (line 4), exit 7. **Open** *10am-5pm Tue-Sun.* **Admission** *free.* **Map** p247 F4.

A money-related museum housed in a gorgeous building that once housed the Bank of Korea. It was designed by Tatsuno Kingo, a man also responsible for Tokyo train station, and built in 1912. Walking into the building's present incarnation, be sure to note the Renaissance-style trimmings on the walls and ceiling; the exhibitions themselves are also quite diverting, particularly those showcasing the production of money, and the collection of rare notes and coins from around the world.

Rodin Gallery

1F Samsung Life Insurance Building, Taepyeongno (2259-7781, www.plateau.or.kr). City Hall subway (lines 1 & 2), exit 8. **Open** *10am-6pm Tue-Sun.* **Map** p254 E4.

One of only a handful of galleries worldwide specially constructed for the display of Rodin's work. Two of his major sculptures – *The Burghers of Calais* and *The Gates of Hell* – are on display in the glass pavilion, a superb, looping construction that was designed around them. Illuminated during twilight hours, it forms a sumptuous pair with the adjacent Namdaemun Gate, which has stood here since the 1390s.

SIGHTS

Dongdaemun & Around

From the mountains to the markets.

Named after Seoul's old eastern gate, the Dongdaemun area is relatively central these days. The wider district stretches all the way from Mount Namsan to the northern peaks, with some terrific sights: these include a cutesy re-creation of a dynastic village, **Namsangol Hanok Village** (*see below*), one of Seoul's most ambitious examples of modern architecture, **Dongdaemun Design Plaza** (*see p66*), and the country's largest market. These form a pleasing contrast with the area's more subtle draws: wooden teahouses, royal burial tombs and Confucian shrines.

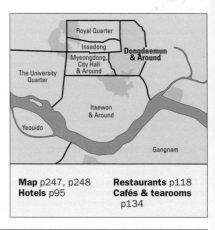

| Map p247, p248 | Restaurants p118 |
| Hotels p95 | Cafés & tearooms p134 |

NAVIGATING THE AREA

The area covered in this section is wide and comparatively tricky to get around, though subway line 4 loosely strings it together. On this line, Chungmuro and Dongdaemun are accessible via stations of the same name; Chungmuro is also on line 3, and Dongdaemun on line 1. Line 4 is also best for Daehangno (via Hyehwa subway station) and Seongbukdong (via Hansung Univ. station). The sights around the latter are fairly scattered, and though they're within walking distance, navigating your way though the hilly lanes can be tricky – it may be best to take a taxi. Also note that Chungmuro is an easy walk from Myeongdong, as is Dongdaemun from Insadong; the banks of Cheonggyecheon stream are the most enjoyable way in which to move between the latter.

CHUNGMURO

Getting there: Chungmuro station (lines 3 & 4).
The area around Chungmuro subway station has long had a somewhat downbeat air, one quite at odds with Myeongdong, just a stone's throw to the west. However, times are changing, and this will soon be home to one of Seoul's largest ever construction projects; *see p68* **All Change on the Jinyang Stretch**. The area's northern end slopes up towards Namsan, a mountain that many choose to attack by foot, bus or taxi from Chungmuro. The one sight of note is **Namsangol Hanok Village**, a cute array of wooden buildings.

FREE Namsangol Hanok Village

Pildong 84-1 (2264-4412). Chungmuro subway (lines 3 & 4), exit 3. **Open** *Apr-Oct* 9am-9pm Mon, Wed-Sun. *Nov-Mar* 9am-8pm Mon, Wed-Sun. **Admission** Free. **Map** p247 G4.
It's certainly worth the trip to Chungmuro to check out this little re-creation of a Joseon-era *hanok* village. The beautiful wooden buildings are actually replicas of those once owned by high-ranking government officials – veritable mansions, at the time. With the building eaves strung with lovely silk lanterns, it's perhaps best to put off a visit until the sun is about to set. The grounds around the village are home to the Namsan Gugakdang performance hall, and rise up to Mt Namsan – it's quite possible to walk up the mountain, using this as your starting base. Also note that Namsangol is used as a focal point during national celebrations such as Chuseok, Seollal and Dano.

SIGHTS

Namsangol Hanok Village.

SIGHTS

For Namsan Gugakdang, see p197. For national holidays, see p165 **A Nation on the Move**.

DONGDAEMUN

Getting there: Dongdaemun subway (lines 1 & 4) or Dongdaemun History & Culture Park subway (lines 2, 4 & 5).

It's quite astonishing to think that Seoul once ended here. Dongdaemun means 'East Great Gate', a reference to the large, ornamental portal built here in the 1390s. The beautiful structure you'll see today only dates from 1869, and is now surrounded on all sides by teeming traffic. Today, however, 'Dongdaemun' is more often used to refer to **Dongdaemun Market** (*see right* **Profile**), a simply gigantic shopping area that has been around for centuries, and starts just to the west. Also here is the **Dongdaemun Design Plaza**, one of the city's more adventurous stabs at civic planning; Dongmyo Shrine, a remnant of the early 17th century, provides a small but pleasing counterbalance, its wooden buildings hemmed in by high-rises.

FREE Dongdaemun Design Plaza

Dongdaemun (3708-2414, http://ddp.seoul.go.kr). Dongdaemun History & Culture Park station (lines 2, 4 & 5), exit 1. **Open** Varies. **Admission** Free. **Map** p248 J3.

Dongdaemun.

One of Seoul's largest civic projects, this plaza and park fills a whole city block. This area was once home to a baseball stadium, floodlights from which tower over the complex. Said to be the shape of cigarette smoke, it was designed by Iraq-born architect Zaha Hadid, though certain elements of the plan had to be ripped up when Joseon-era artefacts were found during excavations. Many of these are now on display in a small museum, while elsewhere in the complex you'll find an art gallery and design library.

DAEHANGNO

Getting there: Hyehwa station (line 4).

This area's name translates as 'University Road', which gives a fair hint as to its predominant demographic. A number of educational institutes are dotted around, the most important of which is **Sung Kyun Kwan University**, which dates back to 1398. Though nothing remains from that time, some buildings on its present-day campus are of century-plus vintage. The roads leading to the university gates from exit 4 of Hyehwa station are packed with cheap snack shacks, bars and shops; in the first few years of the new millennium this area had a decidedly renegade feel to it, though one now diluted with chain stores and restaurants. The one area retaining some flavour is on the other side of the station (exit 2), which has the interesting **Arko Art Gallery** and a whole clutch of small theatres; performances in this area are in Korean only and largely impenetrable to foreign visitors, but you may catch something interesting at **Marronnier Park**, a small outdoor expanse where up-and-coming performers hone their acts. This is also one of the main venues for the Seoul Performing Arts Festival (*see p164*).

Heading north-east along subway line 4, **Hansung University** and **Sungshin Women's University** are accessed via stations of the same name. The former has some particularly cheap bars and chicken restaurants, while the latter also provides access to the **Jeongneung Tombs** – the resting place of several Joseon Dynasty royals.

Arko Art Gallery

Dongsungdong 130-1 (760-4850). Hyehwa station (line 4), exit 2. **Open** 11am-7pm Tue-Sun. **Admission** ₩2,000; more for some exhibitions. **Map** p247 H1.

Just off Marronnier Park and affiliated to the Arts Council of Korea, the striking *hangeul* typography on this large, red-brick building states that 'art makes life more interesting than art itself'. The curators attempt to validate this claim with high-quality exhibitions of local fare. Most of the work is contemporary, although, given the surrounding area, it may come as something of a surprise to see that featured artists are primarily established folk, rather than students.

Profile Dongdaemun Market

Deciphering the indecipherable.

The numbers are staggering. The sprawling market area known as Dongdaemun has no fewer than 20 shopping malls, and more than 30,000 individual shops. It's also a place of residence, manufacture, transport and much more.

Dongdaemun Market is so named because of its proximity to Seoul's old eastern gate. The gate has been around in various guises since 1396, and while the market is not quite of that vintage, it too has stood the test of time. The area has seen trade for centuries, but Dongdaemun's first incarnation as an official market came during the Japanese occupation in 1905. Even then it was the largest such facility on the Korean peninsula, with medicinal herbs, silk clothing, light machinery and even pet monkeys for sale. More or less everything was flattened during the Korean War of 1950-53, but following the ceasefire and the resulting partition of the peninsula, Dongdaemun became a symbol of South Korea's 'can-do' attitude, and resumed its status as the focal point of Seoul's trade.

Today's Dongdaemun can be hard to get one's head around. In fact, to call it a market is to miss the point somewhat: the action takes place over a number of city blocks, both indoors and out. It's a bewildering place, even for those who have been here before, but there is method to the apparent madness. It runs east to west along the man-made Cheonggyecheon stream, whose northern bank is edged with a subsection known as **Gwangjang Market** (*photo p69*). Though a fairly run-of-the-mill section of covered market by day, it comes alive at night when two intersecting alleys burst open to feed the local masses – the atmosphere can be quite

intoxicating. Crossing back over Cheonggyecheon, it will become evident that its southern bank is lined with a snake-like run of indoor markets; these have several levels filled with cheap clothing, though they're mostly aimed at an older crowd.

Youngsters tend to head to Heunginmunno, a busy road that functions as the market area's north–south spine. The west side of the road is a near-continuous run of skyscraper malls: Doosan Tower ('Doota' to its friends) is the tallest, but Migliore, Cerestar and Hello APM are equally busy. Knock-off brand-name goods are a speciality both in and around these buildings. On the other side of the road is the latest Dongdaemun accessory: the Dongdaemun Design Plaza (*see p66*), a futuristic complex designed by Zaha Hadid, and a pretty good indicator of Seoul's architectural intentions.

SIGHTS

Jeongneung Tombs

Jeongneungdong 87-16 (no phone). Sungshin Women's Univ. subway (line 4), exit 5. **Open** *Mar-Oct* 6am-6.30pm Tue-Sun. *Nov-Feb* 6am-5.30pm Tue-Sun. **Admission** Free.

This gorgeous park complex is rarely visited by anyone but those living in the area, making it all the more interesting to explore. It's the resting place of Sindeok, the first of Seoul's many Joseon queens – she was the wife of King Taejo, who was the inaugurator of the Joseon Dynasty in 1392. As with all of Korea's dynastic monarchs, after death she was interred in a grassy burial mound, which now fits quite beautifully into the surrounding area. Sindeok's story actually got more interesting *after* her death; be sure to pick up a pamphlet for the full account.

SEONGBUKDONG

Getting there: Hansung Univ. station (line 4) is the closest to the following sights, though, given their scattered nature, it's much easier to take a cab from the station.

The district of Seongbukdong crawls uphill towards Seoul's northern mountains. This relatively rarified air has long been roping in a more affluent set, which these days includes a fair proportion of Seoul's foreign diplomats – walking around the hilly lanes, you'll see some mansions that would be considered large in any city around the world, and relatively few of the ugly apartment blocks that Seoul is better known for. The oldest and most interesting of these mansions and villas are

All Change on the Jinyang Stretch

The end of an old snake of brutalist buildings.

Seoul doesn't really do retro, and has for years had its gaze steadfastly focused on the future. The area stretching south of Chungmuro station was one of the more appealing slices of Seoul back in the early 1960s, a warren of tight lanes home to dozens of printing presses. But a perfectly straight line of monstrous buildings was built here in 1965, with two full kilometres of gargantuan markets and apartment blocks stretching all the way from Chungmuro's Jinyang Tower to the Jongmyo

Shrine. It was hugely ambitious civil planning, on a scale rarely matched since.

At the time of construction, these were some of the city's largest buildings and visible for miles around, but with so much development since, they have largely been forgotten by modern Seoul; few locals are even aware of their existence. By 2015, the brutalist stretch will have been demolished to make way for a band of parkland, fringed with skyscrapers of chrome and glass: Seoul looking forwards once more.

View from **Jinyang Tower**.

SIGHTS

Gwangjang Market. *See p67.*

used in various ways today: **Seongnagwon** is now open to the public as a beautiful park area; **Suyeon Sanbang** (*see p134*) is now one of Seoul's most atmospheric tearooms; one old mansion complex has been converted into the **Furniture Museum**; and **Samcheonggak** (*see p111*), once a presidential pleasure place, is now a high-end restaurant. Beyond Seongnagwon is **Gilsangsa Temple**, which sits across the road from the famous shop **Hyojae** (*see p155*).

Furniture Museum

Seongbukdong 330-577 (745-0181, www.kofum. com). Hansung Univ. subway (line 4), exit 6. **Open** 1-5pm daily. **Admission** ₩20,000 incl 1 drink.

A real gem, despite ticket prices that are among the highest in the city. The museum is set in a superbly remodelled *hanok* house – the raised walkway is a particularly nice touch, and was once an indication of high status. The building houses a wonderful collection of antique Korean furniture; during the Three Kingdoms period, Korean artesans lent their skills to Japan, which became better known than Korea for its craft work. The styles are similar – restrained, elegant, delightful.

FREE Gilsangsa

Seongbukdong 323 (3672-5945). Hansung University subway (line 4), exit 6. **Open** 24hrs daily. **Admission** Free.

A very pleasant Buddhist temple, whose appearance at the foot of forested hills makes it far closer to the Korean norm than other temples in Seoul. When you've tired of wandering around the dirt tracks, it's quite tempting to fall into the tiny on-site teahouse.

FREE Seongnagwon

Seongbukdong 2-22 (no phone). Hansung Univ. subway (line 4), exit 6. **Open** varies. **Admission** Free.

This large, park-like area receives next to no visitors, but is certainly worth a peep if you're in the area – and if you can find it. The compound has had some illustrious owners. In the past, it housed high-ranking government officials, and, in the early 20th century, even one of King Gojong's sons.

INSIDE TRACK
LITTLE CENTRAL ASIA
AND LITTLE PHILIPPINES

The wider Dongdaemun area is home to two of Seoul's more interesting ethnic communities, both of which remain a mystery to most locals. The area west of Dongdaemun History & Culture Park railway station is often referred to as Russiatown by expats, thanks to the ubiquitous Cyrillic writing; however, most of the traders here are actually Mongolian and Uzbek. The area is best appreciated through restaurants such as **Gostiny Dvor** (*see p118*). Up in Daehangno there's a large Filipino community, which hosts a fascinating Sunday market (9am-6pm) north of Hyehwa Rotary.

The University Quarter

First-class partying

Seoul has dozens of universities, but the concentration of lively students is at its greatest in this small zone just west of the city centre. In Korea, university areas double as the best nightlife zones in almost every single city, but this is particularly in evidence in Seoul: the near-conjoined districts of Hongdae and Sinchon have a simply astonishing number of bars, clubs and other places of entertainment. This is the best-known nightlife centre in the whole country – so get ready to party along three straight kilometres of undiluted pleasure.

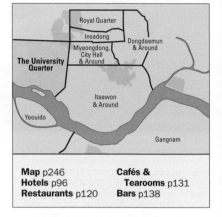

Map p246	**Cafés &**
Hotels p96	**Tearooms** p131
Restaurants p120	**Bars** p138

NAVIGATING THE UNIVERSITY QUARTER

The universities lie clustered around subway line 2. Four successive stations are particularly notable: running from east to west are Ewha Womans University, Sinchon and Hongik University (also referred to as Hongdae) stations. Next is Hapjeong station, within walking distance of which are the only true sights in the area. This is also a stop on line 6; a few further stops west is World Cup Stadium station, good for the stadium and its surrounding parkland. Note that Hongik University is also a stop on the AREX airport line, and the area is particularly popular for backpacker accommodation.

HONGDAE

Getting there: Hongik Univ. station (line 2), Sangsu station (line 6) and Hapjeong station (line 6).

Hongdae is the most famous nightlife district in the whole country. It's centred around **Hongik University**, which caters mainly to the arts. Study, however, is far from the mind of most visitors, who come to eat, drink and be merry: you'll find plenty of recommendations in our

restaurants, bars and nightlife chapters. Actual tourist sights are very thin on the ground – in fact, almost non-existent. The exceptions in Hongdae itself are **Norita Park**, a small triangle of land often humming with music and performances on weekends, and **Sang Sang Ma Dang**, a seven-storey complex with a number of arty attractions. The park also has interesting flea markets on weekend afternoons. Just down by the river, south of Hapjeong station, are a couple of sights pertaining to colonial-era Christian activity in the area – the **Jeoldusan Catholic Martyrs' Shrine** and the **Yanghwajin Foreigners' Cemetery**.

★ FREE Jeoldusan Catholic Martyrs' Shrine

Hapjeongdong 96-1 (3142-4434, www.jeoldusan. or.kr). Hapjeong station (lines 2 & 6), exit 7.
Open 10am-noon, 1-5pm Tue-Sun. **Admission** free; donations welcome.
Centred on a small cliff named Jeoldusan, this pleasant, park-like area conceals a rather gruesome secret, dating back to the 1860s. At the time, Catholicism was taking hold in Korea, partly due to the secret efforts of western missionaries. Nine French missionaries were discovered in 1866 and executed; the

French warships sent in retaliation came up the Hangang River to Jeoldusan, but were eventually forced to retreat. There then followed a purge of Korean Catholics, who were beheaded at the top of the cliff, then thrown on to the rocks below. In all, over 100 martyrs have been made saints, giving Korea one of the world's highest totals. Exactly a century after the executions, a church and memorial hall were built here; the latter has an interesting display about early Korean churches. The site received a couple of high-profile visitors in the 1980s: Pope John Paul II came in 1984, and Mother Teresa the following year.

▶ *For more on Christianity in Korea, see p61.*

FREE Sang Sang Ma Dang

Seogyodong 367-5 (330-6200). Sangsu station (line 6), exit 1. **Open** *Art Square* 10am-11pm daily. *Café* 10am-10pm daily. *Gallery* 1-10pm daily. **Admission** free.

This modern block-style building became one of Seoul's more adventurous slices of modern architecture, following the addition of gooey concrete-and-glass cladding in 2007. The interior is also fascinating: on the ground floor there's a shop selling arty home products, all designed by local university students; a couple of floors up is an interesting gallery; the top floor has a café with good views but awful coffee; and in the basement there's an arthouse cinema (*see p170*). Definitely worth a look if you're in the area.

FREE Yanghwajin Foreigners' Cemetery

Hapjeongdong 144 (332-9174). Hapjeong station (lines 2 & 6), exit 7. **Open** 9am-6pm daily. **Admission** free.

Head towards the river from the martyrs' shrine and you'll come across this small cemetery. It came into

Rooms for a View

The key to Seoul's youth culture.

Seoul is full of user-friendly features – take its rooms for hire, variously equipped so you can sing karaoke, surf the internet or watch a film, any time of day or night. These are particularly prevalent in the university area – students need something to take their minds off study. Most common is the *norae-bang*, which translates as 'song room'. These are karaoke parlours in which couples or small groups rent out a small room, which contains a large television, a book of songs and a few percussion instruments. These rooms typically cost around ₩15,000 per hour;

local men often opt to add female accompaniment (usually above board) for an extra ₩10,000.

Then there are the DVD-*bang*, small rooms in which films can be watched in private – there are whole banks of DVDs to choose from at reception, and a room will cost in the region of ₩12,000. They're extremely popular with courting couples.

Lastly, almost every major road in Seoul features at least one PC-*bang*, or internet café; very few use these for checking their emails – online gaming is the thing here. They usually start at ₩1,000 per hour.

being in 1890 after the death of Presbytarian minister John Heron; Seoul's foreign community was growing at the time, and this area was given over for the burial of non-Koreans. Most of those interred here were missionaries, though a number of diplomats and journalists lie alongside them.

SINCHON & EWHA WOMANS UNIVERSITY

Getting there: Sinchon station (line 2) and Ewha Womans Univ. station (line 2).

The neighbourhood of Sinchon is one of the wildest nightlife spots in the land. Head north from the subway station of the same name and you'll find literally hundreds of bars and restaurants, usually with prices to match their student clientele. The area around Ewha Womans University (usually referred to as E-dae) is equally colourful, though since most students here are female it's more of a shopping district. The only 'sights' as such in these areas are the university buildings, some of which are architecturally interesting.

SIGHTS

School Daze

The race to the top.

There is one dream shared by almost all South Korean parents: that their children attend one of the nation's top universities. And as far as they're concerned, only three universities really matter; Seoul National University, Korea University and Yonsei University (SKY). Admission into one of these is perceived as a means for a family to climb the social ladder and amass wealth, and it's for these reasons that Korean children are subjected to a level of educational pressure and competition that many non-Koreans might consider rather frightening.

Students are expected to study day, night and over the weekend from the time they enter elementary school until their high school graduation. In addition to the normal school day, most children attend private academies called *hakwon*, which were only recently forced by law to end classes before 10pm. Most important is studying for the dreaded university entrance exam, which will more or less determine a student's future – and by extension, that of their family. Some Koreans who fail to enter a SKY university on their first attempt will try over and over again until their score is high enough for acceptance.

For many students, a major source of academic frustration is English. Families spend thousands of dollars a year in extracurricular language education; some provinces have even opened up so-called English Villages, where students can submerge themselves in surroundings that are meant to resemble British or American towns. The demand for language instruction is so high that the South Korean government is funding a project to create English teaching robots in lieu of hiring native speakers from abroad. But as many

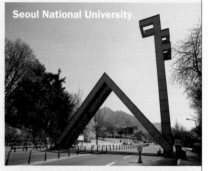
Seoul National University.

visitors to South Korea discover, all the time and money spent on learning English doesn't seem to match the ability of many Koreans to actually speak the language.

In recent years, there's been a backlash against the rigours of Korea's education system. In 2011, a string of suicides at a prestigious engineering school forced many to re-examine the pressure placed on students. Some families don't want their children to be exposed to the competition, and take their kids out of the school system altogether: for those who can afford it, education abroad is a much more attractive option.

That's what 50-year-old Suh Hee-jung thought. She sent both her son and daughter to high school and college in the US so that they wouldn't have to deal with the pressure in Korea. 'The Korean education system is focused only on studying, and only a student's grades are important,' says Suh. 'There's no opportunity for a student to play sports or do other activities. I just don't think kids can have a happy life as a student.'

A short walk from Sinchon station, the campus of **Yonsei University** has a few buildings dating from the 1890s to the 1920s, all elegant structures now cloaked with creeper vines. The statue of an American, Horace Underwood, dates back to 1928 and is said to be the oldest in Seoul – he founded the **Jejungwon**, a hospital within the Yonsei grounds that's also claimed to be the first such facility in the country.

One station further east is **Ewha Womans University** (the spelling and lack of apostrophe is deliberate), whose campus also features a few Gothic buildings from that era. These are augmented by a new wing, whose central, open-air walkway starts above ground and dives far below – a wonderful piece of modern architecture designed by French architect Dominique Perrault.

WEST MAPO

Getting there: World Cup Stadium station (line 6).
The district of Mapo-gu is the westernmost part of Seoul north of the river, and largely made up of uninteresting multi-storey apartment blocks. Tourists most commonly rifle straight through it on their way to the DMZ, but there are a couple of diversions near its western end. This is the location of **Seoul World Cup Stadium**, and its stretch of adjoining parkland.

Seoul World Cup Stadium
Seongsandong 549 (2016-2002, www.seoul worldcupst.or.kr). World Cup Stadium station (line 6), exit 2. **Open** 9am-6pm daily. **Admission** ₩1,000.
Seoul's largest football stadium hosted the semi-finals of the World Cup in 2002, when the surprisingly successful South Korea team of that year finally bowed out to Germany. It also hosted the opening game of the tournament, when Senegal scored a surprise victory over reigning champions France. During the domestic season, it also functions as the home stadium of K-League team FC Seoul. Short tours of the stadium are available, and it's also possible to stay overnight for ₩8,000 at the stadium's *jimjilbang*.
▶ *For more on FC Seoul, see p189. For more on jimjilbangs, see p191.*

FREE World Cup Park
Seongsandong 45-1 (300-5500, www.worldcup park.seoul.go.kr). World Cup Stadium station (line 6), exit 2. **Open** *Haneul Park & Noeul Park* from 9am daily, closing 6.30-8.30pm, varying by mth. *Other parks* 24hrs daily. **Admission** free.
Between the stadium and the north bank of the Hangang River lie several interconnected parks, all confusingly given different names even though they're essentially part of the same whole. Most

Hanuel Park.

interesting by far is Haneul Park, which rises up more than 20 metres above the surrounding plateau. This has nothing to do with the area's geology, but with its interesting recent history – until the mid 1990s, this was Seoul's largest landfill site. Amazingly, given the green charm of the park, tonnes of detritus still lie inside these hills, and some of the methane produced is recycled and used for power at the World Cup Stadium and some nearby apartments. Nearby Noeul Park has a lake and golf course, while in the summer, open-air swimming pools open up in two other park sections.

> ### INSIDE TRACK
> ### DULLING OF THE SENSES
>
> It's ironic that Seoul's most rambunctious quarter has also found fame for silence and darkness. Held every few weekends, the **Silent Disco** (www.silentdisco.co.kr, Korean only) sees a troupe of fun-lovers don headphones in Norita Park, then have a silent-to-others walking party around the Hongdae streets. Only the first 300 to arrive get headphones. Then there's **Dialogue in the Dark** (www.dialogue-in-the-dark.com), which takes place on the ninth floor of the Vertigo building in Sinchon; for ₩30,000 you get to perform various activities in total darkness for an hour or so.

Gangnam

The shinier side of the coin.

Gangnam means 'south of the river', and the name can be used for most of the wide area south of the Hangang. It's far less visited by tourists than areas north of the river, and those who cross the water may feel they've found a different city: the standard of living, already sky-high north of the river, is higher still to the south. People dress differently, eat more non-Korean food, drink more coffee and wine, and spend more on… everything, basically. A visit here allows an insight into a different aspect of Seoul; it's certainly worth crossing the river to see which side of the north–south divide you belong on.

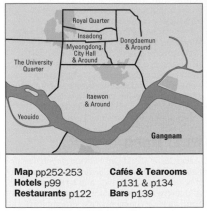

Map pp252-253	Cafés & Tearooms
Hotels p99	p131 & p134
Restaurants p122	Bars p139

NAVIGATING THE AREA

The Gangnam area is pretty large, though well served by both subway and bus. Subway line 3 is particularly handy: it brushes Apgujeong at a station of the same name, then Garosugil at Sinsa station. Gangnam station itself is on line 2, which heads east via Seolleung for the Samneung Tombs, and Jamsil for Lotte World. The suburb of Gwacheon is far from the main Gangnam area, and serviced on subway line 4. However, most locals are far too wealthy to be seen on public transport – taxis are a good option, though avoid the evening rush hour (5.30-7.30pm) at all costs.

APGUJEONG

Getting there: Apgujeong station (line 3), Sinsa station (line 3) or Cheongdam station (line 7).
Apgujeong is often referred to as 'Korea's Beverly Hills' by locals; though the reality is somewhat wide of the mark, it does exude an air of relative affluence. It has precious few sights to speak of, being far more famed for restaurants and shops. There's some particularly fine dining around **Dosan Park**, as well as some superb luxury malls and boutiques. Those in the market for brand names should head instead to **Apgujeongno**, a road on which designer stores curl a twin octave east of Apgujeong station – Gucci, Louis Vuitton, Prada, Jil Sander and friends

are all ready and waiting for your credit cards. This stretch is also notable for one superb piece of design: the west wing of the luxury **Galleria** mall (*see p142*), whose fish scale-like perspex coating hums and glows a colourful show at night (and looks wonderful in the daytime, too). The **Hermès Building** next to Dosan Park is also a treat to look at, and makes an interesting visual statement: essentially a gold-wrapped gift box, it almost audibly says 'buy me'. It's not just of interest to those seeking expensive goodies: one of the upper levels functions as an interesting atelier, while down in the basement level there's a great café (*see p131*) and a stunning museum filled with genuine objets d'art from Mr Hermès himself.

West of Apgujeong proper is another interesting road: **Garosugil**, which means 'tree-lined street'. It does, indeed, sport a fair few gingko trees, which turn a wonderful gold in the autumn. In 2009, Garosugil was almost unanimously thought of as Seoul's 'it' area, but just two years down the line chain stores have moved in and artier sorts are already muttering grumbles of decline.

GANGNAM STATION AREA

Getting there: Gangnam station (line 2), Samseong station (line 2) or Seolleung station (line 2).
The immediate area around Gangnam station fulfils stereotypes of a neon-soaked East Asia:

the streets are lined with pulsating skyscrapers, and packed with vehicles, businessfolk and shoppers dashing between them. As with Apgujeong to the north, the area can only be truly appreciated if you're opening your wallet, though walking around the streets does indeed provide something of an electric thrill. If you're yearning to give some context to the modernity, pop into **Samsung D-light**, a showroom in the headquarters of the Samsung Electronics building, or go to one of the nearby clubs (*see pp186-188*).

Although the area as a whole is more about commerce than sightseeing, there are a couple of gems hidden among the high-rises – the **Samneung Tombs**, a forest-draped park where three Joseon Dynasty royals were laid to rest; and the charming Buddhist temple of **Bongeunsa**. The latter sits above **Coex** (*see p144*), a large underground shopping mall featuring, among other things, an aquarium and the **Kimchi Field Museum**.

All of these sights are located east of Gangnam station. Head west instead and you'll soon come across **Seorae Maeul**, Seoul's 'Frenchtown'. This is much heralded in tourist brochures, but in reality the Gallic air is very faint – it's little more than a regular part of the city with a lycée and a few French restaurants tacked on.

★ FREE Bongeunsa
Samseongdong 73 (514-8061, www. bongeunsa.org). Samseong station (line 2), exit 3. **Open** 24hrs daily. **Admission** free. **Map** p253 O10.

Bongeunsa is a peaceful and interesting oasis set right in the middle of Seoul's wealthiest area. The temple features excellent artworks, authentic architecture and a gigantic standing Buddha statue. Founded in 794 under the name Gyeonseongsa, it was rebuilt under the patronage of Queen Munjeong in 1498 in order to serve as the spiritual guardian of the nearby Samneung Tombs (*see p76*), changing its name to Bongeunsa. By 1550, it had expanded to become a headquarters monastery for the national Jogye Seon Order. Most of its buildings were destroyed in a tragic 1939 fire, and then rebuilt between 1941 and 1982. The *Seonbul-dang* or Hall for Selecting Buddhas was where the national Monastic Exams were held. Surrounded by farms and orchards until the 1960s, Bongeunsa has seen Korea's wealthiest area blossom all around it. This prosperity allowed it to erect a 28m image of Maitreya, the Future Buddha, the tallest stone statue in the nation.

▶ *Bongeunsa offers short educational sessions every Thursday from 2pm to 4pm, and you can also stay overnight as part of the Templestay programme. For more background on Buddhism in Korea, see p77.*

Kimchi Field Museum
Samseongdong 159 (6002-6456, www.kimchi museum.co.kr). Samseong station (line 2), exit 5. **Open** 10am-6pm Tue-Sun. **Admission** ₩3,000. **Map** p253 P10.

Part of the Coex complex, and the name says it all – anything and everything about Korea's spicy national side dish. Most entertaining are the hands-on sessions, in which you get to learn how to make the stuff yourself.

Gangnam.

Samneung Tombs.

SIGHTS

Samneung Tombs

Samseongdong 135-4 (no phone). Seolleung station (line 2), exit 5. **Open** 6am-9pm Tue-Sun. **Admission** ₩1,000. **Map** p253 N11.

The best place in the capital to see how Seoul's royals – or, in fact, anyone of importance – were once laid to rest. The three tombs (the literal translation of 'Samneung') were created to house the remains of King Seongjeong, one of his several wives, and his son King Jungjong. The combined rule of the two kings stretched from 1469 to 1544, and the calm, grassy complex makes it easy to imagine what Seoul must have looked like in those times.

★ FREE Samsung D-Light

Seochodong 3020-10 (2255-2262). Gangnam station (line 2), exit 4. **Open** 10am-7pm Mon-Sat. **Admission** free. **Map** p252 L12.

This showroom is located inside the headquarters of Samsung Electronics, the most international arm of Korea's largest company. It's stuffed full of televisions, mobile phones and other electronic gadgets from Samsung's past, present and future. You'll be able to check your own laptop's content on gigantic screens, play online games from your mobile phone, and make use of whatever developments their boffins have come up with in the last year or so.

JAMSIL

Getting there: Jamsil station (lines 2 & 8) or Mongchontoseong station (line 8).

Located to the east of Gangnam and Apgujeong is Jamsil, which is, essentially, a residential area, and a recently made one at that. You'll be able to divine as much by simply looking

at a map of Seoul… see the semi-circle of unnaturally tight roads, south of the river? That's Jamsil. By and large it's a place to live while you work and have fun somewhere else, but there are a few attractions in the area. Right next to Jamsil station, **Lotte World** is one of the largest theme parks in the country, and a blessing for those travelling with children. To the west of the Jamsil semi-circle is the Olympic Stadium, used for the Seoul Games in 1988. The inauspicious opening ceremony saw thousands of doves released to signify peace – but on the lighting of the Olympic flame, dozens of them were roasted to death on live TV. A week later, Canadian sprinter Ben Johnson broke the men's 100m world record; however, as everyone now knows, he was full of barbiturates at the time. Another notable moment came a stone's throw away in the diving pool, which is where Greg Louganis crashed his head on to the diving board on his way down; after a couple of stitches, he somehow followed this up with a perfect dive to capture gold. On the other side of the Jamsil semi-circle is Olympic Park, also host to many events during the 1988 Games.

Lotte World

Jamsildong 40-1 (411-2000, www.lotteworld.com). Samseong station (line 2), exit 4. **Open** 9.30am-10pm Mon-Thur; 9.30am-11pm Fri-Sun. **Admission** ₩26,000 excl facilities & rides; discounts available for children & after 4pm.

Lotte World is a colossal theme park – in fact, the largest indoor theme park in the world. There's also an outdoor section: Magic Island, connected to the

Buddhism in Korea

The national religion.

Buddhist temples are some of the most rewarding attractions for international visitors to Seoul. Their statues and colourful buildings – with green pines and grey granite cliffs behind them – can make for great photography. Their artworks are often fascinatingly iconoclastic. If you have the opportunity to visit one by hiking up steep mountain trails, don't miss it. They are still relatively isolated from the industrial world, and time seems to move more slowly as you enjoy the views.

Korean Buddhism shares the Northeast Asian Mahayana tradition. It arrived from China in the fifth century, and gave rise to a first Golden Age of artistic and philosophical accomplishment when the Shilla kingdom unified the peninsula in the seventh century. Buddhism became the official national religion during the early Goryeo Dynasty (918-1392), and its cultural expressions rose to a second peak.

Korea turned to neo-Confucianism around 1400, and Buddhism steadily declined to the point where it was barely surviving in the rural mountains by 1900. It then faced challenges from rapidly growing Christianity and modernising governments throughout the 20th century, but instead of fading away entirely it has staged a remarkable comeback. Partly through imitating many of the modern organisational and social techniques of its rival, Christianity, and partly through the inspirational series of more than a dozen great masters of meditation and doctrine who succeeded in reviving and adapting the ancient ways and attitudes, Korean Buddhism has once again become a vibrant factor in Korean society.

Today, roughly a quarter of South Koreans count themselves as Buddhists, the number of temples has increased to over 6,000 and the standards for becoming and remaining a Buddhist monk or nun have increased beyond ancient standards, providing a very effective and dynamic modern clergy.

The writer, David A Mason, is an author and professor of Korean Cultural Tourism at Seoul's Kyung Hee University.

indoor area by monorail. It's also possible to go ice-skating (*see p193*) or bowling (*see p190*) in other parts of the complex.

FREE Olympic Museum

Bangidong 88 (410-1354, www.88olympic.or.kr). Mongchontoseong station (line 8), exit 1.
Open 10am-6pm Tue-Sun. **Admission** free.
A small, diverting museum inside Olympic Park, with a clutch of photographs, exhibitions, mascots and other sights from the history of the Olympic Games. In the lobby, pause for a second to admire *Golden Crown*, a piece of video art by internationally renowned Korean artist Baik Nam Jun.

GWACHEON

Getting there: Seoul Grand Park (line 4) or Seoul Racecourse Park (line 4). Note also that this area is featured on the map on pp244-245.
Nestled between two mountains, this Seoul satellite city is a favourite starting point for hikers and nature-lovers. While a proud city in its own right, Gwacheon's most popular attractions bear the capital's name. For example, **Seoul Racecourse Park** (4566-3333, first of 11-12 races begins around 11am, admission ₩800) offers weekend contests at the nation's biggest (and always packed) horse

track. Also on site is the **Equine Museum** (509-1283, open 9am-6pm daily, admission free). Nearby, the sprawling **Seoul Grand Park** begins at the base of Mt Cheonggyesan and is home to Korea's largest **zoo** and **botanical gardens** (500-7114, open Apr-Oct 9am-7pm daily, Nov-Mar 9am-6pm daily, adult pass ₩3,000) as well as one of the nation's first theme parks, **Seoul Land** (504-0011, open 9.30am-7pm Mon-Thur, 9.30am-8pm Fri, 9.30am-9pm Sat, Sun, closes 1hr early Nov-Mar, admission ₩17,000, day pass ₩31,000). Opened just months before the 1988 Seoul Olympics, the rollercoasters and kitschy Wild West frontier village are awkwardly dated. Also on site is the excellent **National Museum of Contemporary Art** (2188-6000, open 10am-6pm Tue-Fri, 10am-9pm Sat, Sun, admission free). The impressive collection of 4,000-plus items is dominated by Paik Nam June's *The More The Better* media installation – the 18.5m ziggurat made from 1,003 televisions dominates the Core, an atrium surrounded by a winding ramp. West of Seoul Grand Park station is the **Gwacheon National Science Museum** (110 Sanghabeollo, Gwacheon, 023677-1500, open 9.30am-5.30pm, permanent exhibits ₩4,000, planetarium ₩2,000), a family-friendly way to spend an afternoon.

Yeouido

Evenings by the river.

An island sitting just off the Hangang's south bank, Yeouido has a chequered past. Low-lying and marshy, it was largely ignored by the city until the 1960s. It is said that long ago a king, exasperated by the island's lack of usefulness, once asked, 'Are you an island?' Yeouido took its name from this outburst and its Chinese characters actually spell 'You island'. How times have changed, though. Yeouido is now home to Korea's national assembly, and is also the country's largest business district. Indeed, the island's high-rise buildings have given rise to a more contemporary nickname: the Manhattan of Seoul. Yeouido is more about work than play, but spend a summer evening on the riverbank and you may well be fooled into believing that the reverse is true.

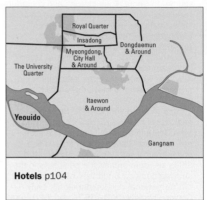

Hotels p104

NAVIGATING THE AREA
Subway lines 5 and 9 criss-cross Yeouido, heading north–south and east–west respectively; lines 1 and 2 make their way through the adjacent area on the south bank of the Hangang.

YEOUIDO

Getting there: Yeouido station (lines 5 & 9), Yeouinaru station (line 5), National Assembly station (line 9) or Saetgang station (line 9).

INSIDE TRACK WHEN TO VISIT

The best time to visit Yeouido Park is in the spring, during the brief flush of cherry blossom. The pretty whitish-pink flowers are only around for a couple of weeks – less than that if there's heavy wind or rain – but locals rush out to enjoy the blossom with *soju* and picnics. The city also organises a few events during this time, under the banner of the **Yeouido Cherry Blossom Festival** (*see p162*). Otherwise, summer is best, if only for the chance to jump into one of the open-air swimming pools on the west of the island.

The main draw of Yeouido island is the **Yeouido Hangang River Park**, a largely paved expanse running along the riverbank. Revamped and upgraded in 2009, this park contains bike and walking trails running parallel to the river. During summer evenings, you'll see lots of couples enjoying some time away from home – and more than a few drinks being passed between the adults. There's no specific must-see-thing in the park, but occasional events take place here – the city's official tourism website (*see p230*) will have information. It's possible to rent bikes (*see p222*), while swan boats are available for hire too. Also note that in summer months, the open-air swimming pools are incredibly popular with young locals.

There are a couple of intriguing sights to the west of Yeouido island: Korea's **National Assembly** and the **Yoido Full Gospel Church**. The latter is, by the sheer numbers that attend, the largest church in the world: imagine a baseball stadium with a Christian cross over the main gate. The church claims over a million members and has services throughout the day on Sunday in six different languages. Senior pastor Cho Yong-gi has presided over the church since its inauguration in 1958. While his views and beliefs have sometimes been controversial, the church continues to grow, seemingly no matter what. Foreigners attending a service will be guided by ushers to specially equipped sections of the church – a distinctly Korean experience complete with multiple cameras, occasional tears and plenty of enthusiasm.

63 City

Yeouidodong 60 (789-5966, www.63.co.kr). Yeouinaru station (line 5), exit 3. **Open** 10am-10pm daily. *IMAX cinema* 10am-8.30pm Mon; 10am-5.30pm Tue-Sun. **Admission** Varies by attraction. Don't go looking for the 63rd floor in the 63 Building – three of the levels from its misleading name are underground. Still, this was the tallest building in Asia when first constructed in 1985, and remained the tallest in Korea until 2002. It's commonly called *yuk-sum* by the locals, after the Korean numbers for six and three, respectively. Most of it is office space, though in the basement and ground levels there are shops and a selection of restaurants – including one

---

Noryangjin Fish Market

Seoul's saltiest market.

A pungent wave of raw fish heralds your arrival at Noryangjin fish market. If you're ready for a look at Korea's earthier side, this is the place to go. First established in downtown Seoul in 1927, this dedicated fish market moved to its present location on the southern fringe of Yeouido in 1971. With 6,000 square metres of floor space, one can just imagine how much seafood is available here. Start with the wholesalers auctioning off their catches during the early hours of the morning, then follow the sellers to their shops – each one a hive of activity. The atmosphere is convivial: there's no hard sell, no pressure to buy, and haggling is part of the game. By lunchtime, most of the vendors are in a relaxed mode, preparing for the after-work crowd with a bottle of *soju* and a late meal of their own: their busiest hours are now behind them. Vendors seem particularly friendly to foreigners, though whatever your nationality it's probably best to avoid showing up in flashy designer clothes – this is a working-class facility.

If you've been itching to try Korean seafood, you can't get much fresher than the fare here, and simply seeing the variety available is beautiful and rather absorbing. Although the ice melts and the aisles do get wet, there's rarely any sense that anything is getting old or stale.

Meander around for long enough and you'll eventually want to buy some fish or king crab and head up to a nearby restaurant, where it will either be cooked or sliced and served up raw. Restaurants also serve side dishes and beverages to go with your main meal. English isn't commonly spoken, but hand gestures and calculators overcome the language barrier on a regular basis. The more exotic types of seafood – snow crab and sea snails – can also be found here, and some places will offer samples of more unusual items. It may sometimes feel like a reality show gone weird, but fortune does indeed favour the brave at Noryangjin – where else will you be able to say you've tried sea cucumber?

SIGHTS

'Buffet Pavilion' and an excellent Japanese restaurant. Also in the basement are the Sea World aquarium, some western-style bowling, and Korea's first IMAX theatre. However, most people are here to head to the observation deck on the 60th floor, 249m (817ft) above ground level. Try to go on a clear day if at all possible.

FREE National Assembly Building

Yeouidodong (788-2865, http://korea.assembly. go.kr). National Assembly station (line 9), exit 1. **Open** 9am-5pm daily. **Admission** free.
Most commonly visited during the springtime blossoming of Yeouido's cherry trees, the National Assembly is where the Korean parliament meets. Consequently, security is present but unobtrusive, watching the facilities and generally keeping order. Completed in 1975, the greenish-blue dome serves as both landmark and a splash of colour that adds to the gardens. The 24 granite pillars are interconnected by the aforementioned dome, apparently representing the opinions of the people coming together as one. Going in for a look around is no problem – just ask

at the visitor's centre. A number of restaurants are within walking distance, as is Yeouido Park.

NORYANGJIN & SEONYUDO

Getting there: Seonyudo station (line 9), Yeongdeungpo station (line 1), Singil station (lines 1 & 5).
There are a few places of note around the island. To the west is a fantastic example of urban engineering: the islet of **Seonyudo**, on which a former water treatment plant has been converted into a delightful park (*see below* **The Garden Island of Seonyudo**). On the southern bank of Yeouido is the district of **Noryangjin**, most famed for its eponymous fish market. This has been around for decades, and it may suffice to say that the surrounding area was appropriate to its salty air – this is changing fast, however, and 2009 saw the opening of **Times Square** (*see p144*), a huge composite of mall, dining and accommodation space.

The Garden Island of Seonyudo

Eco-Seoul.

Sitting pretty in the Hangang, the islet of Seonyudo has an interesting history. Centuries ago, it functioned as a place of escape, where Confucian scholars could paint or write poetry. After everything here was destroyed by floods in 1925, the island was restored, and connected by bridge to Yeouido in 1970. Different times called for different measures – the city's burgeoning population made water treatment essential, and a gigantic water treatment plant was installed on Seonyudo in 1978, taking up most of the island's land area.

How strange that, despite its rather tortured history, Seonyudo is now home to thousands of plants, growing in a maze-like garden. As part of a mammoth rebuilding project, Seonyudo was opened to the public in 2003, the old industrial structures having been integrated into water-based gardens. The end result: an eco-conscious park offering up an odd but pleasant mixture of fresh, healthy plants in some unexpected places. There are places for kids to play on the many wooden boardwalks or by the water – a good place to get one's feet wet. A 468-metre (1,535-foot) footbridge connects the island to the mainland, while another bridge connects things up for the cars. It's quite possible to spend the whole day here: snack shacks and convenience stores keep everybody fed and watered.

Itaewon & Around

Cosmopolitan Korea.

Unlike every other station in the city, most of the people getting off the subway at Itaewon aren't Korean. The area is home to the most diverse group of people you'll find in the whole country; its foreigner-friendly history stems from Yongsan Garrison, a nearby US army base. American troops have been arriving here since the Korean War and, considering their relative wealth in the 1960s and '70s, it's not surprising that an area sprang up serving their needs – the seedier side included. Nowadays, though, things are changing slightly: Itaewon has become substantially more popular with locals on account of its wonderful dining scene. In addition, it's one of the only places in the whole country where homosexuality is openly tolerated.

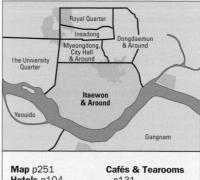

Map p251	**Cafés & Tearooms**
Hotels p104	p131
Restaurants p123	**Bars** p141

NAVIGATING THE AREA

Subway line 6 runs through this area, making consecutive stops at Samgakji, Noksapyeong, Itaewon and Hangangjin. Samgakji is also on line 4, which heads south to service Yongsan and the riverside area before crossing the Hangang.

ITAEWON

Getting there: Itaewon station (line 6).
Every single building on the main Itaewon drag is a shop, bar, restaurant or combination of the above. Most of these were flung up in the 1970s and '80s and some look decidedly worse for wear. However, the road is much improved from years past; façades and storefronts have received a much-needed makeover, while the pavements now feature bronze plaques with dozens of international ways to say hello.

The **Hamilton Hotel** (*see p106*) sits just above the subway station and has been the area's focal point for years. To the east is **Hannamdong**, an up-and-coming area in which the turnaround of restaurants is particularly high; it's also home to the excellent **Leeum Art Museum**. Heading west instead down the Itaewon main road will bring you to Noksapyeong, and the adjacent US Army Garrison. The road splits here, one spur

heading south to Samgakji and the fascinating **War Memorial of Korea**, and the other further west to the intriguing district of Haebangchon. If Itaewon is where Seoul's expat English teachers go to party, Haebangchon is where they actually live. Twice a year, the area showcases local musicians in the 'HBC Fest' – an excellent opportunity to meet creative types in the area. A number of bars and restaurants here are also used in theatrical or musical productions run by the local expat community.

★ Leeum Art Museum

Hannamdong 747-18 (2014-6901, www. leeum.org). Hangangjin station (line 6), exit 1.

INSIDE TRACK TAILORED SUITS

Itaewon is a superb place to buy clothes. Indeed, for years it was the only place in the country in which people of a certain size (for which read foreigners) could do so easily. Nowadays, the best Itaewon investment is tailored clothing – which, though cheap, is of uniformly high quality. For more information on Itaewon tailoring, *see p150*.

SIGHTS

INSIDE TRACK
HOMO HILL & HOOKER HILL

A couple of steep roads south of Itaewon station have achieved cult status. One became jam-packed with brothels catering to the US military, and is now referred to as Hooker Hill. Many of these establishments have now been closed down, but still going strong is Homo Hill, an adjacent road that's now the centre of Korea's gay community. For more on Itaewon's gay life, *see pp176-180.*

Open 10.30am-6pm Tue, Wed, Fri-Sun; 10.30am-9pm Thur. **Admission** ₩10,000. **Map** p251 H7.

The country's largest private museum, Leeum has an excellent collection of modern art – both traditional Korean work and exhibits from around the world. Though the museum only opened in 2004, its reputation as one of the finest art museums in the country is well deserved; it's architecturally interesting, too, with wings designed by international luminaries including Rem Koolhaas. On arrival, take in the eight-legged spider that makes up one of the permanent exhibits, and the randomly changing digital numbers in the floor. Inside, highlights include 13th-century celadon teapots and 18th-century Buddhist mountain paintings. Heading down the spiral staircase to Museum B, you'll find art of a more recent vintage, with a focus on pieces from the 20th and early 21st centuries.

▶ *There are English-language tours of the gallery museum available at 3pm every Saturday and Sunday.*

★ War Memorial of Korea

Yongsandong 1-8 (709-3139, www.war memo.or.kr). Samgakji station (line 6), exit 12. **Open** 9am-6pm Tue-Sun. **Admission** ₩3,000. **Map** p251 E7.

Korea's recent history has been dominated by the Korean War, a conflict that's vividly portrayed in this national memorial. The place is huge, and you'll need at least a couple of hours to see it all. The outdoor exhibits include fighter jets, tanks and other recent tools of war, and sculptures hinting at the possibility of reunification with North Korea. Along parts of the outdoor walls are the names of hundreds of thousands of fallen soldiers engraved in stone, organised by country, region or state. Inside, there are exhibits pertaining to warfare in the Three Kingdoms era, Joseon Dynasty conflicts and the Japanese occupation, and more from the Korean War. There are plenty of materials dedicated to bringing the gruesome latter event to life – including pictures, videos, military gear and much more besides.

MT NAMSAN

Getting there: those with foreign ID can take a taxi to a car park near the top; or yellow bus 2 runs from outside the Hotel Astoria (see p95), near Chungmuro station. It's also possible to take a cable car from Myeongdong (see p59), or walk from Myeongdong, Namsangol or Seoul stations (takes around 20mins).

Historically Seoul's southern mountain, Mt Namsan anchored the south side of the city according to Korea's form of feng shui, known as *poongsu jiri*. Known as Mongmyeoksan (Mt Mongmyeok) in the past, a series of five beacons was installed there to warn the city of danger – the beginnings of an ingenious system that relayed warnings across the country. The city has grown to the extent that the 'South Mountain', as its name means, is now very much in the centre of things. Rubberised hiking trails criss-cross the area, although at 265m, the mountain isn't exactly a hiking challenge – plenty of local women walk the mountain in high heels. Some of the older locals take hiking very seriously; some invest a lot of money in the right shirt, the right shoes, a premium walking stick and, of course, the right backpack. If you take the cable car up to the N Seoul Tower, you'll soar over much of the park – including what's difficult to see from the hiking trails.

N Seoul Tower

Yongsandong 1-3 (3455-9277, www.nseoul tower.net). **Open** 10am-11pm daily. **Admission** ₩7,000. **Map** p247 G5.

Poking out like a needle from Namsan's scalp, the N Seoul Tower is a strong emblem of the city, and one of its most visible icons. Lots of younger Koreans come here for dates – you'll see hundreds of padlocks affixed to the fences, their keys thrown over the precipice as a sign of devotion. A laser show uses the tower as a backdrop every half-hour during the evening, while inside the basement of the complex itself are a souvenir shop, café and snack shack. Most come for the ride to the top of the tower, for which a ticket is necessary. On the upper levels there are also three restaurants offering some of the best tableside views of the city. One of them, the fancy N Grill, rotates to keep the view changing.

YONGSAN

Getting there: Yongsan train, Yongsan station (line 1), Sinyongsan station (line 4) or Seobingo station (Jungang line).

The wide Yongsan area is home to one of the city's two major train stations, and is a hub of local business. It stretches down from Itaewon to the river, and is slated for major renewal – by 2016 it will have been turned inside out, the

War Memorial of Korea.

resulting international business district likely to be focused on the 665-metre **Dream Tower**, designed by Daniel Libeskind. For now, though, there's little to see bar construction cranes, and the superb **National Museum**. The **Banpo Bridge** connects Yongsan to Apgujeong, across the Hangang River; it comes to life with spectacular water shows each evening, best observed from **Banpo Park**.

FREE Banpo Park
Seobingo subway (Jungang line), exit 2. **Open** 9am-6pm Tue, Thur, Fri; 9am-9pm Wed, Sat; 9am-7pm Sun. **Admission** free. **Map** p251 F10.
A riverside park area with walking and cycling trails, as well as stalls renting out jet-skis for rides on the Hangang. Most come in the evenings for the Rainbow Fountain at Banpoaegyo, when Banpo Bridge turns into one giant water show – almost 200 tonnes of water per minute is squirted from the sides of the bridge, and lit on its way down by colourful lights.

★ FREE National Museum
Seobinggoro 135 (2077-9000, www.museum. go.kr). Inchon subway (line 4), exit 2. **Open** 9am-6pm Tue, Thur, Fri; 9am-9pm Wed, Sat; 9am-7pm Sun. **Admission** free; occasional ticket prices for special exhibitions. **Map** p251 F9.
The National Museum is the largest museum in Korea, and the sixth largest in the world. It portrays several thousand years of Korean civilisation across its three huge floors. The collection is arranged chronologically, and starts with Korea's earliest civilisations. Authentic relics include 1,000-year-old Buddhist paintings from the Silla Dynasty, celadon ceramics from the Goryeo Dynasty, and the centre-piece – a 13m marble structure that once served as the Gyeongcheonsa Temple pagoda. Special exhibitions are held on and off throughout the year; in the past they've featured golden Silla Dynasty crowns and pieces from the Silk Road.
► *There are English-language tours of the museum at 10.30am and 2.30pm Tue-Sun.*

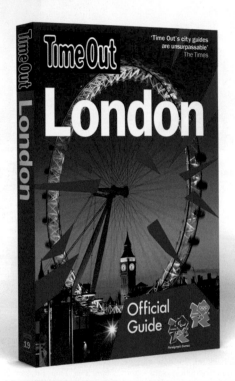

Consume

Noryangjin Fishmarket.
See p79.

Hotels

A regular range, with a few fascinating local idiosyncracies.

It may be a cliché but when it comes to Seoul it's true: this city has a range of accommodation to suit all budgets. However, in Seoul that range is quite markedly skewed towards the lower end of the scale. That's also where you'll find the more interesting hotels: the top end of the market is dominated by international chains, with only a precious few, such as the **Shilla** (*see p96*) and **Park Hyatt** (*see p102*), being particularly notable for their design. In addition, boutique hotels are conspicuous by their absence. However, both of these gaps in the market are filled, in a way, by a

distinctively Korean niche – old wooden *hanok* houses, converted into gorgeous **guesthouses** (*see p90* **Hanok Guesthouses**). Similarly local in style are the city's many **love motels** (*see p100* **The Look of Love**), many of which actually make comfortable (and extremely affordable) places to stay. Visitors also have the chance to overnight at hot spring complexes known as **jimjilbang** (*see p191*).

STAYING IN SEOUL

As an affluent East Asian megalopolis, Seoul has a large, and growing, number of top hotels. As you would expect, standards of service are excellent, and the same can usually be said of the restaurants found on site – the best hotels will have Japanese, Chinese, Korean and Western (usually meaning Italian) to choose from. Rooms are usually very comfortable, though Seoul's sky-high land prices mean that they're usually rather small by international standards. In addition, the city's unfortunate dearth of historic buildings, allied with an insipid (though improving) array of modern designs, means that very few hotels are interesting architecturally. Even the oldest top-end facility in town – the **Westin Chosun** (*see p93*), built in 1914 – has been modernised (although the result is attractive). However, precious few establishments have a distinctive design ethos: the **Shilla** (*see p96*) has given its rooms a rare traditional tweak; the elegant **Imperial Palace** (*see p99*) has had a stab at decadence, while the **Plaza** (*see p91*) and **Park Hyatt** (*see p102*) have benefitted from top-to-bottom renovations orchestrated by international design teams.

The vast majority of the city's rooms lie in its innumerable motels. The very term has negative connotations, and – for obvious

reasons – many foreigners come to refer to them as 'love motels'. However, whatever seaminess exists generally takes place out of audible and visual range, and those who can eschew regular hotel facilities – and tolerate a bit of cheesy decor – will find these Seoul's best-value places to stay.

Note that all hotels are obliged to have no-smoking rooms or floors, though this rule is not always followed to the letter. Motels are another matter: you'll find an ashtray in every single room.

WHERE TO STAY

The vast majority of Seoul's sights are located north of the river, and since hotels here also tend to be far better value than their southern counterparts, it makes sense to stay here. Top-end locations are clustered around **City Hall** and **Myeongdong**; nearby **Insadong** has a few interesting cheapies, while neighbouring **Bukchon** has a clutch of fascinating wooden guesthouses. Myeongdong and **Dongdaemun**

❶ Red numbers given in this chapter correspond to the location of each hotel as marked on the street maps. *See pp246-55.*

to the east are also good for shoppers, though those who prefer their brand names to be real, rather than fake, will find more joy south of the river; the wide **Gangnam** area has plenty of good accommodation.

Gangnam and Myeongdong are two of the city's three main business districts, the other being **Yeouido** island. Backpackers are advised to head straight to **Hongdae**, the country's biggest and busiest nightlife district, and now home to well over a dozen hostels.

PRICES

The prices given in this chapter refer to the rack rates for standard double rooms. Do note that for hotels you'll likely be able to knock a fair chunk off these, especially on weekdays and during the colder months. Motel and hostel prices are consistent year-round. All hotels accept the full range of international cards (American Express, Diners Club, MasterCard and Visa), though any establishment with the words 'motel' or 'hostel' in the review is likely to accept cash only.

TAX AND EXTRA FEES

Unlike almost everything else in the whole country, hotel prices are almost always quoted without tax – 10% will be added to your bill, and, occasionally, the same again as a service charge, so do ask beforehand what the final price will be. Most hotels will also charge for internet access, with a ludicrous ₩20,000 per day the norm; those staying long term or on executive floors may be able to get this for free. Motels are a different story altogether: more and more have internet-ready computers in the rooms (always free to use), and all prices quoted will be final.

BUKCHON & SAMCHEONGDONG

Hanok guesthouses

Anguk Culture House

Angukdong 72-3 (736-8304, www.anguk-house.com). Anguk station (line 3), exit 1. **Rooms** 6. **Rates** ₩70,000. **Map** p254 F2 ➊
Tucked away at the end of a veritable labyrinth of snaking side-alleys, this is perhaps the hardest to track down of Seoul's many guesthouses – which, of course, forms a major part of its appeal. Staff will come to meet you if you call from nearby Anguk station, and once you've made it here the first time doing so again is a piece of cake. Unlike most of the neighbouring *hanok* guesthouses, rooms here have Western-style beds, which may make this charming establishment a better option for some travellers. *Internet (shared terminal).*

Catch a KAL Bus...

Direct from the airport to your hotel.

Comfortable buses head to all corners of Seoul from Incheon airport, but the sky-blue ones operated by Korean Air (KAL) – actually called **KAL Limousine** – head directly to many of the city's top hotels. Tickets cost a standard ₩15,000. Staff at tourist desks in the airport concourse will point the way to the relevant bus stop.
Route 1 Koreana (*see p93*), Plaza (*see p91*), Lotte (*see p93*), Westin Chosun (*see p93*).
Route 2 Best Western Seoul Garden (*see p96*), Millennium Hilton (*see p91*), Grand Hyatt (*see p104*), Shilla (*see p96*).
Route 3A Ritz-Carlton (*see p102*), Novotel Ambassador (*see p102*), Marriott Renaissance (*see p103*).
Route 3B Imperial Palace, Coex InterContinental, Grand InterContinental. (For all, *see p99*.)
Route 4 Sheraton Grande Walkerhill, W Seoul Walkerhill (For both, *see p106*).

Bukchon Guesthouse

Gyedong 72 (743-8530, www.bukchon72.com). Anguk station (line 3), exit 3. **Rooms** 5. **Rates** ₩60,000. **Map** p247 F1 ➋
Simple rooms, a charming courtyard, and a quiet yet easy-to-find location: this ticks all of the main *hanok* guesthouse boxes, and makes for a pleasant place to stay. Pretty and comfortable though the rooms are, they lose marks for lazy renovation work, and service is little more than a pointing out of facilities: perfect for those seeking an unfussy place to sleep. The road outside is also a delectable mix of contemporary and old-fashioned Seoul: small laundrettes and groceries have been joined by a fair number of trendy cafés. *Internet (shared terminal).*

Manaedang

Gyedong 43 (070 4195-9630, www.manaedang. com). Anguk station (line 3), exit 3. **Rooms** 4. **Rates** ₩60,000. **Map** p247 F1 ➌
The smallest and most simple of the Bukchon area's *hanok* guesthouses was converted from a regular local abode in 2008. Its rooms are set around a tiny courtyard, and have been given pleasant splashes of traditional flavour: the Crysanthemum room is particularly pretty, featuring a Joseon Dynasty-style tea sitting area, the gold-and-black floor cushions backed by a folding calligraphic wall of similar colour. Tea ceremonies can, on request, be made part of your stay – the reason behind the somewhat misleading 'Party & Guesthouse' sign leading to the house. *Internet (shared terminal).*

CONSUME

Rakkojae

Gyedong 98 (742-3410, www.rkj.co.kr). Anguk station (line 3), exit 3. **Rooms** *4.* **Rates** ₩275,000. **Map** p247 F1 ❹

A circle of pristine wooden buildings arrayed around a serene dirt courtyard, this is less a place to stay than a work of art. Although far more expensive than all other *hanok* guesthouses in the area, this is the only one that evokes a genuinely dynastic feel – lighting is kept subtle, traditional food and tea are served at appropriate times, and many pieces of furniture are genuine antiques. With a little advance warning, the owners will be able to arrange anything from musical performances to poetry recitals. In addition, all rooms have en-suite facilities, negating the necessity of padding to an outdoor washroom – not exactly traditional, but some things may be best left in the past.

Seoul Guesthouse

Gyedong 135-1 (745-0057, www.seoul110.com). Anguk station (line 3), exit 3. **Rooms** *5.* **Rates** ₩60,000. **Map** p247 F1 ❺

Forget the name – staying at this secluded guesthouse is almost akin to finding oneself in the countryside. Here, Seoul's cacophony of honks and beeps has been diluted down to a surprisingly mute level, allowing the ears to feast on wind chimes, birdsong and other sounds hard to detect in this hectic city. Rooms are Spartan, and the courtyard is filled with greenery.

Internet (shared terminal).

★ Sophia Guesthouse

Sogyeokdong 157-1 (720-5467, www.sophiagh.com). Anguk station (line 3), exit 3. **Rooms** *10.* **Rates** ₩60,000. **Map** p247 F2 ❻

A cheap yet highly appealing *hanok* guesthouse, located just off one of Seoul's most youthfully artsy side streets. Other than pricey Rakkojae (*see above*), it has perhaps the most authentically dynastic feel of the area's guesthouses: the dark-wood structures are Joseon originals, having been built during the 1860s, and the friendly owners have tried hard not to spoil this proud vintage with accoutrements of the modern day; rooms contain traditional paraphernalia such as calligraphic scrolls, pieces of glazed pottery and reproduction Joseon furniture. The courtyard is a great place to take tea. Step outside, though, and you're in modern Seoul, if a winningly tweaked version, with jewellery boutiques, fusion restaurants and contemporary art galleries.

Internet (shared terminal).

Tea Guesthouse

Gyedong 15-6 (3675-9877, www.teaguesthouse. com). Anguk station (line 3), exit 3. **Rooms** *7.* **Rates** ₩90,000. **Map** p247 F1 ❼

The most remote of the Anguk station area's *hanok* guesthouses, lying almost within touching distance of the northern mountains' foothills. Elevation aside, prices here are a little higher than all similar guesthouses bar Rakkojae (*see left*), though the theoretical improvements are not always in keeping with the traditional vibe: computers in the rooms, for example. However, service at Tea Guesthouse is better and more personalised than most competitors – the day's weather forecast, written on a blackboard in two languages, is a good example of the owners' charm and attention to detail. They also give occasional ad hoc, hands-on instruction regarding the creation of *kimchi*, woven fabrics and the like.

Internet (free).

INSADONG

Moderate

Doulos Hotel

Gwansudong 112 (2266-2244, www.doulos hotel.com). Jongno 3-ga station (lines 1, 3 & 5), exit 15. **Rooms** *46.* **Rates** ₩130,000. **Map** p255 G3 ❾

The only genuine hotel on an atmospheric, neon-drenched side street filled with less salubrious accommodation. Ostensibly 'for foreigners only' (though Korean guests are, of course, allowed), it's aimed quite squarely at Japanese budget travellers, who desire little more than clean, quiet rooms, decent showers and a filling breakfast: consider all of these boxes ticked, though said rooms may be a little small for some. Ask about discounts, which can see prices tumble down to under ₩90,000.

Business centre. Concierge. Internet (shared terminals). Restaurant.

Sheel Motel

Gwansudong 137 (2278-9993). Jongno 3-ga station (lines 1, 3 & 5), exit 15. **Rooms** *55.* **Rates** ₩70,000. **Map** p255 G3 ❿

A northern counterpart to the better-known – and far more showy – Jelly Hotel (*see p103*) in Gangnam, the Sheel is what may be referred to as an upper-end love motel. Rooms come in all sorts of shapes and sizes (and many are of a size that would put established hotels to shame), with notable features including hand-painted walls, tables set into the floor, pine bathtubs and karaoke facilities. Staff speak no English, but will be pleased to show you around a few rooms.

Internet (free). Parking (free).

▶ *For more on Korean motels, see p100*
The Look of Love.

Sunbee

Gwanhundong 198-11 (730-3451, www.hotel sunbee.com). Anguk station (line 3), exit 6. **Rooms** *42.* **Rates** ₩90,000. **Map** p255 F2 ⓫

The Sunbee makes a great cheap choice for Seoul sightseers. Rooms are simple (and, for those who may be concerned by such matters, devoid of carpeting), though they somehow manage to squeeze in more or

CONSUME

Hanok Guesthouses

Stay the traditional way.

Rakkojae. *See p89.*

Though decreasing in number with each passing year, Seoul still has a fair few wooden houses known as *hanokjip* (*see p44*). These slate-roofed, pine-beamed structures are most prevalent in the Bukchon area, where whole swathes have been protected by law. This has been a boon for the local heritage, but travellers are also able to reap the rewards, since some *hanokjip* have been converted into tiny guesthouses. They make for fantastic places to stay, especially for those with a love of history: not only are the buildings themselves appealingly traditional (and, in some cases, of genuine dynastic vintage), but they're sandwiched by a pair of royal palaces that were, for centuries, the focal point of the Korean peninsula. Indeed, despite the fact that they're located just a short walk from the modern-day city centre, some of these establishments exude an almost rural air, and a peace hard to find in this pulsating city.

While the structures themselves are traditional in form, concessions have been made to the modern day. Gone are the outdoor toilets, and though facilities are still more commonly shared than en suite, they're all western-style and usuallly scrupulously clean. Gone also, from some rooms, is the sandwich of futon-like blankets that, until the arrival of the bed, enabled most Koreans to sleep on the floor in warm comfort – which is still the way guests sleep at some *hanok* guesthouses. And sleeping on the floor would never have been comfortable in the first place without the ingenious Korean system of underfloor heating known as *ondol*. The warmth once came from pine wood burning beneath the rooms themselves, but with the resulting fires wrecking almost as many *hanok* houses (not to mention temples and palace structures) as war and the Japanese occupation combined, most now have their floors heated with gas.

All of the establishments listed in the Bukchon & Samcheongdong section of this chapter (*see p87*) are *hanok* guesthouses.

less all of the necessaries – look hard enough and you'll find a hairdryer, ironing board, water fountain and a selection of free (non-alcoholic) beverages. In addition, and rather charmingly, guests are also free to make themselves toast at any time of day or night. *Internet (free).*

Tomgi

Nagwondong 134-2 (742-6660). Jongno 3-ga station (lines 1, 3 & 5), exit 4. **Rooms** 55. **Rates** ₩60,000. **Map** p255 G3 ⑫

A quirky love motel, which allows customers to select their room from a bank of illuminated picture-panels – there are various shapes and sizes available. Despite the fact that more people pay for a two-hour 'rest' than a 'stay', rooms are comfortable and adequately soundproofed, and a stay here should sate the appetites of those seeking a slice of idiosyncratic Korea.

Internet (free).

▶*For more on Korean motels, see p100*
The Look of Love.

Budget

Banana Backpackers

Ikseondong 30-1 (3672-1973, www.banana backpackers.com). Anguk station (line 3), exit 4. **Rooms** 14. **Rates** Dorms ₩20,000, doubles ₩55,000. **Map** p255 G2 ⑬

One of Seoul's longest-serving backpacker hostels. A clever location is perhaps the main factor behind its durability – although the hostel lies on a quiet, secluded side street, Insadonggil and four of Seoul's six palaces are within easy walking distance of the premises, as is the nearest subway station. Both the dorms and private rooms have been colourfully decorated, and staff are invaluable sources of travel advice – as, indeed, are the multinational travellers you'll undoubtedly run into in the large, relaxing common room.

Internet (shared terminals).

Biz Motel

Gwansudong 114 (2265-8149). Jongno 3-ga station (lines 1, 3 & 5), exit 15. **Rooms** 26. **Rates** ₩50,000. **Map** p255 G3 ⑭

Pretty good, as far as Korean 'love motels' go. Rooms are cheerfully decorated and kept astonishingly clean; features include adequately comfortable beds, internet-ready computer terminals, piping hot showers and a pouch of free toiletries. Try to check in after 8pm if possible, since after that time prices can fall as low as ₩30,000; on checking out, those with a sweet tooth should be sure to grab one of the free ice-cream bars (melon being the most typically Korean ice-cream flavour, even if melons are hardly grown here). *Internet (free).*

▶*For more on Korean motels, see p100*
The Look of Love.

Saerim Hotel

Gwanhundong 192-17 (739-3377). Anguk station (line 3), exit 6. **Rooms** 60. **Rates** ₩50,000. **Map** p255 F2 ⑮

Officially a hotel, though more like a motel in feel, and with prices to match: for the daily rate at one of Seoul's five-stars, you could stay here for a full week, even more if you factor in the free internet access. The Saerim is ideally located for first-time Seoul tourists – it's just a few paces from Insadonggil and that road's array of traditional restaurants, shops and tearooms, and also within easy walking distance of at least four palaces.

Internet (free).

CITY HALL & MYEONGDONG
Luxury

Millennium Seoul Hilton

Namdaemunno 5-ga 395 (317-3114, www.hilton.com). Seoul station (lines 1 & 4), exit 10. **Rooms** 680. **Rates** ₩410,000. **Map** p247 E5 ⑯

Large, luxurious hotel sitting pretty on Namsan's western flank, and particularly popular with East Asian tourists on account of its adjoining casino. It overlooks the Seoul station area, which is not necessarily a good thing – it may be preferable to opt for a mountain view. Service can feel a little impersonal at times, though the hotel's lofty location has enabled it to build rooms slightly larger than its main competitors. In warmer months, it's hard to turn down the chance of an outdoor barbecue, served in the hotel gardens.

Bar. Business centre. Concierge. Disabled-adapted rooms. Gym. Internet (₩22,000). Parking (free). Pool. Restaurants (5). Room service. Sauna.

★ The Plaza

Taepyeongno 2-ga 23 (771-2200, www.hotel theplaza.com). City Hall station (lines 1 & 2), exit 6. **Rooms** 500. **Rates** ₩435,000. **Map** p254 E3 ⑰

For decades, this hotel made poor use of a great location opposite Seoul Plaza, but a thorough renovation in 2010 – led by Florentine maestro Guido Ciompi – took care of that, with tweaks made to everything from ambient lighting to the cut of staff uniforms. To the surprise of many a Seoulite, this is now one of the most attractive hotels in town, although now with prices to match. The restaurants are particularly arresting, even if their names are a tiny bit confusing: Murasaki is a stunning, pine-lined sushi bar whose name means 'purple' in Japanese – exactly the colour that neighbouring Taoyuen, a Chinese restaurant, has been decked out in.

Bar. Business Centre. Concierge. Disabled-adapted rooms. Gym. Internet (free). Parking (free). Pool. Restaurants (4). Room service. Spa.

CONSUME

Whatever your carbon footprint, we can reduce it

For over a decade we've been leading the way in carbon offsetting and carbon management.

In that time we've purchased carbon credits from over 200 projects spread across 6 continents. We work with over 300 major commercial clients and thousands of small and medium sized businesses, wh rely upon our market-leading quality assurance programme, our experience and absolute commitment to deliver the right solution for each client.

Why not give us a call?

T: London (020) 7833 6000

★ Westin Chosun

Sogongdong 87 (771-0500, www.westinchosun. co.kr). City Hall station (lines 3 & 4), exit 6. **Rooms** 453. **Rates** ₩410,000. **Map** p254 F3 ⑱

Fierce competition between the City Hall area's five-stars has long made it hard for any one establishment to rise to the top of the tree, much less stay there for decades – but that's exactly what the Chosun has done, thanks to its emphasis on recruiting young and incredibly helpful staff, and a clever programme of regular, appropriate renovations. Rooms are as modern as they come: touch-screen monitors dole out useful electronic information about Seoul, there'll be a ready-to-use mobile phone waiting for you on arrival and, almost uniquely for a Korean five-star, internet access is free. This was actually the country's first luxury hotel, having opened up in 1914, just after the end of the Joseon Dynasty from which it took its name; pop into the downstairs bar and you'll see pictures of previous guests, which include several former US presidents and one Marilyn Monroe.

Bar. Business centre. Concierge. Disabled-adapted rooms. Gym. Internet (free). Parking (free). Pool. Restaurants (4). Room service.

Expensive

Koreana

Taepyeongno 1-ga 61-1 (2171-7000, www. koreanahotel.com). Gwanghwamun station (line 5), exit 6. **Rooms** 337. **Rates** ₩190,000. **Map** p254 E3 ⑲

Location and room size are what set the Koreana apart from its competition. The hotel was built in the early 1970s, just before rocketing land prices necessitated the construction of smaller rooms. In addition, it sits proudly on Taepyeongno, a road linking two palaces – Gyeongbokgung and Deoksugung – and City Hall. The standard and superior rooms are somewhat dowdy and a little disappointing, though those on the renovated business and executive floors are worth the extra splurge, and the suites are among the cheapest of Seoul's higher-end hotels.

Bar. Business centre. Concierge. Gym. Internet (₩20,000). Parking (free). Restaurant. Sauna (men only).

Lotte

Sogongdong 1 (771-1000, www.lottehotel.com). Euljiro 1-ga station (line 2), exit 8. **Rooms** 1,120. **Rates** ₩420,000. **Map** p254 F3 ⑳

The Lotte Hotel's twin towers are impossible to miss if you're in the City Hall area, forming part of a colossal, L-shaped complex also sporting a couple of department stores. This is where French star chef Pierre Gagnaire landed when lured in by Seoul, but sadly this gastronomic refinement is not matched by the hotel lobby's overbusy, mall-like atmosphere, or the occasionally atrocious service.

Rooms are also a little small – perhaps no real surprise, given that this hotel has more of them than any other in Korea – but on the plus side prices are often competitive: rack rates are quite high but it's worth asking about discounts.

Bar. Business centre. Concierge. Disabled-adapted rooms. Gym. Internet (₩22,000). Parking (free). Pool. Restaurants (6). Room service.
► *For our review of the Pierre Gagnaire à Séoul restaurant, see p118. For our review of the adjoining Pierre's Bar, see p136.*

Pacific

Namsandong 2-ga 31-1 (777-7811, www.the pacifichotel.co.kr). Myeongdong station (line 4), exit 3. **Rooms** 139. **Rates** ₩190,000. **Map** p255 F4 ㉑

Set back slightly from Myeongdong's main drag, and filling a fork in the road quite nicely, this is one of Seoul's cheaper five-stars, popular with guests from China and Japan. By international standards it's a four-star or less, but the range of on-site facilities is pretty comprehensive, including a relaxing spa, and prices occasionally drop to almost ₩100,000. There's only one restaurant on site, and this is rather shabby, but with Myeongdong's vast culinary possibilities opening up just outside this can be safely ignored.

Bar. Business centre. Concierge. Gym. Internet (free, some rooms only). Pool. Restaurant. Sauna (men only).

Prince

Namsandong 1-1 (752-7111, www.hotelprince seoul.co.kr). Myeongdong station (line 4), exit 2. **Rooms** 100. **Rates** ₩140,000. **Map** p255 F4 ㉒

A tiny bit cheaper than the Pacific (*see above*), its main price rival, the Prince is correspondingly a little poorer in terms of facilities and service, but rooms are spotless (if occasionally a little stuffy), and travellers whose main aim is to get out and see the sights will require little more, since the location is ideal. Rooms are separated not only by category but by colour: red, blue, white and yellow are your choices, and mercifully the interior designers resisted the temptation to go overboard. Lastly, those with energy to burn can hike from the hotel to the top of Namsan mountain – or at least the cable-car entrance.

Internet (shared facilities). Restaurant.

Royal

Myeongdong 1-6 (756-1112, www.royal.co.kr). Myeongdong station (line 4), exit 8. **Rooms** 304. **Rates** ₩220,000. **Map** p255 F3 ㉓

A welcoming hotel right in the thick of the Myeongdong action, meaning that guests can be out sating their shopping (or, indeed, food) addiction in no time. Rooms follow tried-and-tested colour schemes, but note that the owners seem a little confused about what constitutes a 'suite':

CONSUME

CONSUME

Banyan Tree Club & Spa.

some are bedroom only, surely one factor behind their surprisingly cheap prices. As such, it may be a good idea to have a look at a few rooms before making your decision.

Bar. Business centre. Concierge, Internet (₩16,000). Restaurants (2). Room service. Spa.

Sejong

Chungmuro 2-ga 61-3 (773-6000, www.sejong. co.kr). Myeongdong station (line 4), exit 10. **Rooms** 275. **Rates** ₩260,000. **Map** p255 G4 ㉔

Sejong is immensely popular with Japanese tourists; in fact, sitting in the lobby is almost like taking a free trip to Tokyo. The hotel's reputation is well deserved and the place is comfortable, but discounts from the rack rate tend to be minimal, when they exist at all. The location is as good as it gets, with a subway station and airport bus stop just outside, and Myeongdong's shops and restaurants starting around the corner.

Bar. Business centre. Concierge. Gym. Internet (₩20,000). Parking (free). Restaurants (3). Room service.

Moderate

Astoria

Namhakdong 13-2 (2268-7111). Chungmuro station (lines 3 & 4), exit 4. **Rooms** 80. **Rates** ₩99,000. **Map** p255 G4 ㉕

This mid-range hotel underwent substantial renovation work in 2008, though this very evidently focused more on the restaurants, lobby and other common areas, which are now quite attractive, as opposed to the rooms, which remain a little run-down in feel. Do ask to see more than one, as some are rather confusing in shape, and others have less than stellar views. However, prices are fair and the location good. Also note that the on-site bar occasionally puts on a very reasonably priced wine buffet – not vintage selections, of course, but it can be hard to tell after a few glasses.

Business centre. Internet (free, some rooms only). Parking (free). Restaurants (2).

Ibis Ambassador Myeongdong

Myeongdong 59-5 (6361-8888, www.ibis hotel.com). Euljiro 1-ga station (line 2), exit 6. **Rooms** 280. **Rates** ₩120,000. **Map** p254 F3 ㉖

A simple hotel that ticks the main boxes required by most travellers: cheap, comfortable rooms, friendly staff and a superb location on the edge of Seoul's busiest shopping area. In addition, one of the airport bus routes lands immediately outside the main door, and the nearest subway station is literally a stone's throw away. The buffet breakfasts are also excellent. On the down side, rooms are a little small for those travelling in a pair and light sleepers should note that those facing the main road have not been adequately soundproofed.

Bar. Business centre. Concierge. Disabled-adapted rooms. Gym. Internet (free). Parking (free). Restaurant.

▶ *There's a similarly popular, and slightly cheaper, Ibis a few minutes' walk from the Coex complex (3011-8888).*

★ Metro Hotel

Euljiro 2-ga 199-33 (752-1112, www.metrohotel. co.kr). Euljiro 1-ga station (line 2), exit 6. **Rooms** 75. **Rates** ₩120,000. **Map** p254 F3 ㉗

A teeming district of hyper-capitalism it may be, but Myeongdong does have a few quiet side streets, and it's on one of these that the Metro resides. The hotel as a whole has pared common areas and on-site facilities down to an acceptable minimum, though the coffee-coloured rooms are surprisingly large for the price. Some have poor views – ask to see more than one room – and the breakfasts are somewhat meagre, but otherwise this makes an excellent place to stay.

Business centre. Internet (free). Parking (free). Pool. Restaurant.

DONGDAEMUN

Luxury

★ Banyan Tree Club & Spa

Jangchungdong 2-ga 5-5 (2250-8000, www.banyantree.com). Beotigogae station (line 3), exit 1. **Rooms** 36. **Rates** ₩550,000. **Map** p247 H5 ㉘

One of the most exclusive accommodation options in the city, and no mere hotel: as with other properties in the Banyan Tree chain, each room is effectively also a spa, with delightful pools forming part of a large suite, and shower areas equipped with steam rooms and Banyan Tree signature toiletries. From each and every room, the view of Seoul is quite superb – the hotel sits high on the Namsan slopes, and since there are no more than four rooms on each floor, partially panoramic views are guaranteed. Add to this the chain's natural stylings and attention to detail, as well as excellent on-site restaurants, a golf driving range and spa. Another distinction is being both literally and figuratively above the hustle and bustle of the rest of the city, whose already far-away sound is further diluted by the white noise of fountains and water features. The place to come to get away from it all.

Bar. Business centre. Concierge. Gym. Internet (free). Parking (free). Pool. Restaurants (3). Room service. Spa.

▶ *For the on-site Banyan Tree spa, see p158.*

Grand Ambassador

Jangchungdong 2-ga 186-54 (2270-3111, www.grandambatel.com). Dongguk Univ. station (line 3), exit 1. **Rooms** 410. **Rates** ₩410,000. **Map** p247 H4 ㉙

CONSUME

Despite a somewhat poor location in a nothing-area off the north-eastern flank of Namsan, the Grand Ambassador continues to rope in a surprising number of foreign travellers and businessfolk. Most of these end up highly satisfied with the experience, and, cliché though it may be, their satisfaction seems to revolve around small touches – quirky trims on the bedspreads, intriguing pictures on the walls, flowers on the restaurant tables, and staff who genuinely seem unable to frown. In addition, the aforementioned location problem is remedied with free shuttle buses to more interesting parts of northern Seoul.

Bar. Business centre. Concierge. Gym. Internet (₩16,000). Parking (free). Pool. Restaurants (4). Room service. Sauna (closed Sun).

★Shilla
Jangchungdong 2-ga 2-102 (2233-3131, www.shilla.net). Dongguk University station (line 3), exit 5. **Rooms** 463. **Rates** ₩470,000.
Map p248 J4 ③

Excellent restaurants, a superb spa and winning service… all are de rigueur in Seoul's five-star hotels, but the Shilla is unique in that it has made noble efforts to incorporate Korean colours, materials and motifs into its design – witness the almost temple-like roof of the entrance hall, or the oriental bric-a-brac dotted around the corridors. The sleek bedrooms are no different, but while no two are the same, they may feature such paraphernalia as hanging calligraphic scrolls, celadon bowls or furniture inlaid with mother-of-pearl. This bold attempt at traditional flavour should, in theory, prove a winner with foreign travellers and businessfolk. How ironic, then, that the bulk of customers are package tourists enticed by the brand names found in the adjoining duty-free mall.

INSIDE TRACK
ROOMS WITH A VIEW

While the upper floors of almost all top-end hotels are high enough to offer at least a little spectacle, some have particularly good views. North-facing rooms at the **Somerset** (*see p107*) and **Coex InterContinental** (*see p99*) have views over Gyeongbokgung Palace and Bongeunsa Temple respectively, while the **Grand Hyatt** (*see p104*) and **Millennium Hilton** (*see p91*) both benefit from locations part of the way up Namsan mountain. The terrain is flatter south of the Hangang, with the Gangnam area's buzz of night-time neon best viewed from the **Park Hyatt** (*see p102*) or **JW Marriott** (*see p100*); the latter also has good river views from its north-facing rooms.

Bar. Business centre. Concierge. Disabled-adapted rooms. Gym. Internet (₩22,000). Parking (free). Pool. Restaurants (4). Room service. Spa.

Expensive

Eastgate Tower Hotel
Euljiro 6-ga 17-2 (3407-0700, www.eastgate hotel.kr). Dongdaemun station (lines 1 & 4), exit 8. **Rooms** 204. **Rates** ₩210,000.
Map p248 J3 ③

One of the only acceptable hotels in the immediate vicinity of Dongdaemun market, for long a run-down area (if appealingly so), but in recent times subject to some of the city's largest redevelopment projects, including Cheonggyecheon stream and the massive Dongdaemun Design Plaza. The modern, comfortable hotel is tucked away in a maze of side streets, which may make it hard to find; taxi drivers regularly have problems, though directing them towards the Cerestar building – in which the hotel is located – may help. If you're taking the bus or subway, then it's a good idea to print out a map from the hotel website.

Internet (₩10,000). Parking (free). Restaurant.
▶ *For more information on Cheonggyecheon, see p55. For more on Dongdaemun Design Plaza, see p65.*

HONGDAE
Expensive

Best Western Premier Seoul Garden
Dohwadong 169-1 (717-9441, www.best western.com). Mapo station (line 5), exit 3. **Rooms** 362. **Rates** ₩200,000.
Map p250 B7 ③

The most appealing of Seoul's additions to the Best Western chain, with its proximity to Mapo subway station negating some of the issues arising from its slightly out-of-the-way location. But while it may not be the best place to stay for short-term sightseers, with Yeouido and City Hall just a short taxi ride away, it's a practical business base, with good restaurants and innumerable cafés lining the main road outside. Service is amiable, and rooms are well appointed, if a little small.

Bar. Business centre. Concierge. Gym. Internet (free). Parking (free). Restaurants (3). Room service. Sauna.

Lotte City Seoul
Gongdeokdong 467 (6009-1000, www.lotte cityhotel.co.kr). Gongdeok station (line 5), exit 2. **Rooms** 284. **Rates** ₩180,000.
Map p246 C6 ③

The Lotte City Seoul forms part of two futuristic towers, which rise just west of central Seoul. While the immediate surroundings contain nothing of interest, there are dozens of restaurants, cafés and

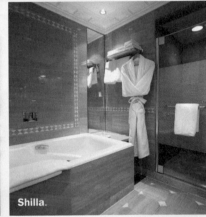

Shilla.

Park Hyatt. *See p102.*

bars within walking distance, as well as a large supermarket. As one may infer from this, the Lotte City is geared towards business travellers rather than tourists; running along a beige-to-coffee spectrum, rooms are pleasant and comfortable enough for a long-term stay, if a little on the small side (a common trait with hotels in Korea, but particularly afflicting those in the Lotte chain). Common areas have been sharply designed and are pleasantly uncluttered.

Bar. Business centre. Concierge. Gym. Internet (free). Parking (free). Pool. Restaurant. Room service. Spa.

Seokyo

Seogyodong 354-5 (330-7777, www.hotelseokyo. co.kr). Hongik Univ. station (line 2), exit 5. **Rooms** 135. **Rates** ₩200,000.

It's debatable which should be more of a surprise – that this is the only bona fide hotel in the wide Hongdae area, or that such an establishment should exist at all. Hongdae's star may be on the wane in terms of fashion, art and more or less anything not related to alcohol, but such is the area's allure that many will find themselves persuaded, in some way, to stay here. It may also appeal to those on extremely tight schedules, being around half an hour closer to

the airport than any comparable facility in City Hall or Gangnam, yet still within a short taxi ride of the city's business districts. The rooms may be slightly worn, but the breakfast buffet will see you gaining weight if forced to stay a while.
Business centre. Concierge. Internet (free). Parking (free). Restaurant.

Budget

Ann's Guesthouse

5F Paradisetel, Donggyodong 159-6 (070 8279-0835, www.annguesthouse.co.kr). Hongik Univ. station (line 2), exit 1. **Rates** *Dorms* ₩20,000.
A cosy little hostel that's perfect for those who want to party – it's in the thick of Hongdae, by far the most hectic part of Seoul by night. Despite this, there's a homely atmosphere, and the comfortable dorm rooms are well shielded from the noise outside.
Internet (shared facilities).

Come Inn

3F Seogyodong 358-91 (1234-5678, www.come innkorea.com). Hongik Univ. station (line 2), exit 5. **Rates** *Dorms* ₩25,000.
A hostel that's every bit as welcoming as its name suggests, and just a few steps away from Hongdae's famed Nolita Park. It's a little homelier and less trendily furnished than some other hostels in the area, but the staff are extremely helpful, and the rooftop is a wonderful place to hang out in warmer months.
Internet (shared facilities).

Hongdae Guesthouse

3F Paradisetel, Donggyodong 159-6 (336-0003, www.hongdaeguesthouse.com). Hongik University station (line 2), exit 1. **Rates** *Dorms* ₩22,000.
In the same building as Ann's guesthouse, and offering more of the same. Each dormitory room has a free-to-use computer, and staff lay on decent breakfasts. It's popular for longer stays – a good place to bunk down if looking for a teaching job.
Internet (shared facilities).

GANGNAM

Luxury

Coex InterContinental

Bongeunsaro 524 (3452-2500, www.seoul. intercontinental.com). Samseong station (line 2), exit 5. **Rooms** 652. **Rates** ₩370,000.
Map p253 O10 ㉟
The mammoth, rectangular Coex complex (*see p75*) is topped and tailed by a pair of InterContinental hotels. This is marginally the more luxurious of the two, and being at the northern end of the rectangle also has tradition to its credit – those with north-facing rooms will be peering straight out over Bongeunsa, one of Seoul's most gorgeous temples.

Try to grab one of the corner suites if possible, as their curved, floor-to-ceiling windows allow in a huge amount of daylight. Various bars and restaurants are arranged around the cavernous lobby, the pick being Asian Live, its open kitchens firing out a mix of authentic Korean, Chinese, Indian and Japanese food.
Bars (2). Business centre. Concierge. Disabled-adapted rooms. Gym. Internet (₩25,000). Parking (free). Pool. Restaurants (3). Room service. Sauna.

★ Grand InterContinental

Teheranno 521 (555-5656, www.seoul. intercontinental.com). Samseong station (line 2), exit 5. **Rooms** 535. **Rates** ₩330,000.
Map p253 P10 ㊱
Also referred to, slightly confusingly, as the Seoul Parnas, this is the southern sibling to the Coex InterContinental (*see left*), located on the opposite end of the large Coex complex. The main differences are that this one is a little cheaper and closer to the subway, though the shoppers worming their way through to the underground Coex mall make the hotel lobby rather busier than it should be. The luxuriant adjoining cafe-bar is quieter, however, and with its location at the bottom of a wide, moodily-lit atrium, it's a wonderfully atmospheric place in which to take coffee or cocktails. Corridors are lined with oriental lanterns and many of the rooms feature traditional Korean paintings or prints, and quirky carpet patterns. Try to get a south-facing room: the views of southern Seoul's vast array of near-identical buildings are unobstructed, and quite tantalising in the light of day.
Bars (2). Business centre. Concierge. Gym.Internet (₩25,000). Parking (free). Pool. Restaurants (6). Room service. Spa. Sauna.

INSIDE TRACK INNOSTEL

Motels (*see p100* **The Look of Love**) may represent Seoul's best-value accommodation, but, conscious of the fact that even the few travellers aware of this fact may be too wary to book a room in one, the city government has roped together the establishments most appropriate to foreign travellers under the clever **Innostel** scheme (www.visit seoul.net). Motels under this umbrella are far less seedy than average, and proprietors have been instructed on the dos and don'ts of putting up – and putting up with – foreign guests. On the website you'll be able to see photos of rooms, and check prices and availablility. In the past, free airport pick-up has even been offered as part of an online deal by some motels – superb value.

★ Imperial Palace

Nonhyeondong 248-7 (3440-8000, www.imperial palace.co.kr). Hakdong station (line 7), exit 1.

Rooms 405. **Rates** ₩330,000. **Map** p252 M10 ⓷

Try not to be fooled by first impressions – the lobby of the Imperial Palace might have looked modish in the 1980s, which makes it all the more surprising that the hotel's rooms are a study in measured opulence. Their lamps, paintings, chandeliers and furniture are, more often than not, souvenirs of the manager's various overseas journeys, lending these wood-and-gold hued rooms an individualised air rare in a Korean five-star; the duplex suites are particularly alluring, with spiral staircases separating baths from beds. The hotel's bars and restaurants are more in keeping with the lobby than the rooms: off-puttingly old-fashioned for some tastes, though appealingly so for others.

Bars (3). Business Centre. Concierge. Disabled-adapted rooms. Gym. Internet (₩25,000). Parking (free). Pool. Restaurants (4). Room service. Sauna.

The Look of Love

The Korean take on the motel.

'Motels' are by far the most common form of accommodation in Seoul, a pattern repeated throughout the country – take a night-time train or bus ride, and you'll see whole clusters of such facilities in the countryside, glowing like miniature cities in a haze of searing neon. But these are motels Korean-style – they're not quite the roadside inns for motorists, often in low-slung blocks, popularised by the US. These motels are often referred to as 'love hotels' by foreign visitors, and they are, indeed, predominantly used for such matters. However, a little clarification is in order. The term hints at gaudily themed rooms dotted with erotic paraphernalia – common in Japan, but almost never the case in Korea.

Rather, motel rooms in Seoul are astonishingly practical: arrayed around the obligatory double bed (twin rooms are almost non-existent) you'll usually find a hot-and-cold water fountain, a couple of free sachets of instant coffee and perhaps some green tea, a hairdryer, tissues and a small refrigerator (usually containing free cans or bottles of sugary drinks). These days, almost all motel rooms also have gigantic flatscreen televisions showing a few international channels, and internet-ready computer terminals are common in newer establishments. Rooms are always en suite, and some bathrooms have a small tub in addition to a shower unit. Here you'll also find shower gel and shampoo, toothpaste (and you'll recieve a toothbrush on check-in), toilet paper and cotton buds. All this comes at a price that, in many cases, will only

JW Marriott

Banpodong 19-3 (6282-6262, www.marriott.com).
Express Bus Terminal station (lines 3, 7 & 9), exit
5. **Rooms** 462. **Rates** ₩310,000. **Map** p252 J11 ⓷⓼
Impossible to miss if you're on the north bank of the
Hangang and looking south, this 34-floor hotel rises
like a monolith from the mammoth express bus terminal complex, which contains not one but three bus
terminals, and a large branch of the Shinsegae
department store. Somewhat surprisingly in a city
almost entirely made up of high-rise buildings, this
is one of the tallest hotels in Seoul (though the tallest
on the Korean peninsula is actually the 105-floor
Ryugyong in Pyongyang). Size and slightly scrubby
environs aside, it's a gorgeous venue with spacious
rooms, friendly, well-trained staff, and a prodigious
number of on-site bars and restaurants. In addition,
it must be said that the office stationery in the rooms
is a lovely idea. Do note that, if coming from the
express bus terminal or its adjoining subway station, signage to the hotel, or indeed anywhere else in
the rambling complex, is quite atrocious.

be a little higher than the daily internet
connection fee in a 'proper' hotel.

Practical they may be, but motels will
not be to every traveller's taste. Their
real *raison d'être* is, for some, all too
apparent – whole sections of the walls
or ceiling are often mirrored, and those
who don't get a free box of condoms at
check-in will likely find one waiting in the
room. The rooms themselves are usually
spotless but you may find a few hairs lying
around. Mercifully, good soundproofing
means that you're unlikely to hear – much
less see – anything untoward going on in
other rooms.

A good way in which to avoid the worst
motels is to book online through **Innostel**
(*see p99* **Inside Track**). Prices tend to be
around ₩30,000-₩50,000 for a room,
though in flashier places such as the **Jelly**
(*see p103*) or **Sheel** (*see p89*) they'll be in
the region of ₩80,000. However, even this
constitutes something of a bargain; if you
feel able to forgo regular hotel facilities
such as currency exchange, breakfast
and English-language service, you'll be
able to enjoy a unique Korean experience,
see through a fascinating window into
contemporary Korean culture, and save
a lot of money too.

CONSUME

Jelly.

Bars (2). Business centre. Concierge. Disabled-adapted rooms. Gym. Internet (₩25,000). Parking (free). Pool. Restaurants (5). Room service. Spa. Sauna.

Novotel Ambassador Gangnam

Yeoksamdong 603 (567-1101, www.novotel.com). Sinnonhyeon station (line 9), exit 4. **Rooms** 332. **Rates** ₩330,000. **Map** p253 O8 ❸

Those able to ignore the blocky, uninviting exterior of this hotel will find that it contains comfy and well-appointed rooms, decorated with a white-and-navy colour scheme. Apart from the larger suites, every room is exactly the same size and shape, so all that remains to be decided is whether you require a north- or south-facing view. The lobby café-bar is pricey and best avoided: you'll find cheaper and more interesting places just down the road.

Bar. Business centre. Concierge. Disabled-adapted rooms. Gym. Internet (free). Parking (free). Pool. Room service. Spa. Sauna.

Oakwood Premier

Samseongdong 159 (3466-8080, www.oakwood premier.co.kr). Samseong station (line 2), exit 5. **Rooms** 280. **Rates** ₩290,000. **Map** p253 P10 ❹

The third hotel in the Coex complex, and less heralded than the InterContinental twins, the Oakwood is worthy of investigation, especially for those staying long term. Its cosy, apartment-style rooms make it suitable for businesspeople or families – studios may suffice for the former, while the latter can choose apartments with up to four bedrooms, or even a rooftop penthouse with its own private garden. All the restaurants, bars, shops and spas one could possibly desire are just downstairs within the underground Coex complex, but for some the real appeal will be the chance to take the lift straight down to the Seven Luck casino – one of very few such facilities in Seoul, or indeed Korea as a whole.

Bar. Business centre. Concierge. Disabled-adapted rooms. Gym. Internet (₩22,000). Parking (free). Pool. Restaurants (2). Room service. Sauna..

★ Park Hyatt

Daechidong 995-14 (2016-1234, www.seoul.park. hyatt.com). Samseong station (line 2), exit 1. **Rooms** 185. **Rates** ₩360,000. **Map** p253 P10 ❹

This is without question the most comfortable and visually appealing hotel on the Korean peninsula: *Time* magazine provided proof of sorts by voting it Asia's best place to be naked. It wasn't actually referencing the rooms – pine-lined affairs with an almost Zen-like use of space – but their adjoining bathrooms, each a space-age granite cavern with commanding views over southern Seoul. The hotel was designed from top to toe by Japanese outfit Super Potato, which threw some pleasingly innovative ideas into the mix – witness the top-floor lobby-with-a-view, or the basement bar built almost

INSIDE TRACK
YOU THOUGHT HOSTELS WERE CHEAP? TRY THE JIMJILBANG

The Hongdae area has a collection of excellent youth hostels, but these aren't actually the cheapest forms of accommodation around. Those staying in double rooms rather than dorms will find lower prices, and greater levels of privacy and comfort, at a cheap motel (*see p100* **The Look of Love**), while for ₩8,000 or so per person – less than half the price of even the cheapest dorm bed – you can spend a night at a sauna-like *jimjilbang* complex (*see p191*).

entirely from old Korean housing. Back in the rooms, floor-to-ceiling windows wring as much light as possible from the outside world; decorative lamps and well-judged spot lighting take over after dark. The service is beyond reproach, and the on-site bars and restaurants superb. *Photo p98.*

Bar. Business centre. Concierge. Disabled-adapted rooms. Gym. Internet (₩26,000). Parking (₩10,000). Pool. Restaurants (2). Room service. Spa. Sauna.

▶ *For coffee and juice bar the Lounge, see p131. For Timber House bar, see p141.*

Ritz-Carlton

Yeoksamdong 602 (3451-8000, www.ritz carlton.com). Sinnonhyeon station (line 9), exit 4. **Rooms** 375. **Rates** ₩420,000. **Map** p252 L11 ❹

The Ritz-Carlton forms a chunky architectural pair with the Novotel (*see above*), just up the road: this is not intended to be a compliment. However, this book is not to be read by its cover, since inside you'll find one of Seoul's more striking hotel lobbies, the entrance hall opening up at its western end to reveal shops, restaurants and a gigantic chandelier. Luxuriant, honeyed tones snake their way from here into the rooms, where they're joined by festive greens, reds and golds, as well as plush carpets, elegant furnishings and highly comfortable beds.

Bar. Business centre. Concierge. Disabled-adapted rooms. Gym. Internet (₩20,000). Parking (free). Pool. Restaurants (4). Room service. Sauna.

Expensive

Blue Pearl

Cheongdamdong 129 (3015-7777, www.hotelblue pearl.com). Cheongdam station (line 7), exit 14. **Rooms** 80. **Rates** ₩200,000. **Map** p253 O8 ❸

A small, simple hotel whose rooms would surely be half the price were they to be found north of the river, rather than within a bag-laden stroll of

Apgujeongno, Korea's prime curl of mega-brand stores. Facilities are (deliberately) bare bones, and rooms are decorated in a basic, understated style, their large windows making visible the teeming roads outside – the setting of the sun turns the grey of the roads into multiple strobes of red and white: a classic image of modern-day East Asia.
Internet (free). Parking (free). Restaurant.

Ellui

Cheongdamdong 129 (514-3535, www.ellui.com). Cheongdam station (line 7), exit 14. **Rooms** 139. **Rates** ₩220,000. **Map** p253 O8 **㊹**
Crying out for renovation it may be, but the Ellui exudes a time-worn charm. Its wood-panelled lobby may look as if it has been steeped in tea for several years, yet ironically it's best suited to the drinking of coffee during the breakfast buffet. Rooms are comfortable and well appointed; get one with a river view if you can.
Business centre. Concierge. Internet (₩20,000). Parking (free). Restaurant. Room service. Sauna.

Marriott Renaissance

Yeoksamdong 676 (553-8118, www.renaissance seoul.com). Yeoksam station (line 2), exit 8. **Rooms** 493. **Rates** ₩260,000. **Map** p253 N11 **㊺**
By far the oldest-looking of Seoul's several additions to the Marriott chain, although the bands of horizontal glass lining its exterior do blend in nicely with surrounding buildings of near-equal vintage. Service is first-class – the *hanbok*-clad attendants are a very nice touch – and the swimming pool one of the most distinctive in Seoul, a quarter-tube of glass providing wonderful views of the high-rise clusters outside; similar sights can be taken in from the rooftop golf driving range. Rooms have also been charmingly decorated.
Bars (2). Business centre. Concierge. Gym. Internet (₩22,000). Parking (free). Pool. Restaurants (5). Room service. Sauna.

Riviera

Cheongdamdong 53-7 (541-3111, www.hotel riviera.co.kr). Cheongdam station (line 7), exit 13. **Rooms** 320. **Rates** ₩230,000. **Map** p253 O9 **㊻**
The most luxurious hotel in the immediate environs of Apgujeongno, and that road's proud collection of luxury flagship stores. Decor is fairly standard hotel beige to coffee – although there are some pretty wild patterned carpets (mercifully these complement, rather than fight, the curtains and bed linen). Those who favour soft beds should know that the ones here are a little hard. Given the charming decor of the rooms, the on-site restaurants are surprisingly ugly, though the Dosan Par and its surrounding clutch of superb eateries is a short taxi ride away.
Bar. Business centre. Concierge. Gym. Internet (₩22,000). Parking (free). Pool. Restaurants (2). Room service. Sauna.

Samjung

Yeoksamdong 604-11 (557-1221, www.samjung hotel.co.kr). Sinnonhyeon station (line 9), exit 4. **Rooms** 159. **Rates** ₩180,000. **Credit** AmEx, DC, MC, V. **Map** p252 M11 **㊼**
Often eschewed by foreign travellers in favour of the neighbouring chain hotels, yet those staying at the Samjung will find its rooms every bit as good, if a tiny bit rough around the edges. The same can be said of the service, though some will find relief in this comparatively less starchy atmosphere. The biggest difference is the price, which often drops as low as ₩130,000 per room – quite a bargain in the pricey Gangnam station area.
Bar. Business centre. Concierge. Gym. Internet (free Wi-Fi). Parking (free). Restaurants (3). Room service. Sauna.

Moderate

★Jelly Hotel

Yeoksamdong 648-7 (553-4737, www.jelly hotel.co.kr). Gangnam station (line 2), exit 8. **Rooms** 41. **Rates** ₩70,000. **Map** p252 M12 **㊽**
The Jelly has become by far the most famous love motel in Seoul, trouncing its innumberable competitors to rise up the ladder of such establishments thanks to the successful exploitation of a hitherto unexplored gap in the local market. Though the model has been faithfully copied many times since, the Jelly became Seoul's first 'upper-end' motel, introducing decorative frills and original styling – some rooms have been designed with Turkish or Chinese themes, while others feature pool tables or heart-shaped bathtubs. The motel scene continues to morph: these days, rooms are not always used for sexual goings-on, and just as often booked by groups of friends here to enjoy a break from family life. Do note that you can't check in until 7pm, and 9pm at weekends.
Internet (free). Parking (free).
▶*For more on Korean motels, see p100* **The Look of Love.**

Popgreen

Sinsadong 614-1 (544-6623, www.popgreen hotel.com). Apgujeong station (line 3), exit 2. **Rooms** 70. **Rates** ₩130,000. **Map** p252 L8 **㊾**
Simple mid-ranger that's as close as you're going to get to Apgujeong's curl of brand-name flagship stores. The location, of course, has an inflationary effect on prices and, although the service is far from five-star, rooms are cosy, and have plenty of room to accommodate your bags of shopping. Note that many of the bathrooms are separated from their adjoining bedrooms by nothing more than frosted glass; if the thought of this makes you uncomfortable it might be best to take a peek at your room before checking in.
Bar. Business centre. Internet (free). Parking (free). Restaurant.

CONSUME

★ Tea Tree Hotel

Sinsadong 535-12 (542-9954, www.teatreehotel. co.kr). Sinsa station (line 3), exit 6. **Rooms** *38.* **Rates** ₩110,000. **Map** p252 L9 ⑩
A wonderful little boutique hotel just off trendy Garosugil – surprisingly, it's the only decent accommodation in this ever more popular area. Rent prices here are among the highest in the whole of Asia, meaning that the rooms aren't colossal; they're actually quite Spartan, too, but have been tastefully designed, with pine flooring and navy wall panels. Try to get one of the Standard Terrace rooms, which come with their own miniature garden. High fences mean that there are no views to enjoy but the little gardens are a highly enjoyable place to take coffee. The upper-level Spa room has a balcony featuring a triangular jacuzzi.
Business centre. Internet (free). Parking (free).

Budget

Richmond

Yeoksamdong 605-17 (562-2151, www.hotel-richmond.co.kr). Sinnonhyeon station (line 9), exit 4. **Rooms** *44.* **Rates** ₩65,000. **Map** p252 M11 ⑪
There are, basically, two forms of accommodation on the hotel-heavy road heading heading east of Sinnonhyeon station: four- and five-star beasts, and cheap, motel-like dives. Hotel by name yet manifestly motel by nature, this establishment is a more than acceptable halfway house, even if its prices lie far towards the cheap end of the scale – a night here costs the same as three days' worth of internet access at some nearby hotels. Some rooms do, indeed, have free-to-use internet terminals of their own, and all have clean en-suite facilities and power showers too.
Internet (free, some rooms only).
▶ *For more on Korean motels, see p100*
The Look of Love.

YEOUIDO

Expensive

Lexington

Yeouidodong 13-3 (6670-7000, www.the lexington.co.kr). Yeouinaru station (line 5), exit 1. **Rooms** *220.* **Rates** ₩240,000.
Many of Seoul's business travellers find themselves based on the island of Yeouido, and the Lexington is one of the better places on Yeouido. The hotel's name was, of course, derived from the famed avenue in Manhattan, and there's other evidence of an attempt at Big Apple stylings: the almost bank-like columns guarding the entrance, the wood panelling in the restaurants, the flowers in the rooms. Less subtle are the New York New York steakhouse, the Broadway café, and a bar called Yanks & Mettz.

Bars (2). Business Centre. Concierge. Gym. Internet (₩17,000). Parking (free). Restaurants (4). Room service.

★Marriott Courtyard

Yeongdeungpodong 442 (2838-3000, www.marriott.com). Yeongdeungpo station (line 1), exit 3. **Rooms** *283.* **Rates** ₩220,000.
The Marriott Courtyard is part of the futuristic Central Park complex, which opened up just south of Yeouido in 2009. Like its neighbouring buildings, its exterior design has a modern beauty rare in cookie-cutter Seoul, but unlike the rest of the complex (particularly the disapointing shopping mall), equal attention has been paid to interior stylings: curved walls and space-age furnishings make the common areas quite pleasing on the eye, while bold patterns and colour schemes do likewise in the rooms. The MoMo clutch of on-site bars and restaurants are worth a hunt around (the pizzas are particularly recommended), but do note that the most direct walking route from Yeongdeungpo subway station will take you through a small red-light district; Mullae station, on line 2, is almost as close.
Bar. Business Centre. Concierge. Gym. Internet (₩15,000). Parking (free). Restaurants (3). Room service.
▶ *For the nearby CGV cinema, see p171.*

Moderate

Yoido

Yeouidodong 10-3 (782-0121). Yeouinaru station (line 5), exit 1. **Rooms** *107.* **Rates** ₩110,000.
Stuck in the wide gulf that separates Seoul's hotels and motels, this budget pick is an acceptable place to stay. It combines a few hotel-like features (very few places at this price level have their own gym, for example) with others more suited to a high-end motel: free-to-use internet terminals, a complimentary can or two of juice, and decor that's adventurous rather than stuffy. It's just a pity that so few rooms have river views – a design flaw, rather than a location issue.
Business Centre. Gym. Internet (free). Parking (free). Restaurant.

ITAEWON

Luxury

Grand Hyatt

Hannam 2-dong 747-7 (797-1234, www. seoul.grand.hyatt.com). Hangangjin station (line 6), exit 1. **Rooms** *601.* **Rates** ₩365,000. **Map** p251 K7 ⑫
The Grand Hyatt is located halfway up Namsan, Seoul's mini-mountain, and as such all of its rooms provide terrific views – those on one side stare

directly at the pine-clad slopes, the remainder back over Itaewon and the river, far beneath. The location does have its drawbacks: you'll need a taxi to get more or less anywhere, though Namsan's spider-web of pleasant walking trails is just a short distance away. Rooms, service and on-site facilities maintain the quality you'd expect from the chain; the restaurants are excellent, with the outdoor poolside barbeque also a winner in warmer months, though a note of caution must be sounded about the downstairs bar (JJ's), which has a somewhat questionable clientele.

Bars (3). Business centre. Concierge. Disabled-adapted rooms. Gym. Internet (₩22,000). Parking (free). Pools (2). Restaurants (6). Room service. Spa.

Expensive

IP Boutique

Hannamdong 737-32 (3702-8000, www.imperial palace.co.kr). Itaewon station (lines 6), exit 2.
Rooms 112. **Rates** ₩220,000. **Map** p251 H7 ⏀
On opening in 2010, this became 'Seoul's first boutique hotel', according to its owners, although others might argue that boutique hotels don't have 112 rooms. The IP's bold design has polarised opinion, with many put off by the lobby: with patterned cushion walls, a resident model knight in armour and other dubious frills, it's a little like walking into an oversized handbag. The rooms themselves are, mercifully, gentler on the eye, with features including iPod docks and pictures painted on to – rather than

Grand Hyatt.

CONSUME

hung from – the walls. Pick your floor carefully, as rooms obey a different colour code on each level. *Business centre. Concierge. Disabled-adapted rooms. Gym. Internet (free). Parking (free). Restaurant. Room service.*

Moderate

Hotel D'Oro
Itaewondong 124-3 (749-6525). Itaewon station (lines 6), exit 2. **Rooms** 40. **Rates** ₩70,000. **Map** p251 G7 🕔

Cheap sleeps in the immediate vicinity of Itaewon station remain popular with American soldiers and their night-time partners, and have long been best avoided. A motel-cum-business hotel with simple but attractive rooms, the D'Oro is a great little exception to the local rule. Set back from the main drag, it's a bit tricky to find – turn left out of the Hamilton, take the second small road on your left, and after 50m or so climb the steps to the right.
Internet (free). Parking (free).
▶*For more on Korean motels, see p100*
The Look of Love.

Hamilton Hotel
Itaewonno 179 (794-0171, www.hamilton.co.kr). Itaewon station (line 6), exit 1. **Rooms** 166. **Rates** ₩130,000. **Map** p251 G7 🕔

Located at the very centre of Itaewon and for some time now that area's most prominent landmark, the Hamilton finds itself fully booked night after night – however, this is less a commentary on the hotel's quality than a reflection of the surrounding area's paucity of quality accommodation. Still, the rooms are fine and represent fair value for the price, while there are good Indian and Chinese restaurants on the complex, and the adjoining shopping mall is a good place to shop for cheap leather shoes or jackets.
Concierge. Gym. Internet (free). Parking (free). Restaurant. Room service. Sauna.

Budget

Kaya Tourist Hotel
Galwoldong 98-11 (798-5101). Namyeong station (line 1), exit 1. **Rooms** 52. **Rates** ₩45,000. **Map** p247 E6 🕔

As with many cheap official 'tourist hotels', the Kaya is merely a less-seedy-than-average motel, replete with the breakfast servings and twin rooms that enable it to exchange an M for an H. The unique selling point here is that it's the closest accommodation to the offices of the USO, whose highly enjoyable tours of the DMZ start at what many travellers find a rather early hour. Staying here will give you an extra half-hour, at least, in bed, and rooms are certainly comfortable enough for a night's stay.
Bar. Internet (free). Parking (free). Restaurant.
▶*For more on Korean motels, see p100*
The Look of Love.

OTHER AREAS
Luxury

Sheraton Grande Walkerhill
Gwangjangdong 175 (455-5000, www.starwood hotels.com). Gwangnaru station (line 5), exit 2. **Rooms** 830. **Rates** ₩450,000.

It's hard to talk about this hotel without referencing the W (*see below*) next door: it may suffice to say that the Sheraton is more of a grown-up's choice. The whole place is rather immaculate, from its scented corridors to the plush carpets and gentle colour schemes of its bedrooms. As with its quirky neighbour, the only real problem is an out-of-the-way location way to the east of Seoul; shuttle buses run every 20 minutes from Gwangnaru station. However, excellent bars and restaurants (and even a juice café) make tempting the more slothful option of staying put.
Bars (2). Business centre. Concierge. Disabled-adapted rooms. Gym. Internet (₩22,000). Parking (free). Pool. Restaurants (7). Room service. Spa. Sauna.

★ W Seoul Walkerhill
Gwangjangdong 175 (465-2222, www.starwood hotels.com). Gwangnaru station (line 5), exit 2. **Rooms** 252. **Rates** ₩460,000.

Highly popular with rich, young Seoulites, the W is surely Seoul's most adventurously designed hotel – even the lifts are worthy of comment, illuminated as they are with luminescent gymnastic rings. An insistent yet sotto voce lounge beat courses through the lobby, and this youthful exuberance carries through to the rooms, many of which could conceivably serve as science fiction sets. Racy furniture and wild colour schemes are standard, but pick the right room and you may also find a heart-shaped bed, or a jacuzzi by the window.
▶*For the Woo Bar, see p141.*
Bars (2). Business centre. Concierge. Disabled-adapted rooms. Gym. Internet (₩22,000). Parking (free). Pool. Restaurants (3). Room service. Spa. Sauna.

SERVICED APARTMENTS
Artnouveau City
Yeoksamdong 701-1, Gangnam (560-9000, www.artnouveaucity.co.kr). Seolleung station (line 2), exit 5. **Rooms** 224. **Rates** ₩260,000. **Map** p253 N11 🕔

Because of its location in the uninteresting Yeoksam station area, the Artnouveau City is of little use as a tourist base, but its proximity to Gangnam's legions of skyscrapers is a bonus for those travelling on business. Rooms are fairly spacious and come equipped with all necessary conveniences; try for one of the duplex suites. In keeping with the promise made by the name, they've been designed with a rare sense of adventure, and the floral motifs on the wallpaper and carpets are quite the tonic in Seoul's blockiest and most modern quarter. Standards of service and cleanliness aren't always as high as they should be, but in general this is a good, and relatively cheap, serviced apartment choice. The owners plan to add more establishments to the chain; see the website for up-to-date details.

Bar. Business centre. Concierge. Gym. Internet (free). Parking (free). Restaurant. Room service. Sauna.

Fraser Place

Uijuro 202 (2220-8888, http://seoul-central. frasershospitality.com). City Hall station (lines 1 & 2), exit 10. **Rooms** 237. **Rates** ₩130,000. **Map** p247 E4 ⑤⑧

This serviced residence also markets itself as Fraser Central, but don't let the name fool you, for it's tucked into a disappointingly uninteresting area to the west of the true city centre. Service is every bit as attentive, and standards of cleanliness as high, as you'd expect from the chain. Monthly rates start at ₩3,500,000 for a simple studio, and though these are comfortable enough they're a bit small; for a little more you'll get a room twice the size, and designed with flair. The unfavourable location necessitates a full run of on-site facilities, including a superb swimming pool and fitness centre, while there's a café adjoining the lobby.

Business centre. Concierge. Disabled-adapted rooms. Gym. Internet (free). Parking (free). Pool. Restaurant. Room service. Sauna.

★ Fraser Suites

Nagwondong 272 (6262-8888, www.seoul. frasershospitality.com). Jongno 3-ga station (lines 1, 3 & 5), exit 5. **Rooms** 213. **Rates** ₩300,000. **Map** p255 F2 ⑤⑨

Colossal, supremely comfortable rooms, impeccable service standards and a full range of facilities make this the most popular serviced residence in Seoul. Monthly rates start at ₩6,500,000, and even these smallest rooms are huge (never less than 52sq m), with gigantic beds; the adjoining living rooms are quite palatial, featuring well-stocked kitchenettes. In addition, the location is quite wonderful: the shops and restaurants of Insadonggil just a few steps away to the west, a three-line subway station similarly close to the east, and a palace at the top of the road. On-site facilities include a well-equipped gym, a rooftop driving range and a (usually empty) swimming pool, while on the ground and basement levels you'll find a cafe, hairdresser and a couple of restaurants.

Business centre. Concierge. Disabled-adapted rooms. Gym. Internet (free). Parking (free). Pool. Restaurants (2). Room service. Sauna.

Han Suites

Samillo 203 (2280-8000, www.hansuites.com), Dongdaemun. Chungmuro station (lines 3 & 4), exit 4. **Rooms** 120. **Rates** ₩90,000. **Map** p255 G4 ⑥⓪

With rates starting at ₩90,000 per day and ₩1,800,000 per month for a simple studio, this is the cheapest decent serviced residence in Seoul. Unfortunately, these cheap prices are not enough to cover things like breakfast and internet access, which cost extra – at ₩22,000 per day, the latter could add a lot to your bill. It's a tiny bit out of the way, but with a location near Myeongdong, and right next to one of the Namsan tunnels, you can jump into a cab and be almost anywhere of note – north or south of the river – in no time. Despite the almost prison block-like layout, rooms are homely; note that most have wood-panelled flooring rather than carpets.

Business centre. Internet (₩22,000). Parking (free). Restaurant.

Marriott Executive Apartments

Yeouidodong 28-3 (2090-8000, www.marriott.com). Yeouido station (lines 5 & 9), exit 2. **Rooms** 103. **Rates** ₩260,000.

The twin glass towers of the Marriott Executive rise proudly from southern Yeouido, staring northwards over the island's vaguely Manhattanesque skyline and the river beyond – a charming view, and one that becomes ever more electric as evening segues into night. The apartments themselves are impeccable, unfussy abodes, with mod cons including flatscreen televisions, Bose sound systems, iPod docks and a rainfall shower, as well as a full range of home appliances. The only real problem is the uninteresting surrounding area, which (rarely, for Seoul) has precious few restaurants; a mercy, then, that the eateries on site are top drawer, the choice including Japanese, Italian and a deli.

Bar. Business centre. Concierge. Disabled-adapted rooms. Gym. Internet (free). Parking (free). Pools (2). Restaurant. Room service.

Somerset

Suseongdong 85 (6730-8000, www.somerset.com). Anguk station (line 3), exit 6, Insadon. **Rooms** 393. **Rates** from ₩4,000,000 per mth. **Map** p254 F2 ⑥①

Superb serviced apartments, offering the high level of comfort required by its mainly long-term visitors. Pick your room carefully, as some peer out over Gyeongbokgung's palatial compound – some of the best views in the whole of Seoul. There's attention to detail (the teddy bears waiting on the bed for new young guests being a particularly nice touch), and those staying a while sometimes find themselves quibbling about such trivial matters as the variety of the breakfast buffet and the depth of the swimming pool – proof of sorts that all of the necessaries are in perfect working order.

Business centre. Concierge. Gym. Internet (free, limited bandwidth). Parking (cost). Pool (outdoor, summer only). Restaurants (3). Room service.

▶ *The Royal Asiatic Society puts on absorbing guest lectures here every second Tuesday. Check www.raskb.com, for information.*

CONSUME

Restaurants

A sizzling surprise around every corner.

Korea's wonderful cuisine is, simply, one of the best reasons for visiting the country. Famously fiery in nature, it has, as yet, failed to truly take hold internationally in the manner of Japanese or Chinese food, but this makes a thorough exploration of the Korean culinary scene even more tempting. With a little bit of courage, you may well find yourself barbecuing your own beef at the table, swallowing seafood you've never seen before, or even eating like the ancient kings of the Joseon Dynasty. However, more than any other city in Korea, Seoul also has a dizzying array of international food, so whatever your taste, disappointment is almost impossible.

BUKCHON & SAMCHEONDONG

Art For Life
Buamdong 29-4 (3217-9364). Gyeongbokgung station (line 3), exit 3. **Open** 11.30am-3pm, 5-10pm daily. **Average** ₩30,000. English menu. **Italian**

Well-made Italian food in the remote – or, at least, remote-feeling – district of Buamdong. The restaurant's name hints at artistic tendencies, and it's a pleasant surprise to see that this is no mere lip service – weekends often see musicians popping by to play a spot of jazz or something similar. In addition, the small garden is full of quirky sculptures.
▶ *For directions to Buamdong, see pp42-50.*

Café Dimi
Tonguidong 1-1 (730-4222), Gyeongbokgung station (line 3), exit 4. **Open** 11am-11pm daily. **Average** ₩15,000. English menu. **Map** p254 E2 ❶ **Italian**

Without a sign, this tiny and charming corner café can be a bit hard to spot. However, despite the diminutive size, it serves a variety of excellent pastas with home-made sauces and fresh noodles, along with a small selection of coffees, wines and beer. Look out for the seasonal drinks, including refreshing summer sangrias and champagne cocktails.

❶ Blue numbers given in this chapter correspond to the location of each restaurant as marked on the street maps. *See pp246-255.*

Cheongsujeong
Samcheongdong 88-23 (738-8288), Anguk station (line 3), exit 1 or Gyeongbokgung station (line 5), exit 5. **Open** 11am-9pm daily. **Average** ₩15,000. **Map** p247 F1 ❷ **Korean**

Situated along the main road in Samcheongdong, this venerable old restaurant specialises in *hanjeongsik* (multi-course) menus and rice with mussels. Try for a seat in the quieter back half of the restaurant, which will allow you to enjoy the savoury rice and impressive spread of side dishes in a more traditional atmosphere.

£ Cheonjin Poja
Sogyeokdong 148-5 (739-6086). Anguk station (line 3), exit 1. **Open** 10am-10pm Tue-Sun. **Average** ₩5,000. **Map** p254 F2 ❸ **Dumplings**

'Cheonjin' is the Korean name for Tianjin, the northeastern Chinese city from which this tiny restaurant's staff hail. The large, juicy dumplings served here are all made fresh. They come in four different styles, and are best served with lashings of soy and ground pepper. They've proven so popular with locals that a sister outlet, this time focusing on noodles, has opened up just a few doors up the road.

★ Chez Simon
Samcheongdong 63-10 (730-1045) Anguk station (line 3), exit 1. **Open** 11.30am-3pm, 5-10pm daily. **Average** ₩25,000. **Map** p247 F1 ❹ **French**

Only in Seoul could you have French cuisine in a wooden *hanok* house. Chez Simon's menu changes regularly, and features the best local ingredients available at the time. The secret to the restaurant's success is the ability of the chef to transform these ingredients into works of art. Each plate is adorned with miniature fireworks of flavour. The lunch or dinner set meals are recommended – with these, you'll get the full range of dishes such as delicious crêpes, steak, pastas and dessert.

Daejangjangi Hwadeok Pizza

Gahoedong 62-1 (765-4298). Anguk station (line 3), exit 2. **Open** noon-10pm daily. **Average** ₩20,000. **No credit cards.** English menu. **Map** p247 F1 ❺ **Pizza**

Pizzas at this secluded, *hanok*-based restaurant have been deemed the best in Seoul by many an expat. Mouthwatering calzoni, capricciosi and other authentic Italian styles are baked in a wood-burning oven, then served on a candle-heated stone slab. The restaurant's unwieldy name – bestowed partly to keep crowds away – means 'Blacksmith's Wood Oven', and there's truth behind each word, since the owners are genuine metalworkers: the light fittings above your table were made by the same chaps who served your pizza.

£ Eat, Rest, Pay, Go

Angukdong 17-18 (723-8089). Anguk station (line 3), exit 1. **Open** 11am-10pm daily. **Average** ₩7,000. **Map** p254 F2 ❻ **Spicy rice cake**

Ddeokbokki, a kind of glutinous rice cake, is a dish that almost every Korean child grows up with. This restaurant specialises in the stuff – its quirky secret is the spicy and savoury red sauce used to cook the delicious rice noodles. You can have it served with a number of toppings: dumplings, mussels, cheese, meat, noodles or egg. There's a long line outside each and every mealtime, so try to get there early.

Eco Bapsang

Jeoksondong 94 (736-9136). Gyeongbokgung station (line 3), exit 4. **Open** 11.30am-2.30pm, 5.30-10.30pm daily. **Average** ₩15,000. English menu. **Map** p254 E2 ❼ **Organic food**

One of very few organic restaurants in Seoul, this quiet, mid-range establishment concentrates on serving high-quality seasonal foods, many of which are vegetarian. In the evening things get a little livelier, with a small drinking menu to go along with *makgeolli*, *soju* and other traditional drinks.

★ £ Jaedong Sundubu

Jaedong 84-10 (747-0011). Anguk station (line 3), exit 2. **Open** 11am-8pm Mon-Sat. **Average** ₩6,000. **Map** p255 F2 ❽ **Tofu stew**

This restaurant takes its name from, and specialises in, an uncurdled tofu stew called *sundubu*. Though tiny, seating maybe 40 people, it sells an impressive 350 bowls of this stuff a day. Unlike most such places, the tofu itself is made in-house, which explains this particular restaurant's popularity with locals. The tofu is soft, creamy and boiled with red pepper paste, clams, mushrooms and onions.

THE BEST RESTAURANTS

For vegetarians
Balwoo. *See p111.*

For retro appeal
31 Sky Lounge Hi-Mart Buffet. *See p117.*

For decadent decor
Palais de Gaumond. *See p123.*

For that royal feeling
Korea House. *See p119.*

For neo-Korean cuisine
Jung Sikdang. *See p122.*

The stew comes to the table bubbling and boiling hot – it's a real favourite on a cold winter day. There might be a queue to get in, but it's certainly worth the wait.

£ Jaedonggol Manim Sundae

Jaedong 46-1 (766-1035). Anguk station (line 3), exit 2. **Open** 9am-10pm daily. **Average** ₩10,000. **Map** p255 F2 ❾ **Noodle sausage**

Sundae is usually a street food, but the version here is miles away from the rubbery sausage you usually get. The mixed *sundae* platter includes Korean-style sausages made fresh with seasonal ingredients, including mugwort, carrots and bellflower root, with a side dish of steamed sweetbreads with a splash of sesame oil. This humble country-style food offers a good pick-me-up for walking around the Samcheongdong and Insadong areas.

£ Jahamun Son Mandu

Buamdong 245-2 (379-2648). Gyeongbokgung station (line 3), exit 3. **Open** 11am-10pm daily. **Average** ₩10,000. English menu. **Dumplings**

With spectacular views of the hills of Buamdong, this elegantly appointed restaurant specialises in North Korean-style dumplings, served in ways ranging from a hearty tri-coloured meat dumpling soup with rice cakes to delicate chilled beef and cucumber dumplings. You can also buy bags of frozen dumplings on your way out for an unusual self-catering option.
▶ *For directions to Buamdong, see pp42-50.*

Keun Giwajip

Sogyeokdong 122-3 (722-9024). Anguk station (line 3), exit 1. **Open** 11.30am-3pm, 6-10pm daily. **Average** ₩40,000. English menu. **Map** p247 F1 ❿ **Korean**

This restaurant serves a variety of different *hanjeongsik* traditional course menus, but the justly famous *ganjang gejang* steals the show. This unusual Korean dish is made by preserving raw

A world
of inspiration

**TIME OUT GUIDES
WRITTEN BY
LOCAL EXPERTS**
visit timeout.com/shop

crab in soy sauce, and is a distinctly delicious and savoury highlight. The old-fashioned interior lends a bit of class and history to the dining experience.

Kim Ssi Doma

Naesudong 74 (738-9288). Gwanghwamun station (line 5), exit 1 or 8. **Open** 11.30am 10pm daily. **Average** ₩15,000. **Map** p254 F2 ⑪

Noodles & meat

Although the basement of a major office tower might not seem the place for it, this noodle and steamed meat restaurant is a traditional-feeling haven right in the middle of downtown. Try any of the excellent noodle dishes for a filling lunch, or stop by in the evening for steamed pork or shark, along with some excellent *makgeolli*.

Mananim Recipe

Anguldong 17-1 (722-2337), Anguk station (line 3), exit 1. **Open** 11am-10pm daily. **Average** ₩15,000. English menu. **Map** p254 F2 ⑫ **Fusion**

Tucked away on a side street, this idiosyncratic little restaurant specialises in home-made organic foods. Most of the menu tilts towards traditional Korean foods like *bibimbap*, but there are also a few pasta dishes. Look out for the home-cured pickles, and cheese made by the charming owner.

Samcheonggak

Seongbuk 2-dong 72-3 (765-3700, www. samcheonggak.or.kr). **Open** noon-3pm, 6-10pm daily. **Average** ₩50,000. English menu.

Korean

Tucked into a mountain fold, this is not just a restaurant; it's a performance house, occasional hotel and a piece of history – it was once a noted *gisaeng* (geisha) entertainment venue, and a favourite of President Park Chung-hee and other military strongmen in the 1970s. The restaurant serves terrific Korean food. There's an à la carte menu, but it may be preferential to pop by for a tea ceremony or *pansori* performance. The website has details.

▶ *Shuttle buses run to Samcheonggak on the hour 10am-10pm, from City Hall station (lines 1 & 2), also stopping at Gwanghwamun (line 5) and Gyeongbokgung (line 3).*

Tosokchon

Chebudong 85-1 (734-5302). Gyeongbokgung station (line 3), exit 2. **Open** 10am-11pm daily. **Average** ₩20,000. English menu. **Map** p254 E2 ⑬ **Chicken and ginseng soup**

Situated in a set of interlocked traditional Korean houses, Tosokchon is widely reputed to have the best *samgyetang* in Seoul. Its best-known (and almost only) menu item is a whole spring chicken stuffed with ginseng, dates, sweet rice and chestnuts, boiled in a thick, rich chicken soup and served with a shot of bracing ginseng liquor. It was a favourite of the late president, Roh Mu-hyeon.

Yongsusan

Samcheongdong 118-3 (739-5599 www.yong susan.co.kr). Anguk station (line 3), exit 1. **Open** 11.30am-3pm, 5-11pm Mon-Sat. **Average** ₩30,000. **Map** p247 F1 ⑭ **Royal cuisine**

A high-end, royal court cuisine restaurant that serves colourful dynastic meals in a sumptuously decorated atmosphere. It offers Kaesong cuisine from the Goryeo Dynasty. This means that you'll get a whole table of traditional dishes such as royal hotpot cooked and served in brassware, meat and vegetable brochettes, marinated beef, grilled fish, and delicate crêpes with a variety of garnishes.

INSADONG

Baekje Gogitjip

Nagwondong 109-1 (745-2224). Jongno 3-ga station (lines 1, 3 & 5), exit 5. **Open** 10am-midnight daily. **Average** ₩15,000. **Map** p255 G2 ⑮ **Beef**

This deceptively plain-looking restaurant holds a couple of fascinating secrets: it's popular with middle-aged gay males (best evidenced, perhaps, by the muscleman calendar on the wall); and it's reputed to occasionally play host to members of the local mafia. However, most customers are simply here for the beef, which, though pricey, is of extremely high quality, and comes in huge portions. As well as barbecue dishes, you can try *yukhoe bibimbap* – raw, steak tartare-like beef, served with a raw egg on a bed of rice, and a bargain at just ₩7,000.

★ Balwoo

Gyeonjidong 71 (2031-2081, www.baru.or.kr). Anguk station (line 3), exit 6. **Open** 11.40am-3pm, 6pm-9pm daily. **Average** ₩30,000. English menu. **Map** p254 F2 ⑯ **Buddhist temple food**

Who needs meat anyway? A question you may well be asking yourself after a meal at this tremendous restaurant, which serves exquisite Buddhist temple food. It's owned and operated by Jogyesa, one of Seoul's most important temples, which sits across the road – quite a view when you're eating your meal. The food itself changes throughout the year, but expect a feast; à la carte items are available, but most plump for the set meals, of which even the smallest has ten individual dishes. Sesame pancakes, bellflower root with pine nut dressing, shiitake mushrooms fried in chilli paste, tofu with salt-pickled herbs, wafer-thin slices of dried orange: a meal that you could eat without saying a word.

▶ *For more information on Jogyesa temple, see p52. For more information on Buddhism in Seoul, see p53.*

Bärlin

Suseongdong 85 (722-5622, www.baerlin.co.kr). Anguk station (line 3), exit 6. **Open** 11.30am-11.30pm Mon-Sat. **Average** ₩50,000. English menu. **Map** p254 F2 ⑰ **German**

A Guide to Korean Cuisine

Tuck into the nation's culinary treasures.

Rice is, and has been since time immemorial, the base of Korean cuisine – the phrase 'have you eaten your rice?' remains a standard Korean greeting. Most dishes here are also given the requisite tang of red pepper paste. But there's so much more to Korean food – you could live in Seoul for years and still know only a fraction of the available dishes.

Koreans tend to eat in groups, and meals here are made for sharing – even if you order individual dishes, they're usually for everyone on the table and expected to be passed around. The traditional way to eat is with legs folded on the floor, which is often heated in colder months.

Below is a short guide to Korea's cuisine, together with some quick recommendations on where to try each type of food listed. For a history of local food, *see p116*. For a glossary of food terms, *see p126* **Korena Menu Reader**.

BARBECUED MEAT

Vegetarians look away now. It would be a mistake for any carnivorous visitor to Seoul to miss out on a traditional meal of barbecued meat, though to take part you may need a local friend – or a bit of pluck. Meals are prepared from raw at the table, usually by the diners themselves, although clueless-looking foreigners will almost always get a helping hand from restaurant staff. Marinated beef or pork, known as

galbi, is the most popular type of meat to grill above the charcoal- or gas-fed flames; while beef can be underdone, ensure that pork is well cooked before eating. Pork belly, *samgyeopsal*, is also widely available, though a little too fatty for some. Lastly, and only available in dedicated restaurants, is chicken *galbi*, served in a large tray.

While it's not the best meat house in the city, **Bulgogi Brothers** (*see p117*) is a superb choice and simplifies the procedure for foreigners.

BIBIMBAP

Bibim means 'mixed' in Korean, and *bap* is the word for rice – this delectable dish sees a blend of roots, leaves, vegetables and spices placed on a bed of rice, usually joined by some meat, egg and spice. The combination is a temple speciality, and is, indeed, a nod to the five colours of Korean Buddhism – yellow for the egg, white for the rice, red for the pepper paste, blue for the meat, and green for the veggies. Vegetarians can ask for the meat to be removed.

Gogung (*see p115*) serves a special variety of the dish, Jeonju *bibimbap*, which hails from Korea's most famed culinary city.

GIMBAP

Gim is lavered seaweed, which is wrapped around rolls of *bap*, or rice, to make a

Galbi.

cylindrical snack. Fillings are numerous, but almost always contain strips of omelette, spam and radish, additions can include the likes of ground beef, kimchi, jalapeños or tuna mayonnaise.

Gimbap is available from **Gimbap Cheonguk** (see p124) and other cheap fast-food restaurants around the city – you'll see it being prepared in the window.

JEON

Jeon are savoury pancakes, made with a variety of ingredients and particularly popular with students, perhaps on account of their grease content, which is good for cutting through alcohol. Most popular are the seafood-heavy haemul pajeon, and the potato-based gamja jeon; similar, though not technically jeon, are mung bean pancakes known as bindaedeok.

Gwangjang Market (see p119) is a terrific place to head for these pancakes.

JEONGSIK

Traditional set meals are known in Korean as jeongsik, and come in innumerable forms. Most are made up of squads of side dishes known as banchan; these always include a kimchi or two, as well as sesame leaves, bamboo shoots and other healthy products. Lastly, there's a bowl of rice, and the main dish of the meal – usually fish, soup or broth.

There are good, traditional jeongsik available at dozens of restaurants in the Insadong neighbourhood.

KIMCHI

There's no doubt at all that kimchi would be Korea's national dish – if only it were a dish at all. The term 'national side dish' may be more apt, since it features as such in every single Korean meal, but is never hunted down specifically or eaten in isolation. Kimchi is a broad term, referring to many varieties of fermented vegetables, including lettuce and radish, and usually – though not always – smothered in red pepper paste.

MANDU

Dumpling purists should note that in Korea, they're not quite as refined as in other Asian nations. However, they certainly make a cheap and tasty snack. Most are

Kimchi.

steamed creations filled with processed meat, veggies or kimchi, but hunt around and you'll also find fried or boiled varieties.

Somandoo in Buamdong has particularly fine dumplings, as well as mountain views from tables on the upper floor. Of the cheapies, it's hard to beat **Mapo Mandu** (see p120).

NAENGMYEON

Quite literally 'cold noodles' and made from buckwheat, naengmyeon is similar to Japanese soba (but spicier, of course – this is Korea, after all), and a perfect summer dish, though one traditionally served in the winter in its homeland of North Korea. It comes in two basic styles: mul naengmyeon sees the noodles swimming with an egg and an ice chunk or two in a spicy, watery soup, while bibim naengmyeon features much the same ingredients but without the soup.

Woo Lae Oak (see p120) is one of the oldest restaurants in the city, and has long been famed for its naengmyeon.

RAMYEON

Though one of the cheapest meals in the country, the spicy noodle soup known as ramyeon is incredibly important to Koreans, who often travel abroad with huge boxes of the stuff. It's usually made with dried, factory-produced noodles, and distinctly less fancy than Japanese ramen, but the red pepper paste provides quite a hit; in restaurants, you can expect onion slices and an egg to be thrown into the mix.

This cheap meal is available at small restaurants all over the city – you can even make your own instant version in a convenience store.

CONSUME

Cooking school: **O'ngo**.

A little bit of German culture, just off ultra-Korean Insadonggil. High ceilings and starched-shirted waiters give a genuine air of European elegance. Simple schnitzels and sausages (the Rostocker is particularly recommended) are available for under ₩30,000, but to actually fill up you'll need a larger meal – order ahead and you can treat yourself to a *haxe* pork shank. Lastly, there are some superb German wines on the menu, as well as Krombacher and Erdinger on tap.

Bongchu Jjimdak
Insadong 25-1 (725-6981). Jongno 3-ga station (lines 1, 3 & 5), exit 5. **Open** 11am-11pm daily. **Average** ₩20,000. **Map** p255 F2 ⑱
Chicken stew
Jjimdak means 'steamed chicken', and that's just what you get at this, Korea's most popular chain for such dishes. Said bird is served in a rich, soy-based sauce, somewhere between a gravy and a stew, with carrots, potatoes and glass noodles. It's a little bit expensive for what you get, though the cheapest portions will easily serve two.

£ Bukchon Sonmandu
Gwanhundong 42-2 (732-1238). Anguk station (line 3), exit 6. **Open** 10am-7pm daily. **Average** ₩5,000. **No credit cards**. **Map** p255 F2 ⑲
Dumplings
Not in the Bukchon area at all, but at least the second word of the name is correct – '*son*' means 'hand' in Korean and '*mandu*' are Korean dumplings. *Mandu* are available everywhere, but the fillings are usually processed. Here, however, you can both

see and taste chunks of exactly what's gone into the mix, and (as if the steaming cauldrons outside the door were not enough) the finger-shaped ridges on the larger dumplings provide further proof that they were made on-site.

Done Zone
Insadong 263 (730-2700). Jonggak station (line 1), exit 3. **Open** 11am-2am daily. **Average** ₩12,000. **Map** p254 F3 ⑳ **Duck & pork belly**
You've had duck. You've had pork belly. Done Zone specialises in the two dishes, and it does them with flair, serving them with a multitude of side dishes and delicious sauces. The thick-cut, smoked pork belly tastes something like grilled bacon – rare in Korea – and the duck has a nice crust. These dishes are often finished off with cold noodles, and go well with *soju*.

★ Doore
Insadong 8-7 (732-2919, www.edoore.co.kr). Anguk station (line 3), exit 6. **Open** noon-4pm, 6-10pm daily. **Average** ₩50,000. English menu. **Map** p255 F2 ㉑ **Dynastic Korean**
One of the most authentically Korean restaurants in the city. Not only is it located in a secluded wooden *hanok* house built in the 1890s, but the often-changing dishes are individually designed by the establishment's chefs. End result: the freshest possible food for each week of each season, and dishes as delicious and healthy as they come. The tableware is beyond reproach, the chunky bowls of brass and handmade earthenware filled with a picturesque, intricately designed array of food. Set

CONSUME

feature an indoor bathroom. This subtle infusion of western sensibilities to local tastes is reflected in the menu today – mouthwatering Korean dishes are served with a sprinkling of Gallic accoutrements. The tableware is also superb, a charming mix of brass and porcelain that blends perfectly with the restaurant's gentle backdrop.

lunches are particularly good value, and there's a modest à la carte selection.

Gogung
B1 Ssamziegil building, Gwanhundong 38 (736-3214, www.gogung.co.kr). Anguk station (line 3), exit 6. **Open** 11am-9pm daily. **Average** ₩15,000. English menu. **Map** p255 F2 ㉒ **Bibimbap**
Bibimbap is, justly, one of Korea's most revered dishes. However, the nation's most acclaimed take on this Buddhist meal hails not from Seoul but Jeonju, a city in the south-western Jeolla province. Artily decorated with tight, colourful bands of traditional rope, Gogung specialises in Jeonju *bibimbap*, which comes surrounded by an even larger than usual army of side dishes. The dish itself has been infused with a few subtle tweaks: sliced jujube, pine nuts, fern bracken and mung bean jelly are among the goodies that may be found if you look hard enough.
▶ *For more information on bibimbap, see p112.*

★ Min's Club
Gyeongundong 66-7 (733-2966). Anguk station (line 3), exit 5. **Open** noon-11pm daily. **Average** ₩50,000. **Map** p255 F2 ㉓ **French-Korean**
To a non-Korean observer, and maybe even most Seoulites today, this gorgeous *hanok* venue would appear to be highly Korean in design. However, on its completion in 1930 it was regarded as one of the city's most adventurous and modern structures. Designed by Gilryong Park, a noted architectural pioneer, it was among the first places in the land to

Namaste
B1 Jongno Tower, Jongno 2-ga 1-1 (2198-3301). Jonggak station (line 1), within station complex. **Open** 11am-10pm daily. **Average** ₩20,000. English menu. **Map** p254 F3 ㉔ **Indian**
Don't be fooled by the unassuming decor, and its location in the ugly 'World Food Court' basement level of Jongno Tower: Namaste is often voted the city's best South Asian restaurant by Seoul's long-term expats. Local businessfolk battle for room on weekday lunchtimes, when ₩10,000 thali menus are on offer – they're superb value for money. However, the Nepali chefs are even prouder of their tandoori dishes, and also make a playful nod to local ingredients with a creamy ginseng lassi.

Nwijo
Gwanhundong 84-13 (730-9301). Anguk station (line 3), exit 6. **Open** 11am-10pm daily. **Average** ₩18,000. **Map** p255 F2 ㉕ **Buddhist temple food**
What a charming setting: tucked away down a winding alley among antique shops, and located in a former noble's house, this restaurant specialises in Buddhist-inspired mountain cuisine. You'll get flavourful salads with wild greens, acorn jelly with spicy cucumber pickles, poached pork, wild sesame porridge and lotus-leaf-wrapped rice. This is a full-course Korean meal that will have you feeling healthy yet full.

£ Pimatgol Jujeom Town
Insadong 30 (723-9046). Jongno 3-ga station (lines 1, 3 & 5), exit 1 or Jonggak station (line 1), exit 3. **Open** 3pm-9pm daily. **Average** ₩10,000. **Map** p255 F2 ㉖ **Traditional Korean**

Spice World

A short history of Korean food.

Ask most people to conjure up their idea of a Korean meal and you'll hear about kimchi, *bulgogi* and how spicy everything is. However, many of what are now Korea's most representative dishes are relatively new in terms of the country's long history, and the food most modern Koreans eat is in many ways quite different from what people would have eaten just a few centuries ago.

Agriculture has been documented in Korea as far back as the Paleolithic Age, with crops such as millet, barley and rice having been the foundation of the diet. These would have been supplemented with meat and fish, as well as locally gathered roots, vegetables and herbs. This prehistoric diet also included fermented foods, and by the Three Kingdoms Period there was already evidence of pickled vegetables. The Baekjae in particular were well known for their love of these early kimchi dishes. Because of the cold, bitter winters, fermentation was an important means of preserving food during the lean season.

The Mongol invasion of the Goryeo Period brought substantial changes to the diet. Prior to that, Koreans were strongly influenced by Buddhism and avoided eating lots of meat. However, the Mongols brought their nomadic foods, which included grilled meats and dishes like *bulgogi*, which even today is cooked on a grill made to resemble the invaders' helmets. It also brought noodles and dumplings into greater prominence in Korean cuisine.

The introduction of New World foodstuffs, including peppers, potatoes, squash, tomatoes and sweet potatoes, had a profound effect on the Korean diet. Sweet potatoes and potatoes helped sustain Korea's poor, rural populations. And while Koreans certainly seasoned and spiced their food long before Jesuit priests supposedly carried peppers with them as they accompanied Hideyoshi's forces in 1593, the new condiment changed the character of Korean food forever.

The cuisine continued to change with the introduction of western foods in the late 19th and early 20th centuries, with the royal court acquiring a taste for coffee, and pork cutlet showing up as a popular restaurant staple. In the latter half of the 20th century, western food chains such as McDonald's and Pizza Hut established a foothold, only to be challenged by local versions like Lotteria and Mister Pizza. The average urban Korean today has an astonishing range of cuisines to choose from, including Indian, Thai, French and Brazilian, as well as traditional Korean favorites. These dishes, too, have now given birth to others, with fusion foods like *bulgogi* pizza, kimchi tacos, and Korean-style fried chicken proving popular.

This is one of the few remaining restaurants with the grit and character of the old Pimatgol alley. It offers only a few options for eating, including an excellent grilled mackerel, acorn salad and savoury pancakes, and a few traditional Korean drinks such as *soju* and *makgeolli*. It's one of the most atmospheric and nostalgic restaurants left from a simpler, bygone era in Korea's modern history.

Restaurant

Sogyeokdong 59-1 (735-8441). Anguk station (line 3), exit 6 or Gyeongbokgung station (line 3), exit 5. **Open** 11am-10pm daily. **Average** ₩50,000. English menu. **Map** p247 F1 **㉗ European**

This modern European-influenced restaurant offers a wide variety of pastas, salads, sandwiches and mains. While on the expensive end of the scale, the quality is a cut above that of most western restaurants in Seoul. The bakery and coffee shop on the first floor also offers some excellent dishes, and makes a good place to stop for a light lunch before braving the galleries of Samcheongdong.

★ Sagwa Namu

Gwanhundong 84-5 (722-5051). Anguk station (line 3), exit 6. **Open** 11.30am-11pm daily. **Average** ₩15,000. English menu. **Map** p255 F2 **㉘ Bangers & mash**

A romantic venue that's extremely popular with local couples, this charming restaurant serves lip-smackingly good bangers and mash – quite at odds with its setting in a secluded *hanok* house, but surprisingly, it works. Korean meals are also available, and in the evening it's also a good place to enjoy a bottle of wine. The restaurant's name means 'apple tree', and there is indeed one in the courtyard – the most atmospheric place to eat, as long as the weather holds.

Sanchon

Gwanhundong 14 (735-0312). Jongno 3-ga station (lines 1, 3 & 5), exit 1 or 5. **Open** 11am-10pm daily. **Average** ₩30,000. English menu. **Map** p255 F2 **㉙ Buddhist temple food**

An old and venerable temple food restaurant, Sanchon was one of the first places to popularise the vegetarian food eaten by Buddhist monks in Korea by turning it from simple food into elaborate multi-dish menus. The restaurant is in a gorgeous and eccentrically decorated *hanok*, and the central space becomes a stage for traditional music and dance performances in the evenings.

Soshim

Gwanhundong 143-1 (734-4388). Anguk station (line 3), exit 6. **Open** 12-9pm daily. **Average** ₩15,000. **Map** p254 F2 **30 Korean country food**

Hidden away in a basement, this quaint restaurant specialises in vegetarian versions of the traditional Korean multi-course meal, with a humble, country-side vibe. Unrefined and unpretentious, it offers a good, meat-free introduction to Korean food, with a few fish dishes available for those who insist.

Tea Talk

Gwanhundong 29-11 (735-8552). Anguk station (line 3), exit 6. **Open** 11am-10pm daily. **Average** ₩12,000. **Map** p255 F2 **31 Ssambap**

This *ssambap* restaurant offers a variety of leaves and bamboo-steamed rice, served with barbecued pork belly and cuts of sirloin beef. After cooking the meat yourself, you should wrap the beef, rice and sauce in leaves and eat. The sauce is unique as well, including everything from pumpkin seeds, garlic, mushrooms, soybean paste and red chilli paste. Service is fast and friendly, and the setting in a traditional house is comforting.

£ Tweet Maru

Insadong 4-2 (739-5683). Jongno 3-ga station (lines 1, 3 & 5), exit 6. **Open** 11am-10pm daily. **Average** ₩6,000. **Map** p255 F2 **32 Bibimbap**

Just outside Jogyesa, this is where the temple's monks like to hang out. Why? Simple: the food is hearty and delicious. Here you get a bowl of barley mixed with rice; this is topped with fresh green vegetables and a salty, earthy soybean paste, the whole shebang mixed up to make a rich, delicious mixed rice dish called *doenjang bibimbap*. The secret is in the sauce, and at lunchtime there is often a line of people waiting to get their bowl.

£ Ttukbegijip

Gwancheoldong 5-1 (2265-5744). Jonggak station (line 1), exit 4 or Jongno 3-ga Station (lines 1, 3 & 5), exit 15. **Open** 6am-9.30pm daily. **Average** ₩4,000. **Map** p255 G3 **33 Broths**

This small restaurant specialises in soups served in an earthenware dish called a *tteukbaegi*. Each order is cooked over a raging gas fire and brought to the table boiling hot. Be sure and try the *urongdwaenjang*, which adds tiny, briny snails to an earthy soybean paste broth, or the intense kimchi soup.

CITY HALL & MYEONGDONG

★ 31 Sky Lounge Hi-Mart Buffet

31F Samil Building (739-4618). Jonggak station (line 1), exit 4. **Open** noon-1am daily; last orders before 9pm. **Average** *Lunch* ₩13,000. *Dinner* ₩18,000. No menu. **Map** p255 F3 **34 Buffet**

Don't be dissuaded by the unwieldy name – this is one of Seoul's most interesting restaurants. It sits on the 31st floor of the Samil Building, whose name means '31'. The number is important to Koreans: 1 March is the anniversary of a noted movement against Japanese rule. This building was completed on that date in 1969, becoming Seoul's first sky-scraper, and the tallest building in Asia at the time. In the 1970s, the top-floor restaurant/club was very much the place to be, and the exclusive reserve of political, military and business bigwigs – Park Chung-hee had a private office here. It's now popular with an older crowd, and exudes a wonderful, worn appeal – and terrific views. The buffet food itself is wonderful, with spaghetti, sushi and tempura worming their way into a largely Korean mix.

★ Bulgogi Brothers

Myeongdong 1-ga 7-1 (319-3351, www.bulgogi bros.com). Euljiro 1-ga station (line 2), exit 5. **Open** 11am-10pm Mon-Fri; 11.30am-10pm Sat, Sun. **Average** ₩30,000. English menu. **Map** p255 F3 **35 Bulgogi**

Marinated rib meat, known in Korea as *galbi*, is surely one of the world's most delightful meals – mainly due to the fact that it's prepared in front of you at the table, typically over a charcoal fire. For new arrivals, this may initially prove a somewhat disconcerting experience, which makes restaurants like Bulgogi Brothers so important. Unlike most such meat houses, menus here are in English, the decor is elegant rather than merely functional, and the meat is superb.

£ Chuncheon Dak Galbi

Gwansudong 143-42 (2274-2170). Jonggak station (line 1), exit 15. **Open** 11am-11pm daily. **Average** ₩10,000. **No credit cards**. **Map** p255 F3 **36 Chicken barbecue**

Chicken *galbi* is prepared a little differently to the pork or beef version (*see p112*), made as it is in a deep pan, rather than over a direct flame. This takes away some of the excitement, for sure, but the meal is no less delicious – lettuce, rice cake and veggies are thrown in with the meat, and just before the end of the meal, those not yet stuffed will get the chance to add some fried rice or noodles to the mix. The restaurant takes its name from the city of Chuncheon.

Goryeo Samgyetang

Seosomundong 55-3 (752-9376). City Hall station (lines 1 & 2), exit 10. **Open** 11am-midnight daily. **Average** ₩15,000. **Credit** All. **Map** p254 E4 **37 Chicken & ginseng soup**

CONSUME

Locals often claim that a soup named *samgyetang* has magical, restorative qualities. To make this dish, a tender young chicken is stuffed with sticky rice, gingko nuts, jujube, liquorice root and ginseng. Here, the broth is carefully coaxed into being by simmering the chicken. The restaurant has a version made with black chicken: a special breed whose skin and meat are both distinctly dark.

★ Kongdu Iyagi

1F Museum of History, Sinmunno 2-ga 2-1 (722-7002). Gyeongbokgung station (line 3), exit 7. **Open** 11am-10pm Mon-Fri; 11am-7pm Sat, Sun. **Average** ₩30,000. English menu. **Map** p254 E3 ❸ **Neo-Korean**

The name of this restaurant translates as 'Beans Story', and assorted legumes do, indeed, make their appearance in most dishes. This is another example of what's becoming known as neo-Korean cuisine, the art of fusing time-honoured ingredients with new and imported tastes or techniques. Here we see the humble *bibimbap* dish given a soybean zing, as well as western-leaning dishes such as mushroom and bean pasta, and halfway houses like seafood tofu steak. It also has a fine line in home-made *makgeolli*.

▶ *For our review of the Seoul Museum of History, see p63.*

£ Myeongdong Dongaseu

Myeongdong 2-ga 59-13 (no phone). Myeongdong station (line 4), exit 6. **Open** 11.30am-9pm daily. **Average** ₩10,000. English menu. **Map** p255 F4 ❸ **Breaded pork cutlet**

Brought from Europe via Japan, the Korean version of breaded pork cutlets is a lunchtime favourite. This respected cutlet house serves only a few basic variations, including one stuffed with cheese, ham and vegetables, but all come out crispy and delicious.

★ Pierre Gagnaire à Séoul

35F Lotte Hotel, Sogongdong 1 (317-7181, www.pierregagnaire.co.kr). Euljiro 1-ga station (line 2), exit 8. **Open** noon-3pm, 6-10pm Mon-Sat. **Average** ₩100,000. English menu. **Map** p254 F3 ❹ **French**

Michelin stars are tricky to come by, but when überchef Pierre Gagnaire swiped three of them, Seoul swiped him. His restaurant sits atop the Lotte Hotel (*see p93*) in downtown Seoul, and the dishes coming out of the kitchen are truly superb – French molecular gastronomy with subtle Korean flourishes. As with his other restaurants, the emphasis here is on colour and form. Such wonderful dishes come at a price, but notable are the lunch deals, a comparative steal at ₩60,000.

Yi Chun Bok Chamchi

Namyeongdong 85-1 (794-4558). Sookmyung Women's Univ. station (line 4), exit 6. **Open** 5pm-2am daily. **Average** ₩30,000. **Map** p247 E6 ❷ **Raw tuna**

An all-you-can-eat tuna restaurant with entertaining chefs who prance around like swashbuckling pirates. The tuna comes in various forms, from blood-red cuts to white abalone and fatty pink belly. If you'd like to encourage the chefs to give you extra service, offer them a shot of *soju* with a ₩10,000 note wrapped around it. In return, you'll get premium cuts of tuna, and a shot of cactus liquor with a tuna eyeball inside.

Zen Hideaway

Myeongdong 2-ga 52-13 (no phone). Myeongdong station (line 4), exit 6. **Open** 11am-11pm daily. **Average** ₩25,000. **Map** p255 F4 ❸ **Italian & Thai**

Thai and Italian cuisine might not seem a perfect match at first, but this trendy restaurant pulls them both off with a bit of flair and fusion. The lunch set menus are excellent value, and the ambiance provides a nice artistic break from the bustle of Myeongdong.

DONGDAEMUN

Gostiniy Dvor

Daehogil 17 (2275-7501). Dongdaemun History & Culture Park station (lines 2, 4 & 5), exit 7. **Open** noon-11pm daily. **Average** ₩20,000. **No credit cards**. English menu. **Map** p247 H3 ❹ **Russian**

This is by far the most visually appealing restaurant in Seoul's 'Little Central Asia', and the food is also a notch above the competition. One favourite, the Julian – cubes of potato and chicken, topped with cheese – is particularly filling, while the classic borscht makes a good addition to any meal. Also notable is the chance to sample some fine Russian and Central Asian alcohol; the various beers from the Russian Baltika label are a cut above Korea's own motley brands.

£ Guksuga

Dongsungdong 130-33 (3673-5798). Hyehwa station (line 4), exit 2. **Open** 10.30am-10.30pm daily. **Average** ₩6,000. **Map** p247 H1 ❺ **Noodles**

When you're ready for something quick and filling but cheap, you can't do any better than this humble noodle house. Try the *janchiguksu* ('celebration noodles') for a dish with nutty, savoury depth, or snack on some of the superb dumplings or rice balls.

★ £ Gwangjang Market

Jongno 5-ga station (line 1), exit 8. **Open** times vary, but generally early morning until midnight. **Average** ₩10,000. **No credit cards**. **Map** p247 H3 ❹ **Market fare**

Not a restaurant at all, but this is the place in Seoul that's most fun for foodies. Most of what's on offer is on display in the market's various covered arcades, though you may well be taking a blind dip into the unknown; striking a balance between safety and adventure are platters of fried comestibles known as *modeum jeon*, mung-bean pancakes called *bindaeddeok*, and *makgeolli* rice wine – the latter is imbibed well into the evening.

Korea House

Pildong 2-ga 80-2 (2266-9101, www.korea house.or.kr). Chungmuro station (lines 3 & 4), exit 3. **Open** noon-2pm, 5-8pm daily. **Average** ₩68,000. Lunch for groups only, reservation essential. English menu. **Map** p255 G4 ❹ **Royal banquets**

The banquet meals served up here are a carbon copy of those enjoyed by the royals of the Joseon Dynasty, and exude centuries of measured refinement. This is Korean cuisine at its finest – the balance of colours, flavours and textures is quite remarkable, with the nine-sectioned *gujeolpan* platter particularly notable. It's impossible to describe the sheer abundance of food, but the prevalence of veggies, roots and shoots ensures that you'll be eating healthily. In addition, for an extra fee you'll be able to enjoy a court performance immediately after your meal.

▶ *Performances at Korea House take place at 7pm and 8.50pm, and last an hour.*

£ Mami Cheonggukjang

Dongsungdong 18-2 (765-0842). Hyehwa station (line 4), exit 1. **Open** 7.30am-10.30pm daily. **Average** ₩6,000. **Map** p247 H1 ❹ **Soybean stew**

Even many Koreans avoid *cheonggukjang*, a strongly odiferous stew made of fermented soybeans, but if you can get past the smell you're in for a delicious, hearty and healthy treat. The kimchi and mushroom versions are the top menu items, and well worth braving the distinctive odour for.

£ Pakganne

Jongno 5-ga 138-10 (2264-0847). Jongno 5-ga station (lines 1, 3 & 5), exit 8. **Open** 11am-midnight daily. **Average** ₩6,000. **Map** p247 H3 ❹ **Mung bean pancakes**

After the Korean War, thousands of displaced North Koreans were left without a home. To make

Pierre Gagnaire à Séoul.

a living, many of them set up food stalls in Gwangjang, a local clothing market. Dating back to that time, Pakganne is famous for its crisp *bindaeddeok* – pancakes made from stone-ground mung beans, mixed with bean sprouts and onions, and fried. It's so well known for the dish that there are queues out of the door at lunchtime, and scores of people order extra to take home. Pakganne also serves excellent banquet noodles and, for the adventurous, the blood sausage known as *sundae*.

Song's Kitchen

Seongbukdong 119-1 (747-1713). Hansung Univ. station (line 4), exit 6. **Open** 11am-11pm daily. **Average** ₩20,000. English menu. **Fusion**
The funky vibe of this converted residence gives a hint of the eclectic menu, which runs from pizza and pasta to spicy rice cakes and served inside a whole baked pumpkin and *patbingsu*, a dessert of shaved ice and sweet red beans. Be sure to try the house drink, *songju*, which combines beer and coffee.

★ Woo Lae Oak

Jugyodong 118-1 (2265-0151). Euljiro 4-ga station (lines 2 & 4), exit 4. **Open** 11.30am-10pm Tue-Sun. **Average** ₩30,000. English menu. **Map** p247/p255 H3 ㊿ **Barbecue & naengmyeon**
This is one of the oldest and most elegant restaurants in Seoul, having started life in 1945, just after the end of Japanese annexation. Many locals have been popping by for decades – the barbecued meat is among the best in Seoul – but since it's rather pricey, regulars usually ask for a bowl of *naengmyeon*, a relative steal at ₩9,000. This is a famous North Korean dish of buckwheat noodles, served in a cold, spicy soup.

HONGDAE

Eurasia

4F Daehyeondong 27-33 (393-7011). Ehwa Womans Univ. station (line 2), exit 1. **Open** 5pm-midnight daily. **Average** ₩15,000. **No credit cards**. English menu. **Russian**
The vast majority of Seoul's few Russian restaurants lie in the alleys south of Dongdaemun market, but here's one smack in the centre of student-heavy Sinchon. This location has made a sleeker, more modern decor almost obligatory, and thankfully the food has not suffered – the ethnic Uzbek staff whip up some particularly fine soups. Of course, it would hardly be a Russian meal without a drink; available here, Armenian cognac is some of the best in the world, and goes well with slices of sugar-covered lemon.

Jangeorang

Changjeondong 6-137 (333-1455, www. jangarang.com). Hongik Univ. station (line 2), exit 9. **Open** 11am-10pm daily. **Average** ₩15,000. **Barbecued eel**

Once you've had freshly barbecued eel, you'll never go for the common, overly slathered stuff you see at every dime-a-dozen sushi shop. Koreans like their eel grilled over a very hot flame, and topped with a seasoned soy-sauce reduction, salt or red chilli paste. The skilled chef will cook it first and then bring it over to your table, where you'll finish the cooking on your own personal barbecue grill. Once the meat is crisp, wrap it with lettuce and top with slivers of raw ginger. It is common to have this with potent, port-like raspberry wine.

Jeong Daepo

Dohwadong 183-8 (713-0710). Gongdeok station (lines 5 & 6), exit 8. **Open** 11am-2am daily. **Average** ₩25,000. English menu. **Barbecue**
A rollicking and rowdy joint for the after-work crowd to gather and blow off steam by eating vast quantities of meat, this Korean barbecue's special attraction is special grill pans with a trench around the outside for cooking omelettes. The meat is good, and goes perfectly with a little kimchi-enhanced egg and a shot of *soju*.

£ Jopok Ricecakes

Seogyodong 355-3 (no phone). Sangsu station (line 6), exit 1. **Open** 2pm-midnight daily. **Average** ₩5,000. **No credit cards**. **Spicy rice cakes**
Jopok is the Korean term for 'mafia', and the staff here are, indeed, reputed to be members of a local racket. Not that there's anything to fear – even if the rumours are true, all you'll notice is a little surliness, of which at least some is for show. Most Koreans come for the ricecakes (a local student staple), but fried goods known as *twigim* are usually far more pleasing to foreign tongues – you'll see them in ranks at the shopfront, so just point at what you want and it'll be refried and smothered in a spicy sauce.

£ Mapo Mandu

Seogyodong 393-1 (333-9842). Hapjeong station (lines 2 & 6), exit 2. **Open** Usually 24hrs daily; closes 10pm Sun. **Average** ₩5,000. **No credit cards**. **Dumplings**
This small chain wrings new tastes from Korea's humble *mandu* dumplings with the addition of one simple ingredient: galbi sauce, which is also used to marinate the beef grilled at barbecue restaurants across the land. Although these are some of Seoul's most distinctive-tasting dumplings, they're also some of the cheapest on offer in the capital, costing just ₩2,500 per portion. Plenty of other simple local rice and noodle dishes are also available, though you'll need a reasonable grasp of Korean to decipher the menu.
▶ *There's another branch of Mapo Mandu a short walk from exit 6 of Chungmuro station (lines 3 & 4).*

CONSUME

Oyori

Seogyodong 409-10 (332-5525). Sangsu station (line 6), exit 1. **Open** 11.30am-9pm daily. **Average** ₩15,000. **No credit cards**. English menu. **Asian fusion**

The owners of this restaurant came up with a terrific idea in 2009. More and more Korean men are marrying women from abroad, and on the many occasions that the marriage does not work out, the ladies in question find it hard to gain meaningful employment in Korea. The entire team here is made up of foreign single mothers, who add their own countries' flavours to the menu; in addition, some of the profits are used to send their kids through school. The restaurant is highly attractive, and the food is excellent.

£ Sak

Sangsudong 310-13 (334-5205). Sangsu station (line 6), exit 1. **Open** 11.30am-10pm daily. **Average** ₩5,000. **Tempura**

Although it seems like nothing more than a little hole-in-the-wall takeaway joint from the outside, inside Sak you'll find people are cramming themselves on to places around the tiny tables to get a chance to eat some of the best snack food to be found in the whole of Seoul. Fresh hot peppers give the *ddeokbokki* an extra kick, but the real star of the show here is the amazingly crispy tempura, including sweet potato, stuffed peppers, shrimp and squid. Enjoy your meal with an imported beer or soda.

Restaurant Etiquette

Toeing the line.

Korea is a nation steeped in Confucian ritual, with dishes, utensils and entire restaurant settings that are alien to many foreigners. It should stand to reason, therefore, that certain rules of culinary etiquette should be observed. Firstly, it's customary to allow the Confucian superior (the eldest male, or simply the one paying for the meal) to both sit first, and take the first few pecks of the meal. Do note that many of the more traditional restaurants seat their customers on the floor at low tables, which newbies may find rather uncomfortable: the trick is to sit strategically next to a wall, which can be discreetly leaned upon in time of need.

Korean meals are also almost always made for sharing – corralling off your own dish is considered unseemly, and you'll often be expected to share bowls of food with others. Then come the chopstick rules: do not poke these through your food or use them to point at anybody. When at rest, they should be placed horizontally on the table or the rim of a bowl; to leave them inside the bowl is a reminder of memorial incense sticks, and thus related to death. Koreans do not expect foreigners to be able to use chopsticks, even those they know to have spent years in the country: those who can use them will be complimented endlessly.

Then, the pouring of drinks. Alcohol is an integral part of eating out, so this is rather important. Rule number one: never pour your own drink. Rule number two: never leave someone with an empty glass. The rules regarding the required hand positions would take some time to explain in full,

but in general try to accept with two hands, and pour with your non-active hand lightly gripping the wrist of your active one. You'll notice that younger people drinking with older people turn their heads 90 degrees when imbibing their drink – again, a mark of Confucian respect, and one largely performed subconsciously.

All this said, Koreans tend to be very forgiving of foreigners regarding culinary customs, and you certainly won't be expected to follow their rules to the letter. Indeed, breaking them time and again can serve to break the ice — fail and you'll have a bit of fun, succeed and you'll win respect. A win-win situation, in other words.

GANGNAM

Gorilla in the Kitchen

Sinsadong 650 (3442-1688, www.gorilla kitchen.co.kr). Apgujeong station (line 3), exit 3. **Open** 11am-11pm daily. **Average** ₩25,000. English menu. **Map** p252 M9 **51**
Health food

Stylish restaurant owned by Bae Yong Joon, an actor who shot to East Asian superstardom after starring in the *Winter Sonata* TV series. He certainly knew how to rope in Apgu's waiflike fashion victims – you'll find calorie counts next to every item on the menu. Pastas and salads sit alongside more interesting dishes, such as the grilled scallop mushrooms with arugula. Some say that the restaurant's popularity has had a negative effect on quality, but it's still a great place to head.

Jung Sikdang

Sinsadong 649-7 (517-4654, www.jung sikdang.com). Apgujeong station (line 3), exit 3.

Open noon-4pm, 6-10pm Mon-Sat; noon-4pm Sun. **Average** ₩55,000. English menu. **Map** p252 M8 **52 Neo-Korean**

Another take on what in-the-know Seoulites now refer to as neo-Korean cuisine, which runs a sketchy grey line from traditional to contemporary. This restaurant sits happily at the latter end of the scale, with foreign ingredients and non-traditional techniques manifest in almost all dishes. Aubergine purée, lime jelly, cinnamon cream and herbal foams will serve as good examples, all arriving artistically laid out on the plate. Then there's the charming view over Dosan Park – a wonderful venue.

★ Palais de Gaumond/Tutto Bene

Cheongdamdong 118-10 (546-8877). Cheongdam station (line 7), exit 9. **Open** 6-11pm daily. **Average** ₩100,000. English menu. **Map** p253 N8 **53 French & Italian**

These two interconnected restaurants are among the classiest in the whole country – over a period of two years, manager Seo Hyun Min designed them

Jung Sikdang.

himself from top to tail; he will be willing to show you the preliminary pencil sketches as proof if necessary. Palais de Gaumond is marginally the more upmarket of the two, serving immaculate French dishes amid chandeliers and huge, angled wall mirrors. Tutto Bene runs along an Orient Express design tangent, and offers Italian cuisine with an empahsis on seafood, the odours mingling with those of fresh flowers.

Star Chef

Dokogdong 417-2 (529-8248). Maebong station (line 3), exit 4. **Open** *4pm-midnight Tue-Sun.* **Average** *₩20,000.* **Fusion**
Formerly head chef at the prestigious Shilla hotel (*see p96*), Ho-nam Kim decided he wanted to open up a bistro in the Gangnam business district, an area more known for wanton bars and clubs than fine dining. His Szechuan/California fusion cuisine quickly became a hit with foodies – particularly recommended are his deep-fried seasonal fish, served whole with a lemon *ponzu* sauce. Also notable are the beef and pine mushroom salad, the gouda omelette, and pretty much any of the daily specials.

★ Sushi Chohi

Sinsadong 650-6 (545-8422). Apgujeong station (line 3), exit 3. **Open** *noon-2.30pm, 6-10pm daily.* **Average** *₩90,000.* English menu. **Map** p252 M9 **54** **Sushi**
Utterly divine sushi, every bit as good as you'd find in Japan. The Tokyo-trained chef has invested heavily in quality equipment, with chopping boards made from Kyushu hardwood and knives costing several thousand dollars. Dinner starts at ₩90,000, and it's worth plonking yourself down next to the chef, who'll tell you exactly where every morsel on your plate was caught; it could be anywhere from Hokkaido to Jeju island. Come for lunch, when the menus are just ₩55,000 but still pretty meaty (in a fishy sense).

ITAEWON

Berlin

Itaewondong 457-1 (749-0903). Noksapyeong station (line 6), exit 1. **Open** *11.30am-2am daily.* **Average** *₩25,000.* English menu. **Map** p251 G7 **55** **East Asian**
An elegant restaurant serving a wide range of Asian and fusion food. Notable examples include delectable green curries from Thailand, samosas in a roasted red pepper sauce, and fish and chips with a wasabi mayo kick. It's also a good place to come for drinks.

£ Chowon Sikdang

Itaewondong 127-18 (no phone). Itaewon station (line 6), exit 3. **Open** *Varies, but usually late morning until at least 2am.* **Average** *₩5,000.* **No credit cards. Map** p251 G7 **56** **Gamjatang**

This little hidey-hole specialises in *gamjatang*, a hearty local broth whose main ingredients are chunks of potato, hunks of succulent pork rib and whole fistfuls of spice. Food aside, don't expect too much refinement here: local working girls and drunken salarymen – all past their prime – form much of the customer base, but it all makes for a rather entertaining spectacle, particularly when viewed over a bottle of *soju*.

★ Copacabana

Itaewondong 119-9 (010 6390-1659). Itaewon station (line 6), exit 1. **Open** *5-10pm Tue-Fri; noon-10.30pm Sat, Sun.* **Average** *₩30,000.* English menu. **Map** p251 G7 **57** **Brazilian barbecue**
All-you-can-eat barbecued meat for ₩29,000: that's Copacabana in a nutshell. Seoul has a fair few *churrasqueiras*, though at this one the owners are actually Brazilian, and the beef is at its freshest and most succulent – just one reason why Ronaldo, Roberto Carlos and other members of the Brazilian football team dropped by during the World Cup in 2002. Mentioning this may be sacrilege of sorts to dedicated carnivores, but the salad bar is also pretty good.

Gecko's Garden

Itaewondong 116-6 (790-0540, www.geckos terrace.com). Itaewon station (line 6), exit 2. **Open** *11am-1am daily.* **Average** *₩40,000.* English menu. **Map** p251 G7 **58** **Mediterranean**
This restaurant has long been popular with Itaewon's upper class, and this is quite apt since its main building was once a mansion. Its tranquil, almost temple-like green ceilings finely augment the classy French, Spanish and Italian dishes whipped up in the kitchen – baked goat's cheese with pineapple relish, salmon steak in kiwi-orange sauce, and a tremendous range of tapas. As evening encroaches, the restaurant morphs into a classy wine and cocktail bar.

Happy House

Itaewondong 127-15 (797-3185). Itaewon station (line 6), exit 3. **Open** *11am-11pm daily.* **Average** *₩15,000.* **No credit cards.** English menu. **Map** p251 G7 **59** **West African**

CONSUME

Itaewon has, for decades, been home to a substantial West African community, the bulk of whom hail from Nigeria. Every single West African in town knows this small restaurant, a regular focus of meeting and eating, thanks to its hearty, authentic food. Polenta-like in consistency, 'grinded rice' forms the basis of most meals here, and can be served with grilled plantain, spicy black-eyed peas or one of a variety of delicious soups.

Kikku

Ichondong 301-162 (794-8584). Ichon station (line 4), exit 3-1. **Open** 11.30am-2.30pm, 5.30-10.30pm daily. **Average** ₩40,000. **Map** p251 F9 ⑥ **Sushi**

Located in Seoul's Little Tokyo, this small sushi restaurant offers exquisitely fresh fish prepared impeccably well and served in authentic Japanese style. The chef's choice lunch set is an absolute steal, costing well under half of what an equivalent meal would cost in one of Seoul's larger sushi houses, and the chefs behind the counter are remarkably responsive to individual customer preferences.

★ La Bocca

Hannamdong 737-37 (790-5907, www.sortinos-seoul.com). Hangangjin station (line 6), exit 3. **Open** 9am-11.30pm Mon-Wed, Sun; 9am-1.30am Thur-Sat. **Average** ₩30,000. English menu. **Map** p251 H7 ⑥ **Italian**

A classy venue serving mouthwatering Italian dishes for dinner, and sandwiches earlier in the day. A wide range of alcoholic drinks makes this an appealing late-night venue, especially when the weather allows use of the outdoor patio area. The table service is excellent, and you're sure to notice the range of wonderful cakes sitting innocently at the counter – almost impossible to resist.

Macaroni Market

Hannam 1-dong 737-50 (749-9181, www.macaronimarket.com). Itaewon station (line 6), exit 2. **Open** 11am-10pm Mon, Sun; 11am-2am Tue-Sat. **Average** ₩25,000. English menu. **Map** p251 H7 ⑥ **Italian**

INSIDE TRACK
GIMBAP HEAVEN

Need a quick bite at a low price? Hunt down the nearest branch of **Gimbap Cheonguk**. Literally meaning '*gimbap* heaven', these orange-fronted fast-food restaurants whip up Korean staple meals in no time – dumplings, breaded pork cutlet, fried rice, noodle soup and (of course) rolls of *gimbap*, all costing ₩5,000 or less, and actually pretty tasty.

Delectable Italian food, and about as authentic as you'll find anywhere in Seoul. The pasta and meat dishes are particularly scrumptious. And, perhaps uniquely in Korea, you'll hear dishes from the menu pronounced correctly, rather than sieved through *hangeul* (the Korean script) – owner Francesco Chu, who once lived in Italy, schools his staff on the correct pronunciation of everything that appears on the menu. The restaurant also functions as a café and deli bar, while the lounge-cum-nightclub out back hosts regular events.

★ OKitchen

Itaewondong 168-14 (797-6420, www.okitchen.kr). Itaewon station (line 6), exit 1. **Open** noon-2pm, 6-9pm Mon-Thur, Sun; noon-2.30pm, 6-9.30pm Fri, Sat. **Average** ₩35,000. English menu. **Map** p251 G7 ⑥ **Fusion**

First things first: the food here is more than just 'OK'. Charming chef Susumu Yonaguni, who hails from the tiny Okinawan island from which his family took their name, has worked in the kitchens of top hotels in London and New York, using these experiences to enrich the menu in his new home city of Seoul. This menu is ever-changing, with many of the ingredients hauled from his remote farm in northern Gyeonggi province, and the remainder bought at Noryangjin fish market. Steaks and sushi are superb, and you'll find quirky dishes such as truffle-glazed polenta, Jeju horse carpaccio and ginseng sorbet. The lunch menu is an astonishing bargain at ₩21,000 for four courses and coffee or tea.

Passion 5

Hannamdong 729-24 (2071-9505). Hangangjin station (line 6), exit 3. **Open** 7.30am-10pm daily. **Average** ₩25,000. English menu. **Map** p251 H7 ⑥ **Brunch & baked goods**

This curious venue is an elaborate, two-layered affair. Downstairs you'll find a superb bakery with adjoining sections for home-made chocolate and ice-cream, and upstairs a brunch café par excellence. Baked goods from the former can be heated and brought to the latter, which, though a little too pretentious for some, serves excellent light meals and filter coffee – don't forget to ask staff for a free refill.

Poom

Huamdong 358-17 (777-9007, www.poomseoul.com). Noksapyeong station (line 6), exit 2. **Open** 11am-8pm Mon-Sat. **Average** ₩70,000. **Map** p247 F5 ⑥ **Neo-Korean**

Specialising in modern takes on familiar Korean dishes, this is one of Seoul's most esteemed restaurants. It uses only high-quality local ingredients and transforms them into delicious delicacies. Diners start their meal with simple daechu berries made into a crisp. Shitake mushroom stuffed with

OKitchen.

shrimp in chicken consommé is another wonderful dish and the sea bream is outstanding as well. Reservations are needed 24 hours in advance.

Suji's

Itaewondong 34-16 (797-3698, www.sujis.net). Noksapyeong station (line 6), exit 1. **Open** 11am-11pm Mon-Fri; 9am-11pm Sat; 9am-10pm Sun. **Average** ₩20,000. English menu. **Map** p251 G7 ⑥ **Diner**

A long-time brunch favourite, looking out over the busy Noksapyeong junction and the military base beyond, Suji's remains popular despite rather high prices. The Manhattan-style menu complements the Manhattan-style decor, and spans the gamut from succulent cheeseburgers to pastas and *huevos rancheros*. It's particularly famed for its pastrami sandwiches, which contain a whopping 200g of meat. Come on a Wednesday evening and an extra 100g is thrown on top for free.

★ T.G.

Itaewondong 305-5 (749-8005). Noksapyeong station (line 6), exit 2. **Open** 11am-10pm Mon-Sat. **Average** ₩14,000. English menu. **Map** p251 G7 ⑦ **Brunch**

This bright and friendly little venue serves excellent brunches. Omelettes, burgers and even chip butties are all available here, but the eggs benedict deserves a special mention: lovingly made, served with a whole squadron of delicious chips, and costing a mere ₩9,000. As could be said of many an item on the menu here, this is half the price charged by most Seoul brunch cafés. The only disappointment is the coffee.

★ Zelen

Itaewondong 116-14 (749-0600). Itaewon station (line 6), exit 1. **Open** noon-3pm, 6pm-midnight daily. **Average** ₩25,000. English menu. **Map** p251 G7 ⑧ **Bulgarian**

If you're unsure what to expect of Bulgarian cuisine, then take a look at a map of Eastern Europe: you'll see that – from a cuisine point of view – the country sits finely poised between the meat- and potato-heavy dishes of the Slavic lands, and the spices, yoghurts and barbecued meats of Turkey and Greece. Some particularly fine and highly diverse food, in other words. The band of Bulgarian brothers who run this restaurant have decorated it with a lot of charm, and their menu is a delight for both vegetarians and meat-eaters.

Korean Menu Reader

RICE DISHES

비빔밥
bibimbap
Vegetables, egg and spice on rice

돌솥비빔밥
dolsot bibimbap
Bibimbap in a hot stone bowl

볶음밥
bokkeumbap
Fried rice

카레/오징어/새우/불고기...
kare/ojingeo/sae-u/bulgogi...
curry/spicy squid/shrimp/
marinated beef...

김치/참치/소고기/샐러드
gimchi/chamchi/sogogi/saelleodeu...
kimchi/tuna/ground beef/salad...

...덮밥
...deopbap
...on rice

...김밥
...gimbap...
...filled rice roll

NOODLE DISHES

라면
ramyeon
Spicy noodle soup

(비빔/물) 냉면
(bibim/mul) naengmyeon
Cold buckwheat noodles
(in a spicy sauce/soup)

우동
udon
Japanese-style udon

MEAT DISHES

소/돼지/닭 갈비
so/dwaeji/dak galbi
Barbecued beef/pork/chicken

삼겹살
samgyeopsal
Barbecued pork belly slices

돈까스
donkkaseu
Breaded pork cutlet

STEWS, SOUPS AND BROTHS

매운탕
maeuntang
Spicy fish soup

계란찜
gyeranjjim
Egg broth

만두국
mandu guk
Dumpling soup

호박죽
hobak juk
Pumpkin porridge

뚝배기불고기
ddukbaegi bulgogi
Beef in a gravy-like broth

김치/된장/순두부 찌개
gimchi/doenjang/sundubu jjigae
Kimchi/soybean/tofu broth

삼계탕
samgyetang
Chicken and ginseng soup

라면
ramyeon
Spicy noodle soup

STREET EATS

튀김
twigim
Fried snacks

떡볶이
ddeokbokki
Rice cake in spicy sauce

고기/김치/군/물…
gogi/gimchi/gun/mul…
Meat/kimchi/fried/boiled…

…만두
…mandu
…Dumplings

호떡
hoddeok
Pancakes filled with cinnamon
and brown sugar

RESTAURANT TYPES

고깃집
gogit-jip
Barbecued meat

시골집
shigol-jip
Country-style restaurant

시장
shijang
Market

횟집
hoet-jip
Seafood restaurant

중국집
jungguk-jip
Chinese restaurant

이탈리안 레스토랑
itallian reseutorang
Italian restaurant

이자카야
ijakaya
Japanese bar-restaurant

패밀리 레스토랑
paemilli reseutorang
Western-style restaurant

TYPES OF ALCOHOL

백세주
baekseju

복분자주
bokbunjaju

동동주
dongdongju

매화수
maehwasu

맥주
maekju
beer

생맥주
saeng maekju
draught beer

막걸리
makgeolli

소주
soju

Cafés & Tearooms

A thousand places to sate your caffeine cravings.

At the turn of the millennium, it was almost impossible to find a decent cup of coffee in Seoul. How times have changed. Nowadays, to say that there's a great café around every corner would only be a slight exaggeration. Café numbers have reached saturation point in neighbourhoods across the city, which has been great news for coffee addicts since such competition has bred a hugely diverse mix of establishments, many of them with Wi-Fi access. Then there are the big chains: Starbucks and Coffee Bean from the US; Pascucci from Italy, and local clones such as Ti-amo and Tom N Toms.

Coffee has almost entirely replaced tea as the city's favourite form of caffeine intake, but there are still a few charming tearooms around, particularly in the traditionally minded Insadong area. Here you can sup green tea from Jeju island or the southern Korean coast, or concoctions made from traditional ingredients such as ginseng, ginger, quince and medicinal herbs.

CAFÉS

The Royal Quarter

Amandier
Angukdong 175-3 (736-9651, www.amandier. co.kr). Anguk station (line 3), exit 1. **Open** 10am-10pm daily. **Map** p254 F2 ①
Chef Ruben Jan Adrian brings his pastry and chocolate expertise to Seoul in a glass-box café. His chocolates are creative and seductive, his macaroons are inspiring, and his cakes raise the bar for pâtisseries in Korea. A true maverick, he takes risks with flavour – whisky chocolate, avocado and banana macaroon, truffle macaroon and Szechuan truffle are all good examples. If sweets are not your thing, there's also strong coffee, sandwiches and freshly baked bread.

Books Cooks
Gahoedong 177-4 (743-4003). Anguk station (line 3), exit 2. **Open** 10am-10pm daily. **No credit cards. Map** p247 F1 ②
A roomy venue with constellations of bare lightbulbs hanging from its high ceiling, and walls lined with interesting books in both English and Korean – if you fancy draining a coffee while learning about red wine, knot-making or the cheese industry, this is the café for you. The other half of its

name comes from the open kitchen, where the cheery, all-female staff cook up fresh scones for ₩4,000. Coffees are a little pricey at ₩7,000 and up, but the elegant cups and saucers make up for this increase in price.

Club Espresso
Buamdong 257-1 (764-8719, www.clubespresso. co.kr). **Open** 9am-6pm daily.
Those who make their way up to the gorgeous Buamdong area could do worse than pop into this pine-lined venue for coffee. As well as the regular roster of lattes, espressos and the like, bags of beans are on sale in their dozens – everything from Aruba to Zanzibar, and all at reasonable prices.

Millimeter Milligram
Angukdong 153 (3210-1604, www.mmmg.net). Anguk station (line 3), exit 1. **Open** 10am-10pm Mon-Sat; 11am-9pm Sun. **No credit cards. Map** p255 F2 ③
Millimeter Milligram is a Korean company selling assorted cutesy trinkets such as decorative stationery, cups and handbags, all designed along youthful, humorous lines. These blend well with the tables and furniture of the Anguk branch, which also functions as a two-floor café – if you like the cup your coffee is served in, you'll find the very same for sale near the front door.

Teas of Korea

Finding your favourite cuppa.

Teas? Yes, you need the 's' because there are such a lot of them in Korea. Almost anything that you can add hot water to and then drink the resulting infusion is called *cha*, which means 'tea'. When you're eating, you'll usually be offered *bori-cha* (warm or cold barley tea) or *oksusu* (maize) tea to accompany your meal. For these drinks, a small quantity of roasted grain is boiled briefly to make a lightly toast-flavoured drink. You can also drink *saenggang* or *daechu* teas, made from ginger and jujube respectively, where the boiling of roots or fruit lasts much longer, yielding a much stronger brew. Sliced fruits such as quince (*mogwa*) or citrus (*yuja*) are preserved in a thick sugar syrup for several months until the full perfume has been extracted, then a small quantity of that is mixed with hot or cold water. There are also teas made using ingredients for herbal medicine, with such a strong medicinal taste that you need slices of candied ginger to help get them down. A summer favourite is cold *omija-cha*, made by letting a cupful of dried *omija* berries soak in a bottleful of cold water overnight. The name means 'five flavours' (sweet, sour, bitter, tart, salty) and it's very refreshing.

Next, we reach the drink that everyone in Japan, China, India and Britain knows as 'tea'. Visitors familiar with Japan or China are usually under the impression that Korea has no 'real' tea, as it is almost totally invisible. You really need to know where to go to be served good Korean tea, either green tea (*nok-cha*), or yellow tea (*hwang-cha*). There are a few 'traditional tearooms' (*see pp132-134*) where such teas are available, but the best thing is to go to

Beautiful Tea Museum. *See p132.*

a temple and be served tea while talking with a monk. Tea in Korea, which in past centuries was widely drunk, has survived almost entirely thanks to monks.

Visitors to Jeju island, or the Boseong area in the south-west, are often taken to visit large tea-fields belonging to one or two companies producing tea in industrial quantities, but the very best tea is made by hand in temples or in private homes around the great Jirisan massif that spans the southernmost region of South Korea.

The finest tea leaves come from bushes growing completely wild. You can only make tea with the new buds growing in April and May, and it's hard work. One kilogram of leaves takes hours to pick and yields only two hundred grams of tea when dried. The drying, too, takes quite some time. But the fragrance emerging as the drying reaches completion, and the intensity of the taste of a brew from newly dried leaves, drunk in the springtime beauty of nature, is one of the greatest joys Korea has to offer. It's worth the journey, as they say.

Writer Brother Anthony of Taizé has lived in Korea since 1980. An expert on tea, he is the author of The Korean Way of Tea *and* Korean Tea Classics *(both published by Seoul Selection). His web page is an excellent source of information:* http://hompi.sogang.ac.kr/anthony/

CONSUME

CONSUME

Remini's Cake House

Gyedong 120-1 (3675-0406, www.reminis cake.com). Anguk station (line 3), exit 3. **Open** 11am-10pm Mon-Sat. **Average** ₩7,000. **Map** p247 F1 ❹

Yun-sun Goo acquired a stellar reputation for her wedding and birthday cakes, and later converted her small bakery into a café. Baking lessons take place in the back room and cakes are still made there too, while in the front of house you can get a slice of delicious cake, a macaroon or a cookie to quell the call of your sweet tooth. The chocolate cake is exceptional here and so are the mini-cheesecakes. However, those able to wait 20 minutes will find the chocolate soufflé even better – straight out of the oven, the chocolate is a gorgeous flux of solid and liquid, sitting on a crisp tart crust of… chocolate. Delicious.

Sajingwan

Gahoedong 1-42 (743-2238). Anguk station (line 3), exit 2. **Open** 10am-midnight daily. **No credit cards. Map** p247 F1 ❺

A charming *hanok* café with an admirably global roster of beans. The tea selection is even greater, with black tea from Ceylon and north-eastern India, green tea from China and Korea, and a number of herbal and fruit concoctions. Caffeine trades places with alcohol as evening encroaches, and the place also functions as a gallery of sorts: the café plays host to rotating exhibitions of photography from around the world.

Sanmotunge

Buamdong 97-5 (391-4737). **Open** 11am-10pm daily. **No credit cards**.

INSIDE TRACK FIRST DENTIST

Visit Sajingwan café (*see left*) and you'll be next door to a piece of history: one door to the north, and actually connected to the café via an off-limits footpath, is Korea's first dental clinic. Amazingly, it's still in operation, the modern equipment quite at odds with its location in a wooden *hanok* house.

Despite the wonderful mountain views from its second-floor balcony, this quirky, out-of-the-way café was largely unknown until it was used as a set in the Korean drama *The Coffee Prince*. For better or worse, it now draws young, arty folk from across the capital and beyond: come on a sunny weekend and you'll be fighting for table space.

Insadong

74

Gyeongundong 34 (732-7488). Anguk station (line 3), exit 5. **Open** 9am-11pm Tue-Sun. **Map** p255 F2 ❻

An odd little place out of keeping with the vast majority of Seoul's cafés – it forgoes the regular American style and Roman characters, using *hangeul*, Korea's own script, for its typography. For such a trendy looking place, the customer base is surprisingly old, though this is quite in keeping with the surrounding area. The only downside: this cafe regularly whips up deliciously gloopy cakes, and places them right next to the till… quite unfair.

Doldamgil.

Hongdae

Bau House
*Seogyodong 405-13 (334-5152). Sangsu station
(line 6), exit 1.* **Open** 10am-6pm Mon-Sat.
No credit cards.
Korea's consumption of dog meat is one of the only
things that the country is known for in the West.
Though the practice does indeed go on today, it's
largely the preserve of older folk in the countryside.
The modern Seoulite is far more likely to own dogs
than eat the poor things, and this bizarre café
provides proof of sorts: over a dozen pooches yelp,
bark and bow-wow enthusiastic greetings to each
and every person that walks through the door.
Customers are, in fact, encouraged to bring their own
dogs along to join the fun.

Café aA
*aA Design Museum, Seogyodong 408-11
(3143-7312, www.aadesignmuseum.com).
Sangsu station (line 6), exit 1.* **Open** noon-
midnight daily.
For all of its artistic invention, Korea has given precious little to the world of furniture: very few university students major in the subject, and the only
real innovations here are the knockoff pieces filling
whole streets around Euljiro 4-ga subway station.
Hail, then, a café that takes its furniture seriously:
every chair is a thing of beauty, and floors above and
below are stocked with products from famed
Scandinavian designers.

Gangnam

Cafe Madang
*Hermès Building, Sinsadong 630-26 (542-6622,
www.hermes.com). Apgujeong station (line 3),
exit 2.* **Open** 11am-9pm Mon-Sat; noon-9pm Sun.
Map p252 M9 ⑦
The products of the Hermès stable may to be well
outside the price range of many visitors, but fear
not: the Seoul flagship also sports a secluded, near-
secretive underground café that gives you a taste
of the brand. All furniture and cutlery used here
are authentic Hermès pieces, making it possible to
buy a little luxury for the price of a latte.
▶ *For more on the Hermès Building, see p74..*

Kring
*Daechidong 968-3 (557-8898, www.kring.
co.kr). Samseong station (line 2), exit 3.*
Open 10am-7pm Mon-Sat; 10am-6pm Sun.
Map p253 P11 ⑧
One of the most distinctive cafés in Seoul – and
that's no great surprise, really, given its location in
one of the city's most adventurously designed
buildings. It shares much of its space with the
Kring complex's on-site gallery, meaning that
there's always something to contemplate over your
espresso; better still is the stand-alone, sky-blue

room on the eastern wall, whose circle-dotted
windows throw magical shapes across the table.

Lounge
*Park Hyatt, Daechi 3-dong 995-14 (2016-1234).
Samseong station (line 2), exit 1 or 2.* **Open**
Drinks 9am-midnight daily. *Full menu* 11am-
midnight daily. **Map** p253 P11 ⑨
Every five-star hotel lobby in Seoul sports a café
open to non-guests. The one in the Park Hyatt is particularly appealing, since its lobby is actually on the
top floor, rather than ground level, and as such provides wonderful views over southern Seoul. There
are few better places to watch the sun set on the
Korean capital, especially when draining one of the
delectable smoothies, designed by superstar sports
nutritionist Patricia Teixeira.
▶ *For our hotel review of the Park Hyatt,
see p102.*

Rosenkavalier
*Sinsadong 29 (512-1466). Apgujeong station
(line 3), exit 2.* **Open** 10am-9pm Mon-Sat.
Map p252 M8 ⑩
This small café has been designed with belle époque
Vienna in mind: think decorative cups and saucers,
elaborate table-lamps and deferring waiters in
starched shirts and dickie-bows. The classical music
wafting from Pung Wol Dang music store next door
enhances the air of sophistication, though it's easy
to blow this to smithereens by giving in to the tempting cake selection – pure decadence.

City Hall & Myeongdong

Doldamgil
*Jeongdong 5-1 (3789-3197). City Hall station
(lines 1 & 2), exit 1.* **Open** 9am-6pm Tue-Sun.
Map p254 E3 ⑪
A small cafe inside Deoksugung, a palace that was,
for a time, home to Korea's first coffee addict, King
Gojong, who fell in love with the beverage in the
1890s, and even constructed a special pavilion in
which to imbibe it. You'll be able to follow in his
regal steps here, and perhaps even treat yourself to
some home-made rice cake.

Itaewon

Indigo
*Daechidong 968-3 (557-8898, www.kring.co.kr).
Noksapyeong station (line 6), exit 2.* **Open**
9am-11.30pm Tue-Sat; 9am-11pm Sun.
Map p251 F7 ⑫
One of the longest-serving cafés in the foreigner-
filled Haebangchon neighbourhood. Much larger
than most neighbouring establishments, it's a comfortable place to relax and read emails or a book for
a few hours; the delectable cakes and panini on offer
also encourage a longer stay. All-day breakfasts go
for around ₩9,000.

CONSUME

CONSUME

INSIDE TRACK BRIDGE CAFÉS

In 2009 and 2010, Seoul livened up its riverbanks with a whole slew of stylish bridge cafés. From west to east, these are located on the Yanghwa and Hangang bridges near Yeouido, the Dongjak and Hannam bridges south of Itaewon, and the Gwangjin and Jamsil bridges near Olympic Park. All are accessible from the riverbanks or by taxi, and open from 11am to 2am, the twinkly views in the latter hours being particularly pretty over a beer or cocktail.

TEAROOMS

The Royal Quarter

Chahyanggi Deudneun Jip

Hwadong 106-2 (720-9691). Anguk station (line 3), exit 1. **Open** 11am-10pm daily. **Map** p247 F1 ⑬
This cleverly converted building manages to mimic a traditional home, despite being a modern structure. While many teahouses offer Korean green teas, this place offers a wider variety of different grades and styles of tea than most, giving visitors a unique chance to sample teas that are rarely available overseas. Koreans consume virtually all the domestically produced tea, making it hard to find elsewhere.

Cha Masineun Tteul

Samcheongdong 35-169 (722-7006). Anguk station (line 3), exit 1. **Open** 11am-10.30pm daily. **Map** p247 F1 ⑭
This elegant teahouse in a 100-year old traditional-style Korean home offers excellent teas, including some harder-to-find brews such as buckwheat tea. Situated in the relaxed and romantic Bukchon neighbourhood, it offers a quiet retreat from the buzz of downtown Seoul, and gorgeous views of either the courtyard or the surrounding area.

Egg

Sogyeokdong 154 (722-8929). Anguk station (line 3), exit 1. **Open** 11am-11pm daily. **Map** p254 F2 ⑮
While not the most traditional of teahouses, Egg's charming colonial building contains a quaint interior. Those needing more substantial snacks and food can sample from the brunch, coffee and wine menus, but those in the know go for the home-made traditional teas, including quince and honey tea, citrus and honey tea, and the tangy-sweet *omija* ('five taste') tea.

Gahwadang

Samcheongdong 35-103 (738-2460). Anguk station (line 3), exit 1. **Open** 11am-10pm daily. **Map** p247 F1 ⑯

Located in the steep hills of Samcheongdong, this small, 50-year-old teahouse is an uncluttered, zen-like space in which to enjoy Korea's traditional drinks, including several kinds of green tea. Be sure to try the rice cakes too.

LN

Hwadong 27-1 (722-7597). Anguk station (line 3), exit 1. **Open** 10am-10pm daily. **Map** p247 F1 ⑰
It may look like an old-fashioned *hanok*, but LN is actually almost brand new, offering all the creature comforts of a modern building with the charm of old Korea. It also serves a wide variety of traditional teas, along with coffee and light snacks.

Margot Café

Wonseodong 129-5 (747-3152). Anguk station (line 3), exit 3. **Open** 11am-10pm Tue-Sun. **Map** p247 G1 ⑱
Located next to a Buddhist temple and across from Changdeokgung Palace, this is a modernised Korean house whose high ceilings and quiet location make it a perfect place to relax. The Korean-style teas such as *omija, yuja*, and lotus root are made from organic ingredients. In summer, staff make a home-made raspberry shaved ice dessert that is mindblowing.

Insadong

Beautiful Tea Museum

Insadong 193-1 (735-6678). Anguk station (line 3), exit 6. **Open** 10.30am-10pm daily. **Map** p255 F2 ⑲
Something of a cross between a store, museum and tearoom, the Beautiful Tea Museum offers a wide variety of traditional Korean and Chinese teas in a modernised *hanok*. The lobby functions as an educational space and store, both providing information on the teas on sale and displaying the tea and tea pots, tea sets and myriad equipment used in the preparation of tea. The courtyard is an exceptionally pleasant place to relax with a cup of tea in warm weather. *Photo p129.*

Jeontong Chatjip Insadong

Gwanhundong 196-5 (723-4909). Anguk station (line 3), exit 6. **Open** 10am-10pm daily. **Map** p255 F2 ⑳
Although it presents an unassuming face to the main street of Insadong, inside, this tearoom is one of the largest in the area, complete with several cosy rooms in the front and a large old *hanok* and courtyard in the back. Try the vibrant sweet-sour *omija* tea, a sweet quince tea, or the soothing mugwort tea as you relax in a traditional setting, and get an order of grilled rice cakes if you need a snack.

Jeontong Dawon

Gwanhundong 30-1 (730-6305). Anguk station (line 3), exit 5. **Open** 10.30am-10.30pm daily. **Map** p255 F2 ㉑

Profile Lee Gyeong-hun

Korean desserts reinvented.

West Meets East. *See p134.*

In 2009, Lee Gyeong-hun opened up dessert café West Meets East, just off Garosugil. He told *Time Out Seoul* about his past influences, his path to current success and his ambitious plans for the future.

'After finishing university, I travelled extensively in Asia, spending many months on the Indian subcontinent,' he explained. 'Trying India's wonderful food made me wonder why the cuisine of my homeland remained so unknown abroad. Although many come to love it, Korean food is simply a little too Korean for many western tastes – lots of aspects are unfamiliar abroad, so these have to be softened a little, just as Indian and Chinese cuisine was when taken to the West.

'I decided to focus on Korean desserts. Korea produces some wonderful, high-quality ingredients, so I tried to fuse these with international styles. Our puddings are all made with local flavours such as green tea, ginseng and black sesame, while we also serve fondue using red bean paste instead of cheese or chocolate – this is eaten with balls of rice cake, dipped in honey or ground walnut. In the evening we also serve *makgeolli*,

a rice wine that Korea is really trying to take abroad.'

The business was not an instant success with Koreans, something Gyeong-hun attributes to a lack of appreciation for local tastes: 'At first, it was very difficult to tempt locals into the café. Koreans have something of an inferiority complex: Garosugil is one of the trendiest roads in the land, but almost every café or restaurant on it is international in nature. We think of desserts and street food as being low-quality: our *hoddeok* pancakes, for example, are usually sold for ₩500 a piece from vans parked on the road. Of course, the hard part was defeating this preconception, and convincing locals to pay ₩8,000 for a high-quality version.' However, the power of modern media was to help turn the business's fortunes around. 'The local media became interested and we were featured on television: suddenly we're full every afternoon.'

With success at home under his belt, Gyeong-hun wants to take his winning formula abroad. 'My long-term aim has been to take these Korean desserts overseas. We've been very popular with Japanese visitors since we opened, so we plan to open up in Tokyo first. Hopefully, you'll see something similar closer to you in the near future.'

CONSUME

TRY THE DESSERTS
For West Meets East, *see p134.*

Visitors to the 'Traditional Teahouse' can try a variety of different teas – including roasted grain powder tea, ginger tea and medicinal teas – in an expansive *hanok* with a beautiful and large outdoor area. Whether you choose to sit inside and enjoy the heated floors on a cold day or go outside and enjoy the sunshine, this is one of the more beautiful places in the city to enjoy a cup of tea.

Min's Club
Gyeongundong 66 (733-2966). Anguk station (line 3), exit 5. **Open** 11am-2.30pm, 6-11pm daily. **Map** p255 F2 ㉒
Housed in one of Korea's most unusual *hanoks*, this half-traditional, half-westernised building dates back to the early 20th century and is an important architectural landmark. Visitors can enjoy a wide variety of traditional teas in the eclectically furnished rooms, or enjoy the courtyard and gardens.

Yetchatjip
2F Gwanhundong 2-2 (722-5019). Anguk station (line 3), exit 6. **Open** 10am-10pm daily. **Map** p255 F2 ㉓
A charming, secluded, second-floor tearoom with a small population of resident birds flying around, including several finches and a couple of curious canaries. A full range of Korean teas is available, and come with delicious traditional sweets. Note that, if you so desire, these can be used to lure the birds to your table.

City Hall & Myeongdong

O'sulloc
Myeongdong 2-ga 33-1 (774-5460, www.sulloc. co.kr). Myeongdong station (line 4), exit 6. **Open** 9am-10pm Mon-Fri; 9am-11pm Sat, Sun. **Map** p255 F4 ㉔
There are several O'sulloc branches located throughout Seoul, but the Myeongdong branch offers both a convenient location and some slight variations on its menu that make it the best one to visit. Most of the teas come from Jeju island's Halla Mountain, and this large, modern teahouse offers black, green and flavoured teas from its own company tea fields. Be sure to check out the desserts, especially the *nokcha patbingsu* – an expensive but wickedly delicious mix of green tea ice-cream and ice shavings.
Other locations throughout the city.

Dongdaemun

Suyeon Sanbang
Seongbukdong 248 (764-1736). Hansung Univ (line 4), exit 6. **Open** 11.30am-10.30pm daily.
One of the most expensive tearooms in Seoul – standard brews go for ₩8,000 and up – but also one of the most attractive. Built in the 1930s, it was once the home of writer Lee Tae-jun, whose grandchildren

converted it into a teahouse. The interiors of the two main wooden buildings have been charmingly decorated, though perhaps the best view is in the tree-shaded garden, looking up at the overhanging wing. A blissful place, though a tiny bit out of the way.

TRADITIONAL DESSERT CAFÉS
O'sulloc (*see left*) is also popular for desserts.

Bukchan & Samcheong

Second Best Place in Seoul
Samcheongdong 28-21 (734-5302). Anguk station (line 3), exit 1. **Open** noon-9pm daily. **No credit cards**. **Map** p247 F1 ㉕
The pace of change on Samcheongdonggil has been quite incredible: almost every establishment has changed hands since the road's rapid transition from 'secret' to 'trendy' in 2004-05. This unassuming place dates back to 1974, making it almost neanderthal in local terms. The first customer to walk through the door ordered a bowl of *patjuk*, and so have most arrivals since: this is a sweet porridge made from red-bean paste and cinnamon, though you'll also encounter such delicious delicacies as jujube slices, rice-cake balls and chunks of chestnut on your way to the bottom of the bowl.

Insadong

Bizeun
Insadong 37 (2128-9726, www.bizeun.co.kr). Jongno 3-ga station (lines 1, 3 & 5), exit 5. **Open** 9am-10pm daily. **Map** p255 F2 ㉖
Delve a little further into this famed Insadonggil rice-cake shop, and you'll find that it's also an excellent dessert café, serving almost nothing but Korean creations in pleasant, chocolate-coloured surroundings. Particularly notable is the *patjuk*, a warm porridge made with red-bean paste and rice-cake balls; it goes well with a ginger latte, and a few glutinous rice products from the shop section.

Gangnam

West Meets East
Sinsadong 518-8 (3445-0919). Sinsa station (line 3), exit 8. **Open** 11am-11pm Mon-Sat; 2-10pm Sun. **No credit cards**. **Map** p252 L9 ㉗
One has to credit this gorgeous little café for its skilful blending of Korean and international ingredients and dishes. Pride of place goes to the *hoddeok*, a pancake made with little bar rice paste, cinnamon, ground walnut and brown suger. It's a wintertime staple all across the land, literally made in the back of a van; here it's created with a little more attention, and served with Häagen-Dazs ice-cream, berries and grilled slices of apple. Heavenly. *Photo p133.*
▶ *For our profile of owner Lee Gyeong-hun, see p133.*

CONSUME

Bars

The best Korean booze, and the best places to drink it.

Seoul's bar scene is always entertaining. With a heady mix of local and international influences, things go in and out of fashion at lightning speed – not just individual bars, but styles, concepts and even entire chunks of the city. **Hongdae** and **Itaewon** are the two mainstays, though: the former is, by and large, a student area, but its appeal extends to artists, expats and trend-setters. Its rival, Itaewon, was once a local byword for sleaze, but the area has been thoroughly spruced up and now features a number of quality establishments. The **Insadong** area is not known for its nightlife, and becomes something of a ghost town at night, but it does boast a few interesting traditional drinking spots. South of the river everything gets much more expensive, though, as often as not, establishments come across as pretentious rather than exclusive.

CONSUME

SEOUL VARIETY

Seoul's range of bar options was not always this wide. As recently as the 1990s, true drinking holes were hard to find, the closest approximation being diner-style restaurant-bars known as *hofs*. These are still absolutely everywhere, though the fact that customers are kept in discrete groups and expected to buy food means that they're not always what visitors are looking for. Nowadays, however, there are other interesting options, including converted *hanok* houses, underground hookah lairs, and a growing range of *makgeolli* bars. For more on Korean drinks, *see p137* **Korean Alcohol**.

BUKCHON & SAMCHEONDONG

Dugahun

Sagandong 109 (3210-2100, www.dugahun.com). Anguk station (line 3), exit 1. **Open** noon-4pm, 6pm-midnight Mon-Sat; noon-4pm Sun. **Map** p254 F2 ❶

A curious venue combining eastern and western sensibilities. It's housed next to a small temple in a wooden *hanok* building, and some seats afford views of Gyeongbokgung Palace. Given such environs, a good wine list may seem too much to ask, but the range is prodigious – some bottles go for thousands of dollars here, but there are far more reasonably priced bottles too. The pinot noir and Bourgogne selections are particularly impressive,

and go down very well indeed with something from the similarly elegant Mediterranean menu.

La Cle

Samcheongdong 95-1 (734-7752). Anguk station (line 3), exit 1. **Open** 6pm-1am daily. **Map** p247 F1 ❷

There's a bit of history to this cellar bar, which functioned as a photography studio during the 1970s and '80s. During these years of dictatorship it also served as a hangout of sorts for various opponents of the regime. Although military rule has long ceased, much of the old furniture in this cosy venue remains, augmented by beer and some decent wine selections.

INSADONG

Baekseju Maeul

Gwancheoldong 256 (720-0055). Jonggak station (line 1), exit 4. **Open** 5pm-1am daily. **Map** p254 F3 ❸

Meaning 'one-hundred year alcohol', *baekseju* is purportedly the healthiest of Korea's many local alcoholic drinks, a sweet, nutty, whisky-coloured infusion with

> ❶ Green numbers given in this chapter correspond to the location of each bar as marked on the street maps. *See pp246-255.*

a slight tang of ginseng. Available in every single convenience store across the land for less than ₩4,000 per bottle, it's made by Guksundang, the country's prime liquor producer, which has also created a small chain of attractive bar-restaurants selling lip-smackingly good draught versions of the stuff, served by the jug.

Other locations Changjeondong 41-14 (323-3103); B1 Seochodong 1317-11 (595-1003).

Meokgeori Chon

Insadong (no number). Anguk station (line 3), exit 6. **Open** varies. **No credit cards.** **Map** p254 F3 ❹

Though their numbers are declining across the city, tent-like snack shacks known as *pojangmacha* still rank among Seoul's most atmospheric places to drink. A whole clutch off Jongno were forced to close by the local authorities, but instead of moving away entirely they all reopened together under one roof – not in tents, this time, but still pretty ramshackle. After a slow start, the place has found favour as an after-work watering-cum-feeding hole for local businesspeople. Nothing's in English, but find somewhere serving savoury pancakes known as *jeon* and you're on to a winner; these go well with *makgeolli* rice wine.

Paldo Ssojeul

Gwancheoldong 12-24 (722-0101). Jonggak station (line 1), exit 4. **Open** 5pm-6am daily. **No credit cards.** **Map** p255 F3 ❺

Though little different in appearance to a regular *hof*, this bar-restaurant has a neat little quirk that sets it apart from the crowd. It specialises in *soju*, Korea's national drink, but eschews the most common labels in favour of regional brews from around the country. Best, perhaps, is Ipseju, which comes from the south-western province of Jeonbuk and contains a smidgeon of maple syrup – a bargain at just ₩4,000 per bottle. This being a *hof*, you'll have to buy food too – try the *golbaengi*, a highly spicy plateful of noodles, greens and boiled river snails.

THE BEST BARS

For views
Pierre's Bar. *See right.*

For beers
Craftworks Taphouse & Bistro. *See p141.*

For local flavour
Pub of the Blue Star. *See right.*

For wine
Naos Nova. *See right.*

For music
Flower. *See p138.*

★ Pub of the Blue Star

Gwanhundong 118-15 (734-3095). Anguk station (line 3), exit 6. **Open** 4pm-midnight daily. **Map** p255 F2 ❻

A charming little *hanok* bar serving several near-unique versions of *makgeolli*: pine needle, mugwort, green tea and more, with all additions 100% natural. The owners, who hail from the Taebaek mountain range near Korea's east coast, ensure that the food served is similar in feel, with the likes of mung-bean pancake, spicy bellflower root and delectable *kimchi*-and-tofu on the menu; since this is written on the wall, in Korean, with calligraphic pens, you may wish to take a local along to decipher them.

Top Cloud

33F Jongno Tower, Jongno 2-ga 1-1 (2230-3000), www.topcloud.co.kr). Jonggak station (line 1), exit 3. **Open** noon-midnight daily. **Map** p254 F3 ❼

Hoisted high above the Insadong streets on a lattice of metal, this restaurant-with-a-view is also a superb place for a sophisticated drink. It may be a little pricey – cocktails here start at just under ₩20,000, while wine prices sail into the stratosphere – but there are few more romantic places to drink in all Seoul.

CITY HALL & MYEONGDONG

★ Naos Nova

Huamdong 448-120 (754-2202, www.naosnova.com). Seoul station (lines 1 & 4), exit 10. **Open** 5pm-1am daily. **Map** p247 E5 ❽

An impeccably designed bar that pays a rare level of attention to its drinks: the presence of an award-winning sommelier means that most customers go for the wine, though the bar's selections of malt whisky and Japanese saké are also first class. Its location on the Namsan slopes, combined with the presence of floor-to-ceiling windows, makes sundown the prime time to visit – the views over Seoul are quite wonderful.

Pierre's Bar

35F Lotte Hotel, Sogongdong 1 (317-7183, www.pierregagnaire.co.kr). Euljiro 1-ga station (line 2), exit 8. **Open** 6pm-2am daily **Map** p254 F3 ❾

Attached to the Pierre Gagnaire restaurant (*see p118*) at the top of the Lotte Hotel, Pierre's offers what might be the finest views of any bar in Seoul. Drinks are not too expensive, considering the Michelin stars that come with the name, and the decor manages to be both soothing and adventurous.

HONGDAE

★ Chin Chin

Seogyodong 343-9 (334-1476). Hongik Univ. station (line 2), exit 9. **Open** 11.30pm-1am daily.

Korean Alcohol

The key to your locally generated hangover.

Beer, spirits, cocktails and wine are available all over Seoul, but it's impossible to truly discover the essence of the city without sampling alcohol of a more traditional nature. Korea has dozens of varieties of alcoholic drinks, many of which are not available in any other country. In addition, they're highly affordable – a large bottle of *makgeolli* costs just over ₩1,000 in a convenience store, while even in a restaurant you're unlikely to pay more than ₩7,000 for a bottle of *baekseju*. Local beer itself is cheap, but pretty awful – most varieties use a preservative closely related to formaldehyde. Here are some more interesting choices:

Baekseju. Often labelled 'Korean wine', and though similar in terms of ABV (alcohol by volume), this drink has nothing to do with grapes. Instead, it's a fermented beverage made from rice, to which a herbal concoction is added – this includes ginseng, ginger, liquorice and cinnamon. The end result is a rum-coloured, pleasantly nutty drink, which goes well with pork and other grilled dishes.
Where to drink: Baekseju Maeul (*see p135*).
Bokbunjaju. A sweet wine made from fermented raspberries, which are primarily grown in the south of the country, and on

Bokbunjaju.

Jeju Island. It's apparently good for sexual stamina, though Koreans say this about a lot of things – if you're interested in testing such contentions to the full, try the drink with some grilled eel.
Where to buy: any convenience store (*see p153* **At Your Convenience**).
Makgeolli. This sweet, milk-coloured rice wine has undergone a surge in popularity since the turn of the millennium. For more, *see p38-40* **Makgeolli Magic**.
Where to drink: Chin Chin (*see left*) for purists, Pub of the Blue Star (*see left*) for the adventurous, and Poseokjeong (*see p138*) for those who want to drink till they drop.
Soju. The national drink, often referred to as 'Korean vodka'. Though only half as strong as its Russian brother at 20 per cent ABV, it's an easy way to get tipsy – you'll see shot after shot being thrown back at any meat restaurant. In theory, it's made from distilled grain or sweet potatoes, though these days most varieties are decidedly chemical in nature. On the whole, North Korean *soju* is far superior, the main exception being the varieties made in the South Korean city of Andong, which are much stronger and far purer than the norm.
Where to drink: Paldo Ssojeul (*see left*). You can also purchase decorative clay bottles of Andong soju at Kwang Ju Yo pottery store (*see p155*).

Baekseju.

CONSUME

INSIDE TRACK
HOW TO ORDER A DRINK

To get the attention of a waiter or waitress in Korean, yell '*cheogi-yo*!' This loosely translates as '*I'm over here*!', which may sound a little rude but is quite fine. Once they're at your table, add *-juseyo*, meaning 'please give me', to the name of the drink you're after. Since Korean numbers vary depending upon whether you'd like a glass, a bottle or a bowl of something, you may have to resort to a bit of finger-mime to communicate the required amount.

One of Seoul's first upscale *makgeolli* bars, and still one of the best, doling out milky concoctions from around the country – the Horangi ('Tiger') brand is particularly delicious, though quite expensive at ₩25,000 per bottle. Elegant vases of more regular *makgeolli* cost around ₩10,000, but whatever you choose, also be sure to grab some of the excellent food: sashimi stands out from a selection of fusion neo-Korean dishes.

Dduktak
Seogyodong 330-17 (336-6883). Hongik Univ. station (line 2), exit 9. Open 5pm-5am daily. No credit cards.
Korea's first *makgeolli* franchise bar. Serious mak-afficionados may turn their noses up at it, but for the newbie it's an awful lot of fun and quite a voyage of discovery – strawberry, kiwi and banana are just three of the flavours on offer, while those with more refined *makgeolli* tastes can ask for the organic Chamsari blend. It's open until late, and those who last the full course will see many falling by the wayside as the clock ticks around to morning.

Flower
Seogyodong 325-1 (no phone). Sinchon station (line 2), exit 8. Open 6pm-midnight daily. No credit cards.
An underground lair that comes to life with music sets each Friday and Saturday night: the owner is a noted local reggae singer and most of the bands here can be safely pigeonholed either inside or close to that genre. While there's barely enough room to breathe during the performances, come during the week and it's extremely quiet – there isn't even a sign outside to let people know there's a bar here, making it a real rarity in neon Seoul.

Nabi
Seogyodong 409-19 (338-4879). Sangsu station (line 6), exit 1. Open 6pm-late daily. No credit cards.
Turkish-style hookah lounges became quite in vogue in the Seoul of 2005, and though the trend has

since subsided somewhat the best places are still kicking around. This one is dark and truly atmospheric, with quiet conversations taking place in the shadows around the petal-spotted central pool. Cocktails are, for most, the way to go, though there are also a few local spirits and beers available.

Oi
Seogyodong 364-26 (334-5484). Hongik Univ. station (line 2), exit 5. Open 6pm-last customers leave daily. No credit cards.
The curiously named Oi bar (pronounced 'oh-aye', rather than 'oy') exudes a sophisticated air rare in the student-packed Hongdae area. Most of the clientele are, indeed, local students – a location just a few paces from the Hongdae University main entrance takes care of that. However, mellow music and floor cushions encourage reserved behaviour, as does the whitewashed, sinuous interior, the cartoonish curves redolent of a Greek island village transported into the future.

Poseokjeong
Changcheondong 52-157 (332-5538). Sinchon station (line 2), exit 3. Open 5.30pm-1am daily, often later at weekends. No credit cards.
Map p246 A4 ⑩
Now, this is dangerous. This apparently unassuming underground lair specialises in *makgeolli* rice wine, and has two interesting tricks up its sleeve. First is the stream of *makgeolli* coursing around the glass-covered main table: the bar is named after a tiny stream in Gyeongju city, on which courtesans of the ancient Silla Dynasty played an elaborate drinking game involving instant lines of poetry and floating cups of wine. Second is the fact that, for three long hours, you're allowed to drink as much from this bar's own stream as you like – for the almost absurd price of ₩4,000. Again… dangerous.

Redemption Reggae Bar
Seogyodong 405-4 (322-5743). Sangsu station (line 6), exit 1. Open 8.30pm-5.30am Fri, Sat; times vary other days. No credit cards.
Known as the 'Re Bar' to regulars, this is one of the only dedicated reggae bars in the city. It hosts regular party nights, but even in between these the atmosphere can be electric, largely thanks to its eccentric customer base – come here to meet some of Seoul's most entertaining misfits.

Shain
Seogyodong 396-22 (338-8969). Hapjeong station (lines 2 & 6), exit 6. Open 6pm-2am Mon-Sat. No credit cards.
Almost no Hongdae bars play independent Korean music, yet this is a pleasing exception, owned as it is by the lead singer of Huckleberry Finn, one of the country's most prominent indie bands. Many of the customers actually belong to other ensembles, though the bar's miniscule size means that

live sets are a rarity here. Instead, it's a good place to down beer or *makgeolli* for as long as you can tolerate the tiny chairs.

▶ For more on Korean indie music, see *p181*.

★ Vinyl
Seogyodong 411-1 (322-4161). Sangsu station (line 6), exit 1. **Open** 6pm-3am daily. **No credit cards.**

Takeaway cocktails may sound like an odd idea, but it's one that's worked ever since this curious hole-in-the-wall bar decided it could increase its income drastically from what it could make from its few tables. It serves a full range of cocktails – they're almost uni-formly strong – in see-through vinyl pouches, enabling customers to amble down the road drinking pina coladas in the manner of an astronaut.

GANGNAM & APGUJEONG

Lound Lounge
Cheongdamdong 83-13 (517-7412, www.74 lound.com). Apgujeong station (line 3), exit 3. **Open** 7pm-4am daily. **Map** p253 N8 ⓫

Hunting down 'it' bars is a favourite pastime of those rich enough to party in the Apgujeong area, making it hard for any one establishment to maintain a con-sistently high level of popularity. Lound has made

Platoon. See p140.

CONSUME

Craftworks Taphouse & Bistro.

a bold attempt to corner the lucrative cocktail market, priding itself on martinis, mojitos and manhattans viewed as the best in the city by its cocktail cognoscenti. The ground floor is essentially a wine bar, albeit one serving good food, with the serious partying done on the second floor, where you can order drinks on distinctive iPod menus.

Off
Samseongdong 9-7 (516-6201). Gangnam District Office station (line 7), exit 1. **Open** *5pm-3am Mon-Sat.* **Map** *p253 N10* ⑫

INSIDE TRACK
CONVENIENCE STORES

Absurd as it may sound, Seoul's seemingly infinite number of convenience stores (*see p153*) actually make for some of the city's best places to drink. In warmer months, most store entrances are surrounded with plastic tables and chairs, filled with locals throwing back bottles or paper cups of cheap alcohol. It can actually be easier to make new friends this way than by heading to a bar or club.

One of the only dedicated whisky bars in Seoul, and as such one of the only places in which the selection dares to venture beyond Ballantine's. There's a pleasing variety to the malt selections, though it's offset by an uninteresting location and slightly drab interior.

Platoon
Nonhyeondong 97-22 (3447-1191, www.kunst halle.com). Apgujeong station (line 3), exit 3. **Open** *11am-1am Mon-Sat.* **Map** *p252 M9* ⑬
The intriguing Platoon arts complex has an appealing ground-floor bar, which attracts arty sorts from all over southern Seoul, particularly on exhibition opening nights. At other, less hectic, times, you'll be able to throw back your beer, wine or cocktails with dishes from the kitchen, which specialises in simple German fare. *Photo p139.*

Rainbow
B1 Seochodong 1308-11 (3481-1869). Gangnam station (line 2), exit 6. **Open** *varies.* **No credit cards**. **Map** *p252 L12* ⑭
A dimly lit underground hookah bar, which, by virtue of being both cheap and unpretentious, defeats the two regular demons that haunt the Gangnam area. A wide variety of tobacco flavours for the hookahs is available, and most customers

take their puffs in between sips of cocktails or draught beer. You'll have to take off your shoes on entry, and place them into a plastic bag – wearing shoes could make the bar's Thai art and fairy lights look a little inappropriate. There's some sort of music on offer most weekend evenings.

Timber House
Park Hyatt Daechi 3-dong 995-14 (2016-1234). **Open** 6pm-2am daily. **Map** p253 P10 ⑮
Timber House is the basement bar in the prestigious Park Hyatt Hotel. Much of its decoration is made from old *hanok* housing, giving the place a pleasant mix of retro and contemporary stylings. Drinks are on the pricey side, though that doesn't seem to concern most of the customers, who prefer to focus on malt and saké lists that rank among the best in Seoul. There's music from 8.30pm every day bar Sunday.
▶ *For a review of the Park Hyatt, see p102.*

ITAEWON

3 Alley Pub/Sam Ryan's
Itaewondong 116-15 (749-3336). Itaewon station (line 6), exit 1. **Open** noon-late daily **Map** p251 G7 ⑯
These two popular expat watering holes sit one above the other on the alley behind the Hamilton Hotel. 3 Alley is the more vociferous of the two, with regular cheap specials and decent food – the chicken wings are a bargain at ₩3,000 for ten. Upstairs is the marginally more refined Sam Ryan's bar, though this, too, can be a cauldron of activity on weekend evenings.

★ Berlin
Itaewondong 457-1 (749-0903). Noksapyeong station (line 6), exit 1. **Open** 11.30am-2am daily. **Map** p251 G7 ⑰
Berlin is really a restaurant, rather than a bar though given its position overlooking the busy Noksapyeong junction it's also a fantastic place to come to enjoy an evening cocktail: the reds and whites of a thousand car lights are finely balanced by gentle candles, making this a prime romantic date location. Weekend DJ sets can also see the place packed out.
▶ *For a review of the restaurant, see p123.*

Bungalow
Itaewondong 112 (793-2344). Itaewon station (line 6), exit 2. **Open** 5pm-3am Mon-Thur; 5pm-5am Fri, Sat; 5pm-2am Sun. **Map** p251 G7 ⑱
Sup cocktails while bathing your feet in an outdoor pool, drink beer on a swing in the sand room, or head to one of the balcony areas to catch the sun: there's rag-tag assortment of seating in this fascinating bar. The drinks themselves aren't always top-notch, but the eclectic environs make for a winning atmosphere, especially in summer months.

INSIDE TRACK
LIVE FOR A HUNDRED YEARS…
OR FIFTY

The nutty flavoured drink *baekseju is* available in almost all meat restaurants and convenience stores. Its name literally means 'hundred-year alcohol', a nod to claims that its healthy ingredients will prolong your lifespan. Some choose to mix the drink with *soju* – a cocktail jokingly referred to as *oshipseju*, or 'fifty-year alcohol'.

Craftworks Taphouse & Bistro
Itaewondong 651 (794-2537, www.craftworks taphouse.com). Noksapyeong station (line 6), exit 2. **Open** 11am-2am daily; can close later Sat, Sun. **Map** p251 G7 ⑲
A quirky little pub with a truly pleasing range of microbrewed beers and ales, the names of which largely revolve around Korean mountains. There's the Geumgang, a dark ale aptly named after the mysterious North Korean mountain; the simple Namsan pilsner; and Halla, a citrus-tasting, golden ale named after an offshore mountain famed for its oranges. They're good enough to make you forget the excellent pub food on offer.

Ggul
Hannamdong (no phone). Hangangjin station (line 6), exit 3. **Open** noon-11pm daily; later on event nights. **No credit cards**. **Map** p251 H7 ⑳
Something of an artists' hangout, this quirky bar is joined to an interesting gallery and plays host to occasional music events. Located in Hannamdong, one of Seoul's most up-and-coming areas, it's a good place to meet people if you're looking for a way into the Seoul art scene. The fact that people are usually sitting on plastic chairs around tables fashioned from traffic cones somehow makes everyone feel more approachable.

ELSEWHERE

Woo Bar
Gwangjangdong 21 (2022-0333). **Open** 10am-2am Mon-Thur, Sun; 10am-3am Fri, Sat.
Way to the east of central Seoul it may be, but the Woo Bar cannot be ignored – located in the lobby of the famed W Hotel (*see p106*), it's one of the most happening places in town (a fact reflected in the prices of the drinks). Weekends see Seoul's top DJs spinning vinyl from a *Space Odyssey*-style booth (*see p188*). The space-age effect continues in the bathrooms: true works of art.
▶ *The Woo Bar is a short taxi ride from Gwangnaru station (line 5); a taxi from central Seoul costs around ₩20,000.*

CONSUME

Shops & Services

There are retail options galore in this 24-hour capital of commerce.

Seoul almost audibly rings with consumerism, the cash registers barely taking a break as the hour hand spools around the clock: as is the case with Seoul's restaurants and bars, many shops and markets are open through the night, making for a thoroughly intoxicating atmosphere. There's quality as well as quantity on offer, most evident in the boutique clothing shops dotting the lanes of Apgujeong, or the affordable bespoke tailors in the Itaewon area. It's also possible to get some local flavour; silky trinkets, colourful rice cakes or a bottle of local liquor will all make charming mementoes of your visit.

General

DEPARTMENT STORES

Galleria
Apgujeongdong 494 (3449-4114, http://dept. galleria.co.kr). Apgujeong station (line 3), exit 1. **Open** *West wing* 10.30am-8.30pm daily. *East wing* 10.30am-8pm daily. **Map** p252 M8.
Facing off across a busy main road, the twin Galleria malls are unianimously regarded by Koreans as the most luxurious in the land. International mega-labels proliferate, though keep an eye out for the works of local designers Suecomma Bonnie (*see p152*), Solidhomme (*see p148*) and Minetani (*see p148*). The west wing – regarded as the more 'budget' of the two – is also viewed by many as the country's most striking piece of modern design, having been cloaked with perspex discs that lend it a snakeskin-like appearance by day, and create a pulsing, *Blade Runner*-style spectacle after sunset.
▶ *For more information on the design of Galleria's west wing, see p74.*

Hyundai
Apgujeongdong 429 (547-2233, www.ehyundai. com). Apgujeong station (line 3), entrance within station complex. **Open** 10.30am-8pm daily. **Map** p252 L8.
Hyundai department stores are sprinkled liberally around Seoul, but the company's Apgujeong outlet is by far the most interesting. While nowhere near as showy or architecturally adventurous as the Galleria stores down the road, this is actually a better place to go hunting for local labels. Particular recommendations include menswear label Solidhomme (*see p148*) and unisex brand Andy & Debb. **Other locations** throughout the city.

Lotte
Sogongdong 1 (771-2500, www.lotteshopping. com). Euljiro 1-ga station (line 2), exit 8. **Open** 10.30am-8pm daily. **Map** p247 F3.
Most of Seoul's many Lotte department stores look near identical, their multiple floors of (mostly female) clothing customarily topped with an expensive food court. The basement levels are good places to shop for western foodstuffs, none more so than the flagship City Hall store, part of a gigantic complex that also contains Lotte Young Plaza (a large mall specialising in cheaper, more youth-oriented labels), the Lotte Hotel (*see p93*), Amore Pacific Spa (*see p158*) and the luxurious, couples-only Charlotte cinema (*see p172*).
Other locations throughout the city.

Shinsegae
Chungmuro 1-ga 52-5 (727-1234, www.shinsegae.com). Hoehyeon station (line 4), exit 7. **Open** 10.30am-8pm daily. **Map** p247 F4.
Unlike Lotte or Hyundai, Korea's two largest department store chains, Shinsegae goes for quality rather than quantity, with each store a unique design rather than a cookie-cutter pressing. The flagship Myeongdong outlet is particularly beautiful, and also a little piece of history: this was Korea's first department store, opening in 1930 under the wing of Japanese giant Mitsukoshi. A large new wing has since been added, but the old store is a superb piece

CONSUME

Going Underground

Seoul's subterranean stalls.

During the 1960s and '70s, Seoul's lightning-fast development necessitated the creation of a large network of tunnels. These were used not only as a means of conveying pedestrians from A to B in the ever busier city centre, but as much-needed retail space in areas where rising rents were driving small shops out of business.

By and large, these are places in which time has stood still. Apart from the addition of a few mobile phone outlets, the small stalls lining the tunnels have remained largely consistent in nature, as have the shoppers themselves: most customers are elderly ladies and gents looking for clothing, jewellery, music or health foods, or dining at hole-in-the-wall snack bars. The clothing deserves a little more explanation, since Korea's older set favour rather bold styles. For the men, there is a vast range of trilbies and flat caps to choose from, as well as colourful cardigans and thousands of eccentric neckties; some are studded with fake gemstones, while others sport tassels or pictures of disembodied cat's heads. Ladies' clothing is no less peculiar, with blouses a particular highlight; these often feature floral motifs but are always extremely garish (some younger Koreans suggest their grandmothers use this as a ploy to detract attention from an ageing face).

Seoul's longest and most interesting tunnel runs for four kilometres from City Hall station to Dongdaemun Design Plaza; an offshoot at the western end heads through the disappointingly modern Lotte complex towards Shinsegae department store. Rising to ground level and 'regular' Seoul is possible at dozens of places along the way, but quite unnecessary; those walking the full length and popping into a few shops on the way will be treated to a full hour of retro Korea, and a free trip back in time.

CONSUME

of annexation-era colonial architecture: its windows glow a delicious lime colour at night, the Christmas decorations are usually among the best in the land, and the interior is home to a large number of interesting local labels, including jeweller Minetani (*see p152*) and women's luxury fashion brand Jardin de Chouette (*see p147*).

Other locations throughout the city.

MALLS

Coex

Coex complex, Samseongdong (www.coex.co.kr). Samseong station (line 2), entrance within station complex. **Open** 10.30am-10pm daily. **Map** p253 P10.

The underground Coex shopping mall has been kicking around since 1979, and to this day is still the default go-to location on rainy days in Seoul. At these times, and on average weekends, it can be uncomfortably overcrowded. The range of shops here is extensive and includes international labels such as Zara, Accessorize and Body Shop, as well as a slew of local favourites, such as Codes Combine (*see p148*). There's also a simple food court, a cinema, a kimchi museum (*see p75*), an aquarium (*see p167*) and a branch of bookshop Bandi & Luni's (*see p145*).

▶ *For the Coex Complex's two Intercontinental hotels, see p99. For the Oakwood Premier, see p102. For Will Spa, see p159.*

Times Square

Yeongdeungpodong 442 (www.timessquare.co.kr). Yeongdeungpo station (line 1), exit 3. **Open** 10.30am-10pm daily.

Times Square, opened in 2010, is Seoul's first real western-style mall. Much of the complex is taken up with a branch of Shinsegae department store (*see p142*). There are plenty of restaurants on the basement levels, while the upper floors contain major international labels such as Zara and the sports giants, and local designers such as Codes Combine (*see p148*). There's also a large branch of Kyobo bookstore (*see p145*). Although the mall is modern and undeniably pretty, the interior layout is poorly signed, as are the pedestrian routes from the surrounding subway stations.

▶ *For the '4D' CGV cinema, see p171. For the Marriott Courtyard hotel, see p104.*

MARKETS

Dongdaemun Market

Dongdaemun station (lines 1 & 4), exit 8. **Open** 24hrs daily. **Map** p247 H3.

To understand Dongdaemun is to understand Seoul, or even the greater concept of Korea. There's simply no better way in which to feel the pulse of the city than by taking a stroll around its largest market, a round-the-clock labyrinth of capitalism that spreads – part indoor, part outdoor – across

several city blocks. It's tempting to think that the entire Korean nation could be fed here, then given a set of new clothes; shopping for food and clothing are, indeed, the two most popular activities with international visitors, but this is the best place in Seoul to scratch beneath the surface.

▶ *For more on Dongdaemun market, see p67.*

Gwangjang Market

Jongno 5-ga station (line 1), exit 7. **Open** Parts open 24hrs daily, most closes before midnight. **Map** p247 H3.

Although essentially part of the mammoth Dongdaemun Market complex, this particular offshoot is the most popular section with visitors to Seoul. Here you'll find Dongdaemun's essentials in microcosm, including two overlapping (and hugely photogenic) lanes of street snacks. These stay open

until at least 11pm, but get here before 6pm and you'll be able to peruse the second-hand clothing section on the second floor.

Nagwon Market

Jongno 3-ga station (lines 1, 3 & 5), exit 5.
Open 8am-9pm daily. **Map** p247 G2.
In modernity-obsessed Seoul, it's a minor miracle that this crumbling complex still exists – the city government has been threatening to tear it down for years. The bulk of the tower is residential, but on the lower levels you'll find the great Seoul Art Cinema (*see p171*) and hundreds of small shops selling musical instruments. Heading further down, the dank basement is a sumptuously grimy, old-fashioned agglomeration of vegetable stalls and street-food shacks.

Namdaemun Market

Hoehyeon station (line 4), exit 5. **Open** Parts open 24hrs daily. **Map** p247 F4.
The second largest market in the land tends to play second fiddle to Dongdaemun, its bigger brother, and is largely overlooked by international travellers. However, those who make it to Namdaemun often find it the more approachable of the two; it's particularly good for spectacles (which can be made up for bargain prices in a matter of hours) and second-hand camera equipment. In addition, the open-air line of snack shacks leading away from exit 5 of Hoehyeon subway station is one of Seoul's most characterful places to eat.

Specialist

BOOKS & MAGAZINES

The shops listed below are the best places to buy English-language books, while the larger stores around Gwanghwamun and Jonggak stations have small sections for Japanese, Chinese and other languages. All have a healthy selection of both novels and non-fiction, as well as colourful guides to Korean history and traditions. They also sell books for language teaching (primarily English) and study (primarily Korean). If you can't get to one of these establishments, head for the nearest department store, which will have a few English-language books kicking around on the top floor.

Most major hotels carry English-language newspapers, usually one or all of the *Korea Times*, *Korea Herald* and *International Herald Tribune*.

Bandi & Luni's

B2 Jongno Tower, Jongno 2-ga 1-1 (2198-3000). Jonggak station (line 1), entrance within station complex. **Open** 10am-10pm daily. **Map** p247 F3.

INSIDE TRACK
SEOUL SUMMER SALE

Every summer, the city hosts the **Seoul Summer Sale**, during which substantial discounts are available in hundreds of shops, restaurants, hotels and more. Precise dates have changed over the years, as has the name of the event. For more information, or to download discount coupons, visit www.visitseoul.net.

A gigantic subterranean bookstore with a large and well-stocked foreign-language section. This is the best place in Seoul in which to find travel guides as well as Korean-language study books, though don't overlook the excellent business and art sections, or the area that's dedicated to Japanese manga.
Other locations Coex complex, Samseongdong (www.coex.co.kr)

Foreign Bookstore

Itaewondong 208 (793-8249). Noksapyeong station (line 6), exit 1. **Open** 10am-9pm daily.
No credit cards. **Map** p251 G7.
Far smaller and more homely than the other bookstores listed here, this atmospheric shop is entirely devoted to foreign-language books (and not just English-language), of which a fair proportion are second-hand cheapies. It's a particularly good bet for guidebooks.

Hank's Bookshop

B1 Sagandong 105-2 (734-9565, www.seoul selection.com). Anguk station (line 3), exit 1.
Open 9.30am-6.30pm Mon-Sat. **Map** p247 F2.
This small English-language bookshop is located across the road from the south-east corner of Gyeongbokgung. It specialises in books on Korean history and architecture, though the second-hand fiction section is worth trawling through – it usually contains a few gems. There's also a small café-cum-tearoom on site: perfect for those who need time to choose their purchases.

Kyobo Bookstore

B1 Kyobo Building, Jongno 1-ga 1 (1544-1900). Gwanghwamun station (line 5), exit 3 & 4.
Open 9.30am-10pm daily. **Map** p247 E3.
The flagship branch of Korea's largest bookshop chain was substantially renovated in 2010. It's crowded at all hours with shoppers and browsers. The foreign-language section is expansive, and a short zig-zag walk leads to a decent music section, a couple of stationery shops and a small food court.
Other locations Times Square, Yeongdeungpodong 442 (www.times square.co.kr).

What the Book?

2F Itaewondong 176-2 (797-2342, www.what thebook.com). Itaewon station (line 6), exit 1.
Open 10am-9pm daily. **Map** p251 G7.

A comfortable store concentrating solely on foreign-language books – its huge popularity with Itaewon's foreign contingent necessitated a move to a much larger location in 2010. As well as dedicated magazine, travel and children's sections, What the Book? also has a range of books in specialist subjects, as well as an admirable selection of second-hand fiction. It's the only major bookstore in Seoul with an English-language website.

Youngpoong Bookstore

B1 & B2 Seorindong 33 (399-5600). Jonggak station (line 1), entrance within station complex.
Open 9am-10pm daily. **Map** p247 F3.

This large bookstore is often overlooked in favour of Bandi & Luni's (*see p145*), just through Jonggak subway station to the north. The foreign-language section here may be smaller than its competitor, but is still well enough stocked to be worth a look.
Other locations Express Bus Terminal (lines 3, 7 & 9), Bangpodong 19-3 (595-4700).

CHILDREN

For children's clothes and toys, it's best to head to the larger **department stores** (*see p142*), which will have dedicated children's sections, dominated by foreign brands, on one of their upper levels. For something a little more local, try **Namdaemun Market** (*see p145*), which features a whole street's worth of kids' clothing. Not to be outdone, **Dongdaemun Market** (*see p144*) has a dedicated 'shoe alley' with plenty of tiny sizes on offer, as well as a good section for toys and stationery. Also worth mentioning are a couple of curiously named local chains, both under the same ownership and dealing in good, if rather expensive, clothes: **Baby Hunt** (infants) and **Hunt Kids** (children).

ELECTRONICS & PHOTOGRAPHY

The home of Samsung and LG, Korea is famed for its electronic goods. However, many visitors

---

INSIDE TRACK
CHILDREN'S SHOES

Korea has no set measurement for shoe sizes; centimetres are most common, but you'll see a mish-mash of international standards on display. If shopping for kids' shoes, having a drawn outline of the feet in question will help matters immensely.

---

find that goods are no cheaper here than in their home countries – surprisingly, this is even the case for goods made by Korean brands. In addition, travellers are unlikely to benefit from Korea's hi-tech mobile phones, since the majority of these cannot be used abroad. Customers are also usually required to sign two-year contracts when buying new models. However, you can rent a mobile phone as soon as you arrive in Korea: booths are dotted around Incheon International Airport. Rates start at around ₩3,000 per day, and there's no fee for incoming calls; outgoing calls typically cost less than ₩1,000 per minute. *See also p228.*

Yongsan Electronics Market (Yongsan train and subway, line 1; open 10am-7.30pm daily) is so large and fascinating that it has become a tourist attraction of sorts. Such is the selection of computer, audio and televisual equipment that you may well walk out with a new toy. Proprietors are used to foreign customers, and many speak English – handy when bargaining, which is worth doing as it will probably knock down prices a tad. This is also the best place to head for computer repairs. **Namdaemun Market** (*see p145*) has a wide selection of used camera equipment.

FASHION

Apgujeongno has its rows of mega-labels, and department stores throughout the city are full of clothing from local and international brands, but Seoul has an encouraging number of up-and-coming designers who are worth tracking down.

Boutiques & designer

Ann Demeulemeester

Sinsadong 650-14 (3442-2570, www.ann demeulemeester.be). Apgujeong station (line 3), exit 2. **Open** 11am-8pm daily.
Map p252 M9.

Take a stroll south of Dosan Park, and you can't miss this superbly designed store, whose exterior – sharply modern yet covered in greenery – brings to mind a space-age apartment swallowed up by the forest. This was the work of local design outfit Mass Studies (also responsible for the interior of nearby multishop Space Mue, *see p151*), who were chosen to create a suitable Korean home for Belgian womenswear designer Ann Demeulemeester, a member of the famed Antwerp Six group of designers. Demeulemeester's designs blend natural elements with fluid modern lines – just like the building. It's somewhat telling that since she opened in Seoul, the same themes have appeared on a number of local labels.

11am

Sinsadong 545-1 (795-5869, www.11am.co.kr).
Sinsa station (line 3), exit 8. **Open** 11am-1pm,
2-6pm Mon-Fri; 11am-1pm Sat. **No credit cards.**
Map p252 L9.
This small shop just off Garosugil sells charmingly
unfussy womenswear – it's quite a contrast with the
glitz lining the main road outside. In addition to
clothing, you'll find earrings, bangles, handbags and
home accessories. Everything is handmade by
11am's small design team.

Jardin de Chouette

Cheongdamdong 25-15 (3444-4007, www.jd
chouette.com). Apgujeong station (line 3), exit 2.
Open 10am-7pm Mon-Sat. **Map** p252 L9.
Exquisite womenswear from designer Kim Jaehyun,
whose talent has made her the envy of the whole
Seoul fashion community. Much of Kim's initial success came from an ingenious pairing of delicate
innerwear and chunky outerwear, and her designs
have also found favour in Japan and the USA. Her
clothing doesn't come cheap – up to ₩2,000,000 for
a jacket – but it's always possible to find something
affordable at her charming boutique. Jardin de
Chouette is also available at Boon the Shop
(*see p151*) and the flagship Shinsegae department
store (*see p142*).

Juun J

Sinsadong 546-4 (515-0351, www.juunj.com).
Sinsa station (line 3), exit 8. **Open** 10am-6pm
Mon-Sat. **Map** p252 L9.
After starting up his Lone Costume label in 1999,
it took a decade for local menswear designer Juun
J's popularity to transcend the Seoul scene. In 2008,
his edgy but elegant clothing caught on abroad,
and he is now a regular feature at Paris Fashion
Week. Indeed, he's now partially based in France,
but his winning mix of classic and street styles continues to prove extremely popular with the affluent
young men of his home city. This shop functions
mainly as a showroom.
▶ *Juun J clothing can also be found in the*
menswear annex branch of Boon the Shop
(see p151).

Lee Young Hee

Sinsadong 665-5 (544-0630, www.leeyoung
hee.co.kr). Sinsa station (line 3), exit 8. **Open**
10am-7pm Mon-Sat. **Map** p252 M8.
Korea's national dress, *hanbok*, has failed to ignite
the international imagination as much as traditional clothing from Japan, China, India or
Vietnam. However, a few Korean designers have
achieved success at home and abroad by stripping
the more vibrant hues from the *hanbok* spectrum,
and adding foreign fabrics and shapes to the mix.
Lee Young Hee is by far the most famous member
of this neo-*hanbok* group, with Hillary Clinton
a regular customer at her New York branch.

Alphabet as Design

Hangeul ties and handbags.

Koreans are extremely proud of *hangeul*,
the highly distinctive local alphabet.
Invented by King Sejong in the 1440s
(*see p54* **Hangeul: a Korean Script**, it
was largely repressed by the Chinese
character-savvy aristocratic elite until
the end of Japanese occupation in 1945.
Nowadays, the repression is more organic:
visitors to Seoul are often surprised that
hangeul is almost non-existent on local
clothing, with the vast majority of Koreans
favouring (occasionally questionable)
English logos or blurbs. Hurrah, then, for
Lee Geon Maan (*see p152*), a designer
whose stylish ties, handbags and purses
all feature abstract hangeul shapes. They
make wonderful souvenirs, and might
convince Koreans that their text can be
more stylish than boring roman letters.

CONSUME

CONSUME

THE BEST FASHION DESIGNERS

Women's clothing
Kim Jae Hyun at **Jardin de Chouette**.
See p147.

Men's clothing
Juun J at **Boon the Shop**. *See p151.*

Ties
Lee Geon Maan. *See p152.*

Shoes
Bonnie Lee at **Suecomma Bonnie**.
See p152.

Handbags
Myounghee Zo at **Stori**. *See p152.*

Off-the-peg designs are available at her Seoul showroom, while a full outfit can be made to measure in a week or so.

Lie Sang Bong

Yeoksamdong 696-26 (553-3380, www.liesangbong.com). Seolleung station (line 2), exit 7. **Open** 10am-8pm Mon-Sat. **Map** p253 N11.
Lie Sang Bong is one of Korea's best-known names in both local and international fashion circles, having found favour with celebrities such as singer Rihanna and skater Kim Yu-na, designed the paintwork of the Korean A1 Grand Prix cars, and affiliated himself with Samsung and other major companies. Lie is based in Paris, where the boldness and originality of his womenswear designs are well rewarded. However, his Korean showroom is aimed squarely at the fortysomething market – which is no bad thing, of course, but adventurous though the clothes may be, their limited age range is proof of a far more conservative domestic scene as far as fashion goes.

Nohke J

Sinsadong 567-26 (6674-4875, www.nohke.com). Apgujeong station (line 3), exit 4. **Open** 10am-6pm Mon-Sat. **Map** p252 L9.
See right **Profile**.

Pushbutton

Hannamdong 745-10 (797-1203, www.pushbutton.co.kr). Hangangjin station (line 6), exit 1. **Open** 10am-6pm Mon-Fri. **Map** p251 H7.
For once, the term 'design lab' seems totally appropriate. This secluded, highly artistic boutique-cum-showroom appears less a shop than a place of creation, best evidenced by the designers who scuttle around clad in lab coats. The clothing itself – all for women – is sold in two lines: Dress Monster is the more conservative label, and sold locally, while Pushbutton is racier and usually made for overseas consumption.

Selfesteem

Sinsadong 545-21 (544-0123, www.selfesteem.co.kr). Sinsa station (line 3), exit 8. **Open** 11am-8pm Mon-Fri. **Map** p252 L9.
Local womenswear designer Mimi Park spent five years studying fashion in London, a fact that becomes quite apparent when taking a look at her collection. Her silky clothing is far bolder and more adventurous than the Korean norm, and finely augmented by the international picks that take up around half the shop space.

Solidhomme

Sinsadong 648-1 (544-8897, www.wooyoungmi.com). Apgujeong station (line 3), exit 2. **Open** 10am-6pm Mon-Sat. **Map** p252 L9.
Rarely is the name of a label truly reflective of the clothes it produces, but Solidhomme says it all: Frenchified menswear, designed along bold, chunky lines. Better known outside Korea as Wooyoungmi, this Korean designer label is also popular in the UK and Japan. In Seoul, the flagship department stores of Galleria and Shinsegae (for both, *see p142*) are the best places to find Solidhomme clothing. The address above operates mainly as a showroom.

General

Codes Combine

Chungmuro 22-1 (776-6385, www.codescombine.co.kr). Myeongdong station (line 4), exit 6. **Open** 10am-10pm daily. **Map** p247 F4.
Affordable unisex label, with stores located all over Seoul. As the brand's name might suggest, its clothes show off intentional clashes of style, with sharp lines dashing all over the place. Asymmetric buttoning is the norm rather than the exception and, combined with zips and/or velcro, this often allows multiple styles to be wrung from a single outfit. There are branches in Coex and Times Square (for both, *see p144*).
Other locations throughout the city.

Uniqlo

Jongno 3-ga 20 (744-0571, www.uniqlo.com). Jongno 3-ga station (lines 1, 3 & 5), exit 2. **Open** 11.30am-9.30pm daily. **Map** p247 G3.
OK, it's a Japanese label, but walk around Seoul and you'll see that many of the city's younger inhabitants wear nothing else. Uniqlo's colourful, youthful designs have become hugely popular since the brand launched in Korea in 2005, and the number of outlets is always growing (there are 20 and counting, in Seoul alone).
Other locations throughout the city.

Profile The New Breed

Seoul's daring fashion designers.

Nohke J.

NOHKE J

Having followed the creed for centuries, Korea is often referred to as the most Confucian nation on earth. From time to time, its tenets took over from those of Buddhism, the state religion, while Confucian scholars – *yangban* – occasionally rose to loftier positions of power than the royal house of Joseon. This legacy remains manifest in many walks of life, even Korea's fashion scene.

Witness, for example, the workings of **Lie Sang Bong** (*see left*), one of the country's most prominent designers and a staple of major international fashion shows. Based in Paris, the designs of this 'Korean McQueen' are extremely popular in France, the US and other western nations – Lindsey Lohan, Beyonce, Rihanna and Lady Gaga are among his many admirers. What a disappointment to step into his Gangnam showroom and see that the Korean versions of his clothes are aimed not at local popstars, but at affluent, middle-aged women. Lie, as his marketing director put it, 'felt that the Korean market was simply not prepared for anything outrageous'. **Juun J** (*see p147*), the most important Korean menswear designer of modern times, is also based in Paris.

Such conservatism clearly cannot last forever. In turn-of-the-20th-century Seoul, it was rare to see skirts that finished above the knee except in red-light districts and the raciest clubs. A few years on, things were quite different, perhaps best exemplified by the typical schoolgirl ruse of taking an extra skirt to class, to change into as soon as the bell rang. Other people feel differently to Lie – perhaps the market is now ready, and just needs a firestarter to set things off...

On the other side of Dosan Park lies the tiny showroom of **Misun Jung**, and her label **Nohke J** (*see p148*). Misun grew up in Jinju, a small and very conservative city on Korea's southern coast. Immediately after graduating in womenswear at Yonsei, a prestigious Seoul university, she set to work on a series of bold designs, hoping they would find acceptance within the local market. As she puts it, 'Koreans are getting less and less conservative with their clothing, because these days they can see all the major international collections online – they wonder why things aren't the same in Seoul.' Her shop opened in 2009, with a silvery, space-age-like theme running through the initial lines. Just a few months later, her clothes had become so popular that plans for a parallel menswear line had to be shelved, perhaps indefinitely. Seoul's own superstars were soon in touch: BoA, one of Korea's most famous singers, put in a personal clothing request for one of her music videos, as did Teen Top, a major local boy band (at the time, anyway). Other similar requests have been turned down, while Lie Sang Bong and others are attending more and more local events. It seems that the Korean fashion scene is about to witness a profound change.

Tailored to Perfection

Korea's Savile Row.

Since the 1970s, male visitors to Seoul have been dragging custom-made suits and shirts home with them. At that time, Seoul was a very poor city by international standards, but, happily for foreign tourists, prices have remained relatively low – you'll be able to get a near-perfect suit or ten decent made-to-measure shirts for under $500. In addition, the quality is far higher than you'd find in Bangkok, Hanoi or other Asian cities famed for their tailoring.

The cosmopolitan district of Itaewon has long been the best place to go hunting for a new jacket; walking down the main road between Itaewon and Noksapyeong stations, foreign men are bound to be invited into at least two or three shops for a measuring. The best shops have customer bases that negate the need for such forms of marketing; the following establishments are particularly recommended.

In business since 1976, **Hamilton Shirts** (Hannamdong 736-9, 798-5693, www.hs76.com) is hugely popular with those looking for tailored shirts. Samples of cotton and silk are present in their hundreds, making the shop's western wall look like a rainbow. Prices start at an incredible ₩35,000 per shirt and, since your measurements will be kept on file, you'll be able to order more from abroad.

A little higher in quality than Hamilton, **Hahn's Custom Tailoring** (Itaewonno 134, 797-0830) also makes excellent shirts, though they actually specialise in suits, employing only the most experienced tailors for this purpose. The materials used are first-rate and the service superb.

Hahn's Custom Tailoring.

Multishops

Åland

Myeongdong 2-ga 53-6 (318-7640,
www.a-land.co.kr). Myeongdong station
(line 4), exit 6. **Open** 9am-11pm daily.
Map p247 F4.

This shop takes its name from the Swedish-speaking Finnish islands and is appropriately quirky, selling a mishmash of designer fashion and household goods, as well as vintage and second-hand clothing. After setting up in Myeongdong in 2006, this curious concept has been such a hit with young Seoulites (and many an expat) that other branches have opened. Local brands to keep an eye out for include sharp unisex designers [blank] and Kimseoryong. For the second-hand bargains (mainly for women, though men might get lucky), head to the top floor.

Other locations Seogyodong 338-36, Hongdae (070/7820-7541); Sinsadong 534-18, Garosugil (070/7820-7549).

Boon the Shop

Cheongdamdong 82-3 (542-8006,
www.boontheshop.com). Apgujeong
station (line 3), exit 2. **Open** 11am-8pm
daily. **Map** p253 N8.

The most prestigious shopping space in the Apgujeong district, Boon the Shop's range of local and foreign luxury labels is augmented by soft lighting, model-like sales staff, a large atrium that plays host to rotating art exhibitions – and prices that shrink the customer base to an affluent few. The main building (also home to a delightful café) has women's clothing only – the likes of Alexander McQueen, Christopher Kane, Stella McCartney and Yohji Yamamoto, as well as local talent Jardin de Chouette (*see p147*). Men have to head down the road to the less spectacular annex.

Other locations Shinsegae, Chungmuro 1-ga 52-5 (727-1234, www.shinsegae.com).

Daily Projects

Cheongdamdong 1-24 (3218-4075,
www.dailyprojects.kr). Apgujeong station
(line 3), exit 2. **Open** 11am-8.30pm daily.
Map p252 M9.

A stylish, one-off shop in which you could spend several hours: first, have a cappucino at the adjoining café, then take time to have a leaf through the miniature library of multinational style magazines, followed by – if you're lucky – a peek at one of the occasional art shows. Then, of course, there's the shopping. The clothing here is aimed at rich young local men; indeed, the store has been something of a winner with aspiring singers and actors. On sale is a mix of Korean and non-Korean menswear, with well-known international brands supplemented by local labels such as Johnny Hates Jazz and Suh Sangyoung.

Space Mue

Cheongdamdong 93-6 (3446-8074,
www.spacemue.com). Apgujeong station
(line 3), exit 2. **Open** 11am-8pm daily.
Map p253 N8.

This unisex multishop boasts quite possibly the most attractive shop interior in all of Korea. Local design team Mass Studies, also responsible for the Ann Demeulemeester building (*see p146*) just to the west, has decked it out like a futuristic beehive, with the hexagonal motifs on the walls, ceiling and floor offset nicely by chunky, polygonal display racks. The appealing design means you may just forget what you were here for in the first place: clothing from some of the world's most heralded designers, including Damir Doma, Martin Margiela and Balenciaga.

Second-hand & vintage

Gwangjang Market

Jongno 5-ga station (line 1), exit 8. **Open** 10am-6pm daily. **No credit cards**. **Map** p247 H3.

Many visitors to Seoul head to Gwangjang for lashings of earthy food and drink, but the market's second floor contains a little secret: reams of quality second-hand clothing, mainly sourced from Japan and the US. This part of the market can be a real chore to track down; the easiest entrance to find is at the market's north-westernmost extremity, just off Jongno.

Momoro Lounge by Romiwa

Seogyodong 339-4 (325-6248, www.romiwa.com).
Hongik Univ. station (line 2), exit 8. **Open** 11am-11pm daily.

This vintage clothing store launched in 2005 after the local owner returned from studying in Australia. You'll find dresses, tops, bottoms, jackets, purses, shoes, belts and jewellery, mostly from the 1970s and '80s. The shop was renovated in late 2010 and now sells books (including one written by the owner, entitled *Special Wardrobe*), CDs, notebooks and other knick-knacks. The interior is decorated with some adorable trinkets, such as vintage Barbies, antique hairdryers and a working phone made of Lego.

FASHION ACCESSORIES

Hats

Luielle

Hwadong 100 (720-6901, www.luielle.com).
Anguk station (line 3), exit 6. **Open** 11am-8pm daily. **Map** p247 F1.

Designer Shirley Chun was the first Asian graduate of the famed CMT millinery school in Paris. Though quality is increasingly falling victim to quantity, her sweet little Samcheongdong boutique remains the best place in the city for hats, berets and the like.

CONSUME

CONSUME

Jewellery

Curious Curious

Itaewondong 455-36 (795-5869, www.curious curious.co.kr). Noksapyeong station (line 6), exit 1. **Open** 1-9pm Tue-Sun. **Map** p251 G7.

A tiny jewellery boutique hovering above Noksapyeong station. It's truly curious that, as is the case with almost every single jeweller in the land, no use has been made of Korea's wonderful historic dynastic designs, which went on to inform the work of Japanese and Chinese artisans. Nevertheless, this is a charming little shop whose beautiful products are handmade on site, and prices are very reasonable.

Minetani

Cheongdamdong 82 (3443-4164). Apgujeong station (line 3), exit 2. **Open** by appointment 10am-6.30pm Mon-Sat. **Map** p253 N8.

An upper-end jewellery label supplying rings, necklaces, bangles and bracelets to Seoul's great and good. A maximum of five pieces are made from any single design, and these have been so successful that Minetani has been asked to make lines for Swarovski, as well as three of Seoul's most luxurious and prestigious stores: Boon the Shop (*see p151*) and the flagship branches of Shinsegae and Galleria (for both, *see p142*) malls. These are generally the best places to see and buy Minetani jewellery, since this small Apgujeong shop is open by invitation only.

Lingerie & underwear

For many years, differences in size and taste meant that Korean lingerie shops were off the radar of many international female travellers. Times are changing, however: plastic surgery and changes in diet have necessitated the introduction of larger bra cup sizes, and colourful designs have pushed the once-prevalent 'skin' colour – a kind of browny-beige – to the margins. International brands are available in department stores, but special mention must also be made of local label **Yes!**, a chain whose branches can be found in all major shopping areas.

Luggage

Gwanhundong 197-4 (733-8265, www.leegeonmaan.com). Anguk station (line 3), exit 6. **Open** 9.30am-8.30pm daily. **Map** p247 F2.

's two Insadonggil stores sell highly distinctive handbags, purses and ties, all featuring abstract characters from the Korean alphabet (for more, *see p147* **Alphabet as Design**) in their design. Lee's designs have proved wildly popular with both visitors and

locals, and he has now opened up an even larger store in Japan, in the Tokyo district of Shibuya.

Stori

Samcheongdong 95 (735-7101, www.storisac.com). Anguk station (line 3), exit 1. **Open** 11am-9pm daily. **Map** p247 F1.

Gorgeous handbags and purses designed by Myeonghee Zo, a Korean woman now resident in London. Her designs make use of traditional Korean fabrics and motifs: mother-of-pearl and tea-dyed hemp make regular appearances, as do patterns featurning tigers (Korea's national animal, though long extinct here). Stori bags are much more popular in the UK, where Zo's designs latched on to the slow-burning oriental fashion trend, than at home.

Shoes

Suecomma Bonnie

Cheongdamdong 96-1 (3443-0217, www. suecommabonnie.com). Apgujeong station (line 3), exit 2. **Open** 11am-9pm daily. **Map** p253 N8.

Women's shoe designer Bonnie Lee is one of the main cogs in the Seoul fashion scene. The fact that she knows everybody who's anybody enables her to keep abreast of local fashion changes, meaning that Bonnie's shoes slide perfectly into each and every seasonal collection. The designs are a little flamboyant for some, though others will find it near impossible to keep their credit cards in their purse. Since most shoes are in the ₩400,000 range, it may be a good idea to check out the season-old bargains at the back of the shops, or shoes bearing the label of budget line SC Bonnie.
► *There's a smaller Suecomma Bonnie boutique just off Samcheongdonggil Hwadong 72 (737-9637), a couple of doors away from the Stori handbag shop (see above).*

FOOD & DRINK

Bakeries

Passion 5

Hannamdong 729-24 (2071-9505). Hangangjin station (line 6), exit 3. **Open** 7.30am-10pm daily. **Map** p251 H7.

This Hannamdong landmark is as well known for its ground-floor bakery as it is for its second-floor brunch café (*see p124*). In fact, the building functions as the headquarters of Paris Baguette's umbrella company, but the goods on offer are a cut above what you'd find at branches of the (only slightly less expensive) chain: moist focaccia and seafood chowder are just a few picks from a truly mouthwatering selection. You should be able to fill up for under ₩10,000, though add another ₩7,000 for a coffee upstairs.

At Your Convenience

Convenience stores epitomise user-friendly Seoul.

Buy the Way.

CONSUME

It's 3am, and you're hungry. In many countries, this would be something of a problem, but not so in Seoul, where the nearest 24-hour convenience store is never – that's *never* – more than a short walk away. At the last count, there were almost 18,000 such establishments across the city, the vast majority belonging to a handful of major chains: **7-Eleven** from the US, **Family Mart** and **Ministop** from Japan, and local chains **Buy the Way** and **GS25**. The goods on offer are fairly similar across the board, but in 2009 Buy the Way gave the market a gentle stir by providing softer lighting in its outlets and serving freshly made coffee; GS25 has since countered with cookies and pastries baked on site.

Sandwiches, crisps and chocolates appease customers with the munchies, while those after more home-grown tastes can try a roll or triangle of *gimbap*: rice filled with kimchi, *bulgogi* beef, tuna mayo or many other ingredients, and wrapped in a layer of lavered seaweed. It's even possible to get something hot: you'll usually find a cylindrical tube of large steamed dumplings next to the counter, and every convenience store sells tubs of instant noodles. The latter can be prepared on the premises as most places have free hot water, and many have seating on which to eat your meal.

The tables and chairs, and the customers using them, migrate outside in warmer months, making convenience stores a great place to drink on the cheap. All sell alcohol around the clock, including beer (such as local brands Cass, OB and Hite) and affordable wines. Then there are the local hooches, such as *soju*, *makgeolli* and *baekseju*. Quite a range of choice, anywhere, and at any hour, day or night... convenient is not the word.

▶ *For more information on Korea's superb array of alcoholic drinks, see p137.*

INSIDE TRACK
BUYING KOREAN ALCOHOL

Seoul's seemingly infinite number of convenience stores all sell a good range of local alcoholic drinks, many of which will taste totally unfamiliar to foreign visitors. Do note, however, that *makgeolli* (rice wine) both spoils and leaks easily, and as such does not make a good souvenir. See *p137* **Korean Alcohol**.

Napoleon

Seongbukdong 35-5 (742-7421). Hansung Univ station (line 4), exit 5. **Open** 8am-10pm daily.
This large, two-floor bakery makes a great starting or finishing point to a tour of the Seongbukdong area. As with most Korean bakeries, the goods may be much sweeter than you'd like, but it's always worth ordering one of the delectable cheesecakes or home-made chocolates.

Retro Oven

Nonhyeondong 252-22 (544-9045) Gangnam District Office (line 7), exit 2. **Open** 11am-8pm Mon-Sat. **Map** p252 M10.
Retro Oven's owner, Pak Cheol-woo, is a born baker: humble, diligent and precise. Every loaf and roll that comes out of his oven feels special. The crusty country loaves and cloud-like ciabattas are highly recommended, as are the German-style soft pretzels, pretzel croissants and the flaky, buttery pains au chocolat.

Wing

Itaewon 2-dong 675 (794-0011). Noksapyeong station (line 6), exit 2. **Open** 9am-9.30pm daily. **Map** p251 G7.
The quality and freshness of the baked items on offer here are evident as soon as you open the door and are, inevitably, hit by an aromatic waft of air. As well as excellent bread, Wing serves cakes and decent coffee.

Wood & Brick

Jaedong 5-2 (747-1592). Anguk station (line 3), exit 1. **Open** 11am-10pm daily. **Map** p247 F1.
The original Wood & Brick was located near Gwanghwamun subway station, and had been dishing out fine baked goods for more than 40 years before the block was demolished in 2010. This wealth of experience has been extended in two new outlets, a stone's throw from each other north of Anguk station. The ciabatta and focaccia have no equal in Seoul, and there's great coffee and cakes too. The deli section sells feta cheese, smoked salmon and other such rarities.

Drinks

High Street Market

Hannamdong 737-24 (790-5450). Itaewon station (line 6), exit 2. **Open** 10am-8pm daily. **Map** p251 H7.
This excellent second-floor market boasts a decent deli counter and bakery, but is perhaps most notable for the wine selection at the back. Red tape and curious tax measures mean that Seoulites generally have to make do with the same old wines, again and again, but the American owners of this establishment manage to source boutique wines from across the globe, explained in full on an informative menu. They also host themed wine events.

Imported food

The basement floor of Lotte's gigantic department store on Sogongdong (*see p142*) has Seoul's best selection of imported food, though the place remains prohibitively busy for most of the day. Rather temptingly, staff dole out free samples of local food – it shouldn't take long to locate some rice cake or fried beef.

Rice cakes

Bizeun

Insadong 37 (2128-9726, www.bizeun.co.kr). Jongno 3-ga station (lines 1, 3 & 5), exit 5. **Open** 9am-10pm daily. **Map** p247 F2.
The sweet, colourful rice cakes sold at this charming Insadonggil outlet make the perfect souvenir: a medium-sized box costs only ₩10,000 or so. Visually striking and quintessentially Korean, the glutinous cakes come in all shapes and sizes, with flavours including green tea, black sesame, red bean and ginger. There are English-language signs dotted around to explain what's what – though even with a description, some flavours may be totally alien to international visitors.
▶ *For Bizeun's adjoining café, see p134.*

INSIDE TRACK
RICE CAKE SHOPS

The old-fashioned **Nagwon Arcade** (*see p159*) is surrounded by small shops selling glutinous rice cake, as well as other Korean sweeties, such as pumpkin taffy, sesame snaps and caramelised sunflower seeds. It would be unfair to single out any particular establishment, since prices and quality are all very similar across the board. Making a brief circuit of the area will probably win you a favourite, since all establishments have highly colourful outdoor displays.

GIFTS & SOUVENIRS
Art & trinkets

Myung Sin Dang
Gwanhundong 18 (736-2466). Anguk station (line 3), exit 6. **Open** *9am-9pm Mon; 9am-8pm Tue-Sun.* **Map** *p247 F2.*

Insadonggil has more art supplies shops than you can shake a paintbrush at, but this was the one that Queen Elizabeth II visited (or, more likely, was dragged to) during her visit to Seoul. The shelves groan under the weight of thousands of brushes, while it's also possible to get a traditional name stamp. Staff can transliterate foreign names into Korean text, and will prepare your name stamp in a matter of minutes.

Ssamziegil
Gwanhundong 38 (736-0088). Anguk station (line 3), exit 6. **Open** *10.30am-9pm Mon-Thur, Sun; 10.30am-10pm Fri, Sat.* **Map** *p247 F2.*

One of Seoul's more striking examples of modern architecture, the Ssamziegil complex is essentially a single, spiral avenue of trinket shops, which curls up for five floors around a central courtyard. All pieces sold here are the work of local designers, and a quick bout of window shopping will reveal everything from jade bangles to handmade paper lanterns. It's a truly mesmerising place, of which Seoul is justly proud. Many of the individual shops take credit cards.

Second Hotel
Hannamdong (no phone). Hangangjin station (line 6), exit 3. **Open** *10am-6pm daily.* **Map** *p247 H6.*

This gift shop sells quirky goods suitable for the home. It moved in 2011 from Apgujeong's Dosan Park area to the trendy Hannamdong area, but kept most of the designers – typically past or present students from the notably artistic Hongdae University. As such, a youthful spirit shines through each and every clock, tablemat and cutlery set on sale here.

Pottery & ceramics

Hankook Chinaware
Cheongdamdong 78-18 (540-6700, www.living hankook.com). Apgujeong station (line 3), exit 2. **Open** *9am-6pm Mon-Fri.* **Map** *p253 N8.*

Forget the ugly name – this shop contains Korean ceramic products of considerable beauty. Hankook is the country's largest producer of ceramics, and this beast of a company runs over a dozen separate lines; you'll find bargains by the door of the store and at the front, but if you're looking for something more refined you should hunt down the Prouna collection, a subtle fusion of European and oriental styles.

Kwang Ju Yo
Gahoedong 203 (741-4801, www.kwangjuyo.com). Anguk station (line 3), exit 2. **Open** *10am-6pm daily.* **Map** *p247 F1.*

Korea led the world in pottery terms for quite some time; the innovations of the Silla and Joseon dynasties saw local artisans reaching heights that remain unscalable even today. Pottery shops are ten-a-penny around the Insadong area, but Kwang Ju Yo is the most prestigious by far, housing its celadon and porcelain creations between beehive-like niches of wood. Its pots, bowls and vases are all made just outside Seoul in Gwangju, a small satellite city that has been a fulcrum of the Korean pottery scene for centuries.

Yido Pottery
Gahoedong 10-6 (744-0704, www.yido.kr). Anguk station (line 3), exit 2. **Open** *10am-9pm Mon-Sat.* **Map** *p247 F1.*

The large Yido shop-gallery provides a wonderful counterpoint to the smaller, more traditional Kwang Ju Yo shop (*see above*) down the road. On display are ceramic wares from a grand roster of Hongdae University graduates, their styles running the gamut from traditional to contemporary – clichéd as it may sound, there really is something for everyone here, and most of it is markedly Korean in nature. Head to the top floors and you'll find a café serving decent sandwiches, as well as a couple of rooms in which pottery classes take place (Korean-language only at the time of writing).

Textiles & bedding

Hyojae
Seongbukdong (720-5393). **Open** *9am-7pm daily, but phone to check.*

Looking at this unassuming, ivy-covered little shop, it's hard to believe that its owner was specially commissioned to make designs for Issey Miyake. Such is the reputation of Lee Hyojae, an expert in Korean textiles, and author of countless books on the subject. The shop sits on a remote, hilly road opposite an appealing temple. Products exude a simple yet refined air; curtains, duvet covers and pillowcases are available, as well as *bojagi*, traditional Korean wrapping cloths made from embroidered silk. *Photo p157.*

Monocollection
Buamdong 306-2 (517-5170, www.mono collection.com). **Open** *Varies. Phone to check.*

The drapery, upholstery and bedding of designer Chang Eung Bogg showcases a pleasant mix of traditional and contemporary Korean colours, fabrics and patterns. The designs are able to sidle into more or less any home, and are particularly popular with affluent Seoulites. Most customers are here for the gorgeous bed linen, although Monocollection's shopping bags also make excellent purchases, and the silk wallpaper is lovely.

CONSUME

Happily, staff are able to arrange international shipping for this and other bulky items. The shop is a little out of the way in Buamdong, but you can also buy the company's products at Korea House restaurant (*see p119*), Yido Pottery (*see p155*) and Incheon International Airport.

HEALTH & BEAUTY
Health

The city of Seoul runs an official medical tourism centre, the **Seoul Medical Tourism Center** (http://eng.seoulmedicaltour.com), which provides a range of treatments and surgery and also gives information on other clinics in the city.

Jaseng Hospital of Oriental Medicine
Sinsadong 635 (3218-2167, www.jaseng.net). Apgujeong station (line 3), exit 2. **Open** International Clinic 9am-6pm Mon-Sat. **Map** p252 M8.
The Jaseng hospital treats dozens of foreign patients every single day, many of whom travel to Korea for this purpose alone – it is by far the most renowned clinic in the land, though with prices to match. Specialising in spine and joint disorders, practictioners speak a variety of languages, and employ a combination of eastern and western schools of medicine.

Kwangdong Oriental Hospital
Samseongdong 161 (2222-4992). Samseong station (line 2), exit 7. **Open** 9am-6pm Mon-Fri; 9am-3pm Sat. **Map** p253 P10.
This hospital offers a wide range of treatments, both eastern and western in nature. The former include several different acupuncture courses, along with facials and massages with Korean herbs and oils, aroma stone therapy and blood circulation programmes. There's a little hint of the orientalist placebo effect here, but in general the standard of care is very high. Not all staff speak English, so it may be best to communicate your wishes through the Korea Tourism Organisation's medical wing (*see p229*).

INSIDE TRACK COSMETICS

The Myeongdong area, accessible via the subway station of the same name (line 4), has more cosmetics shops than it's humanly possible to count, identifiable by hot pants-clad girls trying to drag in (mostly Japanese) customers. Alternatively, there are large cosmetics sections on the ground floor of all the city's department stores (*see p142*).

Migreen Oriental Clinic
Chungmuro 2-ga 63-2 (757-3500, www.mi-green.co.kr). Apgujeong station (line 3), exit 2. **Open** 10am-9pm daily. **Map** p247 F4.
A favourite with local celebrities, on account of its various skincare programmes. Lasting from 30 minutes to two hours, these make use of everything from acupuncture to *makgeolli* (rice wine) packs. Other courses can be tailored to focus on digestive issues, while cupping sessions are also available – and quite a bargain at ₩52,000.

Hairdressers & barbers

Hair & Joy
Donggyodong 168-3 (363-4253). Hongik Univ. station (line 2), exit 4. **Open** 10am-8pm daily. **No credit cards.**
There are several English-speaking stylists at this fashionable salon, some of whom were trained in the UK. Hongdae, the surrounding area, is famed as a centre of youthful experimentation, setting trends that the rest of the country (and, occasionally, the rest of Asia) follows – so this is a great place in which to check out the latest styles.

Zen Hair Salon
Daehyeondong 90-105 (362-4125). Ehwa Womans Univ station (line 2), exit 1. **Open** 10am-8.30pm daily. **No credit cards.** **Map** p246 B4.
This salon specialises in modern female styles – no surprise, given its location right next to Korea's biggest women's university. Many of the stylists have been trained abroad, and the fact that many speak English and are aware of foreign styles and trends is a big plus.

Opticians

Seoul is a great place in which to buy cheap, high-quality spectacles. The best place to go shopping is undoubtedly **Namdaemun Market** (*see p145*), which has outlets by the dozen: ₩35,000 should be enough to land you a good, stylish pair.

Drawing on Face
Sinsadong 651-2 (543-0392). Apgujeong station (line 3), exit 2. **Open** 10am-6pm Mon-Sat. **Map** p252 M9.
Local designer Sunchan Hwang uses titanium to create tailored spectacle frames, each custom-made pair taking around a week to make. Prices start at around $1,000, and those with extra cash can ask for gemstones or gold to be included. Of particular note is the Hana design, made from a single, 80cm length of titanium (*hana* means 'one'), for which Hwang received a Red Dot international design award.

CONSUME

CONSUME

Hyojae. *See p155.*

Pharmacies

There are pharmacies all over Seoul and, although almost none is signed as such in English, you'll usually find an English-speaking staff member. Just ask for the nearest *yakguk*, pronounced 'yak gook'.

Shops

How & What

Gwanhundong 30-7 (730-9210, www.howand what.co.kr). Anguk station (line 3), exit 6. **Open** 10am-6pm Mon-Fri. **No credit cards.** **Map** p247 F2.

Insadong isn't solely about traditional Korean fare, as shown by this women's clothing and aroma boutique. The locally designed clothing, a pastiche of Korean luxury brands, is of moderate interest. But more notable is the 'scent bar' on the left-hand side of the entrance, which sells essential oils from Thailand, as well as apparatus on which to heat them.

Spas & salons

Amore Pacific Spa

10F Avenuel, Namdaemunno 2-ga 130 (2118-6221, www.amorepacific.com). Euljiro 1-ga station (line 2), exit 7. **Open** 10.30am-8.30pm daily. **Map** p247 F3.

Part of the gigantic Lotte complex (*see p142*), this tenth-floor spa provides a rare moment of peace in the heart of one of Seoul's busiest quarters. It's affiliated to Amore Pacific, one of Korea's largest cosmetics brands, and certainly the best known abroad. It's the best place for those wanting to be pampered the local way: Korean ingredients such as green tea leaves, ginseng extract and bamboo sap are used in almost all the products and treatments, and consummate care is taken over the selection of each one. Stone therapy is available for the back, along with specialised treatments for the feet or face.

Banyan Tree Club & Spa

Jangchundong 2-ga 5-5 (2250-8000, www.banyantree.com/en/seoul/overview). Beotigogae station (line 6), exit 1. **Open** 10am-10pm daily. **Map** p247 H5.

A gorgeous venue located on the Namsan slopes, and part of the world-famous Banyan Tree chain of spa-resorts (*see p95*). As with the company's other spas in Phuket, the Seychelles and the Maldives, the service is world-class and the attention to detail sky-high, accented with local nuances. Pan-Asian treatments are available, all making use of natural herbs and spices. Two-hour sessions start at ₩250,000 and facials at just over half that, though it's very tempting to add extras such as the 'Rainmist' steam bath.

INSIDE TRACK GETTING AROUND IN APGUJEONG

The wider Apgujeong area is full of excellent shops, restaurants, cafés and bars, but, unfortunately, the nearest subway station – also known as Apgujeong – is some way from the action. It's best to head by taxi (₩3,000 or so) to Dosan Park, the hub of the area; alternatively, it's a 15-minute walk from the station.

Guerlain

3F Shilla Hotel, Jangchundong 2-ga 202 (2230-1167, www.guerlainspa.com). Dongguk Univ. station (line 3), exit 1. **Open** 7am-10pm daily. **Map** p248 J4.

Based on the third floor of the Shilla Hotel and an oriental offshoot of the French cosmetics brand, this is one of Seoul's more refined spas. Though not quite as showy as its sisters in Paris and the Waldorf in New York, it exudes a gentle style and simplicity, and affords its patrons lovely pine-filled views of Namsan mountain just outside. A full range of treatments, includig facials, footbaths and massages is available, and spa customers are free to use the hotel's excellent swimming pool, sauna and fitness centre.

▶ *For more about the Shilla hotel, see p96.*

Healing Hands

Itaewondong 1-ga (010 3158-5572, www.healinghands.co.kr). Itaewon station (line 6), exit 2. **Open** 11.30am-10pm daily. **Map** p251 G7.

Massage treatments start at ₩60,000 for an hour-long session; and a 20-minute hot-stone massage can be added to any other treatment for an extra ₩10,000. Take your pick from the bright, invigorating Red Room or the relaxing, dark-brown tones of the Zen Room.

Whoo Spa Palace

Cheongdamdong 31-11 (080 022-0303, www.whoo.co.kr). Hakdong station (line 7), exit 8. **Open** 9am-9pm daily. **Map** p253 N9.

This is the most luxurious spa in the land, bar none. Under the same ownership as History of Whoo, one of the country's most vaunted cosmetics labels, it's rarely visited by non-Koreans, and few staff speak English (though this is a place where words seem vulgar and rather unnecessary). Treatments are available by appointment only, meaning that you'll have precious little time to enjoy the lobby's calligraphic scrolls and mother-of-pearl inlaid furniture. In the treatment rooms, you'll be smothered with Chinese herbal lotions, then massaged by what may feel like a dozen hands.

CONSUME

Will Spa
Coex complex, Samseongdong (3466-8100,
www.willspa.co.kr). Samseong station (line 2),
exit 5. **Open** 24hrs daily. **Map** p253 P10.
Deep within the bowels of the Coex complex (*see*
p144) lies this top-notch spa, which is well used to
dealing with foreign folk thanks to the presence of
three five-star hotels in the vicinity. The herbal aro
mas that greet you at the door are a pleasure to
inhale. Then it's on to more serious matters, with
sessions lasting up to three hours; the programme
features intriguing elements such as a ginseng bath,
and a 'chocolate fondue wrap'.

HOUSE & HOME
Antiques

Itaewon has a dedicated 'Antiques Alley'
running south of the station.

Royal Antiques
Hannamdong 736-9 (797-8637, www.royal-
antique.com). Itaewon station (line 6), exit 3.
Open 10am-6pm Tue-Sun. **Map** p251 H7.
The most reputable antiques establishment in Seoul,
as well as one of the oldest, having started life in the
1950s. It's run by the knowledgeable Nam family,
and staff are happy and able to explain the items of
furniture on show in the two-level store. You'll find
both authentic antiques and reproductions from
Korea's Joseon Dynasty, as well as more colourful
offerings from the contemporary Chinese Qing.

General

10 Corso Como
Cheongdamdong 70 (3018-1010, www.10corso
como.co.kr). Apgujeong station (line 3), exit 2. **Open**
Shop 11am-8pm daily. *Café* 11am-11pm Mon-Thur,
Sun; 11am-midnight Fri, Sat. **Map** p253 O9.
The Milanese style label has sent its circles-within-
circles motif to Asia, in the process creating one of
Seoul's most interesting stores. Much of the lower
level is taken up with trendy household goods (some
by local designers), while the second floor also
includes the 10 Corso Como clothing range. Within
the complex is a zany café-bar-restaurant, a near-
monochrome space in which you can enjoy Italian
food and excellent coffee.

MUSIC & ENTERTAINMENT
CDs, records & DVDs

Pung Wol Dang
Sinsadong 657-37 (512-2222, www.pungwol
dang.kr). Apgujeong station (line 3), exit 2.
Open 10am-9pm Mon-Sat. **Map** p252 M8.
Sharing a floor with the Rosenkavalier café (*see*
p131) this shop claims to have the world's largest

collection of classical music. Regardless of the fact
that Korea is also (probably) home to the world's
greatest number of erroneous superlatives, you're
sure to find what you're looking for here. Staff are
knowledgeable, but do not speak English.

Purple Record
Seogyodong 343-5 (336-3023). Sungsu station
(line 2), exit 1. **Open** 11am-11pm daily.
An excellent shop with a commendable range of CDs
and vinyl: look hard enough and you'll find everything from post-rock to Piazzolla. Perhaps more
notably, the relative absence of such outlets in Seoul
means that the customers themselves are also
notable – in a city where the youth subsists almost
entirely on K-pop and generic hip hop, it can be hard
to find locals with independent tastes.

Musical instruments

Nagwon Arcade
3-5F Nagwondong 284, Insadong (no phone).
Jongno 3-ga station (lines 1, 3 & 5), exit 5. **Open**
9am-9pm daily. **No credit cards. Map** p247 F2.
For years, the district government has been threatening to tear down the crusty Nagwon Arcade, a
decaying structure built in 1968. Young local artists
have vociferously campaigned against the arcade's
demolition, particularly because of the musical element: several floors are filled with nothing but tiny
shops selling guitars, drums and other bits of kit.
Even if you're not into music, you'll probably love
this place – just get there before it disappears.

TRAVELLERS' NEEDS
For computer repairs, try Yongsan Electronics
Market (*see p146*). For mobile phone rental, *see*
p228. Advice on shipping largely depends on
where you're sending things to – an internet
search will bring up dozens of operators.

Hanatour
Gongpyeongdong 1 (737-1600 www.hanatour.
com). Anguk station (line 3), exit 4. **Map** p254 F2.
You won't have to walk far to find a branch of
Hanatour, the country's biggest travel agent, and
a good source of train and plane tickets. Few of the
staff speak English, but if you're able to communicate when and where you'd like to go, you'll be
given a price.
Other locations throughout the city.

Mode Tour
Korea Tourism Organisation, Cheonggyecheono
40 (753-9870). Euljiro 1-ga subway (line 2), exit 2.
Open 9am-8pm daily. **Map** p247 F3.
This travel agency has one brilliantly located
branch, inside the Korea Tourism Organisation's
main office. You can guarantee that an English-
speaking member of staff can be tracked down.

CONSUME

Bags packed, milk cancelled, house raised on stilts.

You've packed the suntan lotion, the snorkel set, the stay-pressed shirts. Just one more thing left to do – your bit for climate change. In some of the world's poorest countries, changing weather patterns are destroying lives.

You can help people to deal with the extreme effects of climate change. Raising houses in flood-prone regions is just one life-saving solution.

**Climate change costs lives.
Give £5 and let's sort it** *Here & Now*

www.oxfam.org.uk/climate-change

Be Humankind (X) Oxfa

Arts & Entertainment

Korea House. *See p197.*

Calendar

Seoul's seasons are packed with possibilities.

In Seoul, the non-stop action lasts not only all day long, but all year round. From season to season, the city's culturally minded can enjoy a blistering series of concerts, exhibitions, sports events, festivals and shows. The massive Coex exhibition hall and mega-mall hosts regular events, while Seoul Plaza is the focus of seasonal festivals. And if you begin to tire of the city, you can always travel to rural parts of the country to enjoy their seasonal highlights – the journey from the highest skyscraper in Seoul to the country's remotest temple can be done in a single day.

INFORMATION

The **Seoul Tourism Organisation** website, www.visitseoul.net, will have up-to-date information on times of events.

SPRING

Independence Movement Day

Tapgol Park, Jongno 2-ga 38-1 (731-0534). Jongno 3-ga station (lines 1, 3 & 5), exit 1. **Date** 1 Mar. **Map** p247 G3.

When a group of Korean nationalists published a declaration of independence on 1 March 1919, they were promptly arrested by the Japanese colonial authorities. Fortunately, you won't have to worry about that when you attend the various ceremonies held on this holiday, including a public reading of the declaration, usually held at Tapgol Park.

Seoul International Marathon

Gwanghwamun Plaza to Jamsil Stadium (361-1425, http://marathon.donga.com). **Date** mid Mar. The *Dong-a Ilbo*, one of Korea's most stalwart daily papers, is the sponsor of this race. Don't confuse it with the Joongang Seoul Marathon, organised by a rival newspaper and held in November.

St Patrick's Day Festival

Insadong, Jongno-gu and other venues (iak.co.kr). **Date** 17 Mar or closest Sat.

It may be a cliché, but the Irish do know how to party. The Irish Association of Korea devotes a hefty portion of its yearly budget to the Irish music, Gaelic games, dances and other forms of craic that take up most of the day. After the sun goes down, partygoers retire to local bars for killer deals on Guinness (and killer lines of people waiting for their drink).

Seoul Fashion Week

SETEC (Seoul Trade Exhibition Center), Nambu Sunhwanno 3102 (www.seoulfashionweek.org). Hakyeoul station (line 3), exit 1. **Date** Late Mar, late Oct. **Map** p253 P10.

Join Korean trendsetters, fashionistas and some of the skinniest people in the city for the Fall/Winter and Spring/Summer Seoul collections. Though they're understandably more focused on international events, Korea's top designers usually have stalls here showcasing their work.

► *The work of some of Korea's top designers is highlighted in the Shopping chapter, see p149.*

Beginning of Baseball Season

Date Early Apr.

Koreans have adopted this American pastime as their own, as evidenced by their gold medal finish in the 2008 Olympics in Beijing and a second-place showing against the Japanese team in the World Baseball Classic. Cheerleaders, cheap beer and passionate fans make a trip to the stadium entertaining even for those who aren't devotees of the game.

► *For more on the city's baseball teams, see p189.*

★ Cherry Blossoms in Bloom

Date Early-mid Apr.

Seoul visitors can follow the large crowds to Yeouido, where cars are diverted from the boulevards lined with blossoming trees. For a (somewhat) quieter day, head to Incheon Grand Park or Seoul Grand Park.

World DJ Fest

Gangsang Athletic Park, Gyopyeongni 307, Gangsang-myeon, Yangpyeong District, Gyeonggi Province (www.worlddjfest.com). **Date** early May.

This festival's former location in Nanji Park seemed ideal, but it was frustratingly difficult to actually reach the festival location. Now the organisers have wised up to the headache and the festival has been relocated further up the Hangang at Yangpyeong, an hour east of the city. Subway trains and shuttle buses whisk revellers to the multiple stages, where you'll find crazy crowds dancing to the likes of the Freemasons, Vandalism, Avicci and Dada Life.

Jongmyo Daeje
Jongmyo shrine, Hunjeongdong 159 (765-2124, www.jongmyo.net). Jongno 3-ga station (lines 1, 3 & 5), exit 11. **Date** 1st Sun in May. **Map** p247 G2.
Roughly translating as 'the royal shrine rites', the Jongmyo Daeje were a yearly ritual held at Jongmyo shrine (*see p56*) for the past kings of the Joseon Dynasty. Once the most important ceremony on the calendar, they are a fascinating relic of centuries past.

Hi Seoul Spring Festival
Yeouido Hangang Park, Seoul Plaza and other locations (www.hiseoulfest.org). **Date** Early May.
Despite dramatic budget cuts, the Hi Seoul Festival continues to put on a good show. Events vary by season, but visitors can expect performances by overseas troupes, international food vendors and plenty of good fun. The highlight of the Hi Seoul calendar is definitely the spring festival, held in early May.

★ Lotus Lantern Festival
Jogyesa, Gyeonjidong 45 (2011-1744, www.llf. or.kr). Anguk station (line 3), exit 6. **Date** Early-mid May. **Map** p247 F2.

Religious Koreans are pretty much equally split between Christianity and Buddhism, so it makes sense that the birthdays of both Jesus and Buddha are holidays here. The main form of celebration for the latter is the hanging up of thousands upon thousands of wire-frame 'lotus lanterns'. A particularly spectacular display can be seen at the Jogyesa temple in downtown Seoul; it's also the terminus of an impressive evening parade that winds through much of the surrounding area.

SUMMER

Korean Queer Culture Festival
Jongno-gu and the Cheonggyecheon Stream (303-5626, www.kqcf.org). **Date** early June.
Seoul shows its queer side at this celebration. Alternative lifestyle choices are generally kept under wraps in a culture that can mercilessly punish the slightest infraction against its norms, but at least for a day pride shines with rainbows, face paint, queer film screenings and a parade marching down Jongno and the Cheonggyecheon Stream. Be considerate of camera-shy participants (and somewhat paranoid staff) and leave your camera at home.
▶ *For more on gay and lesbian Seoul, see pp176-180.*

Tea World Festival
Coex Convention Center, Samsung 1-dong 159 (6000-8000, www.teanews.com). Samseong station (line 2), exits 5 & 6. **Date** early June. **Map** p253 P10.
While Koreans may not be as tea-crazy as some of their East Asian neighbours, it's still worth trying

Hi Seoul Spring Festival.

ARTS & ENTERTAINMENT

a cup or two while you're in town, particularly if your visit happens to coincide with this small but entertaining festival.

★ Jisan Valley Rock Festival & Pentaport Rock Festival

Jisan Valley *San Haewolli 28-1, Majang-myeon, Icheon City, Gyeonggi Province (http://valleyrock festival.mnet.com).* **Pentaport** *near Dream Park, Incheon (www.pentaportrock.com).* **Date** Late July.

Until 2009, the Incheon-based Pentaport Rock Festival reigned supreme on the Korean rockers' calendar. But some of the organisers split off after a disagreement and started a second, simultaneous event – the Jisan Valley Rock Festival. Since both festivals take place around the same time as Japan's Fuji Rock Festival, they've been able to draw big acts already on tour in Asia such as Belle & Sebastian, Pet Shop Boys and Oasis.

AUTUMN

Korea International Art Fair

Coex Convention Center, Samsung 1-dong 159 (www.kiaf.org). Samseong station (line 2), exits 5 & 6. **Date** Mid Sept. **Map** p253 P10.

KIAF joins Beijing's CIGE and the Shanghai Art Fair as one of the region's top industry fairs. Even if you're not there to buy, getting a glimpse of art trends in Asia may be reason enough to join the more than 70,000 likely to browse through the booths here.

★ Seoul Drum Festival

Seoul Forest, Seongsu-dong 1-ga 685 (757-2121, www.seouldrum.go.kr). Seongsu 1-ga station. **Date** Late Sept. **Map** p249 N6.

This rhythmic event is a real crowd-pleaser, and its organisers have long been praised for turning spectators into participants. You can listen to world-class drum ensembles from near and far, take lessons on playing the *janggu*, or join in the sprawling percussion parade. Guests who arrive early can chill in the Seoul Forest, an interesting site in itself.

Global Gathering

Nanji Park, Sangamdong 487-257 (323-2838, www.globalgatheringkorea.co.kr). **Date** Early Oct.

The Global Gathering franchise began in England and has brought the joys of clubbing to electronic dance music fans across the world. Though a relative newcomer to the Korean scene, the event has already landed big names like the Prodigy, Fatboy Slim and Armin Van Buuren.

Jarasum Jazz Festival

Jarado, Gapyeong-gun, Gyeonggi Province (031 581-2813, www.jarasumjazz.com). **Date** Early Oct.

From small beginnings, this riverside festival held on the little island of Jarado has become a yearly pilgrimage for patrons of jazz. Past headliners have

included Mike Stern, Joshua Redman, Victor Wooten, George Duke and John Abercrombie. If you're looking for a bite between shows, try out the area's *dakgalbi* – chicken pan-broiled with cabbage, sweet potatoes and rice cake.

Seoul International Fireworks Festival

Han River Park at Yeouido (www.bulnori.com). Yeouinaru station (line 5), exits 2 & 3. **Date** Early Oct.

The fireworks are pretty impressive, but you may find yourself even more surprised at the sheer mass of humanity streaming from Yeouinaru station. Do yourself a favour and get there early to guarantee a seat for when the show barges start unleashing barrage after barrage of bang, dazzle and sparkle.

Grand Mint Festival

Olympic Park, Bangidong 88 (www.mintpaper. com). Olympic Park station (line 5), exit 3. **Date** Mid Oct. **Map** p253 Q9/10.

Take one look at the stage names – Mint Breeze Stage, Loving Forest Garden – and you'll realise this is not your average beer-swilling, mosh pit-rushing music festival. The focus is on relaxing to good music, not partying to hard rock. Korean alternative groups like No Reply, Clazziquai and Kingston Rudieska are the norm here.

Seoul Grand Hilton's Oktoberfest

Grand Hilton Hotel, Hongeundong 201-1 (3216-5656, www.grandhiltonseoul.com). Hongje station (line 3), exit 4. **Date** Early Sept.

The city's biggest Oktoberfest celebration. The fun begins with a massive buffet served up by German chefs, along with all-you-can-drink brews. After the traditional German band finishes its performance on stage, the audience can join in games including nail-the-hammer and beer chug.

Seoul Chungmuro International Film Festival in Seoul (CHIFFS)

Cinemas around Myeongdong (www.chiffs.kr). **Date** Early Sept.

Just east of the shopping district of Myeongdong, Chungmuro was once the centre of the Korean film industry. As the studios saw more success, they expanded and moved to other parts of town. For a couple of days each autumn, the movie spirit returns to the district as more than a hundred films grace local screens. This is a rare chance to catch classic Korean films with English subtitles.

Seoul Performing Arts Festival

Various venues around Daehangno (www.spaf21.com). **Date** Oct.

If you like edgy performance art that pushes the boundaries of what's acceptable on the stage, this may be the festival for you. Previous years have seen the likes of Force Majeure's *The Age I'm In* and Michèle Noiret's *Demain*.

ARTS & ENTERTAINMENT

Haebangchon Music Festival

Various bars at Haebangchon near Itaewon
(www.hbcfest.com). **Date** Late May, late Oct.
Just north-west of Itaewon is Haebangchon, or
'Freedom Village'. The local expat community shows
up in force on the main strip when the area's bars
open their doors to Seoul's finest foreigner bands.

SIWA & Diplomatic
Community Bazaar

Grand Hilton Hotel, Hongeundong 201-1
(www.siwapage.com). **Date** Late Nov.

Hobnob with embassy staff and expats at this huge
bazaar, which sprawls across several halls at one of
Seoul's top hotels. With dozens of countries represented, you can sample a Brazilian caipirinha as you
nibble on a potato covered with melted emmental.
The day's proceeds are donated to local charities.

Seoul Café Show & Fancy Food Fest

Coex Convention Center, Samseong 1-dong 159
(www.cafeshow.co.kr, www.fancyfood.co.kr).
Samseong station (line 2), exits 5 & 6. **Date**
Late Nov. **Map** p253 P10.

A Nation on the Move

Two holidays, one long traffic jam.

For Koreans, holiday time is travel time.
Twice a year, around 20 million Koreans –
nearly half the population – hop in a car
or board a train, and head to the home of
the family patriarch. This mass migration,
known here as *daeidong*, wreaks havoc on
the country's transport system. A road trip
from Seoul to Busan that would ordinarily
take six hours turns into two or even
three times that.

The two holidays to blame for bumper-
to-bumper traffic are Seollal and Chuseok.
Seollal is in late January or early February
at the Lunar New Year, which Koreans
celebrate much like the Chinese. Chuseok,
held on the 15th day of the eighth month
in the Lunar New Year (usually September),
marks the harvest moon and is a time to
give thanks for the bounty of the fields,
somewhat like Thanksgiving in the US.

In many ways, though, Seollal and
Chuseok are the same thing: they both
require families to gather in order to pay
their respects to the departed. This follows
a fairly rigid format: family members put
on traditional *hanbok* clothing and head to
the home of the oldest male. The women
busy themselves with cooking in the
kitchen while the men relax in the living
room. The family performs the *charye*
ceremony, inviting the spirits of the
ancestors to partake of the feast. Then the
living family members chow down on what
the ancestors leave behind. The tribe may
then make a trip to their ancestral grave
to tidy up the site. Finally, people gear up
for another long day on the road. If you
find yourself getting the two holidays
confused, don't be too hard on yourself
– Koreans do the same.

Of course, there are some differences in
the two holidays. During Seollal, families

make *deokguk*, or rice cake soup, which
is offered to the ancestors during *charye*;
while at Chuseok, newly harvested rice is
used. Another Chuseok food is *songpyeon*,
moon-shaped cakes of rice flour,
filled with red beans and chestnuts, and
steamed with pine needles. The other
major difference is the *sebae* bow, which
children offer to their elders at Seollal as
they say '*saehae bok mani badeuseyo*,' or,
'May you receive many blessings in the New
Year'. In return, they receive some wisdom
as well as, more importantly, *sebaedon* –
New Year's cash. This financial incentive
isn't present at Chuseok, making Seollal a
favourite with young members of the family.

Though both of these holidays can be
an awkward time to try to navigate the
country, they are actually not a bad time
to be in Seoul. Because of the mass
exodus of up to 3.5 million Seoulites,
the city is left fairly empty, and most of
those left behind will be involved in family
activities. True, a lot of shops and even
department stores may close for the
holiday, but most historical sites and
palaces remain open. Many will even
offer special holiday activities, including
traditional Korean games like *yutnori*
(a board game played by throwing sticks)
and *jegi chagi* (hacky sack).

Today, more families are making their
permanent residence in Seoul, and the
growing popularity of cremation is resulting
in fewer loved ones being laid to rest in
traditional burial mounds. Some question
whether the holidays will continue to
require the spontaneous movement of
tens of millions of Koreans. But at least
for the present, you'll want to keep an
eye on the lunar calendar before planning
any travel on the peninsula.

ARTS & ENTERTAINMENT

Stock up on treats at these simultaneous food and drink expos. Professionals take part in tournaments including the Korea Barista Championship. But don't forget (and who could?) about the teas, wines, pies, puddings, pizzas, candy, bread, nuts, yoghurt, and the rest of the delicious comestibles here.

WINTER

Christmas

Date 25 Dec.

One of the classics of Korean cinema is titled *Christmas in August*, and that pretty much sets the tone for the cultural accuracy of the holiday. Korean lovers head out on the town while desperate singles call past crushes. Department stores find themselves crowded with shoppers, Santas, wreaths and absurdly large trees.

Seoul Teddy Bear Convention & Festival

Coex Convention Center, Samsung 1-dong 159 (www.bearseoul.com). Samseong station (line 2), exits 5 & 6. **Date** Late Dec. **Map** p253 P10.

Stuffed animal fanatics can hit up the teddy bear museum at N Seoul Tower (*see p82*) any time of the year, but for a truly intense experience with the plushy toys, your only choice is the Teddy Bear Convention – one of the capital's whackier events.

Outdoor Ice Rink at the Seoul Plaza

Seoul Plaza, City Hall. City Hall station (lines 1 & 2), exit 5. **Date** Mid Dec-mid Feb.

A ₩1,000 note will grant you a pair of skates and as much time as you want to twirl around on the ice. The city government sometimes sets up the rink in Gwanghwamun instead, so check in advance to confirm the location.

Bell Tolling for New Year's Eve

Bosingak Belfry, 45-5 Gwancheoldong. Gwanghwamun station (line 5), exit 4 or Euljiro 1-ga station (line 2), exit 3. **Date** 31 Dec. **Map** p247 F3.

In Seoul, the beginning of the New Year is marked by the ringing of a bell. The ponderous bronze bell housed at Bosingak in central Seoul is tolled 33 times on the stroke of midnight as thousands gather to listen. Avoid Jonggak station (the closest stop) since it's typically closed that night – try walking from Gwanghwamun station or Euljiro 1-ga station instead.

Holidays for Sale

It's always time for treats in Korea.

People often complain about the commercialisation of Christmas, but western shoppers can't hold a candle to several Korean holidays that appear to have been conceived at a marketing brainstorming session. First up is Valentine's Day (14 February), when Korean women are expected to buy chocolates for the men they fancy. This favour is returned on White Day (14 March), when guys shower their sweethearts with sweeties and other gifts – which must be at least twice the value of what they were given a month previously. Those left out on both of the preceding months can still gorge themselves on *jajangmyeon* (black noodles) on Black Day (14 April) and forget their sorrows.

Marketers eager to capitalise on this expansion of 14th-based holidays have come up with other concepts for each of the rest of the months. For example, 14 May is Rose Day, when couples give each other the flower of love, and 14 August is Green Day, when lovers commune with nature and drink the potent alcohol *soju* (which comes in green bottles). However, most of these exist in name only and have yet to really catch on.

There is one more shopping day that, though it doesn't fall on the 14th of the month, is quite possibly the most popular of all. This is Pepero Day, which falls on 11 November. On the day that Commonwealth countries recall the sacrifice of those who fell in past wars, Korean youngsters trot out to the nearest convenience store to invest in some of the chocolate-covered crunchy cookie sticks known as Pepero (inspired by Japan's Pocky).

Legend has it that back in 1994, some inspired Busan schoolgirls lined up four Pepero on their desk and connected them with 11 November (the four sticks resemble 11/11). This may be no more than a myth concocted by the marketing geniuses at Lotte Confectionery, the manufacturer of the treats – who may themselves have pinched the idea from Japan, where Pocky has an identical 'festival'. At any rate, each November, supermarkets, convenience stores and stationery shops put out their displays and hawk glitzy boxes filled with multi-flavoured, multi-sized Pepero. And what's there to complain about? Kids and couples love the day – not to mention the Lotte shareholders.

Children

Fun for Seoul's smaller visitors.

Seoul may lack decent parks and pedestrianised areas, but there are still a fair number of ways to keep children amused. The city and its periphery contain some colossal theme parks, most notably **Everland** and **Lotte World**, while **Seoul Park** and **Children's Grand Park** are great for a stroll with the kids. In addition, a number of the city's top museums have dedicated children's areas, and a few – like the **Hello Museum** and **Samsung Children's Museum** – have been designed with young ones in mind; aquariums, zoos and outdoor swimming pools round out the picture.

AMUSEMENT PARKS

★ Everland & Caribbean Bay

Jeondae-ri 310, Pogok-eup, Yongin City, Gyonggi Province (031 320-5000, www.everland.com). **Admission** *Day pass* ₩26,000-₩37,000. *Night pass* (after 5pm) ₩22,000-₩30,000.

Just outside Seoul near Suwon city, South Korea's largest theme park ranks tenth in the world for amusement park attendance. It's home to over 40 exciting rides and attractions. Ride the T-Express and experience Asia's longest and the world's steepest (77 degrees) wooden rollercoaster. The Zoo-topia section features the newly opened Safariland and Herbivore Safari, allowing visitors to get up close to tigers, lions, bears, giraffes, elephants and more. Next door is Caribbean Bay, a water park that boasts the world's longest lazy river ride, wading pools suitable for children, waterslides and a sauna.

▶ *For more about Suwon, including details on how to get there, see p211.*

Lotte World

Jamsildong 40-1 (411-2000, www.lotteworld.com). Jamsil station (lines 2 & 8), exit 4. **Open** 9.30am-8pm Mon-Thur; 9.30am-11.30pm Fri-Sun. **Admission** ₩11,500-₩26,000. *All-access passport* ₩23,000-₩38,000.

Located in the Jamsil area in southern Seoul, Lotte World is one of Asia's top theme parks, hosting over eight million visitors each year. Opened in 1989, the complex is made up of the world's largest indoor theme park; it's centred on Magic Island, an outdoor amusement park on a lake, connected via monorail to shopping malls, a luxury hotel, a traditional folk museum, athletic facilities, an indoor skating rink and movie theatres. A parade takes place every day at 2pm and 7.30pm, and a laser show at 9.30pm.

AQUARIUMS

Coex Aquarium

Samseongdong 159 (6002-6200, www.coex aqua.co.kr). Samseong station (line 2), exits 5 & 6. **Open** 10am-8pm (entrance until 7pm). **Admission** Adults ₩17,500; teens ₩14,500; children ₩11,000. **Map** p253 P10.

This aquarium is handily located in the basement of the Coex Mall (*see p144*), and has six different themed exhibition areas, with 90 exhibition tanks and 140 tanks for breeding. There are about 600 different species on show here, totalling over 40,000 marine creatures altogether – the numbers alone may get young minds racing. The most popular sights for children here are the massive shark tanks, and the Marine Touch area where visitors can pet and play with baby sharks and other creatures.

BABYSITTING & EQUIPMENT RENTAL

Most major hotels in Seoul offer babysitting services, but a couple of options are listed below for those staying longer-term. A number of websites offer equipment rental, including **Total Baby** (www.totalbaby.co.kr), **iBaby Call** (www.ibabycall.co.kr) and **Little Baby** (www.littlebaby.co.kr), but these are in Korean only – call the city information line (120) or ask a local friend to assist.

Ahi wa Omma

1600-4579, www.iwaumma.com. **Office hours**
9am-7pm Mon-Fri. **Rates** ₩28,000 for 3hrs;
₩6,500 for each additional hr; ₩3,000 per hr for
each additional child. Extra charges after 7pm,
weekends & holidays. *English-speaking babysitter*
₩50,000 for 2hrs; ₩20,000 per additional hr;
₩65,000 per hr for 2 children. **No credit cards**.
Ahi Wa Omma, meaning 'baby and mum', has been
providing professional babysitting services since
2001. Babysitters are women aged between 30 and
50 years; all have extensive training and experience.

Happy Helper

989-1279, www.happyhelper.co.kr. **Office hours**
9am-6pm Mon-Fri; 9am-3pm Sat. **Rates** approx
₩45,000 for 5hrs, ₩7,500 for each additional hr,
and ₩3,000 per hr for each extra child. A 20%
surcharge is applied after 8pm, at weekends
& holidays. **No credit cards**. **Map** p248 L8.
Happy Helper provides professional babysitting
services from trained and qualified Korean women

in their 40s and 50s throughout the Seoul area. Full-
and half- day services are available. You can book
online or by phone.

MUSEUMS

★ Hello Museum

*2F Asia Building, Yeoksamdong 688-4
(562-4420, www.hellomuseum.com). Seolleung
station (line 2), exit 5.* **Open** 11am-6pm
Tue-Sat. **Admission** ₩2,000; ₩20,000
2-12s. **Map** p253 N11.
This museum was specially designed for children.
The artwork on display is hung low, and the interactive programmes and activities are hands-on and
educational. Exhibitions and art classes are on rota-
tion, so there is always something new to do, even
for those who have visited before. Special art classes
are offered by director Isaac Kim, who once worked
at the Smithsonian. Special programmes are offered
from Thursday to Sunday. Reservations are recommended as times can change.

Seoul Land.

Samsung Children's Museum

*Sincheondong 7-26 (2143-3600, www.kids.
samsungfoundation.org). Jamsil station (lines
2 & 8), exit 8 or 9.* **Open** 10am-6pm Tue-Sun;
reservations recommended for groups.
Admission ₩5,000-₩6,000.

Specially designed for children up to the age of 12,
this four-storey Samsung Foundation-owned complex provides hands-on educational exhibits for
kids to touch and manipulate. Even though the
descriptions are in Korean, all children can enjoy
the interactive activities, from building a house to
playing music. There are also workshops using
light and photography.

Seoul National Science Museum

*Changgyeonggung 113 (3668-2200, www.ssm.
go.kr). Hyehwa station (line 4), exit 4.* **Open**
9.30am-5.30pm Tue-Sun. **Admission** ₩1,000;
₩500 7-19s. **Map** p247 G1.

Located next to the palace of Changgyeongung, and
as such perfect for incorporating into a wider half-
day trip, this science museum is appealing for both
adults and children, and regularly hosts exhibitions
from around the world. In addition, some of the regular exhibits make maths, space and science fun to
learn. Attractions include a 4D cinema (*see p170*
Inside Track), and creative learning classes for
ceramics, magic and green science. Even the nuclear
energy exhibition is pretty entertaining.

PARKS & ZOOS

★ FREE Seoul Children's Grand Park

*Neungdong 18 (450-9311, www.sisul.or.kr).
Achasan station (line 5), exit 4 for the back
gate, or Children's Grand Park station (line 7),
exit 4 for the main gate.* **Open** *Park grounds*
5am-10pm daily. *Zoo & Botanical Gardens*
10am-6pm daily (subject to weather conditions).
Admission free.

There's plenty for children here at this dedicated
theme park, just east of Seoul, which opened back in
1973. It includes a zoo, botanical gardens and amusement facilities. Some of the most popular venues
include the iLand amusement park, the Marine
Animal House, the Music Fountain, a water playground and a few small sporting facilities.

Seoul Grand Park & Seoul Land

*Makgyedong 33, Gwacheon City, Gyeonggi
Province (02 509-6000, www.seoulland.co.kr).
Seoul Grand Park Station (line 4), exit 2.* **Open**
Seoul Grand Park 9am-6pm daily. *Seoul Land*
9.30am-7pm Mon-Fri; 9.30am-10pm Sat, Sun.

This large park complex is located south of Seoul in
Gwacheon city. The Seoul Land theme park has 40
rollercoasters and a few cinemas, and hosts various
fun festivals each season. Also likely to appeal to
young ones is the zoo, the world's tenth-largest, containing a special children's area.

**INSIDE TRACK
BABY BOOM, BABY BUST**

At the time of writing, South Korea had
one of the world's lowest birth rates, at
just 1.19 children per female – only Macau,
Hong Kong and Belarus had lower rates.
However, the protracted baby boom of the
1950s, '60s and '70s has, somewhat
ironically, also made South Korea one
of the world's most densely populated
countries. Bangladesh is the only country
of any size with a greater number of
inhabitants per square kilometre.

SWIMMING POOLS

Seoul has six outdoor swimming pools
along the Hangang River, which are open
to the public from 30 June to the end of
August. The three most conveniently
located are as follows:

Jamwon Swimming Pool

*Jamwondong 121-8 (536-8263, www.hangang.
seoul.go.kr). Sinsa station (line 3), exit 5.* **Open**
9am-8pm daily. **Admission** ₩5,000; ₩4,000
teens; ₩3,000 4-12s; free under-4s. **Map** p252 J9.

Near Seoul's upscale Apgujeong and Sinsa neighbourhoods, this pool is surrounded by various
sports facilities, including athletics tracks, a football
field and courts for volleyball and tennis. There's
water fun to be had here too, including water-skiing
and motorboating.

Ttukseom Swimming Pool

*Jayang 3-dong 112 (761-8204, www.supia
park.com). Ttukseom Resort station (line 7),
exit 2 or 3.* **Open** 9am-8pm daily. **Admission**
₩5,000; ₩4,000 teens; ₩3,000 4-12s; free under-
4s. **Map** p253 Q8.

The Ttukseom pool is just east of central Seoul, and
has dedicated children's pools. Facilities in the area
include a playground, water fountain, rock climbing facilities, a sunbathing area and food kiosks.

Yeouido Swimming Pool

*82-3 Yeouidodong, Yeongdeungpo-gu
(761-8201, www.supiapark.com. Yeouinaru
station (line 5), exit 2.* **Open** 9am-8pm daily.
Admission ₩5000; ₩4,000 teens; ₩3,000
4-12s, free under-4s.

On the small island of Yeouido, this is the largest outdoor swimming pool in Seoul; a visit here can be combined with a trip to the nearby Beomseom Island and
Ecological Park, or the charming island of Seonyudo
just downstream (*see p80*). The pool area itself contains a playground, water fountains, kiddie pools, a
tanning area, water cannons and food kiosks.

ARTS & ENTERTAINMENT

Film

On the crest of the Hallyu Wave.

Forget food, music or business: Korean film is better known abroad than all three, having spearheaded the 'Hallyu Wave' of K-culture since the local industry crawled out of a government-imposed cinematic dark age in the late 1990s. Korean films have won clutches of awards at Cannes and other major international festivals, with directors such as Kim Ki-Duk and Park Chan-Wook achieving worldwide fame and popularity. Cinemas are everywhere in Seoul, making it easy to catch the newest blockbuster, while local idiosyncrasies such as couple rooms and 'four-dimensional' films are also there to be explored. For more on the local industry and its place in the culture, *see p37* **Making it Big on the Big Screen**.

INFORMATION & FESTIVALS

Going to watch a movie in Seoul is relatively cheap, by international standards – most places charge ₩9,000 or thereabouts. Prominent western films all get an airing here (a far cry from the days of the quota system in place in past decades), and there are a few places in which to catch some artier fare. Unfortunately, very few of the cinemas listed provide information in English, either via telephone, online or in the venues themselves. Another small issue is that only a tiny number of locations screen Korean films with English subtitles – buying DVDs with subtitles remains the best way to get a handle on Korean film in Seoul, and this can be done at any major bookstore (*see p145*). Films in languages other than Korean are almost always shown with Korean subtitles – only children's films suffer the indignity of being dubbed.

CHIFFS, a good local film festival, takes place each September; for more information, *see p164*. There are also a few screenings in early June at the **Korean Queer Culture Festival** (*see p163*), while the arty **Sang Sang Ma Dang** cinema (*see below*) hosts a miniature event of its own in September.

INDEPENDENT

Cinecube
Shinmun-ro 1(il)-ga 226 (2002-7770). Gwanghwamun station (line 5), exit 6.
Tickets ₩8,000. **Seats** 91. **Map** p247 E3.
A tiny cinema just outside the Museum of History (*see p63*). It usually screens two films – mostly European arthouse – at various times throughout the day, rotating the selection each week.

Sang Sang Ma Dang
B3 & B4 Sang Sang Ma Dang Building, Seogyodong 367-5 (330-6263, www.sangsang madang.com). Sangsu station (line 6), exit 1.
Tickets ₩8,000. **Seats** 100.
Forming the lower levels of the fascinating Sang Sang Ma Dang building in Hongdae, this cinema shows a mix of arty Korean and foreign films, usually designed to run in thematic tandem with exhibitions in the third-floor gallery. It also hosts a small

---

INSIDE TRACK 4D FILMS

Although they've been shown in American theme parks in the past, Korea was the first country in the world to screen '4D' films at cinemas. Sensual stimulation is added to the regular three dimensions – at appropriate points in the film, your seat will bank, rise or buzz; small jets of air hit the back of your head; and scents will drop from the ceiling. The CGV cinemas in Yongsan and Yeongdeungpo (*see right*) are equipped for 4D, and more are set to follow.

Directing Talent

The leading lights behind the cameras of the Korean film industry.

Fans of arthouse cinema might tell you that the biting, off-beat films of **Hong Sangsoo** (*HaHaHa*), produced with such regularity that some call him the 'Woody Allen of Korea', or the austere, soul-searching works of **Lee Chang-dong** (*Poetry*) are the best that Korean cinema has to offer. Or those with a taste for controversy might nominate the dark moral tales of **Kim Ki-Duk** (*3-Iron*, *Breath*) or the racy black comedies of **Im Sang-soo** (*A Good Lawyer's Wife*, *The Housemaid*). But if you want to know which Korean directors are on the cusp of making a major impression on the international stage, three names stand out. After building highly successful careers in Korea over the last decade, this troika are setting their sights on the global market.

First, **Park Chan-Wook**. A former philosophy student and cinephile, Park was launched to local fame with the success of blockbuster *JSA* (2000). With *Oldboy*, winner of the Grand Prix at the 2004 Cannes Film Festival, Park created one of the most iconic films of contemporary Korean cinema. Dark, highly stylised and often violent, his films display a mix of genre and arthouse styles. More recently, he directed the vampire movie *Thirst* and the 30-minute work *Night Fishing*, which was shot entirely on an iPhone4 and which won a Golden Bear in the short film competition of the 2011 Berlin International Film Festival. Meanwhile, he is busy preparing his Hollywood debut *Stoker*, featuring a top-notch Hollywood cast and a script written by *Prison Break* star Wentworth Miller.

Like Park, the highly talented **Bong Joon-ho** is influenced, but never constrained by, popular genre conventions. He is perhaps best known internationally for his monster movie *The Host* (2006), about a truck-sized monster that crawls out of the Hangang and begins munching on the citizens of Seoul. Known for his exquisite craftsmanship, Bong's characteristic black humour and penchant for social commentary can also be seen in the crime thrillers *Memories of Murder* (2003), based on a true story of a serial killer, and *Mother* (2009), about a woman trying to prove the innocence of her mentally damaged son. For his next project, *Snow Piercer*, which is to be 80 per cent in English, he is adapting the French sci-fi comic book *Le Transperceneige* – a cue for much international excitement.

Finally, **Kim Jee-woon** has built a career out of directing highly stylised works that, at first glance, look like ordinary genre films, but which reveal unexpected complexities upon closer inspection. His most accomplished and praised films are the horror movie *A Tale of Two Sisters* (2003), noir-gangster film *A Bittersweet Life* (2006) and serial killer flick *I Saw the Devil* (2010), one of the most gruesome Korean films ever made. All thrill on a surface level but are also highly accomplished in their use of space and visual motifs. At the time of writing, Kim was preparing his English-language debut – watch out, Hollywood. *Darcy Paquet is the author of* New Korean Cinema: Breaking the Waves, *and the founder of the website Koreanfilm.org.*

ARTS & ENTERTAINMENT

film festival each September, usually followed by an interesting film music festival later in the year.

▶ *For more about the Sang Sang Ma Dang building, see p71.*

★ Seoul Art Cinema

Nagwondong 284-6 (741-9782). Jongno 3-ga station (lines 1, 3 & 5), exit 5. **Tickets** ₩6,000. **Seats** 300. **Map** p247 F2.

This arty cinema is housed on top of the Nagwon Arcade, and is also known as the Cinematheque; some even refer to it by its old name, Hollywood. Every film shown here is part of a themed series – with focuses ranging from specific directors to studies of whole genres. Some Korean films are shown with English subtitles, but other non-

English films – which form a fair chunk of the progamming – are subtitled in Korean only.

▶ *For more about the Nagwon Arcade, see p145.*

MULTIPLEXES

CGV (tickets ₩8,000; ₩17,000 for 4D films) is a gigantic chain with screens all across Korea. The most notable Seoul venues are in Yongsan (6F I'Park, Hangangno 40-999, 2012-3000) and Yeongdeungpo (Yeongdeungpodong 441-10, 1544-1122, 1544-1122 – both have 4D theatres (*see left* **Inside Track**), and the latter often screens Korean films with English subtitles.

Another chain, **Megabox** (tickets ₩8,000) has screens in most major Seoul districts.

Romance, Seoul-style

Couples' seats and couples' rooms.

Going to the movies is a staple part of dating in many countries, and Korea is no exception, especially Seoul. But Seoul's distinctively practical, user-friendly approach of its movie theatres has led to the popularity of cinemas just for couples. A visit to one of these will make for a quirky and different cinema-going experience.

There are a handful of 'couple seat' cinemas dotted around the city centre. They typically have under 40 seats, all extremely comfortable and set out in pairs. Notable venues with such facilities are **Charlotte**, inside the Lotte complex; and **Cine de Chef** in Apgujeong, which combines Hollywood blockbusters with fine Italian food. For both, *see below.*

A couple of rungs down the culture ladder are Seoul's innumerable DVD rooms, which are primarily used by young couples seeking a degree of privacy unavailable in the city's small homes. For around ₩12,000 you're free to pick out a DVD (there are usually lots of foreign films available), then watch it on a comfy chair in a small room. Tissue boxes and wipe-clean furniture hint at what often goes on here, but there's no harm at all in simply going into one to watch a film – small groups are allowed, too, and you can bring in snacks and alcoholic drinks. DVD rooms are absolutely everywhere, and since most are near-identical it's pointless to single any out for attention. They're usually located on the upper floors of tower blocks, and most common in busier parts of the city – just look for a 'DVD' sign on the sides of such buildings.

COUPLE-SEAT VENUES

Charlotte
7F Avenuel Building, Sogongdong (1544-8855). Euljiro 1-ga station (line 2), exit 1. **Tickets** ₩25,000 Mon-Fri; ₩30,000 Sat, Sun. **Seats** 34. **Map** p247 F3.
Charlotte is a stylish subsection of the sprawling Lotte complex. The ticket price includes two drinks; one is served before the film in an elegant lounge, the other during the screening. After the film, another glass of wine or a cup of coffee is a tempting prospect.

★ Cine de Chef
Sinsadong 602 (3446-0541, www.cinedechef.com). Apgujeong station (line 3), exit 3. **Tickets** ₩40,000. **Seats** 70. **Map** p252 L9.
This two-screen complex actually incorporates one of Seoul's best Italian restaurants, but to dine here you'll be required to purchase a film ticket too. Lunch set meals are around ₩30,000 upwards, and

dinners are double that, but à la carte items are available too. It's also common for couples to share a bottle of wine during the film.

IMAX SCREENS

63 Building
B1 63 Building, Yeouido (2118-5400). Yeouinaru station (line 5), exit 1. **Tickets** ₩8,000. **Seats** 500. **Map** p250 A9.
One of the world's largest IMAX facilities, with seats in a semi-circle in a stylish, red theatre. An increasing number of foreign films are subtitled, not dubbed.

Coex
Samseongdong 159 (6002-1200). Samseong station (line 2), exit 5. **Tickets** ₩8,000. **Seats** 4,218. **Map** p253 P10.
A huge branch of Megabox (*see p171*) in the huge Coex underground mall; it has a couple of screens equipped for IMAX films.

Cine de Chef.

Galleries

From students to masters.

Critics may say that Seoul's modern art scene is often a study in quantity over quality, but the sheer number of galleries at least makes it possible to spend a whole day musing over paintings, photography and sculpture. And, conveniently, many venues lie within walking distance of each other: the lanes of Samcheongdong, Insadong and the Bukchon area are studded with dozens and dozens of galleries, the vast majority of them small and independent in nature. This is the most traditional part of Seoul, and you'll see that today's artists remain informed by the colours, materials and patterns of dynastic Korea.

INFORMATION

Note that most art museums and some other excellent exhibition spaces have been included in our Sightseeing chapters, most pertinently the **Leeum Museum** (*see p82*), the Seoul **Museum of History** (*see p63*), **Seoul Museum of Art** (**SeMA**, *see p62*), the **National Museum of Contemporary Art** (*see p60*), and the slew of small, quirky museums north of Anguk station. However, we have listed the **Daelim Contemporary Art Museum** (*see below*) and the **Kyungin Museum** (*see p175*) here.

It's important to bear in mind that the majority of Seoul's commercial galleries are closed on Mondays. You can find listings of the latest exhibitions in the city's various monthly magazines (*see p227*), but better are the rundowns in Korea's daily English-language newspapers – the *Korea Times* and *Korea Herald*. If you can read Korean (or sequester the services of someone who can), the glossy *Seoul Art Scene* magazine is available at many galleries, and is very comprehensive.

BUKCHON & SAMCHEONDONG

Arario

Sogyeokdong 149-2 (723-6190, www.arario seoul.com). Anguk station (line 3), exit 1. **Open** 10am-7pm Tue-Sun. **Map** p247 F1.
A mainstay of the local scene, the spacious lower level of this gallery is always worth a quick peek: you'll usually find some interesting painting or sculpture. The exhibitions are actually larger and more numerous at Arario's main gallery, which is south of Seoul in the otherwise uninteresting city of Cheonan, an hour's train ride away.

Artsonje Center

Sogyeokdong 144-2 (733-8945, www.artsonje.org). Anguk station (line 3), exit 1. **Open** 11am-7pm Tue-Sun. **Map** p247 E2.
A large, adventurous gallery focusing almost entirely on the younger, edgier side of local art. There are usually only a handful of exhibitions each year, even fewer in the intriguing 'parking lot' space. Even the on-site café is usually roped into the exhibitions somehow; there's also an Indian restaurant on site, and a whole trove of local art books.

Bo An Yeogwan Gallery

Tonguidong 2-1 (720-8409). Gyeongbokgung station (line 3), exit 3. **Open** times vary. **Map** p247 E2.
A truly bizarre place just outside the palace walls, housed inside an old, decaying *yeogwan* – a Korean-style guesthouse largely going the way of the dodo now that motels are around. The building was erected in 1936, and became particularly popular with local poets. Installations are all appropriate to these surroundings and made on spec.

★ Daelim Contemporary Art Museum

Tonguidong 35-1 (720-0667, www.daelim museum.org). Gyeongbokgung station (line 3), exit 3. **Open** 10am-6pm Tue-Sun. **Admission** ₩4,000. **Map** p247 E2.
More gallery than museum, with changing exhibitions, though even the pieces on display from the

permanent collection vary with impressive regularity. The exhibitions themselves are usually photographic in nature, but all sorts of international artists and designers have had their works shown here, including Paul Smit, Dieter Rams and furniture designer Jean Prouve.

Gallery Hyundai

Sagandong 122 (734-6111, www.gallery hyundai.com). Anguk station (line 3), exit 1. **Open** 10am-6pm Tue-Sun. **Map** p247 F2.
The oldest commercial gallery in Korea, established back in the 1960s. A succession of gallerists have walked the tightrope between classic and contemporary local art at Gallery Hyundai, with largely wonderful results. More recent pieces are usually on show in the two smaller halls near the main one – ask at reception for directions and exhibition details.

★ Kukje Gallery

Sogyeokdong 59-1 (735-8449, www.kukje gallery.com). Anguk station (line 3), exit 1. **Open** 10am-6pm Mon-Sat, 10am-5pm Sun. **Map** p247 F1.
Mention the Kukje to any other gallery curator in Seoul, and you'll get a knowing nod of recognition – and, perhaps, resignation. This is the area's most important gallery by far, hawking Korean art around the world while dragging in major artists from overseas; *kukje* does, after all, mean 'international' in Korean. Damien Hirst, Joseph Beuys, Anish Kapoor… to name a just a few.

Sun Contemporary Art Center

Sogyeokdong 66 (720-5789, www.sun contemporary.com). Anguk station (line 3), exit 1. **Open** 10am-6.30pm Mon-Sat. **Map** p247 F1.

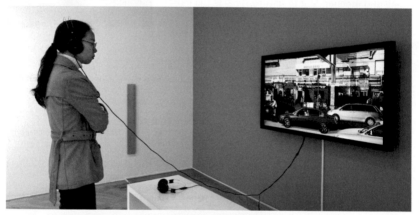

Kukje Gallery.

The contemporary wing of the more illustrious Sun Art Center (*see below*) is spread over a few buildings in the Samcheongdong neighbourhood. While it's not terribly different to other galleries in the area, its floor space alone means it is able to show a fair number of artists, so you'll generally find something interesting. A good place to while away an hour.

INSADONG

Art Center Nabi
4F SK Building, Seorindong 99 (2121-1031, www.nabi.or.kr). Jonggak station (line 1), exit 6. **Open** 10am-5pm Mon-Fri. **Map** p247 F3.
Aiming to bring change and spur creativity in the local culture through the use of new media, this curious centre is more academy than gallery, though it's certainly worth checking out.

★ Insa Art Center
Gwanhundong 188 (736-1020). Anguk station (line 3), exit 6. **Open** 10am-7pm daily. Closes early Tue, open late Wed; times vary, phone to check. **Map** p247 F2.
A gigantic space with seven whole floors of art. There is usually a good mixture of genres, so there's ample chance of finding something you like, though – as is more often than not the case in Insadong – the accent is generally on tradition with a twist. Amazingly, staff change things around once a week; the opening and closing times on Tuesday evening vary depending upon the work involved.

Insa Gallery
Gwanhundong 29-23 (735-2655, www.insa gallery.net). Anguk station (line 3), exit 6. **Open** 10am-6.30pm Mon-Sat; 10.30am-6pm Sun. **Map** p247 F2.
Since opening in 1991, the Insa Gallery has been lassoing together works from some of Korea's most esteemed contemporary artists. Only a selection are on display at any one time, sharing three whitewashed floors with other local and imported pieces.

Kyungin Museum
Gwanhundong 30-1 (733-4448). Anguk station (line 3), exit 6. **Open** 10am-6pm daily. **Map** p247 F2.
A small complex, though one that packs in a fair amount per square inch. There are three main halls and one outdoor hall here, all largely focusing on traditional works. There's also an outdoor space for events (again, largely traditional in nature), a sculpture garden, and even a charming teahouse – in warmer months, you can sup your ginger or chrysanthemum tea outside, while admiring the art.

★ Sun Art Center
Insadong 184 (734-0458, www.sungallery.co.kr). Anguk station (line 3), exit 6. **Open** 10am-6pm Tue-Sun. **Map** p247 F2.

THE BEST ART

Best for international masters
The walls of the **Seoul Museum of Art** (*see p62*) have borne paintings from Picasso, Van Gogh, Monet, Chagall and many other illustrious artists, while the **Kukje Gallery** (*see left*) has done likewise for more recent superstars of the art world.

Best for curiosity value
The odd **Bo An Yeogwan Gallery** (*see p173*) is housed in a decrepit old inn, while the shell of **Platoon/Kunsthalle** (*see below*) is entirely made up of cargo containers.

Best for older art
See paintings from Korean masters of the 20th century at the **Sun Art Center** (*see below*).

Best for architecture
The glass pavilion of the **Rodin Gallery** (*see p63*) is superb, especially when viewed next to the ancient city gate. outside.

It's nice to see an Insadong gallery eschewing the regular fusion of modern and contemporary styles – the Sun is justly proud of its collection, which is mostly made up of works from the early 20th century. Staff will be glad to guide you through this lesser-known period of Korean art.

GANGNAM

CT Gallery
Hwa Su Mok Building, Cheongdamdong 125-24 (3442-4408). Apgujeong station (line 3), exit 2. **Open** 10am-6pm daily. **Map** p253 O8.
An absorbing little space that generally twins the works of a sculptor with that of a photographer or painter – usually one is from Korea and one from the West. There's only one room; walk through and you'll find that it opens up into an expensive wine bar, in which the exhibition continues.

★ Platoon/Kunsthalle
Nonhyeondong 97-22 (3447-1191, www. kunsthalle.com). Apgujeong station (line 3), exit 3. **Open** 11am-1am Mon-Sat. **Map** p252 M9.
A real out-there venue imported from Berlin, its shell made from dozens of interconnected cargo containers. On the inside: a bar serving German beer and snacks, a library of arty books, and a couple of floors' worth of art exhibitions. The latter are usually sponsored by major corporations but can be worth a look; it's not really worth coming here for the art alone, though.

Gay & Lesbian

Where the boys (and girls) are.

You probably won't hear the old 'there are no gay Koreans' mantra any more, thanks to a coterie of LGBT activists and entertainers, such as Hong Seok-cheon and Ha Ri-su. Since the 1990s, the nation's *iban* (queer) community has confronted a society constrained by ideological barriers old and new – from Confucian principles to evangelical Christianity. While South Korea has no history of laws banning homosexuality, most gay Seoulites, both foreign and domestic, keep mum about their sexual orientation at home and at work.

Seoul may not be a gay paradise, then, but that's not to say there's no gay culture: there are over 100 bars of various sizes and themes in the Jongno and Itaewon neighbourhoods (most catering to gay men), a loud and proud queer teen network and one of Asia's longest-running LGBT parades and film festivals.

ARTS & ENTERTAINMENT

NEIGHBOURHOODS

Generally, queer Seoul is packed into three neighbourhoods, each with a distinct vibe. Jongno's **Nagwondong** and **Donuidong** are the oldest. For decades, closeted gay men have congregated in nearly 100 intimate 'member club' bars tucked along narrow alleys. They're secret but not seedy; patrons order *anju* snacks with their booze and schmooze with the owner while queues form for the karaoke stage. Outside, scores of gay men migrate from cafés to a line of food tents outside Jongno 3-ga station (exits 3 and 6). There's also **Starmoon**, a café inside the Fraser Suites building (*see p107*), which draws a young crowd of gay and alternative locals.

In Seoul's premier foreign enclave, **Itaewon**, a curious mix of twentysomething Koreans, off-duty US military and English teachers mingle each weekend on a strip of bars and dance clubs on what's affectionately termed 'Homo Hill'. On summer afternoons, expect to see a conspicuously gay (and gym-fit) crowd of beach bums at the rooftop pool of the **Hamilton Hotel** (*see p106*).

Seoul's handful of lesbian cafés and bars are concentrated in the university areas of **Hongdae** and **Edae** and are strictly off-limits to men, gay or straight. Nearby **Sinchon** has an occasional bar or for gay men.

QUEER INFORMATION

English-language print and online resources about the queer Seoul scene are hard to come by.

The most reliable guide is a 40-odd page booklet published annually by the Korean HIV/AIDS awareness organisation iShap (792-0083, www.ishap.org). The Korean-language safe sex guide also includes maps with simple lists of bars and clubs for major Korean cities.

Net-savvy Koreans flock to queer online portals such as www.ivancity.com and www.tgnet.co.kr for chatting and dating, but registration is essentially limited to Korean nationals. Foreign sites like www.utopia-asia.com provide a frequently updated list of gay and lesbian establishments. For information about the annual Korea Queer Culture Festival (KQCF) parade and film festival, *see p163*.

BARS & CLUBS

Jongno

Bar 79

Donuidong 102 (3673-3478). Jongno 3-ga station (lines 1, 3 & 5), exit 5. Walk 100m, turn left & walk another 100m. **Open** *7.30pm-late daily.* **Map** *p247 G2/p255 G2.*
Opened by two friends, both born in 1979 (hence the name), this casual *soju* bar is popular with customers in their 30s. Much like the nine other tiny pubs that surround an intersection too narrow for vehicle traffic, Bar 79 (*'chill-gu'* in Korean) features just three tables and room for about six at the counter.

★ Bar Friends

*Nagwondong 88-2 (766-5334, http://gofriends.
co.kr). Jongno 3-ga station (lines 1, 3 & 5) exit 5.
Cross the street & turn right into the 1st alley.*
Open 6.30pm-4am daily. **Map** p247 G2/p255 G2.
Located in the shadow of the Nagwon Arcade, this
charming spot combines the best of Seoul's competing
gay bar cultures – the intimacy and friendliness of the
typical Jongno haunt, with stylish decor and freedom
to eschew expensive *anju* snacks. It makes for a comfortable atmosphere to drink a beer or cocktail alone
or with friends, it seats up to 45 (large by Jongno standards) and is one of the few gay bars outside of
Itaewon where you'll occasionally see non-Koreans.

★ Barcode

*2F Myodong 41-1 (3672-0940), Jongno 3-ga
station (lines 1, 3 & 5), across the street from exit
8.* **Open** 7.30pm-3am daily (later when busy).
Map p247 G2/p255 G2.
Opened in 2005, this was the first of Jongno's 'one-
shot' bars, where customers could order beer, wine or
cocktails without paying an obligatory ₩20,000 for
a fruit plate or grilled squid. This unpretentious place,
tailored to gay men in their 30s, is staffed by an affable
owner and bartender. Around 20% of the customers
are foreigners, half of them Japanese. Free Wi-Fi.

Blood G

*4F Nagwondong 218-1 (010 9557-9625). Jongno
3-ga station (lines 1, 3 & 5), exit 5.* **Open** 7.30pm-
late daily. **Map** p247 G2/p255 G2.
Just steps from the subway exit and up four flights
of stairs, this narrow cocktail bar, plastered in red
rose wallpaper, has a friendly feel, despite the
macabre name. It's usually packed at weekends.

The Cola

*B1 Nagwondong 178 (010 762-2822). Jongno
3-ga station (lines 1, 3 & 5), exit 5.* **Open** 7.30pm-
late daily. **Map** p247 G3/p255 G3.
New to the Jongno bar scene, this subterranean spot
may lack sophisticated decor, but it has gained an

ardent following for its great comfort food. There's
something about the smell of fried chicken that
makes one long for a couple of pints of draft beer.
They go well with the upbeat Korean pop music too.

Coyote

*2F Waryongdong 168-1 (070 8946-6448, http://
cafe.daum.net/coyote12). Jongno 3-ga station (lines
1, 3 & 5), exit 6. From the exit, turn left. Walk
200m just past the intersection.* **Open** 7.30pm-late
daily. **Map** p247 G2/p255 G2.
An unabashedly tacky cocktail bar serving an extensive menu of mixed drinks and shots. Enjoy them in
a velvet booth under portraits of Leonardo Dicaprio,
Jude Law and other Caucasian actors/models.

GQ

*2F Nagwondong 147 (010 4003-9192). Jongno
3-ga station (lines 1, 3 & 5), exit 5. Turn left
& left again at the 2nd alley.* **Open** 7.30pm-late
daily. **Map** p247 G2/p255 G2.
Just off the main drag in the heart of gay Seoul's
Nagwondong neighbourhood, GQ is one of a fair
number of bars that cater to bears. Free Wi-Fi and
a mounted LCD television accompany your cocktail.

Kooss

*Sojubang Alley, Donuidong (747-0311). Jongno
3-ga station (lines 1, 3 & 5), exit 5.* **Open**
7.30pm-late daily. **Map** p247 G2/p255 G2.
Among the tiny bars located in the warren of traditional *hanok* houses a few blocks off the main road,
Kooss is owned by an avuncular, bow-tied master
who chats easily with regular customers and newbies
alike. Decorated with vintage Coca-Cola and Chrysler
posters, it's a pleasant break from the typical scene.

Moro

*Donuidong 39-6 (010 3284-8697). Jongno 3-ga
station (lines 1, 3 & 5), exit 4.* **Open** 7.30pm-late
daily. **Map** p247 G2/p255 G2.
A stylish, two-storey bar in a piece of prime real
estate – beside the area's line of popular snack carts.

Bar Friends.

ARTS & ENTERTAINMENT

Customers, most in their early 30s, enter through the rusty brown exterior to order *soju*, whisky and cock-tailsm and a mandatory side dish.

★ Shortbus
Ehwa Building 3F, Myodong 175 (741-0036). Jongno 3-ga station (lines 1, 3 & 5), exit 3. **Open** 7.30pm-late daily. **Map** p247 G2/p255 G2.
One of the best recent additions to the Jongno scene, this third-floor bar is smartly designed, with half a dozen tables set against a row of large windows, a triangular bar and a concrete floor and ceiling. Bartenders speak English and Japanese.

Viva
B1 Jongno 3-ga 12-1 (765-3380, http://cafe. daum.net/barviva). Jongno 3-ga station (lines 1, 3 & 5), exit 2. **Open** 7.30pm-5.30am daily. **Map** p247 G3/p255 G3.
A nice but smoky destination off Seoul's main thor-oughfare. The basement bar pumps Madonna and Lady Gaga into a one-room bar that aggressively markets daily specials, such as salsa lessons and movie nights (bring your ticket stub for one free drink) to its thirtysomething patrons.

Wallpaper
Ikseondong 103 (745-2449). Jongno 3-ga station (lines 1, 3 & 5), exit 6. From the exit, reverse course & turn left. Walk 200m and turn left at intersection. **Open** 7.30pm-late daily. **Map** p247 G2/p255 G2.
Among the most popular of Jongno's many karaoke bars, this one combines a handsome venue and

customers with silver cocktail tables and disco balls. You'll need to arrive early if you plan to sing.

ITAEWON

Almaz
Itaewondong 136-6 (3785-0834). Itaewon station (line 6), exit 3. Turn right at 1st intersection, left at the next. **Open** 7.30pm-late daily. **Map** p251 H7.
One alley north of Homo Hill, this cocktail bar pro-vides a nice counter to the loud and raunchy vibe one block over. A garden entry leads to a dimly lit collection of couches and love seats with groups of handsome men shamelessly eyeing each other. The outdoor seating area is pleasant in warmer weather.

★ Always Homme
Itaewondong 136-40 (798-0578). Itaewon station (line 6), exit 3. Walk 100m & turn right. Take 2nd left. **Open** 8pm-4am Mon-Thur, Sun; 8pm-6am Fri, Sat. **Map** p251 H7.
There's a low-atmosphere at this cosy bar, typically packed at weekends with pre- or post-partiers. The owner, Paul, speaks English and shuttles back and forth between the bar and his Why Not? club (*see p180*) across the alley. The staff – including a tall ex-volleyball player-cum-drag queen – are naughty flirts.

★ Bar Bliss
Itaewondong 72-32 (749-7738, http://barbliss seoul.wordpress.com). Itaewon station (line 6), exit 4. Walk 100m, turn left & go down the stairs. **Open** 7pm-late daily. **Map** p251 G7.

Korea's Legal Trans-formation

All change.

South Korea isn't usually seen as a regional leader when it comes to protecting homosexual rights. But despite its reputation as a conservative society, the country's transgender population has won a series of important victories in the courts since the judiciary endorsed the first legal gender change in 2002, citing an individual's right to dignity and the pursuit of happiness.

The District Court ruling was significant because, while the Korean language generally lacks gender-specific pronouns, every South Korean national is assigned a 13-digit identification number that reveals their sex – a man's seventh number is always a 1 and a woman's is always a 2. Many forms ask for this number, and it can cause awkward or humiliating situations if the number and individual appear not to match. The court's ruling paved the way for transgender Koreans to change their

personal number on a case-by-case basis. Beyond the importance of simply recognising an individual's right to self-identify, however, an official change of sex also enables trans men and women to marry 'opposite sex' partners and makes FTM Koreans eligible and MTF exempt from South Korea's mandatory military service.

Many people attribute the legal gains made by trans Koreans to a prominent celebrity, Ha Ri-su, born Lee Kyung-yup. Ha created a stir with a provocative 2001 television ad that revealed she was biologically male. Her subsequent success as a model, singer and author has raised awareness of trans issues in Korea. Today, other trans figures and activist groups such as Jirung-e are continuing to push against transphobia among gays and straights, and for safer and more widely accessible sex reassignment surgery (SRS).

South Korea's first openly lesbian parliamentary candidate, Choi Hyun-Sook (left).

Why Not?

Itaewondong 137-4 (795-8193). Itaewon station (line 6) exit 3. Walk 100m & turn right. Take the second left. **Admission** ₩10,000 (incl 1 drink). **Open** 8pm-6am daily. **Map** p251 H7.

A dance soundtrack gives way to Korean pop songs and shockingly young patrons mount the stage to show off choreographed dance routines at ths well-known Homo Hill club. Low ceiling, dark interiors and a smoke machine contribute to a somewhat bizarre atmosphere.

Wunderbar

B1 Itaewondong 130-4 (795-2080). Itaewon station (line 6) exit 4. Walk away from Hamilton Hotel & take 1st right down the hill. **Open** 8pm-late daily. **Map** p251 G7.

The space formerly known as Fushigi has traded its moody dark decor for a bright and white look. Famous for its handsome and flirtatious staff, it's a spacious and well-apportioned venue that's a refreshing break from Itaewon's main drag of gay bars and clubs.

THE UNIVERSITY DISTRICT

★ Labris

8F Seogyodong 362-2 (333-5276, http://cafe. naver.com/labris). Sangsu station (line 6), exit 1. Turn around & turn left. Walk about 400m. Club is just before the Hongik University gate. **Open** 7pm-2am Mon-Thur; 7pm-5am Fri-Sun. **Admission** ₩12,000 cover (incl 1 drink & snacks).

Founded in 1997, Labris claims to be Korea's oldest lesbian bar. Classy but unpretentious, the mostly twentysomething clientele enjoy three levels of tables, private rooms and floor space for dancing. Especially busy at weekends, this women-only establishment advises groups to make a reservation at weekends.

Manyeo

1F Seogyodong 362-14 (337-3458, http://cafe. naver.com/mawoman). Sangsu station (line 6) exit 1. From the exit, turn around & turn left. Turn left again at the 3rd alley. Take the first left. **Open** 4.30pm-2am Mon-Thur, Sun; 4.30pm-5am Fri, Sat.

Korean for 'the witch', this girls-only lesbian lounge requires guests to call or send a text message ahead of their visit to ensure somebody lets you in. Once inside, lucky patrons can sit back and enjoy its comfortable environs.

Queer-Bar

B1 Changcheondong 33-17 (333-9225, www.queer-bar.com). Sinchon station (line 2), exit 2. Walk 300m. **Open** 8pm-5am daily. **Admission** ₩15,000 during special parties (incl 1 drink). **Map** p246 A4.

One of two gay bars in the university neighbourhood of Sinchon. The purple-themed Queer-Bar hosts weekend parties with foreign strippers and scantily-clad waiters.

DVD ROOMS & THEATRES

Pagoda DVD Theater

Pagoda Building, Donuidong 76 (744-6997, http://cafe.daum.net/yhy1537). Jongno 3-ga station (lines 1, 3 & 5), exit 5. **Open** 11am-2am Mon-Fri, Sun; 11am-6am Sat. **Admission** ₩5,000. **Map** p247 G2.

A handful of theatres and DVD rooms, most located near Tapgol (Pagoda) Park, provide a seedy venue to watch gay-themed porn flicks and to meet other men. This is one of the more famous ones.

SEX CLUBS

Euphemistically called 'saunas', most of these establishments have minimal (if any) spa-like facilities. They do, however, have dark rooms where men wander in, lie down and let their hands wander.

Equus

4F Ingwang Building, Hannamdong 736-15 (793-6227, www.equuszone.com). Itaewon station (line 6), exit 3. Walk about 350m. **Open** 24hrs daily. **Admission** ₩7,000 7am-7pm; ₩13,000 7pm-7am. **No credit cards**. **Map** p251 H7.

Seoul's most international gay 'sauna' has themed rooms (S&M, prison, and so on), a TV room and sleeping rooms on both floors. Private and group showers are available. Most customers are non-Koreans from other Asian countries.

Prince

3F Hansol Building, Donggyodong 185-18 (334-8245). Sinchon station (line 2), exit 8. Walk 300m. **Open** 24hrs daily. **Admission** ₩5,000 before 7pm; ₩10,000 after 7pm. **No credit cards**.

An easy-to-miss spot located on the road from Sinchon to Hongdae. A simple white sign above a staircase leads to a two-storey complex with showers, lockers and a TV room on the first level and a dozen floors for doubles and groups on the second floor. Most customers are Korean.

Watermill

3F Daeyeong Building, Banpo 1-dong 705-1 (545-9685, www.watermill.co.kr). Nonhyeon station (line 7), exit 4. **Open** 24hrs daily. **Admission** ₩7,000 7am-7pm; ₩13,000 7pm-7am. **No credit cards**. **Map** p252 K10.

A well-decorated single hallway with six curtained rooms with mats on the floor that can each accommodate four to eight people. Shower stalls include two glory holes but most action occurs in the rooms. Customers are almost exclusively young Koreans.

Music

Stepping out of the dark ages.

Music is very big business in Korea. The country's popular output, known as K-pop, has exploded overseas, with singers such as BoA and Rain becoming superstars in Japan, China and Southeast Asia. The same can't be said for alternative fare: rock 'n' roll, punk, jazz and other western genres have enjoyed brief waves of popularity, but local artists have failed to truly take hold at home, much less abroad. However, times may be changing: the nightlife district of Hongdae rocks every night to the sound of live music, and both the quantity and quality of local fare are increasing rapidly. Music festivals now take place each summer (*see p164*), and Korean acts are starting to be farmed out to major events abroad – a golden age may be nigh. For classical and traditional Korean music, *see pp194-198* **Performing Arts**.

ARTS & ENTERTAINMENT

JAZZ

All That Jazz

Itaewondong 68-17 (795-5701, www.allthat jazz.kr). Itaewon station (line 6), exit 1. **Capacity** 70. **Open** 9pm-1am Mon-Thur; 8.30pm-1am Fri; 7pm-2am Sat, Sun. **Admission** ₩5,000-₩10,000. **Map** p251 G7.

This was the first jazz club to open in Korea, in 1976, and has been a staple in the local jazz scene ever since. The country's top jazz musicians perform here regularly. Dinner is available, including the likes of pizza, pasta and risotto.

Club Evans

Seogyodong 407-3, Hongdae (337-8361, www.clubevans.com). Sangsu station (line 6), exit 1. **Capacity** 50. **Open** 7.30pm-2am daily. **Admission** ₩5,000-₩10,000.

The interior of this Hongdae jazz club, especially the yellow bricks that make up the back wall of the stage, makes this one of the most charming jazz clubs in Seoul. There are two sets each night: the first 9-9.50pm and the second 10-11pm. Performers range from jazz students to seasoned musicians. Food, snacks and drinks cost around ₩4,000-₩12,000. *Photo p182.*

La Clé

Samcheongdong 95-2 (734-7752). Anguk station (line 3), exit 1. **Capacity** 50. **Open** 6pm-1am daily. **Admission** ₩3,000.

This rustic jazz bar is located in a basement space in arty Samcheongdong. Its interior is decorated with such objects as old cameras, phonographs and typewriters – this has the effect of making the bar feel something like an old attic. Its cosy ambience makes it a great final destination after a day of shopping and gallery-hopping in the neighbourhood. Musicians perform seven days a week and often tend to be on the younger side. Appetisers, snacks and alcoholic drinks are available.

ROCK & POP

Badable

Donggyodong 18 (4454-2343). Hongik Univ. station (line 2), exit 8. **Capacity** 40-60. **Open** 7pm-11pm Wed-Sun. **Admission** ₩5,000-₩15,000.

'Badabie' is Korean for 'sea rain'. The owner opened this venue in this basement space some years ago to harbour the talents of local musicians. Bands from many different genres perform here, including rock, punk, folk and experimental, and most of the

---

INSIDE TRACK GIGS IN SEOUL

The **Korea Gig Guide** (www.koreagig guide.com) is a tremendously useful English-language resource for finding information about concerts in Seoul. The website also has a detailed map showing the exact location of many of Hongdae's live music venues.

Club Evans. *See p181.*

performers – as well as the audience members – are on the younger side. The interior is pleasingly makeshift, with the audience sitting on benches. Note that drinks are BYO.

Café Bbang
Seogyodong B1 327-18, Hongdae (010 8910-1089, www.cafe.daum.net/cafebbang). Hongik Univ. station (line 2), exit 8. **Capacity** 150. **Open** 6.30-11pm Wed-Sun. **Admission** ₩12,000-₩15,000.
One of the longer running venues in Seoul's indie scene, Bbang first opened its doors in Sinchon in 1994. The club has been based in Hongdae since 2004. A breeding ground for up-and-coming local rock, pop and folk acts, its laidback atmosphere, seated crowds and giant patchwork stage backdrop make it feel like you're hanging out in someone's rec room instead of a live music club.

Chunnyun Dongan Do
Dongsungdong 1-66 (743-5555, www.chunnyun.com). Hyehwa station (line 4), exit 2. **Capacity** 100. **Open** 5pm-3am daily. **Admission** ₩10,000.
This club, whose name means 'For a Thousand Years', has actually been around since the mid 1990s and is located in Daehangno, Seoul's main theatre district. Three local bands perform each night, and food is available, the likes of salads, pasta and steaks. Drinks are around the ₩8,000-₩10,000 mark.

Club Spot
Seogyodong B1 358-34, Hongdae (322-5956, www.cafe.daum.net/clubspot). Hongik Univ. station (line 2), exit 9. **Capacity** 230. **Open** 7-11pm Tue-Sun. **Admission** ₩10,000-₩15,000.
The place to go in Hongdae for punk. Although it delves into the realms of rock, hardcore and hip

hop from time to time, much of Spot's monthly programme focuses on celebrating Seoul's spiky haired and tattooed punks. Live gigs are held at weekends, and occasionally on weekdays as well.

Club Ta
Seogyodong B1 407-6, Hongdae (7621-7835, www.cafe.daum.net/liveclubta). Hongik Univ. station (line 2), exit 9. **Capacity** 200. **Open** 7pm-2am daily. **Admission** ₩10,000-₩20,000.
One of the nicer – and dare we say classier – looking live clubs in Hongdae. Weekends boast a wide range of top-notch rock, pop, folk, funk and bluesy sounds. The club's low stage can make it a bit challenging for people standing at the back to see what's happening during higher profile gigs.

DGBD
Seogyodong B1 395-17, Hongdae (322-3792, www.cafe.daum.net/dgbd). Hongik Univ. station (line 2), exit 9. **Capacity** 250. **Open** varies. **Admission** ₩10,000-₩20,000.
Local music aficionados still call DGBD by its original name, Drug. Drug was a very influential venue in establishing Seoul's indie music scene in the late 1990s. The club was renamed DGBD when it moved to its current location, and although it only features a handful of performances each month, it still remains one of the best live rock music clubs in Hongdae.

FF
Seogyodong B1 407-8, Hongdae (011 9025-3407, www.2005clubff.cyworld.com). Hongik Univ. station (line 2), exit 9. **Capacity** 300. **Open** 8-11pm Tue-Thur, Sun; 6pm-6am Fri, Sat. **Admission** ₩10,000-₩15,000.
Although nothing really stands out about FF, it's one of Hongdae's most popular live clubs. Nightly bills usually feature half-a-dozen (or more) rock and

punk bands. From 11pm to midnight on Friday and Saturday nights FF offers select cocktails for free.

Freebird

Seogyodong 364-22, 2F Geumsan Building, Hongdae (335-4576, www.clubfreebird.com). Hongik Univ. station (line 2), exit 9. **Capacity** 250. **Open** 7pm-1am Mon-Thur, Sun; 7pm-4am Fri, Sat. **Admission** ₩5,000-₩10,000.

Freebird caters mainly to rock and pop groups, but occasionally spotlights blues, folk, punk and electronic acts. Friday and Saturday nights often have an early show that starts at 8pm, and a late gig around 11pm.

Rainbow

Seochodong B1 1308-11 (3481-1869, www.club.cy world.com/peacerainbow). Gangnam station (line 2), exit 6. **Capacity** 100. **Open** 7pm-3am daily. *Gigs* 9pm Fri, Sat. **Admission** free. **Map** p252 L12.

An oriental-style bar, where patrons must remove their shoes and everyone sits on the floor, with a small pond, various percussion instruments for guests to bang away on, and psychedelic mushroom wall hangings. Rainbow has live gigs on Friday and Saturday nights (9pm). Performers range from newbie folk, pop and jazz acts to more seasoned Korean alt-rock veterans.

Sing Your Heart Out

Korean karaoke.

The Japanese invented the concept of the 'empty orchestra' in the early 1970s, and the world came to use the Japanese term – karaoke. It may surprise visitors to Seoul that today karaoke is more popular in Korea than in its country of origin. In fact, it wouldn't be much of an exaggeration to state that every single major road in the city has at least one *noraebang*, or 'singing room', and you'll certainly never be more than a short walk from one.

To westerners, karaoke means solo singers or small groups performing one by one at a bar or club, but in East Asia, the format is somewhat different. Here, the singing takes place in private: groups of friends or colleagues troop into a small room, which is equipped with a large television, a couple of microphones, and usually some tambourines or other form of percussion. Then, of course, there's the songbook – often as large as small phone directories. Most of the songs are, of course, Korean, but every *noraebang* songbook will feature a fair few foreign hits: not just English, but Chinese and Japanese too.

Noraebang rooms usually cost from ₩10,000 to ₩15,000 per hour; unless the place is particularly busy, you'll usually get a few songs' worth of free time tacked on to the end. Seoul's noraebang are near-uniform in nature, but **Luxury Su** (Seogyodong 367-39, 322-3111, www.skysu.com) in Hongdae has found particular renown. All its rooms have been decorated in a fascinating manner, and a few even have floor-to-ceiling windows facing the street – you'll be able to embarrass yourself in full view of Korea's busiest nightlife strip.

ARTS & ENTERTAINMENT

Luxury Su.

Rolling Hall

Seogyodong 402-22, Hongdae (325-6071, www.rollinghall.co.kr). Sangsu station (line 6), exit 1. **Capacity** 250 sitting, 600 standing. **Open** varies. **Admission** ₩15,000-₩70,000.

Rolling Hall hosts a wide range of both local and international performers of many different genres, including rock, metal, punk, hip hop, indie rock, pop, folk and experimental. Such international indie groups as Das Racist, Xiu Xiu, Lymbyc Systym and French Horn Rebellion have played here.

Sang Sang Ma Dang

Seogyodong 367-5, Hongdae (330-6212, www. sangsangmadang.com/concert). Hongik University station (line 2), exit 9. **Capacity** 350. **Open** Varies. **Admission** varies.

Located in the basement of the large Sang Sang Ma Dang arts and cultural complex, this first-rate live music venue boasts arguably the best sound and light systems in Hongdae. No beverages are sold here, so you may want to pick up something to drink at a nearby convenience store. In winter, the third floor of the complex hosts Label Market, an annual exhibition showcasing the wares of local indie artists. There are free acoustic performances each weekend during the event.

▶ *For more on Sang Sang Ma Dang, see p71.*

V-Hall

Seogyodong 356-1, Hongdae (338-0957). Hongik Univ. station (line 2), exit 9. **Capacity** 400. **Open** Varies. **Admission** ₩40,000-₩80,000.

This Hongdae club hosts a wide range of acts, raning from local Korean musicians to international acts such as the Whitest Boy Alive, CocoRosie, Caribou and Do Make Say Think. The venue sometimes operates a bar in the lobby just outside the performance hall.

Sounds of the City

All you need to know about some of the best Korean bands.

Vidulgi Ooyoo

Who are they? A rock quartet formed in 2003, Vidulgi Ooyoo (which means 'Pigeon Milk' in Korean) are one of Korea's most promising indie bands.

Who's in the band? It was started by Lee Jong-seok (guitar, vocals) and Sung Ki-hun (guitar, vocals), with Lee Yong-jun (drums) joining a month later. Ham Ji-hye (guitar, vocals) joined after her old band, Greenish Yellow, broke up, completing the line-up.

Why they're worth a look Vidulgi's performances take audiences into a dream-like world. In the words of guitarist/vocalist Jong-seok: 'We like our performance style to be like a Pink Floyd concept album. We love our music to be like a movie or drama… We transfer from one dream to another.' They play in shoegaze style, so called since it appears that the musicians are constantly gazing at their shoes as they make heavy use of their effects pedals.In 2011, the band was invited to perform at the revered South by Southwest Music Festival in Austin, Texas.

What to listen to *Aero* (2008), their first full-length album, and *Bliss.City.East* and *Vidulgi Ooyoo* (2010), a split EP the band did with the shoegaze band Bliss.City.East from Chicago.

EE

Who are they? EE are a 'total performance art group' that make use of a pop/electronica-based sound, augmented by fine art, fashion, dance and other elements of visual arts in their performances.

Who's in the band? The group consists of vocalist Lee Yun-jeong (who first debuted with Korean punk group Pippi Band) and her husband Lee Hyeon-jun, an installation artist and DJ.

Why they're worth a look EE are much more than a band; they're a performance art group and their colourful, high-energy acts are not only exciting, but usually heavy on pop culture commentary. Also, their music videos are eye-catching and feel as though they were made in another time. Check out the videos for 'Curiosity Kills' and 'High Color Music'. In 2011, the group was invited to perform at the famous Coachella music and arts festival in California.

What to listen to *Imperfect, I'm Perfect* (2009), their first full-length album. The album's title is a reference to Korea's K-pop scene in which most performers lip-synch when they perform, which EE view as a 'sad reality' that is contrary to the image of perfection the K-pop performers are trying to portray. EE disagree with this perfectionist attitude in music and believe that imperfection in music is perfection.

Apollo 18

Who are they? Post-hardcore and post-rock hybrid trio Apollo 18 have quickly emerged as one of the more

Yogiga Expression Gallery
Hapjeongdong 412-1 B1(3141-2603, www.yogiga. com). Hapjeong station (line 2), exit 4. **Capacity** 150. **Open** Varies. **Admission** free-₩15,000.
This welcoming, open-minded art space is rented occasionally for folk, rock and experimental music concerts, but it's best known for its monthly Bulgasari showcase, on the last Sunday of the month (4-7pm). This is an open-mic event of improv, avant-garde and noise music. The free event also occasionally includes painters, *butoh* dancers and belly dancers.

LARGE VENUES

Ax Korea
Gwangjangdong 319-33 (457-5114, www.ax-korea.com). Gwangnaru station (line 5), exit 2. **Capacity** 2,000. **Open** varies. **Admission** ₩99,000-₩110,000.

The sister venue of Shibuya Ax Hall in Tokyo, the Ax is known for having some of the best sound equipment of a larger venue in Korea, and has seating and standing room on two floors. Such acts as Jonsi, Mika, the Flaming Lips, MGMT, Corinne Bailey Rae, John Legend and Kesha have performed here, as well as a whole glut of K-pop stars.
▶ *Gwangnaru station is some way east of central Seoul, about half an hour from Jongno 3-ga.*

Olympic Park Gymnastics Arena
Bangidong 108-2 (410-1684). Jamsil station (lines 2 & 8), exit 10. **Capacity** 11,000 sitting or 12,000 standing. **Open** varies. **Admission** ₩80,000-₩200,000.
This is the only indoor venue in Korea with a 10,000-plus capacity and has welcomed such acts as Santana, Eric Clapton, Black Eyed Peas, Usher, Taylor Swift, Beyoncé, and big K-pop acts such as Rain and JYP.

exciting and innovative players in Korea's burgeoning underground rock scene.
Who's in the band Bassist Kim Dae-inn (who has also released solo music as Jellyboy), guitarist Choi Hyun-seok, and drummer Lee Sang-yun.
Why they're worth a look Apollo 18 were formed in the summer of 2008 and debuted with their post-rock *Red* EP in February 2009. In July of that year they issued the noisier, harder-edged full-length *[0]/The Blue Album*. In January 2010, they re-recorded an expanded version of *Red* and dropped the final piece of their three-disc 'colour' series, the instrumental *Violet*. Their ambitious decision to release three albums in 11 months was applauded by the local music industry. The group won the 2009 Hello Rookie prize, and captured Rookie of the Year at the 2010 Korean Music Awards. In 2009, they became the first band to perform at both of the country's premier summer music events, the Jisan Valley Rock Festival and the Incheon Pentaport Rock Festival (for both, *see p164*). In 2011, Apollo 18 completed their first American tour, playing a remarkable16 concerts in 13 days.
What to listen to Beautiful and powerful, *Red* is an epic listen from start to finish, while the equally strong *[0]/The Blue Album* has been heralded as one of the top Korean albums of the 2000s.

Chang Kiha and the Faces
Who are they? Folk rockers Chang Kiha and the Faces are one of the few local indie bands to be championed by the mainstream media and fans of commercial pop music.
What's their history? Formerly the drummer for modern rock group Nunco Band, Chang began penning solo material while completing his military service. He put out a three-song CD single called *Cheap Coffee* in 2008, and quickly garnered high praise for his insightful, witty lyrics and playful, deadpan delivery. The title track from the disc earned Song of the Year honours at the 2009 Korean Music Awards. Working with a backing band for his album proper, *Chang Kiha and The Faces' Living the Nothing Special Life* surfaced in 2009, and found immediate crossover success. The album has sold in excess of 40,000 copies.
Why they're worth a look Chang Kiha and the Faces are one of the top draws at local music festivals, attracting a mixed crowd of college students and older fans eager to sing along to the act's retro-tinged, folk rock cuts. And while his Korean lyrics are what endear him to the masses, Chang's strong stage presence and intentionally geeky dance choreographies make it fun for all to enjoy the band's live sets.
What to listen to *Living the Nothing Special Life*, Chang Kiha and the Faces' much-lauded full-length debut.

Nightlife

Where to party when the sun goes down.

With a string of posh new venues opening in recent years, Seoul doesn't miss a beat when it comes to partying the night away. From the affluent areas of Apgujeong and Cheongdam for those with money to burn and curves to flaunt, to Hongdae's vibrant streets that attract a much younger, trendier and more energetic crowd, the city has plenty on offer. The number of clubs and lounges is growing rapidly. One thing to keep in mind, though: bouncers at these venues grant access only to those who dress to impress – keep the cargo pants, caps, trainers and shorts tucked safely away at home.

CLUBS

Ark Lounge

Cheongdamdong 84-20 (515-9078). Apgujeong station (line 3), exit 2. **Open** 7pm-4am daily. **Admission** ₩30,000. **Map** p253 N8.

This trendy nightclub lounge has made quite a name for itself – partly thanks to the fact that the cover includes unlimited vodka shots. The horizontal light tubing along the club's walls contribute to a sleek overall style. The house DJs are excellent, and usually spin a collection of progressive and techno house to get the crowd going.

INSIDE TRACK
CLUB DAY & SOUND DAY

Hongdae is busy from dusk until dawn every single night of the year, but once a month it feels as if the whole city has come here to boogie. This is the rather oddly named **Club Day** (www.theclubday.co.kr), when clubbers can buy a ₩20,000 wristband at one of 21 Hongdae clubs – thereby getting free entry to the other 20. A great idea in theory, though in practice clubs are so packed that it's hard to enjoy more than two or three. The event takes place on the last Friday of each month. Less well known is **Sound Day**, which takes place on the third Friday of the month. ₩15,000 will buy you entry to nine live music venues – maps are handed out on the street.

Club Answer

Cheongdamdong 125-16 (548-7115). Cheongdam station (line 7), exit 13. **Open** 9pm-5am Fri, Sat. **Admission** ₩30,000, including 1 drink. **Map** p253 O8.

Located in the ultra-affluent area of Cheongdamdong, Club Answer is widely regarded among Seoulites as *the* place to get down, and with good reason – having had the likes of Kaskade, Paul van Dyke and Benny Benassi spin under its chandeliered ceilings, it is arguably the city's top electro-house club. Cocktails can run anywhere between ₩15,000 and ₩20,000. The VIP area on the second floor is elegant and spacious, with tables costing ₩400,000 (champagne set) or ₩520,000 (vodka and tequila set).

Club Cocoon

Seogyodong 364-26 (no phone). Hongik Univ. station (line 2), exit 9. **Open** 9pm-5am daily. **Admission** ₩15,000.

Hongdae already has a string of popular venues, so for a new club to really stand out from the crowd it has to bring something heavy to the table. Cocoon does just that. With great prices (cocktails range from ₩5,000 to ₩8,000) and one of the most progressive atmospheres in Korea, it remains one of the top draws north of the Hangang river. The club is always packed, especially in August when the venue hosts bikini parties on Friday and Saturday nights.

Club Eden

Ritz Carlton Hotel, Yeoksamdong 602 (6447-0042). Sinnonhyeon station (line 9), exit 4. **Open** 9pm-4am Mon-Thur, Sun; 9pm-6am Fri, Sat. **Admission** ₩30,000, incl 1 drink. **Map** p252 L11.

Opening its doors in December 2008, Club Eden took Korean clubbing to a whole new level. Located in Gangnam, beside the Ritz-Carlton, this incredibly opulent venue houses the city's biggest dancefloor. With a state-of-the-art sound system and elegant interior, Eden is the place of choice for serious party goers. No beatport top-100 dancefloor hits here, only tech house and minimalism. Drinks cost between ₩15,000 and ₩20,000 on the ground floor. Table packages start at ₩360,000 in the upstairs VIP area.

Club Heaven

Yeoksamdong 701-1 (9226-4470). Seolleung station (line 2), exit 5. **Open** 9pm-6am daily. **Admission** ₩30,000, incl 1 drink. **Map** p253 N11.

A relatively recent addition to the city's club circuit, Club Heaven opened its doors in February 2010. One of the top electronic music clubs in the capital, it employs state-of-the-art laser and sound systems to keep its audiophile clientele grooving all night. Some industry heavies have played sets here: Daride, Aaron Moss and Martin Solveig, to name but a few. Sleep isn't your thing? The VIP room – one of the largest in the city – turns into an after-hours club after 4am.

Club Mansion

Seogyodong 368-22 (no phone). Hongik Univ. subway (line 2), exit 6. **Open** 10pm-5am daily. **Admission** ₩20,000.

One of the city's newer venues, Club Mansion is an upscale lounge throughout the week and turns into a trendy club at weekends – the best of both worlds. A stylish interior, spacious bar and relatively cheap drinks make this place hugely popular among those looking for a place with a laid-back atmosphere. It also manages to rope in some pretty heavy hitters in the DJ industry.

Club Mass

Seogyodong 13-8 (599-9215). Gangnam station (line 2), exit 6. **Open** 9pm-6am daily. **Admission** ₩20,000.

Located in the young and affluent Gangnam area, Seoul's self-described 'premier electronic house music club' has a little more of an underground vibe than its larger neighbours, Club Eden and Club Answer. This venue features house and electro music, and regularly welcomes world-renowned DJs.

Club Volume

Crown Hotel, Itaewondong 34 69 (1544-2635, www.clubvolume.com). Itaewon station (line 6),

Club Eden.

ARTS & ENTERTAINMENT

exit 3. **Open** 9pm-6am. **Admission** ₩20,000 before 11pm; ₩30,000 after 11pm. **Map** p251 G8.
The Itaewon area has been making a name for itself of late. Once the stomping ground for a series of expat watering holes, it has since added some pretty swanky venues with more of an affluent vibe. In the basement of the Crown Hotel, this two-storey club has undergone significant renovations with impressive results. The intimate Grey Goose lounge grants great views of the dancefloor and DJ booth, and there's a larger bar on the first level to keep thirsty dancers happy into the late hours. House, electro and tech-house is on the menu for Fridays and Saturdays, with R&B and commercial house served up on Thursdays.

Lound Lounge

Cheongdamdong 83-13 (517-7412, www.74 lound.com). Apgujeong station (line 3), exit 3.
Open 7pm-4am daily. **Admission** Free.
Map p253 N8.
Hugely hyped, this lounge boasts four floors of floor-to-ceiling windows, electronic menus, transparent glass walling and see-through bathroom doors that change colour when you activate the lock. But with such über-extravagance comes über-high pricing. Drinks start at ₩40,000, so if money's no object, you'll be bound to impress. Well-known mixologist Kim Bong-ha dreamed up the impressive cocktail list. There's dining on the first floor.

Woo Bar

W Hotel, Gwangjangdong 21 (2022-0333).
Open 10am-2am Mon-Thur, Sun; 10am-3am Fri, Sat. **Admission** ₩20,000 before 11pm; ₩30,000 after 11pm.
Modern and highly stylish, the Woo Bar remains one of the largest open-space lounges in Seoul. If grabbing great views of the city and chilling among friends in a stunning interior while nursing a signature mojito is your thing, then this is the place for you. Cocktails start at ₩20,000 and the management usually hosts DJ parties and a host of themed events at weekends. Many big names on the global DJ circuit have spun here.
▶ *There are free shuttle buses to the W Hotel every 20mins from Gwangnaru station (line 5).*

A Korean Night Out

Station to station.

Seoul's nightlife scene is becoming more and more western with each passing year – clubs pulse with house and hip hop rhythms, beer and cocktails are the drinks of choice, and old-fashioned Confucian conservatism is slowly going out the window. However, spend a few evenings with some local friends, and you'll surely encounter the old Korean way of going out, which involves stops at hazily defined 'stations'.

Station one is known in Korean as *ilcha*, and usually takes place immediately after work. Socialising with colleagues is an almost obligatory part of office life in Korea, and can even take place on weekend evenings – even in the country with the world's longest working hours, companies see nothing wrong with intruding on their employees' precious free time. *Ilcha* usually takes place at a restaurant, though even here the alcohol flows freely; barbecued meat and *soju* is a long-time favourite combination.

Then it's time for **station two**, known as *icha*. The group, minus a couple of drop-outs (typically those needing to catch trains or buses to the suburbs), will usually head to another restaurant. Alcohol is now the priority, though the purchase of food is still compulsory: traditionally, Korea had no places serving alcohol alone, though times have changed a little now. The most common place for an *icha* is a *hof* – Korea's slightly bizarre take on a pub. Tables are arranged so that the group sticks together; there's no common area, and as such it's almost impossible for an outsider to sneak in. Snack-meals known as *anju* are shared among the group – usually western-style 'fusion' dishes. Beer is the drink of choice, and it's served communally from large plastic tankards; ranging from two to five litres in size, these are often decked with flashing LEDs, and spouting dry ice.

Samcha, or **station three**, is usually the end of the road. This can take place at yet another *hof* or restaurant, though it's also common to head to karaoke-style singing rooms known as *noraebang*. Most of these don't serve alcohol, but most of those that do will also be able to provide ladies to join in the sing-song – a popular add-on if the group has become all-male, and not always totally above board.

It can be hard to remember what other stations there are, though they certainly exist: in certain parts of Seoul, it's possible to see two very different kinds of businessfolk in the mornings – those heading to work, and those finishing up another wild night out.

Sport & Fitness

Global favourites, with a few Asian twists.

Busy Seoul may not seem like the easiest place in which to exercise, but the slender frame of its average inhabitant is not down to diet alone. The city has a wealth of ways in which to keep fit, and has substantial spectator pedigree too, having hosted both the world's two largest sporting events – the World Cup and the Olympic Games. Indeed, it may come as a surprise to know that Korean national teams have performed pretty well in these events: they reached the semi-finals of the World Cup in 2002 and won baseball gold in the 2008 Games. There are thriving local leagues for both football and baseball, and fervent crowds make games quite a spectacle. For something completely different and uniquely Korean, it would be a shame to leave Seoul without a visit to a *jimjilbang*: spa-like affairs that provide a fascinating window on local society.

SPECTATOR SPORTS

Athletics

Korea hosts several marathons (*see p162*) as well as an **IAAF World Challenge** event, which takes place each May in Daegu, about two hours south-east of Seoul by high-speed train.

Baseball

The **Korea Professional Baseball League** has been in operation since 1982, and now has eight teams, and a season running from March to October. Three of the KPBL's teams hail from Seoul: the **Doosan Bears** (www. doosanbears.com), **LG Twins** and **Nexen Heroes**. In addition, the **SK Wyverns** (http://eng.sksports.net) play in the adjacent city of Incheon. The Bears and the Twins are by far the best-supported teams in the city, and both play home games at the **Jamsil Baseball Stadium**. The Wyverns were the country's most successful team in the years following the turn of the millennium, winning the championship in 2007, 2008 and 2010, and finishing as runners-up in 2009. Most players are Korean, although each team has one or two mavericks from the American leagues.

There's baseball on TV most days of the week. Tickets for games are usually very cheap, starting at around ₩5,000.

Jamsil Baseball Stadium

Jamsildong (2240-8864). Sports Complex station (line 2), exit 6. **Capacity** 30,500. **Tickets** ₩6,000 and up. **Map** p253 H10.

The Jamsil Baseball Stadium sits next door to the Seoul Olympic Stadium, and both were host venues for the Summer Games in 1988. Since it's the home of not one but two major teams – the Bears and the Twins – you can expect to find a game here most days during the season.

Football

Football played second fiddle to baseball until 2002, when South Korea co-hosted the FIFA World Cup with Japan. The fact that the national team performed so well in this tournament – losing to Germany in the semi-final – was a boon to the local **K-League** (www.kleague.com), with 16 teams and a season running from late February to December.

Four K-League teams play in and around Seoul. **FC Seoul** (www.fcseoul.com) are the only team in the centre of the city, while **Seongnam Ilhwa** play in the southern suburbs. **Suwon Bluewings** (www.blue wings.kr) and **Incheon United** play in their respective cities, both easily accessible from Seoul. FC Seoul won their first league title in 2010; the preceding decade had been dominated by Suwon and Seongnam, who won seven titles between them. All have competed in the **Asian**

ARTS & ENTERTAINMENT

Champions League (www.the-afc.com), an event won as often as not by Korean teams.

Tickets for games start at ₩10,000. Drinks and snacks are widely available in and around the grounds.

Seoul World Cup Stadium

Seongsandong (2128-2002). World Cup Stadium station (line 6), exit 2. **Capacity** 69,000. **Tickets** from ₩10,000.

Home to FC Seoul, this superb stadium hosted three games in the 2002 World Cup, including South Korea's semi-final defeat. It rarely fills up for league games, and tickets are always available on the door.

Golf

The **Woo Jeong Hills** course hosts a major event on the men's OneAsia tour (www.korea open.com). Some top players came to compete: Sergio Garcia won in 2002, John Daly in 2003 and Vijay Singh in 2007. It's near Cheonan, a city half an hour south of Seoul by high-speed train, and also accessible on subway line 1.

Horse Racing

Races are held on weekends at **Seoul Race Park**, a circuit accessible from Seoul Racecourse Park station on subway line 4. Gambling is technically illegal in Korea, but this is one of the few exceptions to the rule; you'll also be able to watch live feeds from Korea's other two major tracks, and bet on them too. There's a pretty good blog about horse racing in Korea at http://korearacing. wordpress.com.

Ice Hockey

The **Asia Ice Hockey League** (www. ailhockey.com) started life in 2003, and has seven teams. Two are Korean, but neither play in central Seoul – **Anyang Halla** play in the southern suburbs, and **High1** play in the city of Chuncheon, an hour east of Seoul by bus or train. The season runs from September to February.

Martial Arts

The **Kukkiwon** (www.kukkiwon.or.kr) is Korea's main taekwondo centre, but there's rarely much going on at their oversized Gangnam headquarters. Still, pop along and you may get lucky.

Motor Sports

Korea hosted its first **Formula One** race in 2010 at a circuit near Mokpo, a city three

hours south-west of Seoul by high-speed train. Fernando Alonso was the victor on that occasion. The inaugural race was held in October, but this being F1, all can change – see www.koreacircuit.kr for more information.

Tennis

The **Korean Open** (www.hansolopen.com) is a major event on the women's WTA circuit. It's held at Olympic Park each September; to get here head to Olympic Park station (line 5), exit 3.

ACTIVE SPORTS & FITNESS

Baseball

Baseball batting nets are dotted around Seoul, usually costing just ₩1,000 for a dozen balls – these are fired from a machine, and you'll be able to adjust the speed to suit your ability. One highly popular facility is at the southern end of Insadonggil.

Bowling

LCI Bowling

Myeongdong 6-1 (771-2345). Myeongdong station (line 4), exit 3. **Open** 10am-midnight daily. **Tickets** ₩3,000; *shoe hire* ₩1,000. **Map** p247 F3. Simple facilities in the centre of Seoul.

Lotte World

Jamsildong 40-1 (411-4591). Jamsil station (lines 2 & 8), exit 4. **Open** 10am-midnight daily. **Tickets** ₩3,600; *shoe hire* ₩1,500. Large, American-style complex forming part of the gigantic Lotte World complex.

Pierrot Strike

Cheongamdong 85-4 (6007-8008). Apgujeong station (line 3), exit 2. **Open** 10am-midnight daily. **Tickets** ₩5,000; *shoe hire* ₩1,500. Futuristic complex whose alleys are lit with ultra-violet lights.

Cycling

Seoul has grand plans to line the city with bike lanes – a bold endeavour but, given construction schedules and dangerous roads, one that will take some time to come to fruition, if it does at all. However, there are already good bike lanes running along the banks of the Hangang – much of this stretch has been given a park-like makeover, though the highways racing overhead do spoil the atmosphere somewhat.

Bikes can be rented by the hour (₩3,000) from several points along the river. The best and easiest to access is on Yeouido, just down the steps from exit 2 of Yeouinaru station (line 5).

Football

The **Seoul Sunday Football League** (www.ssflkorea.com) has expanded to three divisions, and most teams are almost entirely made up of foreigners. The standard is generally quite high – basically, if you haven't played organised team football before, you're unlikely to get a game.

Gyms

There are fitness centres in most higher-end hotels, though some charge nominal fees for their use. Those staying in Seoul for some time can make use of local gyms – monthly membership rates tend to run from ₩50,000 to ₩80,000, though you'll pay a little more at places equipped with swimming pools. Ask a tourist information office for the closest one to you. Lastly, you'll find simple exercise equipment dotted around the city; such

ARTS & ENTERTAINMENT

Getting Steamy

In at the deep end.

There are few more enjoyable places in which to get a grip on contemporary Korea than the *jimjilbang*. A curious mix of sauna, spa and entertainment facility – and also doubling up as the country's cheapest form of accommodation – these are unique. Most follow the same tried-and-trusted format, so follow the guidelines below and you should look like a regular.

First, put your shoes into a locker, and pay the entry fee: typically around ₩5,000 for the pools and sauna rooms alone, or ₩8,000 if you want to use other facilities or stay the night. Those choosing the latter course of action will be given a T-shirt and a pair of shorts, for use later. Then it's into the changing rooms, which are segregated by gender; here you lock all clothing away, and wander naked into the pool area. After showering, you're free to take your pick of sauna rooms, steam rooms and a variety of pools – some ice-cold, some turned green from gigantic teabags. Those with T-shirts and shorts can put them on and make their way up to the common area; it's a little like pre-school for grown-ups, given the facilities and kindergarten-like attire. Here you'll find a snack bar or restaurant, coin-operated internet terminals, televisions, ice-cold chill rooms, and sometimes even a karaoke room or two (this is Korea, after all). Those wanting to sleep or rest can grab a cushion-like futon and hunt down the quiet room. You can head back to the pools and saunas any time you like, since they're open around the clock – they're particularly refreshing in the morning.

Those who venture into a *jimjilbang* will have to follow a few rules of etiquette. First, it's essential to wash thoroughly before entering the water – the showers are easy to spot, and all have bars of

soap. You'll get extra points for using the abrasive scrubbing flannels, usually located by the door on the way from the changing rooms to the showers. The second major point to note regards entry into the water – diving into the pool is a big no-no. Follow the Korean lead and in no time at all, you'll be relaxing in the most local way possible.

There are *jimjilbang* all over Seoul, and facilities are fairly standard across the board; any local will point you to your nearest one. The most notable facility in town is the gigantic **Dragon Hill** (792-0001), just outside the main entrance of Yongsan train station.

Taekwondo

The world's most popular martial art is Korean.

Taekwondo is based on a belief that, in accordance with the principle of kinetic energy, all movement should be designed to produce maximum power. However, for a sport with such scientific theory behind it, its origins remain shrouded in mystery. Some say that it was a mix of Chinese and Japanese martial arts, others that it was an evolution of traditional Korean forms, suppressed during the Japanese occupation of Korea. Whatever the truth of taekwondo's origins, it officially came into being in the early 1950s, when President Rhee Seungman declared that nine competing systems be integrated as one.

The Korea Taekwondo Association (KTA) was founded in 1960 and assigned many of its masters around the world to teach the new form. Meanwhile, with the sport still in disharmony, two new bodies came into being: in 1966 the International Taekwondo Federation (ITF) was founded, followed by the World Taekwondo Federation (WTF) in 1973. Today, the latter has around 70 million practitioners and a presence in over 192 countries – as many as the United Nations. Taekwondo became an official Olympic sport at the Sydney Games in 2000, the only other martial art besides judo to have an Olympic presence.

Taekwondo is often called the 'kicking' martial art, but it's certainly not limited to kicking. A part of its ideology or credo is that the martial art is to be used only for self-defence, or to serve justice. Unlike many sports that focus solely on physical conditioning, violence and brute force, taekwondo prioritises the balance of mind, body and soul. The soul part comes into play with a strong focus on relaxation and meditation, while conscientiously being a student of respect, discipline, etiquette and justice. Meanwhile, physically, taekwondo focuses on speed, balance, flexibility, precision and strength. And to achieve these, the mental qualities of concentration, focus and technique are critical. It's believed that a marriage of these three areas is necessary to be a good practitioner of taekwondo.

Training takes place in three main areas. First is *pumsae* or 'forms', a systematic series of motions or techniques. These are used as interval training and conditioning to develop mental and physical fortitude.

Then there's *gyeorugi*, also known as sparring, which is what you see in the Olympics. Lastly, there's *gyeokpa*, also known as 'breaking'. Here practitioners often combine their mental and physical strength to break bricks, ice, wooden planks and other items, to demonstrate focus and strength. Grading a practitioner on a combination of these abilities is currently done at the Kukkiwon in central Seoul, which houses administrative staff and certifies instructors and practitioners with *dan* or *pum* certificates. *Dan* is the belt grading system, and *pum* is a grading system for under-16s. There are generally only nine *dans*; a tenth is awarded very occasionally, sometimes posthumously. Holders of the first to fifth black belt are known as masters; those who obtain the sixth to ninth are grandmasters.

Taekwondo has generally kept a low profile in the media, but this hasn't prevented it from becoming the world's most followed martial art. And, in this era of mass media, the WTF plans to launch a series of high profile-initiatives that will catapult taekwondo into the mainstream, while striving to keep a strong foothold in traditional values and beliefs.
The writer, Stream Lee, is director of international business development at the World Taekwondo Federation.

facilities are free to use, open all hours and primarily used by older locals. The best places to find them are on the slopes of Namsan, and the Hangang riverbanks.

Ice Skating

There are a few good ice skating rinks in Seoul. The city also opens up free public facilities in the winter – **Gwanghwamun Plaza** and **Seoul Plaza** both find themselves criss-crossed by legions of merry skaters.

Korea University Ice Skating Rink

Anamdong 1-85 (3290-4243). Korea University station (line 6), exit 2. **Open** 2pm-6pm daily. **Tickets** ₩5,000.

Just a short trek from central Seoul, this ice rink is particularly popular with students from the area's many universities.

Lotte World Ice Skating Rink

Jamsildong 40-1 (411-4591). Jamsil station (lines 2 & 8), exit 4. **Open** 10am-10.30pm daily. **Tickets** ₩13,000.

Large rink able to accommodate 1,000 skaters at a time. It's yet another component of the huge Lotte World complex.

Martial Arts

Seoul city has, in the past, laid on **taekwondo** lessons for foreigners in **Namsangol Hanok Village** – surely one of the most atmospheric places imaginable to study martial arts – every Wednesday and Saturday, except for July and August. Phone 3469-0134 for information. Longer programmes are best organised before arrival – your own national taekwondo or **kendo** (known as *komdo* in Korean) federation will be able to help out.

Rugby

Rugby union is increasing in popularity in Korea, whose national team are usually in the top division of the Asian Five Nations. There are two clubs in the city – **Seoul Survivors** for boys (www.survivorsrfc.com) and **Seoul Sisters** for girls (www.ssrfc.com). They both take part in occasional tournaments, though to join the teams you'll need to be resident in Seoul. However, visitors are welcome to join for weekend practice.

Running

Seoul hosts a **marathon** in March each year, and it's open to the public for an entry fee of ₩40,000. There's another one in October in Gongju (*see p215*), a small city to the south

of Seoul . For more details, see http://marathon.donga.com. For less Olympic distances, the banks of the Hangang are good places for a jog – finding other places to run in the city is tough. Most higher-end hotels have fitness centres with running machines.

Skiing & Snowboarding

There are a fair few ski resorts in the Seoul area; the season usually runs from late November to February. Prices vary depending upon the duration of stay, the time of day, and sometimes even the day of the week – expect to pay in the region of ₩60,000 for a day pass, and ₩40,000 for a part-day pass. Ski or board rental is typically ₩10,000 to ₩15,000.

It's possible to visit any of the following places on a day trip from Seoul, though each resort has accommodation if you'd like to stay the night – booking ahead will certainly be a good idea in winter.

Bears Town

Pocheon City, Naechonmyeon (031 540-5000, www.bearstown.com). **Open** 9am-4am daily.

A large complex that's particularly good for beginners and families – lessons are available, and there's a long sledding hill. There are also more advanced courses, with the 88 Challenger slope by far the most exciting. Also note that it's possible to ski at night.

Jisan Forest Resort

Icheon City, Majangmyeon (031 638-8460, www.jisanresort.co.kr). **Open** 7am-4am daily.

Set in a pine forest 40 minutes from Seoul, this is the most modern facility in the area, with high-speed ski lifts, luxurious condominiums and state-of-the-art snow management systems. Also offers night skiing.

Star Hill Resort

Namnyangju City, Hwado-eup (031 594-1211). **Open** 9am-10.30pm daily.

This resort is located amidst bucolic mountain scenery – yet is only 33km (20 miles) from Seoul, making access a doddle. It's not terribly well set up for foreign visitors, but things are improving.

Yangji Pine Resort

Yongin City, Yangjimyeon (031 338-2001, www.pineresort.com). **Open** 9am-5am daily.

The home of the national skiing championships, this resort also has a wealth of beginners' courses. Night skiing is available, and the facilities are all top-notch.

Water Sports

In the summer, it's possible to get some **jet-ski** action along the Hangang. These cost ₩20,000 per hour to hire, from the park off the northern end of Banpo Bridge.

ARTS & ENTERTAINMENT

Performing Arts

A full roster of spectacular dance and music.

Seoul has a number of important performing arts venues, from gigantic multipurpose complexes to tiny speciality theatres. Although many of its performing arts traditions have been threatened and even become extinct during periods of political upheaval and war, modern Seoul is home to a vibrant theatre scene, impressive musical performances and well-preserved traditional arts performances. Whether looking for mainstream hit musicals, world-class classical music, cutting-edge experimental theatre or the plaintive sounds of traditional *pansori*, Seoul has plenty to offer. For jazz, rock and pop music, *see pp181-185* **Music**.

TICKETS & INFORMATION

Expat magazines *Groove* and *10* both have monthly listings of notable performances, as does the city-affiliated *Seoul Magazine*. Major English-language dailies also usually have information, as do major websites such as Korea4Expats and the Seoul City Blog. Tickets can be bought at venues' box offices, online, or by telephone from ticketing agencies. Leading online vendors include www.ticketlink.co.kr and www.interpark.com, but these can be difficult for non-Koreans to access; you can also make reservations with a foreign credit card at www.visitseoul.net. Another good option is to go through Sejong Belt, an umbrella organisation for 30 different venues, with offices in Gwanghwamun station.

Traditional Korean Performing Arts

Korean performing arts are sadly and undeservedly not as well known as those of neighbouring China and Japan. With everything from slow, elegant court dances to the astounding and evocative vocal techniques of *pansori* singing and the earthy and satirical humour of mask dance dramas, Korea has a remarkable range of arts traditions. Many of these forms have an immediacy of emotion and grace that makes them entrancing and draws people in despite language barriers. While even Koreans have trouble understanding some of the

antiquated language of *pansori* drama, there's no mistaking the deep emotions on display, nor could anyone fail to enjoy the tomfoolery of the indigenous mask dances or be thrilled by the pounding drums of *samulnori*. Court music and dance may not have as much immediate appeal, but do have an undeniable grace and a profound sense of ritual.

In general, Korean performance arts can be divided into those for the court and upper classes and earthier folk performances. The arts that emerged from Korea's ruling aristocracy and court are some of the last vestiges of both a way of life and a political system that was obliterated with the Japanese colonisation and subsequent Korean War. Slow, sometimes even ponderous, their tempo can make them difficult to appreciate at first, but pieces take on a remarkable meditative quality. In contrast, folk performances such as mask dance dramas and *samulnori* – 'farmers' music' – are robust and fast-paced.

There is also a wide variety of religious performances, including Confucian rituals and music and Buddhist and shaman dances. The last of these is particularly colourful, with the shaman taking on new identities and costumes and sometimes performing 'magical' feats such as dancing barefoot on knife blades.

COURT MUSIC & CONFUCIAN RITUAL

Perhaps the most difficult for the casual observer to enjoy, Korean court music was strongly influenced by Confucianism. Measured and slow, it reflects the religion's philosophical

Pansori Rhythms

The story's in the song.

Pansori is a unique form of Korean traditional music that became popular in the 19th century and is still performed today. This exceptionally expressive and emotive form of singing involves a solo performer, called a *soriggun*, who is accompanied by a *gosu*, or drummer. Together, they narrate stories of romantic love, tragedy and filial piety.

Traditionally, *pansori* had a set repertoire of 12 songs, but only five are still being performed today. A full performance of a single story can take up to half a day to complete, but most recitals nowadays are condensed. The singer takes on all the roles and changes their voice, posture and style to reflect the different characters and situations, with an emphasis on portraying emotions. The way each piece is performed also depends on the audience, with a good singer able to read those watching and play up the elements that go down best. Meanwhile, the audience participates by calling out words of encouragement – it's remarkably interactive.

The five stories that are performed are almost all based on Korean folktales, including the romantic favourite *Chunhyang*, which tells of a *gisaeng* who falls in love and marries a high-ranking scholar; *Shimcheong*, the tale of a daughter who sacrifices herself for her blind father and marries a dragon king; and the humorous song of *Heungbu*, a poor but kind man who gets cheated by his evil brother. Along with the *Song of the Red Cliffs* (based on a Chinese tale) and the *Tale of the Dragon King of the Southern Sea*, these stories form the core of most *pansori* performances. Singers learn either the more elaborate *seopyeonjae* 'western' version or simpler *dongpyeonjae* 'eastern' style of each by repeating the song after their teacher. These teachers were often their own parents, and families would travel and perform together.

In the 1970s and '80s the Korean government worked to preserve the tradition, which had been in danger of dying out. While government intervention helped save *pansori*, it might not have done much for its traditional spontaneity and improvisational aspects. However, famed director Im Kwon-taek's masterful film *Seopyeonjae* helped bring more attention to *pansori*, leading to renewed interest from the Korean public. Today, *changjak pansori* – modern compositions that use traditional styles of singing – sit alongside traditional *pansori*. Many of these modern works address the problems of contemporary life and society, using modern Korean to make the songs more accessible to audiences.

ARTS & ENTERTAINMENT

The World of the Gisaeng

Old Korea's cultured courtesans.

Dating back at least to the 11th century, *gisaeng* were a special class of female government slaves who worked principally as entertainers and courtesans. Similar in some ways to Japanese geisha, *gisaeng* were often highly educated and skilled in a variety of areas, able to sing, dance, play instruments and compose poetry. Although they've vanished from modern Korea, their influence on the culture remains.

Most *gisaeng* were either the daughters of *gisaeng*, inheriting the status, or sold into service by poor families. Training at a *gisaeng* school could begin as young as eight, learning to sing, dance, play music, read and write, compose poems and entertain. *Gisaeng* were among the most literate women of their times, and many were renowned for their poetry. Because of their youth (careers peaked in the late teens), intellect, accomplishments and beauty, they have often featured as heroines in popular entertainment, including *pansori*, novels and paintings.

While the majority of *gisaeng* served as court entertainers or at government posts in the provinces, others worked as seamstresses or doctors. They usually retired in their twenties, although this depended on their role and location. Most *gisaeng* had a strong relationship with a particular client or patron, who would help provide for them. The luckiest were able to attach themselves to rich men, who could then buy their contracts and keep them as mistresses or second wives. Many, however, went on to manage local taverns or inns after they were no longer able to entertain.

Gisaeng were some of the most visible and public women in society during the Joseon Dynasty; for a few, their particular intellect, achievements and artistic ability brought fame. One of the best known is Hwang Jini (1520-60). Although many of her works of music and poetry have been lost, the remaining pieces are considered some of the best works of the age. She has become something of a feminist icon for modern Koreans, and has been portrayed in film, opera and TV dramas. Nongae became one of Korea's folk heroes by killing a Japanese general during the Hideyoshi invasion of 1593 during an entertainment session next to the Nam river by embracing him and then jumping off a cliff, dragging them both to their deaths.

Nongae was not the only *gisaeng* to make her mark in national issues. They were often engaged in politics, and were active as spies and supporters of various factions. Many were also involved in the independence movement in the early 20th century. Although no active, classically trained *gisaeng* remain today, they live on in the Korean imagination, and are accorded respect for their role in the development of traditional Korean arts.

emphasis on propriety. Performers often wear elaborate traditional court dress, including gorgeously embroidered chest and shoulder patches, and the dancers in particular are spectacularly costumed. While the best place to experience court music and dance is the **National Gukak Center** (*see p197*), for sheer scale, nothing surpasses the Jongmyo Jeryeak. This revival of Confucian ritual for the royal kings and queens of the Joseon dynasty takes place annually on the first Sunday in May at Jongmyo shrine (*see p56*) in downtown Seoul. The ritual has been declared a UNESCO Masterpiece of the Oral and Intangible Heritage of Humanity. It involves a full traditional orchestra and no fewer than 64 different dances.

RELIGIOUS MUSIC AND DANCE

Buddhist music and dance have an even longer history in Korea. Buddhist chants are still commonly performed daily in temples around the country. More elaborate dances and rituals are still performed on hallowed ground, but also brought to wider audiences in traditional performance venues around the city. Graceful and meditative, they clearly reflect Buddhism's emphasis on peace and harmony. Buddha's Birthday (*see p163*) often brings larger outdoor performances of these dances and rituals.

Korea's native animistic shamans (*see p57*) also have their own sets of chants and dances, some of which have found their way into the repertoires of mainstream traditional performances. The shaman dances in a distinctive, often spectacular way, tending to start slowly and become more and more frantic, reflecting the state of ecstasy that real shamans experience during rituals. While shamanism has suffered suppression and has seemed to have disappeared from Seoul's urbane, modern lifestyle, shaman ceremonies, called *gut*, can still be seen on occasion (particularly on Mt Inhwang, a major centre for Korean shamanism). Many shamanistic dances have been preserved and can be seen as part of traditional performances.

MASK DANCES

Often originating from shamanistic rituals, Korea has a vibrant tradition of masked folk dances. These often satirised the upper classes and religious figures, skewering their self-importance and mocking their hypocritical behaviour. Bickering aristocrats and lewd monks are common characters, along with beautiful maidens, randy widows and village idiots. Along with the earthy humour (one famed dance includes a bull that urinates on the audience before being felled and having its testicles auctioned off) there's a strong religious element, with some dancers taking on the role of village gods and goddesses or representing smallpox and other dangers. The dances were often part of ceremonies to expel demons and bring good luck.

Dancers wear colourful costumes, and the masks are usually made of paper or gourds that are ritually burned at the end of the performance. However, the Andong region uses wooden masks that have been preserved and passed down through the generations; replicas have become popular souvenirs.

PANSORI

See p195 **Pansori Rhythms**.

SAMULNORI & FOLK SONGS

Samulnori music includes four percussion instruments: the kkwaenggari (a small gong), jing (large gong), janggu (hourglass drum), and buk (barrel drum). Led by the kkwaenggari player, who sets the tempo, the four instruments pound out complex rhythms. While stage versions often have the players seated, outdoor performances are usually staged so that the players can move around, leaving room for some very vigorous dancing. Samulnori's older sister, nongak (farmers' music) often adds wind instruments to the mix and can also be seen both on stage at traditional theatres and as part of rural events and festivals. These forms have had a strong influence on many contemporary and popular fusion performances.

Korea's variety of folk music, usually classified by region, is wide. Songs are usually simple and bright, but they convey deep meaning. Many songs have improvised passages, where the singer is expected to spontaneously create a new verse. The influence of these songs can be felt in more modern musical forms, such as the intriguing hybrid 'trot' music, and even in contemporary pop music. Everyone from hip-hop artists to K-pop groups have found that a few bars of indigenous music lend their songs a distinctive Korean touch.

VENUES

Chongdong Theater

Jongdong 8-11 (751-1500). City Hall station (line 1 & 2), exits 1 & 12. **Tickets** From ₩30,000. **Map** p247 F3.

This theatre, beside Deoksogung Palace, hosts the fusion musical *Miso*, which combines a variety of different traditional musical styles, including *samulnori* and *pansori*, to tell the romantic tale of Chunhyang, a *gisaeng* who falls in love with a nobleman.

Gareheon

Sindang 1-dong 387-2 (232-5749). Cheonggu station (lines 5 & 6), exit 1. **Tickets** ₩40,000, incl dinner. **No credit cards. Map** p248 K4.

One of Seoul's most unusual venues, visitors will be surprised to find themselves walking into an old-fashioned Korean home filled with antiques, despite an incongruous location on the fifth floor of an industrial building. Evenings begin with a home-cooked meal, before moving to the small theatre space. The idiosyncratic performance schedule can include everything from pantomime to Buddhist dance to *gayageum* (Korean zither) music to modernised *pansori*. The owner is a skilled singer himself, and the evening usually ends with him leading the audience in a spirited round of folk songs. Performances are held on alternating Thursdays and Saturdays.

Korea House

Pildong 2-ga 80-2 (2266-9101). Chungmuro station (lines 3 & 4), exit 3. **Tickets** ₩50,000. **Map** p247 G4.

Located on the lower slopes of Namsan Mountain in central Seoul, this multipurpose space includes a folk theatre that stages a variety of traditional performances, from *samulnori* to fan dances, and is also a popular venue for weddings and events. There are twice-daily performances from Monday to Saturday, and one performance on Sunday.

National Gukak Center

Seochodong 700 (580-3300). Bangbae station (line 2), exit 1; Nambu Terminal station (line 3), exit 5. **Tickets** Vary; often free.

This massive complex in southern Seoul is dedicated to preserving and promoting Korea's traditional music, and (somewhat fancifully) claims a history dating back to the Shilla court. It is home to some of the country's finest and most renowned performers, and works extensively to train musicians and further traditional musical scholarship.

National Theater of Korea

Jangchungdangil 158 (2288-4120). Dongguk Univ. station (line 3), exit 2. **Tickets** Vary. **Map** p247 H5.

ARTS & ENTERTAINMENT

Home to the National Drama, Changgeuk, Dance, and Orchestra Companies of Korea, this theatre complex hosts a variety of traditional, fusion and modern performances.

Seoul Namsan Traditional Theater

Pildong 2-ga 84-1 (399-1114, http://sngad. sejongpac.or.kr). Chungmuro station (lines 3 & 4), exit 3. **Tickets** Vary. **Map** p247 G4.
Located in the Namsangol Hanok Village, this small theatre stages a variety of traditional musical performances under the management of the Sejong Center for the Performing Arts.
▶ *For more on Namsangol Hanok Village, see p64.*

Classical Music

Koreans are hard-core classical music fans. The city has managed to bring in famed musicians from around the globe, as well as producing some of their own, including pianist and conductor Myung-whun Chung, soprano Sumi Jo, and violinist Kyung-wha Chung. Visitors who want to indulge in a little night music can find it at any number of major venues, including the **Sejong Center for the Performing Arts**, and a new opera house set to open in Yeouido in 2011.

Sejong Center for the Performing Arts

Sejongno 81-3 (399-1111). Gwanghwamun station (line 5) exits 1 & 8. **Tickets** Vary. **Map** p247 E2.
One of the largest performance spaces in the country, this theatre complex sits in the middle of downtown. It hosts a variety of international touring groups and major performances, including traditional, classical, and modern works. It also houses a gallery, chamber orchestra space, and the largest pipe organ in Asia.

Theatre & Musicals

Musicals are very popular in Korea, with international productions swinging by on tour, Korean-language versions of famous musicals, and some locally created musical dramas. Visitors will find everything from an English-language touring production of *The Phantom of the Opera* to K-pop stars in Korean-language adaptations of *The Count of Monte Cristo*.

Western-style theatre is also popular, with major productions being mounted at the main performing arts centres (such as **Sejong Center for the Performing Arts**, *see left*) and larger theatres. However, in addition to these major performance spaces, which tend to attract larger, more classical productions, there's a vibrant experimental scene in the Daehangno area in northern Seoul. Shows are hosted in small, semi-underground venues, from manic comedies to B-boy dance extravaganzas. Despite the language barrier, many of them offer a fascinating glimpse into the cultural interests of Korea's youth.

Korea has also spawned its own unique form of 'nonverbal performance'. Designed specifically to appeal to international crowds by eliminating the language barrier, these productions often use traditional Korean culture as a jumping-off point. The oldest and most famous of these is *NANTA*, which is set in a busy kitchen and uses knives, spoons, pots, pans and even food as percussion instruments, and is based on Korean *samulnori* rhythms. *NANTA* has since been followed by shows like *Jump*, which blends comedy and taekwondo, and *Sachoom*, which brings together a wide variety of different dance styles.

Myeongdong Theater

Myeongdong 1-ga 54 (1644-2003). Euljiro 1-ga station (line 2), exit 6. **Tickets** Vary. **Map** p247 E2.
Housed in a gorgeous and recently restored colonial-period building that was once home to the National Theater, the newly opened Myeongdong Theater hosts a wide range of performances, from modern experimental works to Shakespearean classics.

NANTA

UNESCO Building, Myeongdong 2-ga 50-14 & Jeong Dong Art Hall, Jeongdong (739-8288, nanta.i-pmc.co.kr). Euljiro 1-ga station (line 2), exit 6, & Seodaemun Station (line 5), exit 5. **Tickets** From ₩30,000. **Map** p247 F4.
With performances in two dedicated theatres in Seoul, *NANTA* is one of Korea's biggest theatrical successes. Be prepared to have balls hurled your way, dodge carrot shavings and cabbage chunks, and possibly be hauled on to the stage to participate at either the Myeongdong or Jeongdong venues.

Escapes & Excursions

Bukhansan. *See p201*.

Escapes &
Excursions

0 _____ 50 mile
0 _____ 50 kms
© Copyright Time Out Group 2011

NORTH KOREA

Goseong
Sokcho
Yangyang
East Sea
(Sea of Japan)

The DMZ
(pp204-215)
GYEONGGI-DO
Wacheon
Inje
Mansan
Chuncheon
GANGWON-DO
Gangneung

Ganghwa
Hoecheon
Bukhansan
National Park
(pp201-202)
Hongcheon

The West Sea
Islands
(pp209-211)
Gimpo
SEOUL
Yangsu-ri
(pp202-203)
Yangpyeong
Yeoryang
Donghae

Incheon
(pp205-209)
Suwon
(pp211-215)
Icheon
Wonju

Pyeongtaek
Apsong
Chungju
Jecheon
Damyang
(pp217-218)
Taebaek

Taean
Cheonan
CHUNGCHONGBUK-DO
Uljin

Hongseong
Cheongju
Jeomchon
Yecheon
Yeongju
Andong
Yeongyang

Gongju
(pp215-217)
Daejeon
Sang-ju
GYEONGSANGBUK-DO
Uiseong
Yeongdeo

Bo-ryeong
CHUNGCHEONGNAM-DO
Yeongdong
Gimcheon
Yeongcheon
Pohang

West Sea
(Yellow Sea)
Gunsan
Iksan
Jeonju
Daegu
Gyeongju

Buan
JEOLLABUK-DO
Dagok
Hapcheon
Ulsan

Jeong-eup
Namwon
Namji
Yangsan

Yong-gwang
Danyang
GYEONGSANGNAM-DO
Jinju
Masan
Changwon

Gwangju
Gwacheon
JEOLLANAM-DO
Suncheon
Sacheon
Goseong
Busan

Mokpo
Boseong
Mansong
Korea Strait

Jindo
Gangjin
Goheung

Inset map:
CHINA
Beijing
Pyongyang
NORTH KOREA
SOUTH KOREA
Seoul
East Sea
JAPAN
Tokyo
West Sea
Shanghai
East China Sea
Hanoi
Macau
Taipei
TAIWAN
LAOS
Hong Kong
PACIFIC OCEAN
THAILAND
Vientiane
South China Sea
Bangkok
CAMBODIA
VIETNAM
PHILIPPINES
Phnom Penh
Ho Chi Minh City
Manila
MALAYSIA
BRUNEI
SABAH
Kuala
Lumpur
SARAWAK
Singapore
South-east Asia

Escapes & Excursions

Something special in every direction.

Seoul is, according to some measures, the world's third-largest urban agglomeration, and it's in the top ten whichever way you look at it. The city can be tough to escape, but some fascinating day trips are possible in all directions. To the west: **Incheon**, a city that witnessed the turning point of the Korean War and is surrounded by a spray of delightful islands. To the south: the heritage-listed fortress of **Suwon**, and little **Gongju**, once capital of the Baekje kingdom. To the east: charming **Danyang**, a small town whose periphery includes gigantic caves and one of the country's most astonishing temples. And to the north: the world's most heavily fortified border: the **DMZ**, a four-kilometre-wide band of earth dividing North and South Korea.

Bukhansan

Much of Seoul's northern border with Gyeonggi province is covered by **Bukhansan National Park**. The name Bukhansan refers to ten major mountains located north of the Hangang river. The park combines the rugged **Mt Samgaksan** to the south and **Mt Dobongsan** to the north, with the **Uiryeong Pass** in between. The 30 or so trailheads are concentrated around Samgaksan and eastern Dobongsan, and are meticulously maintained.

This 80-square-kilometre ecological island may be surrounded by Seoul's subway lines and urban sprawl, but Bukhansan remains a wild place where you may be forced to hoist yourself by rope over walls of granite. While bears and tigers no longer roam these forests, there are still more than 1,000 species of plants, as well as pristine streams and natural mineral springs that provide potable water to quench one's thirst (look for the red and blue plastic ladles).

Bukhansan's trails boast remarkable vistas, scores of Buddhist shrines and temples (including Mangwolsa, Doseonsa and Cheonchuksa), and a breath of fresh air just minutes from central Seoul.

Note that Bukhansan's trails are closed from sunset until two hours before sunrise.

BUKHANSAN'S BEST TRAILS

If reaching the summit is a priority, the **Bukhansanseong Fortress Trail** is your best bet. Starting at the Bukhansanseong Park Information Center on the range's west side, this route ascends directly to **Baekundae**, the park's 837-metre (2,740-foot) high point. The three-kilometre trip to the top should take about two hours. Although from afar, Baekundae resembles a whale's smooth dorsal fin, up close it consists of jagged granite crags. After standing atop its windy summit, retrace your steps or consider a 90-minute detour past **Insubong** (which offers some of Asia's best multi-pitch rock climbing; see www.koreaontherocks.com) to **Doseonsa Temple**. The major Buddhist complex is best known for a ten-metre Buddha that, legend says, was magically carved into a cliff by a ninth-century monk, Doseon. On leaving the temple, you can continue around the ridge or grab a bus down to Seoul's Ui-dong neighbourhood. This trail's added perk is seeing what remains of the city's 2,000-year-old, 13-kilometre (eight-mile) fortress wall and gates.

The park's northern end is dominated by Dobongsan. The 'Daoist-Peak Mountain' is said to be the female yin to Samgaksan's male yang. The mountain offers a range of trail types, including the relatively easy **Bomun Range**

Trail that is ideal for novice hikers, children and the elderly. Starting from the Dobong Ranger Station, about 15 minutes from Dobongsan station, the path passes the **Dobong Seowon Confucian School** before turning left on to a 2.5-kilometre route that is highlighted each spring by fields of royal azaleas.

The 90-minute **Sinseondae Trail** is the most direct route to the top. After veering left at the ranger outpost, you'll pass the striking, gold **Neungwonsa Temple**. Shortly after the Dobong Shelter, you'll reach **Cheonchuksa Temple**. Founded in 673, it's one of the mountain's two major Buddhist sites and a popular pitstop for its free cinnamon tea and simple lunch, not to mention its dramatic position beneath Seoninbong's 708-metre (2,325-foot) bald granite head. A few hundred metres along the trail is Madang Bawi, a large rock face where hikers often rest before making the final push to Jaunbong, Dobongsan's 740-metre (2,425-foot) summit. Once again, you can take the same trail back down, or continue northwards to **Mangwolsa Temple** and eventually emerge at the National Park's Dobongsan office.

WHERE TO EAT

★ Jingogae Hanjeongsik
Howondong 229-272, Uijeongbu City (031 873-4100). Mangwolsa station (Seoul Metro line 1), exit 3. **Open** *10am-10pm daily.* **Average** *₩10,000-₩20,000.*
Located just inside the trail head, this restaurant serves a traditional Korean meal accompanied by 18 side dishes, as well as a spicy beef stew (₩15,000) or a full boiled chicken set meal (₩40,000).

Kong Sarang
Dobongdong 411-1, Seoul (955-6016, www.kong sarangdubu.co.kr). Dobongsan station (Seoul Metro lines 1 & 7), exit 1. **Open** *9am-9pm Mon-Fri; 8am-9pm Sat, Sun (July, Aug until 10pm).* **Average** *₩10,000-20,000; ₩14,000 tofu set meal.*

Specialising in soft home-made tofu, this is the perfect place for a tired hiker. Colourful slices of tofu are served alongside skate, pork *bossam* and side dishes.

WHERE TO STAY

Seoul YMCA Campground
Howondong 119, Uijeongbu City (031 873-5624, www.ydarakwon.or.kr). Dobongsan station (Seoul Metro lines 1 & 7), exit 1. **Rates** *₩14,500 per person.* **No credit cards.**
This campsite is about a kilometre from Dobongsan station and provides everything from single bunk to group accommodation. Meals (₩6,000) can be added.

GETTING THERE & AROUND

By train
Reach the Bukhansanseong Fortress Trail via Gupabal station on Seoul Metro line 3, exit 1. Take bus 704 (20mins, ₩1,000 or free with transfer). The Dobongsan area can be reached via Dobongsan station on Seoul Metro lines 1 & 7, exit 1.

TOURIST INFORMATION

In addition to the offices below, there are at least ten tourist information kiosks located at park trail heads, typically open from sunrise to sunset (www.bukhan.knps.or.kr).
Bukhansan National Park Office *Jeongneung 4-dong 1-1 (909-0497). Mia station (Seoul Metro line 4), exit 6.*
Bukhansan National Park Dobong Office *Howondong 229-104, Uijeongbu City, Gyeonggi Province (873-2791). Mangwolsa station (Seoul Metro line 1), exit 3.*

Yangsu-ri

Yangsu-ri is a fast 45-minute drive from Seoul. The confluence of the Hangang river's north and south forks was once a busy way-point for

Bukhansan.

Seoul-bound barges, but when the Paldang Dam tamed the waters in the early 1970s, traffic started moving by land, industry dried up and Yangsu-ri was recast as an ecological destination.

Then as now, this meeting point of rivers (and also, by reputation, lovers) is dominated by **Dumulmeori**, literally 'the head of two waters'. It's reachable via a pleasant, 360-metre (1,180-foot) pathway lined to the left by a river and tiled wall and to the right by acres of lotus ponds. Along the way, enterprising folk serve simple snacks and drinks on picnic-table platforms that jut out over the water. The path ends at a plaza of packed earth surrounding a 500-year-old zelkova tree. Under its bows is a simple altar demonstrating the resilience of Korea's indigenous shamanism. A few metres offshore is a square-sailed skiff – to be photographed, not commandeered. Dozens of photographers head here in the wee hours, especially on crisp autumn mornings, to catch the sunrise over a spooky blanket of fog.

Beside the island is a small peninsula with Yangsu train station on one end, and the sprawling garden of **Semiwon** (031 755-1834, www.semiwon.or.kr, open Mar-Nov 9am-6pm daily, Dec-Feb 10am-4pm daily, admission ₩3,000) on the other. The name means 'a place where water and flowers live together'. The on-site Environmental Training Center argues persuasively for the restoration of the Hangang river's ecosystem. Towards the exit is a shed selling locally grown and organic produce. Summer visitors are advised to arrive early, as the daily number of visitors is limited to 500.

A number of other sites are within easy distance of Yangsu-ri proper. Just 15 minutes by car on the other side of the river's north fork is **Sujongsa Temple** (031 576-8411, open 24hrs, admission free). A winding road leads to a legendary view 610 metres (2,000 feet) above sea level, on **Mt Ungilsan**. The temple's founding in 1460 is also legendary: a ringing bell led King Sejo to discover statues of Buddha's 18 disciples. After exploring the grounds, venture to the summit for great views of Dumulmeori and Seoul.

About eight kilometres upriver are the **KOFIC Namyangju Studios** (031 579-0605, www.studio.kofic.or.kr, open Mar-Oct 10am-6pm Tue-Sun, Nov-Feb until 5pm, admission ₩3,000). Operated by the Korean Film Council and set in a forested valley, they feature several outdoor sets, including the Joseon Dynasty village depicted in Im Kwon-taek's *Chihwaseon*. Another set is a compelling replica of the inter-Korean border that was used for the hit film *JSA* (2000). Above it all is **Undang**, an early 19th-century house that was transported from Seoul in 1994. The sets are complemented by indoor attractions such as the Film Culture Museum, and a warehouse packed floor to ceiling with props and wardrobe items. Free films can be watched at the Cine Movie Theater.

WHERE TO EAT

Sagye
Yongdam-ri 277-4, Yangseo-myeon (031 775-4320). Yangsu station (Jungang line), exit 2. **Open** 11am-2am daily. **Average** ₩10,000-₩20,000.
An upmarket dining option specialising in barbecue, pasta and pizza, this café-restaurant is located on a hill that offers great views and colourful foliage year round, hence its name, meaning 'Four Seasons'.

Yeonbat
Yongdam-ri 514, Yangseo-myeon (031 772-6200). Yangsu station (Jungang line), exit 1. **Open** 11am-9pm daily. **Average** ₩10,000-20,000.
This traditional Korean restaurant has flavoured its popular fish dishes, mung bean pancakes and spicy soups with locally grown lotus leaves.

★ Yukkonginae
Yongdam-ri 430-6, Yangseo-myeon (031 773-6733). Yangsu station (Jungang line), exit 1. **Open** 9am-9pm daily. **Average** ₩10,000; ₩18,000 organic *ssambap* for two.
Organically grown rice and vegetables comprise the bulk of the menu at this traditional Korean eaterie. Several dishes feature mung beans and lotus plants, including fried pancakes, noodles and a popular dried pollack meal.

WHERE TO STAY

Green Hill Hotel
Yongdam-ri 534-12, Yangseo-myeon (031 772-5751). Yangsu station (Jungang line), exit 1. **Rates** ₩80,000 double.
Better described as a motel, Green Hill's big, clean rooms (request a river view) are worth the extra few thousand *won* you'll pay over other accommodation in the area. It has its own mediocre restaurant, but the best perk is its location just opposite Semiwon.

GETTING THERE & AROUND

By train
Dumulmeori and Semiwon are best reached by train – on Seoul's Jungang line – to Yangsu station, exit 1. For Sujongsa Temple, alight at Ungilsan station, one station west of Yangsu; from exit 1, it's a 2.5km walk or a 10min taxi ride (031 576-3944, ₩2,900). A taxi from Ungilsan station to KOFIC Namyangju Studios will cost about ₩6,500 and take about 15mins.

TOURIST INFORMATION

Yangpyeong-gun *Yanggeun-ri 448-8, Yangpyeong-eup (031 773-5101, www.yp21.net). Yangpyeong station (Jungang line), exit 1.* **Open** 9am-6pm daily.

The DMZ

A four-kilometre-wide strip of land runs clean across the Korean peninsula from east to west, dividing the communist North and democratic south. It's known in English as the Demilitarized Zone or DMZ, though this is something of a misnomer – it is by far the most heavily fortified border on the planet, a fact that led to its memorable description by Bill Clinton as the 'scariest place on earth'. Yet, despite this, it's also one of the country's most popular tourist draws.

So, what's to see? Though various sights and lookout points can be reached by public transport, the most interesting sights are only accessible on a guided tour. Precise itineraries vary, but most hit the same spots: an observatory looking out over North Korea, a trip to one of the tunnels beneath the border apparently dug by North Korean infiltrators, and the famed **Joint Security Area** in **Panmunjeom**.

This tiny village came to the fore after the stalemate that brought hostilities to an end in the Korean War; a truce was declared, though

North Korea: Against the Odds

Trouble with the neighbours.

When air raid sirens rang out on 22 November 2010, many of Yeonpyeongdo's 1,500 residents thought it was just another drill on their small island – a notion quickly put to rest when North Korean bombs began to fall on their homes. Two South Korean marines and two civilians lost their lives during the shelling. Yeonpyeongdo is only 11 kilometres (seven miles) from North Korea, across a disputed portion of the Yellow Sea; several months earlier in those same waters, a South Korean naval vessel, the *Cheonan*, exploded, killing 46 sailors. An international investigation held North Korea responsible.

In any other country, such an attack by a foreign power would be considered an act of war. But these two incidents were just the latest in a series of provocations that South Koreans have had to live with since the peninsula was divided in 1945.

One thing most western analysts can agree on is that the North Korean regime has defied the odds since its inception. North Korea was almost wiped off the map during the Korean War once US-led United Nations forces ploughed into its territory in 1950. But thanks to the help of a million-strong Chinese army, it managed to maintain its borders when the war ended in 1953. In the following decades, its ruler, Kim Il Sung, would try to reunite the peninsula once again by force. In 1968, he dispatched commandos to assassinate South Korean president Park Chung-hee, a plot that ended with a shoot-out in downtown Seoul. Kim is also believed to have ordered terrorist attacks against South Korean politicians in Burma in 1983, and the bombing of a Seoul-bound airliner four years later.

As Soviet-backed regimes began to crumble in the early 1990s, many thought North Korea would be the next. Without the help of its allies in Russia, its once stable economy and food distribution system collapsed. The nation was plunged into famine and millions are believed to have starved to death. To make matters worse, Kim Il Sung died in 1994, handing over power to his son, the reclusive Kim Jong Il. However, Pyongyang turned the tables on the international community once again: North Korea proclaimed a Military First Policy and began developing its nuclear weapons programme. Criticism from Washington was met with threats to turn Seoul into a 'sea of fire'; with thousands of pieces of artillery pointed at the South Korean capital, no one wanted to call Pyongyang's bluff.

As the North's economy continued on a downward spiral, South Korea came to its aid. In 1998 President Kim Dae-jung took office, and introduced the Sunshine Policy, the objective of which was the normalising of relations with the North. Inter-Korean industrial and tourism ventures began, bankrolled by the South Korean taxpayer. But Seoul's goodwill was met with deadly naval clashes and, in 2006, Pyongyang detonated an atomic device. The Sunshine Policy was all but forgotten when conservative politician Lee Myung Bak was sworn in as South Korean president in 2008.

The recent upswing in inter-Korean hostilities could be the result of this loss of aid from South Korea. Analysts have long speculated that Kim Jong Il is fatally ill, and is trying to shore up support for his son to succeed him by raising tensions on the peninsula. Whether these are, in fact, the last throws of a failing state is anyone's guess, but for the moment, North Korea doesn't seem to be going anywhere.

not signed by the South Korean government, meaning that the war is still technically going on to this day. Meetings between North and South Korea are still held in three buildings that both sides share. The buildings straddle the border and, on days without scheduled meetings, are open to the public – walk to the opposite side of the room and you'll be able to tell your friends that you've technically been to North Korea. Of course, it's not possible to go any further: the area is crawling with soldiers from both sides, in permanent, tense-muscled defence mode. You'll be escorted to a lookout point, from where you can see clearly into North Korean territory. The view includes **Propaganda Village**, a sham settlement made by the North Korean government, into which a small stream of happy 'residents' arrive by bus every day.

Most tours include a visit to the **Third Tunnel of Agression** (open 9am-3pm Tue-Sun), discovered in 1974 and apparently created by North Korean infiltrators in preparation for a full attack on the south. Other than the excitement of being deep beneath the DMZ, there's not much to see. Before hitting the tunnel, visitors are shown a bizarre movie clip – this is better seen than explained, though have your vomit bag ready. Near the tunnel is **Dorasan Observatory**, which is the only sight in the area accessible without taking a tour: catch a train from Seoul station to Imjingang, at the end of the line, and from there those able to prove their identity with a passport will be able to go one stop further to the unnecessarily huge **Dorasan Station**. You can take a picture of the signs pointing the way to Pyongyang. From the observatory, you'll be able to peep across the border with binoculars (₩500 buys you one minute). For more on the history of the Korean War, see p26.

WHERE TO EAT

There's nowhere special to eat if you're on a DMZ tour; lunch is included with some packages, though you won't have any choice regarding the location. It's worth bringing along a snack or two.

GETTING THERE

Certain parts of the DMZ can be reached on public transport, but for the full experience you'll have to take a tour. There are a bewildering number of operators; you'll almost certainly see pamphlets from at least half a dozen firms in your hotel lobby, or just pop into any Seoul tourist office (see p230). Most tour operators offer essentially the same packages for essentially the same price, and

many will collect you from your hotel. The **USO** (724-7781, www.uso.org/korea) offers excellent tours guided by American infantry for $70, though you'll have to book at least four days in advance. Whichever company you choose, make sure the tour heads to the Joint Security Area, which is by far the most interesting DMZ sight; expect to pay around ₩75,000.

There are a few things to note when taking a tour. First, you must bring your passport. Second, photography is not allowed in particularly sensitive areas – you'll be told when to put your camera away. Third, though this should go without saying, it's highly unwise to play the fool in this area. Do not gesture or shout across the border to any North Korean personnel.

Incheon

Incheon is often overlooked on the Korean travelling itinerary. But this aspiring city – the nation's third largest – on the Yellow Sea aspires to be a global port of call.

In the late 1880s, when it was a fishing village called Jemulpo, Incheon became the Hermit Kingdom's first 'open port', when a fading dynasty allowed Asian and western powers to build discrete settlements – one of which is now Korea's only **Chinatown**. What foreign money managed to create in the brief window before Japanese colonisation represents some of the nation's best early modern architecture. Fifty years later, Incheon's **Wolmido Island** took to the international stage when General MacArthur's amphibious attack turned the tide of the Korean War.

Incheon's highlights aren't limited to its past. The metropolis remains Korea's premier gateway, thanks to **Incheon International Airport**, named the 'world's best' six years running, and the **ferries** that whisk travellers to outlying Korean islands and many Chinese ports. It also boasts the new 21-kilometre (13-mile) **Incheon Bridge**, which links the mainland to the airport; and **Songdo International City**, a $40 billion project to build a brand-new city from the sea. Among the old and new is a typical frenetic Korean city of bright lights, great food and shopping, with its Bupyeong and Arts districts providing some of the most popular watering holes.

SIGHTSEEING

Incheon train station is a convenient starting point for a walking tour of the historic **Jung-gu** district. The grey **Junghwa Gate**, one of three traditional Chinese constructions donated by Weihai city, marks the entrance to **Chinatown**. For now, walk past it and the police station up a narrow alley. The road lined with red lanterns and Chinese row houses is **Jajangmyeon Street**, named after the neighbourhood's contribution to Sino-Korean cuisine. Enjoy a bowl of the famous noodles slathered in sweet, home-made black soybean sauce for ₩8,000 at **Jageumseong**.

As the hill meanders left, head right up stairs painted with pandas, Great Walls and all things Chinese to reach the blue-tiled **Seollin Gate**. Instead of climbing the second staircase, however, make a sharp right turn down the hill to **Mural Street**, which depicts scenes from the third-century Chinese epic, *Records of the Three Kingdoms*. A couple of blocks further on, when the street dips, go left up the hill towards **Chemulpo Club**, a handsome house dating from 1901, where Incheon's first foreigners plotted their exploits.

When the road veers left past the blue-roofed church, you'll probably hear the clucks of a dozen roosters. It's a sure sign that you're approaching Jayu Gongwon, or **Freedom Park**, Korea's first western-style green space. Opened in 1888 as All Nations Park, today it's dominated by tributes to US–Korea ties. In addition to a green cage filled with assorted birds and a hutch

of rabbits, there's a statue of **General Douglas MacArthur**, architect of the 1950 Incheon Landing. The statue overlooks a flower garden and a plaza, from where you can take in the sights and sounds of the working port. A few metres further on is the **Korea–USA Centennial Monument**. Retrace your steps down the brick path and pass the double-level, eight-sided **Palgakjeong** pavilion before exiting the park at Mural Street.

This time around, descend the **Boundary Steps** past the statue of Confucius. The staircase and differing pagodas delineate the old border that separated the Chinese (right) and Japanese (left) concessions. At the bottom, turn left on to the **Street of History & Culture**, two blocks of recently Japanified façades. After passing the district office building on the left, wrap right around the corner into what was old Jemulpo's financial centre. What remains are three regal Japanese banks built in classical and renaissance styles. Among them, the former No.18 Bank was converted into the **Incheon Open Port Modern Architecture Museum**, a worthy stop that explains the area's history.

One block down is the **Incheon Art Platform**, several old brick warehouses converted into a quirky home for the Incheon Foundation for Arts & Culture. Across the street is a small park, the gold **Inhwa Gate** and the imposing **Korean-Chinese Cultural Center**.

If you walk west from the Boundary Steps, you'll pass several historical buildings on your way back to the train station. Once there, if time allows, take a bus (nos.2, 23, 45, 15mins, ₩900) to **Wolmido Island**. No longer an island, it's retained a quirky identity, thanks to a tiny amusement park and charming waterfront promenade. Be sure to sample the local delicacies – prawns caught that morning and deep-fried, or french fry-encrusted corndogs of dubious vintage. Both are delicious.

Alternatively, test your sea legs on a ferry departing for a neighbouring island or China. A 90-minute harbour tour with **Cosmos Cruise** (032-764-1171, www.cosmoscruise.co.kr) provides incredible views of the Incheon Bridge for just ₩15,000. Saturday dinner cruises run to ₩55,000, and other packages are available.

Finally, your Wolmido visit should conclude with a stop at the **Museum of Korean Emigration History**, a sunset snapshot at the lighthouse pier, and a 30-minute hill climb to the **Wolmi Observatory**.

FREE Chemulpo Club
Songhakdong 1-ga 11, Incheon (032 765 0261).
Incheon station (Seoul Metro line 1), exit 1.
Open 9.30am-noon, 1-5.30pm Tue-Sun.
Admission free.

Chinatown, **Incheon.**

This cosy expat clubhouse, built in 1901, was both a social venue and municipal headquarters for Incheon's foreign heavyweights. Today, the large bar is, regrettably, dry. Videos profile the power players of old, and glass cases display a curious collection of 3D paper models of great European and American architecture.

FREE Incheon Art Platform

Haeandong 1-ga 218-3 (032 760-1000, www.inart platform.kr). Incheon station (Seoul line metro 1), exit 1. **Open** 9am-6pm daily. **Admission** free; tickets for performances vary.

This multipurpose arts venue, opened in 2009 and anchored by the Incheon Foundation for Arts & Culture, has managed to revitalise the old city without erasing its history. Twelve brick buildings dating from the 1930s and '40s (and one 100-year-old office) have been turned into exhibition spaces, performance halls and a great café.

Incheon Open Port Modern Architecture Museum

Jungangdong 2-ga 24-1 (032 760-7549). Incheon station (Seoul Metro line 1), exit 1. **Open** 9am-6pm Tue-Sun. **Admission** ₩500.

Scale models and other exhibits show the history of old Incheon's buildings. Models include one of the museum itself: the one-storey former home of the No.18 Bank of Japan was built in 1890 in an eclectic classical style.

FREE Korean-Chinese Cultural Center

Hangdong 1-ga 1-2 (032 760-7860, www.hanjung. go.kr). Incheon station (Seoul line 1), exit 1. **Open** 9.10am-6pm Tue-Sun; theatre open until 10pm during performances. **Admission** free.

This large, garish, four-floor temple to Korea–China relations dominates the neighbourhood. Inside, you'll find Chinese and Korean language classes, special exhibitions and weekend performances. The second floor offers a 'cultural experience zone', where visitors can drink tea, paint and be photographed wearing Chinese attire, while the third floor promotes Incheon's 11 Chinese 'friendship cities'.

FREE Museum of Korean Emigration History

Bukseongdong 1-ga 102-2 (032 440-4710, www.mkeh.incheon.go.kr). Incheon station (Seoul line 1), exit 1, then bus to Wolmido. **Open** 9am-6pm Tue-Sun. **Admission** Free.

Located on the southern end of Mt Wolmisan and completed in 2008, this museum is a fitting installation for Incheon, Korea's first open port for foreigners and departure point for most of Korea's seven million-plus emigrants.

FREE Wolmi Park & Observatory

Bukseongdong 1-ga 97-7 (032 765-4133, wolmi.incheon.go.kr). Incheon station (Seoul line 1), exit 1, then bus to Wolmido. **Open** *Park* Mar-Oct 5am-11pm daily. Nov-Feb 5am-10pm daily. *Garden* 9am-8pm daily. **Admission** free.

About half of Wolmido Island is covered in parkland, including a traditional Korean garden, and trails that lead up to a 24m-high (80ft) observation deck that provides wonderful views of the port and two of the city's modern marvels: Songdo International City and the Incheon Bridge. The half-hour hike is especially popular at sunset.

WHERE TO EAT & DRINK

Café Rip

Incheon Art Platform, Haeandong 1-ga 10-1, Incheon (010 9988-5004). Incheon station (Seoul line 1), exit 1. **Open** 9am-6pm daily. **Average** muffins and bagel ₩2,400; americano ₩3,500.

Located in a bright, glass-encased addition in section H of the Incheon Art Platform (*see left*), this café feels like a modern oasis in a historic setting.

Songdo: Korea's Slice of Dubai

A city emerges from the sea.

Picture a sort of miniature Dubai, built on reclaimed tidal flats. This is **Songdo International City** (www.songdo.com), part of Incheon's Free Economic Zone (FEZ), and a $40 billion private effort to create an international business hub. Located just 35 kilometres west of Seoul, and designed to accommodate 250,000 residents with residential, retail, office and cultural space, the masterplan for this 'insta-city' has features similar – at least in theory – to the boulevards of Paris, New York's Central Park and Venice's canals. Incheon's city of the future can already claim South Korea's tallest building the 305-metre (1,000 foot) Northeast Asia Trade Tower), one of the world's longest bridges and the technological sophistication of a 'ubiquitous city' – all major information systems share data across an integrated network. Although the 2008 global recession took its toll, the world's largest and most expensive private real estate development wrapped up phase one in 2009, with final completion set for 2020.

★ Chungnamseosanjip

Ongnyeondong 550-2 (032 833-1925). Dongchun station (Incheon line 1), exit 1. **Open** 10am-10pm daily. **Average** ₩40,000.

This popular restaurant in Incheon's new Songdo area specialises in live crab plucked from waters off Yeonpyeongdo Island. The spicy soup is enhanced by sweet pumpkin and assorted veggies.

Donghae Haemultang

Bupyeongdong 527-24 (032 514-5649). Bupyeong Market station (Incheon line 1), exit 2. **Open** 10.30am-1am daily. Closed 1st Tue of mth. **Average** ₩10,000-₩20,000; *haemultang* from ₩35,000.

Bupyeong district is famous for its seafood soup street, nicknamed Haemultang-gil. This neighbourhood hotspot combines generous amounts of crab, squid, shrimp, clams, mussels and other marine fare with a spicy broth of bean sprouts.

Jageumseong

Bukseongdong 2-ga 10-2, Incheon (032 761-1688). Incheon station (Seoul line 1), exit 1. **Open** 11am-9.30pm daily. **Average** ₩10,000-₩20,000.

Like most Chinatown restaurants, the specialities here are *jajangmyeon* noodles (₩4,500) and *jjamppong*, a spicy seafood soup. But what sets this place apart is the home-made *chunjang* sauce and lunch specials served until 3pm.

★ Wonbo

Bukseongdong 2-ga 10-13, Incheon (032 773-7888). Incheon station (Seoul line 1), exit 1. **Open** 11am-9pm daily. **Average** dumplings ₩3,500.

Tuck into traditional steamed Chinese dumplings the size of your fist, but grab a napkin before biting into the savoury beef, noodle and cabbage *mandu*.

Yejeon

Bukseongdong 1-ga 98-444, Wolmido Island (032 772-2256). Incheon station (Seoul line 1), exit 1, then bus to Wolmido. **Open** 10.30am-1am daily. **Average** ₩10,000-₩20,000.

Yejeon is located on Wolmido's Culture Street. Locals come here to enjoy breaded pork cutlets and other Japanese dishes in a classy atmosphere, just metres from the waterfront promenade.

GETTING THERE

By train

On Seoul Metro line 1, it takes 68mins (₩1,600 one-way) on an all-stopping train to Incheon station. An express train (same price) will save you approximately 20mins.

TOURIST INFORMATION

The Incheon Tourism Organisation (INTO) operates a number of visitor centres in popular tourist areas. It also has a helpful English-language website (www.into.or.kr) suggesting themed tours.

INTO Incheon International Airport Centre *In front of airport section F (032 743-0011).* **Open** 7am-10pm daily.

INTO Incheon Station Centre *3-61 Bukseongdong 1-ga (032 777-1330). Incheon station (Seoul line 1), exit 1.* **Open** 9am-6pm daily.

INTO Main Office *4F Benikea Premier Songdo Bridge Hotel, 10-2 Songdodong (032 220-5100). University of Incheon station, Incheon line.* **Open** 9am-6pm daily.

INTO Wolmido Island Tourism Centre *98 Bukseongdong 1-ga (032 765-4169). Incheon subway (line 1).* **Open** 6am-6pm daily. In front of the Wolmi Culture Street dock.

West Sea Islands

The Yellow Sea, known as the West Sea in Korea, contains more than 100 islands with spectacular rock formations and lovely beaches. A few are particularly notable. **Ganghwado** repelled foreign invaders for centuries, **Yeongjongdo** is home to Korea's largest airport, and isolated **Baengnyeongdo** is officially part of Incheon, though more than 150 kilometres (93 miles) west of that city's centre. Although these rustic islands hold tremendous tourism potential, their location just south of a maritime border unrecognised by North Korea has caused several deadly naval skirmishes over the years. So, barring a radical détente on the Korean peninsula, they will remain unspoiled destinations for travellers seeking something different.

GANGHWADO

South Korea's fifth largest island is separated from the mainland by a narrow channel, and linked to it by two bridges. Ganghwado is dominated by **Mt Manisan**, a 470-metre-high peak where you'll find **Chamseongdan**, the altar where the mysterious Dangun is said to have founded Korea in 2333 BC. Rites are still performed there every 3 October to mark the nation's foundation holiday.

Korea also boasts the world's largest concentration of dolmen, tombs of massive stones constructed thousands of years ago. Ganghwado has 80 of these sites, which were added to the UNESCO World Heritage List in 2000.

Fast forward to Korea's Goryeo and Joseon royal dynasties, and the island's impressive fortresses. **Gwangseongbo Fortress** repelled attacks by the Mongols, French, Americans and Japanese over the course of seven centuries. In Ganghwa township, three structures from a 17th-century Joseon palace are also worth a look.

An invasion of another sort – British missionaries – resulted in some of Korea's most curious and beautiful places of worship. The **Ganghwa Anglican Church** (250 Gwancheong-ri, Ganghwa-eup, 032 934-6171) was consecrated in 1900. Its lovely turquoise doors contrast sharply with the subdued brown and tan of the **Onsu-ri Anglican Church** (505-3 Onsu-ri, Gilsang-mveon, 032 937-0005), built in 1906. Both demonstrate an attractive fusion of Korean and western architecture.

Not far away is **Jeondeungsa** (635 Onsu-ri, Gilsang-myeon, 032 937-0125, www.jeondeungsa.org), one of Korea's most beautiful temples. The main sanctuary hall (designated a national treasure) was rebuilt in 1621 and is protected by **Samnangseong Fortress**, which repelled France's last-gasp invasion of the island in 1866. Nearby is the **Lotus Lantern International Meditation Center** (85-1 Giljik-ri, Gilsang-myeon, 032 937-7033, www.lotuslantern.net). Founded in 1997, it offers one-, two- and five-night temple stays.

Two more religious sites are accessible by ferry. **Ganghwa Seodo Central Church** is located on Jumundo Island, about 90 minutes from Oepo-ri by boat. Seongmodo Island's **Bomunsa Temple** is a ten-minute boat ride from Oepo-ri or Nae-ri, followed by a shuttle bus. Once there, observe scores of Buddha statues with pretty painted lips.

YEONGJONGDO & MUUIDO

Before it became the site of Korea's largest airport, Yeongjongdo was made up of two separate islands, Yongyudo and Sammokdo. Today's single isle can be reached via two bridges, subway or a short ferry trip from Wolmido Island.

Though the airport is, for many, the be all and end all of Yeongjongdo, it's also famous for its kilometres of thick mud and clams. Beyond the uninspiring **Unseo 'New Town'** cluster of airport hotels are beaches that draw huge crowds each summer. **Eurwangni Beach** (032 751-0015, free admission, but ₩15,000 for an umbrella and mat) is famous for its expansive sands, gorgeous sunsets and nightly fireworks.

A few minutes' walk from **Mashiran Beach** is one of Korea's shortest ferry journeys. Take the ten-minute sailing to beautiful **Muuido Island** to visit its two lovely beaches, **Silmi** and **Hanagae**.

ONGJIN COUNTY

Exactly 100 of Incheon's islands have been lumped together under the banner of **Ongjin County**. About 17,000 people, most employed in the fishing industry, call them home. Despite perennial tension with North Korea, they have become popular destinations for beachcombers and sport fishers. From Yeongjongdo's Sammok Dock, ferries depart hourly for Shindo Dock and sail onward to Jangbongdo Dock. Connected to Shindo via a bridge, Modo Island's **Baemikkumi Beach** is famous for its sensual sculpture park.

Most of Ongjin's outer islands are served by boats that depart from the Incheon Port International Passenger Terminal at Yeonan Wharf. While Jawoldo Island's **Keunmal** and **Jangol beaches** feature dramatic tides that make for great beachcombing, Seungbongdo Island is home to the classy **Dongyang Condominiums** (784 Seungbong-ri, Jawol-myeon, 032 832-1818).

Further afield is Deokjeokdo Island, where you'll find one of the best beaches in the Yellow Sea region: **Seopori Beach**, two kilometres long and surrounded by 200-year-old pine trees. If you'd like to venture even further, it's a two-hour ferry trip to **Yeonpyeongdo Island**, famous for its hiking trails and the majestic **Papillon Cliff**.

It will take four hours by boat to reach South Korea's true island outposts, **Socheongdo**, **Daecheongdo** and **Baengnyeongdo**. **Socheongdo Lighthouse** is located at the end of a bumpy four-kilometre-long road, while Daecheongdo has a pair of beaches – **Jiduri** and **Satandong** – that are popular with families for their shallow water and gentle surf. Baengnyeongdo, set at the mouth of North Korea's Daedongman Bay, is South Korea's north-western frontier. In addition to **Shimcheonggak**, a 360-square-metre pavilion honouring a famous Korean folk opera, there is the **Dumujin** seashore, whose dramatic rock outcroppings are said to resemble a line of military generals. Note that Baengnyeongdo was, in 2010, the site of a North Korean attack (*see p204* **North Korea: Against the Odds**).

WHERE TO STAY & EAT

The region's overnight accommodation varies widely, from a cluster of international transit hotels on Yeongjongdo to guesthouses on the outer islands that are often run by the family next door (or, sometimes more literally, in the next room).

In airport land, if you want a full-service spa, pool and business centre amenities, book a room at the **Hyatt Regency Incheon** (2850 Woounso-dong, Jung-gu, 032 745-1234, www.incheon.regency.hyatt.com, doubles ₩260,0000-₩340,000). A significant step down – but with an ocean view – is the three-star **Ocean Beach Airport Hotel** (773-2 Eulwang-dong, Jung-gu, 032 751-1177, ₩75,000 double). It's close to Eulwangri beach, provides a complimentary airport shuttle and has free wireless internet in public areas. Good food shouldn't be hard to find. **Haesong** (238-3 Eulwang-dong, Jung-gu, 032 747-0073, ₩10,000 *ssambap* set meal) is famous for its hotpot snail *ssambap*. Sashimi lovers should visit **Nonmeori Jayeonsan Hoetjip** (114-1 Deogyodong, Jung-gu, 032 746-8844, around ₩80,000 for a kilogramme of assorted fish).

On Ganghwado, budget travellers have the huge if uninspired **Ganghwa Namsan Youth Hostel** (439-18 Namsan-ri, 032 934-7778, dorms ₩10,000, family rooms also available), located about ten minutes from the Oepo-ri ferry terminal and 20 minutes from the bus terminal. If you'd like to stay in a traditional Korean home, try **Namchwidang Hanok Iyagi Pension** (113 Sagi-ri, Hwado-myeon, 010 9591-0226, www.cafe.naver.com/skacnlekd, two-person room from ₩100,000), which is just east of Mt Manisan.

Ganghwa is renowned for its horse crabs, roasted eel and high-quality ginseng. **Seoul Hoetjip** (032 933-5433, ₩50,000 for two) in

Bomunsa Temple, Seongmodo. *See p209.*

Oepo-ri is famous for its crab stew, while eel restaurants, including **Seonchangjip** (320-3 Sinjeong-ri, Seonwon-myeon, 032 932-7628, ₩60,000 for one kilogramme), are clustered near the Ganghwa Bridge.

To spend the night on Korea's final frontier, Baengnyeong Island, try the comfortable but basic **Island Castle** (316-3 Jinchon-ri, 032 836-6700, www.islandcastle.kr, doubles ₩60,000-₩70,000). For meals, **Sagot Naengmyeon** (528-1 Jinchon-ri, 032 836-0559, ₩5,000) near Sagot Beach is the place for delicious noodles; the sea urchin *kalguksu* is recommended.

GETTING THERE

Yeongjongdo, Muuido & Sindo

From Incheon International Airport, Airport Gate 2 on the third level, you can catch bus no.302 or 306 to Yeongjongdo's Eurwangni Beach (20mins, ₩1,000 or free with transfer). Yongju Marine Transportation operates a ferry between Yeongjongdo and Wolmido (032 762-8880, every 30mins 7am-9pm daily, ₩1,500 adult, ₩6,000 car). A 10min walk from Mashiran Beach is Jamjindo Dock, where Muuido Marine Transportation (032 751-3354, www.muuido.kr) ferries depart for Muuido Island every 15-30mins 7.30am-7pm/7.30pm daily (return ₩3,000 adult, ₩18,000 car). Sejong Shipping Co (032 884-4155, www.sejonghaeun.com) operates ferries from Yeongjongdo's Sammock Dock to Shindo (₩3,600 return) and Jangbongdo (₩5,500 return) islands every hour 7.10am-6.10pm daily. The last ferry back departs Jangbongdo at 6pm and Shindo at 6.30pm.

Ganghwado, Seongmodo & Jumundo

From Seoul, buses leave for Ganghwado from Sinchon Bus Terminal (Seoul line 2's Sinchon station, exit 7, walk 200m) every 10-15mins 5.40am-11.20pm daily (032 934 9811, 70mins, ₩3,400 one-way). From Incheon, buses depart every 15mins 5.20am-9.30pm daily (2hrs, ₩3,500 one-way). On Ganghwado, local buses loop around the major tourist sites.

Ferries to Seongmodo and Jumundo islands depart from Ganghwado's Oepo-ri ferry dock. Seongmodo ferries leave every 30mins 7am-8pm daily in the summer, but stop as early as 6.30pm in the winter (10mins, ₩1,000 adult, from ₩7,000 car), while boats to Jumundo depart just twice daily at 9am and 4pm, with returns at 7am and 2pm (90mins, ₩7,200 adult, from ₩30,000 car).

Outer islands

You can head further afield aboard ferries that depart from Incheon Port International Passenger Terminal at Yeonan Wharf (www.dom.icferry.or.kr).

Ferries to Jawoldo, Seungbongdo and Soijakdo islands (032 887-2891) run once daily Mon-Thur, once or twice on Fri and two or three times Sat &

Sun (70mins, ₩12,100-₩20,000 adult, ₩47,000 car to Jawoldo; ₩11,000-₩18,400 adult, ₩49,000 car to Seungbongdo and Soijakdo).

Ferries to Deokjeokdo Island (02 1577-2891) depart twice daily Mon-Fri with an additional sailing on the weekends (70mins for ₩21,900 or 2hrs for ₩12,100, car ₩54,000).

Ferries Yeonpyeongdo and Soyeonpyeongdo depart once daily (02 1577-2891, 2hrs, ₩44,400 to Yeonpyeongdo, ₩42,300 to Soyeonpyeongdo).

Finally, ferries to Socheongdo, Daecheongdo and Baengnyeongdo leave three times a day (032 887-2891, 4hrs, ₩51,600 to Socheongdo, ₩54,500 to Daecheongdo, ₩57,400 to Baengnyeongdo).

TOURIST INFORMATION

Information about Yeongjongdo and Muuido can be found at the **Incheon Tourism Organisation (INTO)** office at Incheon International Airport (*see p209*).

Ganghwado Tourism Office provides helpful information at its bus terminal location (032 930-3515, open 9am-5pm Mon,Wed-Sun winter, until 6pm summer) and at a small office outside the Oepo-ri ferry dock (Seokpo ri, Samsan-myeon, 032 934-5565).

Ongjin County Office in Incheon (627-608 Yonghyeon-dong, Nam-gu, 032 899-2114) also has information on all the islands, as do brochures you can pick up at the ferry docks. There's also a great English-language website (www.ongjin.go.kr) with details to help you plan your trip.

Suwon

In the late 18th century, King Jeongjo attempted something bold: to move Korea's capital 30 kilometres (19 miles) south, in an effort to escape Seoul's big-city drama. That effort failed and, more than two centuries later, Suwon is merely a provincial capital. Nevertheless, this city of one million functions, for many, as a smaller and rather attractive alternative to Seoul.

Nicknamed the City of Filial Piety, Suwon showcases the Confucianism that still pervades much of Korean culture. The city's most popular landmarks – including its two UNESCO-recognised treasures, the **Hwaseong Fortress** and **Yunggeolleung Royal Tombs**, and the graceful **Hwaseong Haenggung** temporary palace – promote respect for family and authority.

In modern Suwon, however, the head of the household might work at home-grown favourite Samsung Electronics during the week, and on weekends take the family to **World Cup Park**. Once there, fans enthusiastically watch the **Samsung Bluewings** football team kick towards their next national or continental title.

If you don't feel like supporting Korea's biggest conglomerate, perhaps a visit to the attractive **Gyeonggi Arts Center** complex and gardens is a better fit. Or, for the night owl, make your way to the bars and clubs on Rodeo Street, and around the city's 16 colleges and universities.

Also within the Suwon area are the colossal theme park **Everland** (*see p167*) and the intriguing **Korean Folk Village**.

SIGHTSEEING

Suwon may have been Korea's only completely walled city, but long ago its neighbourhoods moved beyond the fortress gates. Nevertheless, the majestic Hwaseong Fortress remains Suwon's focal point, and most of the prime tourist destinations aren't far from it.

From Suwon station, take the pedestrian overpass and walk eastward. A kilometre away is **Suwon Hyanggyo**, a Confucian academy dating from the 13th century that was relocated in the late 1700s when the fortress was under construction. Inside is a large statue of Confucius.

Back on the main street, take a quick look at the **Former Bugukwon Building**, a handsome, three-storey, grey brick structure built in 1916. A few blocks on, turn left at the big intersection and look ahead – the stately **Paldalmun Gate** should come into view. Walk about 300 metres (985 feet) towards it before making a right turn. The brief detour is to pay respects to **Geobuksandang**, a colourful 'turtle shrine' that originated in around 1790 to promote peace and prosperity for **Yeongdong Market**'s merchants. Inside is an altar where offerings of food, flowers and incense are still made every 7 October.

Retrace your steps and make a bee-line for Paldalmun Gate, the southern entrance to **Hwaseong Fortress**. The gate, whose name means 'open in all directions', is protected by a stone *ongseong* semi-circle. The 5.7-kilometre-long wall starts one block west. Follow it up **Mt Paldalsan** and note the various pavilions, gates and sentry towers – of the 48 built along the wall in 1796, 41 remain. Among them, the **Seojangdae** command post and adjacent **Seonodae** crossbow tower are outstanding examples of the integration of western and eastern architectural styles to create a beautiful, yet formidable, bulwark against invasion.

Farther along the ridgeline is the striking **Seobuk Gongsimdon** observation tower. The powerful, three-level, stone and brick edifice is peppered with holes for cannons and archers. Further afield is **Janganmun**; the largest gate ever constructed in Korea, it was destroyed during the Korean War, but rebuilt in 1979.

Korean Folk Village.

At this point, take the road that leads away from Janganmun to **Hwaseong Haenggung Palace**. The largest of the Joseon Dynasty's temporary palaces, it once contained a staggering 576 rooms. The 2010 reconstruction was a dramatic downsizing, but it's still worth a visit. While you're there, stop by **Hwaryeongjeon**, which enshrines King Jeongjo's spirit tablet, and the **Suwon Hwaseong Museum**, which is located across the street just past the Suwoncheon stream. If your feet could do with a rest at this point, why not enjoy Suwon's signature dish – barbecue beef ribs – at **Yeonpo Galbi**. Afterwards, you can hop on the **Dragon Trolley**, which stops outside the palace and five other sites along the wall for just ₩1,500.

Walkers can follow the stream northwards to the wall's **Hwahongmun**. The pavilion (a popular napping spot) spans the waterway atop seven graceful stone arches. As the wall continues eastward, you'll arrive at a large lawn where visitors try their hand at **traditional Korean archery** (five arrows for ₩1,000). From there, the wall makes a direct shot past the **Bongdon** smoke towers to **Jidong Market**, which is just 200 metres from Paldalmun, where you started.

After circumnavigating the fortress, it's time to explore contemporary Suwon. From the bus stop just north of Paldalmun, the southbound no.98 bus goes to **Hyowon Park** and the **Wolhwawon Traditional Chinese Garden**. The two parks make up the top third of a one-kilometre-long civic green belt near City Hall. The central section is home to the expansive **Gyeonggi Arts Center**, while the bottom third is occupied by **Ingye Art Park** and **Suwon Outdoor Concert Hall**.

If time allows, wrap up your Suwon walkabout with a visit to the **Yunggeolleung**

Royal Tombs and nearby **Yongjusa Temple**. Buses depart opposite the concert hall's east entrance and pass Suwon station before reaching the tombs (the journey takes just over an hour). The serene setting is the final resting place for King Jeongjo and his wife, Queen Hyoui. By the king's request, his father's and mother's remains were also moved here. Given the king's broad legacy on Korea, it's a fitting conclusion.

Gyeonggi Arts Center
Ingyedong 1117 (031 230-3200, www.ggac.or.kr). Suwon station (Seoul line 1), exit 1. Open Ticket office 10am-7pm Mon-Fri; 10am-5pm Sat, Sun, holidays. **Tickets** ₩10,000-₩120,000.
A focal point for classical music, dance and performing arts in the province since 1991, this five-floor cultural centre presents high-quality Korean and foreign talent at weekly concerts and musicals.

★ Hwaseong Fortress
Paldallo 2-ga 138 (031 251-4435, http://ehs. suwon.ne.kr). Suwon station (Seoul line 1), exit 1. **Open** *Mar-Oct* 9am-6pm daily. *Nov-Feb* 9am-5pm daily. **Admission** ₩1,000.
One of Korea's greatest architectural treasures, the 5.7km-long wall was completed in 1796 by the kingdom's first paid labourers. The walls were designed to repel future Japanese invasions. Despite extensive damage during the Korean War, most of its majestic gates, sentry towers and pavilions remain, suggesting a powerful and sophisticated era. The fortress was added to UNESCO's World Heritage List in 1997.

Hwaseong Haenggung
Namchangdong 6-2 (031 228-4677, ehs.suwon. ne.kr). Suwon station (Seoul line 1), exit 1. **Open** *Mar-Oct* 9am-6pm daily. *Nov-Feb* 9am-5pm daily. **Admission** ₩1,000.
The Joseon Dynasty's largest temporary palace was fully restored in 2010. Once boasting 576 separate rooms, it was used as a rest stop of sorts for kings on their way to and from Seoul. Over the years, it has also been used for special events and commemorations. A changing of the palace guard ceremony takes place at 2pm every Sunday from April to October. Next door is Hwaryeongjeon, where King Jeongjo's spirit tablet is enshrined.

Hwaseong Museum
21 Poeun Boulevard (031 228-4205, http://hs museum.suwon.ne.kr). Suwon station (Seoul line 1), exit 1. **Open** 9am-6pm Tue-Sun. **Admission** ₩2,000.
A two-floor complex of informative exhibits about the fortress's construction and the many contributions made by its patron, King Jeongjo. In addition to three permanent exhibition venues, there is a kids' experience centre, a cafeteria and a shop. Check out the landscaped roof-top deck for great views of the fortress.

FREE Hyanggyo Confucian Academy
Gyodong 43 (031 245-7639, www.skk-suwon.com). Suwon station (Seoul line 1), exit 1. **Open** 9am-5pm Mon-Fri (groups only Sat). **Admission** free.
The school consists of six buildings on two terraces surrounded by a traditional stone and tile wall. Once used to teach local students the tenets of Korean Confucianism and filial piety, the wall currently holds the memorial tablets of Confucius, Mencius and 25 important men from Korean history.

Praiseworthy Potties

Thrones fit for a king.

Suwon is home to a palace, a fortress... and over 40 world-class public restrooms of ambitious size and design. The latter are thanks to South Korean parliamentarian and two-time former Suwon mayor Sim Jae-duck, a man better known as 'Mr T'. Mr T was passionate about how sanitary toilet facilities and sewer systems could help reduce the two million deaths (mainly of children) that occur worldwide each year following the contraction of waterborne diseases. To that end, he founded the WTO – not the global trade group, but the World Toilet Organisation. After Sim's death in 2009, his widow donated their million-dollar home (toilet bowl-shaped, of course) to the city of Suwon. Today, the colossal commode is also a temple to toilets, as the excellent **Toilet Museum** (186-3 Imokdong, 031 228-4629, open 10am-6pm Tue-Sun, until 5pm Nov-Feb). As you might expect, its own toilet facilities are not to be missed.

ESCAPES & EXCURSIONS

★ Korean Folk Village

Boradong 107, Yongin City, Gyeonggi Province (031 288-0000, www.koreanfolk.co.kr). Suwon station (Seoul line 1), exit 1, then bus. **Open** 9am-6pm daily. **Admission** ₩15,000.

This re-creation of a dynastic village is slightly saccharine but absorbing. Poking around the traditional buildings is quite enjoyable, though everyone is here for the shows, which take place twice a day (11am-1pm, 2.30-4pm). There's a tightrope display and gents firing arrows from prancing horses, though the undoubted highlight is the farmers' dance, in which ribbon-hatted men dance around to a cacophonous drumbeat. Buses leave hourly from Suwon.

World Cup Stadium

Umandong 228 (031 202-2002, www.suwon worldcup.or.kr). Suwon station (Seoul line 1), exit 1. **Open** *Mar-Oct* 9am-6pm daily. *Nov-Feb* 9am-5pm daily. Opening hours of facilities vary. **Admission** *World Cup Memorial Hall* ₩1,000.

This 43,000-capacity stadium was built for the 2002 Korea–Japan World Cup. The roof is said to resemble a flying creature, hence its nickname, the Big Bird. In addition to watching the Samsung Bluewings football team, you can make use of the huge sports centre and sauna, as well as have a poke around the World Cup Memorial Hall soccer museum.

Yunggeolleung Royal Tombs

Hyohaengno 481, Hwaseong City (031 222-0142, http://hwaseong.cha.go.kr). Suwon station (Seoul line 1), exit 1. **Open** *Mar-Oct* 9am-5.30pm Tue-Sun. *Nov-Feb* 9am-4.30pm Tue-Sun. **Admission** ₩1,000.

Among Korea's 40 UNESCO-recognised Joseon royal tomb sites, two joint tombs – those of King Jeongjo and Queen Hyoui, and Jeongjo's father King Jangjo and his queen Heongyeong – are located on a peaceful mountainside not far from Hwaseong Fortress. Colourful T-shaped wooden shrines are set in front of burial mounds protected by stone figures of people and animals.

WHERE TO EAT & DRINK

Jangsu Saenggogi

Ingyedong 1121-4 (031 224-5311). Suwon station (Seoul line 1), exit 1. **Open** 11am-10pm daily. **Average** ₩20,000-₩40,000.

Although the name of a former Chinese restaurant is still visible under the modern neon sign, inside it's no doubt that traditional Korean cuisine in on the menu. The restaurant specialises in delicious slabs of pork belly, but all products – meat, eggs, rice and vegetables – are domestically produced.

Namu Keuneul

Maesanno 1-ga 11-15 (031 257-7806, www. restree.net). Suwon station (Seoul line 1), exit 1. **Open** 11.30am-10pm daily. **Average** ₩3,900 self-service bar.

A popular (and peculiar) chain of coffee shops that offers so much more. Choose from juice, dessert waffles, a dozen organic teas and a dozen yoghurt or shaved ice flavours, as well as a small library, nail care services and even a miniature pool where tiny fish nibble at the dead skin on your toes.

Osatto

Ingyedong 1115-13 (031 233-9811, www.osatto. com). Suwon station (Seoul line 1), exit 1. **Open** 10am-11pm daily. **Average** ₩20,000-₩40,000.

Since 1990 this popular restaurant, located on the periphery of the Gyeonggi Arts Center (*see p213*), has specialised in seafood stews and hotpots packed with clams, prawns, abalone and octopus, as well as the pungent delicacy of raw flower crabs marinated in soy sauce. Dine in or take out.

Yaennaljip

Seryu 3-ga 147-45 (031 223-2534). Suwon station (Seoul line 1), exit 1. **Open** 11.30am-11.30pm daily. **Average** ₩10,000-₩20,000.

If Suwon's countless beef *galbi* restaurants have overwhelmed you, this pork-focused restaurant can provide an alternative treat. It's much beloved locally for its spicy *jokbal* pigs' feet and seasoned *gamjatang* potato soup, served with a rack of pork ribs in a spicy simmering broth.

★ Yeonpo Galbi

Buksudong 25-4 (031 245-5900). Suwon station (Seoul line 1), exit 1. **Open** 10am-10pm daily. **Average** ₩10,000-₩20,000.

The log-cabin façade doesn't quite fit in with its surroundings, but this popular restaurant, located just west of the Suwoncheon stream, serves just about everything *galbi*. Take your pick from a list of barbecue rib meal sets, with beef from Australia, the US or one of Korea's own happy *hanu* heifers.

GETTING THERE

By train

Suwon station on Seoul Metro line 1 can be reached from Seoul station in 63mins (₩1,600 single) on a subway train. Regular trains from Seoul station take only half the time.

TOURIST INFORMATION

The **Suwon Culture & Tourism Office** operates a number of visitor centres, as well as a helpful English-language website (http:// eng.suwon.ne.kr). Given Suwon's limited subway service, Seoul Metro line 1's Suwon station (exit 1) is the nearest rail station to all tour offices.

Hwaseong Haenggung Tourist Information Center *Namchangdong 6-2 (031 228-4480).* Located next to the palace inside the fortress wall. **Main Office** *Ingyedong 1111 (031 228-2068).*

Paldalmun Gate Office *Namchangdong 148-8 (031 228-2765).* One block west of Paldalmun Gate, where the fortress wall begins.

Suwon Station Tourist Information Center *Suwon station, Maesanno 1-ga 18 (031 228-4672). All* **Open** *Mar-Oct* 9am-6pm daily. *Nov-Feb* 9am-5pm daily.

Gongju

Less than an hour and a half from Seoul by bus is Gongju, one of the most delightful small towns in Korea. From 475 to 538, it served as the capital of Baekje, one of Korea's famed Three Kingdoms. Many centuries have since elapsed, but a fair amount of dynastic draws remain and, pleasingly, all are within walking distance of one other. Outside Gongju is rugged Gyeryongsan National Park, which is home to a couple of beautiful Buddhist temples.

SIGHTSEEING

The **River Geumgang** slides through town; on its southern bank you'll see the ancient walls of **Gongsanseong**, a fortress that curls a two-kilometre loop along a caldera-like ridge. Heading directly west on a wide but quiet road, you'll come to the grassy **Royal Tombs**, the park-like final resting place of seven Baekje royals. Just beyond this is **Gongju National Museum**, where hundreds of treasures found in the tombs are displayed. On the way to the museum, you'll pass **Gongju Hanok Village**, a small, replica village of wooden housing that opened in late 2010. It's possible to stay the night here and, given the tranquil environs, doing so is highly recommended.

★ **FREE Gongju National Museum**
Ungjindong 360 (041 854-2205, http://gongju. museum.go.kr). **Open** 9am-6pm Mon-Fri; 9am-7pm Sat, Sun. **Admission** free.
Don't let the name fool you: almost every city in Korea has a 'national museum'. However, this is one of the most enjoyable in the country, and it's certainly the best place in which to see ancient artefacts from the Baekje Dynasty. Pride of place goes to the golden ornaments once worn by Baekje royalty (displayed on the lower level), including flamelike panels once worn on the heads of the kings, and bracelets, necklaces and pendants. On the upper level are pieces of earthenware; as with jewellery, the Baekje kingdom was once Asia's frontrunner in pottery.

★ **Gongsanseong**
Geumseongdong 65-3 (041 856-0331).
Open 9am-6pm daily. **Admission** ₩1,200.

Suwon's Hwaseong (*see p213*) may have its UNESCO badge of recommendation, but for many, Gongsanseong is the best fortress in Korea. Hwaseong's merits are mainly architectural, but its messy interior puts paid to any dynastic atmosphere; the reverse can be said of Gongsanseong, whose perimeter walls contain nought but pine and maple trees, hilly walking paths, a solitary temple and a collection of superbly painted pavilions. Two of these are particularly notable: Imnyugak and Ssangsujeong. The former is visually arresting: climb the wooden staircase, gaze upwards and stare in awe at the soothing, yet highly ornate, squares of painted green. Ssangsujeong is nowhere near as special to look at, but its history is fascinating. It commemorates two trees once located nearby, which were appointed 'high government officials' in the 1620s. Injo, the king at the time, took refuge beneath the trees during a particularly fierce rebellion, and promoted them to leafy positions of power. Sadly, they're no longer around.

Gongsanseong's 2.4km-long perimeter wall was erected shortly after Gongju became the Baekje capital in the fifth century. Back then, the wall was far shorter and made from dirt, though it has been lined with stone since the 17th century. Walking around the wall offers a 360-degree view of Gongju, though the terrain is extremely steep in places – if you have to make a choice, aim for the northern section, which gazes down over the river.

Royal Tombs
Geumseongdong 5-1 (041 856-0331).
Open 9am-6pm daily. **Admission** ₩1,500.
In the days before it became the world's second most densely populated country of any size (Bangladesh is the victor in this particular race), Korea buried its dead on mountain slopes, in small, grass-covered hillocks. This practice still rumbles on today with the rural and/or affluent – basically, the larger the mound, the more important the person. In Baekje times, none was more important than royalty, and the tombs of dynastic kings and queens were often over ten metres in height, and contained carefully selected artefacts from royal life. Just west of central Gongju lie seven such mounds. Despite their size, they remained hidden for centuries and were only rediscovered in the 1920s. The most interesting

INSIDE TRACK
CHANGING OF THE GUARD

In April, May, June and September, try to time your visit to Gongsanseong for early afternoon: at 2pm, a colourful Changing of the Guard ceremony takes place at the western gate. It's also the centre of activity during the **Baekje Festival** in autumn.

The Baekje Kingdom

The rise and fall of a dynasty.

From the time of Christ to the middle of the seventh century, Korea came under the rule of the famed Three Kingdoms: Baekje, Silla and Goguryeo. In these dynastic times, there were no set borders, and the three jostled for power across the peninsula. Baekje was founded in 18 BC, with Onjo its first king; Onjo decided to create his own kingdom after seeing his brother inherit the north-based kingdom of Goguryeo, which had been founded two decades earlier by their father. The first Baekje capital was in Wiryeseong – now swallowed by the sands of time, but almost certainly within the borders of today's Seoul.

At its height, Baekje ruled the western half of present-day South Korea, plus a small chunk of what is now North Korea. Pressure from Goguryeo pushed Baekje south over the years; Gongju (then known as Ungjin) became the capital in 475, giving its crown to the nearby town of Sabi (now Buyeo) in 538. Sabi was the last of the Baekje capitals, for, in 660, the east-based Silla kingdom staged a final attack with their allies from the Chinese Tang Dynasty. Within six years, they would conquer Goguryeo, too, and become the first kingdom to rule over the whole Korean peninsula. Thirty-one Baekje kings had been and gone before their dynastic line was trampled to the ground.

The Baekje kingdom achieved a lot while ruling for more than six centuries. Its influence spread across the country and beyond – and is still in evidence today, particularly in Japan. Although located on the opposite side of the peninsula, Baekje had a strong alliance with the Wa, rulers of Japan at the time; at least one of Baekje's kings was born across the East Sea, and intermarriage took place between Korean and Japanese royalty. Skilled Baekje artisans were sent across the water, and had a highly visible influence on Japanese art. Nowadays, Japan may be far more famed than Korea for jewellery, furniture and fabric, but Baekje supplied its early teachers. However, art pales into insignificance compared with another export; during Sabi's time as the capital, Buddhism made its way across the waves, meaning that Japan has Baekje to thank for every single one of its temples and Buddhist shrines.

tomb, that of King Muryong, was uncovered in 1971, during maintenance work on other tombs. This was the only one of the seven not to have fallen prey to thieves, and the resulting cache of Baekje goodies – almost 3,000 artefacts, seven of which have since been designated National Treasures – makes up much of what you'll see just down the road at the National Museum.

The tombs themselves are now sealed off, though a mock-up has been built for visitors, showing how the interiors would have once looked. Otherwise, there are no sights as such, but the grassy, undulating grounds are a wonderful place for a stroll – the place is quite enchanting under the soft light of dusk.

Out of town

There are two terrific Buddhist temples on the outskirts of Gongju. To the west is **Magoksa**, one of the main temples of Jogye, Korea's largest Buddhist sect, and one of the country's most beautiful temples. The large, sprawling complex is set amid bucolic countryside, around 40 minutes by bus from Gongju – catch the no.7, which runs from the local bus terminal south of the river. Nobody is quite sure of the age of the temple, but most accounts date it from the early 640s, just after Gongju relinquished its status as capital of Baekje. Magoksa's focal point is the Daeungbojeon, a large, two-storey hall overlooking the rest of the site.

East of Gongju is **Gyeryongsan National Park**, whose chunky mountains separate the city from Daejeon (information is available on the Korea National Park Service website, english.knps.or.kr). The park has wonderful temples at both its eastern and western ends. Closest to Gongju is **Gapsa**, founded in 420. It's a gentle 20-minute walk from the road on a tree-lined path; those with some pep in their legs can head further into the mountains, perhaps even as far as **Donghaksa** temple to the east (a tough three-hour walk). To reach Gapsa, take bus no.2 from Gongju bus terminal; it's a half-hour journey. When returning, make sure that you're on the correct no.2 bus – rather ridiculously, the two routes starting from Gapsa both have the same number, but the other one heads to Daejeon. Alternatively, get a taxi from Gongju for around ₩15,000. Note that you'll need to arrange a pick-up time with your driver for the return journey.

WHERE TO EAT

★ Gomanaru

Geumseongdong 184-4 (857-9999). **Open** 9am-10pm daily. **Average** ₩10,000. English menu.
An old favourite, this restaurant has seen its popularity boom recently after featuring in some major Korean food and travel television shows. Its new-found fame is richly deserved, for this is perhaps the best place in the country in which to eat a *ssam-bap* meal. *Ssam* is Korean for 'leaves', and for ₩10,000 per person you get what seems like a whole tree's worth of leaves, as well as no fewer than 20 different side dishes. These include duck meat, quail's eggs, potato salad, grilled gingko nuts, garlic rice, a river fish and much more. For an extra ₩5,000 per head, you can have the whole meal blanketed with edible flowers – one of the most scincillating culinary experiences that Korea can offer. Gomanaru is next to the entrance to Gongsanseong, making it the perfect place to fall into after a tour of the fortress.

Nong Ga

Geumseongdong 192-3 (854-8338). **Open** 10am-10pm daily. **Average** ₩7,000.
A simple eaterie that weaves chestnut – a Gongju speciality, *bam* in Korean – into each and every one of its dishes. The pancakes, dumplings, noodle soups and other items on the Korean-only menu are truly delicious, and prices are extremely reasonable. You can also get a bottle of chestnut *makgeolli* for ₩3,000. The restaurant is on a small side street 50m south of Gomanaru, just across the road from the fortress.

WHERE TO STAY

Gongju's accommodation options are very poor; the town' few international visitors usually drop by on a day trip from Seoul. The only official hotel is the **Hotel Kumgang** (041 852-1071), a short walk west of the bus station. It's essentially a motel, though its twin rooms and provision of a measly breakfast bumps it up a category. All rooms have comfortable beds, internet-ready computers and excellent shower stalls, and prices are very reasonable at ₩40,000 per room. It's surrounded by dozens of far seedier motels, all charging about the same; there are also some cheaper, older guesthouses south of the river.

An interesting place to stay, **Gongju Hanok Village**, just west of the town centre, is a replica village of wooden houses. At the time of writing, only dormitory rooms were available, but spartan double rooms were on the way.

It's also possible to stay at **Magoksa** temple; check the national Templestay website (http://eng.templestay.com) for details.

GETTING THERE

Unusually for a Korean city of any size, there is no railway station in Gongju. The nearest stations are in Daejeon, accessible from Seoul by high-speed train, but it's far faster to take the bus direct to Gongju.

By bus

Buses run along the highway for most of the journey between Seoul and Gongju, making the trip incredibly fast. The official estimate is 90mins, but most buses beat this by ten minutes or so outside peak hours. Services operate from two bus stations in southern Seoul: every 40mins from the Express Bus Terminal (subway lines 3, 7 and 9), and every 20mins from Nambu Bus Terminal (subway line 3). The last bus from the Express Terminal is usually at 11pm, but from Nambu service can dry up before 8pm.

Gongju's bus station is a few hundred metres from the north bank of the Geumgang river. You can walk from the station to all the sights covered here (all of which are south of the river, across a part-pedestrianised, colonial-era bridge), though a ₩4,000 taxi ride will be easier on the legs.

TOURIST INFORMATION

There's a good tourist information booth outside the main entrance of Gongsanseong (*see p215*); staff can give travel advice, dispense maps and book accommodation. Another, far less useful, booth is near the entrance to the Royal Tombs (*see p215*). Some of the basics are also covered – in English – on the city's official tourism homepage (http://tour.gongju.go.kr).

Danyang

A small town in North Chungcheong province, Danyang is located on the fringe of a peninsula that juts into a tranquil lake. River-like in appearance, this is a man-made entity: a dam swallowed the old town whole in 1986. Almost everything you'll see has been built since that time, though an air of decay is already quite apparent – no bad thing, since it merely adds to the town's worn charm. It makes a highly appealing getaway from teeming Seoul. Only two or three of its roads could be described as 'busy', the town-centre bus terminal never has more than a couple of vehicles parked outside, and most restaurants are closed by 9pm.

However, the sights that draw most visitors to Danyang are not in the town at all. Just on the other side of the lake – a ten-minute walk across the bridge – are the **Gosu Caves**, a stunning labyrinthine warren of underground crevices. Half an hour away by bus (take one of the hourly services from the bus station) is **Guinsa**, quite possibly the most visually spectacular temple in the whole of Korea. There's also fun to be had on the lake itself: **cruise boats** head between Danyang and the city of Chungju just to the west, and en route you'll spot a number of huge boulders jutting out of the water.

Gosu Caves

Gosuri (043 422-3072). **Open** 9am-5pm daily. **Admission** ₩5,000.

Just north of Danyang town centre, these limestone caves stretch underground for well over a kilometre. Several major crevices have been made accessible on chunky metal walkways, though only one route will be open on any given day. The caves can be quite tight, and are not suitable for those with a fear of confined spaces. Dozens of restaurants sit outside the cave entrance, and the food is as good as you'll find in the centre of town.

★ FREE Guinsa

Baekjari (043 423-7100). **Open** 24hrs daily. **Admission** free.

Guinsa is the headquarters of the Cheontae sect, an originally Chinese branch of Buddhism that faded into obscurity before being resuscitated in 1945 by Seongwol Wongak, a local monk. He had travelled much of China in order to broaden his knowledge, and this influence is keenly felt in the colour schemes and architectural styles employed in this temple – nowhere else in Korea will you see such bold paintwork or the use of vertical lines. Almost all buildings have been designed with size, rather than beauty, in mind, except for the one at the top of the tight valley in which the complex sprawls; bizarrely, this contains no Buddhist deity, but a huge golden statue of the founding monk, complete with sideburns. The gleaming, golden building has incredibly rich detail in both its paintwork and wooden latticing, though its appearance is spoiled somewhat by the empty, car park-like area immediately outside.

Seeing the entire complex is hard work, given the steepness of the valley. However, making your way up is highly enjoyable. Depending on which path you choose, you'll find yourself burrowing under- and overground; the site is home to what is, surely, the only Buddhist sky path in Korea. You can also stay overnight at the temple; this is best arranged through a tourist office in Seoul (*see p230*). There are also a number of restaurants and cheap guest-houses just down the hill.

WHERE TO STAY & EAT

As is often the case in provincial Korea, Danyang suffers from a near-total dearth of quality accommodation. The only bona fide hotel in town is the **Eidelweiss** (043 421-9988, www.danyanghotel.com), located in an uninteresting area just across the river from the train station. Rooms start at ₩56,000, increasing to ₩85,000 at weekends. It's worth paying around 30 per cent more for the suites, which have been decorated in an ostentatious manner. There's a curl of cheap motels (rooms from ₩30,000) along the lakeside in the town centre. Just past the bridge is the **Motel Luxury** (421-9911), which fulfils most people's expectations of a love hotel: garishly decorated and with no guest services to speak of, though rooms are squeaky clean and actually quite stylish. Rooms start at ₩70,000.

GETTING THERE

By boat

Danyang is accessible by boat from Chungju, an uninteresting city to the west. Times vary by the season and the services have, from time to time, been cancelled altogether; the journey takes two hours, with a ticket costing ₩18,000.

By bus

There's no direct highway from Seoul to Danyang, and traffic on the main roads leading in and out of the capital regularly gets snarled up at weekends. At other times, the journey takes 2.5hrs from Seoul's Express Bus Terminal (subway lines 3, 7 & 9), and a little longer from the Dongseoul bus terminal in the east of the city (Gangbyeon subway, line 2). A ticket costs ₩14,000.

By train

Travelling by train from Seoul's Cheongnyangni station (subway line 1) is undoubtedly the best way of getting to Danyang. There are seven services a day (₩10,300, journey 2-3hrs); the last train back to Seoul leaves at 8.47pm. Danyang station is a fair way from the centre of town; a taxi will cost ₩5,000. Alternatively, it's a beautiful hour-long walk beside the lake, mainly on a sheltered promenade, though there's no direct footpath between the station and the bridge.

TOURIST INFORMATION

Danyang is a small town and almost nobody here speaks English, including staff in the small bus terminal and at most motels. However, there's a pretty good **tourist information booth** (open 9am-6pm) on the end of the bridge.

Directory

Getting Around

ARRIVING & LEAVING

By air

Two airports serve Seoul, with the overwhelming majority of international flights landing at **Incheon International Airport**. Completed in 2001 and generally agreed to be among the world's top airports, it's situated in the West Sea on Yeongjeongdo, an island some 65km (40 miles) west of central Seoul. Most internal flights, as well as a smattering from China and Japan, land at **Gimpo International Airport**, which is located almost exactly halfway between Incheon International Airport and Seoul city centre.

Incheon International Airport

Flight information 032 741-0114, www.airport.kr.

There are several ways to reach central Seoul from the airport, and mercifully all are very simple. Most arrivals use one of the many **airport bus routes** that head into the city – staff at the airport's many information kiosks will be able to advise on which one to take, as well as when and where it will depart from. Buses into Seoul usually depart every 10-20 minutes, and take anywhere between 45 and 90 minutes, depending on their particular destination. Buses are very comfortable. Each journey has a set ticket price, with the cheapest journeys around ₩10,000 and the most expensive ₩15,000 – the latter are generally sky-blue Korean Air buses doing the rounds of top hotels (*see p87*).

Since 2010 it has been possible to head from the airport to central Seoul by **train**. The **A'REX** (www.arex.or.kr) has two classes of service, with wildly different prices – plush 'express' trains depart on the hour; they take 43 minutes to hit Seoul station, with tickets costing ₩13,300. Slower, subway-like 'commuter' services depart every 15 minutes or so; they cost just ₩3,700, yet take only ten minutes more to complete the journey. Trains only hit a few destinations on their way to Seoul, though each is connected to the subway network: Gimpo Airport (lines 5 & 9), Digital Media City (line 2), Hongik Univ. (line 2), Gongdeok (lines 5 & 6), and finally Seoul Station (lines 1 & 4).

Lastly, it's quite affordable to make the journey by **taxi**. Again, fares vary depending upon your exact destination, but prices into central Seoul are usually in the region of ₩65,000. Note that 'deluxe' taxis – black with yellow lights on top – are slightly more comfortable, but will be almost twice as expensive. Extortion is extremely rare in Korean taxis, but it may be easier – and will usually work out cheaper than the meter – to agree on a price beforehand.

Gimpo International Airport

Flight information 02 2660-2114, www.gimpo.airport.co.kr.

Gimpo functioned as Korea's main international airport until being superceded by Incheon in 2001, but has now been largely relegated to an internal flight hub, though with a few connections with China and Japan. Some of the airport bus routes from Incheon airport stop at Gimpo on their way into Seoul, as do A'REX commuter trains.

Bus connections can be confusing, but staff at the airport's information booths will advise on prices, timetables and boarding points. Routes from the arrivals lounge to the **train** tracks are well signposted in Korean, English, Chinese and Japanese; **A'REX** services to Seoul station cost ₩1,200, though from Gimpo it's also possible to take **subway** lines 5 and 9 into the city. Finally, it's also possible to head into central Seoul by **taxi**; prices will vary substantially depending upon your destination, but it'll be around ₩35,000 into the city centre.

By ferry

A number of cities on China's eastern seaboard have ferry connections to Incheon, a city just to the west of Seoul and essentially part of the same urban area. Vessels usually run these routes two or three times per week – journeys all run through the night, and take anywhere from 14 to 24 hours. The cheapest tickets will buy you either a comfy bunk or a floor berth (usually the same price), while you'll pay more for a private room – these are almost all en suite, with one to eight beds. All vessels have vending machines, restaurants and a bar; you can also expect to find karaoke rooms, DVD rental and hot-spring-style bathing facilities.

There are ferries to Incheon from Dalian, Dandong, Lianyungang, Qingdao, Shidao, Weihai, Yantai and Yingkou, as well as the Tanggu port near Tianjin. Ferries arrive at one of Incheon's two international ferry terminals – to head into the capital, it's best to first take a taxi to Dongincheon station, and head from here into Seoul on subway line 1. Alternatively, the journey will be around ₩70,000 by taxi.

It's also possible to arrive in Korea by ferry from Japan – services from Fukuoka and Shimonoseki dock in Busan – the city's train station is within walking distance of the ferry terminal, and has regular high-speed trains to Seoul.

By rail

Almost entirely run by **Korail** (www.korail.com), Korea's small rail network is highly efficient, and relatively cheap by international standards. The main line heads south from Seoul and splits in the city of Daejeon, heading to Mokpo in the south-west and Busan in the south-east. Both of Seoul's two main stations are very central, and connected to the subway network – services from the south-east arrive at **Seoul station** (lines 1 & 4), while those from the south-west arrive at **Yongsan station** (line 1, and very close to Sinyongsan station on line 4).

There are several classes of train running the lines in Korea, with substantial differences in speed and price. Fastest are the high-speed KTX services, which run at speeds of up to 300km per hour; these are followed by Saemaeul and Mugunghwa trains, and finally commuter services heading to Seoul suburbs. Tickets are easy to buy at train stations, though they sometimes sell out at weekends.

By bus

Seoul's three main bus stations are all some distance from the city centre, though two are quite handily located for those based south of the river. Here you'll find the huge **express bus terminal** (subway lines 3, 7 & 9), and the smaller **Nambu bus terminal** (line 3) just to the south. Way to the east of the city is the **Dongseoul bus terminal** (subway line 2). All have information booths, and staff able to advise on onward transport; connections are extremely regular, and it's rare for tickets on any route to sell out. For travel information, however, it's best to dial the dedicated foreign-language information line (02 1330).

PUBLIC TRANSPORT

Seoul has a truly superb public transport network – affordable, clean, efficient, safe, and punctual to a fault. The comprehensive subway network makes getting around surprisingly easy; all stations are signed in English, and usually Chinese and Japanese too. Buses are a slightly different story: route numbers can be confusing, while both at the stops and on board the buses, there's very little non-Korean information. However, if you can read Korean or have become familiar with a particular route, Seoul's buses make a great way to get around.

Subway services start at around 5am, and stop around midnight, or just after 11pm on Saturdays and Sundays. Trains run every 3-10 minutes. Bus hours are a little longer – most routes get going just before 5am, and buses run until 1am on some routes.

If you're in Seoul for more than a couple of days, it'll be worth investing in a pre-paid card – this avoids the need to purchase tickets for every journey, and on any one journey, you'll be able to transfer between buses and subways at no extra cost (*see right*). The **foreign language-information line** (02 1330) will be able to advise on transport practicalities.

Subways

Seoul's subway system has nine main lines, five commuter rail lines, over 300 stations and covers almost a quarter of the country – and it's still growing. All lines are colour-coded, and the main ones are numbered: line 1 (dark blue), line 2 (green), line 3 (orange), line 4 (sky blue), line 5 (purple), line 6 (brown), line 7 (olive), line 8 (pink) and line 9 (gold). These are owned and operated by three separate

organisations (Korail, Seoul Metro and SMRT), though this fact can be safely ignored since the same tickets are valid for all lines, and there are no awkward procedures for transferring from one line to another. Line 2 is a loop line; inside the loop is Seoul's de facto city centre; line 1 is the oldest and follows the national railway tracks for much of its route. The five commuter lines are less useful for travellers, though you may still end up on one at some point.

Each subway station has good city maps – featuring subway lines, of course – on the platforms. Here you'll also find maps of the station area, which will give you an idea of which exit is best for you. It's a piece of cake to find these exits, for dual-language signs leading to them are dotted liberally around each station. You'll also be able to follow these to another line if you're transferring, though do note that routes may be different depending upon which way your connecting train is travelling. To avoid problems, it's best to take a note of the terminal station of your intended train, since these are always named on the signboards.

Buses

The city's bus network is not quite as user-friendly for foreigners as its subway system, but it's still worth learning the ropes if you're in Seoul for anything more than a few days. Buses are colour-coded – green and blue buses run medium-length distances, and are the ones you're most likely to encounter. Red buses head to the suburbs, and yellow ones run short routes. Confusingly, smaller green buses run even shorter routes. At every bus stop you'll see printed lists of stops for each line, your present location typically marked with an arrow facing in the same direction that the bus will be running. Destinations are given in Korean only, with the exception of stops next to subway stations – the station names are given in English, which will often give you an idea as to whether a particular bus route will be heading in the right direction for you.

Buses appear every 5-20 minutes, depending upon the specific route and the time of day.

Tickets & passes

Standard tickets

Subway tickets are only sold at the stations themselves, though a system overhaul in 2009 means that

you're likely to have to buy from a touch-screen machine – although instructions are available in Korean, English, Chinese and Japanese, these machines can be a little confusing at first, though most visitors are able to figure them out before too long. Machines have buttons that you can press if you need human assistance, and in some stations you'll still find staff behind the ticket booths. Ticket prices start at ₩1,000, increasing in increments of ₩100 for every 5km – you'd have to be on the train for more than an hour to pay anything over ₩2,000 for a single journey. When buying from the machines, you have to pay an extra ₩500 deposit, which can be collected from dedicated machines instantly after completing your journey.

There are no tickets for buses. Simply put the required fare into the box next to the driver. For the majority of buses used by foreign visitors, a single fare applies; this is ₩1,800 for red buses, ₩1,000 for blue and green buses, ₩800 for yellow ones, and ₩700 for the small green ones. Do note that change only comes in coin form, and is therefore not usually available from ₩5,000 and ₩10,000 notes – have a few ₩1,000 notes handy.

Pre-paid passes

If you're spending more than a day or two in Seoul, it's worth investing in a pre-paid travel card. These are incredibly useful: you can use them for bus rides and subway rides, and to transfer for free from one to the other; they can also be used for taxi rides, phone calls in specially adapted booths, and even to pay for goods in most convenience stores. Passes negate the need for queueing in subway stations, and provide a discount of ₩100 on each journey.

T-Money is the main type of pass, and you'll be able to buy it for ₩3,000 in subway stations and some street stalls. It's also possible to buy slightly fancier passes in convenience stores – ₩5,000 will get you a dongle that can be attached to a mobile phone.

It's possible to top these passes up in increments of ₩1,000 upwards – every subway station has touch-screen machines that can do the job, as can staff in most convenience stores.

TAXIS

Taxis are a very affordable way of getting around Seoul, and if you're travelling as a group of three or four, they can work out cheaper than buses or subway trains on short journeys. It's almost never necessary to call a taxi, since they're absolutely everywhere. Each taxi has an illuminated panel on its roof, which will be lit up unless the vehicle is on call; it's possible to flag one down by beckoning from the roadside, though note that Koreans do this with their palms facing down. Extortion of foreigners is rare, and almost all drivers will use the meter – if it isn't running, ask your driver to put it on.

There are two types of taxi – regular cabs and 'deluxe' taxis. The latter (which are black, with yellow illuminated panels) are more expensive, and tend to wait outside the airport and major hotels. A flagfall fare of ₩2,400 will take you the first 2km in a regular taxi, with an extra ₩100 added for each 144m travelled; deluxe taxis start at ₩4,500 for the first 3km, the fare increasing by ₩200 every 164m. A special surcharge of 20% applies between midnight and 4am. Tipping is not expected, but it's advisable to get a receipt – the phone number on this will help you track down lost property if you've left something in the cab.

Note that it can occasionally be difficult to find a taxi in the hour or so following the last subway trains. If you get stuck call **Seoul City's official taxi service** on 1644-4842.

CYCLING

Seoul is not a good city to navigate on a bicycle, mainly due to the dangers on the busy city roads, where drivers are not used to dealing with cyclists. However, there are a few good cycle routes dotted around Seoul, particularly along the pedestrianised banks of the Hangang.

Bikes can be rented from any park along the Hangang – the most popular places to pick one up are on the riverbank near World Cup Stadium (subway line 6), and on Yeouido island, just down the steps from Yeouinaru subway station (line 5). Prices are ₩3,000 per hour, and you'll need to leave some photo ID as a deposit. Tandem bikes are also available (for double the price, naturally), and are particularly popular with local couples.

WALKING

Like cyclists, pedestrians are neglected in Seoul – many streets have no pavements, and even those

that exist are regularly taken over by parked cars, or delivery boys on mopeds. In addition, many drivers run red lights, particularly at night. It's also important to note that cars are allowed to make right-hand turns, even when their light is on red – drivers are supposed to give way and almost always do, but always pay attention when crossing the road.

That said, there are a whole clutch of great places for a stroll in Seoul. The capital's five palaces have paths that are wonderful to amble around, its collection of small mountains will put some definition on your calves, Myeongdong is largely pedestrianised and teeming with shoppers, and the banks of Cheonggyecheon Stream offer a rare bit of urban calm.

Guided tours

City Walking Tour
www.visitseoul.net.
Seoul city operates free guided walking tours along 11 routes. Most of these run in and around the palace area, though a few include more far-flung destinations. Tours are divided by theme: ancient culture, Korean traditions, modern culture, and a mix of the three. They're easy to reserve online through the city tourism website – just click on 'walking tours'.

Seoul City Tour Bus *777-6090, http://en.seoulcitybus.com. Tue-Sun.*
Distinctive red-and-white tour buses make laps of Seoul's more interesting quarters, including the palaces, Myeongdong, Dongdaemun, Namsan and the museums around Itaewon. There are two different routes to choose from, with buses appearing every 30 minutes from 8am to 9pm. Day-tickets cost ₩10,000 and are purchased from the driver. There are also cheap night-tours (₩5,000), with buses departing from Gwanghwamun at 8pm, and taking 90 minutes to complete the loop; on all, you'll be given coupons allowing free and discounted entry to Seoul sights.

WATER TRANSPORT

When crossing the kilometre-wide Hangang, you'll notice a distinct absence of river traffic – this can largely be put down to the fact that the river heads into North Korean territory before hitting the sea, and is full of mines to the west of Seoul. However, there is a modicum of river transport within the city

itself, and the aforementioned calm on the waters makes Hangang trips rather pleasurable.

River cruises

A variety of cruise boats operate on the Hangang, with the docks at **Yeouinaru** and **Jamsil** the main hubs; the one on Yeouido is by far the easier to reach, since it's just a short walk down the steps and across the green from Yeouinaru subway (line 5). Boats head off approximately once per hour, generally costing ₩9,000-₩13,000 per person for a trip of around 60 minutes; some return to Yeouido and others do not, so be sure to clarify the schedule beforehand. In addition, some night services come with meals or live music, and are much more expensive – up to ₩60,000 per person.

River taxis

There are over a dozen stop-off points for Seoul's miniature armada of river taxis, which come in a variety of sizes. They've been around since 2007 and are fantastic value, though poor information means that precious few tourists – or even locals – make use of them. It's still best to book through a tour office, and even this can be tough; but persevere and you'll soon be on one of Seoul's most enjoyable trips.

Most popular are the **River Tour** boats, which run in a loop around the river – you'll be able to get on and off as you please. They can accommodate up to seven passengers; and the price determined by where you stop and start; for example, it's ₩18,900 from Yeouido to Banpo Bridge.

Prices are the same for **Direct Service** boats, which take you directly from A to B but have to be reserved in advance.

Lastly, there are clever **Express Shuttle** services designed to help commuters beat the rush-hour traffic; they head from Jamsil to Yeouido every morning, and return in the evening.

The tour boats and direct services operate 10am-10.30pm Mar-Oct, and 10am-9pm Nov-Feb. Outside weekends they take breaks from 5.30pm to 8pm. The commuter boats head from Jamsil every 20 minutes from 7am to 8.30am, and return every 20 minutes from 6.30pm to 8pm. Call 1588-3960 to make a reservation. You'll be able to find up-to-date information at www.pleasantseoul.com.

Resources A-Z

ADDRESSES

Where to start with Korean addresses? The issue is confusing, to say the least. Every street in Seoul does actually have a name, and each building a street number, but these are a very recent introduction – only the major roads have well-known names, and it's no exaggeration to say that most of Seoul's inhabitants do not know the name of their own road.

Instead, rather than having numbers on streets, Korea has long followed a top-down system, starting with the city (Seoul, in this case); this is divided into districts whose names end with '*gu*' (of which there are 25 in Seoul). These are further subdivided into subdistricts whose names end with '*dong*' (of which there are between 10 and 30 in each gu). Specific buildings are demarcated by numbers, but Seoul's rapid growth has rendered these next to useless: they essentially provide more of a chronological idea of how the buildings appeared in the area, rather than where those buildings are actually located. In this guide, we've listed the *dong* and number of each establishment: almost every place listed is in the same few *gu* districts, which make up the heart of central Seoul.

Seoul is currently undergoing a drastic change in terms of addresses. Each will now have a new name with the suffix 'gil'. Of course, the old addresses will continue to be used too. You can read about the new system and find new addressses at www.juso.go.kr/openEngPage.do

Map references to our street maps (*see p246-55*) are used throughout the guide; alternatively, the addresses can also be used to track them down on internet map sites. You can print out maps in English from www.visitseoul.com; http://maps.google.com also has good maps. In addition, taxi drivers will be able to punch addresses into their navigation systems. If all else fails, head into a police station and ask for directions – Koreans have been doing this for decades!

AGE RESTRICTIONS

The Korean age of consent is something of a grey area – 13 is the official legal age, though people have got into serious trouble for having sexual relations with minors of up to 18 years old. The legal ages for drinking, smoking and voting is 19..

ATTITUDE & ETIQUETTE

Korea is one of the world's safest countries, and also probably its most Confucian – it could even be said that social rules are even more important here than national law. Getting to know each facet of the Korean social system would take years, but thankfully locals are usually very tolerant of their visitors' behaviour. However, it would not be remiss to follow a few simple pointers. For business etiquette, *see below*. For details on expected behaviour in a local bathhouse, a *jimjilbang, see p191* **Getting Steamy**. For restaurant etiquette, *see p121*.

BUSINESS

Etiquette

Koreans place great importance on the maintenance of face in business relationships – it is extremely important not to make someone else appear to be in the wrong, even if they clearly are. In addition, it's almost obligatory to socialise after business meetings – this is often a male-only affair, with all that entails. Here are some basic business tips:

● Always carry lots of business cards. These are absolutely essential in Korean business life, and are usually exchanged immediately after an introduction. Cards should be given and received with two hands, and treated with respect – when accepting a card leave it on the table, or keep it in hand, until you can file it away discreetly.

● If you are going to be doing regular business in Korea, it will come in handy to have your name, position and so on translated into Korean, and put on the reverse of your business card. You'll see dozens of places that can do this south of Chungmuro subway station (lines 3 & 4), and in Euljiro Shopping Arcade (*see p143*); bring along a pdf or other electronic file for them to work with.

● Be prepared to sit on the floor in many Korean restaurants – and, occasionally, to drink profuse amounts of *soju*. Never offer to split a bill, but expect to involve yourself in a (good-natured) fight over who should pay. Thank the eventual victor.

● Also be prepared to give out, and ask, information about age, marital status and so on – the former is particularly important in this highly Confucian nation.

● If you intend to give a gift to a host or business partner, ensure that it is professionally wrapped; when receiving a gift, do not unwrap it unless you're asked to do so.

Conventions & conferences

In addition to the facilities listed below, almost all of Seoul's larger hotels have conference rooms for hire, and business centres.
Coex *Samseongdong 159 (6000-1125, www.coex.co.kr). Samseong station (line 2), exit 5.* **Map** p253 O10.

Seoul Convention Bureau *8F Jeodong 1-ga 1-2 (3788-8141, www.miceseoul.com). Euljiro 3-ga station (lines 2 & 3), exit 12.* **Map** p255 G3.

SETEC *Daechidong 514 (2222-3811, www.setec.or.kr). Cheongdam station (line 7), exit 9.* **Map** p253 Q12.

Couriers & shippers

Federal Express *080 023-8000, http://fedex.com/kr_english.*
UPS *1588-6886, www.ups.com/content/kr/en.*

Computer rental

Most of Seoul's major hotels are able to rent out laptop computers to guests, and those that can't should be able to suggest where an alternative solution.

Office hire

Most international arrivals have their office space requirements organised by local contacts. Those who have to organise facilities themselves may find it cheaper to go with a local company – **Office Seoul** (508-2860, www.officeseoul.co.kr) is one such. However, contractual complications mean that it's usually far easier to arrange things via one of the major international websites.

Office services

FedEx Kinko's *566-4491, www.kinkos.co.kr.*
A range of print, copy and express mail services. Check the website for locations – there are 27 in and around Seoul; most are open 24hrs daily.

Couriers & shippers

Federal Express *080 023-8000, http://fedex.com/kr_english.*

Trade Directory

Korea Pages
www.southkoreaages.com.

Useful organisations

American Chamber of Commerce
564-2040, www.amchamkorea.org.
Australian Chamber of Commerce *958-3283, www.austchamkorea.org.*

British Chamber of Commerce
720-9406, www.bcck.or.kr.

Canadian Chamber of Commerce
554-0245, www.canchamkorea.org.

Korea Exchange *051 662-2000, eng.krx.co.kr.*
Korea's stock exchange, the KRX, is actually based in Korea's second city, Busan – part of a plan to farm certain areas of business and administration to the provinces.

Seoul Global Center *3F Seoul Press Center, Sejongdaero 124 (2075-4130, global.seoul.go.kr). City Hall station (lines 1 & 2), exit 4.*
An excellent support centre for foreigners living or doing business in Seoul. Staff can help with business administration and banking; they also offer educational courses, and can even advise on legal issues.

Shinhan Bank Seoul Global Center *Taepyeongno 84 (773-3163). City Hall station (lines 1 & 2), exit 4.* **Map** p254 F3.
Not affiliated to the Seoul Global Center above, this is operated by Shinhan, a major local bank. Their Taepyeongno branch offers a full range of banking and financial services, specially tailored towards foreigners.

CUSTOMS

The duty-free allowances for travellers visiting Korea are 1 litre of alcoholic liquor; 200 cigarettes, 50 cigars or 250g of tobacco; and 56ml (2oz) of perfume. Goods up to the value of US $400 are also allowed to enter Korea duty free; anything above this amount may be subject to tax. There is no limit on the amount of foreign currency that visitors can bring into Korea, though anything above the value of US $10,000 must be declared on entry and exit.

Drug possession is a serious crime in Korea, and penalties can be severe: those found guilty can expect a stay in jail.

For more information, visit the Korea Customs Service website at english.customs.go.kr.

DISABLED

People with disabilities were long ignored in Korean society, but things have certainly improved in Seoul. Most subway stations now have elevators from street-level to platform, and others have mechanisms for the transport of wheelchairs down stairs – these feature a rather demeaning musical jingle, though station staff will be on hand to assist with the apparatus. Buses are a different matter, with only a few designed for wheelchair access; there are, however, priority seats for the elderly or those with difficulty walking. Public toilets are a mixed bag, though the number designed for wheelchair access is increasing.

Most tourist sights offer free or discounted entry for those with disabilities, and the Seoul Tourism Organisation has, in the past, run guided tours specifically for the disabled – check the website (www.visitseoul.net/en) for details.

DRUGS

Very few Koreans use illegal drugs, and they're very hard to find, even in Seoul. Penalties are severe, even for possession of marijuana – you can expect deportation or a spell in jail. Importantly, blood tests are (usually) required when obtaining a work visa. Those with traces of illegal drugs in their system may be prosecuted, even if those substances were taken before entering Korea.

ELECTRICITY

Electric current in Korea runs at 220V, using plugs of the round, two-pinned variety found in much of Europe. However, many older buildings (including cheaper guesthouses in Seoul) run on the old 110V system, and use flat-pinned plugs.

EMBASSIES

Embassies are usually open from 9am to 5pm Monday to Friday, though consular sections usually have shorter working hours.

Australian Embassy *19F Kyobo Building, Jongno 1-ga 1 (2003-0100, www.southkorea.embassy.gov.au).* **Map** p254 E3.

British Embassy *Taepyeongno 40 (3210-5500, ukinrok.fco.gov.uk). City Hall station (lines 1 & 2), exit 3.* **Map** p254 E4.

Canadian Embassy *Jeongdong 16-1 (3783-6000, www.korea.gc.ca). Sodaemun station (line 5), exit 5.* **Map** p254 E3.

Irish Embassy *13F Susongdong 146-1 (774-6455, www.ireland house-korea.com). Gwanghwamun station (line 5), exit 2.* **Map** p254 F2.

New Zealand Embassy *Jeongdong 16-1 (3701-7700, www.nzembassy.com/korea). Sodaemun station (line 5), exit 5.* **Map** p254 E3.

US Embassy *Sejongno 32 (397-4114, seoul.usembassy.gov). Gwanghwamun station (line 5), exit 2.* **Map** p254 E2.

EMERGENCIES

The emergency numbers in Korea are **112** for **police**, and **119** for the **ambulance** or **fire brigade**. In most cases you'll be transferred to an English-speaker if necessary, but since this is not guaranteed it's best to get a Korean-speaker to call if at all possible.

The Foreign Language Information line (02 1330) can help with many enquiries, as can the Dasan 120 Seoul Call Center (120 9). For emergency rooms at hospitals in Seoul, *see below*.

GAY & LESBIAN

See pp176-180.

HEALTH

For Koreans, medical insurance provided by employers or the state covers part of the cost of hospital treatment. This does not apply to visitors, who have to pay the full fee – as always, it's a good idea to make sure that you're fully insured before travel.

Vaccinations are not required for those entering Korea, and there's very little chance of contracting anything peculiar.

Accident & emergency

The following hospitals have clinics with English-speaking staff. In an emergency, you can also call **119**, a line operated by the fire brigade but with staff able to deal with other issues, or the Emergency Medical Information Center on **1339**.

Seoul National University Hospital *Daehangno 101 (2072-2890, www.snuh.org). Hyehwa station (line 4), exit 3.*
This university hospital has an international clinic, and provides 24-hour international-language telephone assistance.

Severance Hospital *Seongsanno 250 (2228-5800, www.yuhs.or.kr). Hyehwa station (line 4), exit 3.*
This university hospital has an international clinic, and provides 24-hour international-language telephone assistance.

Contraception & abortion

Condoms are by far the most common form of contraception in Korea – the Pill is rarely used, and indeed alien to many local females. Condoms are available in almost all convenience stores, and all pharmacies. Abortion was made illegal in 2010, a decision that may be reversed by a future government; in the meantime, this has created a boom time for abortion clinics across the West Sea in Beijing.

Dentists

The following clinics have English-speaking staff.

Hushu International Clinic *Sinsadong 610-5 (1588-7464, english.hus-hu.com). Apgujeong station (line 3), exit 3.* **Open** 10am-7pm Mon-Fri, 10am-4pm Sat. **Map** p252 L8.
This Apgujeong-based clinic also has a dental wing.

Seoul National University Hospital *Daehangno 101 (2072-0753, www.snuh.org). Hyehwa station (line 4), exit 3.* **Open** 24hrs daily.
SNUH also provides dental service, for which it's possible to make appointments online.

Smart Dental *5F Sinsadong 582-10, 3443-2828, www.smart-dental.co.kr, Apgujeong station (line 3), exit 4.* **Open** 10am-7pm Mon-Fri, 10am-4pm Sat. **Map** p252 L8.

Boston University-trained dentist. Night consultations are available.

Doctors

The following clinics have English-speaking staff.
Asan Medical Center *Pungnapdong 388-1 (3010-5001, eng.amc.seoul.kr). Jamsillaru station (line 2), exit 1.* **Open** 9am-5.30pm Mon-Fri.
A large medical centre with a dedicated international clinic. It's east of the centre between the river and Olympic Park.

Samsung Medical Center *Irwondong 50 (3410-0200, www.samsunghospital.com). Irwon station (line 3), exit 1.* **Open** 24hrs daily.
Another large medical centre, located just south of the main Gangnam area.

Opticians

See p156.

Pharmacies

See p156.

HELPLINES

The following helplines offer information in English.

Alcoholics Anonymous *319-5861 (taped message), www.aainkorea.org.*
Emergency Medical Information Center *119 or 1339.*
Immigration Information Centre *1345.*
Korea HIV/AIDS Prevention & Support Center *927-4323, www.khap.org.* **Open** 10am-6pm Mon-Fri.
KHAP, as the organisation is better known, also offers free anonymous testing every Sunday from 10am to 5pm. Call to make an appointment.
Korean National Police Agency *1588-5644.*
Migrants' Center *2632-9933.*
This advice centre deals with work-related problems and can also help with other issues.

ID

Foreigners are legally required to carry their passport at all times, though this is very rarely enforced. Those living or working in Korea should carry their Alien Registration Card, however.

DIRECTORY

INTERNET

Korea is regularly cited as being the most connected country on earth, and most cafes offer high-speed Wi-Fi access. In addition, the number of internet cafes in Seoul is prodigious. Known locally as *'PC-bang'*, there'll always be one within walking distance – just look for the letters 'PC' on a signboard – and they charge just over ₩1,000 per hour.

Most hotels offer high-speed internet access, though those at the top end regularly charge ridiculous rates of over ₩20,000 per day. Motels, on the other hand, often have computers built into their rooms, and these are always free to use.

LANGUAGE

For information on Korean language and pronunciation, and a useful list of words and phrases, *see* p232-35 **Vocabulary**.

Dozens of places offer Korean language classes – ranging from free basics tutorials to semester-long university study programmes. The latter usually cost around ₩1,500,000 for a ten-week intensive course, and are available at **Ehwa University** (elc.ehwa.ac.kr), **Sogang University** (klec.sogang. ac.kr), **Yonsei University** (www.yskli.com) and **Seoul National University** (lei.snu.ac.kr), among others. Of course, these are best arranged in advance.

Easy Korean Academy *Sinsadong 619-2 (511-9314, www.edukorean. com). Apgujeong station (line 3), exit 2.* **Map** p252 L8.
Four-week courses are held on either weekdays (10am-1pm, ₩370,000) or Saturdays (10am-1pm, ₩130,000).

Seoul Global Center *3F Seoul Press Center, Sejongdaero 124 (2075-4130, global.seoul.go.kr). City Hall station (lines 1 & 2), exit 4.*
Free weekday classes, operated in three-month-long courses – participants are expected to attend twice per week. Not available for those on a tourist visa.

YBM Korean Language Institute *Jongno 55-1 (2278-0509, www. kli.ybmedu.com). Jongno 3-ga station (lines 1, 3 & 5), exit 15.* **Map** p255 G3.

A variety of courses, ranging from two hours a day, ten days a month (₩130,000) to four hours a day, 20 days a month (₩480,000). Sessions start at the beginning of each month; private lessons are available for ₩40,000 per hour.

LEGAL HELP

Seoul Global Center *3F Seoul Press Center, Sejongdaero 124 (2075-4130, global.seoul.go.kr). City Hall station (lines 1 & 2), exit 4.*
The centre offers a professional consulting service for areas including business, labour, legal issues and taxes.

Seoul Korean Language Academy *7F Yeoksamdong 649-2 (563-3226, www.seoul-kla.com). Gangnam station (line 2), exit 8.* **Map** p252 M12.
Month-long courses (two hours per day each weekday) are available for ₩370,000.

LIBRARIES

Korea Tourism Organization *40 Cheonggyecheonno (729-9497) Euljiro 1-ga station (line 2), exit 2.* **Open** 9am-5.30pm daily. **Map** p254 F3.
The headquarters of the KTO has a small library in its basement tourist information centre.

Namsan Public Library *Huamdong 30-84 (754-7338, www.namsan lib.go.kr), Express Bus Terminal station (lines 3, 7 & 9), exit 5.* **Open** 9am-7pm Mon-Fri; 9pm-5pm Sat, Sun; closed every 1st & 3rd Mon. **Map** p247 F5.
Up on the Namsan slopes, this library is a pleasant place simply to walk around.

National Library of Korea *Banpodong 664 (535-4142, www.nl. go.kr), Express Bus Terminal station (lines 3, 7 & 9), exit 5.* **Open** 9am-6pm daily; closed every 2nd & 4th Mon. **Map** p252 J11.
Korea's largest library, with over seven million books – of course, only a fraction are non-Korean, but that's still plenty.

LOST PROPERTY

If you've left something behind at a shop, restaurant, cafe or bar, try to call the establishment in question – it will almost certainly still be there. The same can often be said for items left in public spaces. On

public transport, it will obviously be a different matter – try calling one of the following numbers, with the assistance of a Korean speaker if at all possible. It will help to have the bus or subway line number handy, together with the time of travel. In theory, all items lost and recovered on Seoul transport can be tracked on the Integrated Lost and Found Center website, accessible from www.seoul.go.kr.

City Hall Subway Station *6110-1122.*
Incheon International Airport *032 741-0114.*
Seoul Provincial Police *2299-1282.*
Seoul Railway Station *755-7108.*
Seoul Taxi Association *420-6110 (Korean only).*

MEDIA

Magazines

The following Seoul-specialist, English-language monthly magazines are available in hotels and foreigner-oriented bars throughout the city; **Seoul Global Center** (*see left*) is also a good place to pick them up. Some have nominal cover prices, though it's usually possible to get them for free in hotels and bars. For *Newsweek*, *Time* and other foreign magazines, head to one of the major bookshops. Those who can read Korean – or are at least charming enough to glean information from a local – can pick up *Seoul Arts Scene*, a monthly magazine of art listings and maps available at most major galleries.

10 Magazine*10mag.com*.
Excellent magazine blending interesting local stories with up-to-date listings for Seoul and other Korean cities.
Eloquence *www.eloquence.co.kr*.
Aimed at the artier section of the English-speaking magazine market, this specialises in fashion and exhibition listings.
Groove
A little less Seoul-centric than other monthlies listed here, this is nonetheless both a good read and a decent source of information.
Seoul *www.seoulselection.com*.
Well-written, city-run magazine with interesting photo essays and excellent events listings.

Newspapers

The *Chosun Ilbo*, *JoongAng Ilbo* and *Dong-a Ilbo* are the most commonly read newspapers in Korea, each with a daily readership of over two million. The choice is more limited for English speakers: the *Korea Herald*, the near-identical *Korea Times*, and the English-language edition of the *JoongAng Ilbo*, which comes inside local copies of the *International Herald Tribune*. You'll be able to buy these at street stands around the city, though they're more commonly read for free in hotel lobbies and business rooms.

Chosun Ilbo

http://english.chosun.com.
Though not available in print, the *Chosun Ilbo* runs an English-language version of its website. This can be quite entertaining – expats have criticised the paper for printing xenophobic or scaremongering stories about foreigners, English teachers in particular.

Korea Herald

www.koreaherald.com.

Korea Times

www.koreatimes.co.kr.
Affiliated to the *Hankook Ilbo*, a major local daily newspaper.

JoongAng Daily

http://joongangdaily.joins.com.
You'll find this eight-page pullout inside local copies of the *International Herald Tribune*.

Radio

AFN *www.afnkorea.net*.
Radio wing of the US Armed Forces Network – listening can be quite an experience.

KBS World Radio
http://world.kbs.co.kr.

TBS *www.tbsefm.seoul.kr*.
24-hour English-language news and music channel, broadcasting on 101.3MHz.

Television

KBS is the state broadcaster in Korea and runs two main channels, which share the airwaves with major networks **MBC** and **SBS**, which, though officially commercial, are also owned entirely by the government. All are now running programmes in HD. **Arirang TV** is a local English-language channel; it's free-to-air in many countries across the globe, though in Korea itself it usually comes as part of cable packages. Such packages are used in almost all hotels, and also typically feature international channels such as BBC World News, CNN, Discovery and National Geographic, as well as a couple of sports channels.

MONEY

The Korean *won* is not divided into smaller units – no real surprise, since it's one of the least valuable currency units in the world, with even chocolate bars priced in the thousands. It comes in denominations of ₩10, ₩50, ₩100 and ₩500 (coins) and ₩1,000, ₩5000, ₩10,000 and ₩50,000 (notes).

Prices on display should, in theory, include all applicable taxes. The only exceptions are higher-end hotels and restaurants, which often omit a 10 per cent service charge from their listed prices; such hotels also omit VAT of 10 per cent, meaning that in these cases you'll have to add 20 per ent for the real rate.

Korea is still a cash-based society, though credit card use has become very common. All establishments that accept local cards will also accept international ones.

Banks & ATMs

Banks are open 9am to 4pm Monday to Friday, and almost all will be able to exchange foreign currency and travellers' cheques. Most have ATMs capable of dealing with international cards, as do a large proportion of convenience stores and subway stations.

Lost/stolen credit cards

To report lost or stolen cards, dial these numbers:

American Express *2000-8000*.
Diners Club *3015-3607 (office hours); 3015-3608 (outside office hours)*.
MasterCard *0079 811 887 0823*.
Visa *818 0090 88212*.

OPENING HOURS

Seoul is one of the world's most truly open-all-hours cities, and has the longest working hours on earth, but even here things have a limit. Banks are open 9am-4pm Monday to Friday. Government institutions are generally open 9am-6pm Monday to Friday. Post offices are open 9am-6pm Monday to Friday, and 9am-1pm on Saturdays. Most shops and department stores open at 10am; department stores usually close at 8pm, though many regular shops stay open until 11pm and beyond. A fair few restaurants are open all hours, as are all convenience stores.

POLICE

You'd be unfortunate to have to get involved with the police in Seoul, since theft, drug use and violence are extremely rare. However, fights do occasionally break out between foreigners and Koreans (usually in Hongdae and Itaewon), following the consumption of alcohol), and the foreign party is almost systematically held responsible, wherever the real blame lies. A 'blood money' fine is usually administered on the spot, and can run to hundreds of pounds. In other words, it's best to avoid any sort of confrontation – it's also worth noting that every Korean male learns taekwondo as part of their compulsory military service.

The police themselves are usually young pups by international standards, and almost always pleasant to deal with in everyday situations. The **Korean National Police Agency** have an English-language website at (www.police.go.kr), and a 24-hour information line (1588-5644).

POSTAL SERVICES

The national postal system is run by Korea Post (www.koreapost.go.kr). Sending a postcard overseas costs ₩160; letters under 20g cost ₩400 to nearby Asian countries, ₩450 to Southeast Asia, ₩550 to Europe, Australasia or North America, and ₩600 to Africa, South or Central America. Writing addresses in English is acceptable, whether you're sending to a Korean or foreign address, but it's a good idea to use your very clearest handwriting. You can purchase stamps at convenience stores, street stands and post offices.

Post offices

Korean post offices are known locally as *uche-guk*, and fronted by blood-orange coloured panels with a white, bird-like motif. There's one in every city district, and they're usually marked with a red version of the symbol on subway station maps (*see p221*).

The majority of post offices are open 9am-6pm Monday to Friday, and from 9am to 1pm on Saturday.

Gwanghwamun Post Office

Seorindong 154-1 (3703-9011). Gwanghwamun station (line 5), exit 5. **Open** 9am-8pm Mon-Fri, 9am-6pm Sat & Sun. **Map** p254 E3.

DIRECTORY

The most convenient post office for foreign visitors – English is spoken, and the hours longer than usual.

Seoul Central Post Office
Chungmuro 21-1 (6450-1000), Myeongdong station (line 4), exit 5. **Open** 9am-6pm Mon-Fri, 9am-1pm Sat. **Map** p255 G4.
If you're receiving post from abroad, it's almost certain to pass through this building. English-speaking staff can help with telephone enquiries, especially if you've a tracking number to work with.

RELIGION

Christianity – in its various forms – now has more adherants than Buddhism, which was, for centuries, the national religion. For more information on Korean Christianity, *see p61.* For more information on Korean Buddhism, *see p77.* For more information on Shamanist rituals, *see p57.*

SAFETY & SECURITY

Korea is one of the world's safest nations – leave something behind at a restaurant or shop and you'd be very unlucky to return and find that it has gone. Of course, crimes do occur from time to time, and it's best to take the usual precautions. The places in which it pays to be a little careful are Itaewon and Hongdae.

It must also be said that Seoul's road safety record is not on par with that of its general safety. Pay attention when crossing the road, and even when walking on the pavement – motorbikes and parking cars consider this part of their territory, and police rarely take any action.

SMOKING

Smoking is very common among Korean men, and the practice is also taking hold with younger women. Smoking is prohibited in most buildings and public areas, but restrictions are rarely enforced – public toilets are one particularly popular route around the rules, and many cubicles have ashtrays next to the no-smoking signs. However, you'll be free of the smell of smoke in most restaurants and cafes; the latter often have dedicated smoking areas. A new law to prohibit smoking in outdoor public spaces came into force in 2011.

TELEPHONES
Dialling & codes

The country code for Korea is 82. The area code for Seoul is 02, which has been omitted from the numbers in this guide as you will not need to dial it when calling from within the city. If phoning from elsewhere in Korea, or from a mobile phone, you'll need to use the code. If you're phoning from outside Korea, dial the international access code plus 82, then 2 for Seoul, followed by the seven- or eight-digit number.

International calls

Making international calls can be confusing, as each operator has a different international access code. This is 001 for KT, 002 for LG Telecom, 00365 for Onse Telecom, and 00700 for SK Telink. After that, use the regular country (some examples are listed below) and area code minus the zero, plus the main number.

Australia 61
Canada 1
New Zealand 64
Republic of Ireland 353
South Africa 27
UK 44
USA 1

Korea Tourism Organization
40 Cheonggyecheonno (729-9497), Euljiro 1-ga station (line 2), exit 2. **Open** 9am-8pm daily. **Map** p254 F3. The headquarters of the KTO offers offer free international calls – within reason – from its basement tourist information centre.

Public phones & prepaid cards

Sky-blue phone booths are all over the place in Seoul – you'll find them on almost every major road. Most come in pairs, one for coins, one for cards. The latter almost always accept T-Money subway cards (*see p221*), while the former accept ₩10, ₩50, ₩100 and ₩500 coins.

Many subway stations now have large, touch-screen panels with telephone receivers attached – though a little fiddly, these can be used to make free local calls to landlines and mobile phones alike; note that there's a three-minute time limit.

Mobile phones

Korea runs on the 3G network, and many international handsets can

be used in roaming mode. It's not possible to pop a local SIM card into your phone. However, it's possible to rent a mobile phone for the duration of your stay in Korea. The easiest place to do this is at Incheon International Airport. Rates start at around ₩3,000 per day, and there's no fee for incoming calls; those you make from the rented phone typically cost less than ₩1,000 per minute. It's also possible to rent phones from most top-end hotels, typically for rates of around ₩5,000 per day.

Those staying longer in Korea may prefer to purchase a local phone. These can cost as little as ₩20,000 for a bare-bones piece, though for more recent models you'll be looking at ₩100,000 or more. The best place to go hunting is Yongsan Electronics Market (*see p146*), which has a whole floorful of mobile phones – not all are available without a contract, but staff will direct you to appropriate booths.

T-Mobile *Namdaemunno (734-7908), Jongno station (line 1), exit 4.* **Open** 9am-6pm Mon-Fri. **Map** p247 E4. Part of a chain operated by SK Telecom, one of Korea's largest telephone operators. This Jongno branch, located just behind Bosingak belfry, is the only such place in the city that rents out mobile phones to foreigners – rates start at ₩3,000 per day and drop after ten days, with calls charged at ₩600 per minute.

TIME

Korea is nine hours ahead of Greenwich Mean Time (GMT). Daylight Savings Time is not used.

TIPPING

Tipping is not expected in Korea – with the possible exception of taxi drivers, you're likely to be hunted down if leaving even the smallest amount of change in someone's hands. Higher-end hotels and restaurants do sometimes add a ten per cent service charge to the bill.

TOILETS

First, the good news: public toilets are absolutely everywhere in Seoul, and all are free to use. Almost all will have toilet paper, though in some you'll have to spool off a length from a dispenser located near the sinks. Now, the bad news: Korean plumbing systems are often unable to cope with toilet paper, which is more commonly discarded in waste bins next to the toilets – this can look, and smell, a little disgusting.In addition, men often use public toilets as smoking rooms.

Tourist information

There are tourist information booths dotted in convenient places throughout the city, including Seoul and Yongsan train stations, the Express Bus Terminal, and Itaewon subway station. There's also one at the northern end of Insadonggil, and one in the centre of Myeongdong shopping area. All tend to be open daily from 9am to 9pm. Or visit the Seoul Tourism Organisation's website at www.visitseoul.net. Another good sources of information is the **Dasan 120 Seoul Call Center**, which can supply information on almost any aspect of city life. Dial 120 9 for the English-language service.

Korea Tourism Organization
40 Cheonggyecheonno (729-9497), Euljiro 1-ga station (line 2), exit 2. **Open** 9am-8pm daily. **Map** p254 F3. The headquarters of the KTO has an excellent tourist information centre in the basement; though generally focusing on other Korean cities, it can also provide extensive information about Seoul. It also offers advice on medical tourism.

Seoul Global Center *3F Seoul Press Center, Sejongdaero 124 (2075-4130, global.seoul.go.kr). City Hall station (lines 1 & 2), exit 4.* **Open** 9am-6pm Mon-Fri. Though more for services than tourist information, this office has plenty of magazines and pamphlets, and can advise on trips around the city.

Seoul Center for Culture & Tourism *5F M-Plaza, Myeongdong station (line 4), exit 8.* **Open** 9am-8pm daily. **Map** p255 F4. Operated by the Seoul Tourism Organization, this small office is tucked away in Myeongdong's busy lattice of streets, and has a wealth of information for foreign visitors. It also runs hour-long cultural experience programmes, 3-6pm Monday to Friday.

VISAS & IMMIGRATION

Citizens of most countries qualify for a free tourist visa, which is available on arrival at all international airports and ferry terminals. Most will get a three-

month stamp, with notable exceptions including Canadians (six months), Italians and Portuguese (two months), Americans, Taiwanese and South Africans (one month). Citizens of some nations, including China, much of Africa and the former Soviet Union, will have to arrange their visa before travelling to Korea.

It's illegal to do any sort of work in Korea without a proper working visa, though countless people do. Employers will complete most of the necessary paperwork, though requirements seem to vary from month to month – and, frustratingly, even from person to person among staff at the immigration offices. In most cases, you'll need your original degree certificate and a police check from your homeland (which is, of course, far easier and cheaper to arrange at home). All being well, you'll have to exit Korea to pick up your working visa, with Japan the easiest place to head – the charming city of Fukuoka is just three hours by ferry from Busan in south-eastern Korea, and has a highly efficient Korean consulate.

For up-to-date information, check the **Korea Immigration Service** website at www.immigration.go.kr.

WEIGHTS & MEASURES

Korea uses the metric system, though (despite an official replacement with square metres) room sizes are more commonly measured in *pyeong*, a local size equivalent to around 3.3 sq m.

WHEN TO GO

Winters are long and bitter in Seoul, and summers can be uncomfortably sticky, but the ubiquitous use of heating and air-conditioning means that visits are quite feasible year-round. In fact, winters can be very

photogenic, with Seoul's various small mountains covered in a layer of snow; temperatures usually drop below freezing in December, and stay there until February. Spring is decidedly more comfortable and even prettier, with cherry blossom making a brief but spectacular appearance, usually in late March or April. May and June are prime months to visit, while July and August are the hottest (regularly seeing temperatures sailing over 30°C) and wettest of the year. September and October are pleasant, and Seoul's autumn foliage makes this a great time for a spot of hiking in the hills.

Public holidays

Some of Korea's public holidays follow the lunar, rather than the solar, calendar – you'll be able to check dates for the coming years online. For more information on Chuseok and Seollal, Korean equivalents to Lunar New Year and Thanksgiving, respectively – *see p165.*
New Year's Day 1 Jan
Seollal 1st day of 1st lunar month
Independence Day 1 Mar
Children's Day 5 May
Buddha's Birthday 8th day of 4th lunar month
Memorial Day 6 June
Liberation Day 15 Aug
Chuseok 15th day of 8th lunar month
National Foundation Day 3 Oct
Christmas Day 25 Dec

WOMEN

Korea is an extremely safe nation by international standards. It must also be said that women are not, by and large, treated as equals in what is still a highly Confucian society; however, foreign women are usually treated with a little more respect.

THE LOCAL CLIMATE

	High (°C)	Rain (mm)	Sunshine (mm)
Jan	2	20	5.3
Feb	4	25	5.4
Mar	10	45	6.6
Apr	18	75	7.0
May	23	100	7.5
June	27	135	6.3
July	29	325	4.3
Aug	30	350	5.2
Sept	26	140	6.2
Oct	20	50	6.7
Nov	11	50	5.0
Dec	4	25	5.0

DIRECTORY

Further Reference

DIRECTORY

BOOKS

Literature & Fiction

The Dwarf
Cho Se Hui
Twelve mini-stories showing
the social flipside of Korea's
economic boom.

**I Have the Right to
Destroy Myself**
Young-Ha Kim
A Murakami-like 'I' character,
spinning morbid webs of the
mind in Seoul.

Our Twisted Hero
Yi Munyeol
A tale of school bullying,
with not-so-subtle parallels
to Korean politics.

Sketch of the Fading Sun
Park Wan Suh
Collection of short stories.

Who Ate Up All the Shinga?
Park Wan Suh
Semi-autobiographical mother-
daughter tale, set during the
Korean War.

Your Republic is Calling You
Young-Ha Kim
A North Korean spy crosses the
border, and gets mixed feelings
about his return.

Non-Fiction

**The Aquariums of
Pyongyang**
Kang Chol Hwan
Tales from the North Korean
gulags, as told by an escapee.

**A Walk Through the Land
of Miracles**
Simon Winchester
A Brit walks through 1980s Korea
– a truly different land to that of
today – from the southern coast
to the DMZ.

**Everlasting Flower:
a History of Korea**
Keith Pratt
The story of Korea from its
earliest kingdoms, interspersed
with illustrated art features.

Getting Married in Korea
Laural Kendall
Exactly what it says on the cover.

Korea Unmasked
Rhee Won Sok
A comic strip that takes a
sideways glance at the ways
of modern Korean society, as
told by Koreans.

The Korean War
Max Hastings
Acclaimed war historian Max
Hastings takes a fascinating
look at the Korean conflict
of the 1950s.

**The Koreans: Who They Are,
What They Want, Where
Their Future Lies**
Michael Breen
A detailed yet highly accessible
look at Korea's society, history,
economy and politics.

**Korea's Place in the Sun:
A Modern History**
Bruce Cumings
Study of the social changes caused
by Korea's occupation and civil war,
as well as the negative side of its
economic boom.

**The Memoirs of Lady
Hyegyong**
JaHyun Kim Haboush
The best translation of a Joseon-
era scandal that rocked the court.

North Korea: Another Country
Bruce Cumings
Tales from the "other" side of
the Korean conflict, focusing
on the actions of the US and
South Korea.

Under the Black Umbrella
Hildi Kang
Excellent oral history of the
colonial period.

The Zen Monastic Tradition
Robert Buswell
First-hand account of life in a
Korean Zen monastery.

Language

Colloquial Korean
*Danielle Ooyoung Pyun
& Inseok Kim*
The newer editions of this book
from the international *Colloquial*
stable are less riddled with errors
than previous ones.

Speaking Korean
Francis YT Park
The books in this series are not
terribly easy to track down outside
Korea, but they are probably the
best guide to the Korean language
that's available.

Food

Korean Cuisine
Michael Pettid
A comprehensive look at
Korean food.

FILM

3-Iron
Kim Ki Duk (2004)
Odd love story in which a boy
breaks into a house containing
a lonely girl.

Aimless Bullet
Yo Hyun Mok (1960)
Much-loved classic portraying a
day in the life of a salaryman trying
to deal with a delusional mother,
sick wife and crippled child.

Art Museum by the Zoo
Lee Jung Hyang (1998)
Soldier starts a relationship with a
videographer who has moved into
the apartment of his ex; her script
becomes the story within a story.

A Tale of Two Sisters
Kim Ji Woon (2003)
Horror based on a Korean folk tale.

Attack the Gas Station
Kim Sang Jin (1999)
Breezy, ecstatic fun.

Bad Guy
Kim Ki Duk (2001)
Mute gangster starts a relationship
with a girl he tricked into prostitution.

Die Another Day
Lee Tamahori (2002)
Bond comes to Korea – both Koreas,
in fact, since he's imprisoned in the
North and traded across the border.

Forever the Moment
Yim Soon Rye (2008)
Fictional story based on the South
Korean women's handball team,
competing in the 2004 Olympics.

Friend
Kwak Kyung Taek (2001)
This school buddy story was once
the highest-grossing film in Korea,
where it's known as *Chingu*.

Hahaha
Hong Sang Soo (2010)
A Cannes award-winner, this is an
ambitious, interestingly relayed tale
of a mountain encounter.

The Host
Bong Joon Ho (2006)
Monster drama, and the highest-
grossing film in Korean history.

The Housemaid
Kim Ki Young (1960)
Femme fatale destroys a family.
Badly remade in 2010, the original
is worth hunting down.

Inchon!
Terence Young (1982)
Mega-flop starring Laurence Olivier,
and financed by the Moonies.
Cleaned up at the *Razzies*.

The Isle
Kim Ki Duk (2000)
Chiller set in floating huts on
a remote lake.

Joint Security Area
Park Chan Wook (2000)
Film with a backwards storyline,
about a death in the DMZ.

The King and the Clown
Lee Jun Ik (2005)
All-male love triangle involving a
Joseon-dynasty king – set in a Seoul
palace, and partially true.

Memento Mori
Kim Tae Yong (1999)
A groundbreaking film in Korea:
this was one of the first local films
to feature lesbian characters.

My Sassy Girl
Kwak Jae Yong (2001)
A mega hit across Asia, this rom-
com tells a (partially true) story
beginning with a man meeting a
drunk girl on a train.

Northeast of Seoul
David Lowell Rich (1972)
Cringeworthy crime drama set
in Seoul, and most interesting
for the chance to see how the
city has changed.

Nowhere to Hide
Lee Myung Se (1999)
Insane romp around Korea as a
brutish, bumbling detective tries
to track down a ruthless assassin.

Oldboy
Park Chan Wook (2003)
Cannes Award-winning thriller
»that ranks as one of Korea's
best film exports.

Painted Fire
Im Kwon Taek (2002)
Another Cannes winner, about the
fortunes of a real-life 19th century
Seoul artist.

Peppermint Candy
Lee Chang Dong (1999)
Film starting with the suicide of the
protagonist, then running in reverse
to untangle the threads.

The President's Last Bang
Im Sang Su (2005)
Incendiary black comedy about
the assassination of President
Park Chung Hee, and as such
subject to several lawsuits.

Samaritan Girl
Kim Ki Duk (2004)
Two teenage girls sell their bodies
in an attempt to fund a trip to
Europe, with catastrophic results.

Save the Green Planet!
Jang Jun Hwan (2003)
Zany comedy in which the
protagonist kidnaps a businessman
whom he believes to be an alien.

Secret Sunshine
Lee Chang Dong (2007)
An award-winning tale of the
trials of entering middle age,

this film was directed by Korea's
former minister of culture.

Seopyeonje
Im Kwon Taek (1993)
A family of traditional musicians
in 1960s Seoul, this proved an
unexpected success and catapulted
director Im Kwon Taek into
the spotlight.

Shiri
Kang Je Gyu (1999)
Korea's first ever 'Hollywood' film,
about a North Korean girl (later to
star in *Lost*) being hunted down by
the police.

Someone Special
Jang Jin (2004)
A pair of ridiculous, awkward
lovers – this partial spoof is a
great romantic comedy for those
who hate romance films.

**Spring, Summer, Fall,
Winter... and Spring**
Kim Ki Duk (2003)
Beautiful film charting the life of
a monk, set in a remote monastery
on a lake.

Sympathy for Lady Vengeance
Park Chan Wook (2005)
Framed for a murder, a teenage
girl broods in jail then sets about
taking revenge.

Sympathy for Mr Vengeance
Park Chan Wook (2002)
A series of murders get kicked off
by a man searching for a kidney.

The Taebaek Mountains
Im Kwon Taek (1994)
A Berlin Golden Bear nominee,
relaying small-town life in the
years just before the outbreak
of the Korean War.

Take Care of my Cat
Jeong Jae Eun (2001)
Coming-of-age drama, the work
of one of Korea's most prominent
female directors.

Thirst
Park Chan Wook (2009)
A priest falls in love with his friend's
wife, and turns into a vampire. Not
as weird as it sounds.

**Virgin Stripped Bare
by Her Bachelors**
Hong Sang Soo (2000)
An award-winning comic drama,
this sees an arty couple spin an
intricate web of deceit.

The Way Home
Lee Jung Hyang (2002)
Sweet story of a seven-year-old
boy, forced to adapt to life in
the countryside with his mute
grandmother.

Welcome to Dongmakgol
Park Kwang Hyun (2005)
Set during the Korean War, this
sees soldiers from both sides find
themselves cut off from the conflict
in a remote village.

WEBSITES

www.10magazine.asia
Useful blog articles and event
listings, from the magazine folk.

www.aroundseoul.com
Restaurant, club and bar listings.

chingusai.net
Popular local gay & lesbian site
with some English-language
information.

www.cnngo.com/seoul
Focuses on Seoul pop culture.

english.tour2korea.com
English-language version of the KTO
(Korea Tourism Organisation) site.

forums.eslcafe.com/korea
Korean branch of the famed Dave's
ESL cafe, with plenty of Seoul
English-teaching job listings.

innostel.visitseoul.net
City-sponsored site on which you
can search for, and book, cheap
Seoul hotels.

www.jasonstrother.com
Interesting stories from a Seoul-
based radio journalist.

www.korea4expats.com
Good directory and practical
information for expats in Seoul
and beyond.

www.koreagigguide.com
Good site detailing live music in
Korea, with a focus on Seoul.

www.koreaontherocks.com
Rock-climbing possibilities both in
the Seoul area, and across Korea.

www.rjkoehler.com
The 'Marmot's Hole', one of
Seoul's oldest and best-researched
blogs, and particularly good for
architecture, history and politics.

roboseyo.blogspot.com
Quirky blog about Seoul food,
history and culture.

www.seouleats.com
Good food blog with some
superb pictures.

www.seoulgrid.com
The city's premium nightlife blog.

seoulselection.com
Covers most Seoul basics, for
newbies and veterans alike.

www.southkoreapages.com
Trade directory.

www.studyinkorea.com
Ministry of Education site,
giving details of how to enrol
at a Seoul university.

www.utopia-asia.com
This pan-Asian gay & lesbian
site has a good Korea wing.

www.vegetarianinkorea.com
Ultra-valuable resource for
vegetarians in Korea.

www.visitseoul.com
The official Seoul city tourism
guide site.

www.zenkimchi.com
Excellent food blog.

DIRECTORY

Vocabulary

The Korean language is loosely related to Japanese, Mongolian, Finnish, Estonian and Hungarian, though speakers of those languages will notice little similarity on the surface. Korean is extremely tricky to pick up – the syntax used is highly different to western languages, pronunciation is difficult, and it does not lend itself to easy Romanisation. Ironically, the Korean alphabet, hangeul, is one of the world's easiest to pick up; many expats claim to have learnt it on the flight in, and a high proportion of those may well be telling the truth. Locals are amazed to hear foreigners speaking even a word or two of Korean, or reading a bit of hangeul, and your efforts will not go unrewarded.

THE KOREAN ALPHABET

Consonants (pronunciation at end of syllable in brackets)

g (k)　　ㄱ
n　　　　ㄴ
d (t)　　ㄷ
l/r　　　ㄹ
m　　　ㅁ
b (p)　　ㅂ
s (t)　　ㅅ
- (ng)　ㅇ
j (t)　　ㅈ
ch (t)　ㅊ
k　　　ㅋ
t　　　ㅌ
p　　　ㅍ
h　　　ㅎ

Vowels and dipthongs

a　　ㅏ
eo　　ㅓ
o　　ㅗ
u　　ㅜ
eu　　ㅡ
i　　ㅣ
ya　　ㅑ
yeo　　ㅕ
yo　　ㅛ
yu　　ㅠ
ae　　ㅐ
yae　　ㅒ
e　　ㅔ
ye　　ㅖ
wa　　ㅘ
wae　　ㅙ
oe　　ㅚ
wo　　ㅝ
we　　ㅞ
wi　　ㅟ
ui　　ㅢ

THE BASICS

Yes
예/네
ye/ne

No
아니요
aniyo

Please
부탁해요
butak haeyo

Thank you
고마워요/감사합니다(hon.)
gomawoyo/gamsa hamnida

Hello
안녕하세요?/ 안녕하십니까?
annyeong haseyo?/annyeong hashimnikka?

Goodbye
안녕히 계세요(you are leaving)
annyeonghi gyeseyo
안녕히 가세요(they are leaving)
annyeonghi gaseyo

How are you?
어떻게 지냈어요?
eotteokke jinaesseo-yo?

Excuse me (getting attention)
저기요! / 여기요!
yeogi-yo!

Excuse me (to get past)
죄송해요
jeosong haeyo

Sorry
미안해요
mian haeyo

Don't mention it/
no problem
괜찮아요/문제 없어요
gwaenchan-ayo/
munje eopseo-yo

My name is...
내 이름은...이에요
nae ireum-eun... i-eyo

What's your name?
이름이 뭐에요?
ireum-i mwo-eyo?

Pleased to meet you
반가워요/반갑습니다
bangawo-yo/bangapseumnida

Welcome
어서 오십시오
eoseo oshipshiyo

Do you speak English?
영어 할 줄 알아요?
yeong-eo haljul alayo?

I don't speak Korean
나는 한국말 못해요
na-neun hangugmal mot haeyo

Could you speak more slowly?
천천히 말해 주세요
cheoncheonhi malhae jusaeyo

Could you repeat that?
다시 말해 주세요
dashi malhae jusaeyo

I get it
알겠어요
algesseoyo

I don't know
모르겠어요
moreugesseoyo

Where is (...)?
...어디에요?
eodi-eyo?

When is (...)?
...언제에요?
eonje-eyo?

What is (this/that)?
이게/그게 뭐에요?
igeon/geu-ge mwo-eyo?

NUMBERS

Numbers up to 100 have two alternate readings, and confusingly, both may be used within the same term.

1
일/하나
il/hana

2
이/둘
i/dul

3
삼/셋
sam/set

4
사/넷
sa/net

5
오/다섯
o/daseot

6
육/여섯
yuk/yeoseot

7
칠/일곱
chil/ilgop

8
팔/여덟
pal/yeodol

9
구/아홉
gu/ahop

10
십/열
ship/yeol

11
십일/열하나
ship-il/yeol-hana

12
십이/열둘
ship-i/yeol-dul

20
이십/스물
i-ship/seumul

30
삼십/서른
sam-ship/seoreun

40
사십/마흔
sa-ship/maheun

50
오십/쉰
o-ship/sueon

60
육십/예순
yuk-ship/yesun

70
칠십/일흔
chil-ship/ilheun

80
팔십/여든
pal-ship/yeodeun

90
구십/아흔
gu-ship/aheun

100
백/즈믄
baek/jeumeun

200
이백
i-baek

1,000
천
cheon

10,000
일만
il man

100,000
십만
shimman

1,000,000
백만
baengman

DAYS & TIMES

What's the time?
몇시에요?
myeosshi-eyo?

Morning
아침
achim

Afternoon
오후
ohu

Evening
저녁
jeonyeok

Night
밤
bam

Yesterday
어제
eo-je

Today
오늘
oneul

Tomorrow
내일
naeil

Last week
지난 주
jinan ju

Next week
다음 주
daeum ju

Weekend
주말
jumal

Monday
월요일
wol-yoil

Tuesday
화요일
hwa-yoil

Wednesday
수요일
su-yoil

Thursday
목요일
mok-yoil

Friday
금요일
geum-yoil

Saturday
토요일
to-yoil

Sunday
일요일
il-yoil

EATING & DRINKING

For specific dishes, *see p126*
Menu Reader.

Restaurant
식당
sikdang

Barbeque restaurant
고기 굽는 식당
gogi gupneun sikdang

Western restaurant
양식당
yang sikdang

Café
카페
ka-pe

Tearoom
찻집/다방
chatjip/dabang

Bar
술집/호프
suljip/ho-peu

Over here! (to get attention)
저기요!여기요!
jeogi-yo!yeogi-yo!

Can I have a menu?
메뉴 좀 주세요
menyu jom juseyo

Do you have an English menu?
영어 메뉴 있어요?
yeong-eo menyu isseoyo?

How much is it?
얼마에요?
eolma-eyo?

Vocabulary

I'm a vegetarian / I can't eat meat
나는 채식주의자/나는 고기 못 먹
어요
na-neun chaeshik ju-uija/na-neun
gogi mot meogeoyo

Please give me the bill
계산서 주세요
gyesanseo juseyo

ACCOMMODATION

Do you have any rooms?
방 있어요?
bang isseoyo?

single
싱글
singeul

double/queen
더블/퀸
deobeul/kwin

Do you have a room with
two beds?
방에 침대 두 개 있어요?
bang-e chimdae du-ge isseoyo?

Do you have an *ondol* room?
(sleeping on the floor, traditional
Korean Style)
온돌방 있어요?
ondol-bang isseoyo?

Is there … in the room?
방에 … 있어요?
bang-e … isseoyo?

a bath
욕조
yokjo

a shower
샤워기
syawogi

air-conditioning
에어콘
e-eo-kon

a television
텔레비전/TV
tellebijeon/TV

Is breakfast included?
아침식사 포함 되나요?
achim shiksa pohamnayo?

I'll be staying for...
… 잘거에요
...jalgeo-eyo
one night
1박/하룻밤
il-bak/haru

two nights
2박/이틀
i-bak/iteul

three nights
3박/삼일
sambak/sam-il

one week
일주일
il ju il/han ju il

I'm not sure how many nights
I will stay yet.
아직 며칠 있을지 몰라요
ajik myeochil isseulji mollayo

I'd like to stay an extra night.
하룻밤 더 잘게요
haruppam deo jalgeyo

I have a reservation.
예약했어요
yeyak haesseoyo

I do not have a reservation.
예약 안했습니다
yeyak an-haesseoyo

How much is the room?
방이 얼마에요?
bang-i eolma-eyo?

When must I check out by?
체크아웃 시간 몇 시에요?
checkout sigan myeosshi-yeyo?

I would like to pay my bill now.
지금 계산하고 싶어요
jigeum gyesan-hago shipeoyo

Please give me a receipt.
영수증 주세요
yeongsujeung juseyo

MONEY

Money
돈
don

Currency exchange
환전
hwanjeon

I'd like to change some …
…환전하고 싶어요
...hwanjeon-hago shipeoyo

Korean won
한국 원
hanguk won

British pounds
영국 파운드
yeongguk paun-deu

American dollars
미국 불/달러
miguk bul/dalleo

Do you have any change?
잔돈 있어요?
jandon isseoyo?

SHOPPING

I'd like to buy …
…사고 싶어요
...sago shipeoyo

Do you have…?
… 있어요?
...isseoyo?

How much is this/that?
이거/저거 얼마에요?
igeo/jeogeo oelma-eyo?

Can you help me?
도와주세요
dowa juseyo

May I try this on?
입어봐도 돼요?
ibeo bwado doeyo?

Do you have a larger size?
더 큰 사이즈 있어요?
deo keun saijeu isseoyo?

Do you have a smaller size?
더 작은 사이즈 있어요?
deo jageun saijeu isseoyo?

I will buy this.
이것 살게요
igeot salgeyo

No, thank you.
아니에요, 고마워요
anieyo, gomawoyo

Where can I find a …
어디에요?
...eodi-eyo

pharmacy
약국
yakguk

convenience store
편의점
pyeonui-jeom

department store
백화점
baekhwa-jeom

bookshop
서점
seo-jeom

supermarket
슈퍼
syu-peo

market
시장
shijang

camera store
카메라 가게
kamera ga-ge

SIGHTSEEING

Where's the...?
...어디에요?
...eodi eyo?

Tourist office
관광안내소
gwangwang annaeso

Gallery
갤러리
gaelleori

Museum
박물관...
bangmulgwan

Palace
궁
gung

Park
공원
gongwon

Temple
절
jeol

Do you have information on...?
...설명서 있어요?
...seolmyeongseo isseoyo?

Do you have a tour to...?
...에 관광 투어 있어요?
...e gwangwang tu-eo isseoyo?

I'd like to go to the...
...가고 싶어요
...ga-go shipeoyo

Can we get off here?
여기서 내려도 돼요?
yeogiseo naeryeodo doeyo?

Where is the nearest subway station?
가까운 지하철역은 어디에요?
gagga-un jihacheol yeol-eun eodi-eyo?

Am I allowed to take pictures here?
여기서 사진 찍어도 돼요?
yeogi-seo sajin jjik-edo doeyo?

TRANSPORT

Subway
지하철
jihacheol

Train
기차
gicha

Bus
버스
beo-seu

Taxi
택시
taek-shi

Do you have a subway map?
지하철 지도 있어요?
jihacheol jido isseoyo?

One ticket please
한 장 주세요
han jang juseyo

Two tickets please
두 장 주세요
du jang juseyo

Three tickets please
세 장 주세요
se jang juseyo

Four tickets please
네 장 주세요
ne jang juseyo

Can you please call me a taxi?
콜택시 불러 주실 수 있어요?
kol taekshi bulleo jusil-su isseoyo?

I'd like to go to...
...에 가고 싶어요
...e ga-go shipeoyo

Where is the ticket counter?
매표소 어디에요?
maepyoso eodi-eyo?

How much is the ticket?
표 금액이 얼마에요?
pyo geumaegi eolma-eyo?

When will the next one leave?
다음 것 언제 나가요?
daeum cha-neun eon ie chulbal-haeyo?

When will we depart?
언제 출발해요?
eonje chulbal haeyo?

When will we arrive?
언제 도착해요?
eonje dochak-haeyo?

Ticket office
매표소
maepyoso

Ticket vending machine
승차권 발매기
seungcha-gwon balmae-gi

HEALTH

Where is the nearest...
가까운 ...어디에요?
gagga-un ... eodi-eyo?

...hospital
...병원
... byeongwon

...dentist
...치과
...chigwa

...clinic
...의원
ui-won

I'm very sick
많이 아파요
mani apayo

Is there a doctor/dentist who speaks English?
영어 가능한 의사 선생님 계세요?
yeong-eo ganeung-han uisa seonsaeng-nim gyeseyo?

Can the doctor come to see me?
의사 선생님 방문 진료 가능한가요?
uisa-seongaeng-nim bangmun jillyo ganeung hanga-yo??

It's urgent!
급해요!
geup-haeyo!

Help!
도와주세요!
dowa-juseyo!

I have a headache
머리가 아파요
meori-ga apayo

I'm vomiting
토했어요
to-haesseoyo

I'm bleeding
피가 나요
pi-ga nayo

I have a fever
열 있어요
yeol isseoyo

I have diarrhoea
설사해요
seolsa-haeyo

I'm constipated
변비예요
byeonbi-yeyo

It hurts here
여기 아파요
yeogi apayo

I have a toothache
이가 아파요
iga apayo

I've lost a tooth
이가 빠졌어요
iga ppajyeosseoyo

DIRECTORY

Content Index

INDEX

INDEX

Venue Index

INDEX

INDEX

INDEX

Maps

Major sight or landmark	
Hospital or college	
Railway station	
Parks	
River	
Dual carriageway	
Main road	
Main road tunnel	
Pedestrian road	
Steps	
Airport	✈
Church	✚
Metro station	⊘
Area name	INSADONG

Seoul by Area

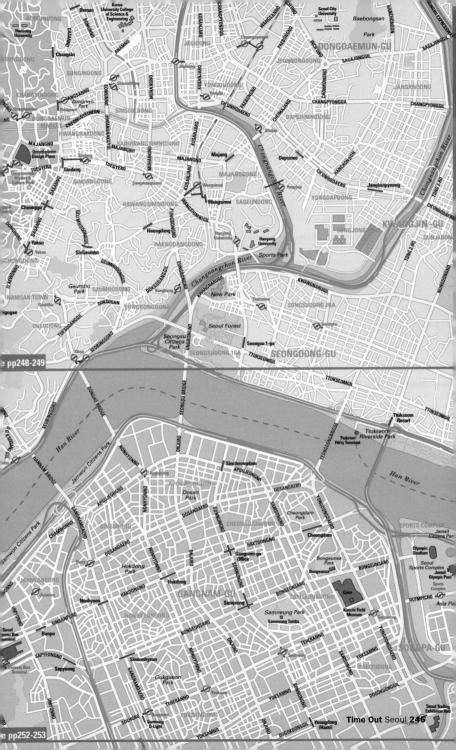

Hotels pp86-107
Restaurants pp108-127
Cafés & Tearooms pp128-134
Bars pp136-141

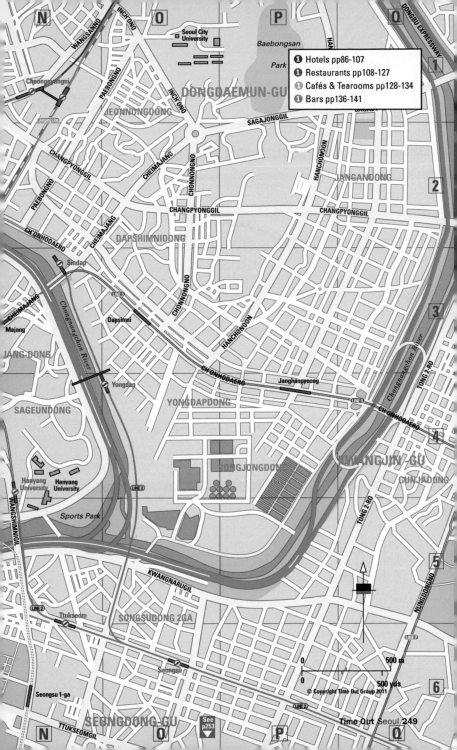

WANGSANNO
INCHONGO
Seoul City University
DONGDAEMUN-GU
Baebongsan Park

❶ Hotels pp86-107
❶ Restaurants pp108-127
❶ Cafés & Tearooms pp128-134
❶ Bars pp136-141

DONGBU EXPRESSWAY

Cheongnyangni
PAEBONGNO
JEONNONGDONG
INCHONGO
SAGAJONGGIL
CHONNONGNO
JANGANDONG

CHANGPYONGGIL
PAEBONGNO
CHEIMAJANG
CHANGPYONGGIL
CHANGPYONGGIL
HANCHONDON

CH'ONHODAERO
CHEIMAJANG
DAPSHIMNIDONG
CHONNONGNO
Sindap
LINE 5

CHEIMAJANG
Dapsimni
Majang
HANCHONDON

JANG-DONG
Chonggyecheon River
CH'ONHODAERO
Janghanpyeong
Chonggyecheon River
Yongdap
CH'ONHODAERO
YONGDAPDONG
LINE 5
KWANGJIN-GU

SAGEUNDONG
GUNJADONG

TONG 2-RO
Hanyang University
Hanyang University
LINE 2
SONGJONGDONG

Sports Park
TONG 2-RO
WANGSIMNIGIL
NUNGDONGNO

KWANGNARUGIL
LINE 2
Ttukseom
SONGSUDONG 2GA

LINE 2
0   500 m
0   500 yds
Seongsu
© Copyright Time Out Group 2011

Seongsu 1-ga
See p253
SEONGDONG-GU
TTUKSEOMGIL
Time Out Seoul 249

N O P Q

N

500 m

500 yds

© Copyright Time Out Group 2011

7

H a n   R i v e r

TTUKSEOMGIL

See p249

TTUKSEOMGIL

Ttukseom Resort

Ttukseom Riverside Park

Ttuksom Ferry Terminal

Ttukseom Riverside Park

8

APGUJEONGNO

53

43 44

DOSANDAERO

46

LINE 7

9

SPORTS COMPLEX

Cheongdam
Park

Jamsil Citizens Park

SAMSONGNO

YONGDONGDAERO

HAKTONGNO

Cheongdam

CHEONGDAMDONG

HAKTONGNO

Gangnam-gu
Office

12

Olympic
Stadium

*Seoul
Sports Complex*

Jamsil
Olympic Pool

Sonneungno

SAMSONGNO

Bongeunsa
Park

BONGEUNSARO

Bongeunsa

Sports
Complex

10

OLYMPICHO

Asia Park

Samjeong

35

40 Coex

YONGDONGDAERO

BONGEUNSARO

SAMSEONGDONG

Kimchi Field
Museum

36

TEHERANNO

45

Samseong

41

9

SONGPA-GU

Samneung Park

Samneung Tombs

SAMSONGNO

SONNEUNGNO

LINE 2

TEHERANNO

YONGDONGDAERO

11

Seolleung

YOKSAMNO

DAECHIDONG

57

45

Bundang Line

YOKSAMNO

SONNEUNGNO

ONJURO

Yeongdong
(Hanti)

DOGOKDONGGIL

DOGOKDONGGIL

YONGDONGDAERO

Seoul Trading
Exhibition Hall

12

Hakyeoul

NAMBUSUNHWANDORO

Time Out Seoul **253**

N O P Q

GYEDONG

YULGONGNO

Unhyeongung

Jongmyo
Royal Shrine

HYOJEDONG

MAREUNNAEGIL

SUPYODARIGIL

JAEHWAGWAN-GIL

Jongno 3-ga

CHANGGYEONGGUNGNO

JONGNO 5GA

SADONG

SAMILNO

Tapgol
Park

Jongmyo
Plaza

4GA

Jongno 3-ga

JUGYODONG

NGNO 3GA

VANCHEOLDONG

LINE 3

CHEONGGYECHEON

STREAM

SUPYODONG

Euljiro 3-ga

LINE 2

Euljiro 4-ga

EULJIRO 4GA

BAEOGAEGIL

EULJIRO 3GA

MAREUNNAEGIL

OJANGDONG

CHEONGGYE

MAREUNNAEGIL

WARYONGNO

SUPYODARIGIL

Myeongdong
Cathedral

LINE 4

TOEGYERO

Chungmuro

TOEGYERO

SOPAGIL

❶ Hotels pp86-107

❶ Restaurants pp108-127

❶ Cafés & Tearooms pp128-134

❶ Bars pp136-141

Namsangol
Hanok Village

Time Out Seoul **255**

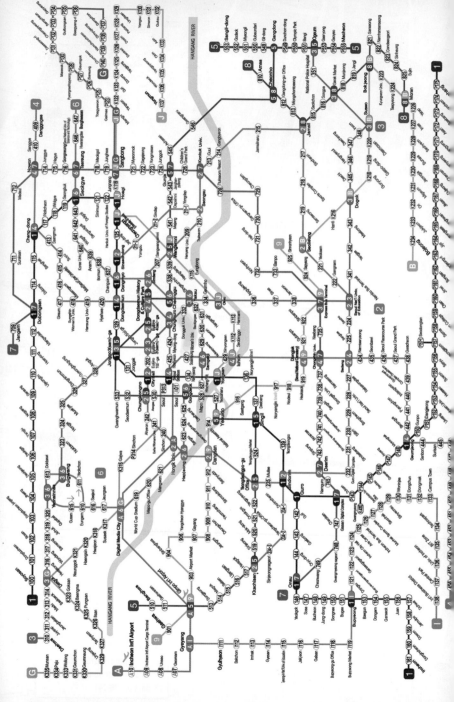

Sanditon & The Watsons

AUSTEN'S UNFINISHED NOVELS

Jane Austen

DOVER PUBLICATIONS, INC.
Mineola, New York

Bibliographical Note

This Dover edition, first published in 2007, is an unabridged republication of the works (both novel fragments from handwritten manuscript pages) as first published in J. E. Austen Leigh's *A Memoir of Jane Austen* (i.e., the second edition, published in 1871 by Richard Bentley and Son, London), and other standard editions. *Sanditon* was written by Jane Austen in 1817, the year of her death, while *The Watsons* was written earlier, c. 1803. Most of the archaic spellings and other minor inconsistencies that derive from the original are retained here for the sake of authenticity, while English punctuation has been Americanized.

The Biographical Note, by Jane Austen's brother Henry (1771–1850), was originally printed as the Preface to the first edition of *Northanger Abbey: and Persuasion*, jointly published posthumously in 1818 by John Murray, London.

Library of Congress Cataloging-in-Publication Data

Austen, Jane, 1775–1817.
 Sanditon ; and, The Watsons / Jane Austen.
  p. cm.
 An unabridged republication of Jane Austen's Sanditon, and The Watsons (both novel fragments from handwritten manuscript pages) as they were first published in J. E. Austen Leigh's A memoir of Jane Austen.
  ISBN-13: 978-0-486-45793-2
  ISBN-10: 0-486-45793-1
 I. Austen, Jane, 1775–1817. Watsons. II. Title.

PR4034.S3 2007
823'.7—dc22

2006102574

Manufactured in the United States of America
Dover Publications, Inc., 31 East 2nd Street, Mineola, N.Y. 11501

CONTENTS

BIOGRAPHICAL NOTE[1]

by Henry Austen

THE FOLLOWING pages are the production of a pen which has already contributed in no small degree to the entertainment of the public. And when the public, which has not been insensible to the merits of *Sense and Sensibility, Pride and Prejudice, Mansfield Park,* and *Emma,* shall be informed that the hand which guided that pen is now mouldering in the grave, perhaps a brief account of Jane Austen [1775–1817] will be read with a kindlier sentiment than simple curiosity.

Short and easy will be the task of the mere biographer.[2] A life of usefulness, literature, and religion, was not by any means a life of event. To those who lament their irreparable loss, it is consolatory to think that, as she never deserved disapprobation, so, in the circle of her family and friends, she never met reproof; that her wishes were not only reasonable, but gratified; and that to the little disappointments incidental to human life was never added, even for a moment, an abatement of goodwill from any who knew her.

Jane Austen was born on the 16th of December, 1775, at Steventon, in the county of Hants. Her father was Rector of that parish upwards of forty years. There he resided, in the conscientious and unassisted discharge of ministerial duties, until he

---

[1] Please see the Bibliographical Note on page ii for detailed information on the provenance of this piece. [ED.]

[2] A somewhat ironic statement from today's perspective, where books about Jane Austen abound. [ED.]

was turned of seventy years. Then he retired with his wife, our authoress, and her sister, to Bath, for the remainder of his life, a period of about four years. Being not only a profound scholar, but possessing a most exquisite taste in every species of literature, it is not wonderful that his daughter Jane should, at a very early age, have become sensible to the charms of style, and enthusiastic in the cultivation of her own language. On the death of her father she removed, with her mother and sister, for a short time, to Southampton, and finally, in 1809, to the pleasant village of Chawton, in the same county. From this place she sent into the world those novels, which by many have been placed on the same shelf as the works of a D'Arblay and an Edgeworth.[3] Some of these novels had been the gradual performances of her previous life. For though in composition she was equally rapid and correct, yet an invincible distrust of her own judgement induced her to withhold her works from the public, till time and many perusals had satisfied her that the charm of recent composition was dissolved. The natural constitution, the regular habits, the quiet and happy occupations of our authoress, seemed to promise a long succession of amusement to the public, and a gradual increase of reputation to herself. But the symptoms of a decay, deep and incurable, began to shew themselves in the commencement of 1816. Her decline was at first deceitfully slow; and until the spring of this present year, those who knew their happiness to be involved in her existence could not endure to despair. But in the month of May, 1817, it was found advisable that she should be removed to Winchester for the benefit of constant medical aid, which none even then dared to hope would be permanently beneficial. She supported, during two months, all the varying pain, irksomeness, and tedium, attendant on decaying nature, with more than resignation, with a truly elastic cheerfulness. She retained her faculties, her memory, her fancy, her temper, and her affections, warm, clear, and unimpaired, to the last. Neither her love of God, nor

---

[3] Novelists Frances Burney d'Arblay (better known as Fanny Burney, 1752–1840) and Maria Edgeworth (1767–1849) [ED.]

of her fellow creatures flagged for a moment. She made a point of receiving the sacrament before excessive bodily weakness might have rendered her perception unequal to her wishes. She wrote whilst she could hold a pen, and with a pencil when a pen was become too laborious. The day preceding her death she composed some stanzas replete with fancy and vigour. Her last voluntary speech conveyed thanks to her medical attendant; and to the final question asked of her, purporting to know her wants, she replied, "I want nothing but death."

She expired shortly after, on Friday the 18th of July, 1817, in the arms of her sister, who, as well as the relator of these events, feels too surely that they shall never look upon her like again.

Jane Austen was buried on the 24th of July, 1817, in the cathedral church of Winchester, which, in the whole catalogue of its mighty dead, does not contain the ashes of a brighter genius or a sincerer Christian.

Of personal attractions she possessed a considerable share. Her stature was that of true elegance. It could not have been increased without exceeding the middle height. Her carriage and deportment were quiet, yet graceful. Her features were separately good. Their assemblage produced an unrivalled expression of that cheerfulness, sensibility, and benevolence, which were her real characteristics. Her complexion was of the finest texture. It might with truth be said, that her eloquent blood spoke through her modest cheek. Her voice was extremely sweet. She delivered herself with fluency and precision. Indeed she was formed for elegant and rational society, excelling in conversation as much as in composition. In the present age it is hazardous to mention accomplishments. Our authoress would, probably, have been inferior to few in such acquirements, had she not been so superior to most in higher things. She had not only an excellent taste for drawing, but, in her earlier days, evinced great power of hand in the management of the pencil. Her own musical attainments she held very cheap. Twenty years ago they would have been thought more of, and twenty years hence many a parent will expect their daughters to be applauded for meaner performances. She was fond of dancing, and excelled in it. It remains now to add a few observations on that which her friends deemed more important, on those endowments which sweetened every hour of their lives.

If there be an opinion current in the world, that perfect placidity of temper is not reconcileable to the most lively imagination, and the keenest relish for wit, such an opinion will be rejected for ever by those who have had the happiness of knowing the authoress of the following works. Though the frailties, foibles, and follies of others could not escape her immediate detection, yet even on their vices did she never trust herself to comment with unkindness. The affectation of candour is not uncommon; but she had no affectation. Faultless herself, as nearly as human nature can be, she always sought, in the faults of others, something to excuse, to forgive or forget. Where extenuation was impossible, she had a sure refuge in silence. She never uttered either a hasty, a silly, or a severe expression. In short, her temper was as polished as her wit. Nor were her manners inferior to her temper. They were of the happiest kind. No one could be often in her company without feeling a strong desire of obtaining her friendship, and cherishing a hope of having obtained it. She was tranquil without reserve or stiffness; and communicative without intrusion or self-sufficiency. She became an authoress entirely from taste and inclination. Neither the hope of fame nor profit mixed with her early motives. Most of her works, as before observed, were composed many years previous to their publication. It was with extreme difficulty that her friends, whose partiality she suspected whilst she honoured their judgement, could prevail on her to publish her first work. Nay, so persuaded was she that its sale would not repay the expense of publication, that she actually made a reserve from her very moderate income to meet the expected loss. She could scarcely believe what she termed her great good fortune when *Sense and Sensibility* produced a clear profit of about £150. Few so gifted were so truly unpretending. She regarded the above sum as a prodigious recompense for that which had cost her nothing. Her readers, perhaps, will wonder that such a work produced so little at a time when some authors have received more guineas than they have written lines. The works of our authoress, however, may live as long as those which have burst on the world with more éclat. But the public has not been unjust; and our authoress was far from thinking it so. Most gratifying to her was the applause which from time to time reached her ears from those who were competent to discriminate. Still, in spite of such applause, so much did she shrink from notoriety, that no accumulation of fame would have induced her, had she lived, to affix her name to any productions of her pen. In the bosom of her own family she talked of them freely, thankful for praise, open to remark, and submissive to criticism. But in public she turned away from any allusion to the character of an authoress. She read aloud with very great taste and effect. Her own works, probably, were never heard to so much advantage as from her own mouth; for she partook largely in all the best gifts of the comic muse. She was a warm and judicious admirer of landscape, both in nature and on canvass. At a very early age she was enamoured of Gilpin on the Picturesque[4]; and she seldom changed her opinions either on books or men.

Her reading was very extensive in history and belles lettres; and her memory extremely tenacious. Her favourite moral writers were Johnson in prose, and Cowper in verse. It is difficult to say at what age she was not intimately acquainted with the merits and defects of the best essays and novels in the English language. Richardson's power of creating, and preserving the consistency of his characters, as particularly exemplified in *Sir Charles Grandison*,[5] gratified the natural discrimination of her mind, whilst her taste secured her from the errors of his prolix style and tedious narrative. She did not rank any work of Fielding quite so high. Without the slightest affectation she recoiled from every thing gross. Neither nature, wit, nor humour, could make her amends for so very low a scale of morals.

Her power of inventing characters seems to have been intuitive, and almost unlimited. She drew from nature; but, whatever may have been surmised to the contrary, never from individuals.

---

[4] *Three Essays: On Picturesque Beauty; On Picturesque Travel; and On Sketching Landscape to Which Is Added a Poem On Landscape Painting*, by William Gilpin (1724–1804), published in 1792. [ED.]
[5] *The History of Sir Charles Grandison* (1753) is a novel by Samuel Richardson (1689–1761). [ED.]

The style of her familiar correspondence was in all respects the same as that of her novels. Every thing came finished from her pen; for on all subjects she had ideas as clear as her expressions were well chosen. It is not hazarding too much to say that she never dispatched a note or letter unworthy of publication.

One trait only remains to be touched on. It makes all others unimportant. She was thoroughly religious and devout; fearful of giving offence to God, and incapable of feeling it towards any fellow creature. On serious subjects she was well-instructed, both by reading and meditation, and her opinions accorded strictly with those of our Established Church.

London, Dec. 13, 1817

Sanditon

CHAPTER 1

A GENTLEMAN & a lady travelling from Tunbridge towards that part of the Sussex coast which lies between Hastings & E. Bourne, being induced by business to quit the high road, & attempt a very rough lane, were overturned in toiling up its long ascent half rock, half sand.—The accident happened just beyond the only gentleman's house near the lane—a house, which their driver, on being first required to take that direction, had conceived to be necessarily their object & had with most unwilling looks been constrained to pass by—. He had grumbled and shaken his shoulders so much indeed, and pitied & cut his horses so sharply, that he might have been open to the suspicion of overturning them on purpose (especially as the carriage was not his master's own) if the road had not indisputably become considerably worse than before, as soon as the premises of the said house were left behind—expressing with a most intelligent portentous countenance that beyond it no wheels but cart wheels could safely proceed. The severity of the fall was broken by their slow pace & the narrowness of the lane, & the gentleman having scrambled out & helped out his companion, they neither of them at first felt more than shaken & bruised. But the gentleman had in the course of the extrication sprained his foot—& soon becoming sensible of it, was obliged in a few moments to cut short, both his remonstrance to the driver & his congratulations to his wife & himself—& sit down on the bank,

1

unable to stand.—"There is something wrong here, said he—
putting his hand to his ancle—But never mind, my dear—
(looking up at her with a smile)—it c^d not have happened, you
know, in a better place.—Good out of evil—. The very thing
perhaps to be wished for. We shall soon get relief.—*There,* I
fancy, lies my cure"—pointing to the neat-looking end of a cottage, which was seen romantically situated among wood on a
high eminence at some little distance—"Does not *that* promise
to be the very place?"—His wife fervently hoped it was—but
stood, terrified & anxious, neither able to do or suggest anything—& receiving her first real comfort from the sight of several persons now coming to their assistance. The accident had
been discerned from a hayfield adjoining the house they had
passed—& the persons who approached, were a well-looking,
hale, gentlemanlike man of middle age, the proprietor of the
place, who happened to be among his haymakers at the time, &
three or four of the ablest of them summoned to attend their
master—to say nothing of all the rest of the field, men, women
& children—not very far off.—Mr Heywood, such was the name
of the said proprietor, advanced with a very civil salutation—
much concern for the accident—some surprise at any body's
attempting that road in a carriage—& ready offers of assistance.
His courtesies were received with good-breeding & gratitude &
while one or two of the men lent their help to the driver in getting the carriage upright again, the travellor said—"You are
extremely obliging, sir, & I take you at your word.—The injury
to my leg is, I dare say, very trifling, but it is always best in these
cases to have a surgeon's opinion without loss of time; and as the
road does not seem at present in a favourable state for my getting up to his house myself, I will thank you to send off one of
these good people for the surgeon." "The surgeon, sir!—replied
Mr Heywood—I am afraid you will find no surgeon at hand
here, but I dare say we shall do very well without him."—"Nay
sir, if *he* is not in the way, his partner will do just as well—or
rather better—. I w^d rather see his partner indeed—I would
prefer the attendance of his partner.—One of these good people
can be with him in three minutes I am sure. I need not ask
whether I see the house; (looking towards the cottage) for
excepting your own, we have passed none in this place, which

can be the abode of a gentleman."—Mr H. looked very much astonished—& replied—"What, sir! are you expecting to find a surgeon in that cottage?—We have neither surgeon nor partner in the parish I assure you."—"Excuse me, sir—replied the other. I am sorry to have the appearance of contradicting you—but though from the extent of the parish or some other cause you may not be aware of the fact;—Stay—Can I be mistaken in the place?—Am I not in Willingden?—Is not this Willingden?" "Yes, sir, this is certainly Willingden." "Then, sir, I can bring proof of your having a surgeon in the parish—whether you may know it or not. Here, sir—(taking out his pocket book—) if you will do me the favour of casting your eye over these advertise-ments, which I cut out myself from the Morning Post & the Kentish Gazette, only yesterday morn^g in London—I think you will be convinced that I am not speaking at random. You will find it an advertisement sir, of the dissolution of a partnership in the medical line—in your own parish—extensive business— undeniable character—respectable references—wishing to form a separate establishment—You will find it at full length, sir,"—offering him the two little oblong extracts.—"Sir,—said Mr Heywood with a good humoured smile—if you were to shew me all the newspapers that are printed in one week throughout the kingdom, you w^d not persuade me of there being a surgeon in Willingden,—for having lived here ever since I was born, man & boy 57 years, I think I must have *known* of such a person, at least I may venture to say that he has not *much business*—To be sure, if gentlemen were to be often attempting this lane in post-chaises, it might not be a bad speculation for a surgeon to get a house at the top of the hill.—But as to that cottage, I can assure you, sir that it is in fact—(in spite of its spruce air at this dis-tance—) as indifferent a double tenement as any in the parish, and that my shepherd lives at one end, & three old women at the other." He took the pieces of paper as he spoke—& having looked them over, added—"I believe I can explain it, sir.—Your mistake is in the place.—There are two Willingdens in this country—& your advertisements refer to the other—which is Great Willingden, or Willingden Abbots, & lies 7 miles off, on the other side of Battel—quite down in the weald. And *we* sir— (speaking rather proudly) are not in the weald."—"Not *down* in the weald, I am sure sir, replied the traveller, pleasantly. It took us half an hour to climb your hill.—Well sir—I dare say it is as you say, & I have made an abominably stupid blunder.—All done in a moment;—the advertisements did not catch my eye till the last half hour of our being in town;—when everything was in the hurry & confusion which always attend a short stay there—One is never able to complete anything in the way of business you know till the carriage is at the door—and accordingly satisfying myself with a brief enquiry, & finding we were actually to pass within a mile or two of a *Willingden*, I sought no farther . . . My dear—(to his wife) I am very sorry to have brought you into this scrape. But do not be alarmed about my leg. It gives me no pain while I am quiet,—and as soon as these good people have succeeded in setting the car^ge to rights & turning the horses round, the best thing we can do will be to measure back our steps into the turnpike road & proceed to Hailsham, & so home, without attempting anything farther.— Two hours take us home, from Hailsham—And when once at home, we have our remedy at hand you know.—A little of our own bracing sea air will soon set me on my feet again.—Depend upon it, my dear, it is exactly a case for the sea. Saline air & immersion will be the very thing.—My sensations tell me so already."—In a most friendly manner Mr Heywood here interposed, entreating them not to think of proceeding till the ankle had been examined, & some refreshment taken, & very cordially pressing them to make use of his house for both purposes.—"We are always well stocked, said he, with all the common remedies for sprains and bruises—& I will answer for the pleasure it will give my wife & daughters to be of service to you & this lady in every way in their power."—A twinge or two, in trying to move his foot disposed the traveller to think rather more than he had done at first of the benefit of immediate assistance—& consulting his wife in the few words of "Well, my dear, I believe it will be better for us."—turned again to M^r H, & said—"Before we accept your hospitality sir,—& in order to do away with any unfavourable impression which the sort of wild goose-chase you find me in, may have given rise to—allow me to tell you who we are. My name is Parker.—Mr Parker of Sanditon; this lady, my wife Mrs Parker.—We are on our road

home from London;—*My* name perhaps—tho' I am by no
means the first of my family, holding landed property in the
parish of Sanditon, may be unknown at this distance from the
coast—but Sanditon itself—everybody has heard of Sanditon,—
the favourite—for a young & rising bathing-place, certainly the
favourite spot of all that are to be found along the coast of
Sussex;—the most favoured by nature, & promising to be the
most chosen by man."—"Yes—I have heard of Sanditon. replied
Mr H.—Every five years, one hears of some new place or other
starting up by the sea, & growing the fashion.—How they can
half of them be filled, is the wonder! *Where* people can be
found with money or time to go to them!—Bad things for a
country;—sure to raise the price of provisions and make the
poor good for nothing—as I dare say you find, sir." "Not at all,
sir, not at all—cried Mr Parker eagerly. Quite the contrary I
assure you.—A common idea—but a mistaken one. It may apply
to your large, overgrown places, like Brighton, or Worthing, or
East Bourne—but *not* to a small village like Sanditon, precluded
by its size from experiencing any of the evils of civilization,
while the growth of the place, the buildings, the nursery
grounds, the demand for every thing, & the sure resort of the
very best company, those regular, steady, private families of
thorough gentility & character, who are a blessing everywhere,
excite the industry of the poor and diffuse comfort & improvement among them of every sort.—No sir, I assure you, Sanditon
is not a place——" "I do not mean to take exceptions to *any*
place in particular sir, answered Mr H.—I only think our coast is
too full of them altogether—But had we not better try to get
you"——"Our coast too full" repeated Mr P.—On that point
perhaps we may not totally disagree; at least there are *enough*.
Our coast is abundant enough; it demands no more.—Every
body's taste & every body's finances may be suited—And those
good people who are trying to add to the number, are in my
opinion excessively absurd & must soon find themselves the
dupes of their own fallacious calculations.—Such a place as
Sanditon, sir, I may say was wanted, was called for.—Nature had
marked it out—had spoken in most intelligible characters—The
finest, purest sea breeze on the coast—acknowledged to be so—
excellent bathing—fine hard sand—deep water 10 yards from

the shore—no mud—no weeds—no slimey rocks—Never was there a place more palpably designed by nature for the resort of the invalid—the very spot which thousands seemed in need of.—The most desirable distance from London! One complete, measured mile nearer than East Bourne. Only conceive, sir, the advantage of saving a whole mile, in a long journey. But Brinshore, sir, which I dare say you have in your eye—the attempts of two or three speculating people about Brinshore, this last year, to raise that paltry hamlet, lying, as it does between a stagnant marsh, a bleak moor & the constant effluvia of a ridge of putrefying sea weed, can end in nothing but their own disappointment. What in the name of common sense is to *recommend* Brinshore?—A most insalubrious air—roads proverbially detestable—water brackish beyond example, impossible to get a good dish of tea within 3 miles of the place—& as for the soil— it is so cold & ungrateful that it can hardly be made to yield a cabbage.—Depend upon it, sir, that this is a faithful description of Brinshore—not in the smallest degree exaggerated—& if you have heard it differently spoken of——" "Sir, I never heard it spoken of in my life before, said Mʳ Heywood. I did not know there was such a place in the world." "You did not!—There, my dear,—(turning with exultation to his wife)—you see how it is. So much for the celebrity of Brinshore!—This gentleman did not know there was such a place in the world.—Why, in truth, sir, I fancy we may apply to Brinshore, that line of the poet Cowper in his description of the religious cottager, as opposed to Voltaire—"*She,* never heard of half a mile from home."— "With all my heart, sir—apply any verses you like to it—But I want to see something applied to your leg—& I am sure by your lady's countenance that she is quite of my opinion & thinks it a pity to lose any more time—And here come my girls to speak for themselves & their mother. (two or three genteel looking young women followed by as many maid servants, were now seen issueing from the house)—I began to wonder the bustle should not have reached *them.*—A thing of this kind soon makes a stir in a lonely place like ours.—Now, sir, let us see how you can be best conveyed into the house."—The young ladies approached & said every thing that was proper to recommend their father's offers; & in an unaffected manner calculated to make the strangers easy—And as M^{rs} P— was exceedingly anxious for relief—and her husband by this time, not much less disposed for it—a very few civil scruples were enough—especially as the carriage being now set up, was discovered to have received such injury on the fallen side as to be unfit for present use.—Mr Parker was therefore carried into the house, and his carriage wheeled off to a vacant barn.—

CHAPTER 2

THE acquaintance, thus oddly begun, was neither short nor unimportant. For a whole fortnight the travellers were fixed at Willingden; Mr P.'s sprain proving too serious for him to move sooner.—He had fallen into very good hands. The Heywoods were a thoroughly respectable family, & every possible attention was paid in the kindest & most unpretending manner, to both husband & wife. *He* was waited on & nursed, & *she* cheered & comforted with unremitting kindness—and as every office of hospitality & friendliness was received as it ought—as there was not more good will on one side than gratitude on the other—nor any deficiency of generally pleasant manners on either, they grew to like each other in the course of that fortnight, exceedingly well.—Mr Parker's character & history were soon unfolded. All that he understood of himself, he readily told, for he was very openhearted;—& where he might be himself in the dark, his conversation was still giving information, to such of the Heywoods as could observe.—By such he was perceived to be an enthusiast;—on the subject of Sanditon, a complete enthusiast.—Sanditon,—the success of Sanditon as a small, fashionable bathing place was the object, for which he seemed to live. A very few years ago, & it had been a quiet village of no pretensions; but some natural advantages in its position & some accidental circumstances having suggested to himself, & the other principal land holder, the probability of its becoming a profitable speculation, they had engaged in it, & planned & built, & praised & puffed, & raised it to something of young renown— and Mr Parker could now think of very little besides.—The facts, which in more direct communication, he laid before them were that he was about 5 & 30—had been married,—very happily married 7 years—& had 4 sweet children at home;—that he was of a respectable family, & easy though not large fortune;—no profession—succeeding as eldest son to the property which 2 or 3 generations had been holding & accumulating before him;—that he had 2 brothers and 2 sisters—all single & all independent—the eldest of the two former indeed, by collateral inheritance, quite as well provided for as himself.—His object in quitting the high road, to hunt for an advertising surgeon, was also plainly stated;—it had not proceeded from any intention of spraining his ankle or doing himself any other injury for the good of such surgeon—nor (as Mr H. had been apt to suppose) from any design of entering into partnership with him—; it was merely in consequence of a wish to establish some medical man at Sanditon, which the nature of the advertisement induced him to expect to accomplish in Willingden.—He was convinced that the advantage of a medical man at hand w^d very materially promote the rise & prosperity of the place—w^d in fact tend to bring a prodigious influx;—nothing else was wanting. He had *strong* reason to believe that *one* family had been deterred last year from trying Sanditon on that account—& probably very many more—and his own sisters who were sad invalids, & whom he was very anxious to get to Sanditon this summer, could hardly be expected to hazard themselves in a place where they could not have immediate medical advice.—Upon the whole, Mr P. was evidently an amiable, family-man, fond of wife, child^n, brothers & sisters—& generally kind-hearted;—liberal, gentlemanlike, easy to please;—of a sanguine turn of mind, with more imagination than judgement. And Mrs P. was as evidently a gentle, amiable, sweet tempered woman, the properest wife in the world for a man of strong understanding, but not of a capacity to supply the cooler reflection which her own husband sometimes needed, & so entirely waiting to be guided on every occasion, that whether he were risking his fortune or spraining his ankle, she remained equally useless.—Sanditon was a second wife & 4 children to him—hardly less dear—& certainly more engrossing.—He could talk of it for ever.—It had indeed the highest claims;—not only those of birthplace, property, and home,—it was his mine, his lottery, his speculation & his hobby horse; his occupation his hope & his futurity.—He was extremely desirous of drawing his good friends at Willingden thither; and his endeavours in the cause, were as grateful & disinterested, as they were warm.—He wanted to secure the promise of a visit—to get as many of the family as his own house w^d contain, to follow him to Sanditon as soon as possible—and, healthy as they all undeniably were—foresaw that every one of them w^d be benefited by the sea.—He held it indeed as certain, that no person c^d be really well, no person, (however upheld for the present by fortuitous aids of exercise & spirits in a semblance of health) could be really in a state of secure & permanent health without spending at least 6 weeks by the sea every year.—The sea air & sea bathing together were nearly infallible, one or the other of them being a match for every disorder, of the stomach, the lungs or the blood; they were anti-spasmodic, anti-pulmonary, anti-septic, anti-billious & anti-rheumatic. Nobody could catch cold by the sea, nobody wanted appetite by the sea, nobody wanted spirits, nobody wanted strength.—They were healing, softening, relaxing—fortifying & bracing—seemingly just as was wanted—sometimes one, sometimes the other.—If the sea breeze failed, the sea-bath was the certain corrective;— & where bathing disagreed, the sea breeze alone was evidently designed by nature for the cure. His eloquence, however could not prevail. M^r & M^{rs} H— never left home. Marrying early & having a very numerous family, their movements had been long limited to one small circle; & they were older in habits than in age.—Excepting two journeys to London in the year, to receive his dividends, Mr H. went no farther than his feet or his well-tried old horse could carry him, and Mrs Heywood's adventurings were only now & then to visit her neighbours, in the old coach which had been new when they married & fresh lined on their eldest son's coming of age 10 years ago.—They had very pretty property—enough, had their family been of reasonable limits to have allowed them a very gentlemanlike share of luxuries & change—enough for them to have indulged in a new carriage & better roads, an occasional month at Tunbridge Wells, & symptoms of the gout and a winter at B— —but the maintenance, education & fitting out of 14 childr n demanded a very quiet, settled, careful course of life—& obliged them to be stationary and healthy at Willingden. What prudence had at first enjoined, was now rendered pleasant by habit. They never left home & they had gratification in saying so.—But very far from wishing their children to do the same, they were glad to promote *their* getting out into the world, as much as possible. *They* stayed at home, that their children *might* get out;—and, while making that home extremely comfortable, welcomed every change from it which could give useful connections or respectable acquaintance to sons or daughters. When M^r & Mrs Parker therefore ceased from soliciting a family-visit, and bounded their views to carrying back one daughter with them, no difficulties were started. It was general pleasure & consent.—Their invitation was to Miss Charlotte Heywood, a very pleasing young woman of two and twenty, the eldest of the daughters at home, & the one who, under her mother's directions had been particularly useful & obliging to them; who had attended them most, & knew them best.—Charlotte was to go,—with excellent health, to bathe & be better if she could—to receive every possible pleasure which Sanditon could be made to supply by the gratitude of those she went with—& to buy new parasols, new gloves, & new broches, for her sisters & herself at the library, which Mr P. was anxiously wishing to support.—All that Mr Heywood himself could be persuaded to promise was, that he would send everyone to Sanditon, who asked his advice, & that nothing should ever induce him (as far [as] the future could be answered for) to spend even 5 shilling at Brinshore.

CHAPTER 3

EVERY neighbourhood should have a great lady.—The great lady of Sanditon, was Lady Denham; & in their journey from Willingden to the coast, Mr Parker gave Charlotte a more detailed account of her, than had been called for before.—She had been necessarily often mentioned at Willingden,—for being his colleague in speculation, Sanditon itself could not be talked of long, without the introduction of Lady Denham & that she was a very rich old lady, who had buried two husbands, who knew the value of money, was very much looked up to & had a poor cousin living with her, were facts already well known, but some further particulars of her history & her character served to lighten the tediousness of a long hill, or a heavy bit of road, and to give the visiting young lady a suitable knowledge of the person with whom she might now expect to be daily associating.—Lady D. had been a rich Miss Brereton, born to wealth but not to education. Her first husband had been a Mr Hollis, a man of considerable property in the country, of which a large share of the parish of Sanditon, with manor & mansion house made a part. He had been an elderly man when she married him;—her own age about 30.—Her motives for such a match could be little understood at the distance of 40 years, but she had so well nursed & pleased Mr Hollis, that at his death he left her everything—all his estates, & all at her disposal. After a widowhood of some years, she had been induced to marry again. The late Sir Harry Denham, of Denham Park in the neighbourhood of Sanditon had succeeded in removing her & her large income to his own domains, but he c^d not succeed in the views of permanently enriching his family, which were attributed to him. She had been too wary to put anything out of her own power—and when on Sir Harry's decease she returned again to her own house at Sanditon, she was said to have made this boast to a friend "that though she had *got* nothing but her title from the family, still she had *given* nothing for it."—For the title, it was to be supposed she had married—& Mr P. acknowledged there being just such a degree of value for it apparent now, as to give her conduct that natural explanation. "There is at times said he—a little self-importance—but it is not offensive;—& there are moments, there are points, when her love of money is carried greatly too far. But she is a goodnatured woman, a very goodnatured woman,—a very obliging, friendly neighbour; a cheerful, independent, valuable character.—and her faults may be entirely imputed to her want of education. She has good natural sense, but quite uncultivated.—She has a fine active mind, as well as a fine healthy frame for a woman of 70, & enters into the improvement of Sanditon with a spirit truly admirable—though now & then, a littleness *will* appear. She cannot look forward quite as I would have her—& takes alarm at a trifling present expense, without considering what returns it *will* make her in a year or two. That is—we think *differently,* we now & then, see things *differently,* Miss H.— Those who tell their own story you know must be listened to with caution.—When you see us in contact, you will judge for yourself."—Lady D. was indeed a great lady beyond the common wants of society—for she had many thousands a year to bequeath, & three distinct sets of people to be courted by; her own relations, who might very reasonably wish for her original thirty thousand pounds among them, the legal heirs of Mr Hollis, who must hope to be more indebted to *her* sense of justice than he had allowed them to be to *his,* and those members of the Denham family whom her 2^d husband had hoped to make a good bargain for.—By all of these, or by branches of them, she had no doubt been long, & still continued to be, well attacked;—and of these three divisions, Mr P. did not hesitate to say that Mr Hollis' kindred were the *least* in favour & Sir Harry Denham's the *most.*—The former, he believed, had done themselves irremediable harm by expressions of very unwise & unjustifiable resentment at the time of Mr. Hollis's death;—the latter, to the advantage of being the remnant of a connection which she certainly valued, joined those of having been known to her from their childhood, & of being always at hand to preserve their interest by reasonable attention. Sir Edward, the present baronet, nephew to Sir Harry, resided constantly at Denham Park; & M^r P— had little doubt, that he & his sister Miss D— who lived with him, w^d be principally remembered in her will. He sincerely hoped it.— Miss Denham had a very small provision—& her brother was a poor man for his rank in society. "He is a warm friend to Sanditon—said Mr Parker—& his hand w^d be as liberal as his heart, had he the power.—He would be a noble coadjutor!—As it is, he does what he can—& is running up a tasteful little cottage ornée, on a strip of waste ground Lady D. has granted him, which I have no doubt we shall have many a candidate for, before the end even of *this* season." Till within the last twelve-month, Mr P. had considered Sir Edw: as standing without a rival, as having the fairest chance of succeeding to the greater part of all that she had to give—but there were now another person's claims to be taken into the account, those of the young female relation, whom Lady D. had been induced to receive into her family. After having always protested against any such addition, and long & often enjoyed the repeated defeats she had given to every attempt of her relations to introduce this young lady, or that young lady as a companion at Sanditon House, she had brought back with her from London last Michaelmas a Miss Brereton, who bid fair by her merits to vie in favour with Sir Edward and to secure for herself & her family that share of the accumulated property which they had certainly the best right to inherit.—Mr Parker spoke warmly of Clara Brereton, & the interest of his story increased very much with the introduction of such a character. Charlotte listened with more than amusement now;—it was solicitude & enjoyment, as she heard her described to be lovely, amiable, gentle, unassuming, conducting herself uniformly with great good sense, & evidently gaining by her innate worth, on the affections of her patroness.—Beauty, sweetness, poverty & dependence, do not want the imagination of a man to operate upon. With due exceptions—woman feels for woman very promptly & compassionately. He gave the particulars which had led to Clara's admission at Sanditon, as no bad exemplification of that mixture of character, that union of littleness with kindness with good sense with even liberality which he saw in Lady D.— After having avoided London for many years, principally on account of these very cousins, who were continually writing, inviting & tormenting her, & whom she was determined to keep at a distance, she had been obliged to go there last Michaelmas with the certainty of being detained at least a fortnight.—She had gone to an hotel—living by her own account as prudently as possible, to defy the reputed expensiveness of such a home, & at the end of three days calling for her bill, that she might judge of her state.—Its amount was such as determined her on staying not another hour in the house, & she was preparing in all the anger & perturbation of her belief in very gross imposition *there*, & an ignorance of where to go for better usage, to leave the hotel at all hazards, when the cousins, the politic & lucky cousins, who seemed always to have a spy on her, introduced themselves at this important moment, & learning her situation, persuaded her to accept such a home for the rest of her stay as their humbler house in a very inferior part of London c^d offer.—She went; was delighted with her welcome & the hospitality & attention she received from every body— found her good cousins the B—— beyond her expectation worthy people—& finally was impelled by a personal knowledge of their narrow income & pecuniary difficulties, to invite one of the girls of the family to pass the winter with her. The invitation was to *one,* for six months—with the probability of another being then to take her place;—but in *selecting* the one, Lady D. had shewn the good part of her character—for passing by the actual *daughters* of the house, she had chosen Clara, a niece,—more helpless & more pitiable of course than any—a dependent on poverty—an additional bur- then on an encumbered circle— & one, who had been so low in every worldly view, as with all her natural endowments & powers, to have been preparing for a situation little better than a nursery maid.—Clara had returned with her—& by her good sence & merit had now, to all appearance secured a very strong hold in Lady D.'s regard. The six months had long been over— & not a syllable was breathed of any change, or exchange.—She was a general favourite;—the influence of her steady conduct & mild, gentle temper was felt by everybody. The prejudices which had met her at first in some quarters, were all dissipated. She was felt to be worthy of trust—to be the very companion who w^d guide & soften Lady D—who w^d enlarge her mind & open her hand.—She was as thoroughly amiable as she was lovely—& since having had the advantage of their Sanditon breezes, that loveliness was complete.

CHAPTER 4

"AND whose very snug-looking place is this?"—said Charlotte, as in a sheltered dip within 2 miles of the sea, they passed close by a moderate-sized house, well fenced & planted, & rich in the garden, orchard & meadows which are the best embellishments of such a dwelling. "It seems to have as many comforts about it as Willingden."—"Ah!—said Mr P.—This is my old house—the house of my forefathers—the house where I & all my brothers & sisters were born & bred—& where my own 3 eldest children were born—where Mrs P. & I lived till within the last 2 years—

till our new house was finished.—I am glad you are pleased with it.—It is an honest old place—and Hillier keeps it in very good order. I have given it up you know to the man who occupies the cheif of my land. *He* gets a better house by it—& I, a rather better situation!—one other hill brings us to Sanditon—modern Sanditon—a beautiful spot.—Our ancestors, you know always built in a hole.—Here were we, pent down in this little contracted nook, without air or view, only one mile & 3 q^{rs} from the noblest expanse of ocean between the South foreland & Land's end, & without the smallest advantage from it. You will not think I have made a bad exchange, when we reach Trafalgar House— which by the bye, I almost wish I had not named Trafalgar— for Waterloo is more the thing now. However, Waterloo is in reserve—& if we have encouragement enough this year for a little crescent to be ventured on—(as I trust we shall) then, we shall be able to call it Waterloo Cresent—& the name joined to the form of the building, which always takes, will give us the command of lodgers—. In a good season we sh^d have more applications than we could attend to."—"It was always a very comfortable house—said Mrs Parker—looking at it through the back window with something like the fondness of regret.—And such a nice garden—such an excellent garden." "Yes, my love, but *that* we may be said to carry with us.—*It* supplies us, as before, with all the fruit & vegetables we want; & we have in fact all the comfort of an excellent kitchen garden, without the constant eyesore of its formalities; or the yearly nuisance of its decaying vegetation.—Who can endure a cabbage bed in October?" "Oh! dear—yes.—We are quite as well off for gardenstuff as ever we were—for if it is forgot to be brought at any time, we can always buy what we want at Sanditon-House.— The gardener there, is glad enough to supply us—. But it was a nice place for the children to run about in. So shady in summer!" "My dear, we shall have shade enough on the hill & more than enough in the course of a very few years;—The growth of my plantations is a general astonishment. In the mean while we have the canvas awning, which gives us the most complete comfort within doors—& you can get a parasol at Whitby's for little Mary at any time, or a large bonnet at Jebb's—and as for the boys, I must say I w^d rather *them* run about in the sunshine than not. I am sure we agree, my dear, in wishing our boys to be as hardy as possible."—"Yes indeed, I am sure we do—& I will get Mary a little parasol, which will make her as proud as can be. How grave she will walk about with it, and fancy herself quite a little woman.—Oh, I have not the smallest doubt of our being a great deal better off where we are now. If we any of us want to bathe, we have not a q^r of a mile to go.— But you know, (still looking back) one loves to look at an old friend, at a place where one has been happy.—The Hilliers did not seem to feel the storms last winter at all.—I remember seeing Mrs Hillier after one of those dreadful nights, when *we* had been literally rocked in our bed, and she did not seem at all aware of the wind being anything more than common." "Yes, yes—that's likely enough. *We* have all the grandeur of the storm, with less real danger, because the wind meeting with nothing to oppose or confine it around our house, simply rages & passes on—while down in this gutter—nothing is known of the state of the air, below the tops of the trees—and the inhabitants may be taken totally unawares, by one of those dreadful currents which do more mischief in a valley, when they *do* arise than an open country ever experiences in the heaviest gale.—But, my dear love—as to gardenstuff;—you were saying that any accidental omission is supplied in a moment by Ly D.'s gardener— but it occurs to me that we ought to go elsewhere upon such occasions—& that old Stringer & his son have a higher claim. I encouraged him to set up—& am afraid he does not do very well—that is, there has not been time enough yet.—He *will* do very well beyond a doubt—but at first it is uphill work; and therefore we must give him what help we can—& when any vegetables or fruit happen to be wanted—& it will not be amiss to have them often wanted, to have something or other forgotten most days;—Just to have a nominal supply you know, that poor old Andrew may not lose his daily job—but in fact to buy the cheif of our consumption of the Stringers.—" "Very well, my love, that can be easily done—& cook will be satisfied—which will be a great comfort, for she is always complaining of old Andrew now, & says he never brings her what she wants.— There—now the old house is quite left behind.—What is it, your brother Sidney says about its being a hospital?" "Oh! my dear Mary, merely a joke of his. He pretends to advise me to make a hospital of it. He pretends to laugh at my improvements. Sidney says any thing you know. He has always said what he chose of & to us, all. Most families have such a member among them I believe Miss Heywood.—There is a someone in most families privileged by superior abilities or spirits to say anything.—In ours, it is Sidney; who is a very clever young man,—and with great powers of pleasing.—He lives too much in the world to be settled; that is his only fault.—He is here & there & every where. I wish we may get him to Sanditon. I should like to have you acquainted with him. And it would be a fine thing for the place!—Such a young man as Sidney, with his neat equipage & fashionable air,—You & I Mary, know what effect it might have: Many a respectable family, many a careful mother, many a pretty daughter, might it secure us, to the prejudice of E. Bourne and Hastings."—They were now approaching the church & village of Sanditon, which stood at the foot of the hill they were afterwards to ascend—a hill, whose side was covered with the woods & enclosures of Sanditon House and whose height ended in an open down where the new builds^{gs} might soon be looked for. A branch only, of the valley, winding more obliquely towards the sea, gave a passage to an inconsiderable stream, & formed at its mouth a 3^d habitable division, in a small cluster of fishermen's houses.—The village contained little more than cottages, but the spirit of the day had been caught, as Mr P. observed with delight to Charlotte, & two or three of the best of them were smartened up with a white curtain & "Lodgings to let"—, and farther on, in the little green court of an old farm house, two females in elegant white were actually to be seen with their books & camp stools—and in turning the corner of the baker's shop, the sound of a harp might be heard through the upper casement.—Such sights & sounds were highly blissful to Mr P.—Not that he had any personal concern in the success of the village itself; for considering it as too remote from the beach, he had done nothing there—but it was a most valuable proof of the increasing fashion of the place altogether. If the *village* could attract, the hill might be nearly full.—He anticipated an amazing season.—At the same time last year, (late in July) there had not been a single lodger in the village!—nor did he remember any during the whole summer, excepting one family of children who came from London for sea air after the hooping cough, and whose mother would not let them be nearer the shore for fear of their tumbling in.—"Civilization, civilization indeed!—cried M^r P—, delighted—. Look, my dear Mary—Look at William Heeley's windows.—Blue shoes, & nankin boots!—Who w^d have expected such a sight at a shoemaker's in old Sanditon!—This is new within the month. There was no blue shoe when we passed this way a month ago.—Glorious indeed!—Well, I think I *have* done something in my day.—Now, for our hill, our health-breathing hill.—" In ascending, they passed the lodge-gates of Sanditon House, & saw the top of the house itself among its groves. It was the last building of former days in that line of the parish. A little higher up, the modern began; & in crossing the down, a prospect House, a Bellevue Cottage & a Denham Place were to be looked at by Charlotte with the calmness of amused curiosity, & by Mr P. with the eager eye which hoped to see scarcely any empty houses.—More bills at the windows than he had calculated on;—and a smaller shew of company on the hill—fewer carriages, fewer walkers. He had fancied it just the time of day for them to be all returning from their airings to dinner—But the sands & the Terrace always attracted some—. And the tide must be flowing—about half-tide now.—He longed to be on the sands, the cliffs, at his own house, & everywhere out of his house at once. His spirits rose with the very sight of the sea & he c^d almost feel his ankle getting stronger already.—Trafalgar House, on the most elevated spot on the down was a light elegant building, standing in a small lawn with a very young plantation round it, about a hundred yards from the brow of a steep, but not very lofty cliff—and the nearest to it, of every building, excepting one short row of smart-looking houses, called the Terrace, with a broad walk in front, aspiring to be the mall of the place. In this row were the best milliner's shop & the library—a little detached from it, the hotel & billiard room—Here began the descent to the beach, & to the bathing machines—& this was therefore the favourite spot for beauty & fashion.—At Trafalgar House, rising at a little distance behind the Terrace, the travellers were safely set down, & all was happiness and joy between Papa & Mama & their children; while Charlotte, having received possession of her apartment, found amusement enough in standing at her ample Venetian window, & looking over the miscellaneous foreground of unfinished buildings, waving linen, & tops of houses, to the sea, dancing & sparkling in sunshine & freshness.—

CHAPTER 5

WHEN they met before dinner, Mᵣ P. was looking over letters.— "Not a line from Sidney!—said he.—He is an idle fellow.—I sent him an account of my accident from Willingden, & thought he would have vouchsafed me an answer.—But perhaps it implies that he is coming himself.—I trust it may.—But here is a letter from one of my sisters. *They* never fail me.—Women are the only correspondents to be depended on.—Now Mary, (smiling at his wife)—before I open it, what shall we guess as to the state of health of those it comes from—or rather what w^d Sidney say if he were here?—Sidney is a saucy fellow, Miss H.— And you must know, he will have it there is a good deal of imagination in my two sisters' complaints—but it really is not so—or very little—They have wretched health, as you have heard us say frequently, & are subject to a variety of very serious disorders.— Indeed, I do not believe they know what a day's health is;—& at the same time, they are such excellent useful women & have so much energy of character that, where any good is to be done, they force themselves on exertions which to those who do not thoroughly know them, have an extraordinary appearance.— But there is really no affectation about them. They have only weaker constitutions & stronger minds than are often met with, either separate or together.—And our youngest b^r— who lives with them, & who is not much above 20, I am sorry to say, is almost as great an invalid as themselves.—He is so delicate that he can engage in no profession.—Sidney laughs at him—but it really is no joke—tho' Sidney often makes me laugh at them all inspite of myself.—Now, if he were here, I know he w^d be offering odds, that either Susan, Diana or Arthur w^d appear by this letter to have been at the point of death within the last month."—Having run his eye over the letter, he shook his head & began—: "No chance of seeing them at Sanditon I am sorry to say.—A very indifferent account of them indeed. Seriously, a *very* indifferent account.—Mary, you will be quite sorry to hear how ill they have been & are. Miss H., if you will give me leave, I will read Diana's letter aloud.—I like to have my friends acquainted with each other—& I am afraid this is the only sort of acquaintance I shall have the means of accomplishing between you.—And I can have no scruple on Diana's account—for her letters shew her exactly as she is, the most active, friendly, warmhearted being in existence, & therefore must give a good impression." He read.—"My dear Tom, we were all much grieved at Your accident, & if you had not described your-self as fallen into such very good hands, I sh^d have been with you at all hazards the day after the rec^{pt} of your letter, though it found me suffering under a more severe attack than usual of my old grievance, spasmodic bile & hardly able to crawl from my bed to the sofa.—But how were you treated?—Send me more Particulars in your next.—If indeed a simple sprain, as you denominate it, nothing w^d have been so judicious as friction, friction by the hand alone, supposing it could be applied *instantly*.—Two years ago I happened to be calling on Mrs Sheldon when her coachman sprained his foot as he was cleaning the carriage and c^d hardly limp into the house—but by the immediate use of friction alone steadily perservered in, (& I rubbed his ankle with my own hand for six hours without inter-mission)—he was well in three days.—Many thanks my dear Tom, for the kindness with respect to us, which had so large a share in bringing on your accident—But pray never run into peril again, in looking for an apothecary on our account, for had you the most experienced man in his line settled at Sanditon, it w^d be no recommendation to us. We have entirely done with the whole medical tribe. We have consulted physician after phy^n in vain, till we are quite convinced that they can do nothing for us & that we must trust to our own knowledge of our own wretched constitutions for any relief.—But if you think it advis-able for the interest of the *place*, to get a medical man there,

I will undertake the commission with pleasure, & have no doubt of succeeding.—I could soon put the necessary irons in the fire.—As for getting to Sanditon myself, it is quite an impossibility. I grieve to say that I dare not attempt it, but my feelings tell me too plainly that in my present state, the sea air w^d probably be the death of me.—And neither of my dear companions will leave me, or I w^d promote their going down to you for a fortnight. But in truth, I doubt whether Susan's nerves w^d be equal to the effort. She has been suffering much from the headache and six leeches a day for 10 days together relieved her so little that we thought it right to change our measures—and being convinced on examination that mach of the evil lay in her gum, I persuaded her to attack the disorder there. She has accordingly had 3 teeth drawn, & is decidedly better, but her nerves are a good deal deranged. She can only speak in a whisper—and fainted away twice this morning on poor Arthur's trying to suppress a cough. He, I am happy to say, is tolerably well—tho' more languid than I like—& I fear for his liver.—I have heard nothing of Sidney since your being together in town, but conclude his scheme to the I. of Wight has not taken place, or we should have seen him in his way.—Most sincerely do we wish you a good season at Sanditon, & though we cannot contribute to your beau monde in person, we are doing our utmost to send you company worth having; & think we may safely reckon on securing you two large families, one a rich West Indian from Surry, the other, a most respectable Girls Boarding School, or Academy, from Camberwell.—I will not tell you how many people I have employed in the business—wheel within wheel.— But success more than repays.—Yours most affec^ly—&c" "Well—said Mr P.—as he finished. Though I dare say Sidney might find something extremely entertaining in this letter & make us laugh for half an hour together I declare *I* by myself, can see nothing in it but what is either very pitiable or very creditable.—With all their sufferings, you perceive how much they are occupied in promoting the good of others!—So anxious for Sanditon! Two large families—One, for Prospect House probably, the other, for N° 2 Denham place—or the end house of the Terrace,—& extra beds at the hotel.—I told you my sisters were excellent women, Miss H———." "And I am sure they must be very extraordinary ones," said Charlotte. "I am astonished at the cheerful style of the letter, considering the state in which both sisters appear to be.—Three teeth drawn at once!—frightful!— Your sister Diana seems almost as ill as possible, but those 3 teeth of your sister Susan's, are more distressing than all the rest.—" "Oh!—they are so used to the operation—to every operation—& have such fortitude!—" "Your sisters know what they are about, I dare say, but their measures seem to touch on extremes.—I feel that in any illness, *I* should be so anxious for professional advice, so very little venturesome for myself or any body I loved!—But then, *we* have been so healthy a family, that I can be no judge of what the habit of self-doctoring may do.—" "Why to own the truth, said Mrs P.—I *do* think the Miss Parkers carry it too far sometimes—& so do you, my love, you know.— You often think they w^d be better, if they w^d leave themselves more alone—& especially Arthur. I know you think it a great pity they sh^d give *him* such a turn for being ill.—" "Well, well— my dear Mary—I grant you, it *is* unfortunate for poor Arthur, that, at his time of life he sh^d be encouraged to give way to indisposition. It *is* bad;—it *is* bad that he should be fancying himself too sickly for any profession—& sit down at 1 & 20, on the interest of his own little fortune, without any idea of attempting to improve it, or of engaging in any occupation that may be of use to himself or others.—But let us talk of pleasanter things.— These two large families are just what we wanted—But—here is something at hand, pleasanter still—Morgan, with his "Dinner on table."—

CHAPTER 6

THE party were very soon moving after dinner. Mr P. could not be satisfied without an early visit to the library, & the library subscription book, & Charlotte was glad to see as much, & as quickly as possible, where all was new. They were out in the very quietest part of a watering-place day, when the important business of dinner or of sitting after dinner was going on in almost every inhabited lodging;—here & there a solitary elderly

man might be seen, who was forced to move early & walk for
health—but in general, it was a thorough pause of company, it
was emptiness & tranquillity on the Terrace, the cliffs, & the
sands.—The shops were deserted—the straw hats & pendant
lace seemed left to their fate both within the house & without,
and Mrs Whitby at the library was sitting in her inner room,
reading one of her own novels, for want of employment.—The
list of subscribers was but commonplace. The Lady Denham,
Miss Brereton, M^r & M^rs P—— Sir Edw: Denham & Miss
Denham, whose names might be said to lead off the season,
were followed by nothing better than—Mrs Mathews—Miss
Mathews, Miss E. Mathews, Miss H. Mathews.—D^r and M^rs
Brown—Mr Richard Pratt.—Lieut: Smith R.N. Capt: Little,—
Limehouse.—Mrs Jane Fisher. Miss Fisher. Miss Scroggs.—
Rev: Mr Hanking. Mr Beard—Solicitor, Grays Inn.—Mrs Davis.
& Miss Merryweather.—Mr P. could not but feel that the list was
not only without distinction, but less numerous than he had
hoped. It was but July however, & August & September were
the months;—And besides, the promised large families from
Surrey & Camberwell, were an ever-ready consolation.—M^rs
Whitby came forward without delay from her literary recess,
delighted to see Mr Parker again, whose manners recommended
him to every body, & they were fully occupied in their various
civilities & communications, while Charlotte having added her
name to the list as the first offering to the success of the season,
was busy in some immediate purchases for the further good of
every body, as soon as Miss Whitby could be hurried down from
her toilette, with all her glossy curls & smart trinkets to wait on
her.—The library of course, afforded every thing; all the useless
things in the world that c^d not be done without, & among so
many pretty temptations, & with so much good will for Mr P. to
encourage expenditure, Charlotte began to feel that she must
check herself—or rather she reflected that at two & twenty
there c^d be no excuse for her doing otherwise—& that it w^d not
do for her to be spending all her money the very first evening.
She took up a book; it happened to be a vol: of *Camilla*. She had
not *Camilla's* youth, & had no intention of having her distress,—
so, she turned from the drawers of rings & brooches repressed

further solicitation & paid for what she bought.—For her particular gratification, they were then to take a turn on the cliff—
but as they quitted the library they were met by two ladies
whose arrival made an alteration necessary, Lady Denham &
Miss Brereton.—They had been to Trafalgar House, & been
directed thence to the library, & though Lady D. was a great
deal too active to regard the walk of a mile as anything requiring
rest, & talked of going home again directly, the Parkers knew
that to be pressed into their house, & obliged to take her tea
with them, would suit her best,—& therefore the stroll on the
cliff gave way to an immediate return home.—"No, no, said her
Ladyship—I will not have you hurry your tea on my account.—
I know you like your tea late.—My early hours are not to put my
neighbours to inconvenience. No, no, Miss Clara & I will get
back to our own tea.—We came out with no other thought.—
We wanted just to see you & make sure of your being really
come—, but we get back to our own tea."— She went on however towards Trafalgar House & took possession of the drawing
room very quietly—without seeming to hear a word of Mrs P.'s
orders to the servant as they entered, to bring tea directly.
Charlotte was fully consoled for the loss of her walk, by finding
herself in company with those, whom the conversation of the
morn^g had given her a great curiosity to see. She observed them
well.—Lady D. was of middle height, stout, upright & alert in
her motions, with a shrewd eye, & self-satisfied air—but not an
unagreeable countenance—& tho' her manner was rather
downright & abrupt, as of a person who valued herself on being
free-spoken, there was a good humour & cordiality about her—
a civility & readiness to be acquainted with Charlotte herself, &
a heartiness of welcome towards her old friends, which was
inspiring the good will, she seemed to feel;—And as for Miss
Brereton, her appearance so completely justified Mr P.'s praise
that Charlotte thought she had never beheld a more lovely, or
more interesting young woman.—Elegantly tall, regularly handsome, with great delicacy of complexion & soft blue eyes, a
sweetly modest & yet naturally graceful address, Charlotte
could see in her only the most perfect representation of whatever heroine might be most beautiful & bewitching, in all the
numerous vol:^{s} they had left behind on Mrs Whitby's shelves.—

Perhaps it might be partly oweing to her having just issued from
a circulating library—but she c^d not separate the idea of a complete heroine from Clara Brereton. Her situation with Lady
Denham so very much in favour of it!—She seemed placed with
her on purpose to be ill-used. Such poverty & dependence
joined to such beauty & merit, seemed to leave no choice in the
business.—These feelings were not the result of any spirit of
romance in Charlotte herself. No, she was a very sober-minded
young lady, sufficiently well-read in novels to supply her imagination with amusement, but not at all unreasonably influenced
by them; & while she pleased herself the first 5 minutes with
fancying the persecutions which *ought* to be the lot of the interesting Clara, especially in the form of the most barbarous conduct on Lady Denham's side, she found no reluctance to admit
from subsequent observation, that they appeared to be on
very comfortable terms.—She c^d see nothing worse in Lady
Denham, than the sort of oldfashioned formality of always
calling her *Miss Clara*—nor anything objectionable in the
degree of observance & attention which Clara paid.—On one
side it seemed protecting kindness, on the other grateful &
affectionate respect.—The conversation turned entirely upon
Sanditon, its present number of visitants & the chances of a
good season. It was evident that Lady D. had more anxiety,
more fears of loss, than her coadjutor. She wanted to have the
place fill faster & seemed to have many harassing apprehensions
of the lodgings being in some instances underlet.—Miss Diana
Parker's two large families were not forgotten. "Very good, very
good, said her Ladyship.—A West Indy family & a school. That
sounds well. That will bring money."—"No people spend more
freely, I believe, than W. Indians," observed Mr Parker.—"Aye—
so I have heard—and because they have full purses, fancy themselves equal, may be, to your old country families. But then,
they who scatter their money so freely, never think of whether
they may not be doing mischeif by raising the price of things—
And I have heard that's very much the case with your West-
injines—and if they come among us to raise the price of our
necessaries of life, we shall not much thank them Mr Parker."—
"My dear Madam, they can only raise the price of consumeable
articles, by such an extraordinary demand for them & such a

diffusion of money among us, as must do us more good than harm.—Our butchers & bakers & traders in general cannot get rich without bringing prosperity to *us*.—If *they* do not gain, our rents must be insecure—& in proportion to their profit must be ours eventually in the increased value of our houses." "Oh!—well.—But I should not like to have butcher's meat raised, though—& I shall keep it down as long as I can.—Aye—that young lady smiles I see;—I dare say she thinks me an odd sort of a creature, —but *she* will come to care about such matters herself in time. Yes, yes, my dear, depend upon it, you will be thinking of the price of butcher's meat in time—tho' you may not happen to have quite such a servants hall full to feed, as I have.—And I do believe *those* are best off, that have fewest servants.—I am not a woman of parade, as all the world knows, & if it was not for what I owe to poor Mr Hollis's memory, I should never keep up Sanditon House as I do;—it is not for my own pleasure.—Well, Mr Parker—and the other is a boarding school, a French boarding school, is it?—No harm in that.—They'll stay their six weeks.—And out of such a number, who knows but some may be consumptive & want asses' milk—& I have two milch asses at this present time.—But perhaps the little misses may hurt the furniture.—I hope they will have a good sharp governess to look after them.—" Poor Mr Parker got no more credit from Lady D. than he had from his sisters, for the object which had taken him to Willingden. "Lord! my dear sir, she cried, how could you think of such a thing? I am very sorry you met with your accident, but upon my word you deserved it.—Going after a doctor!—Why, what sh^d we do with a doctor here? It w^d be only encouraging our servants & the poor to fancy themselves ill, if there was a D^r at hand.—Oh! pray, let us have none of the tribe at Sanditon. We go on very well as we are. There is the sea & the downs & my milch-asses—& I have told Mrs Whitby that if any body enquires for a chamber-horse, they may be supplied at a fair rate—(poor Mr Hollis's chamber-horse, as good as new)—and what can people want for more?—Here have I lived 70 good years in the world & never took physic above twice—and never saw the face of a doctor in all my life, on my *own* account.—And I verily believe if my poor dear Sir Harry had never seen one neither, he w^d have been alive now.—Ten fees, one after another, did the man take who sent *him* out of the world.—I beseech you Mr Parker, no doctors here."—The tea things were brought in.—"Oh, my dear Mrs Parker—you should not indeed—why would you do so? I was just upon the point of wishing you good evening. But since you are so very neigh-bourly, I believe Miss Clara & I must stay."——

CHAPTER 7

THE popularity of the Parkers brought them some visitors the very next morning;—amongst them, Sir Edwd Denham & his sister, who having been at Sanditon H— drove on to pay their compliments; & the duty of letter-writing being accomplished, Charlotte was settled with Mrs P.— in the drawing room in time to see them all.—The Denhams were the only ones to excite particular attention. Charlotte was glad to complete her knowl-edge of the family by an introduction to them, & found them, the better half at least—(for while single, the *gentleman* may sometimes be thought the better half, of the pair)—not unworthy notice.—Miss D. was a fine young woman, but cold & reserved, giving the idea of one who felt her consequence with pride & her poverty with discontent, & who was immediately gnawed by the want of a handsomer equipage than the simple gig in which they travelled, & which their groom was leading about still in her sight.—Sir Edwd was much her superior in air & manner;— certainly handsome, but yet more to be remarked for his very good address & wish of paying attention & giving pleasure.—He came into the room remarkably well, talked much—& very much to Charlotte, by whom he chanced to be placed—& she soon perceived that he had a fine countenance, a most pleasing gentleness of voice, & a great deal of conversation. She liked him.—Sober-minded as she was, she thought him agreeable, & did not quarrel with the suspicion of his finding her equally so, which *would* arise from his evidently disregarding his sister's motion to go, & persisting in his station and his discourse.—I make no apologies for my heroine's vanity.—If there are young ladies in the world at her time of life, more dull of fancy & more careless of pleasing, I know them not, & never wish to know them.—At last, from the low French windows of the drawing room which commanded the road & all the paths across the down, Charlotte & Sir Edw: as they sat, could not but observe Lady D. & Miss B. walking by—& there was instantly a slight change in Sir Edw:'s countenance—with an anxious glance after them as they proceeded—followed by an early proposal to his sister—not merely for moving, but for walking on together to the Terrace—which altogether gave a hasty turn to Charlotte's fancy, cured her of her halfhour's fever, & placed her in a more capable state of judging, when Sir Edw: was gone, of *how* agreeable he had actually been.—"Perhaps there was a good deal in his air & address; and his title did him no harm." She was very soon in his company again. The first object of the Parkers, when their house was cleared of morn^g visitors, was to get out themselves;—the Terrace was the attraction to all;—Every body who walked, must begin with the Terrace, & there, seated on one of the two green benches by the gravel walk, they found the united Denham party;—but though united in the gross, very distinctly divided again—the two superior ladies being at one end of the bench, & Sir Edw: & Miss B. at the other.—Charlotte's first glance told her that Sir Edw:'s air was that of a lover.—There could be no doubt of his devotion to Clara.—How Clara received it, was less obvious—but she was inclined to think not very favourably; for tho' sitting thus apart with him (which probably she might not have been able to prevent) her air was calm & grave.—That the young lady at the other end of the bench was doing penance, was indubitable. The difference in Miss Denham's countenance, the change from Miss Denham sitting in cold grandeur in Mrs Parker's draw^g room to be kept from silence by the efforts of others, to Miss D. at Lady D.'s elbow, listening & talking with smiling attention or solicitous eagerness, was very striking—and very amusing—or very melancholy, just as satire or morality might prevail.—Miss Denham's character was pretty well decided with Charlotte. Sir Edward's required longer observation. He surprised her by quitting Clara immediately on their all joining & agreeing to walk, & by addressing his attentions entirely to herself.—Stationing himself close by her, he seemed to mean to detach her as much as possible from the

rest of the party & to give her the whole of his conversation. He
began, in a tone of great taste and feeling, to talk of the sea &
the sea shore—& ran with energy through all the usual phrases
employed in praise of their sublimity, & descriptive of the *unde-
scribable* emotions they excite in the mind of sensibility.—The
terrific grandeur of the ocean in a storm, its glassy surface in a
calm, its gulls and its samphire, & the deep fathoms of its
abysses, its quick vicissitudes, its direful deceptions, its mariners
tempting it in sunshine & overwhelmed by the sudden tempest,
all were eagerly & fluently touched;—rather commonplace perhaps—but doing very well from the lips of a handsome Sir
Edward,—and she c^d not but think him a man of feeling—till he
began to stagger her by the number of his quotations, & the
bewilderment of some of his sentences.—"Do you remember,
said he, Scott's beautiful lines on the sea?—Oh! what a description they convey!—They are never out of my thoughts when I
walk here.—That man who can read them unmoved must have
the nerves of an assassin!— Heaven defend me from meeting
such a man un-armed."—"What description do you mean?—
said Charlotte. I remember none at this moment, of the sea, in
either of Scott's poems."—"Do not you indeed?—Nor can I
exactly recall the beginning at this moment—But—you cannot
have forgotten his description of woman.—

"Oh! Woman in our hours of ease—"

Delicious! Delicious!—Had he written nothing more, he w^d
have been immortal. And then again, that unequalled, unrivalled address to parental affection—

"Some feelings are to mortals given
With less of earth in them than heaven" &c.

But while we are on the subject of poetry, what think you, Miss
H. of Burns' lines to his Mary?—Oh! there is pathos to mad-
den one!—If ever there was a man who *felt,* it was Burns.—
Montgomery has all the fire of poetry, Wordsworth has the true
soul of it—Campbell in his pleasures of hope has touched the
extreme of our sensations—"Like angel's visits, few & far

between." Can you conceive any thing more subduing, more melting, more fraught with the deep sublime than that line?— But Burns—I confess my sense of his pre-eminence Miss H.— If Scott *has* a fault, it is the want of passion.—Tender, elegant, descriptive—but *tame.*—The man who cannot do justice to the attributes of woman is my contempt.—Sometimes indeed a flash of feeling seems to irradiate him—as in the lines we were speaking of—"Oh! Woman in our hours of ease"—. But Burns is always on fire.—His soul was the altar in which lovely woman sat enshrined, his spirit truly breathed the immortal incense which is her due.—" "I have read several of Burns's poems with great delight," said Charlotte as soon as she had time to speak, but I am not poetic enough to separate a man's poetry entirely from his character;—& poor Burns's known irregularities, greatly interrupt my enjoyment of his lines.—I have difficulty in depending on the *truth* of his feelings as a lover. I have not faith in the *sincerity* of the affections of a man of his description. He felt & he wrote & he forgot." "Oh! no no—exclaimed Sir Edw: in an extasy. He was all ardour & truth!—His genius & his susceptibilities might lead him into some aberrations—but who is perfect?—It were hyper-criticism, it were pseudo-philosophy to expect from the soul of high toned genius, the grovellings of a common mind.—The coruscations of talent, elicited by impassioned feeling in the breast of man, are perhaps incompatible with some of the prosaic decencies of life;—nor can you, loveliest Miss Heywood—(speaking with an air of deep sentiment)—nor can any woman be a fair judge of what a man may be propelled to say, write or do, by the sovereign impulses of illimitable ardour." This was very fine;—but if Charlotte understood it at all, not very moral—& being moreover by no means pleased with his extraordinary stile of compliment, she gravely answered, "I really know nothing of the matter.—This is a charming day. The wind, I fancy, must be southerly." "Happy, happy wind, to engage Miss Heywood's thoughts!—" She began to think him downright silly.—His chusing to walk with her, she had learnt to understand. It was done to pique Miss Brereton. She had read it, in an anxious glance or two on his side—but why he sh^d talk so much nonsense, unless he could do no better, was unintelligible.—He seemed very sentimental, very full of some feelings or other, & very much addicted to all the newest-fashioned hard words—had not a very clear brain she presumed, & talked a good deal by rote.—The future might explain him further—but when there was a proposition for going into the library she felt that she had had quite enough of Sir Edw: for one morn^g, & very gladly accepted Lady D.'s invitation of remaining on the terrace with her.—The others all left them, Sir Edw: with looks of very gallant despair in tearing himself away, & they united their agreeableness—that is, Lady Denham, like a true great lady, talked & talked only of her own concerns, & Charlotte listened—amused in considering the contrast between her two companions.—Certainly, there was no strain of doubtful sentiment, nor any phrase of difficult interpretation in Lady D.'s discourse. Taking hold of Charlotte's arm with the ease of one who felt that any notice from her was an honour, & communicative, from the influence of the same conscious importance or a natural love of talking, she immediately said in a tone of great satisfaction—& with a look of arch sagacity—"Miss Esther wants me to invite her & her brother to spend a week with me at Sanditon House, as I did last summer—But I shan't.—She has been trying to get round me every way, with her praise of this, & her praise of that; but I saw what she was about.—I saw through it all.—I am not very easily taken-in, my dear." Charlotte c^d think of nothing more harmless to be said, than the simple enquiry of—"Sir Edward & Miss Denham?"—"Yes, my dear. *My young folks,* as I call them sometimes, for I take them very much by the hand. I had them with me last summer about this time, for a week; from Monday to Monday; and very delighted & thankful they were.—For they are very good young people, my dear. I w^d not have you think that I *only* notice them, for poor dear Sir Harry's sake. No, no; they are very deserving themselves, or, trust me, they w^d not be so much in *my* company.—I am not the woman to help any body blindfold.—I always take care to know what I am about & who I have to deal with, before I stir a finger.—I do not think I was ever over-reached in my life; & that is a good deal for a woman to say that has been married twice.—Poor dear Sir Harry, (between ourselves) thought at first to have got more.—But, (with a bit of a sigh) he is gone, & we must not find fault with the dead.

Nobody could live happier together than us—& he was a very honourable man, quite the gentleman of ancient family.—And when he died, I gave Sir Edwd his gold watch.—" She said this with a look at her companion which implied its right to produce a great impression—& seeing no rapturous astonishment in Charlotte's countenance, added quickly—"He did not bequeath it to his nephew, my dear—It was no bequest. It was not in the will. He only told me, & *that* but once, that he sh^d wish his nephew to have his watch; but it need not have been binding, if I had not chose it.—" "Very kind indeed! Very handsome!"— said Charlotte, absolutely forced to affect admiration—. "Yes, my dear—& it is not the *only* kind thing I have done by him.— I have been a very liberal friend to Sir Edwd. And poor young man, he needs it bad enough;—for though I am *only* the *dowager,* my dear, & he is the *heir,* things do not stand between us in the way they commonly do between those two parties.— Not a shilling do I receive from the Denham estate. Sir Edw: has no payments to make *me.* He don't stand uppermost, believe me.—It is *I* that help *him.*" "Indeed!—He is a very fine young man;—particularly elegant in his address."—This was said chiefly for the sake of saying something—but Charlotte directly saw that it was laying her open to suspicion by Lady D's giving a shrewd glance at her & replying—"Yes, yes, he is very well to look at—& it is to be hoped that some lady of large fortune will think so—for Sir Edwd *must* marry for money.—He & I often talk that matter over.—A handsome young fellow like him, will go smirking & smiling about & paying girls compliments, but he knows he *must* marry for money.—And Sir Edw: is a very steady young man in the main, & has got very good notions. "Sir Edw: Denham, said Charlotte, with such personal advantages may be almost sure of getting a woman of fortune, if he chuses it."— This glorious sentiment seemed quite to remove suspicion. "Aye my dear—that's very sensibly said," cried Lady D— "And if we c^d but get a young heiress to S! But heiresses are monstrous scarce! I do not think we have had an heiress here, or even a co—since Sanditon has been a public place. Families come after families, but as far as I can learn, it is not one in a hundred of them that have any real property, landed or funded.—An income perhaps, but no property. Clergymen may be, or lawyers from town, or half pay officers, or widows with only a jointure. And what good can such people do anybody?—except just as they take our empty houses—and (between ourselves) I think they are great fools for not staying at home. Now, if we could get a young heiress to be sent here for her health—(and if she was ordered to drink asses milk I could supply her)—and as soon as she got well, have her fall in love with Sir Edward!"—"That would be very fortunate indeed." "And Miss Esther must marry somebody of fortune too—She must get a rich husband. Ah, young ladies that have no money are very much to be pitied!— But—after a short pause—if Miss Esther thinks to talk me into inviting them to come & stay at Sanditon House, she will find herself mistaken.—Matters are altered with me since last summer you know—. I have Miss Clara with me now, which makes a great difference." She spoke this so seriously that Charlotte instantly saw in it the evidence of real penetration & prepared for some fuller remarks—but it was followed only by—"I have no fancy for having my house as full as an hotel. I should not chuse to have my 2 housemaids time taken up all the morn^g in dusting out bed rooms.—They have Miss Clara's room to put to rights as well as my own every day.—If they had hard places, they would want higher wages.—" For objections of this nature, Charlotte was not prepared, & she found it so impossible even to affect sympathy, that she c^d say nothing.—Lady D. soon added, with great glee—"And besides all this, my dear, am I to be filling my house to the prejudice of Sanditon?—If people want to be by the sea, why dont they take lodgings?—Here are a great many empty houses—3 on this very Terrace; no fewer than three lodging papers staring me in the face at this very moment, Numbers 3, 4 & 8. 8, the corner house may be too large for them, but either of the two others are nice little snug houses, very fit for a young gentleman & his sister—And so, my dear, the next time Miss Esther begins talking about the dampness of Denham Park & the good bathing always does her, I shall advise them to come & take one of these lodgings for a fortnight.—Don't you think that will be very fair?—Charity begins at home, you know."—Charlotte's feelings were divided between amusement & indignation—but indignation had the larger & the increasing share.—She kept her countenance & she kept a civil silence. She could not carry her forbearance farther; but without attempting to listen longer, & only conscious that Lady D. was still talking on in the same way, allowed her thoughts to form themselves into such a meditation as this.— "She is thoroughly mean. I had not expected anything so bad.— Mʳ P. spoke too mildly of her.—His judgement is evidently not to be trusted.—His own goodnature misleads him.—He is too kind-hearted to see clearly.—I must judge for myself.—And their very *connection* prejudices him.—He has persuaded her to engage in the same speculation—& because their object in that line is the same, he fancies she feels like him in others.—But she is very, very mean.—I can see no good in her.—Poor Miss Brereton!—And she makes everybody mean about her.—This poor Sir Edward & his sister,—how far Nature meant them to be respectable I cannot tell,—but they are *obliged* to be mean in their servility to her.—And I am mean, too, in giving her my attention, with the appearance of coinciding with her.—Thus it is, when rich people are sordid."—

CHAPTER 8

THE two ladies continued walking together till rejoined by the others, who as they issued from the library were followed by a young Whitby running off with 5 vols. under his arm to Sir Edward's gig—and Sir Edw: approaching Charlotte, said "You may perceive what has been our occupation. My sister wanted my counsel in the selection of some books.—We have many leisure hours & read a great deal.—I am no indiscriminate novel-reader. The mere trash of the common circulating library, I hold in the highest contempt. You will never hear me advocating those puerile emanations which detail nothing but discordant principles incapable of amalgamation, or those vapid tissues of ordinary occurrences from which no useful deductions can be drawn.—In vain may we put them into a literary alembic;—we distil nothing which can add to science.—You understand me, I am sure?" "I am not quite certain that I do.— But if you will describe the sort of novels which you *do* approve, I dare say it will give me a clearer idea." "Most willingly, fair questioner.—The novels which I approve are such as display human nature with grandeur—such as shew her in the sublimities of intense feeling—such as exhibit the progress of strong passion from the first germ of incipient susceptibility to the utmost energies of reason half-dethroned,—where we see the strong spark of woman's captivations elicit such fire in the soul of man as leads him—(though at the risk of some aberration from the strict line of primitive obligations)—to hazard all, dare all, achieve all, to obtain her.—Such are the works which I peruse with delight, & I hope I may say, with amelioration. They hold forth the most splendid portraitures of high conceptions, unbounded views, illimitable ardour, indomitable decision—and even when the event is mainly anti-prosperous to the high-toned machinations of the prime character, the potent, pervading hero of the story, it leaves us full of generous emotions for him;—our hearts are paralysed—. T'were pseudo-philosophy to assert that we do not feel more enwrapped by the brilliancy of his career, than by the tranquil & morbid virtues of any opposing character. Our approbation of the latter is but eleemosynary.—These are the novels which enlarge the primitive capabilities of the heart, & it cannot impugn the sense or be any dereliction of the character of the most anti-puerile man, to be conversant with."—"If I understand you aright—said Charlotte—our taste in novels is not at all the same." And here they were obliged to part—Miss D. being much too tired of them all, to stay any longer.—The truth was that Sir Edw: whom circumstances had confined very much to one spot had read more sentimental novels than agreed with him. His fancy had been early caught by all the impassioned, & most exceptionable parts of Richardson's; & such authors as have since appeared to tread in Richardson's steps, so far as man's determined pursuit of woman in defiance of every opposition of feeling & convenience is concerned, had since occupied the greater part of his literary hours, & formed his character.—With a perversity of judgement, which must be attributed to his not having by nature a very strong head, the graces, the spirit, the sagacity & the perseverance, of the villain of the story outweighed all his absurdities & all his atrocities with Sir Edward. With him, such conduct was genius, fire & feeling.—It interested & inflamed him; & he was always more anxious for its success & mourned over its discomfitures with more tenderness than c^d ever have been contemplated by the authors.—Though he owed many of his ideas to this sort of reading, it were unjust to say that he read nothing else, or that his language were not formed on a more general knowledge of modern literature.—He read all the essays, letters, tours & criticisms of the day—& with the same ill-luck which made him derive only false principles from lessons of morality, & incentives to vice from the history of its overthrow, he gathered only hard words & involved sentences from the style of our most approved writers.—

Sir Edw:'s great object in life was to be seductive.—With such personal advantages as he knew himself to possess, & such talents as he did also give himself credit for, he regarded it as his duty.—He felt that he was formed to be a dangerous man— quite in the line of the Lovelaces.—The very name of Sir Edward he thought, carried some degree of fascination with it.—To be generally gallant & assiduous about the fair, to make fine speeches to every pretty girl, was but the inferior part of the character he had to play.—Miss Heywood, or any other young woman with any pretensions to beauty, he was entitled (according to his own views of society) to approach with high compliment & rhapsody on the slightest acquaintance; but it was Clara alone on whom he had serious designs; it was Clara whom he meant to seduce.—Her seduction was quite determined on. Her situation in every way called for it. She was his rival in Lady D.'s favour, she was young, lovely & dependant.— He had very early seen the necessity of the case, & had now been long trying with cautious assiduity to make an impression on her heart, and to undermine her principles.—Clara saw through him, & had not the least intention of being seduced— but she bore with him patiently enough to confirm the sort of attachment which her personal charms had raised.—A greater degree of discouragement indeed would not have affected Sir Edw:—. He was armed against the highest pitch of disdain and aversion.—If she could not be won by affection, he must carry her off. He knew his business.—Already had he had many musings on the subject. If he *were* constrained so to act, he must naturally wish to strike out something new, to exceed those who had gone before him—and he felt a strong curiosity to ascertain whether the neighbourhood of Timbuctu might not afford some solitary house adapted for Clara's reception;—but the expence alas! of measures in that masterly style was ill-suited to his purse, & prudence obliged him to prefer the quietest sort of ruin & disgrace for the object of his affections, to the more renowned.—

CHAPTER 9

ONE day, soon after Charlotte's arrival at Sanditon, she had the pleasure of seeing just as she ascended from the sands to the Terrace, a gentleman's carriage with post horses standing at the door of the hotel, as very lately arrived, & by the quantity of luggage being taken off, bringing, it might be hoped, some respectable family determined on a long residence.—Delighted to have such good news for M^r and Mrs P., who had both gone home some time before, she proceeded for Trafalgar House with as much alacrity as could remain, after having contending for the last 2 hours with a very fine wind blowing directly on shore; but she had not reached the little lawn, when she saw a lady walking nimbly behind her at no great distance; and convinced that it could be no acquaintance of her own, she resolved to hurry on & get into the house if possible before her. But the stranger's pace did not allow this to be accomplished;— Charlotte was on the steps & had rung, but the door was not opened, when the other crossed the lawn;—and when the servant appeared, they were just equally ready for entering the house.—The ease of the lady, her "How do you do, Morgan?—" & Morgan's looks on seeing her, were a moment's astonishment—but another moment brought Mr P. into the hall to welcome the sister he had seen from the draw^g room, and she was soon introduced to Miss Diana Parker. There was a great deal of surprise but still more pleasure in seeing her.—Nothing c^d be kinder than her reception from both husband and wife. "How did she come? & with whom?—And they were so glad to find her equal to the journey!—And that she was to belong to *them*, was taken as a matter of course." Miss Diana P. was about 4 & 30, of middling height & slender;—delicate looking rather than sickly; with an agreeable face, & a very animated eye;—her manners resembling her brother's in their ease & frankness, though with more decision & less mildness in her tone. She began an account of herself without delay.—Thanking them for their invitation, but *"that* was quite out of the question, for they were all three come, & meant to get into lodgings & make some stay."—"All three come!—What!—Susan & Arthur!—Susan able to come too!—This is better and better."—"Yes—we are actually all come. Quite unavoidable.—Nothing else to be done.—You shall hear all about it.—But my dear Mary, send for the children;—I long to see them."—"And how has Susan borne the journey?—& how is Arthur?—& why do we not see him here with you?"—"Susan has borne it wonderfully. She had not a wink of sleep either the night before we set out, or last night at Chichester, and as this is not so common with her as with *me,* I have had a thousand fears for her—but she has kept up wonderfully.—had no hysterics of consequence till we came within sight of poor old Sanditon—and the attack was not very violent—nearly over by the time we reached your hotel—so that we got her out of the carriage extremely well, with only Mr Woodcock's assistance—& when I left her she was directing the disposal of the luggage, & helping old Sam uncord the trunks.— She desired her best love, with a thousand regrets at being so poor a creature that she c^d not come with me. And as for poor Arthur, he w^d not have been unwilling himself, but there is so much wind that I did not think he c^d safely venture,—for I am *sure* there is lumbago hanging about him—and so I helped him on with his great coat & sent him off to the Terrace, to take us lodgings.—Miss Heywood must have seen our carriage standing at the hotel.—I knew Miss Heywood the moment I saw her before me on the down.—My dear Tom I am so glad to see you walk so well. Let me feel your ankle.—That's right; all right & clean. The play of your sinews a *very* little affected:—barely perceptible.—Well—now for the explanation of my being here.—I told you in my letter, of the two considerable families, I was hoping to secure for you—the West Indians & the semi-nary.—" Here Mr P. drew his chair still nearer to his sister, & took her hand again most affectionately as he answered "Yes, yes;—how active & how kind you have been!"—"The West-Indians, she continued, whom I look upon as the *most* desirable

of the two—as the best of the good—prove to be a Mrs Griffiths
& her family. I know them only through others.—You must have
heard me mention Miss Capper, the particular friend of *my* very
particular friend Fanny Noyce;—now, Miss Capper is extremely
intimate with a Mrs Darling, who is on terms of constant correspondence with Mrs Griffiths herself.—Only a *short* chain, you
see, between us, & not a link wanting. Mrs G. meant to go to the
sea, for her young people's benefit—had fixed on the coast of
Sussex, but was undecided as to the where, wanted something
private, & wrote to ask the opinion of her friend Mrs Darling.—
Miss Capper happened to be staying with Mrs D. when Mrs G.'s
letter arrived, & was consulted on the question; *she* wrote the
same day to Fanny Noyce and mentioned it to her—& Fanny,
all alive for *us*, instantly took up her pen & forwarded the circumstance to me—except as to *names*—which have but lately
transpired.—There was but *one* thing for *me* to do.—I answered
Fanny's letter by the same post & pressed for the recommendation of Sanditon. Fanny had feared your having no house large
enough to receive such a family.—But I seem to be spinning out
my story to an endless length.—You see how it was all managed.
I had the pleasure of hearing soon afterwards by the same
simple link of connection that Sanditon *had been* recommended
by Mrs Darling, & that the West Indians were very much disposed to go thither.—This was the state of the case when I wrote
to you; —but two days ago;—yes, the day before yesterday—I
heard again from Fanny Noyce, saying that *she* had heard
from Miss Capper, who by a letter from Mrs Darling understood
that Mrs G.— has expressed herself in a letter to Mrs D. more
doubtingly on the subject of Sanditon.—Am I clear?—I would
be anything rather than not clear."—"Oh, perfectly, perfectly.
Well?"—"The reason of this hesitation, was her having no connections in the place, & no means of ascertaining that she
should have good accommodations on arriving there;—and she
was particularly careful & scrupulous on all those matters more
on account of a certain Miss Lambe a young lady (probably a
niece) under her care, than on her own account or her daughters.—Miss Lambe has an immense fortune—richer than all the
rest—& very delicate health.—One sees clearly enough by all
this, the *sort* of woman Mrs G. must be—as helpless & indolent,

as wealth & a hot climate are apt to make us. But we are not all born to equal energy.—What was to be done?—I had a few moments indecision;—whether to offer to write to *you*,—or to Mrs Whitby to secure them a house?—but neither pleased me.—I hate to employ others, when I am equal to act myself— and my conscience told me that this was an occasion which called for me. Here was a family of helpless invalids whom I might essentially serve.—I sounded Susan—the same thought had occurred to her.—Arthur made no difficulties—our plan was arranged immediately, we were off yesterday morn^g at 6—, left Chichester at the same hour today—& here we are.—" "Excellent!—Excellent!—cried Mr Parker.—Diana, you are unequal'd in serving your friends & doing good to all the world.—I know nobody like you.—Mary, my love, is not she a wonderful creature?—Well—and now, what house do you design to engage for them?—What is the size of their family?—" "I do not at all know—replied his sister—have not the least idea;—never heard any particulars;—but I am very sure that the largest house at Sanditon cannot be *too* large. They are more likely to want a second.—I shall take only one however, & that, but for a week certain.—Miss Heywood, I astonish you.—You hardly know what to make of me.—I see by your looks, that you are not used to such quick measures."—The words "unaccount-able officiousness!—activity run mad!"—had just passed through Charlotte's mind—but a civil answer was easy. "I dare say I do look surprised, said she—because these are very great exertions, & I know what invalids both you & your sister are." "Invalids indeed.—I trust there are not three people in England who have so sad a right to that appellation!—But my dear Miss Heywood, we are sent into this world to be as extensively useful as possible, & where some degree of strength of mind is given, it is not a feeble body which will excuse us—or incline us to excuse ourselves.—The world is pretty much divided between the weak of mind & the strong—between those who can act & those who can not, & it is the bounden duty of the capable to let no opportunity of being useful escape them.—My sister's com-plaints & mine are happily not often of a nature, to threaten existence *immediately*—& as long as we *can* exert ourselves to be of use to others, I am convinced that the body is the better, for the refreshment the mind receives in doing its duty.—While I have been travelling, with this object in view, I have been perfectly well."—The entrance of the children ended this little panegyric on her own disposition—& after having noticed & caressed them all,—she prepared to go.—"Cannot you dine with us?—Is not it possible to prevail on you to dine with us?" was then the cry; and *that* being absolutely negatived, it was, "And when shall we see you again? And how can we be of use to you?"—and Mr P. warmly offered his assistance in taking the house for Mrs G.—"I will come to you the moment I have dined, said he, & we will go about together."—But this was immediately declined.—"No, my dear Tom, upon no account in the world, shall you stir a step on any business of mine.—Your ankle wants rest. I see by the position of your foot, that you have used it too much already.—No, I shall go about my house-taking directly. Our dinner is not ordered till six—& by that time I hope to have completed it. It is now only ½ past 4.—As to seeing *me* again today—I cannot answer for it; the others will be at the hotel all the even^g, & delighted to see you at any time, but as soon as I get back I shall hear what Arthur has done about our own lodgings, & probably the moment dinner is over, shall be out again on business relative to them, for we hope to get into some lodgings or other & be settled after breakfast tomorrow.— I have not much confidence in poor Arthur's skill for lodging-taking, but he seemed to like the commission.—" "I think you are doing too much, said Mr P. You will knock yourself up. You sh^d not move again after dinner." "No, indeed you should not, cried his wife, for dinner is such a mere *name* with you all, that it can do you no good.—I know what your appetites are.—" "My appetite is very much mended, I assure you, lately. I have been taking some bitters of my own decocting, which have done wonders. Susan never eats I grant you—& just at present *I* shall want nothing. I never eat for about a week after a journey—but as for Arthur, he is only too much disposed for food. We are often obliged to check him."—"But you have not told me any thing of the *other* family coming to Sanditon, said Mr P. as he walked with her to the door of the house—the Camberwell Seminary; have we a good chance of *them?*" "Oh, certain—quite certain.—I had forgotten them for the moment, but I had a letter 3 days ago from my friend Mrs Charles Dupuis which assured me of Camberwell. Camberwell will be here to a certainty, & very soon.—*That* good woman (I do not know her name) not being so wealthy & independent as Mrs G.—can travel & chuse for herself.—I will tell you how I got at *her.* Mrs Charles Dupuis lives almost next door to a lady, who has a relation lately settled at Clapham, who actually attends the seminary and gives lessons on eloquence and belles lettres to some of the girls.—I got that man a hare from one of Sidney's friends— and he recommended Sanditon;—Without *my* appearing however—Mrs Charles Dupuis managed it all.—"

CHAPTER 10

IT WAS not a week, since Miss Diana Parker had been told by her feelings, that the sea air w^d probably in her present state, be the death of her, and now she was at Sanditon, intending to make some stay, & without appearing to have the slightest recollection of having written or felt any such thing.—It was impossible for Charlotte not to suspect a good deal of fancy in such an extraordinary state of health.—Disorders & recoveries so very much out of the common way, seemed more like the amusement of eager minds in want of employment than of actual afflictions & relief. The Parkers, were no doubt a family of imagination & quick feelings—and while the eldest brother found vent for his superfluity of sensation as a projector, the sisters were perhaps driven to dissipate theirs in the invention of odd complaints.— The *whole* of their mental vivacity was evidently not so employed; part was laid out in a zeal for being useful.—It should seem that they must either be very busy for the good of others, or else extremely ill themselves. Some natural delicacy of constitution in fact, with an unfortunate turn for medicine, especially quack medicine, had given them an early tendency at various times, to various disorders;—the rest of their sufferings was from fancy, the love of distinction & the love of the wonderful.—They had charitable hearts & many amiable feelings—but a spirit of restless activity, & the glory of doing more than anybody else, had their share in every exertion of benevolence—and there was vanity in all they did, as well as in all they endured.—M^r &

Mrs P. spent a great part of the even^g at the hotel; but Charlotte had only two or three views of Miss Diana posting over the down after a house for this lady whom she had never seen, & who had never employed her. She was not made acquainted with the others till the following day, when, being removed into lodgings & all the party continuing quite well, their brother & sister & herself were entreated to drink tea with them.—They were in one of the Terrace houses—& she found them arranged for the even^g in a small neat drawing room, with a beautiful view of the sea if they had chosen it,—but though it had been a very fair English summer-day,—not only was there no open window, but the sofa & the table, and the establishment in general was all at the other end of the room by a brisk fire.—Miss P.— whom, remembering the three teeth drawn in one day, Charlotte approached with a peculiar degree of respectful compassion, was not very unlike her sister in person or manner— tho' more thin & worn by illness & medicine, more relaxed in air, & more subdued in voice. She talked however, the whole evening as incessantly as Diana—& excepting that she sat with salts in her hand, took drops two or three times from one, out of several phials already at home on the mantelpiece,—& made a great many odd faces & contortions, Charlotte could perceive no symptoms of illness which she, in the boldness of her own good health, w^d not have undertaken to cure, by putting out the fire, opening the window, & disposing of the drops & the salts by means of one or the other. She had had considerable curiosity to see Mr Arthur Parker; & having fancied him a very puny, delicate-looking young man, the smallest very materially of not a robust family, was astonished to find him quite as tall as his brother & a great deal stouter—broad made & lusty—and with no other look of an invalide, than a sodden complexion.— Diana was evidently the chief of the family; principal mover & actor;—she had been on her feet the whole morning, on Mrs G.s' business or their own, & was still the most alert of the three.—Susan had only superintended their final removal from the hotel, bringing two heavy boxes herself, & Arthur had found the air so cold that he had merely walked from one house to the other as nimbly as he could,—& boasted much of sitting by the fire till he had cooked up a very good one.—Diana, whose exer-

cise had been too domestic to admit of calculation, but who, by
her own account, had not once sat down during the space of
seven hours, confessed herself a little tired. She had been too
successful however for much fatigue; for not only had she by
walking & talking down a thousand difficulties at last secured a
proper house at 8^g p^r week for Mrs G.—; she had also opened so
many treaties with cooks, housemaids, washer-women &
bathing women, that Mrs G. would have little more to do on her
arrival, than to wave her hand & collect them around her for
choice.—Her concluding effort in the cause, had been a few
polite lines of information to Mrs G. herself—time not allowing
for the circuitous train of intelligence which had been hitherto
kept up,—and she was now regaling in the delight of opening
the first trenches of an acquaintance with such a powerful discharge of unexpected obligation. M^r & Mrs P.— & Charlotte had
seen two post chaises crossing the down to the hotel as
they were setting off,—a joyful sight—& full of speculation.—
The Miss Ps— & Arthur had also seen something;—they
could distinguish from their window that there *was* an arrival at
the hotel, but not its amount. Their visitors answered for two
hack-chaises.—Could it be the Camberwell Seminary?—No—
No. Had there been a 3^d carriage, perhaps it might; but it was
very generally agreed that two hack chaises could never contain
a seminary.—Mr P. was confident of another new family.—
When they were all finally seated, after some removals to look
at the sea & the hotel, Charlotte's place was by Arthur, who was
sitting next to the fire with a degree of enjoyment which gave a
good deal of merit to his civility in wishing her to take his
chair.—There was nothing dubious in her manner of declining
it, and he sat down again with much satisfaction. She drew back
her chair to have all the advantage of his person as a screen, &
was very thankful for every inch of back & shoulders beyond her
preconceived idea. Arthur was heavy in eye as well as figure, but
by no means indisposed to talk;—and while the other 4 were
chiefly engaged together, he evidently felt it no penance to have
a fine young woman next to him, requiring in common polite-
ness some attention—as his b^r, who felt the decided want of
some motive for action, some powerful object of animation for
him, observed with considerable pleasure.—Such was the influ-

ence of youth & bloom that he began even to make a sort of apology for having a fire. "We sh^d not have had one at home, said he, but the sea air is always damp. I am not afraid of anything so much as damp.—" "I am so fortunate, said C. as never to know whether the air is damp or dry. It has always some property that is wholesome & invigorating to me.—" "*I* like the air too, as well as any body can; replied Arthur, I am very fond of standing at an open window when there is no wind—but unluckily a damp air does not like *me*.—It gives me the rheumatism.— You are not rheumatic, I suppose?—" "Not at all." "That's a great blessing.—But perhaps you are nervous." "No—I believe not. I have no idea that I am."—"*I* am very nervous.—To say the truth nerves are the worst part of my complaints in *my* opinion. My sisters think me bilious, but I doubt it.—" "You are quite in the right, to doubt it as long as you possibly can, I am sure.—" "If I were bilious, he continued, you know, wine w^d disagree with me, but it always does me good.—The more wine I drink (in moderation) the better I am.—I am always best of an even^g.—If you had seen me today before dinner, you w^d have thought me a very poor creature.—" Charlotte could believe it—. She kept her countenance however, & said—"As far as I can understand what nervous complaints are, I have a great idea of the efficacy of air & exercise for them:—daily, regular exercise;—and I should recommend rather more of it to *you* than I suspect you are in the habit of taking."—"Oh, I am very fond of exercise myself—he replied—& mean to walk a great deal while I am here, if the weather is temperate. I shall be out every morning before breakfast—& take several turns upon the Terrace, & you will often see me at Trafalgar House."—"But you do not call a walk to Traf: H. much exercise?—" "Not, as to mere distance, but the hill is so steep!—Walking up that hill, in the middle of the day, would throw me into such a perspiration!— You would see me all in a bath by the time I got there!—I am very subject to perspiration, and there cannot be a surer sign of nervousness.—" They were now advancing so deep in physics, that Charlotte viewed the entrance of the servant with the tea things, as a very fortunate interruption.—It produced a great & immediate change. The young man's attentions were instantly lost. He took his own cocoa from the tray,—which seemed provided with almost as many teapots &c as there were persons in company, Miss P. drinking one sort of herb-tea & Miss Diana another, & turning completely to the fire, sat coddling and cooking it to his own satisfaction & toasting some slices of bread, brought up ready-prepared in the toast rack—and till it was all done, she heard nothing of his voice but the murmuring of a few broken sentences of self-approbation & success.—When his toils were over, however, he moved back his chair into as gallant a line as ever, & proved that he had not been working only for himself, by his earnest invitation to her to take both cocoa & toast.—She was already helped to tea—which surprised him— so totally self-engrossed had he been.—"I thought I should have been in time, said he, but cocoa takes a great deal of boiling."— "I am much obliged to you, replied Charlotte—but I *prefer* tea." "Then I will help myself, said he.—A large dish of rather weak cocoa every evening, agrees with me better than any thing."—It struck her however, as he poured out this rather weak cocoa, that it came forth in a very fine, dark-coloured stream—and at the same moment, his sisters both crying out,—"Oh! Arthur, you get your cocoa stronger & stronger every even^g"—, with Arthur's somewhat conscious reply of "*Tis* rather stronger than it should be tonight"—convinced her that Arthur was by no means so fond of being starved as they could desire, or as he felt proper himself.—He was certainly very happy to turn the conversation on dry toast, & hear no more of his sisters.—"I hope you will eat some of this toast, said he, I reckon myself a very good toaster; I never burn my toasts—I never put them too near the fire at first—& yet, you see, there is not a corner but what is well browned.—I hope you like dry toast."—"With a reasonable quantity of butter spread over it, very much—said Charlotte— but not otherwise.—" "No more do I—said he exceedingly pleased—We think quite alike there. So far from dry toast being wholesome, *I* think it a very bad thing for the stomach. Without a little butter to soften it, it hurts the coats of the stomach. I am sure it does.—I will have the pleasure of spreading some for you directly—& afterwards I will spread some for myself.—Very bad indeed for the coats of the stomach—but there is no convincing *some* people. It irritates & acts like a nutmeg grater.—" He could not get command of the butter however, without a struggle; his sisters accusing him of eating a great deal too much, & declaring he was not to be trusted;—and he maintaining that he only eat enough to secure the coats of his stomach;—& besides, he only wanted it now for Miss Heywood.—Such a plea must prevail, he got the butter & spread away for her with an accuracy of judgement which at least delighted himself; but when her toast was done, & he took his own in hand, Charlotte c^d hardly contain herself as she saw him watching his sisters, while he scrupulously scraped off almost as much butter as he put on, & then seize an odd moment for adding a great dab just before it went into his mouth.—Certainly, Mr Arthur P.'s enjoyments in invalidism were very different from his sisters—by no means so spiritualized.—A good deal of earthy dross hung about him. Charlotte could not but suspect him of adopting that line of life, principally for the indulgence of an indolent temper—& to be determined on having no disorders but such as called for warm rooms & good nourishment.—In one particular however, she soon found that he had caught something from *them.*— "What! said he—Do you venture upon two dishes of strong green tea in one even^g?—What nerves you must have!—How I envy you.—Now, if *I* were to swallow only one such dish—what do you think its effect would be upon me?—" "Keep you awake perhaps all night"—replied Charlotte, meaning to overthrow his attempts at surprise, by the grandeur of her own conceptions.— "Oh, if that were all!—he exclaimed.—No—It acts on me like poison and w^d entirely take away the use of my right side, before I had swallowed it 5 minutes.—It sounds almost incredible— but it has happened to me so often that I cannot doubt it.—The use of my right side is entirely taken away for several hours!" "It sounds rather odd to be sure—answered Charlotte coolly—but I dare say it would be proved to be the simplest thing in the world, by those who have studied right sides & green tea scientifically & thoroughly understand all the possibilities of their action on each other."—Soon after tea, a letter was brought to Miss D. P.— from the hotel.—"From Mrs Charles Dupuis—said she—some private hand."—And having read a few lines, exclaimed aloud, "Well, this is very extraordinary! very extraordinary indeed!—That both should have the same name.—Two Mrs Griffiths!—This is a letter of recommendation & introduc-

tion to me, of the lady from Camberwell—& *her* name happens
to be Griffiths too.—" A few lines more however, and the colour
rushed into her cheeks, & with much perturbation she added—
"The oddest thing that ever was!—a Miss Lambe too!—a young
West-Indian of large fortune.—But it *cannot* be the same.—
Impossible that it should be the same."—She read the letter
aloud for comfort.—It was merely to "introduce the bearer,
Mrs G.— from Camberwell, & the three young ladies under
her care, to Miss D. P.'s notice.—Mrs G.— being a stranger at
Sanditon, was anxious for a respectable introduction—& M^{rs} C.
Dupuis therefore, at the instance of the intermediate friend, pro-
vided her with this letter, knowing that she c^d not do her dear
Diana a greater kindness than by giving her the means of being
useful.—Mrs G.'s chief solicitude w^d be for the accommodation &
comfort of one of the young ladies under her care, a Miss
Lambe, a young W. Indian of large fortune, in delicate health."—
"It was very strange!—very remarkable!—very extraordinary"
but they were all agreed in determining it to be *impossible* that
there should not be two families; such a totally distinct set of
people as were concerned in the reports of each made that
matter quite certain. There *must* be two families.—Impossible to
be otherwise. "Impossible" & "Impossible," was repeated over &
over again with great fervour.—An accidental resemblance of
names & circumstances, however striking at first, involved
nothing really incredible—and so it was settled.—Miss Diana
herself derived an immediate advantage to counterbalance her
perplexity. She must put her shawl over her shoulders, & be running about again. Tired as she was, she must instantly repair to
the hotel, to investigate the truth & offer her services.—

CHAPTER 11

IT would not do.—Not all that the whole Parker race could say
among themselves, c^d produce a happier catastrophe than that
the family from Surrey & the family from Camberwell were one
& the same.—The rich West-Indians, & the young ladies' seminary had all entered Sanditon in those two hack chaises. The
Mrs G. who, in her friend Mrs Darling's hands, had wavered as to
coming & been unequal to the journey, was the very same

Mrs G. whose plans were at the same period (under another representation) perfectly decided & who was without fears or difficulties.—All that had the appearance of incongruity in the reports of the two, might very fairly be placed to the account of the vanity, the ignorance, or the blunders of the many engaged in the cause by the vigilance & caution of Miss Diana P—. *Her* intimate friends must be officious like herself, & the subject had supplied letters & extracts & messages enough to make everything appear what it was not. Miss D. probably felt a little awkward on being first obliged to admit her mistake. A long journey from Hampshire taken for nothing—a brother disappointed— an expensive house on her hands for a week, must have been some of her immediate reflections—& much worse than all the rest, must have been the sort of sensation of being less clearsighted & infallible than she had believed herself.—No part of it however seemed to trouble her long. There were so many to share in the shame & the blame, that probably when she had divided out their proper portions to Mrs Darling, Miss Capper, Fanny Noyce, Mrs C. Dupuis & Mrs C. D's neighbour, there might be a mere trifle of reproach remaining for herself.—At any rate, she was seen all the following morn^g walking about after lodgings with Mrs G.—as alert as ever.—Mrs G. was a very well-behaved, genteel kind of woman, who supported herself by receiving such great girls & young ladies as wanted either masters for finishing their education, or a home for beginning their displays.—She had several more under her care than the three who were now come to Sanditon, but the others all happened to be absent.— Of these three, & indeed of all, Miss Lambe was beyond comparison the most important & precious, as she paid in proportion to her fortune.—She was about 17, half mulatto, chilly & tender, had a maid of her own, was to have the best room in the lodgings, & was always of the first consequence in every plan of Mrs G.— The other girls, two Miss Beauforts were just such young ladies as may be met with, in at least one family out of three, throughout the kingdom; they had tolerable complexions, shewy figures, an upright decided carriage & an assured look;— they were very accomplished & very ignorant, their time being divided between such pursuits as might attract admiration, & those labours & expedients of dexterous ingenuity, by which they could dress in a stile much beyond what they *ought* to have afforded; they were some of the first in every change of fashion—& the object of all, was to captivate some man of much better fortune than their own.—Mrs G. had preferred a small, retired place, like Sanditon, on Miss Lambe's account—and the Miss Bs—, though naturally preferring any thing to smallness & retirement, yet having in the course of the spring been involved in the inevitable expense of six new dresses each for a three days visit, were constrained to be satisfied with Sanditon also, till their circumstances were retrieved. There, with the hire of a harp for one, & the purchase of some drawing paper for the other & all the finery they could already command, they meant to be very economical, very elegant & very secluded; with the hope, on Miss Beaufort's side, of praise & celebrity from all who walked within the sound of her instrument, & on Miss Letitia's, of curiosity & rapture in all who came near her while she sketched—and to both, the consolation of meaning to be the most stylish girls in the place.—The particular introduction of Mrs G. to Miss Diana Parker, secured them immediately an acquaintance with the Trafalgar House-family, & with the Denhams;—and the Miss Beauforts were soon satisfied with "the circle in which they moved in Sanditon" to use a proper phrase, for every body must now "move in a circle,"—to the prevalence of which rotatory motion, is perhaps to be attributed the giddiness & false steps of many.—Lady Denham had other motives for calling on Mrs G. besides attention to the Parkers.— In Miss Lambe, here was the very young lady, sickly & rich, whom she had been asking for; & she made the acquaintance for Sir Edward's sake, & the sake of her milch asses. How it might answer with regard to the baronet, remained to be proved, but, as to the animals, she soon found that all her calculations of profit w^d be vain. Mrs G. would not allow Miss L. to have the smallest symptom of a decline, or any complaint which asses milk c^d possibly releive. "Miss L. was under the constant care of an experienced physician;—and his prescriptions must be their rule"—and except in favour of some tonic pills, which a cousin of her own had a property in, Mrs G. never did deviate from the strict medicinal page.—The corner house of the Terrace was the one in which Miss D. P. had the pleasure of settling her new friends, & considering that it commanded in front the favourite lounge of all the visitors at Sanditon, & on one side, whatever might be going on at the hotel, there c^d not have been a more favourable spot for the seclusion of the Miss Beauforts. And accordingly, long before they had suited themselves with an instrument, or with drawing paper, they had, by the frequency of their appearance at the low windows upstairs, in order to close the blinds, or open the blinds, to arrange a flower pot on the balcony, or look at nothing through a telescope, attracted many an eye upwards, & made many a gazer gaze again.—A little novelty has a great effect in so small a place; the Miss Beauforts, who w^d have been nothing at Brighton, could not move here without notice; —and even Mr Arthur Parker, though little disposed for supernumerary exertion, always quitted the Terrace, in his way to his brother's by this corner house, for the sake of a glimpse of the Miss Bs—, it was ½ a q^r of a mile round about, & added two steps to the ascent of the hill.

CHAPTER 12

CHARLOTTE had been 10 days at Sanditon without seeing Sanditon House, every attempt at calling on Lady D. having been defeated by meeting with her beforehand. But now it was to be more resolutely undertaken, at a more early hour, that nothing might be neglected of attention to Lady D. or amusement to Charlotte.—"And if you should find a favourable opening my Love, said Mr P. (who did not mean to go with them)—I think you had better mention the poor Mullins's situation, & sound her ladyship as to a subscription for them. I am not fond of charitable subscriptions in a place of this kind—It is a sort of tax upon all that come—Yet as their distress is very great & I almost promised the poor woman yesterday to get something done for her, I believe we must set a subscription on foot—& therefore the sooner the better,—& Lady Denham's name at the head of the list will be a very necessary beginning.—You will not dislike speaking to her about it, Mary?"—"I will do whatever you wish me, replied his wife—

but you would do it so much better yourself. I shall not know what to say."—"My dear Mary, cried he, it is impossible you can be really at a loss. Nothing can be more simple. You have only to state the present afflicted situation of the family, their earnest application to me, & my being willing to promote a little subscription for their releif, provided it meet with her approbation.—" "The easiest thing in the world—cried Miss Diana Parker who happened to be calling on them at the moment—. All said & done, in less time than you have been talking of it now.—And while you are on the subject of subscriptions Mary, I will thank you to mention a very melancholy case to Lady D. which has been represented to me in the most affecting terms.—There is a poor woman in Worcestershire, whom some friends of mine are exceedingly interested about, & I have undertaken to collect whatever I can for her. If you w^d mention the circumstances to Lady Denham!—Lady Denham *can* give, if she is properly attacked—& I look upon her to be the sort of person who, when once she is prevailed on to undraw her purse, w^d as readily give 10^{Gs} as 5.—And therefore, if you find her in a giving mood, you might as well speak in favour of another charity which I & a few more, have very much at heart—the establishment of a Charitable Repository at Burton on Trent.—And then,—there is the family of the poor man who was hung last assizes at York, tho' we really *have* raised the sum we wanted for putting them all out, yet if you *can* get a Guinea from her on their behalf, it may as well be done."—"My dear Diana! exclaimed Mrs P.— I could no more mention these things to Lady D.— than I c^d fly."—"Where's the difficulty?—I wish I could go with you myself—but in 5 minutes I must be at Mrs G.— to encourage Miss Lambe in taking her first dip. She is so frightened, poor thing, that I promised to come & keep up her spirits, & go in the machine with her if she wished it—and as soon as that is over, I must hurry home, for Susan is to have leaches at one o'clock—which will be a three hours business,—therefore I really have not a moment to spare—besides that (between ourselves) I ought to be in bed myself at this present time, for I am hardly able to stand—and when the leaches have done, I dare say we shall both go to our rooms for the rest of the day."—"I am sorry to hear it, indeed; but if this is the case I hope Arthur will come to us."—"If Arthur takes my advice, he will go to bed too, for if he stays up by himself, he will certainly eat & drink more than he ought;—but you see Mary, how impossible it is for me to go with you to Lady Denham's."— "Upon second thoughts Mary, said her husband, I will not trouble you to speak about the Mullins's.—I will take an opportunity of seeing Lady D. myself.—*I* know how little it suits you to be pressing matters upon a Mind at all unwilling."—*His* application thus withdrawn, his sister could say no more in support of hers, which was his object, as he felt all their impropriety & all the certainty of their ill effect upon his own better claim.—Mrs P. was delighted at this release, & set off very happy with her friend & her little girl, on this walk to Sanditon House.—It was a close, misty morn^g, & when they reached the brow of the hill, they could not for some time make out what sort of carriage it was, which they saw coming up. It appeared at different moments to be everything from the Gig to the Pheaton,—from one horse to 4; & just as they were concluding in favour of a tandem, little Mary's young eyes distingished the Coachman & she eagerly called out, "T'is Uncle Sidney Mama, it is indeed." And so it proved.— Mr Sidney Parker drinking his servant in a very neat carriage was soon opposite to them, & they all stopped for a few minutes. The manners of the Parkers were always pleasant among themselves— & it was a very friendly meeting between Sidney & his sister in law, who was most kindly taking it for granted that he was on his way to Trafalgar House. This he declined however. "He was just come from Eastbourne, proposing to spend two or three days, as it might happen, at Sanditon—but the hotel must be his quarters—He was expecting to be joined there by a friend or two."—The rest was common enquiries & remarks, with kind notice of little Mary, & a very well-bred bow & proper address to Miss Heywood on her being named to him—and they parted, to meet again within a few hours.— Sidney Parker was about 7 or 8 & 20, very good-looking, with a decided air of ease & fashion, and a lively countenance.—

This adventure afforded agreeable discussion for some time. Mrs P. entered into all her husband's joy on the occasion, & exulted in the credit which Sidney's arrival w^d give to the place. The road to Sanditon H. was a broad, handsome, planted approach, between fields, & conducting at the end of a q^r of a mile through second gates into the grounds, which though not extensive had all the beauty and respectability which an abundance of very fine timber could give.—These entrance gates were so much in a corner of the grounds or paddock, so near one of its boundaries, that an outside fence was at first almost pressing on the road—till an angle *here,* & a curve *there* threw them to a better distance. The fence was a proper park paling in excellent condition; with clusters of fine elms, or rows of old thorns following its line almost every where.—*Almost* must be stipulated—for there were vacant spaces—& through one of these, Charlotte as soon as they entered the enclosure, caught a glimpse over the pales of something white & womanish in the field on the other side;—it was something which immediately brought Miss B. into her head—& stepping to the pales, she saw indeed—& very decidedly, in spite of the mist; Miss B— seated, not far before her, at the foot of the bank which sloped down from the outside of the paling & which a narrow path seemed to skirt along;—Miss Brereton seated, apparently very composedly—& Sir E. D. by her side.—They were sitting so near each other & appeared so closely engaged in gentle conversation, that Ch. instantly felt she had nothing to do but to step back again, & say not a word.—Privacy was certainly their object.—It could not but strike her rather unfavourably with regard to Clara;—but hers was a situation which must not be judged with severity.—She was glad to perceive that nothing had been discerned by Mrs Parker; if Charlotte had not been considerably the tallest of the two, Miss B.'s white ribbons might not have fallen within the ken of *her* more observant eyes.—Among other points of moralising reflection which the sight of this tete a tete produced, Charlotte c^d not but think of the extreme difficulty which secret lovers must have in finding a proper spot for their stolen interviews.— Here perhaps they had thought themselves so perfectly secure

from observation!—the whole field open before them—a
steep bank & pales never crossed by the foot of man at their
back—and a great thickness of air, in aid—. Yet here, she had
seen them. They were really ill-used.—The house was large &
handsome; two servants appeared, to admit them, & every
thing had a suitable air of property & order.—Lady D. valued
herself upon her liberal establishment, & had great enjoyment
in the order and the importance of her style of living.—They
were shewn into the usual sitting room, well-proportioned &
well-furnished;—tho' it was furniture rather originally good &
extremely well kept, than new or shewey—and as Lady D. was
not there, Charlotte had leisure to look about, & to be told by
Mrs P. that the whole-length portrait of a stately gentleman,
which placed over the mantlepiece, caught the eye immediately, was the picture of Sir H. Denham—and that one among
many miniatures in another part of the room, little conspicuous, represented Mr Hollis.—Poor Mr Hollis!—It was impossible not to feel him hardly used; to be obliged to stand back
in his own house & see the best place by the fire constantly
occupied by Sir H. D.

The Watsons

———

THE first winter assembly in the town of D. in Surrey was to be held on Tuesday, Octr 13th, & it was generally expected to be a very good one; a long list of country families was confidently run over as sure of attending, & sanguine hopes were entertained that the Osbornes themselves would be there.—The Edwards's invitation to the Watsons followed, of course. The Edwards's were people of fortune, who lived in the town & kept their coach; the Watsons inhabited a village about 3 miles distant, were poor & had no close carriage; & ever since there had been balls in the place, the former were accustomed to invite the latter to dress, dine & sleep at their house, on every monthly return throughout the winter.—On the present occasion, as only two of Mr W.'s children were at home, & one was always necessary as companion to himself, for he was sickly & had lost his wife, one only could profit by the kindness of their friends; Miss Emma Watson who was very recently returned to her family from the care of an aunt who had brought her up, was to make her first public appearance in the neighbourhood; & her eldest sister, whose delight in a ball was not lessened by a ten years enjoyment, had some merit in cheerfully undertaking to drive her & all her finery in the old chair to D. on the important morn^g.—As they splashed along the dirty lane Miss Watson thus instructed & cautioned her inexperienc'd sister.—"I dare say it will be a very good ball, & among so many officers, you will hardly want partners. You will find Mrs Edwards's maid very willing to help you, and I would advise you to ask Mary Edwards's opinion if you are at all at a loss for she has a very good taste.—If Mr E. does not lose his money at cards, you will stay as late as you can wish for; if he does, he will hurry you home perhaps—but you are sure of some comfortable soup.—I hope you will be in good looks—. I should not be surprised if you were to be thought one of the prettiest girls in the room, there is a great deal in novelty. Perhaps Tom Musgrave may take notice of you—but I would advise you by all means not to give him any encouragement. He generally pays attention to every new girl, but he is a great flirt & never means anything serious." "I think I have heard you speak of him before, said Emma. Who is he?" "A young man of very good fortune, quite independent, & remarkably agreeable, an universal favourite wherever he goes. Most of the girls hereabout are in love with him, or have been. I believe I am the only one among them that have escaped with a whole heart, and yet I was the first he paid attention to, when he came into this country, six years ago; and very great attention did he pay me. Some people say that he has never seemed to like any girl so well since, tho' he is always behaving in a particular way to one or another."—

"And how came *your* heart to be the only cold one?"—said Emma, smiling. "There was a reason for that—replied Miss W. changing colour.—I have not been very well used Emma among them, I hope you will have better luck."—"Dear sister, I beg your pardon, if I have unthinkingly given you pain."—"When first we knew Tom Musgrave, continued Miss W. without seeming to hear her, I was very much attached to a young man of the name of Purvis a particular friend of Robert's, who used to be with us a great deal. Every body thought it would have been a match." A sigh accompanied these words, which Emma respected in silence—but her sister after a short pause went on.—"You will naturally ask why it did not take place, & why he is married to another woman, while I am still single.—But you must ask him—not me—you must ask Penelope.—Yes, Emma, Penelope was at the bottom of it all.—She thinks everything fair for a husband; I trusted her, she set him against me, with a

view of gaining him herself, & it ended in his discontinuing his
visits & soon after marrying somebody else.—Penelope makes
light of her conduct, but *I* think such treachery very bad. It has
been the ruin of my happiness. I shall never love any man as I
loved Purvis. I do not think Tom Musgrave should be named
with him in the same day."—"You quite shock me by what you
say of Penelope—said Emma. Could a sister do such a thing?—
Rivalry, treachery between sisters!—I shall be afraid of being
acquainted with her—but I hope it was not so. Appearances
were against her."—"You do not know Penelope.—There is
nothing she w^d not do to get married—she would as good as tell
you so herself.—Do not trust her with any secrets of your own,
take warning by me, do not trust her; she has her good qualities, but she has no faith, no honour, no scruples, if she can
promote her own advantage.—I wish with all my heart she
was well married. I declare I had rather have her well-married
than myself."—"Than yourself!—Yes, I can suppose so. A heart,
wounded like yours can have little inclination for matrimony."—
"Not much indeed—but you know we must marry.—I could do
very well single for my own part—A little company, & a
pleasant ball now & then, would be enough for me, if one could
be young for ever, but my father cannot provide for us, & it is
very bad to grow old & be poor & laughed at.—I have lost
Purvis, it is true but very few people marry their first loves. I
should not refuse a man because he was not Purvis—. Not that
I can ever quite forgive Penelope."—Emma shook her head
in acquiescence.—"Penelope however, has had her troubles—
continued Miss W.—she was sadly disappointed in Tom
Musgrave, who afterwards transferred his attentions from me
to her, & whom she was very fond of; but he never means anything serious, & when he had trifled with her long enough, he
began to slight her for Margaret, & poor Penelope was very
wretched—. And since then, she has been trying to make some
match at Chichester; she wont tell us with whom, but I believe
it is a rich old Dr Harding, uncle to the friend she goes to see;—
& she has taken a vast deal of trouble about him & given up a
great deal of time to no purpose as yet.—When she went away
the other day she said it should be the last time.—I suppose

you did not know what her particular business was at Chichester—nor guess at the object which could take her away, from Stanton just as you were coming home after so many years absence."—"No indeed, I had not the smallest suspicion of it. I considered her engagement to Mrs Shaw just at that time as very unfortunate for me. I had hoped to find all my sisters at home; to be able to make an immediate friend of each."—"I suspect the D^{r} to have an attack of the asthma,—& that she was hurried away on that account—the Shaws are quite on her side.—At least I believe so—but she tells me nothing. She professes to keep her own counsel; she says, & truly enough, that 'too many cooks spoil the broth.'"—"I am sorry for her anxieties, said Emma,—but I do not like her plans or her opinions. I shall be afraid of her.—She must have too masculine & bold a temper.—To be so bent on marriage—to pursue a man merely for the sake of situation—is a sort of thing that shocks me; I cannot understand it. Poverty is a great evil, but to a woman of education & feeling it ought not, it cannot be the greatest.—I would rather be teacher at a school (and I can think of nothing worse) than marry a man I did not like."—"I would rather do any thing than be teacher at a school—said her sister. *I* have been at school, Emma, & know what a life they lead; *you* never have.—I should not like marrying a disagreeable man any more than yourself,—but I do not think there *are* many very disagreeable men;—I think I could like any good humoured man with a comfortable income.—I suppose my aunt brought you up to be rather refined." "Indeed I do not know.—My conduct must tell you how I have been brought up. I am no judge of it myself. I cannot compare my aunt's method with any other person's, because I know no other."—"But I can see in a great many things that you are very refined. I have observed it ever since you came home, & I am afraid it will not be for your happiness. Penelope will laugh at you very much." "*That* will not be for my happiness I am sure.—If my opinions are wrong, I must correct them—if they are above my situation, I must endeavour to conceal them.—But I doubt whether ridicule,—Has Penelope much wit?"—"Yes—she has great spirits, & never cares what she says."—"Margaret is more gentle I imagine?"—"Yes—especially in company; she is all gentleness & mildness

when anybody is by.—But she is a little fretful & perverse
among ourselves.—Poor creature! she is possessed with the
notion of Tom Musgrave's being more seriously in love with her,
than he ever was with any body else, & is always expecting him
to come to the point. This is the second time within this twelve-
month that she has gone to spend a month with Robert and Jane
on purpose to egg him on, by her absence—but I am sure she is
mistaken, & that he will no more follow her to Croydon now
than he did last March.—He will never marry unless he can
marry somebody very great; Miss Osborne perhaps, or something in that stile.—" "Your account of this Tom Musgrave,
Elizabeth, gives me very little inclination for his acquaintance."
"You are afraid of him, I do not wonder at you."—"No indeed—
I dislike & despise him."—"Dislike & despise Tom Musgrave!
No, *that* you never can. I defy you not to be delighted with him
if he takes notice of you.—I hope he will dance with you—& I
dare say he will, unless the Osbornes come with a large party, &
then he will not speak to any body else.—" "He seems to have
most engaging manners!—said Emma.—Well, we shall see how
irresistible Mr Tom Musgrave & I find each other.—I suppose I
shall know him as soon as I enter the ball-room; he *must* carry
some of his charm in his face."—"You will not find him in the
ballroom, I can tell you, you will go early, that Mrs Edwards may
get a good place by the fire, & he never comes till late; & if the
Osbornes are coming, he will wait in the passage, & come in
with them.—I should like to look in upon you, Emma. If it
was but a good day with my father, I w^d wrap myself up, &
James should drive me over, as soon as I had made tea for him;
& I should be with you by the time the dancing began." "What!
Would you come late at night in this chair?"—"To be sure I
would.—There, I said you were very refined;—& *that's* an
instance of it."—Emma for a moment made no answer—at last
she said,—"I wish Elizabeth, you had not made a point of my
going to this ball, I wish you were going instead of me. Your
pleasure would be greater than mine. I am a stranger here, &
know nobody but the Edwardses; my enjoyment, therefore
must be very doubtful. Yours, among all your acquaintance, w^d
be certain.—It is not too late to change. Very little apology cd.
be requisite to the Edwardses, who must be more glad of your

company than of mine, & I sh^d most readily return to my father; & should not be at all afraid to drive this quiet old creature home. Your cloathes I would undertake to find means of sending to you."—"My dearest Emma cried Eliz: warmly—do you think I would do such a thing?—Not for the universe—but I shall never forget your goodnature in proposing it. You must have a sweet temper indeed;—I never met with any thing like it!—And w^d you really give up the ball, that I might be able to go to it!—Believe me Emma, I am not so selfish as that comes to. No; tho' I am nine years older than you are, I would not be the means of keeping you from being seen.—You are very pretty, & it would be very hard that you should not have as fair a chance as we have all had, to make your fortune.—No Emma, whoever stays at home this winter, it shan't be you. I am sure I sh^d never have forgiven the person who kept me from a ball at 19." Emma expressed her gratitude, & for a few minutes they jogged on in silence.—Elizabeth first spoke.—"You will take notice who Mary Edwards dances with."—"I will remember her partners, if I can—but you know they will be all strangers to me." "Only observe whether she dances with Capt. Hunter, more than once; I have my fears in that quarter. Not that her father or mother like officers, but if she does you know, it is all over with poor Sam.—And I have promised to write him word who she dances with." "Is Sam. attached to Miss Edwards?"— "Did not you know *that*?"—"How should I know it? How should I know in Shropshire, what is passing of that nature in Surrey?— It is not likely that circumstances of such delicacy should make any part of the scanty communication which passed between you & me for the last 14 years." "I wonder I never mentioned it when I wrote. Since you have been at home, I have been so busy with my poor father and our great wash that I have had no leisure to tell you anything—but, indeed I concluded you knew it all.—He has been very much in love with her these two years, & it is a great disappointment to him that he cannot always get away to our balls—but Mr Curtis won't often spare him, & just now it is a sickly time at Guildford—" "Do you suppose Miss Edwards inclined to like him?" "I am afraid not: you know she is an only child, & will have at least ten thousand pounds."—"But still she may like our brother." "Oh, no—. The

Edwards look much higher. Her father & mother w^d never consent to it. Sam is only a surgeon you know.—Sometimes I think
she does like him. But Mary Edwards is rather prim & reserved;
I do not always know what she w^d be at."—"Unless Sam feels on
sure grounds with the lady herself, it seems a pity to me that he
should be encouraged to think of her at all."—"A young man
must think of somebody, said Eliz:—& why should not he be as
lucky as Robert, who has got a good wife & six thousand
pounds?" "We must not all expect to be individually lucky
replied Emma. The luck of one member of a family is luck to
all.—" "Mine is all to come I am sure—said Eliz: giving another
sigh to the remembrance of Purvis.—I have been unlucky
enough, & I cannot say much for you, as my aunt married again
so foolishly.—Well—you will have a good ball I dare say. The
next turning will bring us to the turnpike. You may see the
church tower over the hedge, & the White Hart is close by it.—
I shall long to know what you think of Tom Musgrave." Such
were the last audible sounds of Miss Watson's voice, before they
passed thro' the turnpike gate & entered on the pitching of the
town—the jumbling & noise of which made farther conversation most thoroughly undesirable.—The old mare trotted
heavily on, wanting no direction of the reins to take the right
turning, & making only one blunder, in proposing to stop at
the millener's before she drew up towards Mr Edward's door.—
Mr E. lived in the best house in the street, & the best in the
place, if Mr Tomlinson, the banker might be indulged in calling
his newly erected house at the end of the town with a shrubbery
& sweep, in the country.—Mr E.s house was higher than most of
its neighbours with two windows on each side the door, the windows guarded by posts and chains, and the door approached by
a flight of stone steps.—"Here we are—said Eliz:—as the carriage ceased moving—safely arrived,—& by the market clock,
we have been only five & thirty minutes coming,—which *I* think
is doing pretty well, tho' it would be nothing for Penelope.—Is
not it a nice town?—The Edwards's have a noble house you see,
& they live quite in stile. The door will be opened by a man in
livery with a powder'd head, I can tell you."

Emma had seen the Edwardses only one morn^g at Stanton,
they were therefore all but strangers to her, & tho' her spirits

were by no means insensible to the expected joys of the evening, she felt a little uncomfortable in the thought of all that was to precede them. Her conversation with Eliz: too giving her some very unpleasant feelings, with respect to her own family, had made her more open to disagreeable impressions from any other cause, & increased her sense of the awkwardness of rushing into intimacy on so slight an acquaintance.—There was nothing in the manner of M^{rs} or Miss Edwards to give immediate change to these ideas;—the mother, tho' a very friendly woman, had a reserved air, & a great deal of formal civility—& and the daughter, a genteel looking girl of 22, with her hair in papers, seemed very naturally to have caught something of the stile of the mother who had brought her up.—Emma was soon left to know what they could be, by Eliz.'s being obliged to hurry away—& some very, very languid remarks on the probable brilliancy of the ball, were all that broke at intervals a silence of half an hour before they were joined by the master of the house.— Mr Edwards had a much easier, & more communicative air than the ladies of the family; he was fresh from the street, & he came ready to tell what ever might interest.—After a cordial reception of Emma, he turned to his daughter with, "Well Mary, I bring you good news.—The Osbornes will certainly be at the ball tonight.—Horses for two carriages are ordered from the White Hart, to be at Osborne Castle by 9.—" "I am glad of it— observed Mrs E., because their coming gives a credit to our assemblies. The Osbornes being known to have been at the first ball, will dispose a great many people to attend the second.—It is more than they deserve, for in fact, they add nothing to the pleasure of the evening, they come so late & go so early;—but great people have always their charm."—Mr Edwards proceeded to relate every other little article of news which his morning's lounge had supplied him with, & they chatted with greater briskness, till Mrs E.'s moment for dressing arrived, & the young ladies were carefully recommended to lose no time.—Emma was shewn to a very comfortable apartment, & as soon as Mrs E.'s civilities could leave her to herself, the happy occupation, the first bliss of a ball, began.—The girls, dressing in some measure together, grew unavoidably better acquainted; Emma found in Miss E.— the shew of good sense, a modest unpretending mind, & a great wish of obliging—& when they returned to the parlour where Mrs E. was sitting respectably attired in one of the two satin gowns which went thro' the winter, & a new cap from the milliner's, they entered it with much easier feelings & more natural smiles than they had taken away.—Their dress was now to be examined; Mrs Edwards acknowledged herself too old-fashioned to approve of every modern extravagance however sanctioned—& tho' complacently viewing her daughter's good looks, w^d give but a qualified admiration; & Mr E. not less satisfied with Mary, paid some compliments of good humoured gallantry to Emma at her expense.—The discussion led to more intimate remarks, & Miss Edwards gently asked Emma if she were not often reckoned very like her youngest brother.—Emma thought she could perceive a faint blush accompany the question, & there seemed something still more suspicious in the manner in which Mr E. took up the subject.—"You are paying Miss Emma no great compliment I think, Mary, said he, hastily—. Mr Sam Watson is a very good sort of young man, & I dare say a very clever surgeon, but his complexion has been rather too much exposed to all weathers, to make a likeness to him very flattering." Mary apologized, in some confusion. "She had not thought a strong likeness at all incompatible with very different degrees of beauty.—There might be resemblance in countenance; & the complexion, & even the features be very unlike."—"I know nothing of my brother's beauty, said Emma, for I have not seen him since he was 7 years old—but my father reckons us alike." "Mr Watson!—cried Mr Edwards, Well, you astonish me.— There is not the least likeness in the world; Y^r brother's eyes are grey, yours are brown, he has a long face, & a wide mouth.—My dear, do *you* perceive the least resemblance?"—"Not the least.—Miss Emma Watson puts me very much in mind of her eldest sister, & sometimes I see a look of Miss Penelope—& and once or twice there has been a glance of Mr Robert—but I cannot perceive any likeness to Mr Samuel." "I see the likeness between her & Miss Watson, replied Mr E.—, very strongly— but I am not sensible of the others.—I do not much think she is like any of the family *but* Miss Watson; but I am very sure there is no resemblance between her & Sam."—

This matter was settled, & they went to dinner.—"Your father, Miss Emma, is one of my oldest friends—said Mr Edwards, as he helped her to wine, when they were drawn round the fire to enjoy their desert,—We must drink to his better health.—It is a great concern to me I assure you, that he should be such an invalid.—I know nobody who likes a game of cards in a social way, better than he does; & very few people that play a fairer rubber.—It is a thousand pities that he should be so deprived of the pleasure. For now we have a quiet little whist club that meets three times a week at the White Hart, & if he c^d but have his health, how much he w^d enjoy it." "I dare say he would sir— & I wish with all my heart he were equal to it." "Your club w^d be better fitted for an invalid, said Mrs E. if you did not keep it up so late."—This was an old grievance.—"So late, my dear, what are you talking of; cried the husband with sturdy pleasantry—. We are always at home before midnight. They would laugh at Osborne Castle to hear you call *that* late; they are but just rising from dinner at midnight."—"That is nothing to the purpose,— retorted the lady calmly. The Osbornes are to be no rule for us. You had better meet every night, & break up two hours sooner." So far, the subject was very often carried;—but M^r & Mrs Edwards were so wise as never to pass that point; and Mr Edwards now turned to something else.—He had lived long enough in the idleness of a town to become a little of a gossip, & having some curiosity to know more of the circumstances of his young guest than had yet reached him, he began with, "I think Miss Emma, I remember your aunt very well about 30 years ago; I am pretty sure I danced with her in the old rooms at Bath, the year before I married—. She was a very fine woman then—but like other people I suppose she is grown somewhat older since that time.—I hope she is likely to be happy in her second choice."

"I hope so; I believe so, sir—said Emma in some agitation.—" "Mr Turner had not been dead a great while, I think?" "About 2 years sir." "I forget what her name is now."—"O'Brien." "Irish! Ah! I remember—& she is gone to settle in Ireland.—I do wonder that you should not wish to go with her into *that* country Miss Emma—but it must be a great deprivation to her, poor lady!—After bringing you up like a child of her own."—"I was not so ungrateful, sir, said Emma warmly, as to wish to be any-where but with her.—It did not suit them, it did not suit Capt. O'brien that I sh^d be of the party."—"Captain!—repeated Mrs E. the gentleman is in the army then?" "Yes ma'am."—"Aye—there is nothing like your officers for captivating the ladies, young or old.—There is no resisting a cockade my dear."—"I hope there is."—said Mrs E. gravely, with a quick glance at her daughter;— and Emma had just recovered from her own perturbation in time to see a blush on Miss E.'s cheek, & in remembering what Elizabeth had said of Cap. Hunter, to wonder & waver between his influence & her brother's.—

"Elderly ladies should be careful how they make a second choice." observed Mr Edwards.—"Carefulness—discretion— should not be confined to elderly ladies, or to a second choice added his wife. It is quite as necessary to young ladies in their first."—"Rather more so, my dear—replied he, because young ladies are likely to feel the effects of it longer. When an old lady plays the fool, it is not in the course of nature that she should suffer from it many years." Emma drew her hand across her eyes—& Mrs Edwards on perceiving it, changed the subject to one of less anxiety to all.—

With nothing to do but to expect the hour of setting off, the afternoon was long to the two young ladies; & tho' Miss Edwards was rather discomposed at the very early hour which her mother always fixed for going, that early hour itself was watched for with some eagerness.—The entrance of the tea-things at 7 o'clock was some relief—& luckily M^r and Mrs Edwards always drank a dish extraordinary, & ate an additional muffin when they were going to sit up late, which lengthened the ceremony almost to the wished-for moment. At a little before 8, the Tomlinsons carriage was heard to go by, which was the constant signal for Mrs Edwards to order hers to the door; & in a very few minutes, the party were transported from the quiet and warmth of a snug parlour, to the bustle, noise, & draughts of air of the broad entrance-passage of an inn.—Mrs Edwards carefully guarding her own dress, while she attended with yet greater solicitude to the proper security of her young charges' shoulders & throats, led the way up the wide staircase, while no sound of a ball but the first scrape of one violin, blessed the ears

of her followers, & Miss Edwards, on hazarding the anxious
inquiry of whether there were many people come yet was told
by the waiter as she knew she should, that "Mr Tomlinson's
family were in the room." In passing along a short gallery to the
assembly-room, brilliant in lights before them, they were
accosted by a young man in a morning dress & boots, who was
standing in the doorway of a bedchamber, apparently on purpose to see them go by.—"Ah! M^{rs} E— how do you do?—How
do you do Miss E.?—he cried, with an easy air;—You are determined to be in good time I see, as usual.—The candles are but
this moment lit"—"I like to get a good seat by the fire you know,
Mr Musgrave," replied Mrs E. "I am this moment going to dress,
said he—I am waiting for my stupid fellow.—We shall have a
famous ball, the Osbornes are certainly coming; you may
depend upon *that* for I was with Ld Osborne this morn^g—"

The party passed on—M^{rs} E's satin gown swept along the
clean floor of the ball-room, to the fireplace at the upper end,
where one party only were formally seated, while three or four
officers were lounging together, passing in & out from the
adjoining card-room.—A very stiff meeting between these near
neighbours ensued—& as soon as they were all duly placed
again, Emma in the low whisper which became the solemn
scene, said to Miss Edwards, "The gentleman we passed in the
passage, was Mr Musgrave, then?—He is reckoned remarkably
agreeable I understand.—" Miss E. answered hesitatingly—
"Yes—he is very much liked by many people.—But *we* are not
very intimate."—"He is rich, is not he?"—"He has about 8 or
900£ a year, I believe.—He came into possession of it, when he
was very young, & my father & mother think it has given him
rather an unsettled turn.—He is no favourite with them."—The
cold & empty appearance of the room & the demure air of the
small cluster of females at one end of it began soon to give way;
the inspiriting sound of other carriages was heard, & continual
accessions of portly chaperons, & strings of smartly-dressed girls
were received, with now & then a fresh gentleman straggler,
who if not enough in love to station himself near any fair creature seemed glad to escape into the card-room.—Among the
increasing number of military men, one now made his way to
Miss Edwards, with an air of empressément, which decidedly

said to her companion, "I am Capt. Hunter."—& Emma, who could not but watch her at such a moment, saw her looking rather distressed, but by no means displeased, & heard an engagement formed for the two first dances, which made her think her brother Sam's a hopeless case.—

Emma in the meanwhile was not unobserved, or unadmired herself.—A new face & a very pretty one, could not be slighted —her name was whispered from one party to another, & no sooner had the signal been given, by the orchestra's striking up a favourite air, which seemed to call the young men to their duty, & people the centre of the room, than she found herself engaged to dance with a brother officer, introduced by Capt. Hunter.—Emma Watson was not more than of the middle height—well made & plump, with an air of healthy vigour.— Her skin was very brown, but clear, smooth & glowing—; which with a lively eye, a sweet smile, & an open countenance, gave beauty to attract, & expression to make that beauty improve on acquaintance.—Having no reason to be dissatisfied with her partner, the even^g began very pleasantly to her; & her feelings perfectly coincided with the reiterated observation of others, that it was an excellent ball.—The two first dances were not quite over, when the returning sound of carriages after a long interruption, called general notice, & "the Osbornes are coming, the Osbornes are coming"—was repeated round the room.— After some minutes of extraordinary bustle without, & watchful curiosity within, the important party, preceded by the attentive master of the inn to open a door which was never shut, made their appearance. They consisted of Ly. Osborne, her son Ld Osborne, her daughter Miss Osborne; Miss Carr, her daughter's friend, Mr Howard formerly tutor to Ld Osborne, now cler-gyman of the parish in which the castle stood, Mrs Blake, a widow-sister who lived with him, her son, a fine boy of 10 years old, & Mr Tom Musgrave; who probably imprisoned within his own room, had been listening in bitter impatience to the sound of the music, for the last half-hour. In their progress up the room, they paused almost immediately behind Emma, to receive the compt^s of some acquaintance, & she heard Ly. Osborne observe that they had made a point of coming early for the gratification of Mrs Blake's little boy, who was uncommonly fond of dancing.—Emma looked at them all as they passed—but chiefly & with most interest on Tom Musgrave, who was certainly a genteel, good looking young man.—Of the females, Ly. Osborne had by much the finest person; tho' nearly 50, she was very handsome, & had all the dignity of rank.—

Ld Osborne was a very fine young man; but there was an air of coldness, of carelessness, even of awkwardness about him, which seemed to speak him out of his element in a ball-room. He came in fact only because it was judged expedient for him to please the borough—he was not fond of women's company, & he never danced.—Mr Howard was an agreeable-looking man, a little more than thirty.—

At the conclusion of the two dances, Emma found herself, she knew not how, seated amongst the Osborne set; & she was immediately struck with the fine countenance & animated gestures of the little boy, as he was standing before his mother, wondering when they should begin.—"You will not be surprised at Charles's impatience, said Mrs Blake, a lively pleasant-looking little woman of 5 or 6 & 30, to a lady who was standing near her, when you know what a partner he is to have. Miss Osborne has been so very kind as to promise to dance the two 1st dances with him."—"Oh! yes—we have been engaged this week, cried the boy, & we are to dance down every couple."—On the other side of Emma, Miss Osborne, Miss Carr, & a party of young men were standing engaged in very lively consultation—& soon afterwards she saw the smartest officer of the sett, walking off to the orchestra to order the dance, while Miss Osborne passing before her, to her little expecting partner hastily said—"Charles, I beg your pardon for not keeping my engagement, but I am going to dance these two dances with Col^n Beresford. I know you will excuse me, & I will certainly dance with you after tea." And without staying for an answer, she turned again to Miss Carr, & in another minute was led by Col. Beresford to begin the set. If the poor little boy's face had in its happiness been interesting to Emma, it was infinitely more so under this sudden reverse;—he stood the picture of disappointment, with crimson'd cheeks, quivering lips, & eyes bent on the floor. His mother, stifling her own mortification, tried to soothe his, with the prospect of Miss Osborne's second promise;—but tho' he contrived to utter, with an effort of boyish bravery, "Oh! I do not mind it"—it was very evident, by the unceasing agitation of his features, that he minded it as much as ever.—Emma did not think, or reflect;—she felt & acted—. "I shall be very happy to dance with you, sir, if you like it," said she, holding out her hand with the most unaffected good-humour.—The boy in one moment restored to all his first delight, looked joyfully at his mother; and stepping forwards with an honest & simple "Thank you, ma'am," was instantly ready to attend his new acquaintance. The thankfulness of Mrs Blake was more diffuse;—with a look most expressive of unexpected pleasure & lively gratitude, she turned to her neighbour with repeated & fervent acknowledgments of so great and condescending a kindness to her boy. Emma, with perfect truth, could assure her that she could not be giving greater pleasure than she felt herself—& Charles being provided with his gloves & charged to keep them on, they joined the set which was now rapidly forming,—with nearly equal complacency.—It was a partnership which c^d not be noticed without surprise. It gained her a broad stare from Miss Osborne and Miss Carr as they passed her in the dance. "Upon my word, Charles, you are in luck," said the former, as she turned him; "you have got a better partner than me"; to which the happy Charles answered "Yes."—Tom Musgrave, who was dancing with Miss Carr, gave her many inquisitive glances; and after a time Ld Osborne himself came, & under pretence of talking to Charles, stood to look at his partner.—Tho' rather distressed by such observation, Emma could not repent what she had done, so happy had it made both the boy & his mother; the latter of whom was continually making opportunities of addressing her with the warmest civility.—Her little partner, she found, tho' bent chiefly on dancing, was not unwilling to speak, when her questions or remarks gave him anything to say; & she learnt, by a sort of inevitable enquiry, that he had two brothers & a sister, that they & their mamma all lived with his uncle at Wickstead, that his uncle taught him Latin, that he was very fond of riding, & had a horse of his own given him by Ld Osborne; & that he had been out once already with Ld Osborne's hounds.—At the end of these dances, Emma found they were to drink tea;—Miss E. gave her a caution to be at hand, in a manner which convinced her of Mrs E.'s holding it very important to have them both close to her when she moved into the tearoom; & Emma was accordingly on the alert to gain her proper station. It was always the pleasure of the company to have a little bustle & croud when they adjourned for refreshment;—the tearoom was a small room within the cardroom, & in passing thro' the latter, where the passage was straightened by tables, Mrs E. & her party were for a few moments hemmed in. It happened close by Lady Osborne's cassino table; Mr Howard who belonged to it spoke to his nephew; & Emma, on perceiving herself the object of attention both to Ly. O. & him, had just turned away her eyes in time, to avoid seeming to hear her young companion delightedly whisper aloud, "Oh! uncle, do look at my partner. She is so pretty!" As they were immediately in motion again however Charles was hurried off without being able to receive his uncle's suffrage.—On entering the tearoom, in which two long tables were prepared, Ld Osborne was to be seen quite alone at the end of one, as if retreating as far as he could from the ball, to enjoy his own thoughts, & gape without restraint.— Charles instantly pointed him out to Emma.—"There's Lord Osborne—let you & I go & sit by him.—"No, no, said Emma laughing you must sit with my friends."

Charles was now free enough to hazard a few questions in his turn. "What o'clock was it?"—"Eleven."—"Eleven!—And I am not at all sleepy. Mamma said I should be asleep before ten.— Do you think Miss Osborne will keep her word with me, when tea is over?" "Oh! yes.—I suppose so."—tho' she felt that she had no better reason to give than that Miss Osborne had *not* kept it before.—"When shall you come to Osborne Castle?"— "Never, probably.—I am not acquainted with the family." "But you may come to Wickstead & see mamma, & she can take you to the castle.—There is a monstrous curious stuff'd fox there, & a badger—anybody would think they were alive. It is a pity you should not see them."—

On rising from tea, there was again a scramble for the pleasure of being first out of the room, which happened to be increased by one or two of the card parties having just broken up & the players being disposed to move exactly the different way. Among these was Mr Howard—his sister leaning on his arm—& no sooner were they within reach of Emma, than Mrs B. calling her notice by a friendly touch, said "Your goodness to Charles, my dear Miss Watson, brings all his family upon you. Give me leave to introduce my brother—Mr H." Emma curtsied, the gentleman bowed—made a hasty request for the honour of her hand in the two next dances, to which as hasty an affirmative was given, & they were immediately impelled in opposite directions.—Emma was very well pleased with the circumstance;—there was a quietly-chearful, gentlemanlike air in Mr H. which suited her—& in a few minutes afterwards, the value of her engagement increased, when as she was sitting in the cardroom somewhat screened by a door, she heard Ld Osborne, who was lounging on a vacant table near her, call Tom Musgrave towards him & say, "Why do not you dance with that beautiful Emma Watson?—I want you to dance with her— & I will come & stand by you."—"I was determining on it this very moment my lord, I'll be introduced & dance with her directly."—"Aye, do—& if you find she does not want much talking to, you may introduce me by & bye."—"Very well my lord—. If she is like her sisters, she will only want to be listened to.—I will go this moment. I shall find her in the tearoom. That stiff old Mrs E. has never done tea."—Away he went,— Ld Osborne after him—& Emma lost no time in hurrying from her corner, exactly the other way, forgetting in her haste that she left Mrs Edwards behind.—"We had quite lost you—said Mrs E.— who followed her with Mary, in less than five minutes.— If you prefer this room to the other, there is no reason why you should not be here, but we had better all be together." Emma was saved the trouble of apologizing, by their being joined at the moment by Tom Musgrave, who requesting Mrs E. aloud to do him the honour of presenting him to Miss Emma Watson, left that good lady without any choice in the business, but that of testifying by the coldness of her manner that she did it unwillingly. The honour of dancing with her, was solicited without loss of time—& Emma, however she might like to be thought a beautiful girl by lord or commoner, was so little disposed to favour Tom Musgrave himself, that she had considerable satisfaction in avowing her prior engagement.—He was evidently surprised & discomposed.—The stile of her last partner had

probably led him to believe her not overpowered with applications.—"My little friend Charles Blake, he cried, must not
expect to engross you the whole evening. We can never suffer
this—It is against the rules of the assembly—& I am sure it will
never be patronised by our good friend here Mrs E.; she is by
much too nice a judge of decorum to give her license to such a
dangerous particularity."—"I am not going to dance with Master
Blake sir." The gentleman a little disconcerted, could only hope
he might be more fortunate another time—& seeming unwilling
to leave her, tho' his friend Ld Osborne was waiting in the doorway for the result, as Emma with some amusement perceived—
he began to make civil enquiries after her family.—"How comes
it, that we have not the pleasure of seeing your sisters here this
evening?—Our assemblies have been used to be so well treated
by them, that we do not know how to take this neglect."—"My
eldest sister is the only one at home—& she could not leave my
father"—"Miss Watson the only one at home!—You astonish
me!—It seems but the day before yesterday that I saw them all
three in this town. But I am afraid I have been a very sad neighbour of late. I hear dreadful complaints of my negligence wherever I go, & I confess it is a shameful length of time since I was
at Stanton.—But I shall *now* endeavour to make myself amends
for the past."—Emma's calm curtsey in reply must have struck
him as very unlike the encouraging warmth he had been used to
receive from her sisters, & gave him probably the novel sensation of doubting his own influence, & of wishing for more attention than she bestowed. The dancing now recommenced; Miss
Carr being impatient to *call,* everybody was required to stand
up—& Tom Musgrave's curiosity was appeased, on seeing
Mr Howard come forward and claim Emma's hand—"That will
do as well for me"—was Ld Osborne's remark, when his friend
carried him the news—& he was continually at Howard's elbow
during the two dances.—The frequency of his appearance
there, was the only unpleasant part of her engagement, the only
objection she could make to Mr Howard.—In himself, she
thought him as agreeable as he looked; tho' chatting on the com-
monest topics he had a sensible, unaffected, way of expressing
himself, which made them all worth hearing, & she only
regretted that he had not been able to make his pupil's manners

as unexceptionable as his own.—The two dances seemed very short, & she had her partner's authority for considering them so.—At their conclusion the Osbornes & their train were all on the move. "We are off at last, said his lordship to Tom— How much longer do *you* stay in this heavenly place?—till sunrise?"—"No faith! my lord, I have had quite enough of it. I assure you—I shall not shew myself here again when I have had the honour of attending Ly. Osborne to her carriage. I shall retreat in as much secrecy as possible to the most remote corner of the house, where I shall order a barrel of oysters, & be famously snug." "Let us see you soon at the castle; & bring me word how she looks by daylight."—Emma & Mrs Blake parted as old acquaintance, & Charles shook her by the hand & wished her "goodbye" at least a dozen times. From Miss Osborne & Miss Carr she received something like a jerking curtsey as they passed her; even Ly. Osborne gave her a look of complacency— & his lordship actually came back after the others were out of the room, to "beg her pardon," & look in the window seat behind her for the gloves which were visibly compressed in his hand.—

As Tom Musgrave was seen no more, we may suppose his plan to have succeeded, & imagine him mortifying with his barrel of oysters, in dreary solitude—or gladly assisting the land-lady in her bar to make fresh negus for the happy dancers above. Emma could not help missing the party, by whom she had been, tho' in some respects unpleasantly, distinguished, & the two dances which followed & concluded the ball, were rather flat, in comparison with the others.—Mr E. having play'd with good luck, they were some of the last in the room.—"Here we are, back again I declare—said Emma sorrowfully, as she walked into the dining room, where the table was prepared, & the neat upper maid was lighting the candles—"My dear Miss Edwards—how soon it is at an end!—I wish it could all come over again!—" A great deal of kind pleasure was expressed in her having enjoyed the even^g so much—& Mr Edwards was as warm as herself, in the praise of the fullness, brilliancy & spirit of the meeting, tho' as he had been fixed the whole time at the same table in the same room, with only one change of chairs, it might have seemed a matter scarcely perceived.—But he had won 4 rubbers out of 5, & everything went well. His daughter felt the advantage of this gratified state of mind, in the course of the remarks & retrospections which now ensued, over the welcome soup.—"How came you not to dance with either of the Mr Tomlinsons, Mary?"—said her mother. "I was always engaged when they asked me." "I thought you were to have stood up with Mr James, the two last dances; Mrs Tomlinson told me he was gone to ask you—& I had heard you say two minutes before that you were *not* engaged."—"Yes—but—there was a mistake—I had misunderstood—I did not know I was engaged.—I thought it had been for the 2 dances after, if we stayed so long—but Capt. Hunter assured me it was for those very two.—"

"So you ended with Capt. Hunter Mary, did you?" said her father. And who did you begin with?" "Capt. Hunter" was repeated, in a very humble tone—"Hum!—That is being constant however. But who else did you dance with?" "Mr Norton, & Mr Styles." "And who are they?" "Mr Norton is a cousin of Capt. Hunter's."—"And who is Mr Styles?" "One of his particular friends,"—"All in the same reg^t added Mrs E.—Mary was surrounded by red coats the whole even^g. I should have been better pleased to see her dancing with some of our old neighbours I confess.—" "Yes, yes, we must not neglect our old neighbours—. But if these soldiers are quicker than other people in a ball room, what are young ladies to do?" "I think there is no occasion for their engaging themselves so many dances beforehand, Mr Edwards."—"No—perhaps not—but I remember my dear when you & I did the same."—Mrs E. said no more, & Mary breathed again.—A great deal of goodhumoured pleasantry followed—& Emma went to bed in charming spirits, her head full of Osbornes, Blakes & Howards.—

The next morn^g brought a great many visitors. It was the way of the place always to call on Mrs E. on the morn^g after a ball, & this neighbourly inclination was increased in the present instance by a general spirit of curiosity on Emma's account, as everybody wanted to look again at the girl who had been admired the night before by Ld Osborne.—

Many were the eyes, & various the degrees of approbation

with which she was examined. Some saw no fault, & some no beauty—. With some her brown skin was the annihilation of every grace, & others could never be persuaded that she were half so handsome as Eliz: Watson had been ten years ago.—The morn^g passed quietly away in discussing the merits of the ball with all this succession of company—& Emma was at once astonished by finding it two o'clock, & considering that she had heard nothing of her father's chair. After this discovery she had walked twice to the window to examine the street, & was on the point of asking leave to ring the bell & make enquiries, when the light sound of a carriage driving up to the door set her heart at ease. She stepd again to the window—but instead of the convenient but very un-smart family equipage perceived a neat curricle.—Mr Musgrave was shortly afterwards announced;—& Mrs Edwards put on her very stiffest look at the sound.—Not at all dismayed however by her chilling air, he paid his comp^{ts} to each of the ladies with no unbecoming ease, & continuing to address Emma, presented her a note, which he had the honour of bringing from her sister; but to which he must observe a verbal postscript from himself w^d be requisite.—"

The note, which Emma was beginning to read rather *before* Mrs Edwards had entreated her to use no ceremony, contained a few lines from Eliz: importing that their father in consequence of being unusually well had taken the sudden resolution of attending the visitation that day, & that as his road lay quite wide from R., it was impossible for her to come home till the following morn^g, unless the Edwardses w^d send her which was hardly to be expected, or she c^d meet with any chance conveyance, or did not mind walking so far.—She had scarcely run her eye thro' the whole, before she found herself obliged to listen to Tom Musgrave's farther account. "I received that note from the fair hands of Miss Watson only ten minutes ago, said he—I met her in the village of Stanton, whither my good stars prompted me to turn my horses heads—she was at that moment in quest of a person to employ on the errand, & I was fortunate enough to convince her that she could not find a more willing or speedy messenger than myself—. Remember, I say nothing of my disinterestedness.—My reward is to be the indulgence of conveying you to Stanton in my curricle.—Tho' they are not written down,

I bring your sister's orders for the same.—" Emma felt distressed; she did not like the proposal—she did not wish to be on terms of intimacy with the proposer—& yet fearful of encroaching on the Edwardses, as well as wishing to go home herself, she was at a loss how entirely to decline what he offered.—Mrs E. continued silent, either not understanding the case, or waiting to see how the young lady's inclination lay. Emma thanked him—but professed herself very unwilling to give him so much trouble. "The trouble was of course, honour, pleasure, delight. What had he or his horses to do?"—Still she hesitated. "She believed she must beg leave to decline his assistance—she was rather afraid of the sort of carriage—. The distance was not beyond a walk.—" Mrs E. was silent no longer. She enquired into the particulars—& then said, "We shall be extremely happy Miss Emma, if you can give us the pleasure of your company till tomorrow—but if you cannot conveniently do so, our carriage is quite at your service, & Mary will be pleased with the opportunity of seeing your sister."—This was precisely what Emma had longed for; & she accepted the offer most thankfully; acknowledging that as Eliz: was entirely alone, it was her wish to return home to dinner.—The plan was warmly opposed by their visitor. "I cannot suffer it, indeed. I must not be deprived of the happiness of escorting you. I assure you there is not a possibility of fear with my horses. You might guide them yourself. *Your sisters* all know how quiet they are; they have none of them the smallest scruple in trusting themselves with me, even on a race course.— Believe me—added he, lowering his voice—*you* are quite safe, the danger is only *mine*."—Emma was not more disposed to oblige him for all this.—"And as to Mrs Edwards's carriage being used the day after a ball, it is a thing quite out of rule I assure you—never heard of before—the old coachman will look as black as his horses—. Won't he Miss Edwards?"—No notice was taken. The ladies were silently firm, & the gentleman found himself obliged to submit.

"What a famous ball we had last night!—he cried, after a short pause. "How long did you keep it up, after the Osbornes & I went away?"—"We had two dances more."—"It is making it too much of a fatigue I think, to stay so late.—I suppose your set was not a very full one."—"Yes, quite as full as ever, except the

Osbornes. There seemed no vacancy anywhere—& everybody danced with uncommon spirit to the very last."—Emma said this,—tho' against her conscience.—"Indeed! perhaps I might have looked in upon you again, if I had been aware of as much;—for I am rather fond of dancing than not.—Miss Osborne is a charming girl, is not she?" "I do not think her handsome." replied Emma, to whom all this was chiefly addressed. "Perhaps she is not critically handsome, but her manners are delightful. And Fanny Carr is a most interesting little creature. You can imagine nothing more *naive* or *piquante*; & what do you think of Ld Osborne Miss Watson?" "That he would be handsome even, tho' he were *not* a lord—& perhaps—better bred; more desirous of pleasing, & shewing himself pleased in a right place.—" "Upon my word, you are severe upon my friend!—I assure you Ld Osborne is a very good fellow.—" "I do not dispute his virtues—but I do not like his careless air.—" "If it were not a breach of confidence, replied Tom with an important look, perhaps I might be able to win a more favourable opinion of poor Osborne.—" Emma gave him no encouragement, & he was obliged to keep his friend's secret.—He was also obliged to put an end to his visit—for Mrs Edwards's having ordered her carriage, there was no time to be lost on Emma's side in preparing for it.—Miss Edwards accompanied her home, but as it was dinner hour at Stanton, staid with them only a few minutes,—"Now my dear Emma, said Miss W., as soon as they were alone, you must talk to me all the rest of the day, without stopping, or I shall not be satisfied. But first of all Nanny shall bring in the dinner. Poor thing!—You will not dine as you did yesterday, for we have nothing but some fried beef.—How nice Mary Edwards looks in her new pelisse!—And now tell me how you like them all, & what I am to say to Sam. I have begun my letter, Jack Stokes is to call for it tomorrow, for his uncle is going within a mile of Guildford the next day.—" Nanny brought in the dinner;—"We will wait upon ourselves, continued Eliz: & then we shall lose no time.—And so, you would not come home with Tom Musgrave?"—"No. You had said so much against him that I could not wish either for the obligation, or the intimacy which the use of his carriage must have created—. I should not even have liked the appearance of it.—" "You did very right; tho' I wonder at your forbearance, & I do not think I could have done it myself.—He seemed so eager to fetch you, that I could not say no, tho' it rather went against me to be throwing you together, so well as I knew his tricks;—but I did long to see you, & it was a clever way of getting you home; besides it won't do to be too nice.—Nobody could have thought of the Edwardses letting you have their coach,—after the horses being out so late.—But what am I to say to Sam?"—"If you are guided by me, you will not encourage him to think of Miss Edwards.—The father is decidedly against him, the mother shews him no favour, & I doubt his having any interest with Mary. She danced twice with Capt. Hunter, & I think shews him in general as much encouragement as is consistent with her disposition, & the circumstances she is placed in.—She once mentioned Sam, & certainly with a little confusion—but that was perhaps merely oweing to the consciousness of his liking her, which may very probably have come to her knowledge."—"Oh, dear yes—she has heard enough of that from us all. Poor Sam!—He is out of luck as well as other people.— For the life of me Emma, I cannot help feeling for those that are cross'd in love.—Well—now begin, & give me an account of everything as it happened.—" Emma obeyed her—& Eliz: listened with very little interruption till she heard of Mr H. as a partner.—"Dance with Mr H.—Good heavens! You don't say so! Why—he is quite one of the great & grand ones;—did you not find him very high?" "His manners are of a kind to give *me* much more ease & confidence than Tom Musgrave's." "Well—go on. I should have been frightened out of my wits, to have had anything to do with the Osborne's set."—Emma concluded her narration.—"And so, you really did not dance with Tom M. at all?— But you must have liked him, you must have been struck with him altogether."—"I do *not* like him, Eliz:—. I allow his person & air to be good—& that his manners to a certain point—his address rather—is pleasing.—But I see nothing else to admire in him.—On the contrary, he seems very vain, very conceited, absurdly anxious for distinction, & absolutely contemptible in some of the measures he takes for becoming so.—There is a ridiculousness about him that entertains me—but his company gives me no other agreeable emotion." "My dearest Emma!— You are like nobody else in the world.—It is well Margaret is not

by.—You do not offend *me*, tho' I hardly know how to believe
you. But Marg^t w^d never forgive such words." "I wish Marg^t could
have heard him profess his ignorance of her being out of the
country; he declared it seemed only two days since he had seen
her.—" "Aye—that is just like him, & yet this is the man, she *will*
fancy so desperately in love with her.—He is no favourite of
mine, as you well know, Emma;—but you must think him agreeable. Can you lay your hand on your heart, & say you do not?"—
"Indeed I can, both hands; & spread to their widest extent."—
"I should like to know the man you *do* think agreeable." "His
name is Howard." "Howard! Dear me. I cannot think of *him*, but
as playing cards with Ly Osborne, & looking proud.—I must
own, however, that it *is* a relief to me, to find you can speak as
you do, of Tom Musgrave; my heart did misgive me that you
would like him too well. You talked so stoutly beforehand, that I
was sadly afraid your brag would be punished.—I only hope it
will last;—& that he will not come on to pay you much attention;
it is a hard thing for a woman to stand against the flattering ways
of a man, when he is bent upon pleasing her.—" As their quietly-
sociable little meal concluded, Miss Watson could not help
observing how comfortably it had passed. "It is so delightful to
me, said she, to have things going on in peace & goodhumour.
Nobody can tell how much I hate quarrelling. Now, tho' we have
had nothing but fried beef, how good it has all seemed.—I wish
everybody were as easily satisfied as you—but poor Marg^t is very
snappish, & Penelope owns she had rather have quarrelling
going on, than nothing at all."—Mr Watson returned in the
evening, not the worse for the exertion of the day, & consequently pleased with what he had done, & glad to talk of it, over
his own fireside.—

Emma had not foreseen any interest to herself in the occurrences of a visitation—but when she heard Mr Howard spoken
of as the preacher, & as having given them an excellent sermon,
she could not help listening with a quicker ear.—"I do not know
when I have heard a discourse more to my mind—continued
Mr W. or one better delivered.—He reads extremely well, with
great propriety & in a very impressive manner; & at the same
time without any theatrical grimace or violence.—I own, I do
not like much action in the pulpit—I do not like the studied air

& artificial inflexions of voice, which your very popular & most admired preachers generally have.—A simple delivery is much better calculated to inspire devotion, & shews a much better taste.—Mr H. read like a scholar & a gentleman."—"And what had you for dinner sir?"—said his eldest daughter.—He related the dishes & told what he had ate himself. "Upon the whole, he added, I have had a very comfortable day; my old friends were quite surprised to see me amongst them—& I must say that everybody paid me great attention, & seemed to feel for me as an invalid.—They would make me sit near the fire, & as the partridges were pretty high, Dr Richards would have them sent away to the other end of the table, that they might not offend Mr Watson—which I thought very kind of him.—But what pleased me as much as anything was Mr Howard's attention;— There is a pretty steep flight of steps up to the room we dine in—which do not quite agree with my gouty foot—& Mr Howard walked by me from the bottom to the top, & would make me take his arm.—It struck me as very becoming in so young a man, but I am sure I had no claim to expect it; for I never saw him before in my life.—By the bye, he enquired after one of my daughters, but I do not know which. I suppose you know among yourselves."—

On the 3^d day after the ball, as Nanny at five minutes before three, was beginning to bustle into the parlour with the tray & the knife-case, she was suddenly called to the front door, by the sound of as smart a rap as the end of a riding-whip c^d give—& tho' charged by Miss W. to let nobody in, returned in half a minute with a look of awkward dismay, to hold the parlour door open for Ld Osborne & Tom Musgrave.—The surprise of the young ladies may be imagined. No visitors would have been welcome at such a moment; but such visitors as these—such a one as Ld Osborne at least, a nobleman & a stranger, was really distressing.—He looked a little embarrassed himself,—as, on being introduced by his easy, voluble friend, he muttered something of doing himself the honour of waiting on Mr Watson.— Tho' Emma could not but take the compliment of the visit to herself, she was very far from enjoying it. She felt all the inconsistency of such an acquaintance with the very humble stile in which they were obliged to live; & having in her aunt's family been used to many of the elegancies of life, was fully sensible of all that must be open to the ridicule of richer people in her present home.—Of the pain of such feelings, Eliz: knew very little;—her simpler mind, or juster reason saved her from such mortification—& tho' shrinking under a general sense of inferiority, she felt no particular shame.—Mr Watson, as the gentlemen had already heard from Nanny, was not well enough to be down stairs;—with much concern they took their seats—Ld Osborne near Emma, & the convenient Mr Musgrave in high spirits at his own importance, on the other side of the fireplace, with Elizth.— *He* was at no loss for words; but when Ld Osborne had hoped that Emma had not caught cold at the ball, he had nothing more to say for some time, & could only gratify his eye by occasional glances at his fair neighbour.—Emma was not inclined to give herself much trouble for his entertainment—& after hard labour of mind, he produced the remark of its being a very fine day, & followed it up with the question of, "Have you been walking this morning?" "No, my lord. We thought it too dirty." "You should wear half-boots."—After another pause, "Nothing sets off a neat ankle more than a half-boot; nankin galoshed with black looks very well.—Do not you like half-boots?" "Yes—but unless they are so stout as to injure their beauty, they are not fit for country walking."—"Ladies should ride in dirty weather.—Do you ride?" "No, my lord." "I wonder every lady does not.—A woman never looks better than on horseback.—" "But every woman may not have the inclination, or the means." "If they knew how much it became them, they would all have the inclination, & I fancy Miss Watson—when once they had the inclination, the means w^d soon follow."—"Your lordship thinks we always have our own way.—*That* is a point on which ladies and gentle^n have long disagreed—but without pretending to decide it, I may say that there are some circumstances which even *women* cannot controul.—Female economy will do a great deal my lord, but it cannot turn a small income into a large one."—Ld Osborne was silenced. Her manner had been neither sententious nor sarcastic, but there was a something in its mild seriousness, as well as in the words themselves which made his lordship think;—and when he addressed her again, it was with a degree of considerate propriety, totally unlike the half-awkward, half-fearless stile of his former remarks.—It was a new thing with him to wish to please a woman; it was the first time that he had ever felt what was due to a woman, in Emma's situation.—But as he wanted neither in sense nor a good disposition, he did not feel it without effect.—"You have not been long in this country I understand, said he, in the tone of a gentle^n. I hope you are pleased with it."—He was rewarded by a gracious answer, & a more liberal full view of her face than she had yet bestowed. Unused to exert himself, & happy in contemplating her, he then sat in silence for some minutes longer, while Tom Musgrave was chattering to Elizth, till they were interrupted by Nanny's approach, who, half-opening the door & putting in her head, said, "Please, ma'am, master wants to know why he be'nt to have his dinner."—The gentlemen, who had hitherto disregarded every symptom, however positive, of the nearness of that meal, now jumped up with apologies, while Elizth called briskly after Nanny "to tell Betty to take up the fowls."—"I am sorry it happens so—she added, turning good-humouredly towards Musgrave— but you know what early hours we keep.—" Tom had nothing to say for himself, he knew it very well, & such honest simplicity, such shameless truth rather bewildered him.—Ld Osborne's parting comp^{ts} took some time, his inclination for speech seeming to increase with the shortness of the term for indulgence.—He recommended exercise in defiance of dirt—spoke again in praise of half-boots—begged that his sister might be allow'd to send Emma the name of her shoemaker—& concluded with saying, "My hounds will be hunting this country next week—I believe they will throw off at Stanton Wood on Wednesday at 9 o'clock.— I mention this, in hopes of y^r being drawn out to see what's going on.—If the morning's tolerable, pray do us the honour of giving us your good wishes in person.—

The sisters looked on each other with astonishment, when their visitors had withdrawn. "Here's an unaccountable honour! cried Eliz: at last. Who would have thought of Ld Osborne's coming to Stanton.—He is very handsome—but Tom Musgrave looks all to nothing, the smartest & most fashionable man of the two. I am glad he did not say anything to me; I w^d not have had to talk to such a great man for the world. Tom was very agree-

able, was not he?—But did you hear him ask where Miss
Penelope & Miss Marg^t were, when he first came in?—It put
me out of patience.—I am glad Nanny had not laid the cloth
however, it w^d have looked so awkward;—just the tray did not
signify.—" To say that Emma was not flattered by Ld Osborne's
visit, would be to assert a very unlikely thing, & describe a very
odd young lady; but the gratification was by no means unal-
loyed; his coming was a sort of notice which might please her
vanity, but did not suit her pride, & she w^d rather have known
that he wished the visit without presuming to make it, than have
seen him at Stanton.—Among other unsatisfactory feelings it
once occurred to her to wonder why Mr Howard had not taken
the same privilege of coming, & accompanied his lordship—but
she was willing to suppose that he had either known nothing
about it, or had declined any share in a measure which carried
quite as much impertinence in its form as goodbreeding.—
M^r W was very far from being delighted, when he heard what
had passed;—a little peevish under immediate pain, & ill disposed to be pleased, he only replied— "Phoo! Phoo!—what
occasion could there be for Ld O.'s coming? I have lived here 14
years without being noticed by any of the family. It is some
foolery of that idle fellow T. Musgrave. I cannot return the
visit.—I would not if I could." And when T. Musgrave was met
with again, he was commissioned with a message of excuse to
Osborne Castle, on the too-sufficient plea of Mr Watson's infirm
state of health.—

A week or ten days rolled quietly away after this visit, before
any new bustle arose to interrupt even for half a day, the tranquil & affectionate intercourse of the two sisters, whose mutual
regard was increasing with the intimate knowledge of each
other which such intercourse produced.—The first circumstance to break in on this serenity, was the receipt of a letter
from Croydon to announce the speedy return of Margaret, & a
visit of two or three days from M^r & Mrs Robert Watson, who
undertook to bring her home & wished to see their sister
Emma.—It was an expectation to fill the thoughts of the sisters
at Stanton, & to busy the hours of one of them at least—for as
Jane had been a woman of fortune, the preparations for her
entertainment were considerable, & as Eliz: had at all times

more good will than method in her guidance of the house, she could make no change without a bustle.—An absence of 14 years had made all her brothers & sisters strangers to Emma, but in her expectation of Margaret there was more than the awkwardness of such an alienation; she had heard things which made her dread her return; & the day which brought the party to Stanton seemed to her the probable conclusion of almost all that had been comfortable in the house.—Robert Watson was an attorney at Croydon, in a good way of business; very well satisfied with himself for the same, & for having married the only daughter of the attorney to whom he had been clerk, with a fortune of six thousand pounds.—Mrs Robt was not less pleased with herself for having had that six thousand pounds, & for being now in possession of a very smart house in Croydon, where she gave genteel parties, & wore fine clothes.—In her person there was nothing remarkable; her manners were pert and conceited.—Margaret was not without beauty; she had a slight, pretty figure, & rather wanted countenance than good features;—but the sharp & anxious expression of her face made her beauty in general little felt.—On meeting her long-absent sister, as on every occasion of shew, her manner was all affection & her voice all gentleness; continual smiles & a very slow articulation being her constant resource when determined on pleasing.—

She was now so "delighted to see dear, dear Emma" that she could hardly speak a word in a minute.—"I am sure we shall be great friends,"—she observed, with much sentiment, as they were sitting together.—Emma scarcely knew how to answer such a proposition—& the manner in which it was spoken, she could not attempt to equal. Mrs R. W. eyed her with much familiar curiosity & triumphant compassion;—the loss of the aunt's fortune was uppermost in her mind, at the moment of meeting;—& she cd. not but feel how much better it was to be the daughter of a gentleman of property in Croydon, than the niece of an old woman who threw herself away on an Irish captain.—Robert was carelessly kind, as became a prosperous man & a brother; more intent on settling with the post-boy, inveighing against the exorbitant advance in posting, & pondering over a doubtful halfcrown, than on welcoming a sister, who was no longer likely to have any property for him to get the

direction of.—"Your road through the village is infamous, Eliz:;
said he; worse than ever it was. By Heaven! I would endite it if
I lived near you. Who is surveyor now?"—There was a little
neice at Croydon, to be fondly enquired after by the kind-
hearted Elizabeth, who regretted very much her not being of
the party.—"You are very good—replied her mother—& I
assure you it went very hard with Augusta to have us come away
without her. I was forced to say we were only going to church &
promise to come back for her directly.—But you know it would
not do, to bring her without her maid, & I am as particular as
ever in having her properly attended to." "Sweet little darling!—
cried Marg^t—It quite broke my heart to leave her.—" "Then
why was you in such a hurry to run away from her? cried
Mrs R.— You are a sad shabby girl.—I have been quarrelling
with you all the way we came, have not I?—Such a visit as this,
I never heard of!—You know how glad we are to have any of you
with us—if it be for months together.—& I am sorry, (with a
witty smile) we have not been able to make Croydon agreeable
this autumn."—"My dearest Jane—do not overpower me with
your raillery.—You know what inducements I had to bring me
home,—spare me, I entreat you—. I am no match for your arch
sallies.—" "Well, I only beg you will not set your neighbours
against the place.—Perhaps Emma may be tempted to go back
with us, & stay till Christmas, if you don't put in your word."—
Emma was greatly obliged. "I assure you we have very good
society at Croydon.—I do not much attend the balls, they are
rather too mixed,—but our parties are very select & good.—I
had seven tables last week in my drawingroom. Are you fond
of the country? How do you like Stanton?"—"Very much"—
replied Emma, who thought a comprehensive answer, most
to the purpose.—She saw that her sister in law despised her
immediately.—Mrs R. W. was indeed wondering what sort of a
home Emma c^d possibly have been used to in Shropshire, & setting it down as certain that the aunt could never have had six
thousand pounds.—"How charming Emma is!—" whispered
Marg^t to Mrs Robert in her most languishing tone.—Emma was
quite distress'd by such behaviour;—& she did not like it better
when she heard Marg^t 5 minutes afterwards say to Eliz: in a
sharp quick accent, totally unlike the first—"Have you heard

from Pen. since she went to Chichester?—I had a letter the other day.—I don't find she is likely to make anything of it. I fancy she'll come back 'Miss Penelope,' as she went.—"

Such, she feared would be Margaret's common voice, when the novelty of her own appearance were over; the tone of artificial sensibility was not recommended by the idea.—The ladies were invited upstairs to prepare for dinner. "I hope you will find things tolerably comfortable, Jane"—said Eliz^th as she opened the door of the spare bedchamber.—"My good creature, replied Jane, use no ceremony with me, I intreat you. I am one of those who always take things as they find them. I hope I can put up with a small apartment for two or three nights, without making a piece of work. I always wish to be treated quite "en famille" when I come to see you—& now I do hope you have not been getting a great dinner for us.—Remember, we never eat suppers."—"I suppose, said Marg^t rather quickly to Emma, you & I are to be together; Eliz^th always takes care to have a room to herself."—"No—Eliz^th gives me half hers."—"Oh!—(in a soften'd voice, & rather mortified to find that she was not ill used) "I am sorry I am not to have the pleasure of your company—especially as it makes me nervous to be much alone."

Emma was the first of the females in the parlour again; on entering it she found her brother alone.—"So Emma, said he, you are quite the stranger at home. It must seem odd enough for you to be here.—A pretty piece of work your Aunt Turner has made of it!—By Heaven! A woman should never be trusted with money. I always said she ought to have settled something on you, as soon as her husband died." "But that would have been trusting *me* with money, replied Emma, & *I* am a woman too.—" "It might have been secured to your future use, without your having any power over it now.—What a blow it must have been upon you!—To find yourself, instead of heiress of 8 or 9000 £, sent back a weight upon your family, without a sixpence.—I hope the old woman will smart for it." "Do not speak disrespectfully of her—She was very good to me; & if she has made an imprudent choice, she will suffer more from it herself, than *I* can possibly do." "I do not mean to distress you, but you know every body must think her an old fool.—I thought Turner had been reckoned an extraordinary sensible, clever man.—How

the devil came he to make such a will?"—"My uncle's sense is
not at all impeached in my opinion, by his attachment to my
aunt. She had been an excellent wife to him. The most liberal &
enlightened minds are always the most confiding.—The event
has been unfortunate, but my uncle's memory is if possible
endeared to me by such a proof of tender respect for my
aunt."—"That's odd sort of talking!—He might have provided
decently for his widow, without leaving every thing that he had
to dispose of, or any part of it at her mercy."—"My aunt may
have erred—said Emma warmly— she *has* erred—but my
uncle's conduct was faultless. I was her own niece, & he left to
herself the power & the pleasure of providing for me."—"But
unluckily she has left the pleasure of providing for you, to your
father, & without the power.—That's the long & short of the
business. After keeping you at a distance from your family for
such a length of time as must do away all natural affection
among us & breeding you up (I suppose) in a superior stile, you
are returned upon their hands without a sixpence." "You know,
replied Emma struggling with her tears, my uncle's melancholy
state of health.—He was a greater invalid than my father. He c^d
not leave home." "I do not mean to make you cry,—said Robt
rather softened—& after a short silence, by way of changing the
subject, he added—"I am just come from my father's room, he
seems very indifferent. It will be a sad break-up when he dies.
Pity, you can none of you get married!—You must come to
Croydon as well as the rest, & see what you can do there.—I
believe if Marg^t had had a thousand or fifteen hundred pounds,
there was a young man who w^d have thought of her." Emma was
glad when they were joined by the others; it was better to look
at her sister in law's finery than listen to Robert, who had equally
irritated & grieved her.—Mrs Robert exactly as smart as she had
been at her own party, came in with apologies for her dress—"I
would not make you wait, said she, so I put on the first thing I
met with.—I am afraid I am a sad figure.—My dear Mr W.—(to
her husband) you have not put any fresh powder in your hair."—
"No—I do not intend it.—I think there is powder enough in my
hair for my wife & sisters."—"Indeed you ought to make some
alteration in your dress before dinner when you are out visiting,
tho' you do not at home." "Nonsense."—"It is very odd you

should not like to do what other gentlemen do. Mr Marshall & Mr Hemmings change their dress every day of their lives before dinner. And what was the use of my putting up your last new coat, if you are never to wear it?"—"Do be satisfied with being fine yourself, & leave your husband alone."—To put an end to this altercation, & soften the evident vexation of her sister in law, Emma (tho' in no spirits to make such nonsense easy) began to admire her gown.—It produced immediate complacency.— "Do you like it?—said she.—I am very happy.—It has been excessively admired;—but sometimes I think the pattern too large.—I shall wear one tomorrow that I think you will prefer to this.—Have you seen the one I gave Margaret?"—

Dinner came, & except when Mrs R. looked at her husband's head, she continued gay & flippant, chiding Elizth for the profusion on the table, & absolutely protesting against the entrance of the roast turkey—which formed the only exception to "you see your dinner."—"I do beg & entreat that no turkey may be seen today. I am really frightened out of my wits with the number of dishes we have already. Let us have no turkey I beseech you."— "My dear, replied Eliz. the turkey is roasted, & it may just as well come in, as stay in the kitchen. Besides if it is cut, I am in hopes my father may be tempted to eat a bit, for it is rather a favourite dish." "You may have it in my dear, but I assure you I shan't touch it."—

Mr Watson had not been well enough to join the party at dinner, but was prevailed on to come down & drink tea with them.—"I wish we may be able to have a game of cards tonight," said Eliz. to Mrs R. after seeing her father comfortably seated in his arm chair.—"Not on my account my dear, I beg. You know I am no card player. I think a snug chat infinitely better. I always say cards are very well sometimes, to break a formal circle, but one never wants them among friends." "I was thinking of its being something to amuse my father, answered Elizth—if it was not disagreable to you. He says his head won't bear whist—but perhaps if we make a round game he may be tempted to sit down with us."—"By all means my dear creature. I am quite at your service. Only do not oblige me to chuse the game, that's all. *Speculation* is the only round game at Croydon now, but I can play anything.—When there is only one or two of you at home, you must be quite at a loss to amuse him—why do not you get him to play at cribbage?—Margaret & I have played at cribbage, most nights that we have not been engaged."—A sound like a distant carriage was at this moment caught; everybody listened; it became more decided; it certainly drew nearer.—It was an unusual sound for Stanton at any time of the day, for the village was on no very public road, & contained no gentleman's family but the rector's.—The wheels rapidly approached;—in two minutes the general expectation was answered; they stopped beyond a doubt at the garden gate of the parsonage. "Who could it be?—It was certainly a postchaise.—Penelope was the only creature to be thought of. She might perhaps have met with some unexpected opportunity of returning."—A pause of suspense ensued.—Steps were distinguished, first along the paved footway, which led under the windows of the house to the front door, & then within the passage. They were the steps of a man. It could not be Penelope. It must be Samuel.—The door opened, & displayed Tom Musgrave in the wrap of a travellor.— He had been in London & was now on his way home, & he had come half a mile out of his road merely to call for ten minutes at Stanton. He loved to take people by surprise, with sudden visits at extraordinary seasons; & in the present instance had had the additional motive of being able to tell the Miss Watsons, whom he depended on finding sitting quietly employed after tea, that he was going home to an 8 o'clock dinner.—As it happened however, he did not give more surprise than he received, when instead of being shewn into the usual little sitting room, the door of the best parlour a foot larger each way than the other was thrown open, & he beheld a circle of smart people whom he c^d not immediately recognize arranged, with all the honours of visiting round the fire, & Miss Watson sitting at the best Pembroke table, with the best tea things before her. He stood a few seconds in silent amazement.—"Musgrave!"— ejaculated Margaret in a tender voice.—He recollected himself, & came forward, delighted to find such a circle of friends, & blessing his good fortune for the unlooked-for indulgence.—He shook hands with Robert, bowed & smiled to the ladies, & did everything very prettily; but as to any particularity of address or emotion towards Margaret, Emma who closely observed him,

perceived nothing that did not justify Eliz.'s opinions tho'
Margaret's modest smiles imported that she meant to take the
visit to herself.—He was persuaded without much difficulty to
throw off his greatcoat, & drink tea with them. "For whether
he dined at 8 or 9, as he observed, was a matter of very little
consequence,"—and without seeming to seek, he did not turn
away from the chair close by Margaret which she was assiduous
in providing him.—She had thus secured him from her sisters—
but it was not immediately in her power to preserve him from
her brother's claims, for as he came avowedly from London, &
had left it only 4. hours ago, the last current report as to public
news, & the general opinion of the day must be understood,
before Robert could let his attention be yielded to the less
national, & important demands of the women.—At last however
he was at liberty to hear Margaret's soft address, as she spoke
her fears of his having had a most terrible, cold, dark dreadful
journey.—"Indeed you should not have set out so late.—"
"I could not be earlier, he replied. I was detained chatting at the
Bedford, by a friend.—All hours are alike to me.—How long
have you been in the country Miss Marg^t?"—"We only came this
morn^g.—My kind brother & sister brought me home this very
morn^g.—'Tis singular, is not it?" "You were gone a great while,
were not you? a fortnight I suppose?"—"*You* may call a fortnight
a great while Mr Musgrave, said Mrs Robert smartly—but *we*
think a month very little. I assure you we bring her home at
the end of a month, much against our will." "A month! Have
you really been gone a month! 'tis amazing how time flies.—"
"You may imagine, said Marg^t in a sort of whisper, what are my
sensations in finding myself once more at Stanton. You know
what a sad visitor I make.—And I was so excessively impatient
to see Emma;—I dreaded the meeting, & at the same time
longed for it.—Do you not comprehend the sort of feeling?"—
"Not at all, cried he, aloud. I could never dread a meeting with
Miss Emma Watson,—or any of her sisters." It was lucky that
he added that finish.—"Were you speaking to me?"—said
Emma, who had caught her own name.—"Not absolutely—he
answered—but I was thinking of you,—as many at a greater distance are probably doing at this moment.—Fine open weather
Miss Emma! charming season for hunting." "Emma is delightful,

is not she?—whispered Marg^t. I have found her more than answer my warmest hopes.—Did you ever see anything more perfectly beautiful?—I think even *you* must be a convert to a brown complexion."—He hesitated; Margaret was fair herself, & he did not particularly want to compliment her; but Miss Osborne & Miss Carr were likewise fair, & his devotion to them carried the day. "Your sister's complexion, said he, at last, is as fine as a dark complexion can be, but I still profess my preference of a white skin. You have seen Miss Osborne?—she is my model for a truly feminine complexion, & she is very fair."—"Is she fairer than me?"—Tom made no reply.—"Upon my honour, ladies, said he, giving a glance over his own person, I am highly endebted to your condescension for admitting me, in such dishabille into your drawing room. I really did not consider how unfit I was to be here, or I hope I should have kept my distance. Ly. Osborne w^d tell me that I were growing as careless as her son, if she saw me in this condition."—The ladies were not wanting in civil returns; & Robert Watson stealing a view of his own head in an opposite glass,—said with equal civility, "You cannot be more in dishabille than myself.—We got here so late, that I had not time even to put a little fresh powder in my hair."—Emma could not help entering into what she supposed her sister in law's feelings at the moment.—When the tea-things were removed, Tom began to talk of his carriage—but the old card table being set out, & the fish & counters, with a tolerably clean pack brought forward from the buffet by Miss Watson, the general voice was so urgent with him to join their party, that he agreed to allow himself another quarter of an hour. Even Emma was pleased that he would stay, for she was beginning to feel that a family party might be the worst of all parties; & the others were delighted.—"What's your game?"—cried he, as they stood round the table.—"Speculation, I believe, said Elizth—My sister recommends it, & I fancy we all like it. I know *you* do, Tom."—"It is the only round game played at Croydon now, said Mrs Robert—we never think of any other. I am glad it is a favourite with you."—"Oh! me! cried Tom. Whatever you decide on, will be a favourite with *me*.—I have had some pleasant hours at speculation in my time—but I have not been in the way of it now for a long while.—Vingt-un is the game at

Osborne Castle; I have played nothing but vingt-un of late. You would be astonished to hear the noise we make there.—The fine old, lofty drawing-room rings again. Ly Osborne sometimes declares she cannot hear herself speak.—Ld Osborne enjoys it famously—and he makes the best dealer without exception that I ever beheld—such quickness & spirit! he lets nobody dream over their cards—I wish you could see him overdraw himself on both his own cards—it is worth anything in the world!"—"Dear me!—cried Marg^t why should not we play at vingt-un?—I think it is a much better game than speculation. I cannot say I am very fond of speculation." Mrs Robert offered not another word in support of the game.—She was quite vanquished, & the fashions of Osborne-Castle carried it over the fashions of Croydon.—"Do you see much of the parsonage family at the castle, Mr Musgrave?—" said Emma, as they were taking their seats.—"Oh! yes—they are almost always there. Mrs Blake is a nice little good-humoured woman, she & I are sworn friends; & Howard's a very gentlemanlike good sort of fellow!—You are not forgotten I assure you, by any of the party. I fancy you must have a little cheek-glowing now & then Miss Emma. Were you not rather warm last Saturday about 9 or 10 o'clock in the even^g—? I will tell you how it was.—I see you are dieing to know.—Says Howard to Ld Osborne—" At this interesting moment he was called on by the others, to regulate the game & determine some disputable point; & his attention was so totally engaged in the business & afterwards by the course of the game as never to revert to what he had been saying before;—& Emma, tho' suffering a good deal from curiosity, dared not remind him.—He proved a very useful addition to their table; without him, it w^d have been a party of such very near relations as could have felt little interest, & perhaps maintained little complaisance, but his presence gave variety & secured good manners.—He was in fact excellently qualified to shine at a round game; & few situations made him appear to greater advantage. He played with spirit, & had a great deal to say & tho' with no wit himself, c^d sometimes make use of the wit of an absent friend; & had a lively way of retailing a common-place, or saying a mere nothing, that had great effect at a card table. The ways, & good jokes of Osborne Castle were now added to his ordinary means of entertainment;

he repeated the smart sayings of one lady, detailed the over-
sights of another, & indulged them even with a copy of
Ld Osborne's stile of overdrawing himself on both cards.—The
clock struck nine, while he was thus agreeably occupied; &
when Nanny came in with her master's bason of gruel, he had
the pleasure of observing to Mr Watson that he should leave him
at supper, while he went home to dinner himself.—The carriage
was ordered to the door—& no entreaties for his staying longer
c^d now avail,—for he well knew, that if he staid he must sit down
to supper in less than ten minutes—which to a man whose heart
had been long fixed on calling his next meal a dinner, was quite
insupportable.—On finding him determined to go, Marg^t began
to wink & nod at Elizth to ask him to dinner for the following
day; & Eliz. at last not able to resist hints, which her own hos-
pitable, social temper more than half seconded, gave the invitation: "Would he give Robt the meeting, they should be very
happy?" "With the greatest pleasure"—was his first reply. In
a moment afterwards—"That is, if I can possibly get here in
time—but I shoot with Ld Osborne, & therefore must not
engage—You will not think of me unless you see me."—And
so, he departed, delighted with the uncertainty in which he had
left it.—

Marg^t in the joy of her heart under circumstances, which she
chose to consider as peculiarly propitious, would willingly have
made a confidante of Emma when they were alone for a short
time the next morn^g; & had proceeded so far as to say—"The
young man who was here last night my dear Emma & returns
today, is more interesting to me, than perhaps you may be
aware—" but Emma pretending to understand nothing extraordinary in the words, made some very inapplicable reply, &
jumping up, ran away from a subject which was odious to her
feelings.—

As Marg^t would not allow a doubt to be repeated of Musgrave's
coming to dinner, preparations were made for his entertainment
much exceeding what had been deemed necessary the day
before; and taking the office of superintendance intirely from
her sister, she was half the morning in the kitchen herself
directing & scolding.—After a great deal of indifferent cooking,

& anxious suspense however they were obliged to sit down without their guest.—T. Musgrave never came, & Marg^t was at no pains to conceal her vexation under the disappointment, or repress the peevishness of her temper—. The peace of the party for the remainder of that day, & the whole of the next, which comprised the length of Robert & Jane's visit, was continually invaded by her fretful displeasure, & querulous attacks.—Eliz. was the usual object of both. Marg^t had just respect enough for her b^r & s^{rs} opinion, to behave properly by *them,* but Eliz. & the maids c^d never do anything right—& Emma, whom she seemed no longer to think about, found the continuance of the gentle voice beyond her calculation short. Eager to be as little among them as possible, Emma was delighted with the alternative of sitting above, with her father, & warmly entreated to be his constant comp^n each even^g—& as Eliz. loved company of any kind too well, not to prefer being below, at all risks, as she had rather talk of Croydon with Jane, with every interruption of Marg^t's perverseness, than sit with only her father, who frequently c^d not endure talking at all, the affair was so settled, as soon as she could be persuaded to believe it no sacrifice on her sister's part.—To Emma, the change was most acceptable, & delightful. Her father, if ill, required little more than gentleness & silence; &, being a man of sense and education, was if able to converse, a welcome companion.—

In *his* chamber, Emma was at peace from the dreadful mortifications of unequal society,& family discord—from the immediate endurance of hard-hearted prosperity, low-minded conceit, & wrong-headed folly, engrafted on an untoward disposition.— She still suffered from them in the contemplation of their existence; in memory & in prospect, but for the moment, she ceased to be tortured by their effects.—She was at leisure, she could read & think,—tho' her situation was hardly such as to make reflection very soothing. The evils arising from the loss of her uncle, were neither trifling, nor likely to lessen; & when thought had been freely indulged, in contrasting the past & the present, the employment of mind, the dissipation of unpleasant ideas which only reading could produce, made her thankfully turn to a book.—The change in her home society, & stile of life in consequence of the death of one friend and the imprudence of another had indeed been striking.—From being the first object of hope & solicitude of an uncle who had formed her mind with the care of a parent, & of tenderness to an aunt whose amiable temper had delighted to give her every indulgence, from being the life & spirit of a house, where all had been comfort & elegance, & the expected heiress of an easy independance, she was become of importance to no one, a burden on those, whose affection she c^d not expect, an addition in an house, already overstocked, surrounded by inferior minds with little chance of domestic comfort, & as little hope of future support.—It was well for her that she was naturally chearful;—for the change had been such as might have plunged weak spirits in despondence.—

She was very much pressed by Robert & Jane to return with them to Croydon, & had some difficulty in getting a refusal accepted; as they thought too highly of their own kindness & situation, to suppose the offer could appear in a less advantageous light to anybody else.—Elizth gave them her interest, tho' evidently against her own, in privately urging Emma to go.— "You do not know what you refuse Emma—said she—nor what you have to bear at home.—I would advise you by all means to accept the invitation, there is always something lively going on at Croydon, you will be in company almost every day, & Robt & Jane will be very kind to you.—As for me, I shall be no worse off without you, than I have been used to be; but poor Marg^t's disagreeable ways are new to *you,* & they would vex you more than you think for, if you stay at home.—" Emma was of course un-influenced, except to greater esteem for Elizth, by such representations,—& the visitors departed without her.—